Lecture Notes
in Business Information Processing   99

Series Editors

Wil van der Aalst
Eindhoven Technical University, The Netherlands
John Mylopoulos
University of Trento, Italy
Michael Rosemann
Queensland University of Technology, Brisbane, Qld, Australia
Michael J. Shaw
University of Illinois, Urbana-Champaign, IL, USA
Clemens Szyperski
Microsoft Research, Redmond, WA, USA

T0178130

Florian Daniel
Kamel Barkaoui
Schahram Dustdar (Eds.)

Business Process Management Workshops

BPM 2011 International Workshops
Clermont-Ferrand, France, August 29, 2011
Revised Selected Papers, Part I

 Springer

Volume Editors

Florian Daniel
University of Trento
Povo, Italy
E-mail: daniel@disi.unitn.it

Kamel Barkaoui
CNAM-CEDRIC
Paris, France
E-mail: kamel.barkaoui@cnam.fr

Schahram Dustdar
Vienna University of Technology
Vienna, Austria
E-mail: dustdar@infosys.tuwien.ac.at

ISSN 1865-1348   e-ISSN 1865-1356
ISBN 978-3-642-28107-5   e-ISBN 978-3-642-28108-2
DOI 10.1007/978-3-642-28108-2
Springer Heidelberg Dordrecht London New York

Library of Congress Control Number: 2011945866

ACM Computing Classification (1998): J.1, H.4, D.2

Typesetting: Camera-ready by author, data conversion by Scientific Publishing Services, Chennai, India

Printed on acid-free paper

Springer is part of Springer Science+Business Media (www.springer.com)

Foreword

These volumes collects the proceedings of the workshops held on August 29, 2011, in conjunction with the 9th International Conference on Business Process Management (BPM 2011), which took place in Clermont-Ferrand, France. The proceedings are so-called post-workshop proceedings, in that the authors were allowed to revise and improve their papers even after the workshops, so as to take into account the feedback obtained from the audience during their presentations.

Due to its interdisciplinary nature, which naturally involves researchers and practitioners alike, the BPM conference has traditionally been perceived as a premium event to co-locate a workshop with – both by academia and by industry. The 2011 edition of the conference was no exception: its call for workshop proposals attracted 17 proposals with topics ranging from (among others) traditional BPM concerns like design and analysis to novel, emerging concerns like social BPM and compliance. Given the high quality of the submissions, selecting candidate workshops and assembling the best mix of workshops was not an easy task. Eventually, the following 12 workshops were selected for co-location with BPM 2011:

- *7th International Workshop on Business Process Design (BPD 2011)* – organized by Marta Indulska, Michael Rosemann, and Michael zur Muehlen.
  BPD 2011 focused on the design, innovation, evaluation, and comparison of process improvement techniques and tools to comprehensively cover process enhancement approaches such as, for example, TRIZ, reference (best practice) models, process innovation, or resource-based approaches to process improvement.
- *7th International Workshop on Business Process Intelligence (BPI 2011)* – organized by Boudewijn van Dongen, Diogo Ferreira, and Barbara Weber.
  BPI 2011 aimed to bring together practitioners and researchers from different communities such as BPM, information systems research, business administration, software engineering, artificial intelligence, process and data mining with the goal to provide a better understanding of techniques and algorithms to support a company's processes at build-time and the way they are handled at run-time.
- *4th International Workshop on Business Process Management and Social Software (BPMS2 2011)* – organized by Selmin Nurcan and Rainer Schmidt.
  The objective of BPMS2 2011 was to explore how social software interacts with business process management, how business process management has to change to comply with weak ties, social production, egalitarianism and mutual service, and how business processes may profit from these principles.
- *Second International Workshop on Cross-Enterprise Collaboration (CEC 2011)* – organized by Daniel Oppenheim, Francisco Curbera, Frank Leymann, Dimka Karastoyanova, Alex Norta, and Lav R. Varshney.

CEC 2011 explored the management, coordination, and optimization of complex end-to-end processes carried out collaboratively by people across enterprise boundaries. The goal of the workshop was to foster research in the emerging area of cross-enterprise collaboration.

- *Second International Workshop on Empirical Research in Business Process Management (ER-BPM 2011)* – organized by Bela Mutschler, Jan Recker, and Roel Wieringa.

ER-BPM 2011 stimulated empirical research aimed at the better understanding of the problems, challenges, and existing solutions in the BPM field. The workshop provided an interdisciplinary forum for both researchers and practitioners.

- *5th International Workshop on Event-Driven Business Process Management (edBPM 2011)* – organized by Nenad Stojanovic, Opher Etzion, Adrian Paschke, and Christian Janiesch.

edBPM 2011 continued its tradition of previous editions in exchanging novel ideas, methods, tools, and solutions for event-driven BPM, with the main goal to connect research and industry in better understanding what can be done from the research point of view and what is the need from the industry/business point of view.

- *First International Workshop on Process Model Collections (PMC 2011)* – organized by Hajo Reijers, Marcello La Rosa, and Remco Dijkman.

PMB 2011 aimed to attract novel research in the area of business process model collections. Among its topics, we find concerns related to process model repositories such as version management, efficient storage, querying, and retrieval of process models.

- *First International Workshop on Process-Aware Logistics Systems (PALS 2011)* – organized by Nejib Ben Hadj-Alouane, Ramzi Hammami, Samir Tata, and Moez Yeddes.

PALS 2011 dealt with problems related to the design and optimization of global logistics systems, from a business process management perspective. It is dedicated to exploring and mastering the tools needed for operating, reconfiguring and, in general, making decisions within logistics-based systems.

- *4th International Workshop on Process-Oriented Information Systems in Healthcare (ProHealth 2011)* – organized by Mor Peleg, Richard Lenz, and Manfred Reichert.

ProHealth 2011 focused on the potential and the limitations of IT support for healthcare processes. The workshop provided a forum wherein challenges, paradigms, and tools for optimized process support in healthcare were debated.

- *Second International Workshop on Reuse in Business Process Management (rBPM 2011)* – organized by Marcelo Fantinato, Maria Beatriz Felgar de Toledo, Itana Maria de Souza Gimenes, Lucinéia Heloisa Thom, and Cirano Iochpe.

rBPM 2011 focused on exploring any type of reuse in the BPM domain at its various levels: the basic service-oriented foundation level; the service composition level; the management and monitoring upper level; and, the quality of service and semantics orthogonal level.

- *Second International Workshop on Traceability and Compliance of Semi-Structured Processes (TC4SP 2011)* – organized by Francisco Curbera, Frank Leymann, Hamid Motahari Nezhad, and Beth Plale.

TC4SP 2011 focused on processes whose lifecycle is not fully driven by a formal process model and a business process management system (BPMS). These processes do not benefit from the advantages of BPMSs, but have the same need for transparency, monitoring, compliance management, and root cause analysis capabilities as fully structured processes.

- *First International Workshop on Workflow Security Audit and Certification (WfSAC 2011)* – organized by Rafael Accorsi and Wil van der Aalst.

WfSAC 2011 brought together researchers working on innovative, well-founded methods for workflow security audit and certification and industry applying these methods in practical cases.

With these 12 workshops, the BPM 2011 workshop program was the largest workshop program in the history of the conference. Yet, as the unexpectedly large participation in the workshop day testifies (more than 210 registered attendees for all the workshops together), the selected workshops formed an extraordinary and balanced program of high-quality events. We are confident the reader will enjoy this volume as much as we enjoyed organizing this outstanding program and assembling its proceedings.

Of course, we did not organize everything on our own. Many people of the BPM 2011 Organizing Committee contributed to the success of the workshop program. We would particularly like to thank the General Chairs, Farouk Toumani and Mohand-Said Hacid, for involving us in this unique event, the Organizing Chairs, Michel Schneider and Raoul Medina, for the smooth management of all on-site issues, the workshop organizers for managing their workshops and diligently answering the wealth of emails we sent around, and, finally, the authors for presenting their research and work at the BPM 2011 workshops and actually making all this possible.

September 2011   Florian Daniel
                                                       Kamel Barkaoui
                                                     Schahram Dustdar

Preface

The following preface is a collection of the prefaces of the post-workshop proceedings of the individual workshops. The actual workshop papers, grouped by event, form the body of these volumes.

7th International Workshop on Business Process Design (BPD 2011)

Organizers: Marta Indulska, Michael Rosemann, and Michael zur Muehlen

The 2011 International Workshop on Business Process Design (BPD) was the seventh consecutive workshop in its series, organized in conjunction with the 9th International Conference on Business Process Management, held in Clermont-Ferrand, France, 2011. The workshop was born out of the recognition that designing a process that improves organizational performance is a challenging task that requires a plethora of inputs (for example, organizational strategies, goals, constraints, and IT capabilities, to name a few). This task is the most value-adding step in the process lifecycle, yet it has attracted only limited academic contributions thus far. Accordingly, since the workshop's inception in 2005, the workshop has provided a forum for researchers interested in all aspects of design, innovation, evaluation, and comparison of process improvement techniques and tools.

The BPD 2011 proceedings represent a collection of six excellent research papers that were presented in extended presentation and discussion sessions during the BPM2011 conference. The paper selection was based on a rigorous double-blind process, which resulted in a 32% acceptance rate. As Organizing Chairs of the BPD workshop, we would like to sincerely thank the Program Committee for their thorough reviews of BPD2011 submissions. We would like to extend our thanks to the authors for their presentations, and to all participants of the workshop for their comments on the presented papers. We would also like to thank Hajo Reijers, Eindhoven University of Technology, Germany, for his insightful keynote presentation.

September 2011

Marta Indulska
Michael Rosemann
Michael zur Muehlen

Program Committee

7th International Workshop on Business Process Intelligence (BPI 2011)

Organizers: Boudewijn van Dongen, Diogo R. Ferreira, and Barbara Weber

Business process intelligence (BPI) is an area that is quickly gaining interest and importance in industry and research. BPI refers to the application of various measurement and analysis techniques in the area of business process management. In practice, BPI is embodied in tools for managing process execution quality by offering several features such as analysis, prediction, monitoring, control, and optimization.

The goal of this workshop is to promote a better understanding of the techniques and algorithms to support business processes at design-time and the way they are handled at run-time. We aim to bring together practitioners and researchers from different communities, e.g., business process management, information systems, database systems, business administration, software engineering, artificial intelligence, and data mining, who share an interest in the analysis and optimization of business processes and process-aware information systems. The workshop aims at discussing the current state of ongoing research and sharing practical experiences, exchanging ideas, and setting up future research directions that better respond to real needs. In a nutshell, it serves as a forum for shaping the BPI area.

The seventh edition of this workshop attracted 16 international submissions. Each paper was reviewed by at least three members of the Program Committee. From these submissions, the top five were accepted as full papers and, in addition, another five interesting submissions were accepted as short papers for presentation at the workshop.

The papers presented at the workshop provide a mix of novel research ideas, practical applications of BPI, as well as new tool support. Ailenei, Rozinat, Eckert, and van der Aalst are motivated by the need for a systematic comparison of existing process mining tools, and their work presents a list of process mining use cases as a first step toward an evaluation framework. Swinnen, Depair, Jens, and Vanhoef present a case study on the use of process mining together with association rule mining for analyzing deviating cases. Clase and Poels describe a method to merge separate log files coming from different systems. Trkman et al. investigate the relationship between business analytics and supply chain performance. Ferreira and Alves present an approach for finding communities in the social network of process participants by means of clustering. Barba, Weber, and Del Valle introduce an approach for assisting users during process execution through a recommendation system that considers both the control-flow and the resource perspectives. Aiolli, Burratin, and Sperduti propose a metric for the comparison of business process models, which is based on the relations defined for the algorithm. Leyer and Moormann suggest the combination of process mining techniques and statistical methods to evaluate customer integration in service processes. Luengo and Sepúlveda apply clustering for the detection of different versions of a business process. Finally, Damer, Jans, Depaire, and Vanhoof propose a new compliance analysis approach based on clustering the log into homogeneous groups.

For the first time this year, the workshop was accompanied by a challenge, for which researchers and practitioners were asked to apply any BPI technique of their disposal to a real-life dataset of a Dutch academic hospital in order to get insights into the treatment processes of that hospital. We invited a jury to rank the proposals and our sponsors – Pallas Athena and Futura Process Intelligence – provided the prizes for the two best submissions.

The BPI challenge attracted three international submissions which were ranked by a jury consisting of practitioners and researchers, as well as the owner of the dataset. The jury unanimously ranked the submissions, which resulted in Filip Caron and J.C. Bose winning the challenge and receiving an iPad 2 each. These proceedings contain a two-page abstract of the two winning submissions. The jury particularly liked the fact that both authors stepped outside of the BPI domain and included knowledge from the medical domain in order to come to certain conclusions. This clearly showed that real-life analysis cannot be done only from within the academic walls, but that the strong relation between researchers and practitioners is and will stay particularly important in the field of BPI.

These proceedings additionally contain the Process Mining Manifesto, which has been jointly developed by more than 70 scientists, consultants, software vendors, and end-users in the BPI area. As part of this workshop, a meeting of the IEEE task-force was held, during which the content of the Process Mining Manifesto was discussed. This document aims to promote the area of process mining and provides a set of guiding principles and challenges.

As with previous editions of the workshop, we hope that reader will find this selection of papers useful to keep track of the latest advances in the area of BPI, and we look forward to keep bringing new advances in future editions of the BPI workshop.

September 2011   Boudewijn van Dongen
                                            Diogo R. Ferreira
                                            Barbara Weber

Program Committee

Wil van der Aalst	Eindhoven University of Technology, The Netherlands
Ana Karla Alves de Medeiros	Capgemini Consulting, The Netherlands
Gerardo Canfora	University of Sannio, Italy
Malu Castellanos	HP, USA
Peter Dadam	University of Ulm, Germany
Boudewijn van Dongen	Eindhoven University of Technology, The Netherlands
Diogo R. Ferreira	Technical University of Lisbon, Portugal
Walid Galoul	Insitut Telecom, France
Gianluigi Greco	University of Calabria, Italy
Daniela Grigori	University of Versailles, France
Antonella Guzzo	University of Calabria, Italy
Joachim Herbst	DaimlerChrysler Research and Technology, Germany
Chen Li	University of Twente, The Netherlands
Jan Mendling	Humbolt University, Germany
Jürgen Moormann	Frankfurt School of Finance and Management, Germany
Oscar Pastor Lopez	Universidad Politécnica de Valencia, Spain
Manfred Reichert	University of Ulm, Germany
Anne Rozinat	Fluxicon, The Netherlands
Pnina Soffer	Haifa University, Israel
Alessandro Sperduti	University of Padua, Italy
Barbara Weber	Innsbruck University, Austria
Hans Weigand	Infolab, Tilburg University, The Netherlands
Ton Weijters	Technical University of Eindhoven, The Netherlands
Mathias Weske	Hasso Plattner Institute at University of Potsdam, Germany

4th International Workshop on Business Process Management and Social Software (BPMS2 2011)

Organizers: Selmin Nurcan and Rainer Schmidt

Social software[1] is a new paradigm that is spreading quickly in society, organizations, and economics. Social software has created a multitude of success stories such as wikipedia.org and the development of the Linux operating system. Therefore, more and more enterprises regard social software as a means for further improvement of their business processes and business models. For example, they integrate their customers into product development by using blogs to capture ideas for new products and features. Thus, business processes have to be adapted to new communication patterns between customers and the enterprise: for example, the communication with the customer is increasingly a bi-directional communication with the customer and among the customers. Social software also offers new possibilities to enhance business processes by improving the exchange of knowledge and information, to speed up decisions, etc.

Social software is based on four principles: weak ties, social production, egalitarianism, and mutual service provisioning.

- *Weak Ties*[2]: Weak ties are spontaneously established contacts between individuals that create new views and allow combining of competencies. Social software supports the creation of weak ties by supporting the creation of contacts on impulse between non-predetermined individuals.
- *Social Production*[3,4]: Social production is the creation of artifacts, by combining the input from independent contributors without predetermining the way to do this. By this means it is possible to integrate new and innovative contributions not identified or planned in advance. Social mechanisms such as reputation assure quality in social production in an a posteriori approach by enabling a collective evaluation by all participants.
- *Egalitarianism*: Egalitarianism is the attitude of handling individuals equally. Social software highly relies on egalitarianism and therefore strives to give all participants the same rights to contribute. This is done with the intention to encourage a maximum of contributors and to get the best solution fusioning

---

[1] R. Schmidt and S. Nurcan, "BPM and Social Software," Business Process Management Workshops, 2009, pp. 649-658.

[2] M.S. Granovetter, "The Strength of Weak Ties," American Journal of Sociology, vol. 78, 1973, S. 1360.

[3] Y. Benkler, The Wealth of Networks: How Social Production Transforms Markets and Freedom, Yale University Press, 2006.

[4] J. Surowiecki, The Wisdom of Crowds, Anchor, 2005.

a high number of contributions, thus enabling the wisdom of the crowds. Social software realizes egalitarianism by abolishing hierarchical structures, merging the roles of contributors and consumers, and introducing a culture of trust.

– *Mutual Service Provisioning*: Social software abolishes the separation of service provider and consumer by introducing the idea that service provisioning is a mutual process of service exchange. Thus both service provider and consumer (or better prosumer) provide services to one another in order to co-create value. This mutual service provisioning contrasts with the idea of industrial service provisioning, where services are produced in separation from the customer to achieve scaling effects.

To date, the interaction of social software and its underlying paradigms with business processes have not been investigated in depth. Therefore, the objective of the workshop was to explore how social software interacts with business process management, how business process management has to change to comply with weak ties, social production, egalitarianism and mutual service, and how business processes may profit from these principles.

The workshop discussed three topics:

1. New opportunities provided by social software for BPM
2. Engineering next generation of business processes: BPM 2.0?
3. Business process implementation support by social software

Based on the successful BPMS2 2008, BPMS2 2009, BPMS2 2010 workshop, the goal of this workshop was to promote the integration of business process management with social software and to enlarge the community pursuing the theme.

We wish to thank all authors for having shared their work with us, as well as the members of the BPMS2 2011 Program Committee and the workshop organizers of BPM 2011 for their help with the organization of the workshop.

September 2011   Selmin Nurcan
                                                                   Rainer Schmidt

Program Committee

Ilia Bider	IbisSoft, Sweden
Jan Bosch	Intuit, Mountain View, California, USA
Dragan Gasevic	Athabasca University, Canada
Rania Khalaf	IBM T.J. Watson Research Center, USA
Ralf Klamma	RWTH Aachen, Germany
Agnes Koschmider	Karlsruhe Institute of Technology, Germany
Sai Peck Lee	University of Malaya, Kuala Lumpur, Malaysia
Gustaf Neumann	Vienna University of Economics and Business Administration, Austria
Selmin Nurcan	University Paris 1 Pantheon Sorbonne, France
Andreas Oberweis	Karlsruhe Institute of Technology, Germany
Gil Regev	EPFL & Itecor, Switzerland
Michael Rosemann	Queensland University of Technology, Australia
Rainer Schmidt	University of Applied Sciences, Aalen, Germany
Miguel-Ángel Sicilia	University of Alcalá, Madrid, Spain
Pnina Soffer	University of Haifa, Israel
Markus Strohmaier	Graz University of Technology, Austria
Karsten Wendland	University of Applied Sciences, Aalen, Germany

Second International Workshop on Cross-Enterprise Collaboration (CEC 2011)

Organizers: Alexander H. Norta, Daniel V. Oppenheim, Lav R. Varshney, Francisco Curbera, Dimka Karastoyanova, and Frank Leymann

On August 29, 2011, the Second International Workshop on Cross-Enterprise Collaboration (CEC) was held as part of the 9th International Conference on Business Process Management (BPM 2011) in Clermont-Ferrand, France.

Cross-enterprise collaboration (CEC) occurs when two or more organizations collaborate to realize a common goal. The move of process, work, and operations from an organization-centric environment to a collaborative ecosystem of partners and providers is becoming pervasive because many organizations find they can no longer develop all the required innovation in-house or lack necessary capabilities. Sharing the financial cost and overall risk is another important incentive for collaboration, especially in projects with a high degree of uncertainty that may require frequent change and adaptation.

The workshop focused on how to reconcile the continuum from rather informal to very strongly formalized CEC models in which the collaborating organizations utilize organization-bridging choreographies to connect with partner and/or provider in-house business processes for carrying out sourced transactions to achieve the collaboration's goal. The workshop goal was to provide a venue for academics and practitioners to establish a community for CEC with future expansion potential. Consequently, the workshop identified the state of the art, core research challenges, enterprise-collaboration models, corresponding architectures, frameworks, or methodologies.

The first workshop keynote was presented by Hamid Motahari Nezhad from HP Labs, Palo Alto, who discussed CEC in the context of multi-sourced service engagements and outlined a vision and conceptual architecture for offering the supporting technology for CEC as a service. Then there was a keynote presentation by Alex Kass from Accenture Technology Labs. This talk identified collaboration between people and between systems as two pillars of any CEC and presented a vision for a CEC platform in which technology support for knowledge sharing, process sharing, and data coupling has to be offered. The final part of the keynote talks was from Alex Norta on the completed EU-FP6 CrossWork research project on which a recently published book in the Springer *Information Systems* series was based. In this approach external processes could be defined and utilized by the collaborating organizations and then mapped to individual organizations through a layer of conceptual processes.

The subsequent paper presentations covered the following areas. First, an approach was shown by Christian Pichler et al. for creating conflict-free updates of UN/CEFACT-based cross-organizational modeling consensus. The second presentation by Jorge Roa et al. was about using colored Petri-net notation for designing collaborative business processes. The advantage of this approach is the availability of established formal verification techniques. Finally, a paper by Stefan Mutke et al. about a service-provision framework based on prior analysis and deconstruction of customer requirements focused on how to set up enterprise collaborations from the logistics domain.

September 2011

Alexander H. Norta
Daniel V. Oppenheim
Lav R. Varshney
Francisco Curbera
Dimka Karastoyanova
Frank Leymann

Program Committee

Ram Akella	University of California, Santa Cruz, USA
Rama Akkiraju	IBM Research, USA
Vasilios Andrikopoulos	Tilburg University, The Netherlands
Christoph Dorn	Vienna University of Technology, Austria
Marta Indulska	University of Queensland, Australia
Alex Kass	Accenture Technology Labs, USA
Jim Laredo	IBM Research, USA
Grace Lewis	Carnegie Mellon University, USA
Heiko Ludwig	IBM Research, USA
Daniel Schall	Vienna University of Technology, Austria
Jianwen Su	University of California, Santa Barbara, USA
Liang Zhang	Fudan University, China

Second International Workshop on Empirical Research in Business Process Management (ER-BPM 2011)

Organizers: Bela Mutschler, Jan Recker, and Roel Wieringa

In an effort to manage and improve business processes to enable business benefits, *business process management* (BPM) heavily relies on the use of IT-based systems. Past years have seen the emergence of holistic enterprise resource planning systems, automated workflow systems, process design tools, expert systems, virtual collaboration systems and business rule systems as process-aware information systems that enable process change and management and thereby contribute to business value generation.

BPM research has traditionally taken one of two forms. One vein of BPM research has focused on the development and extension of associated tools, methods, standards, and technologies. The other vein of BPM research has been concerned with evaluating the suitability of existing BPM technology, to build informed opinions about qualities and deficiencies of BPM practices and tools.

Over recent years, we have witnessed a growing demand for insights or evaluations of BPM technology based on dedicated empirical research strategies. Such research has only recently gained prominence in the community but is now firmly established as an important strand of research around the use of BPM, as evidenced, for example, by dedicated journal special issues on this topic[5]. The benefits of empirical research include improved problem understanding and improved insight into the performance of techniques in practice. These benefits have been demonstrated in areas like software engineering (e.g., in the context of software development processes or code reviews), information systems (e.g., in the form of theories of acceptance and use of information systems), or, indeed, business (e.g., in studies of organizational performance) for a long time, we believe, and are still under-represented in the academic field of BPM, notwithstanding the efforts made to date.

The Workshop

The Second International Workshop on Empirical Research in Business Process Management (ER-BPM 2011) set out to be a premier forum for researchers to address the demand for further empirical research, and sought to stimulate

---

[5] Recker, J., Mutschler, B., Wieringa, R.: Empirical Research in Business Process Management: Introduction to the Special Issue. in: *Inf. Syst. E-Business Management*, 9(3), pp. 303-306 (2011).

empirical research that, in turn, can contribute to a better understanding of the problems, challenges, and existing solutions in the BPM field.

In particular, the workshop provides an interdisciplinary forum for both researchers and practitioners to improve the understanding of BPM-specific requirements, methods and theories, tools and techniques. Therefore, the workshop deals with different facets of applying and using BPM methods and technologies and strives to provide new insights into the challenges, applications, and perspectives emerging for BPM technology.

ER-BPM 2011 was the follow-up workshop of a very successful first ER-BPM workshop that took place in Ulm (Germany) in conjunction with BPM 2009. The papers from this workshop appeared as part of a dedicated book series[6], and the best papers were also published as extended articles as part of a journal special issue[1].

The Papers in a Nutshell

At ER-BPM 2011, we accepted six papers for presentation. These articles provide a snapshot of current examples for how empirical research in BPM can be conducted, and what insights such research can uncover.

The paper by Houy et. al investigates theoretical foundations of empirical BPM research based on conceptual considerations and a review of empirical BPM literature. Their analysis clearly shows that empirical BPM research is only to a certain extent guided by existing theory. Furthermore, it can be seen that the investigated contributions often refer to theories originating from other different fields of research, like economics or sociology.

The paper by Michelberger et. al investigates fundamental issues related to process-oriented information logistics based on two exploratory case studies in the automotive and the clinical domain. Additionally, they present results of an online survey with 219 participants supporting the case study findings. Their research does not only reveal different types of process information, but also allows for the derivation of factors determining its relevance. Understanding such factors, in turn, is a fundamental prerequisite to realize effective process-oriented information logistics.

In the third paper, Luebbe and Weske present a new technique for process co-creation with domain experts called tangible business process modeling. More specifically, they present not only results of a laboratory experiment in which the method is applied, they also illustrate how they used action research in two further studies in which groups modeled BPMN and EPCs using tangible tiles on a table.

Soffer et. al propose to study the process of process modeling based on problem-solving theories. Specifically, their work takes the approach that problems are first

---

[6] Rinderle-Ma, S., Sadiq, S.W., Leymann, F.: Business Process Management Workshops - BPM 2009 International Workshops. in: Lecture Notes in Business Information Processing, 43, Springer, Ulm (2009).

conceptualized as mental models, to which solution methods are applied. The paper then suggests that investigating these two phases can help understand and hence improve the semantic and syntactic quality of process models. Specifically, the paper reports on an empirical study addressing the mental model created during process model development, demonstrating the feasibility of such studies. It then suggests designs for other studies that follow this direction.

The paper by Pinggera et. al introduces the formal concept of a phase diagram through which the modeling process can be analyzed, and a corresponding implementation to study a modeler's sequence of actions. In an experiment building on these assets, they observed a group of modelers engaging in the act of modeling. Collected data are used to demonstrate their approach for analyzing the process of process modeling.

Finally, the paper by Pichler et. al investigates in an experimental setting whether either the imperative or the declarative process modeling approach is superior with respect to process model understanding. Their study finds that imperative process modeling languages appear to be connected with better understanding.

September 2011

Bela Mutschler
Jan Recker
Roel Wieringa

Program Committee

Jorg Becker	European Research Center for Information Systems, Germany
Ralph Bobrik	Universität Ulm, Germany
Maya Daneva	University of Twente, The Netherlands
Peter Fettke	German Research Center for Artificial Intelligence, Germany
Wolfram Höpken	University of Applied Sciences Ravensburg-Weingarten, Germany
Marta Indulska	University of Queensland, Australia
Ralf Laue	University of Leipzig, Germany
Stephanie Meerkamm	University of Bayreuth, Germany
Jan Mendling	Vienna University of Economics and Business Administration, Austria
Bela Mutschler (Co-chair)	University of Applied Sciences Ravensburg-Weingarten, Germany
Michael Prilla	Ruhr-Universität Bochum, Germany
Jan Recker (Co-chair)	Queensland University of Technology, Australia
Manfred Reichert	University of Ulm, Germany
Hajo A. Reijers	Eindhoven University of Technology, The Netherlands
Stefan Seidal	Universität Liechtenstein, Liechtenstein
Roel Wieringa (Co-chair)	University of Twente, The Netherlands
Barbara Weber	Innsbruck University, Austria

5th International Workshop on Event-Driven Business Process Management (edBPM 2011)

Organizers: Opher Etzion, Adrian Paschke, Christian Janiesch, and Nenad Stojanovic

Event-driven computing is gaining ever-increasing attention from industry and the research community and this workshop shows its importance in the business process management domain. We had more than 15 submissions almost uniformly spread over industry and academic communities. Topics ranged from modeling data-intensive processes to various types of monitoring business processes. Events have become first-class citizens in BPM, enabling novel real-time applications on top of the business process execution. However, there is still much to be done, especially in the context of unified terminology and conceptualization (e.g., what is an event in BPM).

We selected nine papers for presentation although, almost all of the submissions contained very interesting material for this kind of workshop and we would like to thank all authors for their great job.

We also thank to the members of the Program Committee for very constructive reviews, which helped authors improve their work.

September 2011

Opher Etzion
Adrian Paschke
Christian Janiesch
Nenad Stojanovic

Program Committee

Rama Akkiraju	IBM Research, USA
Alexandre Alves	Oracle Corp., USA
Pedro Bizarro	University of Coimbra, Portugal
Schahram Dustdar	Vienna University of Technology, Austria
Dimka Karastoyanova	University of Stuttgart, Germany
Agnes Koschmider	Karlsruhe Institute of Technology, Germany
Jim Laredo	IBM Research, USA
Mack Mackenzie	Starview, USA
Gregoris Mentzas	National Technical University of Athens, Greece
Prabir Nandi	IBM Research, USA
Marco Seiriö	RuleCore, Sweden
Guy Sharon	IBM Research, USA
Ljijana Stojanovic	Karlsruhe Institute of Technology, Germany
Jan Vanthienen	Katholieke Universiteit Leuven, Belgium

First International Workshop on Process Model Collections (PMC 2011)

Organizers: Hajo Reijers, Marcello La Rosa, and Remco Dijkman

Nowadays, as organizations reach higher levels of business process management maturity, they tend to collect large repositories of business process models. It is quite common that such collections of industry-strength business process models include thousands of activities and related business objects such as data, applications, risks, etc. These models are increasingly published over an intranet to a large number of stakeholders with varying skills and responsibilities. In that sense, it may not come as a surprise that many organizations struggle to manage such high volumes of complex process models. The problem is exacerbated by overlapping content across models, poor version management, process models that are used simultaneously for different purposes, the use of different modeling notations such as EPCs, BPMN, etc. In light of these challenges, the aim of the First Workshop on Process Model Collections was to present and discuss novel research in the area of business process model collections.

Topics and Papers

The workshop attracted 14 paper submissions. Each of these submissions was reviewed by at least three Program Committee members. After receiving the reviews, eight papers were accepted for presentation at the workshop. In addition a keynote speaker was invited.

The papers address various topics in the area of process model collections, in particular:

- Similarity of process models
- Clustering of process models
- Variability management and consolidation of process model collections
- Configurable models as a means to consolidate process model collections
- Process log collections in addition to process model collections
- Novel concepts and technology to share process model collections
- Navigating process model collections
- Relations between process models
- Frameworks to organize process model collections
- Searching process models in a collection

The keynote (1) on "Consolidated Management of Business Process Variants" by Marlon Dumas compares three different approaches for consolidating a collection of similar process models: consolidation based on shared subprocesses, consolidation based on configurable process models, and consolidation based on model synchronization. "Towards Cross-Organizational Process Mining in Collections of Process Models and Their Executions" by Joos Buijs, Boudewijn van Dongen, and Wil van der Aalst (2) presents a means to join process model collections

Table 1. Topics of the workshop and related papers

Topic	1	2	3	4	5	6	7	8	9
Similarity	X				X				
Clustering			X						
Consolidation	X					X			
Configurable Models	X					X			
Log Collections		X							
Sharing Models				X					
Navigation									X
Process Relations								X	
Organizing Models							X		
Search		X							

with process log collections. By joining these two, questions can be answered like "Which process model in the collection best reflects the behavior of my organization." "Activity-Oriented Clustering Techniques in Large Process and Compliance Rule Repositories" by Stefanie Rinderle-Ma, Sonja Kabicher, and Thao Ly (3) presents techniques for clustering both process models and rules. Clustering allows more efficient checking of rules on a process model collection. "An Open Process Model Library" by Rami-Habib Eid-Sabbagh, Matthias Kunze, and Mathias Weske (4) presents novel concepts and techniques for sharing process model collections, which it calls "process libraries." "Analyzing Differences Between Business Process Similarity Measures" by Michael Becker and Ralf Laue (5) presents an analysis of 22 different process similarity metrics that have been proposed until now. "Comparing Business Processes to Determine the Feasibility of Configurable Models: A Case Study" by Jan Vogelaar, Eric Verbeek, Borana Luka, and Wil van der Aalst (6) presents an analysis of the extent to which process similarity metrics can be used to determine how process models in a collection can be consolidated by means of configurable process models. "Industry Operations Architecture for Business Process Model Collections" by Jorge Sanz, Ying Tat Leung, Ignacio Terrizzano, Valeria Becker, Susanne Glissmann, Joseph Kramer, and Guang-Jie Ren (7) presents a framework for organizing process model collections. "On Formalizing Inter-process Relationships" by Tri Kurniawan, Aditya Ghose, Lam-Son Lê, and Hoa Khanh Dam (8) discusses and formalizes the different relations that process models in a collection can have with each other. "Navigating in Process Model Collections: A New Approach Inspired by Google Earth" by Markus Hipp, Bela Mutschler, and Manfred Reichert (9) presents a novel way to navigate process model collections. Thus, the papers that are presented at the workshop address the topics outlined above as shown in Table 1.

September 2011

Hajo Reijers
Marcello La Rosa
Remco Dijkman

Program Committee

First International Workshop on Process-Aware Logistics Systems (PALS 2011)

Organizers: Nejib Ben Hadj-Alouane, Ramzi Hammami, Samir Tata, and Moez Yeddes

The PALS workshop spanned one day and intended to bring together researchers and practitioners from BPM and logistics systems communities to discuss the key issues related to the design and optimization of global logistics systems, from a BPM perspective. It was dedicated to exploring and mastering the tools needed for operating, reconfiguring, and, in general, making decisions within logistics-based systems, in order to provide the customers and system users with the greatest possible value.

Operationally, the PALS workshop was grouped into two topics: BPM in logistics systems and optimization of global logistics systems using BPM.

BPM in Logistics Systems

The first topic of the workshop included three full papers.

- On the Modeling of Healthcare Workflows Using Recursive ECATNets
- Negotiating Deadline Constraints in Inter-Organizational Logistic Systems: A Healthcare Case Study
- Configurable Process Models for Logistics: Case Study for Customs Clearance Processes

The first paper claims that logistic processes in healthcare systems (or careflows) are highly flexible and extremely dynamic. To deal with theses issues, the authors proposed to take advantage of the description power of recursive ECATNets for realizing flexible workflows in the healthcare domain. The benefit of such modeling is that soundness verification of these workflows can be obtained via model checking techniques.

The second paper argues that current logistics methods are more focused on strategic goals and do not deal with short-term objectives, such as, reactivity and real-time constraints. The authors propose to apply inter-organizational workflows for automating logistic procedures in a collaborative context. As a proof of concept they consider a case study of a healthcare process and focus on the negotiations aspects of temporal constraints in critical situations.

The third paper discusses the main challenges for the use of configurable process models in logistics systems and describes some future work. It proposes to use configurable process models in logistics systems and analyzes and creates a set of process models for customs clearance services for import and export processes and delivers the configurable process model out of these models.

The Optimization of Global Logistics Systems Using BPM

The second topic of the workshop included five full papers.

- A Formal Framework for Cooperative Logistics Management
- Linear Integer Programming for the Home Healthcare Problem
- Evolutionary Algorithm for Scheduling Production Jobs and Preventive Maintenance Activities
- On the Modeling of Logistics Decisions Impact on Product Greenness: Sensitivity Analysis
- A Mathematical Model for Global Supplier Selection

The first paper discusses transportation sharing and vehicle routing within the context of green cooperative logistics for the purpose of reducing carbon emissions and satisfying product delivery deadlines. The author addresses the use of a symbolic calculus permitting users of a large logistics-sharing system to reason about vehicle routes and delivery demands while being aware of carbon emission reductions. We note that this calculus bares resemblance to declarative workflow languages.

The second paper discusses business processes that address vehicle routing and nurse assignment for the purpose of providing healthcare services, at home, for the elderly, and/or disabled persons. This paper addresses a problem that is increasingly gaining importance in today's modern societies. The paper gives a mathematical model for the process and addresses resource assignment and scheduling issues. The third paper discusses a scheduling problem combining production operations as well as preventive maintenance tasks. The paper provides an evolutionary heuristics for producing schedules that aim to reduce the cost of maintenance while optimizing the completion dates of the production operations.

The fourth paper addresses the problem of providing a model for global supply chains that aims to optimize the environmental impacts of production, within the context of current legislation, while still maximizing profit making. A nice application of the model is provided for the case of a textile manufacturing operation. The paper focuses on issues related to the sensitivity of the results with respect to small changes in the problem parameters.

The last paper in this second workshop topic deals with the problem of supplier selection within the context of global logistics chains. The paper deals with this problem by providing a framework for integrating inventory and transportation activities. A multi-stage process is provided for dealing with the supplier selection problem.

Concluding Remarks

At the end of the workshop we conducted a brainstorming session inviting PALS participants to identify research issues and ideas which they consider to be at the forefront of attention when considering process-aware logistics systems. The main areas of research that stemmed from this discussion are the following:

- Focusing on suitable business process models integrating activities and re- sources, suitable for capturing logistics systems and problems
- Identifying appropriate workflow patterns for modeling logistics
- Developing tools for transforming workflow models, semi-automatically, into mathematical models that allow for the application of optimizations techniques

The participants showed considerable enthusiasm related to inciting research in the business process area that has a direct impact on modern industrial environments.

We thank all our authors and participants for their valuable contributions. We are also grateful to our Program Committee members who helped us in evaluating the papers for this workshop. Furthermore, we would like to thank the BPM Workshop Chairs and all the BPM organizers for making this event possible.

September 2011

Nejib Ben Hadj-Alouane
Ramzi Hammami
Samir Tata
Moez Yeddes

Program Committee

Michele Angelaccio	University of Rome, TorVergata, Italy
Karim Baïna	ENSIAS of Rab, Morocco
Atidel Ben Hadj Alouane	ENIT, Tunisia
Saif Benjaafar	University of Minnesota, USA
Malika Boukala	USTHB of Alger, Algeria
François Charoy	Nancy University, France
Naoufel Cheikhrouhou	EPFL, Switzerland
Anis Chelbi	ESSTT, Tunisia
Maria Di Mascolo	University of Grenoble, France
Alexandre Dolgui	Ecole des Mines de Saint-Etienne, France
Schahram Dustdar	Vienna University of Technology, Vita Lab, Austria
Samir Elhedhli	University of Ottawa, Canada
Yannick Frein	INPG, Grenoble, France
Walid Gaaloul	Institut Telecom, Telecom SudParis, France
Sveinn Gudmundsson	Toulouse Business School, France
Fatma Gzara	University of Waterloo, Canada
Mohamed Jmaiel	University of Sfax, Tunisia
Imed Kacem	Université Paul Verlaine Metz, France
Mohamed Khalgui	Xidian University, China
Kais Klai	University of Paris 13
Nikolay Mehandjiev	University of Manchester, UK
Sébastien Mitraille	Toulouse Business School, France
Uche Okongwu	Toulouse Business School, France
Olivier Perrin	University of Nancy 2, France
Sumitra Reddy	West Virginia University, USA
Nidhal Rezg	University of Metz, France
Ingo M. Weber	University of New South Wales, Australia

4th International Workshop on Process-Oriented Information Systems in Healthcare (ProHealth 2011)

Organizers: Mor Peleg, Richard Lenz, and Manfred Reichert

Healthcare organizations and providers are facing the challenge of delivering high-quality services to their patients, at affordable costs. A high degree of specialization of medical disciplines, prolonged medical care for the ageing population, increased costs for dealing with chronic diseases, and the need for personalized healthcare are prevalent trends in this information-intensive domain. The emerging situation necessitates a change in the way healthcare is delivered to the patients and healthcare processes are managed.

BPM technology provides a key with which to implement these changes. Though patient-centered process support has become increasingly crucial in healthcare, BPM technology has not yet been broadly used in healthcare environments. This workshop elaborated on both the potential and the limitations of IT support for healthcare processes. It further provided a forum wherein challenges, paradigms, and tools for optimized process support in healthcare could be debated. We wanted to bring together researchers and practitioners from different communities (e.g., BPM, information systems, medical informatics, e-health) who share an interest in both healthcare processes and BPM technologies.

The success of the first three ProHealth Workshops, which were held in conjunction with the 5th, 6th, and 7th International Conferences on Business Process Management (BPM 2007, BPM 2008, and BPM 2009), demonstrated the potential of such an interdisciplinary forum to improve the understanding of domain-specific requirements, methods and theories, tools and techniques, and the gaps between IT support and healthcare processes that are yet to be closed, providing insights into the social and technological challenges, applications, and perspectives emerging for BPM in this context.

Enterprise-wide process-oriented information systems have been demanded by healthcare institutions for over 20 years and terms like "continuity of care" have even been discussed for over 50 years. Yet, healthcare organizations are currently using a plethora of specialized non-standard information systems and continue to focus on the development of systems for specialized departments that frequently only focus on their internal processes. Many of the successful existing information systems focus on non-process-oriented systems, such as imaging, drug order-entry, laboratory test result storage, storage of diagnoses and progress notes in electronic medical records, alerts and reminders, and billing applications.

Information systems and decision-support systems for managing patient care processes, however, are still scarcely developed; most often only by a small number of university-led teams. Such patient care management systems are highly complex and pose many challenges: they require availability of encoded data coming from different sources, flexibility in deviating from the encoded process at the discretion of the physician user, and may involve a team of clinical users that together take care of a patient in a coordinated way.

The recent trend toward healthcare networks and integrated care even increases the need to effectively support interdisciplinary cooperation along with the patient treatment process. Recent studies discussing the preventability of adverse events in medicine recommend the use of information technology, since insufficient communication and missing information turned out to be among the major factors contributing to adverse events. Yet, there is still a discrepancy between the potential and the actual usage of IT in healthcare.

The ProHealth 2011 workshop was held in Clermont-Ferrand, France, in conjunction with the 8th BPM Conference. It focused on IT support of high-quality healthcare processes. It addressed topics including the modeling of healthcare processes, conformance and compliance checks of clinical guidelines, adaptive healthcare processes, and process quality improvement as well as healthcare process security.

The workshop received 14 papers from Germany (7), South Korea (2), Canada (1), UK (1), Italy (1), Spain (1), and a paper with authors from the USA and The Netherlands. Papers had to clearly establish their research contribution as well as their relation to healthcare processes. Eight full papers were selected to be presented in the workshop according to their relevance, quality, and originality.

In his keynote paper "Context, Retrospection, and Prospection in Healthcare Process Definitions," Leon Osterweil from the Department of Computer Science at the University of Massachusetts, Amherst, discussed the execution of precise and complete formal definitions of healthcare processes in the Little-JIL formalism, focusing on how the process definition can be used to provide run-time information to guide process participants. This new focus has made it clear that more thought must be given to how to communicate with participants in order to assure more effective guidance. The work suggests that participants, especially human participants, will require that process-provided guidance be accompanied by context, history, and prospective information if the guidance is to be credible, acceptable, and ultimately useful.

The following three papers focus on conformance and compliance checks of clinical guidelines. The paper entitled "Reusing a Declarative Specification to Check the Conformance of Different CIGs" by Adela Grando, Wil van der Aalst, and Ronny Mans explored formal methods for checking whether computer-interpretable guidelines (CIGs) expressed in formal languages such as PROforma (previous work) and GLIF conform to declarative specifications of constraints that the guideline should obey. They started with a GLIF CIG that was automatically translated into a colored Petri net (CPN) and used CPN model-checking tools to establish conformance to a DECLARE specification of the guideline.

In the paper entitled "Conformance Checking of Executed Clinical Guidelines in Presence of Basic Medical Knowledge" Bottrighi, Chesani, Mello, Montali, Montani, and Terenziani explore the interaction between clinical guideline knowledge and basic medical knowledge from the viewpoint of the adherence of an observed CIG execution trace to both types of knowledge. They propose an approach based on the GLARE language to represent clinical guidelines, and on a homogeneous formalization of both clinical guidelines and basic medical knowledge using event calculus and its Prolog-based implementation REC, focusing on a posteriori conformance evaluation.

In the paper "Compliance-Oriented Process Management Using the Example of Clinical Trials," Jörg Schlundt and Stefan Jablonski provide an overview of compliance management in clinical trials, analyzing current scientific approaches and their shortcomings. To overcome the deficiencies, they present a framework for process-oriented compliance management, in which the extraction and modeling of compliance requirements are done in a process-oriented way. In addition they present a matching operator by which different compliance standards can be made comparable.

The next three papers focus on adaptive healthcare processes from different perspectives. Christoph Neumann, Peter Schwab, Andreas Wahl, and Richard Lenz present the "α-Adaptive" approach, which is intended to support runtime adaptability of metadata for document-based decentralized process management. The approach extends the α-Flow approach, which uses distributed case files (α-Docs) as a coordination platform for ad hoc cooperation among different healthcare organizations. The authors demonstrate how the metadata to annotate α-Docs can be extended on demand.

In the paper "Guarded Process Spaces (GPS): A Navigaton System Towards Creation and Dynamic Change of Healthcare Processes from the End-User's Perspective," Claudia Reuter, Peter Dadam, Stephan Rudolph, Wolfgang Deiters, and Simon Trillsch introduce a framework that enables user-defined processes based on a predefined set of possible processes. A guarded process space is to be seen as a roadmap that contains all possible processes. Specifying and modifying clinical pathways can be assisted based on that paradigm, as it is essentially just navigating through that roadmap.

The paper "Enabling YAWL to Handle Dynamic Operating Room Management" by Sebastian Schick, Holger Meyer, Markus Brandt, and Andreas Heuer addresses yet another approach to flexibility. The approach is aimed at achieving flexibility by monitoring data changes and specifying where corresponding process changes should take effect. The last two papers focus on process quality improvement and access control. In the paper "Developing a Process Quality Assessment Questionnaire – A Case Study on Writing Discharge Letters," Robert Heinrich, Barbara Paech, Antje Brandner, Ulrike Kutscha, and Bjoern Bergh propose a systematic approach to creating a questionnaire intended to detect business process quality problems. The approach is based on comprehensive standard catalogs of quality criteria for both processes and data. The case-based reduction of these criteria and the deduction of appropriate questions is exemplified by a case study on writing discharge letters.

The paper "A Personalized Access Control Framework for Workflow-Based Health Care Information" by Nazia Leyla and Wendy McCaull finally addresses the important issue of data security in healthcare. The approach presented in the paper is based on the assumption that patients should decide themselves who is allowed to see which data. The authors explain how such individual constraints can be enforced within the NOVA Workflow Management System.

We would like to thank all authors who submitted a paper to the ProHealth Workshop, including those whose papers were not accepted for presentation. We particularly thank the invited speaker as well as the members of the Program Committee and the reviewers for their efforts in selecting the papers (in αbetical order): Joseph Barjis, Oliver Bott, Adela Grando, Stefan Jablonski, Wendy Mc-Caull, Ronny Mans, Bela Mutschler, Oystein Nytro, Lee Osterweil, Hajo Reijers, Shazia Sadiq, Danielle Sent, Yuval Shahar, Ton Spil, Annette ten Teije, Paolo Terenziani, Lucineia Thom, Dongwen Wang, and Barbara Weber. They helped us to compile a high-quality program for the ProHealth 2011 workshop and contributed to improving the initial submissions by their recommendations to the authors. We would also like to acknowledge the splendid support of the local organization and the BPM 2011 Workshop Chairs.

We hope you will find the papers of the ProHealth 2011 workshop interesting and stimulating.

September 2011

Mor Peleg
Manfred Reichert
Richard Lenz

Program Committee

Joseph Barjis	Delft University of Technology, The Netherlands
Oliver Bott	Fachhochschule Hannover, Germany
Stefan Jablonski	University of Bayreuth, Germany
Adela Grando	University of Edinburgh, United Kingdom
Richard Lenz	Friedrich-Alexander University, Erlangen-Nuremberg, Germany
Wendy MacCaull	St. Francis Xavier University, Canada
Ronny Mans	Eindhoven University of Technology, The Netherlands
Silvia Miksch	Vienna University of Technology, Austria
Bela Mutschler	University of Applied Sciences Ravensburg-Weingarten, Germany
Oystein Nytro	Norwegian University of Science and Technology, Norway
Leon Osterweil	University of Massachusetts, USA
Mor Peleg	University of Haifa, Israel
Manfred Reichert	University of Ulm, Germany
Hajo Reijers	Eindhoven University of Technology, The Netherlands
Shazia Sadiq	University of Queensland, Australia
Danielle Sent	Universiteit van Amsterdam, The Netherlands

Second International Workshop on Reuse in Business Process Management (rBPM 2011)

Organizers: Marcelo Fantinato, Maria Beatriz Felgar de Toledo, Itana Maria de Souza Gimenes, Lucinéia Heloisa Thom, and Cirano Iochpe

The current complexity inherent in the corporative world demands a great dynamism from the IT infrastructure in order to provide technical solutions for conducting business. Business process management (BPM), including its service-oriented foundation, has been providing important technological support to improve organization competitiveness. In order to increase dynamism and competitiveness, BPM can benefit from reuse approaches and techniques at several stages of the business process life cycle.

The Second International Workshop on Reuse in Business Process Management was dedicated to exploring any type of reuse in the BPM domain. Therefore, it was a forum in which to discuss systematic reuse applied to BPM at its various levels:

1. The basic service-oriented foundation level—including issues such as service development, description, publication, discovery and selection
2. The service composition level—encompassing service negotiation and service aggregation
3. The management and monitoring upper level—including business process modeling, execution, monitoring, and contract establishment and enactment
4. The Quality of Service and Semantics orthogonal level

Moreover, the impact of reuse on business- and service-oriented engineering as well as how it can help in the design of more high-quality process models were very important topics to be discussed in this workshop.

Different existing reuse approaches and techniques can be extended to be applied to this fairly new domain, including: software product line or software product families; variability descriptors; design patterns such as feature modeling; aspect orientation; and component-based development. In addition, completely new approaches and techniques can be proposed. Their use must also be discussed, preferably under experimentation as well as results analysis.

We would like to thanks the PNPD and the SticAmSud Programs of the Coordenao de Aperfeioamento de Pessoal de Nivel Superior (CAPES) from the Brazilian government.

September 2011

Marcelo Fantinato
Maria Beatriz Felgar de Toledo
Itana Maria de Souza Gimenes
Lucinéia Heloisa Thom
Cirano Iochpe

Program Committee

Akhil Kumar	Penn State University, USA
Antonio Ruiz-Cortés	University of Seville, Spain
Alessandro F. Garcia	Pontifical Catholic University of Rio de Janeiro, Brazil
Barbara Weber	University of Innsbruck, Austria
Bertram Ludäscher	University of California at Davis, USA
Christoph Bussler	Saba Software, Inc., USA
Daniel A. Menasce	George Mason University, USA
Dennis Smith	Carnegie Mellon University, USA
Fernanda A. Baião	Federal University of Rio de Janeiro State, Brazil
Flávia M. Santoro	Federal University of Rio de Janeiro State, Brazil
Hajo Reijers	Eindhoven University of Technology, The Netherlands
Heiko Ludwig	IBM T.J. Watson Research Center, USA
Jaejoon Lee	Lancaster University, UK
Jan Bosch	Intuit, Inc., USA
Jan Mendling	WU Vienna, Institute for Information Business, Austria
João Porto de Albuquerque	University of São Paulo, Brazil
José Palazzo M. de Oliveira	Federal University of Rio Grande do Sul, Brazil
Luciano A. Digiampietri	University of São Paulo, Brazil
M. Brian Blake	University of Notre Dame, USA
Manfred Reichert	University of Ulm, Germany
Masao J. Matsumoto	Kyushu Sangyo University, Japan
Miriam A.M. Capretz	The University of Western Ontario, Canada
Peter Green	The University of Queensland, Australia
Renata de M. Galante	Federal University of Rio Grande do Sul, Brazil
Sergiu Dascalu	University of Nevada, USA
Stefanie Rinderle-Ma	University of Ulm, Germany
Tammo van Lessen	University of Stuttgart, Germany
Wil M.P. van der Aalst	Eindhoven University of Technology, The Netherlands

Second International Workshop on Traceability and Compliance of Semi-Structured Processes (TC4SP 2011)

Organizers: Francisco Curbera, Frank Leymann, Hamid Motahari Nezhad, and Beth Plale

Semi-structured processes are those business or scientific processes whose life cycle is not fully driven by a formal process model. Often, an informal description of the process is available in the form of a process graph, flow chart, or an abstract state diagram, but the execution is not completely controlled by a central entity (such as a workflow engine), if at all. Instead, a variety of IT and human-centric mechanisms are used, including email, content management systems, Web-based forms, custom applications, or a combination thereof.

Examples of semi-structured processes are collaborative and case-oriented processes as well as most end-to-end line of business processes in commercial enterprises. Even when there is a formally managed process in place, there are often exceptional situations that fall outside the purview of the workflow engine, making measuring compliance against desired business and regulatory policies difficult. In spite of the widespread adoption of BPM technology, semi-structured processes are commonplace in today's commercial and governmental organizations.

Semi-structured processes do not benefit from most advantages provided by business process management systems (BPMSs). In particular, one major advantage of process management is oversight through the inherent provenance of data and actions. Being able to answer the question "Who did what when and how?" makes processes transparent and reproducible, supports compliance monitoring and root cause analysis, and provides the means for deep mining of activities and information.

The goal of the TC4SPs workshop is to investigate how to extend the oversight, traceability, and compliance management of traditional BPMSs to semi-structured processes through techniques and algorithms to gather, correlate, analyze, and persist provenance data of processes. The workshop aims to bring together practitioners and researchers from different communities – such as business process management, scientific workflow, complex event and compliance monitoring, data and process mining – who share an interest in semi-structured processes. We encourage submissions that report the current state of research in the area and share practical experiences.

Workshop Program

The program of the 2011 edition of the TC4SP workshop included an invited keynote talk and four papers selected among the submissions to the workshop.

Keynote, Social BPM: opening organizational processes to social interactions.
Piero Fraternali, Politecnico di Milano.

Abstract: The talk overviews the motivations, background disciplines, scientific and technical challenges of social BPM, defined as the emerging effort of bringing together the methodological rigor of structured business process management and the flexibility and communication power of social software. The approach of the BPM4People project (www.bpm4people.org) is illustrated, which exploits model-driven architectures and generative software production to support the rapid prototyping and deployment of BPM solutions integrated with social interaction platforms.

Accepted Papers

Four submitted contributions were presented during the second edition of the workshop focusing on the topics of compliance, noisy provenance capture, and runtime support for semi-structured process execution.

Building on a review of recent research on the topic of governance, risk, and compliance (GRC) in business process management, Thomas Schäfer, Peter Fettke, and Peter Loos trace the high number of failures in compliance enforcement for business processes to three main complexity drivers: the increased complexity of the regulatory environment, the growing complexity of major business processes in an organization, and the high frequency of change of the processes themselves. The authors identify the need for new tools and a new methodology to deal with GRC requirements in BPM practice. Awareness of the three complexity drives they identify is likely to drive a new focus on the economic aspects of compliance management and its impact on processes and organizations.

The need to manage the risk exposure derived from an organization's business processes is the topic of the paper by Yurdaer Doganata and Francisco Curbera. Building on previously published work on the performance of automated auditing tools, the paper first examines the factors that determine the effectiveness of automated auditing tools, and considers the economic returns that an organization can expect form investments in an automated tool providing a certain amount of risk reduction. The design of an auditing tool providing a target level of risk reduction is addressed in the second part of the paper, which gives criteria for how to select the parameters affecting the tool's performance to reach the desired risk reduction.

Provenance databases capture records of process execution to support compliance checking, historical analysis, ensure repeatability, etc. One of the main challenges when analyzing provenance data is that the provenance captured in most real-world use cases is noisy and incomplete. This challenge motivates the paper by You-Wei Cheah, Beth Plale, Joey Kendall-Morwick, David Leake, and Lavanya Ramakrishnan. They discuss the process of creating a large (10 GB) noisy provenance database based on realistic scientific workflows and exhibiting specific rates of certain failure types, and they analyze its performance characteristics. The data are then used to test two analysis techniques that work on noisy data, one assessing the quality of captured provenance traces, and the other using a case reasoning technique to repair broken provenance.

The paper by Bernardo Oliveira Pinto and António Rito Silva considers the problem of enabling and supporting a more flexible execution paradigm of semi-structured processes. They propose an architecture that combines the prescriptive aspects of activity-centric workflows with the flexibility and guidance provided by a goal-based model. The proposed "blended workflow" architecture allows deviation from prescribed activities through a set of predefined, goal-centric operations, and uses a shared data model to maintain consistency between the activity and goal-based sides of the process. The blended architecture provides a seamless extension of the traditional activity models to support a flexible, ad-hoc execution that is semi-structured in nature.

September 2011

Francisco Curbera
Frank Leymann
Hamid Reza Motahari Nezhad
Beth Plale

Program Committee

Fabio Casati	University of Trento, Italy
Schahram Dustdar	TU Wien, Austria
Olaf Hartig	Humboldt University of Berlin, Germany
Dimka Karastoyanova	University of Stuttgart, Germany
Geetika Lakshmanan	IBM Research, USA
Paolo Missier	University of Manchester, UK
Sudha Ram	University of Arizona, USA
Florian Rosenberg	IBM Research, USA
Satya Sahoo	Wright University, USA
Heiko Schuldt	University of Basel, Switzerland
Mathias Weske	University of Potsdam, Germany

First International Workshop on Workflow Security Audit and Certification (WfSAC 2011)

Organizers: Rafael Accorsi and Wil van der Aalst

The automation of business processes by means of workflow management systems enables the flexible adjustment of enterprise systems to the current demand, which is highly appreciated at managerial level. Technically, it also provides for a systematic separation of processes and IT-architectures, allowing, for example, the seamless outsourcing of process fragments to a cloud or the selection of different service sets for process execution.

Despite these immediate advantages, enterprises are still reluctant in fully relying on automated workflows. For instance, a recent survey carried out in Germany shows that merely 23% of the enterprises employ workflow management systems, whereas security, privacy, and compliance concerns are the main inhibitors for new deployments [7]. While research, methodologies, and corresponding tool support lying at the intersection of business process management, security and privacy, and (formal) analysis could provide an appropriate basis for tackling these issues, the current state of the art fails to do so [8].

Certification to provably attest and control workflow adherence to properties and *auditing* to detect violations happening at runtime are essential instruments to achieve reliably secure process-aware information systems. The WfSAC Workshop series on Workflow Security Audit and Certification brings together researchers and practitioners investigating and applying preventive and detective analyses to check security and compliance requirements for workflow models and the corresponding management systems.

Scientific Program

The program of WfSAC addresses these topics. WfSAC included two invited speakers, five long papers, and three short papers. The balance of authors from academia and industry shows that the topics addressed at WfSAC are of relevance to both communities, indicating a high potential to transfer research techniques into commercial tools.

Keynotes: The *academic* keynote of Ernesto Damiani (Milan University) presented the current state of the art and challenges on service certification, thereby

---

[7] L. Lowis and R. Accorsi. Finding vulnerabilities in SOA-based business processes. *IEEE Transactions on Service Computing*, 4(3):230–242, August 2011.

[8] Statistisches Bundesamt. *Unternehmen und Arbeitstätten. Nutzung von Informations- und Kommunikationstechnologien in Unternehmen (in German)*. Statistisches Bundesamt, 2011.

summarizing the efforts in the EU-funded project ASSERT4SOA. The *industry* invited speech given by Mieke Jans (Hasselt University / Deloitte) addressed the use of process mining [9] in audits. Dr. Jans focused on the current technical limitations and economical inhibitors encountered in the application of process mining techniques in large-scale audits, indicating research topics to improve this situation.

Long Papers

- K. Haller (Swisscom, Switzerland): *Data-Privacy Assessments for Application Landscapes: A Methodology*
- J. Crampton (Royal Holloway, UK), M. Huth (Imperial College, UK): *On the Modeling and Verification of Security-Aware and Process-Aware Information Systems*
- S. Burri (ETH Zurich, Switzerland), G. Karjoth (IBM Research Zurich, Switzerland): *Flexible Scoping of Authorization Constraints on Workflows with Loops and Parallelism*
- A. Baumgraß et al. (Vienna WU, Austria): *Conformance Checking of RBAC Policies in Process-Aware Information Systems*
- E.P. Santos et al. (Curitiba Catholic University, Brazil): *Modeling Business Rules for Supervisory Control of Process-Aware Information Systems*

Short Papers

- E. Ramezani et al. (Furtwangen HS, Germany): *Separating Compliance Management and Business Process Management*
- S. Schefer et al. (Vienna WU, Austria): *Checking the Satisfiability of Binding Constraints in a Business Process Context.*
- T. Stocker (Freiburg University, Germany): *Time-Based Trace Clustering for Evolution-aware Security Audits.*

September 2011

Rafael Accorsi
Wil van der Aalst

---

[9] W. van der Aalst. *Process Mining – Discovery, Conformance and Enhancement of Business Processes.* Springer, 2011.

Program Committee

The WfSAC organizers would like to thank the PC members for their great job producing detailed reports on the submitted manuscripts.

Achim Brucker	SAP Labs, Germany
Fabio Casati	Trento University, Italy
Jason Crampton	London University, UK
Isao Echizen	NII, Japan
Aditya Ghose	Wollongong University, Australia
Jana Koehler	Lucerne University, Switzerland
Niels Lohmann	Rostock University, Germany
Heiko Ludwig	IBM Research, USA
Alexander Mädche	Mannheim University, Germany
Raimundas Matulevicius	Tartu University, Estonia
Birgit Pfitzmann	IBM Research, USA
Silvio Ranise	FBK, Italy
Stefanie Rinderle-Ma	Vienna University, Austria
Shazia Sadiq	Queensland University, Australia
Pierangela Samarati	Milan University, Italy
Christian Schlaeger	Ernst &Young, Germany
Steffen Staab	Koblenz University, Germany
Thomas Stocker	Freiburg University, Germany
Barbara Weber	Innsbruck University, Austria
Jan Martijn van der Werf	Eindhoven TU, The Netherlands
Nicola Zannone	Eindhoven TU, The Netherlands

Table of Contents – Part I

4th International Workshop on Business Process Management and Social Software (BPMS2 2011)

2nd International Workshop on Cross Enterprise Collaboration (CEC 2011)

2nd International Workshop on Empirical Research in Business Process Management (ER-BPM 2011)

5th International Workshop on Event-Driven Business Process Management (edBPM 2011)

Table of Contents – Part II

1st International Workshop on Process Model Collections (PMC 2011)

1st International Workshop on Process-Aware Logistics Systems (PALS 2011)

4th International Workshop on Process-Oriented Information Systems in Healthcare (ProHealth 2011)

2nd International Workshop on Reuse in Business Process Management (rBPM 2011)

2nd International Workshop on Traceability and Compliance of Semi-Structured Processes (TC4SP 2011)

1st International Workshop on Workflow Security Audit and Certification (WfSAC 2011)

Towards Classification Criteria for Process Fragmentation Techniques*

Michele Mancioppi**, Olha Danylevych, Dimka Karastoyanova,
and Frank Leymann

Institute of Architecture of Application Systems (IAAS),
University of Stuttgart, Germany
{firstname.lastname}@iaas.uni-stuttgart.de

Abstract. Process fragmentation is the foundation of many state-of-the-art techniques for supporting management, reuse and change of process models. Such techniques vary greatly in terms of which types of processes they are applicable to, what they aim at accomplishing, how they define the resulting process fragments, etc. The comparison, analysis, reuse and selection of the available process fragmentation techniques are hindered by the lack of a common terminology and classification criteria, and by the large discrepancy in the characteristics that are covered when presenting novel fragmentation techniques. This work starts addressing this issue by investigating classification criteria for process fragmentation techniques based on the "seven Ws", namely Why, What, When, Where, Who, Which, and how. The presented classification criteria are applied to some of the process fragmentation approaches available in the literature. In addition to enabling the classification of fragmentation techniques, the classification criteria here presented form a "checklist" for authors of future works in the field of process fragmentation.

Categories: Process improvement techniques and tools.

1 Introduction

One broad category of changes applied during the maintenance of process models foresees their *fragmentation* (also referred to as *modularization*, see e.g. [1], or *decomposition*, e.g. [2]), i.e. the creation of *process fragments* that group some of the process model's elements (activities, control flows, data flows, etc.). Fragmentation of process models is performed for a variety of reasons, such as enabling the distributed execution of the process models by dividing them in process fragments that are executed separately in different locations [3], possibly with the

---

* The research leading to these results has received funding from the European Community's Seventh Framework Programme under the Network of Excellence S-Cube - Grant Agreement n° 215483.
** Part of this research has been conducted by Michele Mancioppi while working at the European Research Institute in Services Science (ERISS), Tilburg University, The Netherlands.

F. Daniel et al. (Eds.): BPM 2011 Workshops, Part I, LNBIP 99, pp. 1–12, 2012.
© Springer-Verlag Berlin Heidelberg 2012

goal of optimizing non-functional Quality of Service (QoS) characteristics [4,5], abstracting process models as simplified ones that show only the most important process elements [6] and enabling the reuse of parts of existing process models in others [7,8].

The state of the art lacks reference frameworks for comparing process fragmentation techniques, which hinders their analysis, combination and reuse. Depending on the focus and motivation of the research, different works that propose techniques for process fragmentation often discuss some characteristics like the impact of the technique in the process's lifecycle, and neglect others, e.g. the computational complexity of that fragmentation technique. Our goals are twofold. First of all, we wish to establish the foundation for classifying the state of the art of process fragmentation. Secondly, we aim at providing researchers with a "check-list" of aspects to treat when presenting novel process fragmentation techniques. To reach our goals, we investigate classification criteria for process fragmentation techniques based on the seven "Ws", i.e. why, what, when, where, who, which, and how. The classification criteria here proposed are applied to some process fragmentation techniques available in the literature, namely [3,2,5,9,10,4,11,6].

The paper is structured as follows. Section 2 establishes the basic terminology and definitions that are adopted in this work. Section 3 presents the criteria for the classification of process fragmentation techniques. Section 4 discusses the classification criteria presented in Section 3 and exemplifies them by applying them to a number of works in the state-of-the-art. Finally, Section 5 concludes the paper by presenting our final remarks and directions for future work.

2   Definitions

This section introduces the terminology that is adopted in the remainder of the paper.

A *process model* is the specification, by means of a process-modeling language, of the structure of a particular process. A *process-modeling language*, e.g. Web Services Business Process Execution Language (WS-BPEL), defines the syntax for specifying process models and their (operational) semantics. Process-modeling languages provide *constructs* that are instantiated in the process models as *process elements*. For example, WS-BPEL provides constructs for specifying several types of activities, event handlers, compensation handlers, etc. The activity INVOKE AMAZON WS is a process element of the process model BUY BOOKS ON AMAZON, and it is obtained by instantiating the WS-BPEL construct Invoke Activity in the BUY BOOKS ON AMAZON model. In other words, a process model is an aggregation of process elements that result from the instantiation of constructs provided by the adopted process-modeling language. A more detailed discussion on the relations among process-modeling languages, constructs, process elements and the like is provided in [12].

In the scope of this work a *process fragment* is an *arbitrary subset* of the process elements comprised within a process model. That is, a process fragment can be any selection, possibly even empty, of the process elements comprised in a process model. Our definition of process fragments is, on purpose, extremely generic and it allows for empty process fragments because (while not particularly interesting in real-world scenarios) they are useful abstract concepts, e.g. in the scope of change operators (see e.g. [13]). In practice, process fragments tend to satisfy some *structural constraints* (also called *semantic conditions* [14]) that depend on their intended usage, i.e. the goals they fulfil such as reuse or distributed execution, and the adopted process modeling languages. Examples of constraints are well-formedness and soundness in Petri-Nets. For the sake of generality, such structural constraints are not accounted for in the above definition of process fragment. A specific classification criterion is dedicated to the structural constraints of process fragments (see Section 3).

Fragmentation is the act of creating process fragments out of one process model by applying a *fragmentation technique*. A fragmentation technique is a method to perform fragmentations according to some *fragmentation criteria*, i.e. the rationale underpinning the fragmentation technique. The fragmentation criteria may be described in natural language, e.g. "the resulting process fragments group the activities according to who executes them", or formally, e.g. using Set Theory.

3 Classification Criteria for Fragmentation Techniques

This section presents the classification criteria that we identify on fragmentation techniques for process models. The classification criteria are shown in Figure 1. What input, What output and How, are further refined in sub-criteria that capture their different aspects. How these classification criteria have been elicited is discussed in Section 4.1.

3.1   What Input Is Given to the Fragmentation

The What input criterion investigates the characteristics of the process models in input to the fragmentation technique. The different aspects of the input process models are:

Process-modeling language denotes which process-modeling language is used to specify the process models (see Section 2).

The Structural constraints sub-criterion specifies which requirements are imposed on the structure of the process model (see Section 2). Some recurring examples are *soundness* or *well-formedness* (the actual definitions of which depend on the process modeling language that is employed).

3.2   Why Is the Process Model Fragmented

The Why criterion specifies the goals that motivate the fragmentation of the process model, e.g. enabling the distributed execution or the reuse of process fragments. Providing an exhaustive list of motivations for fragmenting process

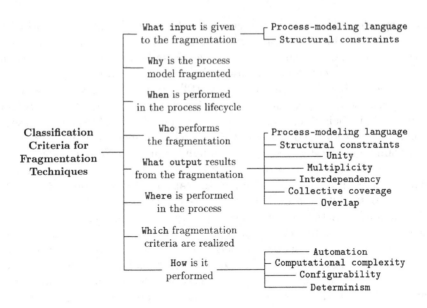

Fig. 1. The classification criteria for fragmentation techniques of process models

models is beyond the reach of this work, and better suited for an extensive survey of the literature. However, some examples may help the reader. During the research that has led to this work, the most recurrent motivations for fragmenting process models were:

Distributed Execution: The goal is to enable the execution on different sites of different parts of a "monolithic" process model. Often the reason for pursuing distributed execution lies in the possibilities for Quality of Service optimization it yields. Compliance is another motivator for distributed execution, i.e. when some of the activities of a process cannot be executed in the same site as others. Moreover, sometimes distributed execution is necessary for fulfilling functional requirements of the processes, e.g. accessing multiple data sources, each of them accessible only on particular sites.

Abstraction: Process models in their entirety are not always suited for all audiences. In some cases it is preferable to hide some parts of a model (e.g. its technical details or too fine-grained activities) to increase its understandability.

Reuse: Process fragmentation can also be used to isolate recurring parts of process models for future reuse in others. However, reuse is not only limited to streamlining the design of future process models, but it supports their modularization. Similarly to the case of source code of software, having the implementation of shared logic defined only once in a fragment (e.g. a sub-process) that is referred to by multiple process models simplifies their maintenance.

Analysis: Several techniques for structural (i.e. at design time) analysis of process models hinges on their fragmentation, e.g. [2].

3.3 When Is the Fragmentation Performed in the Process Model Lifecycle

The When criterion regards in which phases of the process model lifecycle takes place the fragmentation. The particular lifecycle to be considered depends on the process models that are fragmented. For example, the lifecycle for business processes presented in [15] comprises the following phases: Goal Specification, Process Design, Process Implementation, Process Enactment, Process Monitoring and Process Evaluation. Usually, the fragmentation of a process model may be performed during Process Design or Process Implementation (e.g. to abstract the process model and provide its outlook to the modeler), Process Enactment (e.g. the engine that runs the process model divides it in process fragments that are executed in a distributed fashion), Process Monitoring (for example to show the execution of which process fragments has produced certain logs) or Process Evaluation (e.g. highlighting which parts of the process models constitute bottlenecks).

3.4 Who Performs the Fragmentation

The fragmentation of a process model may be performed by actors playing different roles in the enterprise, e.g. business process analysts or business process architects [16]. Actors that perform fragmentations are not necessarily humans, but may also be systems (e.g. an application server or a development tool), e.g. in case of automatic fragmentation techniques (see the Automation sub-criterion of How in Section 3.8).

It is interesting to notice that the value of the Who criterion for a particular fragmentation technique is closely related with When (see Section 3.3). The reason is that the available alternatives for Who are the human actors, systems and software involved in the process model lifecycle phases in which the fragmentation is performed (e.g. the business analyst and the Integrated Development Environment at Process Design time).

3.5 What Output Results from the Fragmentation

Generally, the outcome of the fragmentation of a process model is zero or more process fragments. The properties of the process fragments generated through different fragmentations vary greatly. The sub-criteria that characterize the properties of the process fragments can be grouped according to the type of the property they capture, namely (1) sub-criteria defined on the basis of each single process fragment and (2) those based on all the process fragments cumulatively.

Sub-criteria based on properties of single process fragments: These criteria consider the properties of process fragment considered separately.

The `Process-modeling language` and `Structural constraints` sub-criteria are "duplicates" from `What input`. The definitions of these sub-criteria is exactly the same as their homonyms' under `What input`, except that they apply to the process fragments instead of the process model that is fragmented. Their description is here omitted for reasons of space. It is of course possible that for one fragmentation technique the value of the `Process-modeling language` and `Structural constraints` sub-criteria under `What input` and `What output` may differ. For example, one fragmentation technique might get in input WS-BPEL models and create Petri-Net fragments. Similarly, the fragmented process model might be assumed to be well-formed and deadlock-free, but the resulting process fragments might not be required to satisfy those structural constraints.

In general terms, unity is defined as "the state of being united or joined as a whole" [17]. In the case of a process fragment, `Unity` specifies whether it is still "physically" comprised in the process model. `Unity` is "*preserved*" if the process fragment is fundamentally a "high-lighted area" of the process model. Otherwise, `Unity` is "*disrupted*" in fragmentation techniques that create process fragments that are independent from the original process model, e.g. if the process fragments themselves are separate process models or instances.

Sub-criteria based on properties of all the process fragments cumulatively: The following criteria focus on properties that arise from comparing the process fragments with each other and with the process model.

`Multiplicity` specifies how many process fragments result from the fragmentation. The values of the criterion `Multiplicity` may be specified as ranges, e.g. between m and n, extremes included. Often, however, the uppen and lower bounds cannot be identified a priori, but instead depend on the particular process models that are fragmented. Therefore multiplicities as in regular grammars, namely 0, 1, + (i.e. more than 1), or* (i.e. an specified number) are likely more common.

`Interdependency` defines which kind of dependencies (if any) exist among the process fragments. Different fragmentation techniques are likely to define different types of dependencies, e.g. control- and data dependencies [5] and co-ordination protocols [3] in the case of fragmentation techniques for enabling distributed execution of the process models.

The extent to which the process fragments cumulatively comprise all the process elements of the original process model is treated by the `Collective coverage` criterion. "*Full*" coverage is achieved if every process element of the process model is contained in at least one of the process fragments, and no process fragment contains process elements not originally present in the process model. "*Partial*" coverage occurs when the union of the process fragments contains a proper subset of the process elements of the process model. The coverage is additionally labeled "*-extended*" if the process fragments collectively contain process elements that were not part of the original process model. "*Null*" coverage means that all the process fragments are empty. While this type of coverage has little relevance for real-world applications of fragmentation techniques, it must be taken into account for reasons of consistency.

Finally, the criterion Overlap denotes the extent to which different process fragments produced by one fragmentation share process elements. The alternatives are defined as pair-wise relations between process fragments. In [12] we provide a framework that provides process-modeling language agnostic definitions relations mentioned in the remainder of this section (here omitted for reasons of space). "*Full overlap*" is when the two process fragments comprise exactly the same process elements. Since process fragments are defined as sets of process elements, "*full overlap*" denotes an identity relation. "*Nesting*" is the case in which one process fragment is a proper subset of another. "*Partial overlap*" is when two process fragments have in common at least one process element, but neither process fragment is a subset (proper or improper) of the other. Finally, process fragments that do not share any process element have "*no overlap*". The classification of a fragmentation technique should list all the cases that may occur in fragmentations. If all the alternatives listed above are possible, the classification may report "*any*" for brevity.

3.6 Which Fragmentation Criteria Are Realized

The Which criterion describes the rationale underpinning the fragmentation technique in terms of which fragmentation criteria it implements (see Section 2). For example, a process fragmentation technique for enabling distributed execution of processes may have a criterion such as "Group process elements into process fragments according to the location where those elements need to be executed".

It should be noted that, while the Why criterion explains the motivations that lead to the fragmentation, the Which criterion explains how these goals are to be achieved. The reason of the distinction between Which and Why is that similar goals may be achieved by different techniques, and vice-versa.

3.7 Where Is the Fragmentation Performed in the Process Model

The Where criterion treats the *scope* of the fragmentation, i.e. the regions of the process model that are processed during and affected by the fragmentation. If the fragmentation takes into account the entirety of the process model, its scope is "*global*", and "*partial*" otherwise.

The sub-criterion Collective coverage of What output and the Where criterion are related. On one hand, not all the process elements processed during a fragmentation end up in some process fragments (i.e. global scope does not imply full coverage). On the other hand, a process element that is not processed cannot be included in any process fragment.

3.8 How Is the Fragmentation Performed

The How criterion classifies the fragmentation techniques according to the technical characteristics of the algorithms they employ. (Instead, their rationale is described by Which, which is a stand-alone criterion for underlining its importance.)

`Automation` refers to which extent the fragmentation techniques are automated. There are three possibilities. *"Manual"* fragmentation techniques are performed entirely by humans. *"Automatic"* fragmentations are executed entirely by computerized systems, with no human intervention required. Finally, *"semiautomatic"* fragmentation techniques are partly manual and partly automatic, in that some activities of are manual and some automatic.

`Computational complexity` is the evaluation of the complexity of the fragmentation technique, for example, according to the size of the input (i.e. the number of process elements in the process model) [18]. An example of computational complexity is $O(n)$, i.e. the fragmentation requires at most linear amount of time with respect to n, i.e. the size of the input. Alternatively, complexity classes may also be used as values, e.g. P, NP or `EXP-TIME`.

`Configurability` is the capability of the fragmentation technique to be customized in terms of scope, properties of the resulting process fragments (e.g. upper- and lower bounds for granularity, see Section 3.5), etc.

`Determinism` reports whether the fragmentation technique always produces the same process fragments as output given the same process model and configurations in input.

4   Discussion

In this section we discuss the elicitation and completeness of the classification criteria (Section 4.1), and draw some observations by applying them to selected works in the state of the art (Section 4.2).

4.1   Elicitation and Completion of the Classification Criteria

To elicit the criteria presented in this section, we have firstly performed an extensive survey of the literature on process modeling, process fragments and process fragmentation. After this first phase we conjugated each "W" separately to the fragmentation techniques we had reviewed earlier, which has resulted in the eight questions that form the first level of the classification criteria (see Figure 1).

The second phase of our research focused on identifying sub-criteria for further refining the previously identified classification criteria. We proceeded by examining again the literature on process fragmentation, this time with the goals of (1) classifying the information each work provides under one of the eight criteria, and (2) making sure that each piece of information could be classified under one of the eight main criteria (i.e. making sure we did not miss any criterion). Often one article would highlight some aspect that, while fitting into some of the criteria, had not been explicitly covered by others works, e.g. the computational complexity of the proposed fragmentation techniques. Each of these aspects eventually resulted in a sub-criterion.

In addition to the iterative refinement process, the classification criteria have been influenced by feedback of authors of works on fragmentation techniques in the scope of the European Network of Excellence in Software Services and Systems (S-Cube), where a preliminary version has been employed as the foundation of [19].

In general, proving the completeness of classification criteria, i.e. that the criteria we have elicited capture all the relevant aspects of fragmentation techniques, is obviously impossible. However, we believe we have capture criteria that (1) sufficiently distinguish different techniques and (2) are applicable to every fragmentation technique irrespective of its aim, algorithms it employs, process-modeling languages it assumes, etc. Specifically, in this work we refrained from introducing (sub-)criteria without a suitable level of generality, i.e. criteria applicable only to a niche of the fragmentation techniques in the state of the art. Of course, the classification criteria here presented may be further extended and specialized for particular categories of fragmentation techniques. For example, one might want to classify fragmentation techniques that aim at enabling distributed executions on the basis of the overhead they introduce at runtime.

4.2 Application of the Classification Criteria to the State of the Art

Table 1 presents the outcome of the application of the classification criteria to [3,2,5,9,10,4,11,6]. The classified approaches have been selected for their heterogeneity in terms of goals, techniques employed and assumed process modeling notations (in particular, making sure that the selection covered both "industrial" process-modeling languages like WS-BPEL and formalisms like Petri-Nets). Unfortunately, for reasons of space we cannot provide an overview of the classified works.

The entries in Table 1 are divided in three categories:

1. Those whose evaluation is based on explicit statements found in the work. That is, entries in this category where straightforward to classify. In Table 1, there is no special marker to identify these entries (i.e. it is the "default" category).
2. Entries whose evaluation is not based on information explicitly stated by the paper, but that we could infer on the basis of the information therein provided. For example, the authors of [9] do not explain how their fragments are related with each other, but in the scope of distributed execution of their fragments it is clear that it is necessary to have coordination mechanisms to enforce consistent consumption of tokens in public places across the different locations.
3. Entries that could neither be evaluated nor implied because of the lack of pertinent information in the work. These entries are marked as *Unspecified*.

For reasons of space we must refrain from analysing in great detail the classification data provided in Table 1. Moreover, such analyses would be undermined by the relatively small sample of works here analysed. However, there is one interesting observation that can be drawn at first sight: There are large discrepancies

Table 1. Classification of some of the fragmentation techniques [values marked with * are implied by us]

	Khalaf [3]	Vanhatalo et al. [2]	Danylevych et al. [5]	Tan and Fan [9]	Zhai et al. [10]	Nanda et al. [4]	Ivanovic et al. [11]	Polyvyanyy et al. [6]
What input is given to the fragmentation								
Process-modeling language	WS-BPEL	Workflow graphs	Workflow graphs	CFW Nets	WS-BPEL	WS-BPEL	Logic-based workflow notation	Workflow graphs
Structural constraints	Well-formedness, "no write and a read that are in parallel write to the same location", suppress.Join.Failure set to yes, exactly one correlation set, a single top level "flow" activity, "receive" and "reply" couples must be placed in the same participant	Well-formedness	No cycles in the global transaction	Well-formedness & Soundness	Unspecified	Unspecified	Unspecified	Unspecified
Why is the process model fragmented	Distributed execution	Soundness Analysis	QoS Optimization	Distributed execution	Distributed execution	Distributed execution for QoS Optimization (maximized throughput)	Abstraction, QoS Optimization	Abstraction
When is the fragmentation performed in the process lifecycle	Unspecified	Unspecified	* [15]: Process Design, Process Implementation	* [15]: Process Enactment	Unspecified	Unspecified	* [15]: Process Design, Process Enactment	Unspecified
Who performs the fragmentation	Human process designer	Unspecified	Modeling tool	Unspecified	Unspecified	Unspecified	Analyst, Automated tools	Unspecified
What output results from the fragmentation								
Process-modeling language	WS-BPEL	Workflow graphs	Workflow graphs	CFW Nets	WS-BPEL, skeletons [3]	WS-BPEL	Logic-based workflow notation	Workflow graphs
Structural constraints	Well-formedness	Well-formedness, SESE	No cyclic dependencies among fragments	Well-formedness & Soundness	Unspecified	Unspecified	Unspecified	Unspecified
Unity	Disrupted	Preserved	Preserved	Unspecified	Disrupted	Disrupted	Preserved	Disrupted
Multiplicity	1+	1+	1+	2+	2+	2+	1+	1
Interdependency	Yes (Messaging, coordination protocols)	Yes (Process Structure Tree)	Yes (Stratification graph)	* Yes (Coordination of creation and consumption of tokens in duplicated places)	Yes (Messaging among running instances of process fragments)	Yes (Messaging among running instances of process fragments)	Yes (Messaging among running instances of process fragments)	No
Collective coverage	Partial-extended	Partial	* Full-extended	Full-extended (places may be duplicated)	Unspecified	Full-extended	Full	Partial
Overlap	No (the processes are partitioned)	Nesting or No	No (the strata are partitions)	Yes (duplicated places)	Unspecified	Yes (if cycles exist in the process model)	* No	Partial
Where is the fragmentation performed in the process	Global	Global	Global	Global	Global	Global	Global or partial	Global
Which fragmentation criteria are realized	Process fragments group activities so that "conflicting writes between multiple activities are resolved in a manner that respects the explicit control order"	Group adjacent process elements in SESE fragments	Group activities in fragments that optimize costs and QoS of the execution of the process model	Group activities by locations where they are executed	Partition activities to optimize the data flow on the basis of the generated PPG	Partition activities based on the process model's PDG to optimize throughput	Shared-based independence	Discriminate important process elements from irrelevant on the basis of criteria such as relative probability, relative effort of a process activity, etc.
How is the fragmentation performed								
Automation	Automated	Automated	Automated	Automated	Automated	Automated	Automated	Automated
Determinism	* Yes	* Yes	* No	* Yes	* Yes	* Yes	* Yes	* Yes
Configurability	Yes (assign activities to locations)	No	Yes (QoS aspects to optimize)	Yes (assignment of activities to locations)	No	Yes (choice among multiple heuristics)	Yes (Different objectives)	Yes (granularity of the abstraction selected through the slider's threshold)
Computational complexity	Unspecified (the complexities mentioned are about how many activities are added, not how much it takes to fragment)	Linear to input size	Unspecified	Unspecified	$O(4n^2)$; n = number of nodes in the PPG generated from the original WS-BPEL process model	$O(e^2p)$; e = max number of def-use edges per portable node, p = number of portable nodes in the process model	Depends on the precision of the analysis	Unspecified

in the types of characteristics that are treated when presenting fragmentation techniques. Every work makes it explicit e.g. which process-modeling languages they assume, the fragmentation criteria they employ, or whether their techniques can be configured or not. This is not surprising given the fact that those data are fundamental to the exposition of the fragmentation technique.

However, there are categories of information much less consistently provided. This is the case, for example, of the computational complexity of the fragmentation techniques. Roughly half of the works in our sample explicitly discuss the computational complexity of the fragmentation techniques therein presented, and we find this very surprising given its relevance from both the scientific and practical perspective. Similarly, only three out of eight works discusses when the proposed technique should or could be applied in the lifecycle of the process model, and none of them do it by referencing a concrete lifecycle like [15]. The same situation applies to "who performs the fragmentation": it would be very interesting to know if the authors envision their techniques to be built-in, for example, in Integrated Development Environments (IDEs) or execution engines, or instead embedded in middleware like Enterprise Service Buss (ESBs); however this type of information is only seldom provided.

Given the inconsistent record of characteristics covered in the literature, we believe that the classification criteria here presented will serve as a valuable "check-list" for authors of novel fragmentation techniques besides their primary function of enabling the comparison of existing techniques, and therefore their selection and reuse.

5   Conclusions

Fragmentation techniques are important tools for changing process models in response to evolving requirements. However, the lack of a consistent taxonomy for classifying the different fragmentation techniques and the properties of the process fragments they produce has hindered their comparison and reuse. At the best of our knowledge, this work is the first attempt to investigate the characteristics of fragmentation techniques for process models and the properties of the resulting process fragments. The classification criteria presented in this work provide (1) a basis for classifying existing fragmentation techniques, hence supporting their comparison, selection and reuse, and (2) a "check-list" of what authors should explicitly specify about the novel fragmentation approaches they introduce. We have exemplified the application the classification criteria to selected fragmentation techniques in the state of the art.

The future work foresees an exhaustive survey and classification of the state of the art of process fragmentation using the criteria here presented. We believe that an analysis of the outcome of the classification of the state of the art may yield insights on how our criteria can be further refined and validated. Moreover, an overview of the characteristics of the process fragments that are produced during fragmentation may lead to a fine-grained taxonomy of their types which, in turn, would provide a more reliable and consistent terminology than the one currently adopted in the literature.

References

1. Reijers, H.A., Mendling, J., Dijkman, R.M.: Human and automatic modularizations of process models to enhance their comprehension. Inf. Syst. 36(5), 881–897 (2011)
2. Vanhatalo, J., Völzer, H., Leymann, F.: Faster and More Focused Control-Flow Analysis for Business Process Models Through SESE Decomposition. In: Krämer, B.J., Lin, K.-J., Narasimhan, P. (eds.) ICSOC 2007. LNCS, vol. 4749, pp. 43–55. Springer, Heidelberg (2007)
3. Khalaf, R., Kopp, O., Leymann, F.: Maintaining data dependencies across bpel process fragments. Int. J. Cooperative Inf. Syst. 17(3), 259–282 (2008)
4. Nanda, M.G., Chandra, S., Sarkar, V.: Decentralizing execution of composite web services. In: OOPSLA, pp. 170–187. ACM (2004)
5. Danylevych, O., Karastoyanova, D., Leymann, F.: Optimal stratification of transactions. In: ICIW, pp. 493–498. IEEE Computer Society (2009)
6. Polyvyanyy, A., Smirnov, S., Weske, M.: Process model abstraction: A slider approach. In: EDOC, pp. 325–331. IEEE Computer Society (2008)
7. Weber, B., Rinderle, S., Reichert, M.: Change Patterns and Change Support Features in Process-Aware Information Systems. In: Krogstie, J., Opdahl, A.L., Sindre, G. (eds.) CAiSE 2007 and WES 2007. LNCS, vol. 4495, pp. 574–588. Springer, Heidelberg (2007)
8. Ma, Z., Leymann, F.: Bpel fragments for modularized reuse in modeling bpel processes. In: Mauri, J.L., Giner, V.C., Tomas, R., Serra, T., Dini, O. (eds.) ICNS, pp. 63–68. IEEE Computer Society (2009)
9. Tan, W., Fan, Y.: Model Fragmentation for Distributed Workflow Execution: A Petri Net Approach. In: Ramos, F.F., Larios Rosillo, V., Unger, H. (eds.) ISSADS 2005. LNCS, vol. 3563, pp. 207–214. Springer, Heidelberg (2005)
10. Zhai, Y., Su, H., Zhan, S.: A data flow optimization based approach for BPEL processes partition. In: ICEBE, pp. 410–413. IEEE Computer Society (2007)
11. Ivanovic, D., Carro, M., Hermenegildo, M.V.: Automatic Fragment Identification in Workflows Based on Sharing Analysis. In: Maglio, P.P., Weske, M., Yang, J., Fantinato, M. (eds.) ICSOC 2010. LNCS, vol. 6470, pp. 350–364. Springer, Heidelberg (2010)
12. Mancioppi, M., Danylevych, O., Papazoglou, M.P., Leymann, F.: A language-agnostic framework for the analysis of the syntactic structure of process fragments. Technischer Bericht Informatik 2010/2007. University of Stuttgart (November 2010)
13. Weber, B., Reichert, M., Rinderle-Ma, S.: Change patterns and change support features - enhancing flexibility in process-aware information systems. Data Knowl. Eng. 66(3), 438–466 (2008)
14. Harel, D., Rumpe, B.: Modeling languages: Syntax, semantics and all that stuff (part i: The basic stuff). Technical report, Weizmann Science Press of Israel (2000)
15. zur Mühlen, M., Ho, D.T.-Y.: Risk Management in the BPM Lifecycle. In: Bussler, C.J., Haller, A. (eds.) BPM 2005. LNCS, vol. 3812, pp. 454–466. Springer, Heidelberg (2006)
16. Kajko-Mattsson, M., Lewis, G.A., Smith, D.B.: A framework for roles for development, evolution and maintenance of soa-based systems. In: SDSOA 2007, p. 7. IEEE Computer Society, Washington, DC (2007)
17. Abate, F.R. (ed.): The Oxford Dictionary and Thesaurus. Oxford University Press (1996)
18. Papadimitriou, C.H.: Computational complexity. Addison-Wesley (1994)
19. Danylevych, O.: CD-JRA-2.2.3: Algorithms and techniques for splitting and merging service compositions. Technical report, S-Cube Consortium (2009)

Harmonization of Business Process Models

Heidi Romero, Remco Dijkman, Paul Grefen, and Arjan van Weele

Eindhoven University of Technology, The Netherlands
{h.l.romero,r.m.dijkman,p.w.p.j.grefen,a.j.v.weele}@tue.nl

Abstract. When multiple similar business processes must be designed, a trade-off is necessary between designing a single, standardized, process or designing multiple, specific, processes. Standardization, on the one hand, helps to benefit from re-use of resources and to reduce redundancy. Specificity, on the other hand, helps to tailor the processes to specific needs. The activity of deciding on this trade-off is called harmonization. This paper operationalizes the notion of process harmonization, identifies aspects that determine harmonization and defines metrics to determine the level of harmonization. Furthermore, it presents the factors that influence the level of harmonization that can be achieved in a company. The harmonization aspects and factors are extracted from case studies in practice. Together the metrics, aspects and factors can be used to determine the current and optimal level of harmonization for a company.

1 Introduction

When designing business processes, often multiple processes with the same goal have to be addressed. For example, most companies maintain different processes for procurement of services, procurement of product-related goods and procurement of non-product-related goods. Also, many companies maintain multiple different processes for different, geographically separate, locations.

When this is the case, a trade-off is necessary between designing the processes as generic (standardized) as possible or as specific as possible. Note that we consider a process to be standardized, only if it is followed precisely by all business organizational units to which it applies; it must not be the case that some business units never perform certain paths in the process. For example, consider the situation in which one business unit takes care of procurement of services and another of procurement of goods and, as a consequence, they always follow different paths in the procurement process. In this case we say that there are two processes that apply to the different business units: one for procurement of services and one for procurement of goods. Standardization provides several advantages, acknowledged in the literature, including an improvement in efficiency, reduction of complexity and further decrease of operating costs [1,2,3]. However, full standardization is not always possible, for example, because of legal or cultural differences between different locations or because of differences regarding the types of cases that the processes deal with. In addition, when using a technique such as configurable reference models [4], a process does not have

F. Daniel et al. (Eds.): BPM 2011 Workshops, Part I, LNBIP 99, pp. 13–24, 2012.

to be designed completely standardized or completely specific; the trade-off can lead to a degree of standardization/specificity. We call the activity of making this trade-off *harmonization*. We call the result of this trade-off, the degree of standardization/specificity, the *level of harmonization*.

What remains is to determine what the 'optimal' level of harmonization is, at which a company should design its business processes. To assist in making this decision, this paper presents a conceptual framework for harmonization of business processes. This framework consists of metrics for quantifying the level of harmonization, characteristics of processes and aspects with respect to which a trade-off should be made and factors that determine what the optimal level of harmonization can be.

The research approach that was used to develop the harmonization framework, was to:

1. determine variants of a number of business processes from three large organizations;
2. through interviews, identify factors that cause differences between these variants;
3. establish metrics for measuring the level of harmonization through literature study; and
4. determine the correlation between the presence or absence of factors and the level of harmonization.

The remainder of this paper is structured as follows. Section 2 describes the conceptual framework used to define harmonization. Section 3 shows the metrics developed to measure the level of harmonization of a collection of business process variants. Section 4 explains two case studies in which different factors were identified and linked with their level of harmonization. Section 5 briefly describes related work and Section 6 concludes.

2   Process Harmonization

The benefits of business processes harmonization are well documented specially by practitioners at consultancy firms. They range from improving the efficiency, decreasing operating costs, increasing internal control, to facilitating the interoperability between different companies with a uniform user of IT systems [2]. The reduction in the number of process variants increases the agility towards process changes and also lowers the costs of process maintenance [5]. The internal control increases because the harmonization provides a good basis for comparing the performance between different process variants.

One of the most promising advantages of the harmonization is how it facilitates the information exchange among systems. Therefore, it is a topic of high interest especially for organizations and IT solutions providers, considering that the amount of information managed by firms nowadays is enormous and they need to rely on information systems. When companies look for IT solutions they are looking for a full support of their processes and they found out that they cannot support all the variety of processes existent across business units, products lines and regions. Process variants are expensive to configure and difficult to maintain. The business process harmonization reduces process variability across organizations [6].

However, there is little research in the field of business process harmonization. As a consequence there is also not a uniform definition. Some authors treat business process harmonization like process standardization [7,8], while others distinguish these two concepts. In particular, it was suggested that harmonization does not propose one standard process, but multiple process variants without attempting to make them all uniform [5]. It is emphasized that harmonization of business processes refers to the identification of differences between processes and to setting bounds to their degree of variation. Also in the context of inter-organizational business processes, harmonization does not impose standardized routing in the domain of a collaborating party. It allows a consumer to ensure the presence of desired service content and behavior in different degrees from a supplier [9].

In this study, we interpret the relation between standardization and harmonization as follows. In line with the work on configurable reference models [10,4], we say that a standard process can describe multiple process variants. The number of variants indicates the level of harmonization. Therefore, harmonization is defined as the activity of designing a (configurable) reference model with an optimal number of variants. This optimal number of process variants can vary between process collections depending on different factors, but the aim is always to define one standard process with as little variation as possible. Therefore, in this context one standard process is the optimal level of harmonization achievable by a set of business processes.

To further operationalize the concept of harmonization, we developed the conceptual framework shown in Figure 1. This framework presents that the harmonization level of a collection of processes can be measured using different metrics ($\mathcal{Y}i$). These metrics describe the variability among the processes within this collection. We also suggests that the level of harmonization can be influenced by different factors ($\mathcal{X}i$), as described in the literature [11].

Among the factors that were identified, are: differences in legal systems, differences in business practices from one culture to another and differences in business culture with regard to management authority and control mechanisms. These factors make the harmonization a challenge. The challenge arises with the identification of an appropriate level of commonality between the different process variants [11]. However, the influence exerted by these factors is not the same, therefore we include a variable ai that indicates the weight of the influence exerted by each factor in the level of harmonization measured by $\mathcal{Y}i$.

Clearly, the level of harmonization can differ for different processes ($\mathcal{P}\rangle$). In addition, different aspects ($\mathcal{Z}k$) of process modeling are often considered, such as the activities that are performed, the relations between these activities and the IT applications that are used to perform the activities [12]. In order to define the number of process variants of a collection of business processes, it is necessary

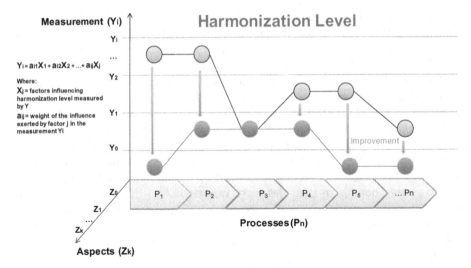

Fig. 1. Framework Business Process Harmonization

to define with respect to which aspect those processes differ. The differentiation of each of these aspects (activities, relations and applications) can provide a deeper insight into the collection of processes offering greater opportunities for improvement. This suggests the need to differentiate the harmonization level of a set of business processes with respect to different aspects, considering that each one of them offers a different perspective on the problem.

3   Level of Harmonization

This section defines three metrics that can be used to measure the level of harmonization of each of the aspects that are defined in Section 2. Clearly, any number of metrics can be envisioned and the goal of this section is not to define one final set of metrics. Instead, the goal is to define metrics that provide an indication of the level of harmonization that appeals to process designers. With that goal in mind, we defined metrics to meet the following criteria:

Understandability. The most important criterion is that a metric must be simple to understand in order to be usable by people from practice to determine the level of harmonization of their processes.

Meaningfulness. As a consequence a metric must also be meaningful; a practitioner must be able to understand why a metric represents the level of harmonization of a certain business process aspect well. For example, 'number of process variants' is a good metric, because to a practitioner it is a clear indicator of the level of harmonization of his collection of processes, considering that each process variant must be managed and supported separately. Thus, it is easy to understand that less variance means a higher level of standardization.

Uniformity. To further improve the understandability of the metrics, they should be applicable as broadly as possible to measure the level of harmonization for each of the different aspects.

In the future, research will be done to determine empirically, which metrics are the most appealing to the process designers.

3.1   Harmonization Metrics

Using the criteria outlined above, we defined three metrics.

The first way of measuring the level of harmonization is by counting the number of process variants in the collection. Two processes are defined as process variants when they differ in at least one element of one of the aspect under evaluation. Figure 2 shows an example of three process variants of a tendering process. They differ with respect to several aspects. They differ with respect to the activities, because it can be observed that the activity *Make short list* is present in variant 1 but not in variant 2 and 3. Also variants 2 and 3 differ with respect to the activity *Prepare RFP*. In this case, we can conclude that with respect to the activity aspect, there are three process variants. However, if we evaluate the number of process variants with respect to the departments involved, we can observe that three departments are involved in the three processes (procurement, internal customer and supplier), therefore the number of process variants with respect to the department aspect is 1. Concluding, the number of process variants depends on the aspects that are considered.

The second way of measuring the level of harmonization is by computing how often, on average, each distinct element appears in a process variant. As such, it is an indication of the similarity of process variants. This metric is represented as a percentage and can be computed by counting the number of process variants (for all aspects) in which a distinct element appears divided by the number of processes. This value is divided by the number of distinct elements. A distinct element is an element that can be used to describe process variants. It can appear in multiple variants. For example, Figure 2 contains the distinct (activity) element 'create supplier's list'. This distinct element appears in two variants. Let the set of distinct elements that we are interested in be E, the process variants in which an element $e \in E$ appears be *Appearances(e)* and the set of process variants be V. Then the average number of appearances of an element per process variant is:

$$\text{AVG}_{e \in E} \frac{|Appearances(e)|}{|V|}$$

As an example, the Figure 2 contains three roles, each of which appears in all three process variants. So the average number of role appearances per process variant is 1.0. This metric evaluates the variety of elements per process variants in the collection.

The third way of measuring the level of harmonization is by computing how often each activity, on average, is associated with the same element of a particular

Table 1. Metric to evaluate the level of harmonization of a collection of processes

Aspects	Elements	Number P.variants	Appearances per p.variants	Commonality
General	Processes	✓		
Activities	Activities	✓	✓	
Control-flow	Splits (decisions)	✓	✓	
Control-flow	And (parallelism)	✓	✓	
Applications	IT Applications	✓	✓	✓
Resources	Roles	✓	✓	✓
Resources	Departments (groups)	✓	✓	✓
Resources	Companies (groups)	✓	✓	✓

kind. As such, it is an indication of the similarity of process variants. This metric can assume values ranging from 0 to 1, and be expressed as a percentage. It differs from the previous one in the sense that it indicates not only if the distinct elements are common between processes but also if they are attached to the same activities. For instance, it is possible that two different processes share the same IT applications, however some of this applications are not used to perform the same activities between those processes. In this case the average number of appearances of a distinct element per process variant is equal to 1, but the commonality will be less than 1.

Given an element type (such as departments), the commonality determines for each activity, how often that activity is associated with the same element of that type. The maximum number is divided by the total number of appearances of the activity. For example, in figure fig:figexample, the activity 'define evaluation criteria' is associated twice with the 'procurement' department and once with the 'internal customer' department. The maximum number, therefore, is 2. The is computed as the average over all activities. If $AppearancesPer(E, A)$ returns the number of appearances of a distinct element (of a certain type) as associated with a distinct activity. Then the commonality is:

$$\text{AVG}_{a \in A} \frac{\text{MAX}_{e \in E} AppearancesPer(e, a)}{|Appearances(a)|}$$

Each of these metrics is applied to the following aspects: activities, control-flow, applications and resources. Some aspects can also be decomposed into different elements that provide different information about the differences between processes in the collection. In this study we consider two elements in the control-flow aspect: decisions and parallelism. We use a 'split-nodes' to measure decisions and 'and-nodes' to measure parallelism. For example, in variant 3 of Figure 2, after having the evaluation criteria defined and the received the tenders, there is one decision to be made. We also consider three elements within the resource aspect: roles, departments and companies. A role is an abstraction of the resources performing an activity within the company. A department is a functional unit within the company, and a company is an organizations involved in the process. For instance some processes include suppliers or external organizations to which specific activities within the process are subcontracted.

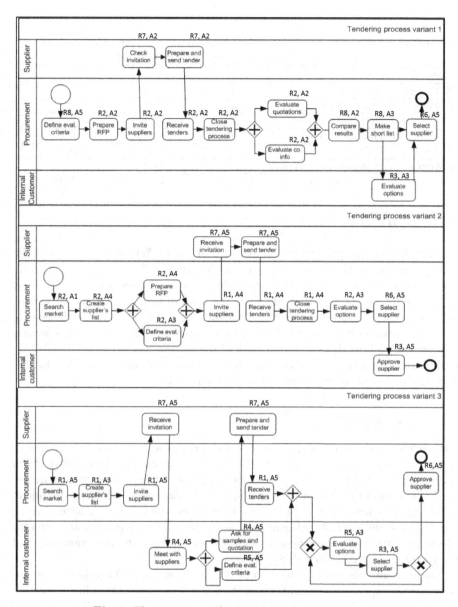

Fig. 2. Three variants of a supplier selection process

Although the ideal is to apply the metrics to the different aspects of harmonization as uniformly as possible, not each possible application of a metric to an aspect is meaningful. Table 1 shows each of the aspects of harmonization that we identified in Section 2. A check-mark in a cell represents that the corresponding metric is meaningful for each aspect.

For completeness, table 2 shows the values for each of the possible metrics for the example from figure 2.

Table 2. Metric applied to a supplier selection process

Aspects	Elements	Number p.variants	Appearances per p. variants	Commonality
General	Processes	3	—	—
Activities	Activities	3	0.65	—
Control-flow	Splits (decisions)	2	0.33	—
Control-flow	And (parallelism)	1	1.00	—
Applications	IT Applications	3	0.60	0.79
Resources	Roles	3	0.63	0.77
Resources	Departments (groups)	1	1.00	0.92
Resources	Companies (groups)	1	1.00	1.00

4   Empirical Studies

An exploratory case study was conducted using two different cases. For real-life business processes this is a suitable methodology to follow in order to identify the different factors [13]. Two case studies were performed with the goals of: (i) identifying the factors that influence the level of harmonization that can be achieved; and (ii) exploring the effect that these factors could have on the level of harmonization, as it is measured using the metrics from Section 3. This section first presents a brief description for both of the cases, it then presents the factors that were identified in the cases and explores the relation between the factors and the level of harmonization that can be achieved.

4.1   Case Descriptions

Two different companies were selected in terms of the harmonization challenge that they are facing with respect to the different aspects identified before. Each company is treated as a case and each case focuses on the procurement processes (with their variants). We did not include all the processes within procurement, but a significant set that includes comparable processes per case. Several interviews were conducted at each company with commodity managers and director of the procurement department to identify the different process variants, and the factors underlying their differences.

The company names are substituted for confidentiality. Therefore, they are refer in this paper as Case A and Case B. Case A is a company which produces medical systems. The process variants were collected from two facilities, located in two different countries. The type of process analyzed in this case includes the acquisition of production related products. This process involves 3 different departments, 2 companies, 3 roles and 2 IT applications in place. To perform some activities no IT applications are not required. Case B is a company from the automotive industry. It is part of a multinational company, but only one location for manufacturing of its products was chosen. It was chosen considering the complexity of its processes and its involvement in new product development. During the data collection, process variants related to both production and non-production related products and services were included. This process involves 4 different departments, 2 companies, 6 roles and 2 IT applications.

4.2 Identified Factors

The main factors identified in the case studies, influencing the variability in the processes collected are shown in Table 3. The factors were identified through semi-structured interviews. First, in a series of interviews, the processes of the companies were modeled and differences between the processes were identified. Second, in a series of interviews, reasons (factors) for the identified differences were determined.

Table 3. Factors of variability in procurement processes

Case	Case A	Case B
Factors	- Legal requirements - Level of definition of specifications - Different Locations	-Legal requirements -Product type: (production related or not) - Level of definition of specs - Relation with suppliers

4.3 Relation between Factors and Level of Harmonization

To determine how the factors affect the level of harmonization exactly, the metrics from Section 3 were applied to the collections of processes identified per case. The results are shown in Table 4.

Table 4 clearly shows that the level of harmonization of a set of processes differs per aspects as hypothesized in the conceptual framework defined in Section 2. For example, there is a difference between the level of harmonization as measured through *the appearances per process variants* with respect to IT applications than with respect to roles and departments.

This table also shows that there is a difference in the level of harmonization of case A and case B. There is a clear difference between the two cases with respect to the level of harmonization with respect all aspects. We will study the possible causes for these differences, using the factors from Subsection 4.2 as explanation.

We can observe that in both cases the *number of process variants* in general is directly linked with the *number of process variants* with respect to the activities. Also the factor *legal requirement* and *level of definition of the specifications* are shared by both cases. Therefore we can derive that these factors impose the addition of specific activities to a process. For example, if the specifications of the product are well known and defined, then the number of activities to be perform can be reduced compare to the process expected when those specifications are not known and maybe more interaction with suppliers is required.

Two aspects that show interesting relations are roles and IT applications. The *the appearances per process variants* with respect to IT applications is 1.00 for case A, compared to 0.75 for case B. In contrast to the commonality, in which

Table 4. Metric to evaluate the level of harmonization of a collection of processes

Cases	Aspects	Elements	Number variants	Appearances per variant	Commonality
Case A	General	Processes	2	—	—
	Activities	Activities	2	0.60	—
	Control-flow	Splits (decisions)	2	0.50	
	Control-flow	And (parallelism)	1	0	
	Applications	IT Applications	1	1.00	0.95
	Resources	Roles	2	0.83	0.98
	Resources	Departments (groups)	1	0.67	0.95
	Resources	Companies (groups)	1	0.50	1.00
Case B	General	Processes	8	—	—
	Activities	Activities	8	0.50	—
	Control-flow	Splits (decisions)	1	1.00	—
	Control-flow	And (parallelism)	2	0.75	—
	Applications	IT Applications	2	0.75	0.98
	Resources	Roles	5	0.71	0.80
	Resources	Departments (groups)	3	0.69	0.83
	Resources	Companies (groups)	1	1.00	1.00

case B has a higher *level of commonality*(0.98) compared to case A with 0.95. Considering that in both cases they use two different IT applications, we can derive that when specific applications are use for specific activities within the process (*commonality*), like in case B, and activities are not shared between processes, then the *the appearances per process variants* with respect to the IT applications is low (0.75) but the commonality is high (0.98).

This difference can be partly explained by the fact that case A has different locations in different countries, while case B only has one location. Interestingly, although the differences in applications used is high in case A, the commonality of applications used is also high (0.95). The interpretation of this number is that, for activity appearances that the two locations have in common, they also use the same application to a large extent. Looking at the case in more detail, we can see that the locations have few activities in common. This is caused by different legal requirements in the countries in which the departments are located. So, in this case the level of commonality is high (0.95) because many activities are not shared between locations, while for the few activities that are shared, the same application are in used. Consequently, the different locations can be looked at as a cause for a strong difference in activities that are performed and applications that are used. The different legal requirements can cause a further difference in the activities that are performed.

The *commonality* with respect to the roles differ between cases. It means that common activities among processes in case A also have common roles, while common activities in case B have less common roles. Looking at the factors, we can see that in case B we studied processes that differed with respect to the types of product that were procured, while in case A we only studied processes that concern a single type of product. Looking at the processes in more detail, it is indeed the case that different types of products require different departments and different roles to be involved in the execution of the processes. Consequently, the factor of 'product type' can be looked at as an explanatory factor when differences between roles or departments are found.

This striking relations between the presence or absence of certain factors and the effect on the level of harmonization, show that the framework is promising as a direction for measuring and understanding process harmonization. To determine a clear correlation between the presence or absence of certain factors and the level of harmonization, more research is necessary.

5 Related Work

Harmonization is strongly related to previous research in the field of (configurable) reference models [10,4] and process comparison [14].

The work on (configurable) reference models also addressed variability between different process models with the same goal. The work on harmonization complements this work by providing tools to determine the optimal level of harmonization (i.e.: the reference model that fits the organization best).

The work on process comparison deals with determining similarity and differences between process models. The work on harmonization complements this work by not only focusing on determining similarity and differences, but also determining the level of similarity (harmonization) that would be optimal for an organization.

6 Conclusions

This paper presents a framework that can help practitioners determine how standardized or how specific they should design their business processes. This trade-off is called harmonization. To determine the optimal level of harmonization, different aspects of business processes are considered separately, including: activities, resources, control-flow and IT applications. In addition, causal factors are identified that influence the level of harmonization that can be achieved.

In two exploratory case studies, the factors that influenced the level of harmonization the most were identified as: case type and legal requirements. The case type influenced the level of harmonization that could be attained with respect to the resource aspect. This was caused by the fact that different types of resources (i.e.: roles and departments) were required to handle different types of cases. The legal requirements influenced the level of harmonization that could be attained with respect to the IT application aspect. This was caused by the fact that different legal requirements required differences between IT applications.

The work in this paper is exploratory, presenting the framework and showing it's possible merit by applying it to two case studies. The first results that are obtained in this way, show that the framework is promising as a tool to explain the cause for variation between similar processes.

In future work the framework must be refined by performing more case studies. In this way, more, and also more precise, factors will be identified that influence the possible level of harmonization. In addition, the influence exerted by each factor on the possible level of harmonization will be determined more precisely, using a quantitative research method.

References

1. Muenstermann, B., Eckhardt, A., Weitzel, T.: The performance impact of business process standardization. Business Process Management Journal 6, 29–56 (2010)
2. Davenport, T.: The coming commoditization of processes. Harvard Business Review 83, 100–108 (2005)
3. Wöllenweber, K., Beimborn, D., Weitzel, T., König, W.: The impact of process standardization on business process outsourcing success. Information Systems Frontiers 10, 221–224 (2008)
4. Gottschalk, F., van der Aalst, W., Jansen-Vuller, M., La Rosa, M.: Configurable Process Models: Experiences from a Municipality Case Study. In: van Eck, P., Gordijn, J., Wieringa, R. (eds.) CAiSE 2009. LNCS, vol. 5565, pp. 486–500. Springer, Heidelberg (2009)
5. Richen, A., Steinhorst, A.: Standardization or harmonization? you need both. In: European Health Informatics (November 2005)
6. Tay, J., Parker, R.: Measuring international harmonization and standardization. Abacus 28, 217–220 (1992)
7. Welch, J., Kordysh, D.: Seven keys to erp success. Strategic Finance 89, 40–47 (2007)
8. Darshana, S., Dey, S.: Everyone is different! exploring the issues and problems with ERP enabled shared service initiatives. In: Proc. of ACIS 2007, pp. 93–98 (2007)
9. Norta, A., Eshuis, R.: Specification and verification of harmonized business process collaborations. Information Systems Frontiers 12, 457–479 (2009)
10. Gottschalk, F., van der Aalst, W., Jansen-Vuller, M., La Rosa, M.: Configurable workflow models. IJCIS 17, 177–221 (2008)
11. Gulla, J., Mollan, R.: Implementing SAP R/3 in a multi-cultural organization. In: Proc. of EMRPS 1999, pp. 127–134 (1999)
12. Tumay, K.: Business process simulation. In: Proc. of Conf. on Winter Simulation, pp. 93–98. IEEE Computer Society (1996)
13. Schafermeyer, M., Grgecic, D., Rosenkranz, C.: Factor influencing business process standardization. In: Proc. of HICSS 2010, pp. 3–10. IEEE Computer Society (2010)
14. Dijkman, R.: Diagnosing Differences Between Business Process Models. In: Dumas, M., Reichert, M., Shan, M.-C. (eds.) BPM 2008. LNCS, vol. 5240, pp. 261–277. Springer, Heidelberg (2008)

A Blended Workflow Approach

António Rito Silva

INESC-ID/IST/Technical University of Lisbon
Rito.Silva@ist.utl.pt

Abstract. Semi-structured workflow approaches are being recognised
as essential to support collaboration whenever ad-hoc work needs to be
performed due to the occurrence of unanticipated events in dynamic
environments. However, semi-structured workflows need to balance the
support of unexpected situations with guidance for the situations where a
standard behaviour is wanted. The blended workflow approach proposes
an integration of two distinct workflow specifications, the activity-based
specification, which precisely defines how to coordinate work for expected
situations, and a goal-based specification, which empowers people to accomplish the business process goals using their tacit knowledge. In this
paper we describe the blended workflow approach, illustrate it with an
example, and identify the compliance properties that a blended workflow
approach needs to have to integrate activity and goal specifications.

Keywords: Activity-based workflow, Goal-based workflow, Semi-
structured workflows, Flexible workflows.

1 Introduction

Today's mainstream workflow systems are activity-based. They focus on how
activities can be coordinated using control flow primitives, as sequential and
parallel execution, to achieve the business process goals [1,2]. Activity-based
workflows prescribe the activities execution order but lack flexibility to handle
unexpected situations for which they were not codified.

A new set of workflow approaches is emerging which fosters end users collaboration to deal with unexpected situations, e.g., ActionBase [3]. These workflows
support ad-hoc behaviour and delegate to end users the responsibility to guarantee that the business process goals are achieved. However, they lack the guidance
provided by activity-based workflows.

In this paper we propose a new approach, called blended workflow, which
intends to bridge the gap between completely structured workflows and ad-hoc
workflows. The idea behind the blended workflow approach is that a workflow
management system should allow end users to deviate from the structured execution whenever it is necessary, yet may allow them to regain the guidance
provided by structured workflows once the unexpected situation is dealt with.
To do so, blended workflow proposes the coexistence of two workflow specifications, a prescriptive activity-based specification and a descriptive goal-based

F. Daniel et al. (Eds.): BPM 2011 Workshops, Part I, LNBIP 99, pp. 25–36, 2012.

specification, and the execution of their workflow instances according to both specifications.

In the next section we introduce the blended workflow approach by using an example to illustrate it. Section 3 extends the example with the description of two unexpected situations to illustrate how a blended workflow allows deviations without giving up guidance, and section 4 identify the compliance qualities that need to be preserved between the two specifications and their workflow instances. Related work is described in section 5 and, finally, we conclude and propose future work in section 6.

2   Blended Workflow

The blended workflow approach integrates an activity-based and a goal-based specification. The rational behind it is that an activity-based specification is an over-specification of the behaviour necessary to achieve the business process goals. Usually, this over-specification describes a standard behaviour that organisations want to enforce, though it is not mandatory when unexpected situations occur. Actually, the standard behaviour prescribed by the activity-based specification often hinders the reaction to unexpected situations. Therefore, blended workflow considers another specification, a goal-based specification, which is declarative and empowers people to decide what business goals are appropriate to achieve when an unexpected situation occurs, and how to achieve them.

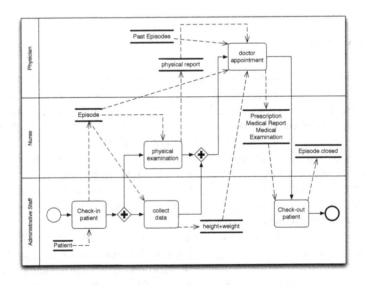

Fig. 1. Activity-based specification of the medical episode

To illustrate the blended workflow approach consider an example of a medical episode. The activity-based specification of a medical episode is defined in

Figure 1. This specification integrates control flow with data flow. To be executed an activity needs to be enabled by both flows, control and data, represented by activity inward arrows, respectively, solid and dashed.

Data flow is defined by activities pre- and post- conditions. The input data required by an activity to execute is its pre-condition, e.g. the existence of a height data value for Doctor Appointment activity, and the state expected after an activities execution is its post-condition, e.g. a physical report data value for Physical Examination activity. The data produced by an activity, defined by its post-condition, may, eventually, be required by another's activity pre-condition, hence establishing data flow dependences. For instance, physical report data value defines a data flow dependence between Physical Examination and Doctor Appointment. Note that we consider the existence of data as a condition itself, but more complex conditions may be specified, e.g., height > 0.

In the blended workflow approach control flow is independent of pre- and post-conditions[1]. This clear separation of data flow from control flow allows to identify which parts of the activity-based specification are explicitly related to the goal-specification. Therefore, we say that an activity is enabled by control flow when it can execute considering the control flow patterns [5]. However, to execute, following the blended workflow approach, it is also required that its pre-condition holds: the activity should also be enabled by data flow.

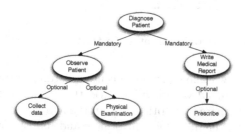

Fig. 2. Goal-based specification of the medical episode

Figure 2 describes the medical episode goal-based specification. A goal is represented by a condition on data. For instance, Write Medical Report goal requires the existence of a Medical Report object that contains a diagnosis written by the doctor. The goals are structured as a tree and the edges represent goal dependences: it represents a goal decomposition structure where the super goal comprises its subgoals. Two kinds of goal dependences are considered, mandatory, where the super goal requires the achievement of the subgoal, and optional, where the super goal can be fulfilled without requiring the subgoal

---

[1] Note that for the sake of simplicity we are ignoring activities pre- and post- conditions which are used for control flow [4]. However, in a complete specification we would distinguish pre- and post- conditions for control flow from pre- and post- conditions for business goal achievement.

achievement. For instance, `Write Medical Report` can be achieved without requiring the optional goal `Prescribe` to be fulfilled.

The activity-based specification has to comply with the goal-based specification. This means that any successful execution following the activity-based specification must fulfil the super goal and all mandatory subgoals it depends transitively on. Therefore, to support this compliance the blended workflow approach considers a third specification: a data specification. The data specification describes the data entities that are required by both specifications, in particular by goal conditions and activities pre- and post- conditions.

Figure 3 depicts a data specification for the medical episode case. A `Patient` has a record of past `Episodes`. During workflow execution a new `Episode` object is created and linked to a new `Medical Report` object. It is the existence of the new `Medical Report` object that is required by both conditions, `Doctor Appointment` post-condition and `Write Medical Report` goal condition.

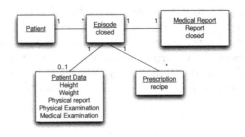

Fig. 3. Data specification for the medical episode

The execution of a workflow instance occurs according to two views: activity and goal. For each blended workflow instance, there is an instance of the data specification which is shared by both views. In the activity view, an activity can be executed when it is enabled by control flow and its pre-condition holds. As result of the activity execution, if it is correctly implemented, the shared data is changed and thus the post-condition will also hold. To fulfil a goal, in the goal view, it is necessary to make its condition true, which means that the shared data needs to be changed accordingly. Consequently, whenever the shared data changes it is necessary to re-synchronise the views according to the new workflow instance data state. When an activity is executed, the goal conditions may be re-evaluated to identify if some goals are fulfilled as result. Similarly, when a goal is fulfilled, it is necessary to identify which activities post-conditions became true and, thus, do not need to execute anymore.

The data specification and the conditions – goal, pre- and post- – define a mapping between activity- and goal- based specifications. This mapping needs to ensure that end users can consistently interact with the blended workflow through any of the views. Section 4 details how goal and the activity views are kept consistent using the shared data.

3   Flexibility

In addition to activity execution and goal fulfilment, the blended workflow allows activities and goals to be skipped, and the creation of new goals. Hence, for the sake of flexibility, the execution of a blended workflow supports three new types of operations:

- *Skip activity.* End users can skip the execution of an activity. When an activity is skipped the blended workflow identifies the set of goals that may be skipped as well, if any. On the other hand, when an activity is skipped, the control flow proceeds as if the activity has been executed, yet its post-condition is not fulfilled. Consequently, activities that became enabled by control flow may require data values produced by the skipped activity and, thus, they can not execute. Therefore, to regain the guidance provided by the activity-based specification, the blended workflow generates a pre-activity for each activity that is enabled for execution by control flow but which pre-condition does not hold. The pre-activity requests the end user to enter the data necessary to enable the pre-condition and, thus, to allow the execution to proceed according to the specification. As an alternative, the end user can decide to skip some of the activities which pre-conditions do not hold.
- *Skip goal.* End users can decide to skip a goal achievement. When a goal is skipped, all its subgoals, which were not fulfilled yet, are also skipped. Additionally, the blended workflow analyses the activities post-conditions to identify the set of activities that may be skipped as well.
- *Add goal.* End users can decide to define a new goal for a particular workflow instance. To create a new goal, they have to define a new condition. Additionally, it may be necessary to define new data entities and attributes, which are required by the condition and were not defined yet. The achievement of a new goal does not have impact on the activity-based specification since the goal is not implemented by the specification.

The blended workflow approach does not support an add activity operation because it would require the end user to redefine the activities control flow, which is not a trivial operation. On the other hand, the add goal operation does not require from the end user any particular modelling skill but to understand the business goals. These rules are central in how the blended workflow approach addresses flexibility; "disruptive" flexibility is handle by the goal-based specification while the activity-based specification is preserved to keep the standard behaviour. Note that skipping an activity preserves the standard behaviour because execution continues according to the control flow, if as the activity had been executed.

Two unexpected situations are described next to illustrate how activities and goals can be skipped, and when goals can be created.

Administrative strike. Consider the situation where administrative staff go on strike. `Check-in Patient`, `Collect Data`, and `Check-out Patient` activities cannot be executed and are skipped. Consequently, the `Collect Data` goal becomes skipped as well because the state of attributes `height` and `weight` was set to skipped by `Collect Data` activity and the `Collect Data` goal requires the existence of `height` and `weight` values for the patient. Additionally, when a nurse intends to execute the `Physical Examination` activity, he has to execute a pre-activity to create an instance of the `Episode` entity because the activity's pre-condition requires the existence of an `Episode` instance. On the other hand, the new `Patient Data` object defined in the `Physical Examination` post-condition, has to be linked with the `Episode` object. Similarly, the doctor needs to execute a pre-activity to collect data because `Doctor Appointment` pre-condition requires the existence of `height` and `weight` values. As result of pre-activities execution, the workflow execution can now follow the standard activity-based specification.

However, it can be the case that the doctor decides not to follow the prescribed activity-based specification, and the associated standard behaviour, and tries to achieve the main goal by following the goal specification: she observes the patient and writes the medical report. Actually, she needs to create a new `Medical Report` object. Hence, the main goal is achieved and later on, when the strike ends, the administrative staff can execute the activity `Check-out Patient`. Note that in this situation, the doctor is empowered to decide how she can achieve the main goal, and, afterwards some of the skipped activities can be executed to provide some of the missing information and comply with standard procedures. Note as well that `Observe Patient` goal is achieved without requiring the optional goals to be achieved.

Second opinion. It can be the case that a doctor, when examining a patient, decides that she needs a colleague's second opinion before she writes the medical report. To do so, she creates a new goal, `Second Opinion`, and associate it as a mandatory subgoal of `Write Medical Report`. To create the new goal she also needs to define a new entity, `Second Opinion Report`, and associates it to `Medical Report` entity. The `Second Opinion` goal's condition requires the existence of a `Second Opinion Report` instance linked with the `Medical Report` instance. Note that in this situation, the deviation does not have a direct impact on the activity view. Moreover, the changes done to the goal view only have impact on this particular workflow instance and do not change the goal specification of other instances.

4 Compliance

The compliance quality allows to smoothly integrate a guided execution of the workflow, which is defined by an activity-based specification, with end users empowerment to deviate execution when unexpected situations occur. After a deviation has occurred, it should be possible to proceed execution following the activity-based specification.

The activity-based specification contains more goals than the goal-based specification. We refer to the latter as business goals. Business goals constitute a subset of the activity-based specification goals. The additional goals in the activity-based specification are embedded in the control flow, yet they are not necessary to achieve the business goals: they define how the business goals can be achieved. However, in the examples that illustrate deviations, there is a case where the goal specification has a business goal which is not considered by the activity specification. This occurs when a new business goal is created during execution. The end user is empowered to define a new business goal when an exceptional situation occurs, like in the second opinion case. Therefore, we refer to the business goals that are implemented by the activity-based specification as the *initial set of business goals*.

To represent the impact of skipped activities and goals on the shared data we introduce the notion of *skipped* state. Hence, a data value can be in one of three kind of states, *exists*, *empty*, and *skipped*. The *exists* state occurs when a value was explicitly assigned to the data entity and the *empty* state when its value is undefined. The *skipped* state indicates that the end user intentionally decided not to assign a value to the data. The latter indicates that the end user skipped an activity or a goal. Conditions evaluation follow a three-valued logic with values: true, false and skipped. An atomic condition over a data entity, e.g. exists(height), in the *skipped* state returns the *skipped* logic value. The *skipped* logic value is an absorbing element for conjunction and a neutral element for disjunction.

In this section we sketch a formal demonstration on how both views of a workflow instance can be kept synchronised. We show intuitively how this synchronisation can be achieved by describing the dependences among specifications and, inductively, how the execution of each possible operation keep the views synchronised.

4.1 Dependences

The three proposed specifications hold a set of constraints which can restrict workflow execution. In this section we address each one of the dependences and discuss them in terms of their impact during execution.

Control flow dependences. The control flow dependences are used to determine which activities are enabled for execution, given the set of activities that have already finished. An end user can skip an activity only if it is enabled by control flow. Similarly, when a goal is skipped, only the activities that are enabled by control flow, and which post-conditions became skipped, can be, automatically, skipped as a result. Control flow dependences do not impact on goal achievement, so it is possible for an end user to fulfil any goal he wants, independently of the control flow dependences.

Data flow dependences. Pre- and post- conditions define a set of data dependences in the activity-based specification. When an activity's pre-condition holds true, its activity is enabled for execution by the data flow. We say that an activity-based specification is well-formed if when an activity is enabled by control flow it is also enabled by data flow. However, when there are data values in the *skipped* state, due to skipped activities or goals, it may be possible that some activities enabled by control flow are not enabled by data flow, their preconditions evaluate as *skipped*. If this is the case, either the end user decides to skip the activity, or the automatic generation of pre-activities allows the update of data values from *skipped* to *exists* state and, thus, the execution can proceed according to the activity specification.

Goal dependences. The subgoal relationship defines the dependences among goals. These dependences can be mandatory or optional. To fulfil a goal, it is necessary that all its mandatory sub-goals are already achieved. The creation of a new goal may include the definition of new data entities and data relationships. These changes to the data specification may have impact on the goal-based execution, as explained below.

Data dependences. The data specification is a UML like specification of entities, attributes and relationships. Conditions, either activity's pre- and post- conditions or goal conditions, depend on data. Conditions can use several predicates. When applied to a data entity the `exists` predicate holds true if the data value is in state *exists*, skipped if the data value is in state *skipped* and false it it is in state *empty*. The entities relationships define data dependences. For instance, if there is a one to many relationship between two entities, an instance of the first entity has to exist when an instance of the second entity is created. This kind of dependence restricts the order by which goals can be achieved. Therefore, the goal execution order can also depend on the data structure, which has some similitude with the product-based approaches [6].

4.2   Workflow Specification Qualities

Well-formed Activity Specification. An activity-based specification is well-formed when any sequence of activities that is enabled by control flow is also enabled by data flow. This means that whenever an activity is enabled by control flow its pre-condition should hold true. The sequences of activities of well-formed activity specifications which first activity can execute in the workflow initial state are called *correct sequences*.

Prove that an Activity Specification is Well-formed. Consider a sequence of activities that are enabled by control flow, and that the first activity can execute in the workflow initial state. Consider the set of activities that are enabled for execution by control flow, after the execution of the given sequence of activities. For each one of these activities we have to show that the composition of the sequence activities post-conditions generates a shared state where the activity pre-condition holds true.

Blended Workflow Specification Compliance. Given a well-formed activity-based specification and an initial set of business goals, we say that the activity-based specification complies with a goal-based specification if every successful execution of the activity-based specification, brings the workflow instances to a state where the initial set of business goals hold. In this case we say that the activity-based specification implements the goal-based specification.

Prove of Compliance for a Blended Workflow Specification. For each correct sequence of activities of the well-formed activity specification, which execution brings the workflow to a final state (*correct final sequence*), it is necessary to show that the composition of the activities post-conditions generate a state where the initial set of mandatory business goals hold true. Additionally, it is necessary to show that for each optional business goal, in the initial set of business goals, there is at least one correct final sequence which execution generates a state where the optional business goal holds true.

4.3   Workflow Instances Synchronisation

Synchronised Execution. The two views, activity and goal, of a blended workflow instance are synchronised when the end user has the same amount of information about goal achievement in either of the views. Additionally, the end user can proceed execution on any of the views, to achieve the business goals, without being asked to redo what was already done in the other view.

Synchronisation of Blended Workflow Views. The synchronised execution of the activity and goal views can be explained by induction on the blended workflow operations. Hence, for each operation we need to show how the data shared by both views is changed and how the views reflect these changes.

Consider the blended workflow operations:

– *Execute activity.* After an activity's execution its post-condition holds, considering that the activity is correctly implemented. Therefore, the shared data was changed accordingly. The goals conditions are re-evaluated and the goals that hold true are set as fulfilled.
– *Fulfil goal.* Similarly, when a goal is achieved its condition holds true because the shared data was changed accordingly. The post-conditions of all activities that are enabled for execution by the control flow are re-evaluated. For the activities post-conditions which hold true, the respective activities are marked as executed and the control flow re-evaluated to identify if there are new activities that became enabled for execution. If any, their post-conditions are re-evaluated and the procedure repeated.
– *Skip activity.* When an activity is skipped, the activity view changes according to the control flow, as if the activity has been executed. However, the activity is marked as *skipped* and the data entities, which are accessed by atomic conditions of the activity's post-condition, are set to the *skipped* state if they are in the *empty* state. Therefore, some of the goals can become *skipped*. In the activity view the pre-conditions of the activities that were enabled for execution by control flow are re-evaluated. For those pre-conditions which evaluate as *skipped* a pre-activity is generated.

- *Skip goal.* When a goal is skipped, the data entities accessed by its condition are set to the *skipped* state if they are in the *empty* state. For each activity which is enabled for execution by control flow, its post-conditions are re-evaluated, and if it evaluates as *skipped* the activity is marked as skipped, and the execution proceeds according to the control flow.
- *Add goal.* Adding a goal, and executing a goal that does not belong to the initial set of business goals does not have impact on the activity view.

5 Related Work

As far as we know this is the first proposal that proposes the integration of activity-based with goal-based specifications. However, there is some research work that is related to ours. Some of the work on goal-based business process models [7,8] propose methodologies to design business processes by decomposing goals. A similar methodology can be applied in the blended workflow approach do design both specifications, activity-based and goal-based. There is also a research trend on object-centric business processes [6,9,10,11]. The blended workflow approach relies on a data specification to synchronise the two views. However, it also considers activity and goal specifications as valuable artefacts because they support different kinds of behaviour, respectively, standard and unplanned.

There has been work on workflow flexibility. The work by Dadam and Reichert [12] supports a powerful set of mechanisms that allow deviations. However, end users behaviour is hindered by an activity-based specification which limits the set of possible deviations. On the other hand, ad hoc and semi-structured workflows, e.g. ActionBase [3], do not provide guidance on how end users can accomplish their work.

The work on declarative workflows, e.g. Declare [13], propose the use of temporal logic to define the control flow between activities. Although, it avoids an over-specification of the control flow, it does not prescribe a standard behaviour. The blended workflow goal view also follows an declarative approach, but the conditions are used to define what are the business goals instead of the activities execution order.

The blended workflow approach has some similarities with the case handling approach [14,15]. Both approaches consider that context tunnelling hinders knowledge workers to perform their work and use conditions to describe which goals need to be achieved. However, in the blended workflow we explicitly consider two separate specifications which can evolve separately, providing different levels of flexibility. Additionally, in blended workflow, activities' pre- and post- conditions do not add extra-semantics to the activity-based specification; an workflow instance can execute only using the control flow of the activity-based specification. Pre- and post- conditions are necessary to keep both views, goal- and activity-based, synchronised.

6   Conclusions

In this paper we present a blended workflow approach which integrates an activity-based with a goal-based specification. This approach empowers end users to deviate from the standard workflow specification whenever an unexpected situation occurs, but allow them regain the guidance of an activity-based workflow once the exceptional situation is dealt with.

The paper presents the main concepts and qualities that a blended workflow approach must have and sketches a proposal for formalisation. In future work we intend to define a complete formalisation of the blended workflow approach. On the other hand, we intend to define an architecture for the blended workflow implementation that can integrate existing activity-based engines as external modules.

We also intend to classify the different kinds of goals, and allow a discretionary achievement of goals dependent on which aspects changed in the environment. For instance, by separating organisational goals from business goals we empower end users to focus on business goals achievement when the organisational structure changes. This classification will also contribute to the definition of a set of modelling guidelines. Additionally, the guidelines should also help modellers in the definition of well-formed activity specifications that comply with its goal specification. Even though being an open issue, we believe that centring the modelling activities in the data specification will help on the identification of goal and activities conditions. Currently, we are modelling a large real case to assess the blended workflow applicability.

Acknowledgements. The author would like to thank Arthur ter Hofstede and de Marcello La Rosa from the Queensland University of Technology for the insightful discussions on the blended workflow idea. This work was supported by FCT (INESC-ID multiannual funding) through the PIDDAC Program funds.

References

1. Russell, N., ter Hofstede, A., van der Aalst, W.: Newyawl: Designing a workflow system using coloured petri nets. In: Proceedings of the International Workshop on Petri Nets and Distributed Systems, PNDS 2008 (2008)
2. OMG: Business process modelling notation (October 2009),
   http://www.bpmn.org/
3. Base, A.: Human process management system. Technical report, Action Base (2009)
4. Russell, N., ter Hofstede, A.H.M., Edmond, D., van der Aalst, W.M.P.: Workflow Data Patterns: Identification, Representation and Tool Support. In: Delcambre, L.M.L., Kop, C., Mayr, H.C., Mylopoulos, J., Pastor, Ó. (eds.) ER 2005. LNCS, vol. 3716, pp. 353–368. Springer, Heidelberg (2005)
5. van der Aalst, W., ter Hofstede, A., Kiepuszewski, B., Barros, A.: Workflow patterns. Distributed and Parallel Databases 14(1), 5–51 (2003)
6. van der Aalst, W.: On the automatic generation of workflow processes based on product structures. Computers In Industry 39(2), 97–111 (1999)

7. Kueng, P., Kawalek, P.: Goal-based business process models: creation and evaluation. Business Process Management Journal 3(1), 17–38 (1997)
8. Lapouchnian, A., Yu, Y., Mylopoulos, J.: Requirements-Driven Design and Configuration Management of Business Processes. In: Alonso, G., Dadam, P., Rosemann, M. (eds.) BPM 2007. LNCS, vol. 4714, pp. 246–261. Springer, Heidelberg (2007)
9. Künzle, V., Reichert, M.: Towards object-aware process management systems: Issues, challenges, benefits. In: Proceedings of the 10th International Workshop on Business Process Modeling, Development, and Support (2009)
10. Künzle, V., Reichert, M.: Integrating users in object-aware process management systems: Issues and challenges. In: 5th International Workshop on Business Process Design (2009)
11. Chao, T., Cohn, D., Flatgard, A., Hahn, S., Linehan, M., Nandi, P., Nigam, A., Pinel, F., Vergo, J., Wu, F.Y.: Artifact-Based Transformation of IBM Global Financing. In: Dayal, U., Eder, J., Koehler, J., Reijers, H.A. (eds.) BPM 2009. LNCS, vol. 5701, pp. 261–277. Springer, Heidelberg (2009)
12. Dadam, P., Reichert, M.: The adept project: a decade of research and development for robust and flexible process support. Computer Science - R&D 23(2), 81–97 (2009)
13. van der Aalst, W., Pesic, M., Schonenberg, H.: Declarative workflows: Balancing between flexibility and support. Computer Science - Research and Development 23(2), 99–113 (2009)
14. van der Aalst, W.M., Weske, M., Grünbauer, D.: Case handling: A new paradigm for business process support. Data and Knowledge Engineering 53 (2005)
15. Guenther, C.W., Reichert, M., van der Aalst, W.M.: Supporting flexible processes with adaptive workflow and case handling. In: Proceedings WETICE 2008 - 3rd IEEE Workshop on Agile Cooperative Process-aware Information Systems, ProGility 2008 (2008)

Role Assignment in Business Process Models

Agnes Koschmider[1], Liu Yingbo[2], and Thomas Schuster[3],

[1] Institute of Applied Informatics and Formal Description Methods
Karlsruhe Institute of Technology, Germany
agnes.koschmider@kit.edu
[2] School of Software, Tsinghua University, Beijing 100084, China
lyb01@mails.tsinghua.edu.cn
[3] FZI Forschungszentrum Informatik, Germany
schuster@fzi.de

Abstract. Business processes are subject to changes due to frequently fluctuating opportunities. The changes has as result a modification of business process models and also the organizational model since both models are jointly linked through the assignment of roles to process activities. A consistent adaptation of both model types (due to changes) still poses challenges. For instance, varying competences and skills are insufficiently considered for the (re-)assignment of roles to process activities. As a consequence, tasks are performed inefficiently. In this paper we will present an organizational model that considers resources' competences, skills and knowledge. Based on this model the hidden Markov model is applied to efficiently assign roles to process activities. The improvement in task processing through automated role assignment is a significant contribution of this approach.

1 Introduction

A business process model consists of activities that are performed by roles or respectively by organizational units. The assignment of roles to process activities depends on the roles' skills and competences and should ensure that information is allocated to proper persons. For instance, a secretary should be assigned to tasks doing preliminary work for seniors. A salesperson should be assigned to tasks supporting the interaction with customers.

Changes in information system requirements or new business opportunities may require modifications of process activities and the assignment of roles to them. Role assignment tends to be complicated because roles might be assigned to hundreds of activities as illustrated by the following example. In the past the following observations were made in enterprises [1, 2], e.g., *Enterprise A* had 48 roles and 922 process activities; in *Enterprise B* 102 roles were allocated to 399 process activities and in *Enterprise C* 81 roles were allocated to 256 activities. Advanced business process model experiences are required in order to understand and rapidly assign appropriate roles to business process activities. Therefore, assisting process modelers to efficiently assign roles to activities is of great value.

F. Daniel et al. (Eds.): BPM 2011 Workshops, Part I, LNBIP 99, pp. 37–49, 2012.

We aim to improve the assignment of roles to process activities through an advanced meta-model for resources that considers roles' competences, skills and knowledge. Based on this model we are capable to efficiently retrieve appropriate roles to perform a task. The retrieval and assignment rely on the hidden Markov model [3]. The advantage of using a hidden Markov model instead of other approaches (like data mining based approaches) is the ability to consider role's competences and workflow history data for role assignment. Additionally, the model allows considering the relationship between different process activities (described via control flow) rather than focusing on a single activity.

The approach presented in this paper can be applied twofold. Assume the process modeler is creating a process model and she is uncertain which role to assign to a process task. Based upon our approach recommendations of appropriate role assignment can be made. On the other hand our approach is suitable to support exhaustive process model reuse. Before creating a new process model by assembling already designed process models, the process builder can use our approach to update the reused process model. As soon as a process builder reuses a process model, the role assignment of the model is matched with our algorithm.

The meta-model for organizational units is summarized in the next section. Section 3 illustrates our approach of role assignment to process activities. The application of our approach is demonstrated in Section 4. Section 5 compares our approach with related work and Section 6 concludes the paper with an outlook on future research.

2   Modeling Foundation

In this section we illustrate the requirements and modeling foundation of our proposed solution. Therefore we will outline a meta-model for the description of resources that can be utilized in business processes. The meta-model defines the resource modeling language (RML), which is introduced by [21]. Within the following subsection we illustrate the core of RML defined by the human resource meta-model (HRMM).

2.1   Organizational Meta-model

HRMM is a MOF-compliant meta-model, modeled as ecore model [20]. An overview of the HRMM is given in Figure 1. Central concepts of HRMM are: *HumanResource*, *Role*, *OrganizationalUnit* and the competence related modeling objects *Competence*, *Skill* and *Knowledge*. In utmost related approaches competence concepts are not modeled explicitly, although different studies revealed that roles and human resources depend on competences [11, 16]. To tackle this issue HRMM integrates competence descriptions and associates them to roles and human resources, thus allowing for enhanced assignment strategies. In HRMM this is represented by the model elements *Competence*, *Skill* and *Knowledge*. In order to enable a sound assignment of activities to resources, we will reveal relationships of competence models and resource models (a business process view) that can be modeled in RML.

HRMM is part of the RML meta-model and combines approaches known by other resource meta-models in business process management [11] with competence descriptions as utilized in human resource management [17, 18]. The meta-model allows definitions of organizational aspects and hierarchies; furthermore it allows an explicit extension of these structures by descriptions of competences (in particular competences, skills and knowledge). The competences can be modeled independently and may be reused for further specifications of roles and human resources (as shown below). With the intention of empowering assignment strategies, it is essential to know that competences, skills and knowledge can be detailed by a level of proficiency (as given in EQF [17]); furthermore competences may require other competences, skills and knowledge, while skills can require other skills and knowledge. Additionally competences can be prioritized by a correlation coefficient.

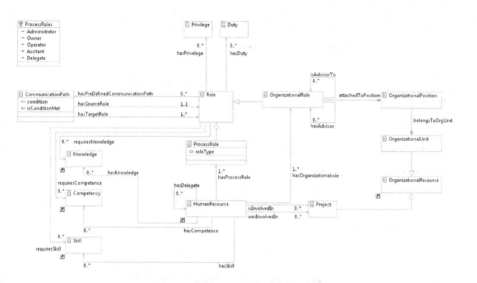

Fig. 1. Human Resource Meta Model (HRMM)

Human resources (*HumanResource*) are used to depict manpower. To represent their integration in organizational structures human resources can be associated to organizational roles (*OrganizationalRole*) and positions (*OrganizationalPosition*). Organizational hierarchies are detailed and reflected by the elements *OrganizationPosition*, *OrganizationalUnit* and their associated relationships *hasAdvisor* and *isAdvisorTo* of *OrganizationalRole*. Roles may be detailed by rights (*Privilege*), obligations (*Duty*) and predefined communication channels (*CommunicationPath*), e.g., to model escalation mechanisms. Furthermore organizational roles can be used to determine appropriate resources for task execution. Figure 2 illustrates an instance of a human resource model given in RML. While it is obvious that the organizational structure is basically given graphically, the box at the right hand side of the figure reveals that a lot of properties are modeled as non-graphical attributes of a model element.

The description of a delegate is given as non-graphical attribute (in this case *Architect B* – with associated organizational role *Chief Designer* – is a delegate of *Manager A* – with associated organizational role *Project Manager*). Furthermore the description of competences, skills and knowledge is also modeled as non-graphical attributes. The competences given in Figure 2 are competences suggested by the European standard e-CF [17].

Obviously the combination of the concepts states above bridges the gap between business process management and human resource management. Consequently, not only details about the modeled resources and their competences are revealed, but also decision support for a multitude of questions is facilitated. Decisions which can be supported by this modeling technique are (1) Recruitment of new resources, (2) Identification of core competences or (3) Task allocation.

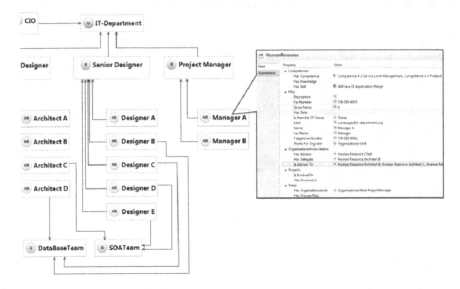

Fig. 2. Cut-Out of a RML Instance

The first two points are strongly related to HR planning and business partner selection. Task allocation finally is a common issue during business process execution – usually solved by the definition of declarative constraints (at modeling time) and specialized algorithms to match appropriate resources (at runtime). In the following sections task allocation is addressed by assignment of roles to process activities instead of particular resources. Thereby the process model is kept independent of changes in the organizational model.

3 Automatic Role Assignment Based on the Hidden Markov Model

In this section we suggest to solve the assignment of roles to activities by means of hidden Markov model inference [4].

3.1 Hidden Markov Model Inference

The hidden Markov model (HMM) is a statistical Markov model in which the system being modeled is assumed to be a Markov process with unobserved (hidden) states. These states are not directly visible, but output, dependent on the state, is visible. Each state has a probability distribution over the possible output events. Therefore the sequence of events generated by the HMM gives some information about the sequence of states. Note that the adjective 'hidden' refers to the state sequence through which the model passes, not to the parameters of the model; even if the model parameters are known exactly, the model is still 'hidden' [3].

Formally, a HMM can be defined by a set of parameters $\lambda = (N, M, T, E, \pi)$:
- N, is a set of hidden states,
- M, is a set of events,
- $T_{|N| \times |N|}$, is a transition matrix that determines the state transition probability,
- $E_{|N| \times |M|}$, is a matrix that denotes the emission probability that the event will be observed for any given state $n \in N$,
- π, is an initial vector that denotes the probability of each state in the first beginning.

For a given sequence of events with t observations $y_{1..t} \in M$, and a hidden Markov model with parameter λ, an inference associated to this HMM [4] is to find a probability distribution over hidden states for a point in time in the past, i.e. to compute $P(x_k|y_{1..t})$, for $k < t$. This inference problem can be solved by the so called "forward-backward algorithm", which is an efficient method for computing the smoothest values for all hidden state variables [5].

3.2 Building Hidden Markov Model

In our approach the set of hidden states N describes the set of possible roles, which may be attached to activities in a workflow model. The set of observable events M relates to a set of workflow activities. The inference associated to HMM can be described as the probability distribution over roles (hidden state) and activities of a given activity sequence (observed events) in a process model and a hidden Markov model. By this probability distribution the likelihood of the assignment of roles to activities can be determined. Hence, an ordered list of role assignments can be recommended to the process modeler according to the probability distribution.

As we mentioned before, if parameter λ of HMM is defined the probability distribution over roles and activities can be easily obtained by the "forward-backward algorithm". In conclusion determining the parameter λ has to be done; therefore we present an approach to fulfill this task:
- Let all candidate roles (plus a start and an end role) be the set of hidden states, namely N,
- Let all activities (including a start and an end activity) be the set of events, namely M,

-   Transition matrix T can be obtained from event logs of the workflow by analyzing the sequence frequency of role transitions. The entry T_{ij} represents the probability of transition from role i to role j, thus T_{ij} can be calculated as:

$$T_{ij} = \frac{freq(R_i \rightarrow R_j)}{freq(R_i \rightarrow *)} \qquad (1)$$

$freq(R_i \rightarrow R_j)$ refers to the number of transitions from *role i* to *role j* in the log file, and $freq(R_i \rightarrow *)$ refers to all transitions from *role i*.

-   Emission matrix E can be specified according to the competence and skills of roles for a given activity, which allows answering the following question: "according to the knowledge and skill of a *role i* what kind of activities are suitable to be performed by this *role*?". This competence value can be obtained by the measurement of the human resource meta-model (see Section 2).

$$E_{ij} = Competence\ of\ role\ i\ to\ activity\ j \qquad (2)$$

-   Finally, the initial vector π is (1, 0, ..., 0); which indicates that the start activity is always performed by the start role.

Before calculating the role assignment probability, we need to uncover similar process activities in order to avoid inconsistencies in the workflow event log. To find synonyms, homonyms and different abstraction levels of activity labels, we use the similarity measures presented in [22]. After this similarity match process, activities in the new workflow model can be easily mapped to events in the hidden Markov model.

3.3   Calculating Role Assignment Probability Matrix

After obtaining the parameters of the HMM and uncovering similar process activities, the final step is to determine the probability of roles being appropriate to be assigned to activities. However, in real world a workflow model usually contains various control flow structures such as e.g., *joins* and *forks*, which eventually result in multiple observed sequences of activities in the same workflow model. Such observed sequences may generate multiple probability distributions over roles for activities, when HMM inference is applied. Therefore, it is essential merging different probability matrixes for each observed activity sequences.

Assume that the workflow model is a directed acyclic graph (DAG) of activities. For each activity $a_i \in M$ let probability distribution p_i be a vector of probability with ||N|| entries. Each entry in p_i refers to the probability of one role for activity a_i. Based on a workflow model, an activity sequences set S can be generated by enumerating all paths from the start activity to the end activity.

For each activity sequence $s \in S$, a probability matrix P_s of roles over activities can be computed by means of the "forward-backward algorithm" namely $P_s = (p_1, p_2, ...p_n)$, n=||M||. Note if activity a_j is not in the given sequence s, then the corresponding probability distribution vector $p_j=0$ is $P_s = (p_1, p_2 ...p_{j-1}, 0, p_{j+1} ...p_n)$. In addition, if the occurrence probability of an activity sequence is different, a weight w_s can also be assigned to the activity sequence s. Once the probability matrix for any activity sequence has been computed, the probability distribution matrix P of roles over activities in the workflow model can be obtained by calculating the weighted average probability matrix of all the probability matrixes and normalizing each column vector in order to ensure that each column sum equals 1.

$$P = normalize\left(\frac{\sum_{s \in S} w_s P_s}{\sum_{s \in S} w_s}\right) \tag{3}$$

Based upon the role assignment probability matrix, the role assignment for any given activity can be easily performed by retrieving the most appropriate role for a specific activity.

4   Assignment Demonstration

In order to demonstrate the applicability of our approach, we present an example in this section. Let the following process model with seven activities (design activity, verify activity, review prototype, approve design, classify documents and additionally a start and end activity as postulated in Section 3.1.) be given as depicted in Figure 3.

Fig. 3. Example process of engineering design process

There are six roles that can be assigned to these activities {Start Role, Senior Designer, Chief Designer, Project Manager, Secretary, End Role}. Skills and competences of roles are listed in Table 1. Note that the activities {Start, End} and roles {Start Role and End Role} are added in order to facilitate following analysis.

Table 1. Role Information

#	Role	Skill	Competence
R1	Start Role	Start workflow	
R2	Senior Designer	create drawing, classify documents	service
R3	Chief Designer	create drawing, review drawing	design architecture
R4	Project Manager	review drawing, approve design	product planning
R5	Secretary	classify documents	contract management
R6	End Role	End Workflow	

Furthermore we assume that there are ten completed cases in the event log, the case information and related performers' role for each activity are listed in Table 2.

In order to build the hidden Markov model, we perform the following steps. Firstly, let the set of hidden states be the set of candidate roles namely N = {start role(R1), senior designer(R2), chief designer(R3), project manager(R4), secretary(R5), end role(R6)}. Secondly, the event set M is built by observable activities in the process model namely M = {start, design activity, verify activity, review prototype, approve design, classify document, end}.

The transition matrix can also be obtained from the workflow event log by counting the frequency of direct role transition during execution. For example in Table 2 there are 10 direct role transitions from R1 to others (the entries with underscore), 7 out of these 10 transitions are from R1 to R2, and 3 out of these 10 transitions are from R1 to R3. Therefore the entries $T_{1,2}$ and $T_{1,3}$ in transition matrix T are $T_{1,2}=7/10$ and $T_{1,3}=3/10$. Table 3 illustrates the transition matrix calculated out of the workflow log shown in Table 2.

Table 2. Workflow Event Log

	Start	Design Activity	Verify Activity	Review Prototype	Approve Design	Classify Documents	End
1	R1	R2	R2	R3	R4	R5	R6
2	R1	R2	R3	R3	R4	R5	R6
3	R1	R2	R2	R3	R4	R5	R6
4	R1	R2	R2	R3	R4	R5	R6
5	R1	R2	R2	R4	R4	R3	R6
6	R1	R2	R2	R3	R4	R5	R6
7	R1	R2	R2	R3	R4	R5	R6
8	R1	R3	R2	R3	R4	R5	R6
9	R1	R3	R3	R3	R4	R2	R6
10	R1	R3	R3	R4	R4	R5	R6

Table 3. Transition Matrix from Workflow Event Log

	R1:Start Role	R2:Senior Designer	R3:Chief Designer	R4:Project Manager	R5:Secretary	R6:End Role
R1:Start Role	0	7/10	3/10	0	0	0
R2:Senior Designer	0	6/15	7/15	1/15	1/15	0
R3:Chief Designer	0	1/15	4/15	9/15	1/15	0
R4:Project Manager	0	1/12	1/12	2/12	8/12	0
R5:Secretary	0	0	0	0	0	1
R6:End Role	0	0	0	0	0	1

The emission matrix shows probabilities of generating observable events when the system is in a hidden state. In workflow staff assignment observable events are workflow activities, hidden states are roles. Hence event emission probability means the likelihood of roles to complete certain activities. Apparently, this likelihood is determined by role's skills and competences, therefore the emission matrix can be created by domain experts. Table 4 shows an example emission matrix where each column represents an activity (observable event) and each row represents a role (hidden state). As shown in Table 4, it is most likely for senior designers to complete the "Design Activity" (0.7), while it is quite unlikely to perform the activity of "Approve Design" (0.01).

The initial state vector defines the probability of choosing the first state when the transition starts. Since workflows always start with the start activity the initial role is always the start role; hence the initial state vector is (1, 0...). Once parameters of HMM are defined, role assignment can be easily performed as follows. Assume the process designer tends to reuse process artifacts without assigned roles (in general: appropriate role have to be assigned to modeled process activities). Then all sequences of activities (start to end) are enumerated. Initially, similar activities are uncovered (for instance the activity "Verify Specification" is matched to "Verify Activity", see Figure 4). Subsequently, resulting activity sequences are $s_1=\{$Start, Design Activity, Verify Activity, Approve Design, Classify Documents, End$\}$ and $s_2=\{$Start, Design Activity, Review Prototype, Approve Design, Classify Documents, End$\}$.

Table 4. Emission Matrix for Roles to Activities

	start	Design Activity	Verify Activity	Review Prototype	Approve Design	Classify Documents	end
R1:Start Role	1	0	0	0	0	0	0
R2:Senior Designer	0	0.7	0.2	0.05	0.01	0.04	0
R3:Chief Designer	0	0.2	0.2	0.4	0.15	0.05	0
R4:Project Manager	0	0.05	0.05	0.2	0.65	0.05	0
R5:Secretary	0	0	0	0	0	1	0
R6:End Role	0	0	0	0	0	0	1

With the parameter of HMM defined in the previous discussion, the probability distribution matrix for observed sequence can be computed by means of the "forward/backward algorithm". Table 5 and Table 6 show the probability distribution matrix of s_1 and s_2. Note that for s_1 the review activity is not available, therefore corresponding probability distribution over roles for "Review" in table 5 is 0. Accordingly, probability distribution of activity "Verify" in table 6 is also 0.

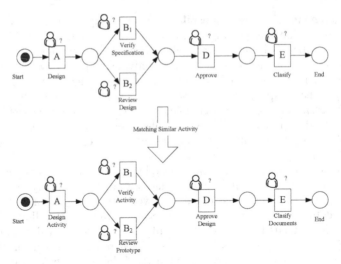

Fig. 4. Target workflow model after matching similar activity

Table 5. Probability distribution of roles over activities with s_1

	Start	Design Activity	Verify Activity	Review Prototype	Approve Design	Classify Documents	End
Start Role	1.000	0.000	0.000	0.000	0.000	0.000	0.000
Senior Designer	0.000	0.9438	0.0113	0.000	0.0007	0.0014	0.000
Chief Designer	0.000	0.0562	0.9572	0.000	0.0002	0.0008	0.000
Project Manager	0.000	0.000	0.0315	0.000	0.9990	0.000	0.000
Secretary	0.000	0.000	0.000	0.000	0.000	0.9978	0.000
end role	0.000	0.000	0.000	0.000	0.000	0.000	1.000

Table 6. Probability distribution of roles over activities with s_2

	Start	Design Activity	Verify Activity	Review Prototype	Approve Design	Classify Documents	End
Start Role	1.000	0.000	0.000	0.000	0.000	0.000	0.000
Senior Designer	0.000	0.9525	0.000	0.0852	0.0024	0.0025	0.000
Chief Designer	0.000	0.0475	0.000	0.9000	0.0005	0.0016	0.000
Project Manager	0.000	0.000	0.000	0.0148	0.9972	0.000	0.000
Secretary	0.000	0.000	0.000	0.000	0.000	0.9959	0.000
end role	0.000	0.000	0.000	0.000	0.000	0.000	1.000

Finally, the probability distribution over roles for all activities can be computed by calculating the normalized weighted average of table 5 and table 6. The result is shown in table 7. With probability distribution shown in table 7, the most suitable role assignment for activities in the new workflow model is shown in figure 5.

Table 7. Probability distribution of roles over all Activities

	Start	Design	Verify	Review	Approve	Classify	End
Start Role	1.000	0.000	0.000	0.000	0.000	0.000	0.000
Senior Designer	0.000	0.9482	0.0113	0.0852	0.0015	0.0019	0.000
Chief Designer	0.000	0.0518	0.9572	0.9000	0.0003	0.0012	0.000
Project Manager	0.000	0.000	0.0315	0.0148	0.9981	0.000	0.000
Secretary	0.000	0.000	0.000	0.000	0.000	0.9969	0.000
end role	0.000	0.000	0.000	0.000	0.000	0.000	1.000

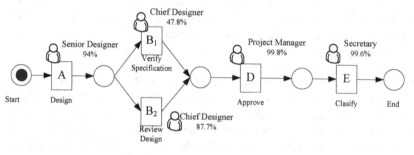

Fig. 5. Suggested role assignment

5   Related Work

The purpose of our work is to automate the part of resource assignment. In particular, we used a probabilistic approach to realize our idea. Therefore it is related to the efforts of automating process resource assignment. Automating resource assignment is very important in workflow resource management [7]. Early work on automating resource assignment in process management is based upon rules [8, 9, 10]. However, rule based approaches of automating resource assignment require knowledge of organization and business, which is not likely to be obtained in the first beginning. In [11] zur Muehlen envisioned the idea of applying knowledge discovery approach to help process resource assignment, later on, in [12] Ly et al. have shown that the problem of deriving resource assignment rules using information from event log data and organizational information as input can be interpreted as an inductive learning problem. Therefore, machine learning techniques can be adapted in order to solve the problem. In particular they use decision tree methods to find those assignment rules [13]. In [14] Liu et al. further developed the approach using new machine learning approaches and evaluated the practical validity using three enterprises' data set. In [15] Huang et al. proposed a reinforcement learning based approach to allocate resource to workflow with performance optimization consideration. They introduce a mechanism in which the resource allocation optimization problem is modeled as Markov decision processes and solved using reinforcement learning. The proposed mechanism observes its environment to learn appropriate policies, which optimize resource allocation in business process execution. The hidden Markov model based approach is also used in [6] by Yang et al. to allocate the most proficient set of employees for a whole business process based on workflow event logs.

6   Conclusion

The assignment of roles to process activities is a time-consuming task and requires a certain amount of business process model experiences. In this paper we have first introduced a meta-model for the description of resources that can be utilized in business processes. The advantage of this model is an exhaustive consideration of roles' skills and competences, thus allowing to allocate appropriate resources (persons that fulfill specific roles) to given activities of workflow models. Based upon this meta-model we used the hidden Markov model inference to provide recommendation for the assignment of roles to process activities. Assisting process modelers to efficiently assign roles to activities is of great value.

Work that is in progress is to integrate a formalism that allows checking role conflicts (if roles are assigned to activities, which are not able to perform the task). Furthermore the consideration of actual resource capacities (number of resources attached to roles) and instance properties (instantiation of workflow instances based on probability distributions) would be valuable and is also part of current research activities.

References

1. Liu, Y., Wang, J., Sun, J.: A Machine Learning Approach to Semi-Automating Workflow Staff Assignment. In: The 22nd Annual ACM Symposium on Applied Computing (SAC 2007), Seoul, Korea (2007)
2. Liu, Y., Wang, J., Sun, J.: Mining Workflow Event Log to Find Parallel Task Dispatching Rules. In: The 4th International Workshop on Computer Supported Activity Coordination (CSAC 2007), Funchal, Madeira - Portugal (2007)
3. Rabiner, L.R.: A Tutorial on Hidden Markov Models and Selected Applications in Speech Recognition. Proceedings of the IEEE 77(2), 257–286 (1989)
4. Cappé, O., Moulines, E., Rydén, T.: Inference in Hidden Markov Models. Springer, Heidelberg (2005)
5. Durbin, R., Eddy, S., Krogh, A., Mitchison, G.: Biological Sequence Analysis (1998)
6. Yang, H., Wang, C., Liu, Y., Wang, J.: An Optimal Approach for Workflow Staff Assignment Based on Hidden Markov Models. In: Meersman, R., Herrero, P. (eds.) OTM-WS 2008. LNCS, vol. 5333, pp. 24–26. Springer, Heidelberg (2008)
7. Russell, N., ter Hofstede, A.H.M., Edmond, D., van der Aalst, W.M.P.: Workflow Resource Patterns. Eindhoven University of Technology, Eindhoven (2005)

8. Du, W., Shan, M.-C.: Enterprise Workflow Resource Management. In: HP Labs Technical Reports (1999)
9. Huang, Y.-N., Shan, M.-C.: Policies in a Resource Manager of Workflow Systems: Modeling, Enforcement and Management. In: HP Labs Technical Reports (1999)
10. Reis, C.A.L., Reis, R.Q., Schlebbe, H., Nunes, D.J.: A Policy-Based Resource Instantiation Mechanism to Automate Software Process Management. In: Proceedings of the 14th International Conference on Software Engineering and Knowledge Engineering. ACM Press, Ischia (2002)
11. zur Muehlen, M.: Organizational Management in Workflow Applications – Issues and Perspectives. Information Technology and Management 5(3-4), 271–291 (2004)
12. Ly, L.T., Rinderle, S., Dadam, P., Reichert, M.: Mining Staff Assignment Rules from Event-Based Data. In: Bussler, C.J., Haller, A. (eds.) BPM 2005. LNCS, vol. 3812, pp. 177–190. Springer, Heidelberg (2006)
13. Rinderle-Ma, S., van der Aalst, W.: Life-Cycle Support for Staff Assignment Rules in Process-Aware Information Systems, Technical Report, TU Eindhoven (2007)
14. Liu, Y., Wang, J., Yang, Y., Sun, J.: A Semi-Automatic Approach for Workflow Staff Assignment. Comput. Ind. 59(5), 463–476 (2008)
15. Huang, Z., van der Aalst, W., Lu, X., Duan, H.: Reinforcement Learning Based Resource Allocation in Business Process Management. Data & Knowledge Engineering (2010)
16. van der Aalst, W.M.P., Kumar, A., Verbeek, H.M.W.: Organizational modeling in UML and XML in the context of workflow systems. In: Proceedings of the 2003 ACM Symposium on Applied Computing, Melbourne, Florida, pp. S. 603–S. 608 (2003)
17. European e-Competence Framework, "European e-Competence Framework 2.0 – A commom European Framework for ICT Professionals in all industrie sectors". In: CEN Workshop Agreement, European Commission (2010)
18. HR-XML Consortium: Competencies, HR-XML Version 3.0 (2011), http://www.hr-xml.org/
19. OASIS: Web Services – Human Task (WS-HumanTask) Specification Version (November 2009)
20. Object Management Group: Meta Object Facility (MOF) Core Specification OMG Available Specification Version 2.0 (January 2006), http://www.omg.org/docs/formal/06-01-01.pdf
21. Oberweis, Schuster, T.: A meta-model based approach to the description of resources and skills. In: 16th Americas Conference on Informaction Systems, AMCIS 2010 Proceedings (2010)
22. Ehrig, M., Koschmider, A., Oberweis, A.: Measuring Similarity between Semantic Business Process Models. In: Proceedings of the Fourth Asia-Pacific Conference on Conceptual Modelling (APCCM 2007), pp. 71–80. Australian Computer Science Communications, Ballarat (2007)

RAL: A High-Level User-Oriented Resource Assignment Language for Business Processes*

Cristina Cabanillas, Manuel Resinas, and Antonio Ruiz-Cortés

Universidad de Sevilla, Spain
{cristinacabanillas,resinas,aruiz}@us.es

Abstract. An important task of business process design is the definition of what and how members of an organization are involved in the activities of the business processes developed within it. In this paper we analyse the capabilities of BPMN 2.0, the de-facto standard for business process modelling, in this regard. The conclusion is that, although it provides some mechanisms to assign resources to business process activities, they present several drawbacks. On the one hand, it does not provide a clear way to relate the assignment of resources with a model of the structure of the organization. On the other hand, it relies on XPath as the default language to assign resources to activities. The consequence is that it has limitations regarding the expressiveness of resource assignment expressions. Furthermore, it makes resource assignment not easy to learn and use since XPath has not been designed for that purpose. To overcome these drawbacks we introduce RAL (Resource Assignment Language), a DSL based on a well-known organizational metamodel that can be used together with BPMN 2.0. RAL provides more expressiveness to the resource assignments and it uses a high-level sintaxis defined to be used by technically unskilled users.

Keywords: resource-aware business process design, resource assignment, RAL, BPMN, workflow resource pattern.

1 Introduction

Business processes and the organization in which they are developed are closely related, since the human resources[1] of the company (i.e., its members) play an indispensable role both as supervisors of the execution of automatic activities and as performers of software-aided and/or manual activities. Consequently, an important task in business process design is the definition of which members of an organization are involved in each of the activities of the business processes developed within it.

* This work has been partially supported by the European Commission (FEDER), Spanish Government under the CICYT project SETI (TIN2009-07366); and projects THEOS (TIC-5906) and ISABEL (P07-TIC-2533) funded by the Andalusian Local Government.

[1] From now on we will use the term *resource* to refer to *human resources*.

F. Daniel et al. (Eds.): BPM 2011 Workshops, Part I, LNBIP 99, pp. 50–61, 2012.

Nowadays, most business process modelling languages provide some mechanism to carry out such a task. In this work we focus on BPMN 2.0 because it is the current standard notation for business process modelling. We have studied its capabilities to manage resources in business process models and we have realized that, although the graphical representation of resource assignments is not possible in BPMN, it does provide a textual way to assign resources to the activities of the process models. Specifically, it provides two different methods, one focused on selecting resources of a concrete type (e.g. a role or a group) and applying filters over that type to decide the potential performers of the activity, and another open to allow free assignments on any basis. In both cases, it relies on XPath[2] as the default language to either define filters or assignments. However, these methods present several drawbacks regarding expressiveness, relation with the organizational structure and ease of use.

As far as expressiveness is concerned, sometimes the assignment of the resources that can do a certain activity is quite straightforward, e.g., "Activity *Design process* must be performed by a business process analyst". However, it is not hard to find assignments that are more complex to express. For instance, "Activity *Supervise Code* must be performed by an expertised technician (with at least three years of experience) or by a consultant". In this regard, Russell et al. have described a set of *workflow resource patterns* that intend to capture the various ways in which resources are represented and utilised in workflows [1]. In particular, the *creation patterns* focus on different ways resources can be assigned to activities and constitute the main set of workflow resource patterns expressing things configurable at the level of process models, such as for instance "Activity *Deploy Application* must be undertaken by someone that reports work to the *Project Manager*, preferably the person that carried out activity *Supervise Code*". Unfortunately, the use of XPath as the default language limits the expressiveness to specify resource assignment expressions, as detailed in Section 3.

As can be seen from the previous examples, relating the organizational structure with the process models is necessary in order to be able to deal with some of these patterns. Besides being unable to express such type of constraints, the lack of consideration of the organizational structure regarding resource assignment may cause execution problems such as delays and/or blocks. For instance, two parallel activities could be associated with the same role, meaning that persons playing that role must perform them at run time. If only one person of the organization has that role, there may be delays in the process execution. This problem could be solved with different resource management. However, if the process model is not explicitly related to a model of the structure of the organization, which is the case of BPMN, it is much harder to analyse and detect this kind of situations.

Finally, one of the goals of BPMN is to provide a notation that is understandable by non-technical users, allowing to reduce the gap between business and IT. However, XPath is a language oriented exclusively to technical users and it has a very different purpose than to assign resources to activities. This makes

---

[2] http://www.w3.org/TR/xpath20/

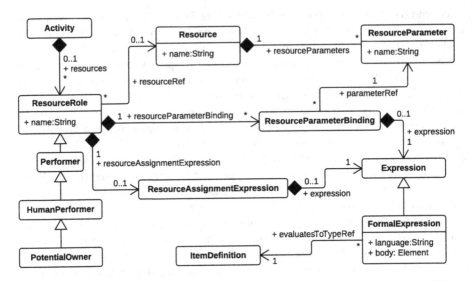

Fig. 1. Excerpt of the BPMN 2.0 metamodel regarding resource assignment [2]

it certainly hard for a non-technical user to understand such a type of resource assignment.

We have defined a Domain Specific Language (DSL) called RAL (Resource Assignment Language) with the aim of easing the way resources are assigned in BPMN, while providing high expressiveness due to its basis on a well-known organizational metamodel [1]. In this paper we will explain what can be expressed with RAL and how it can be used inside of BPMN 2.0.

Section 2 contains a detailed explanation of how BPMN 2.0 allows resource assignment in business process models. In Section 3 we present RAL. Section 4 shows the expressiveness of RAL by applying it to some creation patterns and to an example use case. Some related work can be found in Section 5, and a set of conclusions are presented in Section 6.

2   Resource Management Capabilities of BPMN 2.0

BPMN is the de-facto standard for business process modelling. It has been improved in its current version (2.0) as for the assignment of resources to activities of a business process [2]. However, the definition of *resource* BPMN 2.0 provides and the use of this term are still a little imprecise and hard to use. On the one hand, it allows the definition of elements of type *Resource*, but resource types are not set (so a resource can be anything, from a person to an organization), no relationships can be established between them and there is not a metamodel supporting them. On the other hand, the procedure proposed by BPMN is not oriented to modellers without technical skills, since the default language to define resource assignment expressions is XPath, which is far from easy-to-use.

Figure 1 shows an excerpt of the BPMN 2.0 metamodel regarding the assignment of resources to activities [2]. Each activity can have zero or more instances of *ResourceRole* assigned, which can be seen as potential performers or potential resources responsible for the activity at run time (class *PotentialOwner*). The metamodel contains two alternatives to assign the so-called potential owners.

Queries over a Specific Resource Type. As stated in [2], "a *Resource* can be *Human Resources* as well as any other resource assigned to activities during process execution time. The definition of a resource is *abstract* [...]". The BPMN specification indicates that *the name* of the resource type we want to assign to an activity must be set in class *Resource*, e.g., a specific role. We can then configure the assignment giving values to the resource parameters, such as country or age, by means of class *ResourceParameterBinding*. This class will contain an *Expression* that defines constraints on the values of the parameters to reduce the number of potential owners. Class *ResourceParameterBinding* can only be used if in conjunction with *Resource*.

In order to define the filtering expression BPMN proposes by default the use of XPath. The language has been extended to provide functions that ease some tasks such as reading information from data objects connected to the activities of the process. A brief example of this resource assignment method is shown in [2]. As can be deduced from the XML code of the example, expressing queries this way may become quite complicated and, besides, although the name of the resource type is textually specified, the process actually knows nothing about what type of resource it is (i.e., it could be a role, a group, etcetera), so the actual resource type is something transparent to the process.

Free Resource Assignment. BPMN allows less restrictive resource assignment as well, permitting to write any XPath expression to define the assignment by means of class *ResourceAssignmentExpression*. In this case, the XPath expression does not have to be stuck to a previously fixed resource type. This total freedom may be positive because no constraints are set beforehand but, at the same time, it makes it difficult for users not familiarized with XPath to define complex resource assignments in an easy and high-level way. We remind the reader that the main goal of BPMN is to allow non-technical users to design or, at least understand business process models. From this perspective, we believe the current resource assignment language provided by BPMN is not the best option.

It is important to stress that the two methods are incompatible with each other, i.e., the selection of potential owners is made either with the mechanism based on *Resource* or with a *ResourceAssignmentExpression*. Our proposal constitutes an alternative to XPath that must be used in the second resource assignment method aforementioned.

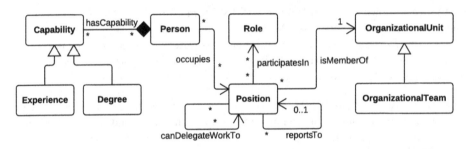

Fig. 2. Excerpt of the organizational metamodel described by Russel et al. [1]

3   RAL (Resource Assignment Language)

RAL is a DSL developed to ease the assignment of resources to the business process activities. It uses the entities and relationships defined by Russell et al. in the organizational metamodel shown in Figure 2 to define the way assignment expressions can be built. As depicted in the figure, the organizational metamodel basically consists of persons, positions, roles and organizational units. A person can have a set of capabilities, such as his/her professional experience. The metamodel is extensible to include new capabilities. Each person occupies one or more positions within an organization. In turn, a position can participate in several roles and belong to an organizational unit, which can be, for instance, an organizational team. Some relationships between positions are also established.

RAL expressions should be placed in class *FormalExpression* of the BPMN metamodel (cf. Figure 1), setting attribute *language* to RAL and writing the RAL expression in attribute *body*. As described below, RAL allows expressing from simple assignments based on a specific person or role to assignments as complex as desired by means of the compound expressions. Its EBNF notation is shown in Language 1. We next explain RAL expressions, using the term *group resource* to refer to anything but persons, i.e., positions, roles and organizational units. Persons are sometimes called *individual resources*.

Expression *IS PersonConstraint* allows expressing that an activity must be performed by someone indicated in a *PersonConstraint*: (i) a specific person; (ii) the person who performed another activity; or (iii) the person indicated in a data field.

HAS GroupResourceType groupResourceName allows assigning an activity to a given group resource, or to one read from a field of a data object.

SHARES Amount GroupResourceType WITH PersonConstraint is used to assign persons that share some or all position(s), role(s) or organizational unit(s) with the person indicated in a *PersonConstraint*.

Expression *HAS CAPABILITY CapabilityConstraint* allows expressing constraints based on personal capabilities, such as *years of experience* or *reputation*[3]. These constraints may consist of the existence of certain capability

---

[3] We can also consider issues such as *age* or *origin* capabilities.

Language 1. Expression assignment EBNF language definition

```
Expression := IS PersonConstraint
   | HAS GroupResourceType GroupResourceConstraint
   | SHARES Amount GroupResourceType WITH PersonConstraint
   | HAS CAPABILITY CapabilityConstraint
   | IS ASSIGNMENT IN ACTIVITY activityName
   | RelationshipExpression
   | CompoundExpression

RelationshipExpression := ReportExpression
   | DelegateExpression

ReportExpression := REPORTS TO PositionConstraint Depth
   | IS Depth REPORTED BY PositionConstraint

DelegateExpression := CAN DELEGATE WORK TO PositionConstraint
   | CAN HAVE WORK DELEGATED BY PositionConstraint

CompoundExpression := NOT (Expression)
   | (Expression) OR (Expression)
   | (Expression) AND (Expression)
   | (Expression) AND IF POSSIBLE (Expression)

PersonConstraint := personName
   | PERSON IN DATA FIELD dataObject.fieldName
   | PERSON WHO DID ACTIVITY activityName

GroupResourceConstraint := groupResourceName
   | IN DATA FIELD dataObject.fieldName

CapabilityConstraint := capabilityName
   | CapabilityRestriction

PositionConstraint := POSITION namePosition
   | POSITION OF PersonConstraint

Amount := SOME        GroupResourceType := POSITION
   | ALL                             | ROLE
                                     | UNIT
Depth := DIRECTLY
   | λ
```

or of the holding of certain condition on the value of a capability. We are not detailing the *CapabilityRestriction* for space reasons, since it is based on mathematical and logical operators and its use is easily understandable.

Expression *IS ASSIGNMENT IN ACTIVITY activityName* is used to indicate that an activity has the same RAL expression as another activity. This avoids having to re-write several times the same assignment, at the same time as it helps saving time and effort and prevents typing errors.

RelationshipExpression is set to allow expressing constraints such as "Activity *Fill Travel Authorization* must be performed by someone that reports to the *Project Coordinator*", according to the relationships between positions depicted in Figure 2.

CompoundExpression allows expressing combination and negation of the aforementioned expressions. Furthermore, the conditional expression *AND IF POSSIBLE* has been included to let the modeller express preferences/priorities. For instance, by stating that, *if possible*, an activity has to be carried

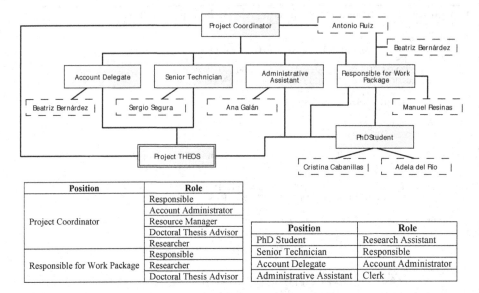

Fig. 3. Excerpt of the organizational model of ISA Group from a project perspective

out by certain role, we are meaning that that is the first assignment we have to try when actually allocating the activity to an individual resource (at run time). In case preferences are not fulfilled, they are just ignored.

Note that some of these expressions could be analysed at design time and a set of potential owners would be obtained (cf. Section 2), from which the actual owner/performer and, thus, the person in charge of the activity, would be selected at run time. However, sometimes the allocation has to be directly deferred until run time because some running information is required and it is missing at design time, e.g. those assignments depending on data field values.

It is important to notice that we have restricted RAL to expressions involving *a single instance* of a business process. The history of resource allocations and past process executions are not considered for now. Some specific examples of the language usage are described in Section 4 with the help of a use case.

4   Application of RAL. Examples

Imagine we belong to an organization with the structure shown in Figure 3. This figure contains an instantiation of the organizational metamodel described in Section 3. Specifically, it is an excerpt of the *ISA Research Group* of the University of Seville from a research project perspective. There are six positions (Project Coordinator, Account Delegate, Senior Technician, Administrative Assistant, Responsible for Work Package and PhD Student) that are members of one organizational unit (Project THEOS), and seven persons occupying these positions. Each position of the model can delegate work to any inferior position

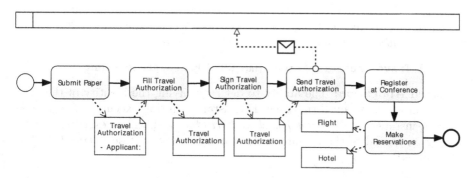

Fig. 4. Simplified process for Conference Travel Management

and report work to its immediately upper position. The relationship *participatesIn* of the metamodel is summarized in a table. For instance, individual *Beatriz Bernárdez* belongs to positions *Responsible for Work Package* and *Account delegate*. As a responsible for work package she has three roles: *Responsible*, *Researcher* and *Doctoral Thesis Advisor*. On the other hand, her other position gives her the role *Account Administrator*. Both positions are in turn linked to the *Project THEOS*, which is an organizational unit. A table with the *hasCapability* relationship should also be specified.

The business process in the BPMN model of Figure 4 may represent some work developed in our organization. The figure illustrates a simplified version of the process to manage the trip to a conference (according to the rules of the University of Seville), from the submission of the final version of an accepted paper to the booking of the transport tickets and the accommodation. It starts with the submission of the Camera Ready version of a paper, and it continues when one of the authors fills up a form requesting for authorization both to travel to the venue place and to take the funds from some funding source. This authorization must be approved by some person in charge of account management related to the applicant. The travel authorization is sent for revision to an external entity, where someone might sign the document. Then, the attendant must register at the conference and make the appropriate reservations.

We are going to show examples of resource assignments to the activities of the business process in Figure 4 using RAL language. We are using as example some workflow resource patterns. Specifically, the patterns we are most interested in are the creation patterns, as they are mainly focused on information that must/can be specified at design time, as is the case of RAL.

Direct Allocation: The ability to specify at design time the identity of the resource that will execute a task. For instance, the *Sign Travel Authorization* task must only be undertaken by *Antonio*:

```
Sign Travel Authorization: IS Antonio
```

Role-Based Allocation: The ability to specify that a task can only be executed by resources with a given role. For instance, instances of the *Fill Travel Authorization* task must be executed by a *Research Assistant*:

```
Fill Travel Authorization: HAS ROLE ResearchAssistant
```

Deferred Allocation: The ability to defer specifying the identity of the performer of a task until run time. For instance, during execution of the process, instances of the *Send Travel Authorization* task will be executed by the person named in the resource field *Applicant* of data object *Travel Authorization*:

```
Send Travel Authorization:
    IS PERSON IN DATA FIELD TravelAuthorization.Applicant
```

Authorization: The ability to specify the range of resources that are authorized to execute a task. For instance, only a *Researcher* and a *Research Assistant* are authorized to execute instances of the *Submit Paper* task:

```
Submit Paper:
    (HAS ROLE Researcher) OR (HAS ROLE ResearchAssistant)
```

Separation of Duties: The ability to specify that two tasks must be allocated to different resources in a given workflow case. For instance, instances of the *Sign Travel Authorization* task must be allocated to a different person from that who executed the *Fill Travel Authorization* task:

```
Fill Travel Authorization:
    NOT (IS PERSON WHO DID ACTIVITY SignTravelAuthorization)
Sign Travel Authorization:
    NOT (IS PERSON WHO DID ACTIVITY FillTravelAuthorization)
```

In this case, we assume at design time we do not know the real execution order of the activities and, thus, we set the constraint in both of them.

Case Handling: The ability to allocate the activities within a given workflow case to the same resource. For instance, all tasks assigned to position *PhD Student* are allocated to the same person.

```
Assigned to some activities: (HAS POSITION PhDStudent) AND
    (IS PERSON WHO DID ACTIVITY FillTravelAuthorization)
```

The second part of the composition is not necessary for the first task that has been assigned the position *PhdStudent*. Please, note that the example exposed is this case is fictitious and will not be considered later in this paper.

Retain Familiar: Where several resources are available to undertake an activity, the ability to allocate an activity within a given workflow case to the same resource that undertook a preceding activity. For instance, any *PhD Student* available can undertake the *Register at Conference* task, but it should be allocated to the same person that undertook the *Submit Paper* task.

```
Register at Conference: (HAS POSITION PhDStudent)
AND IF POSSIBLE (IS PERSON WHO DID ACTIVITY SubmitPaper)
```

Capability-based Allocation: The ability to offer or allocate instances of a task to resources based on their specific capabilities. For instance, instances of the *Submit Paper* task must be allocated to someone with a degree:

```
Submit Paper: HAS CAPABILITY Degree
```

Organizational Allocation: The ability to offer or allocate instances of a task to resources based on their position within the organization and their relationship with other resources. For instance, the *Sign Travel Authorization* task must be allocated to someone that is reported by (the position of) the person that undertook the *Fill Travel Authorization* task:

```
Sign Travel Authorization: IS REPORTED BY POSITION OF
PERSON WHO DID ACTIVITY FillTravelAuthorization
```

Please note that we have not included workflow resource pattern *history-based allocation* because we are focused on a single business process instance and disregard previous executions, as aforementioned. Pattern *automatic execution* is not included either because no resource assignment is required in this case.

The final resource assignment of every activity of the business process in Figure 4 are those depicted in Figure 5. Note that the last assignment does not belong to the previous examples and has been specified here to show how Language 1 allows expressing quite complex constraints.

5   Related Work

The need of including organizational aspects in business process design can be seen in [3], where Künzle et al. present a set of challenges that should be addressed to make business processes both data-aware and resource-aware.

In 1999, Bertino et al. defined a language to express constraints in role-based and user-based assignments to the tasks of a workflow [4]. They got to check whether the configured assignments were possible at runtime and to plan possible resource allocation based on the assignments. They considered also dynamic aspects for these checks. The language was based on functions and was more complex and hard to use than RAL, since its goal was wider.

In 2007, Russell et al. described a set of workflow resource patterns aimed at explaining the requirements for resource management in workflow environments [1]. They analysed the support provided by some workflow tools, BPMN 1.0 among others, but they did not provide a specific way to assign resources to workflow activities. These patterns were used by Grosskopt to analyse the ability of BPMN 1.0 again and to propose solutions to extend the number of patterns addressed by the standard [5]. However, he did not consider nor included organizational information in the process models and, hence, he could not establish assignments on the basis of the resource capabilities or their relationships.

```
Submit Paper:
((HAS ROLE Researcher) OR (HAS ROLE ResearchAssistant))
AND (HAS CAPABILITY degree)

Fill Travel Authorization:
(HAS ROLE ResearchAssistant) AND
(NOT (IS PERSON WHO DID ACTIVITY SignTravelAuthorization))

Sign Travel Authorization:
(IS Antonio) AND ((NOT(IS PERSON WHO DID ACTIVITY
FillTravelAuthorization)) AND (IS REPORTED BY POSITION OF PERSON
WHO DID ACTIVITY FillTravelAuthorization))

Send Travel Authorization:
IS PERSON IN DATA FIELD TravelAuthorization.Applicant

Register at Conference:
(HAS POSITION PhDStudent) AND IF POSSIBLE (IS PERSON WHO DID
ACTIVITY SubmitPaper)

Make Reservations:
(NOT (IS Antonio)) AND ((SHARES SOME ROLE WITH Antonio)
OR (HAS ROLE ResearchAssistant))
```

Fig. 5. Resource assignments of the process activities in Figure 4

During 2008, Meyer worked on the extension of BPMN 1.1 to manage resource allocation in business process models and he presented the results in his Master's Thesis [6]. He revised the metamodel and task lifecycle of BPMN and proposed a formal representation of the resource perspective, together with a prototypical implementation for Oryx[4].

In 2009, Awad et al. used the workflow resource patterns again as a reference framework to study the resource management in BPMN 1.2 and proposed a metamodel extension [7]. They focused on the creation patterns but, unlike our approach, they played with swimlanes by giving specific meaning to lanes, so the process models grew as more roles were involved in the processes. Furthermore, they did not consider the organizational structure and proposed OCL[5] as constraints language. They extended Oryx with a prototype that included graphical representation for the creation patterns, but we believe defining new constraints is very complex due to the use of OCL.

To the best of our knowledge, there is not yet an approach that tries to improve resource management in BPMN 2.0 without changing its metamodel and oriented to users technically unskilled.

---

[4] http://bpt.hpi.uni-potsdam.de/Oryx/
[5] http://www.omg.org/spec/OCL/

6   Conclusions and Future Work

In this paper we have explained the current mechanism BPMN 2.0 proposes to assign resources to the activities of a business process, concluding that:

- It allows expressing quite a lot of constraints regarding resources, but the use of XPath makes it problematic the expression of constraints containing conjunctions, disjunctions and/or negations referring to resource types.
- In the current approach the process model is always kept out of the organizational structure of the company, so it does not know about roles, positions or persons, and, hence, assignments considering relationships between the potential owners cannot be made. That may be the reason why most of the tools for business process execution (e.g., jBPM, Activiti) use only resource assignments based on individual resources or groups.
- Its basis on XPath also makes it difficult for users with no technical knowledge about coding to learn how to work with resource assignments in BPMN model activities. A higher-level user-oriented language would be useful.

We have intended to overcome these three drawbacks of BPMN with RAL, by providing a notation close to natural language, and expressive enough to build complex assignments considering both the business process and the organizational model. In the future we plan to define a graphical notation for RAL and we will explain how we have managed to analyse resource assignments and extract useful information from resource-aware business process models by mapping RAL into an OWL ontology.

References

1. Russell, N., van der Aalst, W.M.P., ter Hofstede, A.H.M., Edmond, D.: Workflow Resource Patterns: Identification, Representation and Tool Support. In: Pastor, Ó., Falcão e Cunha, J. (eds.) CAiSE 2005. LNCS, vol. 3520, pp. 216–232. Springer, Heidelberg (2005)
2. "Bpmn 2.0," recommendation, OMG (2011)
3. Künzle, V., Reichert, M.: Integrating Users in Object-Aware Process Management Systems: Issues and Challenges. In: Rinderle-Ma, S., Sadiq, S., Leymann, F. (eds.) BPM 2009 Workshops. LNBIP, vol. 43, pp. 29–41. Springer, Heidelberg (2010)
4. Bertino, E., Ferrari, E., Atluri, V.: The specification and enforcement of authorization constraints in workflow management systems. ACM Trans. Inf. Syst. Secur. 2, 65–104 (1999)
5. Grosskopf, A.: An extended resource information layer for bpmn. tech. rep., BPT (2007)
6. Meyer, A.: Resource perspective in bpmn - extending BPMN to support resource management and planning. Master's thesis, Hasso Plattner Institute, Potsdam, Germany (2009)
7. Awad, A., Grosskopf, A., Meyer, A., Weske, M.: Enabling resource assignment constraints in BPMN. tech. rep., BPT (2009)

*f*QDF: A Design Framework for *fine-granular* Quality Control of Business Process Outcomes

Vikram Jamwal and Hema Meda

Tata Consultancy Services
{vikram.jamwal,hema.meda}@tcs.com

Abstract. To assure quality in a Business Service it is imperative to engineer quality into the process that produces it. We introduce *f*QDF: a Quality Design Framework for *fine-granular* quality control of business process outcomes. The framework defines a Quality Breakdown Structure (QBS) that provides a fine-granular quality definition for process outcomes. QBS is used to derive a Process Breakdown Structure (PrBS) ensuring that the process is engineered-in for quality outcomes. Deploying *f*QDF results in a quality-aware business process, where the quality is designed-in up-front rather than it being an afterthought. We introduce and explain the concepts of *f*QDF and their impact on quality-building in the context of a real-life case study viz., a Document Processing Service.

Keywords: Quality, Quality Design Framework, Quality Model, Human Centric Business Process, Business Services.

1 Introduction

Business Organizations utilize the services of a Business Service Provider to enhance their efficacy. They wish that the service is delivered at the desired level of quality. Our experience shows that when a Business Service is complex in nature, service quality specifications are either *amiss or* are *implicit*. This implies that we do not have a clear basis for quality control. Another major challenge that arises is how a Service Provider ensures that the business process is *designed-in* or *engineered-in* to deliver quality outcomes.

In this paper we present a design framework for designing a fine-granular quality-aware business process (refer Section 3) which we refer to as *f*QDF. *f*QDF helps to alleviate both of the above challenges: it makes the quality specifications explicit for a business process and helps to provide fine-granular control over the quality of business process outcomes. Deploying *f*QDF results in a quality-aware business process, where the quality is designed-in up-front rather than it being an afterthought.

*f*QDF unfolds in the form of three structures:

1. *Product Breakdown Structure (PBS)*, which determines how a product or a service is composed from its components.
2. *Quality Breakdown Structure (QBS)*, which determines how the quality characteristics of product components (or service components) result in quality attributes of a product (or a service).

F. Daniel et al. (Eds.): BPM 2011 Workshops, Part I, LNBIP 99, pp. 62–74, 2012.

3. *Process Breakdown Structure (PrBS)*, which determines how an overall process for producing a product or a service can be created from the process components.

One of the novel features of these three breakdown structures is that, together, they enable *fine-granular control* over the quality of the process outputs. In this paper we also provide a generic approach to designing such quality-aware business processes (refer Section 4).

We have deployed these concepts in a business process of a major consulting company, which we shall refer to in this paper as ABC (AB Consulting). The concepts in this paper and the impact of *f*QDF on quality building is explained in the context of this process that produces a business service, viz., Document Processing Service (DPS). In Section 2 we give an overview of DPS. We describe the core process of document processing and explain the complexity and quality challenges in the process. In Section 5 we provide implementation details and in Section 6 we compare our approach with other related approaches to quality modeling and quality building in practice and literature. In Section 7 we conclude our discussion and indicate future directions of our work.

2   Case Study Overview: Document Processing Service (DPS)

In this section we give an overview of DPS, which serves as a *case-study* for our Quality Design Framework. ABC consultants need to present various forms of reports[1] to their clients. The consultants ideally like to concentrate on the content and depend upon a Document Processing Service (DPS) to enhance and format the documents to comply with ABC brand guidelines and their requirements. The DPS process involves the steps as shown in Fig. 1. ABC Consultants, from different geographies (over 22), send in the raw documents along with the *to-be-applied* formatting requirements. At the Service Provider end, a Team Leader (TL) estimates the processing time for each request and assigns the request to a processing team member (PTM). Depending on the size of request and the urgency of task completion, one or more PTMs process the document. Once the document is formatted, it is reviewed by a Quality Control (QC) team. The QC member may send the document for rework, if necessary, along with her feedback. Finally, the formatted document is delivered back to the customer. The whole process may go through a number of iterations if the customer is not satisfied with the output, or if customer has new additional requirements. The process gets complex with: large number of customer requests, multiple types of documents (~ 22), variable sized requests, variable loads during the course of a year (e.g., from Feb to May, document loads were: 2290, 3832, 2958, and 1950), and off-shore teams (~ 125 FTE) which work in different shifts.

The core of the process is Document Processing, where a human processor formats a raw document. This is indicated in Fig. 1 by circle marks. For the purpose of

---

[1] Proposals, RFPs / Sales Pitch Documents, Audit Reports, Financial Reports, Presentations (Screenable, Printable), Brochures, Hand-outs, Placemats, Newsletters, Posters, etc.

discussion in this paper, we shall concentrate mainly on this portion of the process. This seemingly single step in the DPS process, in reality, expands into a very complex process which is difficult to model. It is *knowledge intensive* and the processing steps happen primarily in the human processor's mind.

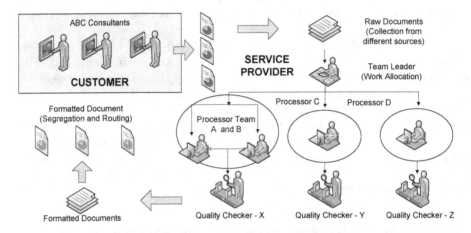

Fig. 1. Document Processing Service

It becomes imperative that Quality is accounted for in the process in a more systematic manner so that despite dependence on the ability of an individual processing expert, quality outcomes can be consistently produced across process instances. In the subsequent sections we discuss various aspects of the *f*QDF and illustrate the concepts in the context of DPS.

3   Our Approach: *f*QDF

As discussed above, building a quality process outcome[2] (product or service) can be a real challenge unless '*what is the desired quality*', '*what determines that quality*', and '*how do we devise a process that builds that quality*' is properly understood. Quality Design Framework (*f*QDF) becomes a means for answering these questions.

3.1   Quality Specification

Before building any model, we have to answer the question: Which quality concerns us? It has been well understood that the 'quality that matters' is determined by the stakeholders viewpoint [7, 8]. A stakeholder uses the product in her context and

---

[2] Henceforth in our discussion we shall use the term *product* to signify both kinds of process outcomes – product and service.

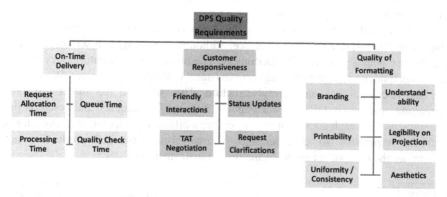

Fig. 2. Quality Attributes relevant to DPS

experiences the 'In-Use Quality' of the product [7]. It is the context of a stakeholder that determines her viewpoint. Once we have factored in all the relevant stakeholders viewpoints, we are left with a set of Quality Attributes for the product in use. These requirements are then converted into features [10] or quality characteristics that a product should support. This set of features serves as the Quality Specification for the product. **DPS Quality Attributes:** From ABC Consultant's perspective, *quality of formatting* plays an important role in the quality of output documents. It determines the effectiveness of ABC Consultant in the market. Any client dissatisfaction on this account also has an adverse business impact for ABC. In addition, Consultants would also like to receive the formatted document within an assured turn-around-time (TAT). Overall, for a good service experience, responsiveness to customers by the persons working on documents is a critical factor. Fig. 2 expands on these *quality attributes* for the DPS Service. Further in this paper, as discussed in Section 2, we concentrate only on the most critical quality attribute of DPS, viz., Quality of Document Formatting.

Having specified the required Quality Characteristics of a service, it is imperative from DP Service Provider perspective, that there are no Service Level Agreement (SLA) misses on the above parameters. In the subsequent sections, we explain the production side (Service Provider side) of the process, where we expound on our approach to articulate the quality of a product or a service through componentization.

3.2   Product Breakdown Structure (PBS)

A product (or service) is usually constructed from more than one part. The intermediate components are composed (or assembled) to build a final product. The components are determined by: the nature of domain, the ease of manufacturing components, and ease of composing the product from the components. PBS unfolds in the form of a tree structure (e.g. refer Fig. 4), where a higher level component is composed from its immediate child components.   The bottommost (leaf-level) components are atomic components, i.e., they are (i) readily available, off-the-shelf, or (ii) constructed atomically, i.e., a further component breakdown is not important from the modeling and production perspective.

As mentioned in previous section our main concern in this case-study is the *Quality of Document Formatting Service*. Although formatting is a service, still it is closely tied with a product, viz., Document. The objective of formatting service is to transform a document, from the *unformatted-state* to the *formatted-state*. We observe that the document has an internal structure. This structure has direct affect on formatting process. In DPS there are about 22 *types* of documents, and based on this internal structure, each document would require a different formatting process. Thus it becomes imperative to consider the internal composition of product, which determines the component level (formatting) transformations.

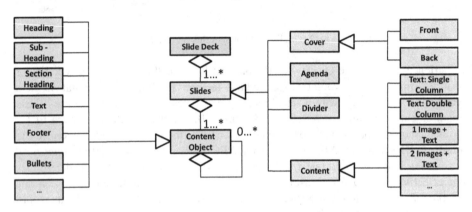

Fig. 3. Product Breakdown Structure for *Screenable-Printable*

Let us consider a document type, *Screenable-Printable*. We shall use this document type to explain the concepts in this paper and our approach. A *Screenable-Printable* type implies that the document has to be formatted in a way that it is suitable for viewing after projection on screen, and printouts of the formatted document are suitable for reading. For the *Screenable-Printable* document type, suitable components[3] that logically evolve from formatting perspective are: cover slide, table of contents, section dividers, slides containing the content of the presentation and finally the back cover. Content in a document can appear in many forms - text, images, illustrations, charts, schematic diagrams, tables, etc. and in any order. We call each of these content types as *content objects*. Some content objects, e.g. diagrams, may be identified as composite content objects, i.e., they are composed from other content objects. We refer to Fig. 3 for the PBS for *Screenable-Printable*. In the next section we discuss the quality imperatives for a product and its components.

---

[3] Note that a product can have different component breakdown structures, depending upon various user perspectives[12]. It is semantics of domain that determines the suitable form for decomposition.

3.3 Quality Breakdown Structure (QBS)

We observe that for constructing a product (or fulfilling a service), at each node of a PBS tree, we have two associated tasks: (i) Construction (or Transformation) of each child component, and (ii) Composition of (transformed) child components. Each component exhibits certain quality characteristics. The quality characteristics of components at a lower level determine the quality characteristics of a component at the higher level [4]. In addition, composition of components may result in the emergence of new quality characteristics.

Hence we emphasize on two types of quality: (i) Component Quality: quality characteristics directly associated with, or, inherent in the components, (ii) Assembly Quality: quality characteristics that come into play when the components are put (assembled/composed) together; we indicate these quality characteristics as $Quality_{Across}$ (or Q_{Across}).

QBS for Screenable-Printable Document Type.

We now build a QBS to capture what determines the quality of *Screenable-Printable* document from the document processing service perspective. Let D be the document which is under consideration. If $D_1, D_2,...,D_n$ be the components, let $Q(D)$ define the Quality of Document D after correct formatting, and $Q(D_x)$, define the quality of component D_x after the correct formatting. In practice, the composition of two or more individual components might have influence on the overall aggregate quality. To account for this we introduce a new term called Q_{Across}. Then the Quality of entire Document at top level can be considered as:

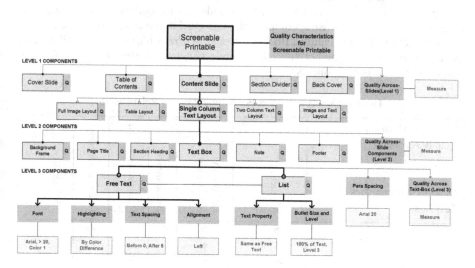

Fig. 4. Quality Breakdown for a section of *Screenable-Printable* Document Type

$Q(Screenable\text{-}Printable) = \ Quality\_Compose\ (Q(Table\ of\ Contents),\ Q(Cover\ Slide),$
$\sum Q(Content\ Slide),\ \sum Q(Section\ Dividers),\ Q(Back\ Cover),\ Q_{Across})$

Now Q_{Across} can be a complex composition. It can come from the composition of $Q(D_1)$ and $Q(D_2)$, or any other two sub-components taken at a time, or $Q(D_1)$, $Q(D_2)$, $Q(D_3)$ or any other three components taken at a time, and so on. For our purposes, we highlight the need for capturing such quality in composition. In the above case, Q_{Across} accounts for: for example, page setup, consistency across slides, uniform branding across all slides etc. Onus is on process-designer to enlist all the relevant cases that account for Q_{Across}.

For each Quality Attribute that is relevant to a process outcome, we need to determine:

(i)   Nodes on PBS that contribute to the quality-attribute build-up
(ii)   Quality characteristics of the component (or component-composition) that contribute to the quality-attribute build-up
(iii)   Measures of these quality characteristics

Only when every component and its composition at a lower level yields desired quality characteristics for a higher level component, do we have the assurance that the component assembly would result in a quality process-outcome.

For example, Table 1 indicates the influence of each of the quality characteristics of Text Box on the resultant Quality of the *Screenable-Printable* document type. Such influence mapping has to be identified for the entire PBS of *Screenable-Printable*. The designer of the component quality also has to define a measure for each of these characteristics. In *Screenable-Printable* case, content object 'Text Box' can be treated as leaf-level component. Fig. 4 indicates the quality characteristics and their measures for a 'Text Box' component. The QBS designer has to ensure that for the entire set of desired qualities, PBS of *Screenable-Printable* document will ensure: Quality attributes of a higher (top) level node can be achieved from the Quality characteristics of its components.

Table 1. Quality Attribute, Formatting Property Relationship

Formatted Document Quality Attributes → Quality Characteristics of Text Box ↓	Aesthetics	Uniformity/ consistency	Brand image	Readability on Projection	Understandability	Printability
Highlighting through color	↑	↑	↑		↑	
Alignment	↑	↑			↑	
Line/para spacing	↑	↑			↑	
Font size	↑	↑		↑		↑
Color (Text, fill color, background)	↑	↑	↑	↑		↑

To summarize: For each Quality Attribute of a product we need to construct a QBS. This QBS specifies the Quality Characteristics of components and their composition at all relevant levels. If we are unable to do this for a particular Quality Attribute, it implies that we cannot aim for a fine-granular control over that particular Quality Attribute. Each Quality Attribute provides a specification as well as imposes a certain constraint on a component characteristic. The final QBS results from trade-offs of values resulting from the entire set of Quality Attributes.

3.4 Process Breakdown Structure (PrBS)

Finally, we consider the process that has to ensure that we build the product with requisite quality characteristics. Once we have designed a PBS and QBS that results in final desired outcome quality, we now have only to devise a process that ensures:

- Each of the subcomponents has requisite quality characteristics
- Component composition takes place in a manner that the higher level component has the requisite quality characteristics.

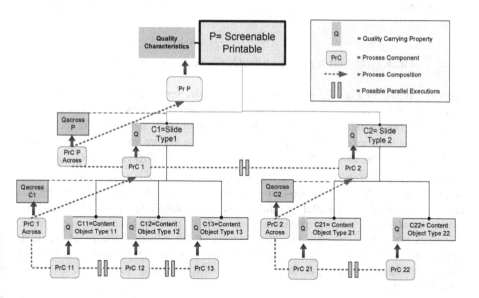

Fig. 5. Process Composition for *Screenable-Printable* Document Type

This implies that we take care of building both – Component quality and the Q_{Across} for those Components. We define each part of the process that contributes towards composing a component with given quality characteristics as *Process Component (PrC)*. An overall process (Refer Fig. 5) that results from combining these PrCs then yields us the overall process for development of a quality product.

For example, Formatting Process for *Screenable-Printable* can be organized on the following levels:

- Level 1 - Format Document. This is achieved by: Format (Level 2) + Build Q_{Across} for Level 1; this includes, for example, page setup (portrait or landscape), margins, header and footer, etc.
- Level 2 - Format Page/Slide. This is achieved by: Format (Level 3) + Build Q_{Across} for Level 2; this includes spacing between content objects, their arrangement, etc.
- Level 3 - Format Content Object. As a Content object can be composite, the subsequent levels emerge by applying action 'Format Content Object' recursively.

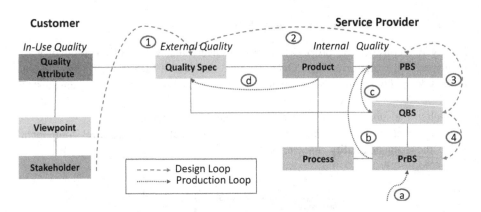

Fig. 6. Framework for *fine-granular* Quality control in a Business Process

QBS as shown in Fig. 4 for *Screenable-Printable*, serves as a specification from where the PrBS can be derived. It lays down rules that serve as constraints for composing the overall formatting process. For example, as shown in Fig. 5, we can create multiple process configurations, as long as we ensure sequencing constraints:

Config 1: PrC 22->PrC 21->PrC 2_{Across} ->PrC 12->PrC 13->PrC 11->PrC 1_{Across} ->PrC$_{Across}$

Config 2: PrC 11->PrC 12->PrC 13->PrC 1_{Across} ->PrC 21->PrC 22->PrC 2_{Across} -> PrC$_{Across}$

Note that at each level, the process components (For example, PrC 11, PrC 12, PrC 13) can be executed in parallel if they have no interdependencies. Further, the management can create an overall optimized DPS process by optimizing people, resources, and tools, against various products. PrBS becomes the basis for such optimization. We conclude that by organizing the process (e.g. *formatting* in DPS) in the above manner, we provide an assured means for building quality into a Product (or a Service).

4   Methodology for Applying *f*QDF

The Design Framework *f*QDF describes various models - PBS, QBS, PrBS, and their inter-relationships for a business process. As shown in Fig. 6, these models are created during the design phase (Steps 1, 2 3, 4) of a particular business process. These models then serve as Quality Engineering tools, during the production phase (Steps a, b, c, d) of that process. The generic methodology for creating models for a particular business process can be stated as:

1. Identify the Quality Attributes for process outcomes considering the viewpoints of all classes of Stakeholders. This constitutes the *In-Use* quality.
2. Convert these Quality Attributes into Quality Specification for the process outcomes. This constitutes the *External-Quality* of the product (or service).
3. Look for the (natural) breakdown of the process outcomes such that: *"Quality characteristics of a higher-level component results from Quality characteristics of its sub-components and Quality emerging during the sub-component composition."*
4. Devise a process that ensures: *"Each component meets its Quality Specification and the component assembly process accounts for Q_{Across}."*

When we are able to achieve the above, we can say that we have a process that ensures that the Quality is *designed-in*, or the Quality is *engineered-in* the service or a product. This process design approach results in a preventive approach for building quality into products, as opposed to the curative approach [9]. It leads to a Process which produces Quality Products or Services by design.

5 Implementation and Discussion on the Benefits of Solution

At present we have applied *f*QDF to DPS for 5 document types. The Quality Models (Quality Specification Model and Processing Model) for DPS have been implemented with the help of an Excel based tool. The tool exports the models in the form of easily navigable and hyperlinked Web-enabled models which are referenced by the formatting persons during document processing. Processing Model (derived from PrBS) uses a basic subset of BPMN that is easy to use and familiar to most users. A Processing Model will typically contain 20-25 process components. The Processing Models at different levels are hyper-linked for easy cross-navigation.

Quality Models for DPS led to significant improvement in the quality of formatting work. This was mainly due to: (i) *Explication* of Quality Specifications and Processing Practices, (ii) *Standard/uniform definition of quality* across processors, QC teams, brand guideline creators, and ABC management, and (iii) Accurate and fine-granular measures of quality resulting in *more precise quality models*. We are also planning the quantitative measures for these improvements in near future. The other long term expected benefits are expedited *training of new employees and subject matter experts, systematized change management, and best practice building*.

6 Comparison with Related Work

We compare our work with some of the other approaches to quality building in business processes and product development.

Six sigma: Six sigma methodology is widely used in the business process outsourcing industry for improving the quality of process outcomes. Six sigma [3] employs a problem solving approach to improving the quality of process outcomes. Thus it begins by identifying a Critical To Quality (CTQ) metric of the process that is undergoing improvement. Thereafter appropriate six sigma tools and methods are used to determine the cause of the problem or defect and for rectifying the problem so as to achieve improvement in the CTQ metric. The motivation behind our work was to capture componentization inherent in a service or a product. We specify the quality requirements for all the components that make the product or service. These quality models become fine-granular in their approach towards quality control. Thus they can serve as base models for applying the six sigma methodology to improve quality in processes, where outcomes are complex in nature. In addition, we also provide an approach for composing processes for building products having desired quality attributes.

Business Process Quality Management: Quality models have been proposed in [11,13]. These models identify quality characteristics of a business process along four dimensions - activities, inputs and outputs, human and non-human resources. The framework (QoBP) is used to design quality-aware business processes by capturing and specifying high-level quality requirements along these four dimensions. The framework also includes a measurement model for specifying metrics of quality characteristics along the four dimensions.

The Quality Breakdown Structure, as presented in this paper, models quality requirements mainly for process outcomes. However, we believe that the approach can be extended to include the four dimensions of quality as proposed in the above framework. In our approach, we provide a means for capturing quality requirements at different levels of detail. We show that by capturing quality requirements in such a fashion, we can derive finer level tasks in the process. Thus the Process Breakdown Structure provides a basis for identifying and organizing the finer level tasks in the process.

Software quality models: Quality models have been proposed for improving quality of software products. Related work in this area includes that of [4-8]. Dromey's work has some closeness to our approach of modeling quality. Dromey [4] suggests that a product's internal properties determine its external quality attributes. Thus the internal properties must be built into the product in order for it to exhibit the desired external quality attributes. This approach is similar to the way we build QBS. They propose a generic quality model consisting of: product properties that influence quality, a set of high-level quality attributes, and a means of linking them. They present an approach to constructing quality models. Other quality models such as McCall [6], Boehm [5] and ISO [7,8] present a top down approach for organizing and structuring quality characteristics of a software product into a hierarchy of quality factors. In comparison to these approaches on software product quality, our work, in addition introduces Process Breakdown Structures that are useful in designing process models that will build the desired quality into the process outcomes. This leads to standardized way of capturing best practices.

Work Breakdown Structures and Product Structure Diagrams: A Work Breakdown Structure (WBS) is defined as a deliverable-oriented hierarchical decomposition of the work to be executed by the project team to accomplish the project objectives and create the required deliverables [1]. These are used in project management. The smaller chunks of work can be assigned, monitored and managed more easily. Time schedules and cost estimates can be reliably assigned to the lowest level packages of work. In the manufacturing scenario, the Product Structure Diagram

(PSD) is used for capturing the physical components of a product. These diagrams are used to show the relationship of each component part to its parent component (or assembly) and the grouping of parts that make up as subassembly [2]. Feature-driven software projects use a similar technique to arrive at a feature breakdown structure [10]. The PBS and QBS breakdown structures have a similarity to WBS and PSD with respect to componentizing; though they vary in their purpose. Primary purpose of WBS is to make estimation, assignment and management of work units easier. The focus of QBS is on defining the customer-desired specifications of quality. It may be said that QBS approach extends work breakdown structures to account for deliverable quality explicitly. PBS has close proximity to PSD; both deal with defining the structure of a product from its components. However, PBS as discussed in this paper can be used for both service and product componentization. Moreover, the product that is implied in PBS is usually a product whose state is transformed by a business process rather than being constructed by a manufacturing process.

7   Conclusion

In this paper we presented a design framework, *f*QDF, for creating quality-aware business processes. *f*QDF provides a means for: (i) Building the Quality Specification for a business process outcome, (ii) Describing how a product or a service is composed from its components, (iii) Specifying how the quality characteristics of the components and their composition result in quality characteristics of a higher level component, and (iv) Specifying how an overall process for producing a service (product) can be created from the process components that build components with right quality characteristics. Our approach has the novel feature that it provides a means of specification of quality characteristics at different levels of granularity. This enables more precise control over the process outcome quality. Moreover, quality breakdown (QBS) by design ensures that the components will have requisite quality characteristics that ensure a final product with desired quality attributes. The approach is geared especially towards Human Centric Processes - it provides the human processor with reference models to build quality into the components of the product or service that she is responsible towards.

We discussed the benefits from implementing *f*QDF for a large outsourced business service. We believe that similar benefits will accrue for other processes where the process outcomes (product or service) are complex and are amenable to componentization.

References

1. Project Management Institute: A Guide to the Project Management Body of Knowledge, PMBOK Guide (2004)
2. Russell, R., Taylor, B.: Operations Management. Prentice Hall (2002)
3. Brue, G.: Six Sigma for Managers. McGraw-Hill (2002)
4. Dromey, R.G.: Cornering the Chimera. J. IEEE Software 13(1), 33–43 (1996)

5. Boehm, B.W., Brown, J.R., Kaspar, H., Lipow, M., McLeod, G., Merritt, M.: Characteristics of Software Quality. Elsevier (1978)
6. McCall, J.A., Richards, P.K., Walters, G.F.: Factors in Software Quality. National Tech. Information Service 1, 2, 3 (1977)
7. Int'l Organization for Standardization: Software Product Evaluation - Quality Characteristics and Guidelines for Their Use, ISO/IEC Standard, ISO-9126 (1991)
8. IEEE Standard for Software Quality Metrics Methodology: IEEE 1061-1998 (1998)
9. Dromey, G.R.: Software Quality - Prevention Versus Cure. Software Quality Control 11(3), 197–210 (2003)
10. Kang, K., Cohen, S., Hess, J., Nowak, W., Peterson, S.: Feature-Oriented Domain Analysis (FODA) Feasibility Study, Technical Report, CMU/SEI-90-TR-21
11. Heravizadeh, M.: Quality-aware Business Process Management, PhD Thesis, Queensland University of Technology (2009)
12. Tarr, P.L., Ossher, H., Harrison, W.H., Sutton Jr., S.M.: N Degrees of Separation: Multi-Dimensional Separation of Concerns. In: ICSE, pp. 107–119 (1999)
13. Heravizadeh, M., Mendling, J., Rosemann, M.: Dimensions of Business Processes Quality (QoBP). In: Ardagna, D., Mecella, M., Yang, J. (eds.) Business Process Management Workshops. LNBIP, vol. 17, pp. 80–91. Springer, Heidelberg (2009)

Definition and Validation of Process Mining Use Cases

Irina Ailenei[1], Anne Rozinat[2], Albert Eckert[3], and Wil M.P. van der Aalst[1]

[1] Eindhoven University of Technology, P.O. Box 513, NL-5600 MB,
Eindhoven, The Netherlands
i.m.ailenei@student.tue.nl, w.m.p.v.d.aalst@tue.nl
[2] Fluxicon Process Laboratories
anne@fluxicon.com
[3] Siemens AG, Corporate Technology, Munich, Germany
albert.eckert@siemens.com

Abstract. Process mining is an emerging topic in the BPM marketplace. Recently, several (commercial) software solutions have become available. Due to the lack of an evaluation framework, it is very difficult for potential users to assess the strengths and weaknesses of these process mining tools. As the first step towards such an evaluation framework, we developed a set of process mining use cases and validated these use cases by means of expert interviews and a survey. We present the list of use cases and discuss the insights from our empirical validation. These use cases will then form the basis for a detailed evaluation of current process mining tools on the market.

Keywords: Business Process Intelligence, Process mining, Use cases, Evaluation framework.

1 Introduction

The area of Process Mining has attracted the attention of both researchers and practitioners. As a consequence, a significant number of algorithms and tools were developed. For instance, the academic process mining tool ProM Version 5.2 contains more than 280 pluggable algorithms, developed to provide a wide range of functionalities and techniques. Additionally, commercial process mining tools have emerged on the market and often use their own standards and naming. For a potential user, this situation is quite confusing and it is difficult to choose the most suitable process mining tool or algorithm for the task at hand.

Our goal is to develop an evaluation framework that can be used to assess the strengths and weaknesses of different process mining tools. We will then apply this evaluation framework to compare commercial process mining tools that are currently available on the market. Therefore, the main questions of this project are:

1. What are typical process mining *use cases*?
2. Which *process mining tools* are suitable for which use case?

As *process mining tool* we consider any software that is able to extract process models from raw event logs (without having to manually create a model beforehand).

F. Daniel et al. (Eds.): BPM 2011 Workshops, Part I, LNBIP 99, pp. 75–86, 2012.

Fig. 1. Use cases for process mining may vary depending on the context

As process mining *use cases* we consider typical applications of process mining functionality in a practical situation.

Consider Figure 1, which illustrates that the use of any process mining tool will be carried out in a certain context. We can assume that the context of the person using process mining has an influence on which type of functionality is considered most important. For example, the role or function a person fulfills in their organization might impact the type of analysis that the user is interested in (e.g., an auditor would be more interested in checking the compliance of processes whereas a process analyst will be mostly focused on process improvement). Another example is the type of project: In a process improvement project a user is likely to be more focused on diagnosing process bottlenecks and inefficiencies whereas in an IT re-implementation project the main goal might be to extract the current processes in an executable process modeling language such as BPMN. Even within one project, process mining could be used in different phases (e.g., as a quick-scan in the beginning of an improvement project or as a means to validate the actual improvements at the end of the project).

In this paper, we address the first question of the project by reporting on the development of an evaluation framework by defining and categorizing use cases for process mining. To ensure that the list of use cases is as complete and as relevant as possible, we validate these use cases by expert interviews with practitioners and a survey. During the validation, we also capture information about the context of the user to find out how their role affects the importance they give to the different use cases. These use cases will then form the basis for a detailed evaluation of current process mining tools in the market. The definition of the evaluation criteria and the results obtained are, however, outside the focus of this paper.

The remainder of the paper is organized as follows. Section 2 discusses related work. Section 3 describes the approach that we followed to define and validate the process mining use cases. Section 4 introduces our list of process mining use cases in detail. In Section 5, we then describe how we validated these use cases through expert interviews and a survey. Finally, in Section 6 we give an outlook on how we are currently detailing and applying our evaluation framework for the assessment of different commercial process mining tools.

2   Related Work

As process mining is an emerging topic, little work has been done on the systematic identification of use cases. Lion's share of process mining literature focuses on process discovery. Several authors describe how to evaluate discovered process models [10,4,5,6,8,7]. For example, in [8] an evaluation framework is defined. The framework provides an extended set of tests to judge the quality of process mining results. One of the problems is a lack of commonly agreed upon benchmark logs. This year's Business Processing Intelligence Challenge (BPIC) aims to address this problem by providing a reference log.

Unlike the approaches aiming to judge the quality of the discovered process model [4,5,6,8,7], we focus on the different functionalities related to process mining. Clearly, this extends beyond pure control-flow discovery.

Our approach to define and validate use cases is related to [9] (e.g., conducting interviews with BPM experts). However, in [9] the focus is on business process model abstraction rather than process mining. Also related are the evaluations done in the context of the workflow patterns [2].

3   Approach

One of the challenges of our study was to decide which approach we are going to follow in defining and validating the list of use cases to be used for the tools evaluation. Since there was no standard reference for process mining use cases, we followed an inductive approach, similar to the one described in [9], which aimed at defining a list of process mining functionalities needed in practice that is as complete and relevant as possible. Figure 2 illustrates the sequence of steps that constitute the approach we followed.

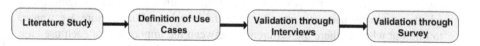

Fig. 2. The four phases of the approach

Literature Study. The purpose of the literature study was to get an overview about the existing functionality available in the context of process mining. In order to do this, we looked at the functionality provided by the process mining tool ProM [1] and focused our attention on academic articles about process mining techniques as well as on marketing brochures and descriptions of a couple of commercial process mining tools present on the web.

Definition of Use Cases. The next step was the definition of an initial list of process mining use cases. We consider a use case to represent the use of a concrete process mining functionality with the goal to obtain an independent and final result. Therefore, actions performed before the actual analysis, like the import of the event log or filtering, are not included in our list. When defining the list of use cases, we used the classification of process mining techniques described in [10]. Figure 3 is a simpler representation of this classification and also shows our scope in relation with the entire classification. The definition of use cases is thus restricted to the offline analysis and does not include any techniques that deal with prediction, detection or recommendation. This limitation was introduced due to the inability of evaluating the systems participating in the study in an online analysis environment. The description and examples of each use case are introduced in Section 4.

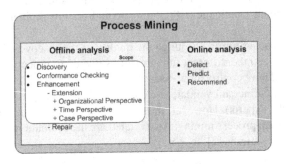

Fig. 3. The project's scope in the context of process mining

Validation through Interviews. The great number of existing process mining techniques and the lack of a standard list of use cases led to the need of validating the defined list. We started our validation phase by conducting a series of ten semi-structured interviews with practitioners having process mining expertise. First, we wanted to verify the understandability of the descriptions of the use cases by asking them to provide examples with situations in which each use case would be useful. Second, the goal of the interviews was to validate the list of use cases by removing the use cases that the participants considered irrelevant, and by determining whether there are use cases missing from the initial set. Furthermore, we wanted to find out whether there are differences between the importance of each use case for different categories of end users. One lesson learnt from the interviews was that participants have the tendency of saying that all use cases are equally important. As a result of this observation, we deviated from the approach described in [9], where use cases were just classified as important or not important, and instead used the sorting method for *ranking* the use cases based on their importance. The findings of the interviews are presented in detail in Section 5.1.

Validation through Survey. Distributing a survey among people familiar with the field of process mining was the most suitable method to collect a larger number of responses for the validation phase. In total, we obtained 47 responses. The main goals of the survey were to capture the context of the respondents by asking for their role and domain, get the use cases rankings, and find out what additional functionality not covered by the list of use cases is considered important and should be included in our tool evaluation. The results of the survey are discussed in Section 5.2.

The list of validated use cases will serve as a basis for a detailed evaluation of a couple of commercial process mining systems. For this purpose, an evaluation framework has been developed. This framework incorporates next to the description and the example for each use case, also related assumptions and a set of acceptance criteria used to decide whether the use case is supported or not by a tool.

4 Use Cases

This section introduces the list of process mining use cases by providing a short description of each use case. A more complete presentation, containing in addition a practical example for every use case, is given in [3]. The use cases are grouped into the categories described in [10]. Section 4.1 contains use cases belonging to the process discovery part, subsection 4.2 focuses on the conformance checking use cases, while sections 4.3, 4.4, 4.5 present the use cases related to the organizational, the time, and the case perspective.

4.1 Discovery

The use cases belonging to this category are focused on the control flow perspective of the process. The user gets a clear understanding of the analyzed process by looking at its structure, frequent behavior and at the percentages of cases following every discovered path.

Use case 1: Structure of the process. Determine the structure of an unknown process or discover how a process looks like in practice.

Use case 2: Routing probabilities. Get a deeper understanding of the process by looking at the probabilities of following one path or another after a choice point.

Use case 3: Most frequent path in the process. Discover what is the path in the process that is followed by the highest percentage of cases.

Use case 4: Distribution of cases over paths. Discover common and uncommon behavior in the process by looking at the distribution of cases over the possible paths in the process.

4.2 Conformance Checking

This category consists of use cases which have the purpose of checking whether the process has the intended behavior in practice. The use cases pertaining to this category have in common that in order to execute them one needs an additional input besides the event log of the process to be analyzed. This input may be a reference model of the process or a rule which the discovered process has to be checked against.

Use case 5: Exceptions from the normal path. Discover the outliers of the process by looking at the exceptional behavior observed in practice.

Use case 6: The degree in which the rules are obeyed. Check whether the rules and regulations related to the process are obeyed.

Use case 7: Compliance to the explicit model. Compare the documented process model with the real process as observed in the event log.

4.3 Enhancement - Extension - Organizational Perspective

The focus of the use cases included in this category is on the organizational analysis. The outcome of executing these use cases provides the user with an insight in the issues related to the resource perspective of the process.

Use case 8: Resources per task. Discover the relation between resources and tasks.

Use case 9: Resources involved in a case. Discover the group of resources involved in solving a particular case.

Use case 10: Work handovers. Manage resource location or determine possible causes for quality and time issues by looking at how work is transferred between resources.

Use case 11: Central employees. Determine who the central resources for a process are by analyzing the social network based on handovers of work.

4.4 Enhancement - Extension - Time Perspective

As performance-related insights are most valuable, most of the use cases related to enhancement correspond to the time perspective.

Use case 12: Throughput time of cases. Determine the time that passed since the start of a case in process until its completion.

Use case 13: Slowest activities. Discover potential time problems by looking at the slowest activities in the process.

Use case 14: Longest waiting times. Determine delays between activities by analyzing the waiting times before each activity.

Use case 15: Cycles. Learn whether additional delays occur in the process due to cycles.

Use case 16: Arrival rate of cases. Determine the frequency with which new cases arrive in the process.

Use case 17: Resource utilization rate. Determine what are the utilization rates of the resource i.e, measure the fraction of time that a resource is busy.

Use case 18: Time sequence of events. Get a deeper understanding on the organization of a process by looking at the time sequence of activities for a specific case. (e.g. Gant-graph for activities).

4.5 Enhancement - Extension - Case Perspective

The case perspective of the process is represented by a single use case.

Use case 19: Business rules. Discover what are the process attributes that influence the choice points and what are the conditions for following one branch or another.

5 Validation of the Use Cases

The use cases were validated by conducting ten interviews (Section 5.1) and by distributing a survey (Section 5.2) among process mining users and experts.

5.1 Interviews

We conducted in total ten interviews with process mining users and domain experts. The interviews can be divided into two categories:(1) interviews aimed at gaining some qualitative feedback on the understandability of the use cases and (2) interviews which were focused on obtaining a ranking of the use cases based on their importance for the interviewees and on identifying missing use cases.

(1) Based on the feedback received from the first type of interviews (in total: four) two non-relevant use cases were removed from the list, the descriptions of a couple of use case were refined and a short motivation was added for each remaining use case. The two irrelevant use cases referred to the possibility of identifying the paths in the process taking most time and to the possibility of visualizing the list of process attributes stored in the event log. The aim of refining the use case descriptions and of adding the motivation dimension was to increase the understandability and clarity of what each use case is about and what its practical purpose is.

(2) In the second type of interviews (in total: six) we asked the interviewees to sort the list of cases in the order of their importance in practice and on discovering any missing use cases. Moreover, we were interested in gaining additional insights on what are the functionalities that a process mining tool should provide to its users. These interviews were structured in three parts. The first part aimed at getting information about the experience of the interviewee in the context of process mining and about the added value that process mining brings to their work. Secondly, the interviewees were shown the list of use cases and were asked to assign to each use case a score from 1 to 19 based on its importance (1 being the most important). The last part of the interview was meant to summarize the discussion, to learn about possible use cases missing from the initial list and about additional functionality that interviewees consider useful in a process mining tool. The complete summary of the outcomes of these six interviews can be found in [3].

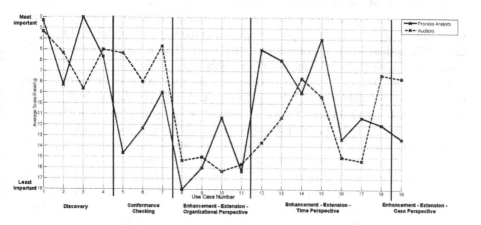

Fig. 4. Use cases ranking results from the interviews with process analysts and auditors

Table 1. Top 5 and Bottom 5 Use Cases for Process Analysts

Top 5 Use cases	Bottom 5 Use Cases
U3. Most frequent path in the process	U8. Resources per task
U1. Structure of the process	U11. Central employees
U15. Cycles	U9. Resources involved in a case
U12. Throughput time of cases	U5. Exceptions from the normal path
U4. Distribution of cases over paths	U16. Arrival rate of cases U19. Business rules

Table 2. Top 5 and Bottom 5 Use Cases for Auditors

Top 5 Use cases	Bottom 5 Use Cases
U1. Structure of the process	U10. Work handovers
U7. Compliance to the explicit model	U11. Central employees
U4. Distribution of cases over paths	U8. Resources per task
U2. Routing probabilities	U17. Resource utilization rate
U5. Exceptions from the normal path	U9. Resources involved in a case U16. Arrival rate of cases

The six interviews we conducted were balanced from the point of view of the interviewee's role in the context of using process mining techniques. Three of the persons interviewed were process analysts and the other three were auditors. The second dimension we took into account when selecting the interviewees was the domain they belong to. In this context we aimed at having a broader range of domains and therefore we talked with people working in the banking industry, healthcare, public sector, and business process consulting.

Figure 4 depicts the profiles of process analysts and auditors based on the use case rankings collected from our interviews. On the x-axis we refer to use case numbers, while the y-axis represents the averages of the scores the use cases were assigned during the interviews. The graphic shows there are some differences in ranking the use cases based on the profile of the respondents. For instance, use case 12 (Throughput time of cases) is one of the most important use cases according to the process analysts group, while the auditors consider this quite irrelevant in practice. The opposite holds for use case 5 (Exceptions from the normal path), which is ranked as highly important by the auditors and less important by the process analysts.

Furthermore, the top five and bottom five use cases were extracted for each category of respondents (cf. Table 1 and Table 2). Our expectations regarding the difference in needs of people having different roles are confirmed by comparing the top five use cases for each category. The contents of the top rankings are quite different, except for two use cases that are considered important by all: discovering the structure of a process and looking at the distribution of cases over the paths in the process.

When comparing the rankings of the least interesting use cases, one can also identify some similarities. Four use cases are common for both rankings. Respondents, independent of their role, consider that determining the group of resources performing a task and the group of resources involved in a case, as well as looking at the central employees of a process and at the arrival rate of cases in the process are less relevant use cases.

5.2 Survey

As a next step, we designed and distributed a survey to collect a larger number of responses. The survey contained all the questions addressed during the interviews, but also additional ones, which serve the purpose of capturing more detailed information about the end user's need in terms of process mining functionality. The contents of the survey and the complete results are given in [3].

This section presents the results obtained for a selection of the questions asked. We focus on the role and activity domain of the respondents, the ranking of the use cases, the identification of missing use cases and the possible functionality important for a process mining tool but not covered in the list of use cases.

From this survey, we received 47 responses. Although this number of responses is not enough to obtain statistically significant results, nor to generalize them, the survey results can provide useful qualitative feedback to validate our use cases. The highest percentages of responses we received are from people working in domains like academia (43%, 20 responses), information technology(21%, 10 responses), business process management consulting (19%, 9 responses), and banking (6%, 3 responses). The distribution over the roles shows a high percentage of researchers (51%, 24 responses), followed by process analysts (28%, 13 responses), process managers (9%, 4 responses), and consultants (6%, 3 responses).

The scores obtained by each use case based on the rankings were computed both over all responses and based on the role of the respondent. The score of a use case is the average of all scores registered from all rankings of the respondents belonging to the same role (the lower the score the more important is the use case). Based on these scores, we generated the graph depicted in Figure 5, which presents the profiles of the four most representative roles among the respondents.

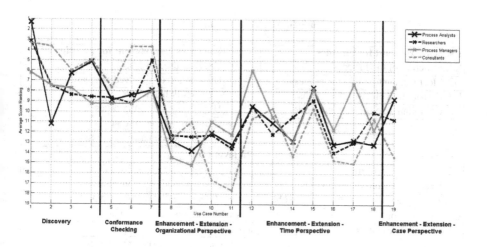

Fig. 5. Use cases ranking results based on respondents roles

Again, the results confirmed our expectation that the way users rank the use cases differs based on the role they have. It is interesting to see that use case 6 (The degree in which rules are obeyed) is considered medium important by researchers, process analysts and process managers while consultants view it as an essential use case. The same observation holds for use case 17 (Resource utilization rates); process managers view it as a highly relevant use case, while the respondents belonging to the other categories have a different opinion.

However, similarities in the ranking are also quite frequent. For instance, use case 1 (Structure of the process) is graded as one of the most important use cases by all the roles. Similarly, use cases 3 (Most frequent path in the process) and 7 (Compliance to the explicit model) are present in the tops of all rankings. The lower parts of the four rankings also share common use cases. Examples are use case 11 (Central employees) and use case 16 (Arrival rate of cases).

The rankings obtained for the use cases were also grouped based on the domains of activity of the respondents. The results show few differences between the three domains considered (academia, information technology and business process management consulting). The profiles of the domains are shown in [3].

Table 3 presents the results of rankings of the use cases based on the survey responses. We make the distinction between use cases relevant for all the roles, use cases less relevant for all the roles and use cases relevant only for some specific roles. This distinction was made by considering relevant the top nine use cases from the aggregated rankings of each role and less relevant the remaining ten use cases.

Four use cases (U1, U3, U4, and U7) are considered important by all the groups of respondents, while six use cases (U8, U9, U10, U14, U16, and U18) are rated as less important by all the groups. It is interesting to note that there are two use cases (U13 and U17) that are relevant for only one of the categories of respondents. The opposite holds for use cases U5, U6, U12, and U15, which resulted to be important for three out of the four categories of respondents.

Table 3. Aggregated results survey

Uses case relevant for all roles	Use cases less relevant for all roles
U1. Structure of the Process	U8. Resources per task
U3. Most frequent path in the process	U9. Resources involved in a case
U4. Distribution of cases over paths	U10. Work handovers
U7. Compliance to the explicit model	U14. Longest waiting times
	U16. Arrival rate of cases
	U18. Time sequence of events

Use case	Relevant for
U2. Routing probabilities	researchers, pr managers, consultants
U5. Exceptions from the normal path	researchers, pr analysts, consultants
U6. The degree in which the rules are obeyed	researchers, pr analysts, consultants
U12. Throughput time of cases	researchers, pr analysts, pr managers
U13. Slowest activities	consultants
U15. Cycles	researchers, pr analysts, pr managers, consultants
U17. Resource utilization rate	pr managers
U19. Business rules	pr analysts, pr managers

For the question asking whether there are any missing use cases, 58% of the respondents answered no, while 42% suggest new use cases. Among these suggestions, the measurement of different KPIs (cost, quality, flexibility, etc), the creation of a simulation model, and the online analysis of an event log with the purpose of making predictions were mentioned. Since our scope is limited to the process mining techniques that perform an offline analysis of processes and the last two indications we received are related to the online type of analysis, they are not considered for new use cases. The suggestion related to the KPIs measurement does however fit in our scope, but at the moment is too vague and general to be transformed in a testable use case.

The answers regarding the additional functionalities that a process mining system should offer to its users can be grouped into the following categories: input and output capabilities, the ability to filter and cluster data, the integration with external systems like databases, BPM tools, ERP, CRM, etc, animation capabilities, and the support for large input event logs. This information will be used as basis for the extended evaluation of the process mining tools in the following phases of the project.

5.3 Conclusions of the Validation Phase

The use cases ranking results derived from the survey are in line with the ones resulted from the interviews, in the sense that respondents having different roles have different needs in terms of process mining functionality. This is reflected in the scores assigned to the use cases. Another similarity between the results of the two validation steps is the fact that use case 1 (Structure of the process) was considered overall the most important one, while use cases 11 (Central employees) and 16 (Arrival rate of cases) are the least significant ones.

Based on the feedback received during the validation phase of our approach, we removed two irrelevant use cases, we rephrased all the use cases descriptions that were unclear, and we obtained a classification of use cases based on their importance for different roles.

The outcome of the interviews and survey was the validated list of process mining use cases. By validated, we mean use cases properly formulated, understandable, and corresponding to the needs of process mining users. Additional developments of the use cases needed for the practical tool evaluation are described in section 6.

6 Future Work

In this paper we presented the method we used to define and validate a list of process mining use cases. We employed an exploratory approach to collect a comprehensive set of process mining functionalities needed in practice. We started by looking at the literature in the domain of process mining and the functionality available in ProM. The next step was the definition of a set of use cases grouped according to the classification of process mining techniques given in [10]. We then validated the use cases by means of ten semi-structured interviews with domain experts and process mining users and by a survey.

The outcome of this study, namely the validated list of process mining use cases, is a part of a broader project that aims at evaluating a set of commercial process mining systems. The evaluation is done by judging whether a system provides support for each of the use cases in the list.

To do this, the use cases are currently further refined by assumptions and detailed acceptance criteria to allow for an unambiguous and repeatable evaluation. For example, use case 1 (Structure of the process) will be tested based on detailed acceptance criteria that determine which kinds of behavioral patterns [2] can be discovered by the tool. Additional to the complete use cases framework, we developed a set of benchmark event logs as part of our experimental setup for the evaluation.

So far we used our framework to evaluate two process mining tools: Futura Reflect by Futura Process Inteligence and ProcessAnalyzer by QPR. Based on the use cases we created a comprehensive set of event logs to test the functionality. Our initial findings show that the approach indeed reveals relevant strengths and weaknesses of the different tools. Currently, we are working on the evaluation of two other systems: ARIS Performance Process Manager (PPM) by Software AG and Flow by Fourspark.

Acknowledgements. We want to thank the practitioners who were willing to support us in an expert interview and everyone who took the time to fill out our survey.

References

1. Process Mining, http://www.processmining.org/
2. van der Aalst, W.M.P., ter Hofstede, A.H.M., Kiepuszewski, B., Barros, A.P.: Workflow Patterns. Distributed and Parallel Databases 14(1), 5–51 (2003)
3. Ailenei, I., Rozinat, A., Eckert, A., van der Aalst, W.M.P.: Towards an evaluation framework for process mining systems. Technical Report BPM Center Report BPM-11-13, BPMcenter.org (2011)
4. Alves de Medeiros, A.K., Günther, C.W.: Process mining: Using CPN tools to create test logs for mining algorithms. In: Proceedings of the Sixth Workshop and Tutorial on Practical Use of Coloured Petri Nets and the CPN Tools (2005)
5. Goedertier, S., Martens, D., Vanthienen, J., Baesens, B.: Robust Process Discovery with Artificial Negative Events. Journal of Machine Learning Research 10, 1305–1340 (2009)
6. Muñoz-Gama, J., Carmona, J.: A Fresh Look at Precision in Process Conformance. In: Hull, R., Mendling, J., Tai, S. (eds.) BPM 2010. LNCS, vol. 6336, pp. 211–226. Springer, Heidelberg (2010)
7. Rozinat, A., van der Aalst, W.M.P.: Conformance Checking of Processes Based on Monitoring Real Behavior. Information Systems 33(1), 64–95 (2008)
8. Rozinat, A., Alves de Medeiros, A.K., Günther, C.W., Weijters, A.J.M.M., van der Aalst, W.M.P.: The Need for a Process Mining Evaluation Framework in Research and Practice. In: Castellanos, M., Mendling, J., Weber, B. (eds.) Informal Proceedings of the International Workshop on Business Process Intelligence (BPI 2007), pp. 73–78. QUT, Brisbane (2007)
9. Smirnov, S., Reijers, H.A., Nugteren, T., Weske, M.: Business Process Model Abstraction: Theory and Practice. Technical report, Hasso Plattner Institute Postdam (2010)
10. van der Aalst, W.M.P.: Process Mining - Discovery, Conformance and Enhancement of Business Processes. Springer, Heidelberg (2011)

A Process Deviation Analysis – A Case Study

Jo Swinnen, Benoît Depaire, Mieke J. Jans, and Koen Vanhoof

Hasselt University, Agoralaan Building D, 3590 Diepenbeek, Belgium

Abstract. Processes are not always executed as expected. Deviations assure the necessary flexibility within a company, but also increase possible internal control weaknesses. Since the number of cases following such a deviation can grow very large, it becomes difficult to analyze them case-by-case. This paper proposes a semi-automatic process deviation analysis method which combines process mining with association rule mining to simplify the analysis of deviating cases. Association rule mining is used to group deviating cases into business rules according to similar attribute values. Consequently, only the resulting business rules need to be examined on their acceptability which makes the analysis less complicated. Therefore, this method can be used to support the search for internal control weaknesses.

Keywords: Association Rule Mining, Business Rules, Fuzzy Miner, Internal Control, PAIS, PredictiveAPriori, Process Mining.

1 Introduction

Operations within a company contain all kinds of automated processes which are carried out by one or more process aware information systems (PAIS) like ERP, CRM and workflow systems. Mostly, a preliminary designed process model is created for each process. However, to assure the necessary flexibility within a company, the settings of the related information systems are often loosened to allow deviating behavior in a process. Not all these deviations are depicted in the designed process model to avoid a complicated representation of the process and since they are not always generally accepted. To manage and control processes within a company, a good internal control system is indispensable, especially after the introduction of legislations such as the *Sarbanes-Oxley Act of 2002* [5]. Analyzing deviations in a process on their acceptability is an excellent way to find possible weaknesses in the internal control system.

Deviations can be classified into three categories: 'explicit exceptions', 'implicit exceptions' and 'anomalies'. *Explicit exceptions* are well-established guides implemented by every employee. These exceptions are generally accepted within a company. However, there are no generally accepted guides for *implicit exceptions*, but in certain circumstances these exceptions can be applied. Both explicit and implicit exceptions guarantee the necessary flexibility within a company to react fast and to operate effectively. A third category, *anomalies*, indicates unknown deviations which can correspond to errors, flaws or even fraud. For internal control purposes, it is urgent to detect these anomalies. Likewise, exceptions

F. Daniel et al. (Eds.): BPM 2011 Workshops, Part I, LNBIP 99, pp. 87–98, 2012.
© Springer-Verlag Berlin Heidelberg 2012

need a profound examination to check whether they comply with required exception guides. That way, possible weaknesses in the internal control system of an organization can be detected.

Until recently, it was not possible to discover all this deviating behavior and the designed process model often shows only the expected process flow. Nowadays, information of processes as they take place are widely recorded by PAIS in so-called '*event logs*'. An event log contains information about the events, i.e. activities of a process. For each event, the *process instance*, the *originator* and the *timestamp* are registered. *Process mining* allows these event logs to be analyzed [2]. One of the main process mining approaches is process discovery to extract a process model of the real life event logs. Since the event logs capture information of the actual process, unknown process behavior is revealed directly. Consequently, process discovery is a good starting point to analyze real process behavior, including deviations. *Heuristics Miner* [23] and *Fuzzy Miner* [10] are two algorithms which can visualize processes with unstructured and conflicting behavior. It is possible that a variety of deviations is exposed and that a lot of cases follow a deviating path. To verify whether certain deviations are allowed, these cases actually need to be examined case-by-case in order to check whether prescribed conditions are met. This case-by-case analysis requires a lot of resources and a new approach to simplify this analysis would be appropriate.

This paper suggests a new method to semi-automate the analysis of deviations in a process by clustering deviating cases into corresponding business rules through use of process mining and association rule mining techniques. *Business rules* can simplify the investigation of deviating cases in a business process by controlling or influencing process behavior. Ross (2003) defines a business rule as '*a directive intended to influence or guide business behavior*' [15]. Business rules can help to analyze deviating cases in a process by defining on which conditions a certain deviating path is followed by a case. In this way only the business rules need to be examined on their acceptability.

The remainder of this paper is organized as follows. Section 2 presents the new method to analyze deviations in a process. In section 3 the proposed method is applied in a real life case study. Related work is covered in section 4 and finally section 5 concludes the research.

2   Process Deviation Analysis

The *process deviation analysis* presented in this paper strives to simplify the examination of deviations from the prescribed process model. In order to apply this method a couple of assumptions need to be made in advance. This method assumes the presence of a PAIS which makes it possible to collect an event log of the underlying process. Mostly an event log refers to a case, an activity, a timestamp and a performer. Here the additional assumption is made that the event log also contains other attributes, which can help to analyze the deviations. This technique assumes that there are only execution logs available and therefore does not consider the existence of change logs like in adaptive PAIS

[9, 21, 22]. Further, a PAIS is aware of the underlying process but the settings of the information systems are not always very strict in order to allow flexibility within the company. In this way, deviating behavior can occur. As a last assumption, the number of cases following a deviation need to be large enough to apply rule mining. Deviations followed by just a few cases can be checked manually. The presented methodology comprises three main steps:

1. Find the main deviations with fuzzy miner
2. Applying association rule mining to discover business rules
3. Discussion with a business expert

Find the Main Deviations with Fuzzy Miner. Fuzzy Miner [10] is a process discovery algorithm which enables users to interactively explore processes from event logs. The main problem tackled by Fuzzy Miner is the visualization of 'spaghetti-like' real life processes, since this miner is suitable for visualizing less-structured processes [14]. For these essential features Fuzzy Miner has been picked out as starting point of this analysis.

A Fuzzy Miner visualization contains two main components, i.e. nodes and edges. Each *node* represents an event class in the process model and the nodes are linked to each other with *edges* to depict relations between these event classes. The interactive feature of Fuzzy Miner is then established by the use of two fundamental metrics to simplify and visualize complex, less-structured processes: (1) *significance* and (2) *correlation*. These metrics make sure that decisions can be made whether to show a very detailed process model or to show only the most significant information of the process. More detailed information about the metrics can be found in Günther et al. (2007).

The default settings of Fuzzy Miner result in a condensed view of the main process behavior. By loosening the *cut-off* parameter of the edges, the view can gradually reveal details and show less significant and correlated edges. If these edges are not part of the expected process flow, these can be considered as possible deviations. Subsequently, the number of cases that follow such a deviation, can be found by using *LTL checker* [18]. By running the rule '*Eventually Activity A Next B*' the existence of the direct relation between activity A and B, in this case the deviation, can be tested. Each deviating path is analyzed separately.[1]

Applying Association Rule Mining to Discover Business Rules. After the selection of a deviation, a label is assigned to each case to indicate whether the deviation exists (label = '1') or not (label = '0'), resulting in supervised data. The cases and their corresponding label are further summarized in a data table, which also contains other relevant attributes in order to find associations between these attributes and the label. Association rule mining is chosen since it searches for all kinds of patterns in the data and for each individual case different rules can be found. The output can subsequently be used to formulate

---

[1] The process mining techniques are plug-ins of the open-source software ProM: www.processmining.org

business rules which can correctly group the cases following and not following the deviation. Consequently, the business rules can be used as a control mechanism to examine this deviation.

Association rule mining aims at finding rules that meet a certain degree of *support* and *confidence*. The *support* is an indicator for the number of cases for which a rule applies. The *confidence*, on the other hand, indicates in how many cases the rule predicts a correct attribute value in proportion to the number of cases for which it makes any prediction. *PredictiveAPriori* [17] is selected as algorithm, because it only uses one measure, i.e. *accuracy*, to define the reliability of the rule. Instead of only calculating the confidence of a rule, the accuracy corrects for how frequently the rule occurs in the data set, the support. Since it was introduced, PredictiveAPriori has been succesfully used in various other methodologies [4, 7] and applications [6, 8][2].

Discussion with a Business Expert. Finally, the involvement of a business expert is necessary to analyze the business rules on their acceptability. This analysis can be done according to the previously defined categories of deviations.

3   Case Study

3.1   Running Example: Procurement Process

The presented methodology is applied to a real life data set provided by a company, ranked in the top 20 of European financial institutions. The selected business process is procurement, for which the data was extracted from their SAP system. The *process instance* which is analyzed in the procurement process is a purchase order item line. The steps of process selection and data preparation are adopted from [11] and will not be discussed into detail, since it goes beyond the scope of this paper. Interested readers may refer to [11] where a framework for internal fraud risk reduction was introduced.

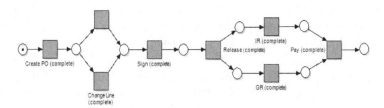

Fig. 1. Designed process model of the procurement process

The designed process model of the procurement process is represented in Figure 1. This figure represents the expected process behavior of a purchase order. Exceptions are not taken into account. First, the purchase order (PO) with a number of item lines is created. Before it can be released, it needs to be

---

[2] The data mining tool being used is Weka: http://www.cs.waikato.ac.nz/ml/weka/

signed. After the release, the goods (GR) and the corresponding invoices (IR) are received. The last step in the process, the payment, can be fulfilled when these two steps are completed. After the creation of the purchase order, a side path exists to change line of a PO. In some cases, it happens that the PO is created first and afterwards products are added to this PO. If a change line occurs and a release follows, a new sign is required in between.

The related event log of this process contains 26,185 cases for which 181,845 events are executed. 304 different sequences of activities are revealed in the whole event log, which is a lot for such a straightforward designed process model. This diverse behavior makes it an interesting event log to look at deviating paths and their corresponding cases.

3.2   Application of the Method

Step 1. Find the Main Deviations with Fuzzy Miner. In a first step, Fuzzy Miner is applied to detect deviations of the expected process path. Figure 2 depicts the process model by applying the default settings of Fuzzy Miner. The depicted patterns cover 71% (18,563 cases) of the total event log and resemble exactly to the designed process model. This means that there is still 29% (7,622 cases) left that follow a different path. The main question now is: '*Are these cases to be worried about?*'

By loosening the cut-off, additional relations will appear gradually. The first relation appearing is 'Change Line-Release' as depicted in Figure 3. This means that there could be cases for which there is no 'Sign' after a change of the purchase order before it was released again. To check whether this deviation indeed occurred, LTL-checker is used to verify whether there are cases where these two events directly followed each other. Apparently, in 2,790 cases a direct flow between 'Change Line' and 'Release' shows up, which means that the required 'Sign' in between is missing. By loosening the cut-off further, more deviations appear in the Fuzzy Miner visualization. In Table 1 the first four supplementary deviations with their corresponding number of cases are given. For the first three deviations, this methodology can help to analyze the corresponding cases since the number of cases is too large to check them case-by-case. The deviation 'Sign - GR' is only followed by 11 cases, so a manual check is sufficient. This case study will focus on the first deviation 'Change Line-Release'. The analysis of the other deviations is analogous.

Table 1. Cut-off values with their corresponding flows

Cut-off	Extra Flows	Occurences
0.2	Create PO - Sign - Release - GR - IR - Pay	11,608
	Create PO - Change Line - Sign - Release - GR - IR - Pay	6,955
0.4	... - **Change Line - Release** - ... **(No Sign)**	2,790
0.5	... - Release - IR - ... (No GR)	4,973
0.55	... - Create PO - Release - ... (No Sign)	739
0.75	... - Sign - GR - ... (No Release)	11

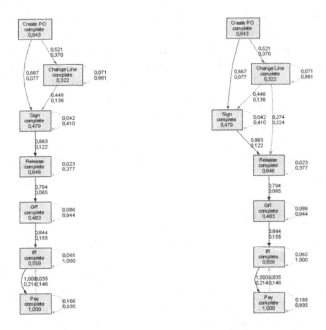

Fig. 2. Fuzzy Miner results with default settings (0.2)

Fig. 3. Fuzzy Miner results with cut-off of 0.4

Step 2. Applying Association Rule Mining to Discover Business Rules.
The focus of this step is on the deviation 'Change Line-Release'. Deviations in a process model are often acceptable under specific conditions, but if there are a lot of deviating cases it becomes hard to verify whether these deviating cases are acceptable or not. By discovering and grouping these cases into business rules, it becomes easier by only examining the business rules on their acceptability.

First, a label is assigned to each case to record whether the deviation 'Change Line-Release' appears (label = '1') or not (label = '0'). Further, a data table (Table 2) is created with all relevant attributes from the event log for each case. Each PO has a corresponding 'CaseID', 'GR', 'Purchase_Group', 'Supplier', 'Unit', 'PO_Value' and 'Creator_PO'. Further, since the deviation implies no sign between 'Change Line' and 'Release', it is interesting to see whether a sign is present before or after this deviation. By applying LTL-checker, a new attribute 'Sign' could be created which indicates whether there is a sign in the remaining part of the trace or not. For a certain document type, the company has a prescribed policy related to the PO value. If the PO value is under a certain threshold, a sign is not required. The attribute 'PO_Value_Above_Threshold' consequently records whether the PO value is underneath this threshold or not. There are 6 different document types and only one of them has the policy related to the PO value. This document type is considered as a higher risk than others and therefore needs more caution. 'Doc_Type' indicates whether for the corresponding document type the threshold for the PO value is applied (TRUE) or not (FALSE). These attributes are deduced from the corresponding event log.

Table 2. Attributes of a case

CaseID	The ID related to the purchase order item line
Label	The label that indicates whether there is a deviation 'Change Line - Release' (label = '1') or not (label = '0')
Sign	Indicator if there is a 'Sign' event before 'Change Line' or after 'Release' for this case
GR	Indicator whether 'Goods Receipt' is present (a service) or not
Doc_Type	Indicator whether the document type is risky or not
Purchase_Group	The purchase group corresponding to the purchase order line
Supplier	The supplier of the ordered goods or services
PO_Value	Value of the purchase order
PO_Value_Above_Threshold	Indicator if the PO value is above a certain threshold for which there always needs to be a sign
Unit	The unit of the quantity
Creator_PO	The person who created the purchase order in the first place

After the creation of the data table, the extraction of appropriate business rules can begin. The first problem arising, is the enormous difference between the number of cases with label '1' and '0', respectively 2,790 and 23,398 cases which causes a huge bias towards the cases with label '0'. Consequently, if a rule miner is applied to the whole data set, the cases with label '1' do not even show up in the first 100 rules. To solve this problem, a random sample is taken to make sure that the number of cases with label '0' corresponds roughly to the 2,790 cases with label '1'.

The number of association rules retrieved with PredictiveAPriori is 250. Out of 250 association rules, 176 rules are related to the deviation. Since, a lot of these association rules overlap, they can be summarized in more abbreviated rules. PredictiveAPriori generates association rules that can be generalized as much as possible, therefore these rules can be extended with additional conditions according to other attribute values. Since the goal of this analysis is to summarize the deviating cases into business rules, these additional conditions are added in the business rules to provide the business experts with as much information as possible. Table 3 shows the resulting rules, which can be used as business rules to verify whether they are acceptable or not[3]. The first column is a summary of the discovered business rules. For each rule the number of cases with the deviation is given and the confidence of this rule is calculated by dividing the number of cases with the deviation by the total number of cases following this rule (label '1' and '0'). The resulting business rules cover 2,777 cases out of 2,790 cases, which means only these 10 business rules and 13 remaining cases need to be examined on their acceptability. 4 rules have a confidence of 100% which means that all covered cases deviate from the designed process. The confidence can be related to *type I errors* in hypothesis testing. If the confidence is less than 100%, it means that the rule sometimes predicts *false-positive*, i.e. the label is predicted falsely.

Step 3. Discussion with a Business Expert. In a last step, the business rules for the deviation 'Change Line-Release' are discussed with a business expert. It is possible that for some cases 'Sign' and/or 'GR' are not required, but these cases

---

[3] The ID's for the purchase groups and suppliers are anonymized to ensure confidentiality.

Table 3. Extracted Business Rules

	PredictiveAPriori Rules	Label = 1	Label={0,1}	Confidence
1	IF Supplier = {1, 2, 3, 4, 5, 6, 7, 8, 9, 10, 11, 12, 13, 14, 15, 16, 17, 18, 19, 20, 21, 22, 23, 24, 25, 26, 27, 28, 29, 30, 31, 33, 34, 35, 36, 37, 38, 39, 40, 41, 42, 43, 44, 45, 46, 47, 48, 49, 50} AND Sign = FALSE AND GR = FALSE AND Doc_Type = TRUE AND Creator_PO = BATCH AND Unit = BL THEN Label = 1	2171	2216	98%
2	IF Supplier = 32 AND GR = FALSE AND Doc_Type = TRUE AND Creator_PO = BATCH AND Unit = BL THEN Label = 1	17	17	100%
3	IF Purchase_Group = {B, C, D, E, F, G, H, I, J, K, L, M, N, O, P, Q, R, S, T, U, V, W, X, Y, Z, AA} AND Sign = FALSE AND GR = FALSE AND Doc_Type = TRUE AND Creator_PO = BATCH AND Unit = BL THEN Label = 1	2631	2687	98%
4	IF Purchase_Group = A AND Sign = FALSE AND GR = FALSE AND Doc_Type = TRUE AND Unit = BL THEN Label = 1	36	37	97%
5	IF Purchase_Group = BB AND Sign = TRUE THEN Label = 1	89	95	94%
6	IF Purchase_Group = V AND Sign = FALSE AND GR = FALSE AND Doc_Type = TRUE AND Creator_PO = BATCH AND Unit = BL AND Value_PO_Above_Threshold = TRUE THEN Label = 1	174	174	100%
7	IF Purchase_Group {M, N, U} AND Sign = FALSE AND GR = FALSE AND Doc_Type = TRUE AND Creator_PO = BATCH AND Unit = BL AND Value_PO_Above_Threshold = FALSE THEN Label = 1	69	77	90%
8	IF Supplier = {6, 22, 27, 32} AND Sign = FALSE AND GR = FALSE AND Doc_Type = TRUE AND Creator_PO = BATCH AND Unit = BL AND Value_PO_Above_Threshold = TRUE THEN Label = 1	126	132	95%
9	IF Supplier = 6 AND Purchase_Group = M AND Sign = FALSE AND GR = FALSE AND Doc_Type = TRUE AND Creator_PO = BATCH AND Value_PO_Above_Threshold = TRUE THEN Label = 1	12	12	100%
10	IF Supplier = 51 AND Purchase_Group = CC AND Sign = FALSE AND GR = FALSE AND Doc_Type = TRUE AND Creator_PO = BATCH AND Unit = BL AND Value_PO_Above_Threshold = TRUE THEN Label = 1	6	6	100%

need to meet certain conditions. For instance, 'Sign' is not required provided that the following two conditions are met. The PO must concern a certain document type (Doc_Type = TRUE) and the value of the PO needs to be underneath a prescribed threshold (PO_Value_Above_Threshold = FALSE). These conditions are generally known guides in the company and can therefore be categorized as an 'explicit exception'. A business rule confirming this explicit exception would be expected. Rules 1, 3-4 AND 6-10 all have 'Doc_Type' = TRUE and no sign which normally is allowed if the PO value stays underneath the threshold. But the expected supplementary condition 'PO_Value_Above_Threshold' = FALSE is apparently missing for rule 1 and 3-4. Analyzing the corresponding cases shows that the explicit exception is violated frequently since there are a lot of cases that have a PO value exceeding the threshold. It is possible that for certain suppliers or purchase groups this threshold is not taken into account because normally the threshold is not exceeded for these particular suppliers or purchase groups. This violation truly needs a profound examination.

A following finding can be drawn from the confidence of the business rules. The rules having a confidence of 100% imply that for the defined attribute values in these business rules the cases always have the deviation 'Change Line-Release' in their trace for certain purchase groups and suppliers. Since no explicit exceptions apply here, a possible explanation can be that these are 'implicit exceptions'. Therefore, the completion of the PO's for the corresponding suppliers and purchase groups needs to be examined. If these business rules indeed are implicit exceptions, a decision can be made whether they will be used as explicit exceptions in the future or not. In case these business rules are not implicit exceptions, it needs to be verified whether they need to be categorized as unacceptable 'anomalies' instead of exceptions.

Subsequently, rule 5, covering 89 cases, is the only rule with the condition 'Sign' = TRUE. This means that before 'Change Line' or after 'Release' one or more signs are present. It is possible that the sign is registered at a wrong moment or is done in a different way for this purchase group. It needs to be examined why this particular purchase group 'BB' systematically changes lines. Rules 6 and 8-10 all have a PO value above the threshold and document type 'TRUE', so normally a sign is required as defined in the above explicit exception. The additional condition 'Sign' = FALSE in these rules contradicts this explicit exception. These rules, covering 318 cases, therefore violate the regulations of the company. They can be classified as anomalies and need a very close examination.

Finally, the 13 remaining cases need to be examined case-by-case to verify their acceptability. There are for instance two cases which have a document type that does not support the explicit exception of the PO threshold. Since there is no 'Sign' for these cases, this again is a violation of the explicit exception, i.e. an anomaly. A closing remark needs to be made concerning 'GR'. Except for rule 5, 'GR' is marked as not present in all the business rules. This implies the purchase of services which can be considered as risky since, next to 'Sign', another control element is omitted. There is no registration of GR and it is not possible to check whether these services are delivered or not.

Summary. These findings result in some suggestions towards the case company. The absence of a sign and GR in most of the business rules signify a loss of two important control points in the procurement process. Consequently, the chance for internal control weaknesses is enhanced. The fact that the threshold for the PO value is violated in already 318 cases indicates a serious anomaly in the process. It implies actually non-compliance with the explicit exception for 'Doc_Type' = TRUE stating that a sign is necessary if the PO value exceeds the threshold. This can indicate once again a significant internal control weakness which needs to be examined very closely. The first 5 rules can also be examined more closely in this matter by looking at the attribute for the PO threshold. It is further recommended to look deeper into the discovered rules above to assure that explicit and implicit exception rules are followed correctly. Perhaps, it needs to be verified whether the possible implicit rules, i.e. the rules with 100% confidence but no explicit guides within the company, can be made more explicit by using these business rules.

The deviation analysis was also applied to the second and third deviation of Table 1 to make sure that this method can be generalized to other deviations. The last deviation in this table is an example of a deviation that needs to be checked manually since there are only 11 cases. The deviation for which there is no 'GR' between 'Release' and 'IR' is followed by 4,973 cases and the deviation for which there is no 'Sign' between 'Create PO' and 'Release' by 739 cases. The process deviation analysis results into 20 and 9 business rules respectively. Additionally, for the deviation 'no GR', there are 1,438 remaining cases left. It is possible to generate more business rules with PredictiveAPriori to lower the number of remaining cases, but that is at the expense of a lower accuracy level. Here the choice was made to provide only business rules with an accuracy above 95%.

Instead of analyzing 8,513 deviating cases case-by-case for these 4 deviations, only 39 business rules and 1,462 remaining cases need to be investigated. In this way, the analysis of deviating cases becomes more efficient and less time-consuming.

4 Related Work

The presented technique to analyze deviations in a process assumes the presence of a PAIS. Nowadays, there exist also adaptive PAIS, which have both execution logs and change logs. In adaptive PAIS, processes can deviate from the prescribed process model according to a changed situation. These changes are registered in the change logs. In this way deviations can exist, but can also be analyzed through the change logs [9, 21, 22]. In this paper, only execution logs are used to analyze deviations since not all PAIS have these change logs.

The combined use of process mining and business rules was already presented by [3]. Crerie et al. (2009) use process mining and data mining to discover two types of business rules, i.e. *condition action assertions* and *authorization action assertions*. The process deviation analysis leans on the discovery of condition action assertions. Instead of focusing on business rules that define normal behavior in a process, this analysis is used to examine whether deviating cases are acceptable or not. The use of business rules to analyze deviating cases can further be seen as a type of *decision point analysis*. A decision point analysis algorithm was already presented by [16]. This algorithm can be used to analyze how data attributes influence the path which is followed by a certain case. It supports data analysis for business processes in a direct way and it can be used to extend the designed process model afterwards.

The idea of extending internal control with process mining was already mentioned in previous research [11, 13, 20]. A first case study to extend internal auditing with process mining is given in [12], where the usefulness of deviation analysis is already pointed out. In [1] the opportunities and challenges for process mining in a audit context are clarified. The different aspects, i.e. *process discovery, conformance checking* and *extension* of process mining can enrich internal control and therefore auditing in several ways. In [19], conformance checking is suggested in the context of *online auditing* to check whether processes are executed conform integrated business rules in the information systems of a company. By applying the proposed process deviation analysis, it becomes possible to enrich or perhaps change these integrated business rules according to real life information about deviating paths expressed in additional business rules. This methodology can also be seen as an extension of *process diagnostics*, a methodology proposed in [2]. The third step, control flow analysis, can be further enriched with information about the deviating patterns in the real process behavior.

5   Conclusions

This paper presents a new method to analyze deviating behavior in a process. The process deviation analysis comprises three main steps resulting in business rules which cluster cases following a deviating path in the process. A business expert only needs to analyze these business rules on their acceptability. The included case study shows the usefulness of the method by analyzing one deviating path of a real life process. Consequently, the analysis of this deviating path by using the business rules is much more efficient than a case-by-case analysis. An analysis of the business rules by a business expert raised quickly a lot of questions round the internal control system of the procurement process.

This methodology provides an efficient way to analyze deviations in a process by grouping deviating cases into a limited set of business rules. These business rules can be used to check whether explicit exceptions comply with their prescribed conditions. Further, unknown process behavior, like implicit exceptions and anomalies, can be made visible and accessible by applying this methodology. Implicit exceptions on the one hand are made explicit and can therefore also be checked on their compliance. On the other hand, anomalies in a process and consequently internal control weaknesses can be detected.

References

[1] Alles, M., Vasarhelyi, M.: Process Mining of Event Logs in Auditing: Opportunities and Challenges. In: 1st International Symposium on Accounting Information Systems, Orlando (2010)

[2] Bozkaya, M., Gabriels, J., van der Werf, J.M.: Process Diagnostics: a Method Based on Process Mining. In: Proceedings of the International Conference on Information, Process, and Knowledge Management: Eknow 2009, pp. 22–27 (2009)

[3] Crerie, R., Baião, F.A., Santoro, F.M.: Discovering Business Rules through Process Mining. In: Halpin, T., Krogstie, J., Nurcan, S., Proper, E., Schmidt, R., Soffer, P., Ukor, R. (eds.) BPMDS 2009 and EMMSAD 2009. LNBIP, vol. 29, pp. 136–148. Springer, Heidelberg (2009)

[4] Depaire, B., Vanhoof, K., Wets, G.: ARUBAS, An Association Rule Based Similarity Framework for Associative Classifiers, vol. 8, pp. 692–699 (2008)

[5] Dobre, M.M.: Studies Bucharest Academy of Economic. Disclosure of Internal Control Deficiencies under the Sarbanes_Oxley Act of 2002. In: Amis 2010 - Proceedings of the 5th International Conference, Accounting and Management Information Systems, pp. 13–37 (2010)

[6] Drymonas, E., Zervanou, K., Petrakis, E.G.M.: Unsupervised Ontology Acquisition from Plain Texts: The OntoGain System. In: Hopfe, C.J., Rezgui, Y., Métais, E., Preece, A., Li, H. (eds.) NLDB 2010. LNCS, vol. 6177, pp. 277–287. Springer, Heidelberg (2010)

[7] García, E., Romero, C., Ventura, S., de Castro, C.: Using Rules Discovery for the Continuous Improvement of e-Learning Courses. In: Corchado, E., Yin, H., Botti, V., Fyfe, C. (eds.) IDEAL 2006. LNCS, vol. 4224, pp. 887–895. Springer, Heidelberg (2006)

[8] García, E., Romero, C., Ventura, S., de Castro, C.: Evaluating Web Based Instructional Models Using Association Rule Mining. In: Houben, G.-J., McCalla, G., Pianesi, F., Zancanaro, M. (eds.) UMAP 2009. LNCS, vol. 5535, pp. 16–29. Springer, Heidelberg (2009)

[9] Günther, C.W., Rinderle, S., Reichert, M., van der Aalst, W.: Change Mining in Adaptive Process Management Systems. In: Meersman, R., Tari, Z. (eds.) OTM 2006. LNCS, vol. 4275, pp. 309–326. Springer, Heidelberg (2006)

[10] Günther, C.W., van der Aalst, W.M.P.: Fuzzy Mining – Adaptive Process Simplification Based on Multi-perspective Metrics. In: Alonso, G., Dadam, P., Rosemann, M. (eds.) BPM 2007. LNCS, vol. 4714, pp. 328–343. Springer, Heidelberg (2007)

[11] Jans, M.: A Framework for Internal Fraud Risk Reduction: The IFR Framework. PhD thesis, Hasselt University (2009)

[12] Jans, M., Depaire, B., Vanhoof, K.: Does Process Mining Add to Internal Auditing? An Experience Report. In: Halpin, T., Nurcan, S., Krogstie, J., Soffer, P., Proper, E., Schmidt, R., Bider, I. (eds.) BPMDS 2011 and EMMSAD 2011. LNBIP, vol. 81, pp. 31–45. Springer, Heidelberg (2011)

[13] Jans, M., Lybaert, N., Vanhoof, K.: Business process mining for internal fraud risk reduction: results of a case study. In: Proceedings of Induction of Process Models (2008)

[14] Li, J.: Tutorial fuzzy miner plug-in 1.2.2 (2010)

[15] Ross, R.G.: Principles of the Business Rule Approach. Addison-Wesley Information Technology (2003)

[16] Rozinat, A., van der Aalst, W.M.P.: Decision Mining in ProM. In: Dustdar, S., Fiadeiro, J.L., Sheth, A.P. (eds.) BPM 2006. LNCS, vol. 4102, pp. 420–425. Springer, Heidelberg (2006)

[17] Scheffer, T.: Finding association rules that trade support optimally against confidence. Intelligent Data Analysis 9(4), 381–395 (2005)

[18] van der Aalst, W.M.P., de Beer, H.T., van Dongen, B.F.: Process Mining and Verification of Properties: An Approach Based on Temporal Logic. In: Meersman, R. (ed.) OTM 2005. LNCS, vol. 3760, pp. 130–147. Springer, Heidelberg (2005)

[19] van der Aalst, W.M.P., van Hee, K., van der Werf, J.M., Kumar, A., Verdonk, M.: Conceptual model for online auditing. Decision Support Systems 50(3), 636–647 (2011)

[20] van der Aalst, W.M.P., van Hee, K.M., van der Werf, J.M., Verdonk, M.: Auditing 2.0: Using process mining to support tomorrow's auditor. Computer 43(3), 90–93 (2010)

[21] Weber, B., Reichert, M., Rinderle-Ma, S., Wild, W.: Providing integrated life cycle support in process-aware information systems. International Journal of Cooperative Information Systems 18(1), 115–165 (2009)

[22] Weber, B., Wild, W., Lauer, M., Reichert, M.: Improving Exception Handling by Discovering Change Dependencies in Adaptive Process Management Systems. In: Eder, J., Dustdar, S. (eds.) BPM Workshops 2006. LNCS, vol. 4103, pp. 93–104. Springer, Heidelberg (2006)

[23] Weijters, A., van der Aalst, W.M.P.: Rediscovering workflow models from event-based data using little thumb. Integrated Computer-Aided Engineering 10(2), 151–162 (2003)

Merging Computer Log Files for Process Mining: An Artificial Immune System Technique

Jan Claes and Geert Poels

Department of Management Information Systems and Operations Management
Faculty of Economics and Business Administration
Ghent University, Tweekerkenstraat 2, 9000 Ghent, Belgium
{jan.claes,geert.poels}@ugent.be

Abstract. Process mining techniques try to discover and analyse business processes from recorded process data. These data have to be structured in so called *computer log files*. If processes are supported by different computer systems, merging the recorded data into one log file can be challenging. In this paper we present a computational algorithm, based on the Artificial Immune System algorithm, that we developed to automatically merge separate log files into one log file. We also describe our implementation of this technique, a proof of concept application and a real life test case with promising results.

Keywords: Business Process Modelling, Process Mining, Process Discovery, Log File Merging.

1 Introduction

Process mining techniques [1] are used to discover and analyse business processes in a semi-automatic way. Starting from all kinds of recorded process data (called *log files*) process mining tries to automatically discover the structure and properties of the business processes, which can be visualised in business process models.

Traditionally, business process models were made by domain experts, based on their experience and perceptions in the organisation. This manual task of modelling is subjective and time-consuming. In contrast, process mining techniques start from recorded actual process data and therefore the main benefits of process mining relate to correctness (no errors), completeness (no missing paths) and speed. [2]

However, the first step of gathering the recorded data is still a primarily manual task and thus the results of process mining techniques can be tempered if no optimal set of data is collected.

Three actions have to be taken before process discovery and analysis techniques can be performed: searching for data in the IT support systems, structuring these data (i.e. identifying single process steps (events) and groups of process steps that belong to the same process execution (process instances)), and converting these data to the format required by the process mining tool. If process data are found in different sources, then a fourth action is required: merging the data into one computer log file.

F. Daniel et al. (Eds.): BPM 2011 Workshops, Part I, LNBIP 99, pp. 99–110, 2012.

In this paper we present an automated technique for merging already collected, structured and converted process data according to an Artificial Immune System (AIS) algorithm, which is based on the features and behaviour of the vertebrate immune system. By automating this fourth action of the preparation step, we try to broaden the benefits of process mining to an extended part of the overall process mining procedure, because the automation makes the merge step in the preparation phase faster (speed), the use of data from multiple systems is facilitated (completeness) and the way these data are merged is less subjective than when performed manually (correctness).

We start with a description of the problem of log file merging for process mining and discuss related research topics in Section 2. The Artificial Immune System algorithm and its technical implementation details are presented in Section 3. Experiment results of a proof of concept application using a generated test case are described in Section 4. As a minimal form of validation the AIS merging technique was also applied to a real case. The results of this realistic exercise can be found in Section 5. To end the paper, a conclusion is provided in Section 6.

2   Problem Description

2.1   Process Mining

The starting point for process mining techniques is a single computer log file. This file often does not exist at the beginning of the analysis, but must be constructed out of the actual recorded process data. These data have to be *collected* first from databases or files (e.g. SAP audit trails, web service log file) (Fig. 1). When all relevant data are collected, they have to be *structured* before analysis can start. A process is normally executed over and over again and thus the data set contains information of multiple executions of the same process. Different event records that belong to the same execution of a process are grouped into *traces*. Usually, one log file will contain information of only one process, but otherwise the traces are again grouped per process. A last preparation step, before process mining can be applied, is the *conversion* of the structured data set into the proper format, mostly according to a selected tool. This is a pure syntactical exercise and should be possible in a (semi-) automated way.

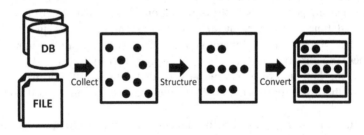

Fig. 1. Preparation steps before process mining techniques can be performed

2.2   Log File Merging

In the nineties many business process tasks were being automated or supported by IT systems. Many tools were developed and nowadays, in many cases, processes are supported by multiple IT systems with no clear relation to each other [3]. For this reason recorded process data is scattered across several databases or files and merging these data into one consistent data set can be challenging [3].

In this paper we present as a solution for this challenge a technique for automated merging of data from different sources. Our approach is implemented in ProM[1], a well known academic process mining tool, which implies that for our implementation we assume the different data sets are first separately structured and converted to the ProM file format[2] (e.g. with Nitro[3], a tool mainly made for this purpose).

Fig. 2 shows the steps for our solution implementation. First, data is collected, structured and converted into a series of ProM compatible computer log files (e.g. using Nitro). Second, our Artificial Immune System Merger plug-in in ProM is used to merge the files into one computer log file. Third, this log file is used as input to discover and analyse the business process with the other plug-ins included in ProM.

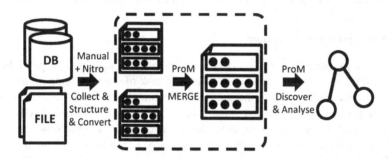

Fig. 2. Merging data of different sources can be performed after structuring and converting to a tool-specific file format. We implemented our merge technique in the ProM analysis tool itself.

2.3   Related Research

We are not aware of any literature reporting on research of automated log file merging techniques. Nevertheless the same kind of problem is studied in other research areas (e.g. data matching [4]) or in other contexts (e.g. introducing RFID technology for consistent case numbering in supply chains [5], matching related activities in different process models [6]).

In the field of process mining similar research is performed for *event correlation* problems [7, 8]. This subarea is concerned about finding a way to automatically structure log files (i.e. to determine which events belong to the same process execution and have to be put together in the same trace in the log files). For example *event cluster-*

---

[1] ProM can be downloaded at http://www.processmining.org/prom/downloads.

[2] More information about the ProM file format (xes) can be found at http://xes-standard.org

[3] Nitro can be downloaded for trial at http://fluxicon.com/nitro.

ing techniques (e.g. [9]) usually calculate a proximity function that is used to decide if events belong together [7]. Where these techniques focus on finding out which *events* belong together, this paper describes a technique to find out which *traces* (groups of events) of different computer log files belong together.

3   Solution Design

The merging of two computer log files consists of two steps: (i) linking together traces of both logs that belong to the same process execution and (ii) merging these traces into one trace to be stored in a new log file. We assume reliable and comparable timestamps are available in the original logs causing the second step to be a simple exercise of chronological ordering of all the events of linked traces into one new trace in the resulting merged log file. Therefore our solution description focuses on the first step of finding traces in both log files that belong together. In our opinion, more than one factor can indicate that two traces should be linked (see 3.2.1). We looked for existing techniques that incorporate multiple indicators in their solution procedure and found our inspiration in the Artificial Immune System algorithm [10].

3.1   Artificial Immune System

An Artificial Immune System (AIS) is a computational algorithm inspired by the vertebrate immune system (see Fig. 3). The main task of the vertebrate immune system is to discover and eliminate disease causing elements (called *antigens*). The cells responsible for this task are called *immune cells*. There are two types: B-cells recognise antigens by the molecules on their surface and T-cells require other accessory cells that in their place recognise the antigens. Our solution implementation is based on the B-cells which directly recognise antigens. The B-cells are covered with receptor molecules (called *antibodies*) which can bind with the antigen surface molecules. The strength of a binding is related to the affinity between an antigen surface molecule and the antibody in the binding. If this affinity reaches a certain threshold value, the immune system is activated and the antigen is destroyed.

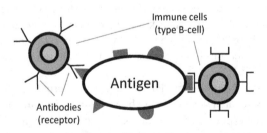

Fig. 3. Antigen (disease causing element) and immune cells (of type B-cell) with their antibodies (receptor molecules). (inspired by Fig. 1(a) in [10]).

The real strength in the immune system lies in the principles of clonal selection, hypermutation and receptor editing. When antibodies connect with antigens with a high affinity, they clone themselves in high volumes. The higher the affinity, the higher the amount of clones. This principle of *clonal selection* causes the immune system to be highly resistant to the found antigens and become 'immune' to them.

After cloning, the antibodies are subject to random changes (*hypermutations*) and a more diverse population of antibodies is created. Because only the ones with the highest affinity with discovered antigens are cloned, the antibody population becomes better in recognising and killing antigens. The hypermutations are random, but the amount of changes depends on the binding affinity: the higher the affinity, the less changes.

Because the cloning, amount of mutations, but also the life span of the antibodies depend on the affinity with an antigen, the antibodies with the lowest affinity tend to leave the population and make room for newly formed antibodies, which is called *receptor editing*.

3.2   Implementation Details

Fig. 4 shows the steps in our AIS algorithm implementation. The algorithm starts with a total random population (RANDPOP) of solutions. Each solution is nothing more than a set of links between (a part of) the traces in both logs. To quantify the affinity of each set of links in the population, a fitness function score is calculated for every solution in the population. The solutions in the random population are next sorted according to their fitness function score. The actual population used throughout the algorithm is smaller than RANDPOP in size and therefore the initial population (INITPOP) is constructed out of the best solutions in RANDPOP (i.e. with the highest fitness function score). The AIS algorithm then iterates over three steps until a certain stop condition is met: clonal selection, hypermutation and receptor editing.

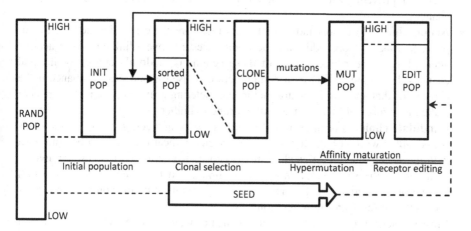

Fig. 4. Steps in our Artificial Immune System algorithm implementation (inspired by Fig. 1 in [11])

Clonal selection

The solutions in the population (INITPOP) are sorted according to their fitness function score. The top p_{clone} percentage solutions with the highest scores are selected to build up the next population. This new population (CLONEPOP) contains as much elements as the previous one and for this reason multiple clones of the same element will be included. The chance that a solution from the selected top p_{clone} solutions will be chosen for cloning depends on the fitness function score of that solution.

Hypermutation

Every solution in CLONEPOP is then altered (mutated) to build a new population MUTPOP. The amount of mutations on each solution depends again on the fitness function score, but this time, the higher the score, the less mutations. The amount of mutations for solution s (num_s) is calculated with formula (1):

$$num_s = \max \left(1, \frac{\left(100-100e^{-0,05(bestScoreSoFar-score_s)}\right) numLinks}{100}\right) \tag{1}$$

Each particular mutation on a certain solution follows the next four steps:

- **Indicator factor choice**. The goal of mutations is to find solutions which would get a higher fitness function score. As this score is the sum of a number of indicator factors (see 3.2.1), we choose a factor to be improved by this mutation. In the next three steps we try to improve our solution for this selected indicator factor, but it is possible that the overall score will decrease (due to the other factors in the function). At the start, there is an equal chance for each indicator factor to be selected, but also for a total random change (i.e. not aimed at improving a specific factor) to be selected. If at a time a mutation for a specific indicator did decrease the overall fitness score, this factor gets only half the chance of the other factors to be chosen in the next mutations. If it is again chosen and leads to an overall improvement this time, the chance is reset to be equal to the other factor chances.
- **Action choice**. For most indicator factors there are three possible actions to improve that factor score: add a link between traces, remove a link between traces or alter a link between traces. One of these actions is randomly chosen with equal chances. For some indicators a certain action is useless and has no chance to be chosen for that specific indicator factor (e.g. deleting a link between traces cannot make the number of links with a certain property higher).
- **Candidate choice**. For the selected indicator factor and action a set of candidates is assembled with all links for which the selected indicator factor can be optimised with the selected action. A random link is chosen from this set. Because a previous mutation on the same solution can have diminished the overall fitness function score, priority is given to all touched links in previous mutations on the same solution in the current algorithm iteration.
- **Improvement choice**. For the selected indicator factor, action and candidate link a set of improvements (new links) is built. A random improvement is chosen from this set.

Receptor editing

The solutions in MUTPOP are sorted according to their fitness function score. The top p_{edit} percentage solutions with the highest score are selected to be part of the next population (EDITPOP). This new population has to contain as much elements as the previous one and for this reason new solutions are picked from the initial random population (RANDPOP) to fill up the new population. The chance to be selected is again related to the fitness score of each solution: All solutions of RANDPOP have a chance to be selected for the new generation of POP, but the solutions with a higher fitness score still get a higher chance than the solutions with a lower fitness score.

Stop condition

The resulting population (EDITPOP) serves as input for another cycle of clonal selection, hypermutation and receptor editing. This iterating algorithm stops when a certain stop condition is met. Then the best solution of all generated populations (which is continuously updated) is the proposed solution. In our implementation a fixed amount of iterations can be set (*numIter*). If in *numIterNoOpt* consecutive iterations no improvement of the overall best solution is achieved, the algorithm stops earlier. The algorithm parameters (size of RANDPOP, size of the other populations, p_{clone}, p_{edit}, *numIter* and *numIterNoOpt*) can be modified by the user to be optimised for a certain combination of input logs.

Fitness function

The fitness function determines the affinity of a certain solution. This fitness function score is used throughout the whole algorithm as every step is influenced by the affinity. Because different factors can indicate that traces in both logs belong together, the fitness function is built up from different indicator factors:

$$f = w_1 \sum STI_i + w_2 \sum EAV_i + w_3 \sum ET_j + w_4 \sum MT_j + w_5 \sum TD_i \qquad (2)$$

In the next part of this text we will use the terms *first trace* and *second trace*. With these terms we mean a trace from one of both logs and a trace from the other log respectively. Notice that the input order of the log files to be merged is not important.

Same trace identifier (STI$_i$)

A first indicator for two traces to belong together is if they have the same trace identifier (i.e. the process execution is consistently identified in both logs). In this case the problem is rather trivial, because it's almost certain how to link the traces from the two logs. But this is no reason to exclude the factor from our fitness function. If, exceptionally, two traces with the same trace identifier do not belong together (e.g. a customer number that matches with an invoice number), then another solution should score higher due to the other indicator factors of the fitness function.

Equal attribute values (EAV$_i$)

In many processes a reference number or code is used throughout the entire process. This is most probably the trace id. But maybe other numbers are passed from event to event. If this number is logged, we should search for matching values of event attributes. Note that attribute names do not need to correspond. The name for this number can be different in both logs (e.g. "invoice number" and "reference number") and matching attribute names is more challenging [12]. Also note that some attribute values may have equivalents in lots of traces (for example status *completed*). This would make barely any difference between different solutions, because almost all possible solutions would score higher.

Extra trace (ET$_j$)

It is possible that a first trace should be linked to multiple second traces (e.g. one order handling causes two deliveries), but we think the number of second traces linked to the same first trace should be rather low. If too many second traces are linked to the same first trace, this indicator factor makes the overall fitness function score decrease (unless other factors have a greater positive effect indicating that there should be more than one trace linked to the current trace).

Missing trace (MT$_j$)

Analogically, we think a solution with traces of both logs that are not linked is probably less correct. If there are second traces that are not linked to a first trace, this indicator factor makes the overall fitness function score decrease to encourage traces to participate in links between the two logs. The combination of this factor and the extra trace factor should lead to an even spread of links between the traces in both logs.

Time difference (TD$_i$)

A last indication in our implementation for two links to belong together is the time difference. In our opinion smaller time differences are more probable then higher differences, which is represented by a higher score for smaller time differences. The time difference for a certain link in a certain solution is defined as the difference between the times of the first events of both logs.

Each indicator factor has a weight that can be changed by the user to give the opportunity to influence the algoritshm with his insights on the log file merging problem. At the end an overview of the individual indicator scores for the solution is presented to the user which also gives him the chance to gain insight and to start over with new indicator scores.

Some of the factors are calculated for each individual link in the solution (STI$_i$, EAV$_i$ and TD$_i$). Therefore in RANDPOP we also include two special solutions which we think can be a good starting point for the optimal solution: one for which we linked every first trace to the second trace with which it has the highest individual link score and one for which we linked every second trace to the best first trace.

4   Proof of Concept

We have tested our technique with a simulated example. The benefit of using simulation is that the correct solution (i.e. the process to be discovered) is known. Another advantage is that properties like time difference or noise can be controlled.

The example model we used in our experiments (see Fig. 5) is based on the same example model as in [13]. We generated two log files with 100 random executions of the process where the executions of tasks A, E, and F were logged in a first log file and the executions of tasks B, C and D in the second file. We initially did not include noise, the executions did not overlap in time, and there was no structural unbalance in choosing one or the other path first for the AND-split (B and C) or selecting the path to be followed for the OR-split (A or E). Because there is no unbalance in choosing paths in the OR-split, the second log ends up with about 50 traces. Time differences between consecutive events were also random.

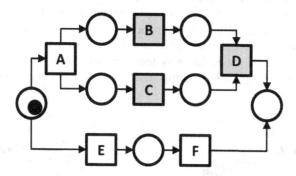

Fig. 5. Process model for our back-end IT support process example

We then also generated different log files with different properties:

- We added noise in the same way as described in [14]. One of four options is randomly selected: (i) delete minimum one and up to one third of events from the beginning of a trace, (ii) from the middle of a trace, (iii) from the end of a trace, or (iv) switch places of two random events in a trace. The noise percentage determines the chance a trace is influenced by noise in one of the four ways.
- Another property we varied is overlap. The overlap percentage determines the chance of each execution to start during the previous execution. With 10% overlap 10% of traces started before the previous ones ended.
- Finally, we repeated each test with two log files without matching trace identifiers.

The results of our tests with matching trace identifiers were perfect (in all our tests a perfect set of links was found and both log files were correctly merged). The results of our tests without matching trace identifiers can be seen in Table 1. Our implementation always found the correct *number* of links, but when traces run partly in parallel, there seems to be too little information left to find the right links. The amount of noise in the logs seems to have little impact on the correctness of the identified links. The duration for all our tests was about 300-400 milliseconds on a 3,45GB RAM 2,39 GHz laptop.

Table 1. Test results for non-matching identifiers with varying noise and overlap percentage (percentage of correct links in relation to total links identified)

No matching id	Overlap						Mean
Noise	0%	10%	20%	50%	75%	100%	
0%	100%	94%	80%	68%	46%	48%	73%
10%	100%	88%	85%	68%	53%	52%	74%
20%	100%	92%	88%	54%	45%	42%	70%
50%	100%	91%	87%	71%	58%	49%	76%
Mean	100%	91%	85%	65%	50%	48%	

5   Validation

We also tested our new AIS algorithm on a real test case in a university in Belgium. The payroll process of a specific type of employees is shown in Fig. 6: Different users register payroll information in an SAP application (step 1), the data is stored in the SAP database (step 2), data is extracted to transfer files (step 3) that are imported and processed in the old salary calculation system in Oracle (step 4 to 6) and get back to the SAP database and applications through other transfer files (step 7 to 9).

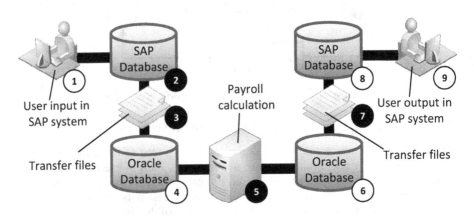

Fig. 6. Main steps in the payroll process

The steps where we extracted logs are shown in black circles (step 2, 3, 5, and 7). The constructed log files for step 2, 5 and 7 contained recorded information of 1.032 employees and used the same trace identifier. The constructed log file for step 3 contained information of 8.242 employees and used another trace identifier (although we were able to check our merge solution because the trace identifier used in the other three log files could be derived from an attribute in the log for step 3).

We merged the log from step 2 with the log from step 3, the resulting merged log was then merged again with the log from step 5 and finally the overall resulting merged log was again merged with the log from step 7. The results of these merge exercises are shown in Table 2.

Because the merged log files never have the same trace identifiers, results are average (the amount of links between the files is correct, but there are 32-39% incorrect links). The durations of the merging on a 3,45GB RAM 2,39GHz laptop are also presented in Table 2 (6-10 minutes). We did an extra test to merge only the log files from step 5 and step 7 (with matching trace identifiers) and noted that results were considerably better (4% incorrect links) and faster (53 seconds).

We discovered that for all our tests the fitness function score for the right solution would have been lower than the score of the proposed solution. This suggests our algorithm finds a solution with an optimal score, but the errors were made due to an imperfect fitness function (missing indicator factors, obsolete factors or suboptimal fixed factor scores).

Table 2. Results for our real life test case experiment

Merging	Number of traces	Number of linked traces	Number of correct linked traces	Duration of merge
2 & 3	1032 & 8242 = 8242	1032/1032 (100%)	700/1032 (68%)	6 min.
23 & 5	8242 & 1032 = 8242	1032/1032 (100%)	697/1032 (68%)	9,5 min.
235 & 7	8242 & 1032 = 8242	1032/1032 (100%)	627/1032 (61%)	10,3 min.
5 & 7	1032 & 1032 = 1032	1032/1032 (100%)	990/1032 (96%)	53 sec.

6   Conclusion

In this paper we presented a technique for log file merging using an Artificial Immune System algorithm. All the steps in this algorithm are influenced by a fitness function, which determines the quality of discovered parts of the solution. To calculate the fitness function score a set of factors is defined that indicate if parts of the two logs belong together. The sum of all factors has to lead the algorithm to an optimal solution. We implemented the algorithm in ProM, a well known academic process mining tool and tested our solution with a set of generated files with varying characteristics and a real life test case.

One of the indicators to decide if a trace of one log matches with a trace of the other log is the *trace identifier*. If the identifier of two traces is equal, it is almost certain that both traces belong together. For all our tests with matching trace identifiers the log files were correctly merged. If the traces of both logs had different identifiers, our implementation struggled with log files with many overlapping traces, but had few problems with log files with much noise. Our future research includes optimising our implementation (in speed and correctness) and validating our solution with extended case studies.

References

1. Van Der Aalst, W.M.P.: Process Mining: Discovery, Conformance and Enhancement of Business Processes. Springer, Heidelberg (2011)
2. Rozinat, A., Mans, R.S., Song, M., Van der Aalst, W.M.P.: Discovering Simulation Models. Information Systems 34, 305–327 (2009)

3. Georgakopoulos, D., Hornick, M.: An overview of workflow management: from process modeling to workflow automation infrastructure. Distributed and Parallel 3, 119–153 (1995)
4. Shvaiko, P., Euzenat, J.: A Survey of Schema-Based Matching Approaches. In: Spaccapietra, S. (ed.) Journal on Data Semantics IV. LNCS, vol. 3730, pp. 146–171. Springer, Heidelberg (2005)
5. Gerke, K., Claus, A.: Process Mining of RFID-Based Supply Chains. Commerce and Enterprise, 285–292 (2009)
6. Weidlich, M., Dijkman, R., Mendling, J.: The iCoP Framework: Identification of Correspondences between Process Models. In: Pernici, B. (ed.) CAiSE 2010. LNCS, vol. 6051, pp. 483–498. Springer, Heidelberg (2010)
7. Motahari-Nezhad, H.R., Saint-Paul, R., Casati, F., Benatallah, B.: Event correlation for process discovery from web service interaction logs. The VLDB Journal (2010)
8. De Pauw, W., Hoch, R., Huang, Y.: Discovering Conversations in Web Services Using Semantic Correlation Analysis. In: ICWS 2007, pp. 639–646 (2007)
9. Ferreira, D., Zacarias, M., Malheiros, M., Ferreira, P.: Approaching Process Mining with Sequence Clustering: Experiments and Findings. In: Alonso, G., Dadam, P., Rosemann, M. (eds.) BPM 2007. LNCS, vol. 4714, pp. 360–374. Springer, Heidelberg (2007)
10. De Castro, L.N., Timmis, J.: Artificial immune systems: A novel paradigm to pattern recognition. In: Artificial Neural networks in pattern Recognition, pp. 67–84 (2002)
11. Van Peteghem, V., Vanhoucke, M.: An Artificial Immune System for the Multi-Mode Resource-Constrained Project Scheduling Problem. In: Cotta, C., Cowling, P. (eds.) EvoCOP 2009. LNCS, vol. 5482, pp. 85–96. Springer, Heidelberg (2009)
12. Wang, J.R., Madnick, S.E.: The inter-database instance identification problem in integrating autonomous systems. In: Data Engineering, pp. 46–55. IEEE (2002)
13. Van der Aalst, W.M.P., Weijters, A.J.M.M.: Process Mining: A Research Agenda. Computers in Industry 53, 231–244 (2004)
14. Weijters, A.J.M.M., Van der Aalst, W.M.P.: Rediscovering Workflow Models from Event-based Data Using Little Thumb. Integrated Computer-Aided Engineering 10, 151–162 (2003)

Business Analytics, Process Maturity and Supply Chain Performance

Peter Trkman[1], Marcelo Bronzo Ladeira[2], Marcos Paulo Valadares De Oliveira[3], and Kevin McCormack[4]

[1] University of Ljubljana, Kardeljeva pl. 17, 1000 Ljubljana, Slovenia
[2] Universidade Federal de Minas Gerais, Universidade
Av. Antonio Carlos, 6627 Belo Horizonte - Minas Gerais, Brazil
[3] Universidade Federal do Espírito Santo, Rua Ludwik Macal 809/501, Jardim da Penha
Vitória-ES-Brazil, 29060-030
[4] DRK Research Institute, 5425 Willow Bridge Lane Fuquay Varina, NC 27526 USA
peter.trkman@ef.uni-lj.si, marcelobronzo@cepead.face.ufmg.br,
{marcos,kmccormack}@drkresearch.org

Abstract. The paper investigates the relationship between analytical capabilities in the plan, source, make and deliver area of the supply chain and its performance. The effects of analytics on different maturity levels are analyzed with various statistical techniques. A sample of 788 companies from the USA, Europe, Canada, Brazil and China was used. The results indicate the changing impact of business analytics use on performance, meaning that companies on different maturity levels should focus on different areas. The theoretical and practical implications of these findings are thoroughly discussed.

Keywords: BPM Maturity, business analytics, Supply Chain Management, Performance, SCOR.

1 Introduction

Business analytics ("BA") can be an important tool to improve the organization's efficiency. An important area of BA use is in supply chain management ("SCM") since an improvement in SCM can considerably improves performance of single companies and supply chain ("SC") as a whole [1]. The organizational factors that influence the impact of BA on SC performance remain unclear. Although an investment in BA has been statistically proven to be beneficial [2], it means a considerable undertaking for any organization. Due to the finite nature of their resources, companies are pressed to prioritize their efforts and identify those areas where positive effects of the development of BA capabilities are most likely.

In this sense, a company may not be able to make simultaneous efforts in different areas of SCM. Thus it is needed to investigate which factors influence the magnitude of BA impact on performance. We argue that the effect of BA on performance

F. Daniel et al. (Eds.): BPM 2011 Workshops, Part I, LNBIP 99, pp. 111–122, 2012.
© Springer-Verlag Berlin Heidelberg 2012

depends on the supply chain process maturity of the organization. Accordingly, the main contribution of our paper is the statistical analysis of the impact of the use of BA in different areas of the SC (based on the Supply Chain Operations Reference ('SCOR') model) on the performance of the SC. Further, the mediating effects of two important constructs, namely information systems ('IS') support and business processes orientation ('BPO'), are examined. The first part of the statistical analysis [2] used a sample 310 companies from different industries from the USA, Europe, Canada, Brazil and China, while further 478 companies were surveyed for the second part of our study.

The structure of the paper is as follows: first, the importance of BA and its influence on the SC performance is established. The moderating effect of BPO maturity is discussed. The research model is presented. Then the methodology and results obtained are presented. The findings are thoroughly discussed along with the limitations of our research and potentially interesting topics for further research.

2   The Influence of BA on Performance

The use of BA can have a profound influence on performance on operational, tactical and even strategic levels [3]. The professional press has thus quickly touted BA as an approach to achieve faster cycle times, greater flexibility and a higher "metabolism" for processing information [4]. This applies to SC as well - monitoring and improving the performance of a SC has namely become an increasingly complex task. A complex performance management system includes many management processes such as identifying measures, defining targets, planning, communication, monitoring, reporting and feedback [5]. Properly implemented and used, BA can increase performance in each of these processes [2].

However, the positive impact of a BA investment in SCM operations should not be taken for granted. Despite major investments in SCM in the last decade, businesses are struggling to achieve a competitive advantage [6]. Companies or individual decision makers are not necessarily able to derive value from the growing amount of information [7].

A compelling and specific vision for how an organization will use information to improve their performance is needed [8]. This further increases the need to analyze in which area the impact of BA may be most beneficial. Many organizations with systems already in place to collect data and gather information find themselves in a situation where they have no roadmaps to put their vast data and information into use [9]. An improper investment in an early stage of implementing BA may hinder further development. On the other hand, successful efforts may lead to a long-term continuous increase in performance since the path dependency and irreversibility in the development make it difficult to imitate [10].

2.1   Ways of Business Analytics Influence

As shown, the potential positive impact of BA on SC performance is well established; however, the potential ways and moderating influences of this impact are not so well-understood. Most previous research papers have used SCM as an umbrella term to analyze this impact. Yet it should not be forgotten that SCM is quite a broad term and encompasses the integration of organizational units and business processes along a SC to coordinate materials, information and financial flows in order to fulfil customer demands [11]. SCM is therefore still largely eclectic with little consensus on its conceptualization [12] and can basically encompass every business activity in a company. In this sense, a more precise reference is needed to analyze the impact of BA.

Since SCOR has been widely employed for SC optimization in recent years (see e.g. [5]), it was used as a framework for our study. SCOR has often been recognized as a systematic approach to identifying, evaluating and monitoring supply chain performance [5, 13]. In the SCOR model, a balanced performance measurement system at multiple levels, covering four core SC processes (Plan, Source, Make, Deliver, later Return was also added), was developed [5]. SCOR is supposed to be the most promising model for SC strategic decision-making [14]. It provides a common SC framework, standard terminology and metrics that can be used for evaluating, positioning and implementing SC processes [14].

Several examples of BA use in various areas were previously reported [2]. In general, improvements in any of the four areas can considerably increase the SC performance [13]. However, the influence of BA in each of these four areas on different process maturity levels has not been analyzed.

The positive impact of BA is however not self-assured but has to be moderated by IS support and by the BPO. Modern BA tools have namely not only been successfully incorporated into existing organizational ISs but have also become an integral part of organizational business processes [15]. The link between IT use and the simultaneous design of business processes is a vital ingredient to bring a benefit from such development efforts. In fact, in practice it is often difficult to separate the origin of the benefit, whether it has derived from IT, a process change, or both [16].

Although both effects are obviously connected, it may still be important to identify which are the moderating effects of each of them separately. The moderating effect of BPO is discussed in the next section while the effect of IS support is described in [2].

2.2   Moderating Effect of Business Process Orientation

The main question is how to assure that BA will indeed be used to improve the operation of a SC. Our hypothesis is that the BPO [17] has a moderating effect between BA use and SC performance. Therefore, both BPO and BA maturity have to increase in order to lead to improved business performance. This could mean that companies that are more process-oriented are in a better position to utilize BA to improve their performance. This is in line with the previous finding that BA systems have to be process-oriented to link across functions/break the functional perspective at both the strategic and tactical levels [18].

Several reasons make BPO especially important. Since most firms offer similar products and use comparable technologies, business processes are among the last remaining points of differentiation with BA optimizing their value [19]. Further, in order to fully use BA companies need to undergo thorough business process changes, apply change management practices and focus on changing downstream decision-making and business processes [20]. Thus a proper level of maturity of business processes (see e.g. [17, 21]) may be determine a proper focus of investment of BA; in our case, which of the SCOR areas needs to be improved.

Management is thus faced with a complex set of operating issues and challenges that often necessitates the making of trade-offs [22]. Even further: efforts to improve business processes must shift their emphasis over time [22]. Obviously, companies have limited time/resources and a tension arises between quick/efficient decision-making and the careful analysis of data before decisions are taken. The key to managing this tension is to spend time understanding the critical issues and indicators surrounding a decision context, and to really focus on the few ones that make most of the difference [23]. Managers need to better understand what really makes the difference and draw an improvement roadmap optimizing the use of the firm's resources. Hence, the successful implementation of BA must focus first on specific business needs [6]. These business needs may change with the change in BPO. This paper aims to evaluate this relationship using descriptive statistics to illustrate how BA impacts performance considering the different maturity levels and SCOR process areas of Plan, Make, Source and Deliver.

For the purpose of this research, the Supply Chain Process Management Maturity Model – SCPM3 [24] is used to provide the classification of levels and the respective characterization. Although various stage models may differ in terms of the number of stages and what the stages are called, they are all similar in that they break down a phenomenon's evolution into a series of distinct phases [25].

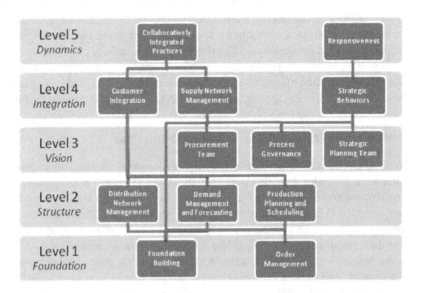

Fig. 1. SCPM3 – Supply Chain Process Management Maturity Model [24]

The SCPM3 model (shown in Figure 1) was chosen since previously developed maturity models only outline the general path towards achieving greater maturity, whereas SCPM3 provides a clearer identification of important areas on each of the five levels. Further, while most maturity models (see a review in [26]) are built on anecdotal evidence or consulting practice SCPM3 was derived from a statistical analysis. As illustrated in Figure 1, the model is composed of 13 groups of capabilities hierarchically interrelated and classified on five levels of maturity.

Squared boxes (fig. 1) are groups of capabilities that are configured under hierarchical relationships that are represented by the links between the boxes. For example a firm that wants capabilities related with "Collaboratively Integrated Practices" need to develop "Customer Integration" and "Supply Network Management" capabilities. Those hierarchical relationships are not a necessary condition but firms that develop such capabilities at previous levels are able to get a better return of investment from higher level capabilities.

3   Methodology

3.1   Data Collection

The survey instrument was developed using a 5-point Likert scale measuring the frequency of practices consisting of: 1 – never, or does not exist; 2 – sometimes; 3 – frequently; 4 – mostly; and 5 – always, or definitely exists. The initial survey was tested within a major electronic equipment manufacturer and with several SC experts. Based upon these tests, improvements in wording and format were made to the instrument and several items were eliminated.

The Supply Chain Council board of directors also reviewed the initial survey instrument. Based on this review, the survey was slightly reorganized to better match the SCOR model. The whole questionnaire is provided in [2]. The questions focus on decision-making in the key SCM decision categories for each of the four SCOR decision areas. The whole data set can be obtained from the authors by email.

3.2   Sample

The sample for the first part of the study was composed of respondents whose functions are directly related to SCM processes from 310 different companies with headquarters in the USA, Europe, Canada and China. The sample deliberately included companies from different industries since various industry settings need to be investigated in the context of global supply chains [27].

The study participants were selected from several sources:

1. The membership list of the Supply Chain Council. The "user" or practitioner portion of the list was used as the final selection since this represented members whose firms supplied a product, rather than a service, and were thought to be generally representative of supply chain practitioners rather than consultants.

2. Firms that were interested in measuring their supply chain maturity and developing an improvement plan. These firms responded to an email solicitation recruiting participants for a global research project on Supply Chain Maturity.

For the second part of the research a larger sample was needed since the companies in the sample had to be divided according to their maturity level. Thus the survey was repeated with additional questions added using the companies formally associated with IMAM. IMAM is a recognized logistics education and consultancy institution in São Paulo, Brazil. By accessing the mailing list of this institution, the sample composition evolved: manufacturing firms; construction firms; retail businesses; graphic industries; extractive firms; communication and IT providers; gas, water and electricity productive facilities and distribution services. 478 additional cases were thus included in the sample.

3.3   Data Analysis

The whole sample was divided by considering the companies' maturity levels based on the scores obtained when using the SCPM3 classification. After pre-processing the sample, generating the new variables and identifying the five sets, one for each maturity level, 52 companies were identified as belonging to maturity level 1, 156 to level 2, 206 to level 3, 233 to level 4, and 141 to level 5.

The SC performance construct is a self-assessed performance rating for each of the SCOR decision areas. The construct is based on perceived performance, as determined by the survey respondents. It is represented as a single item for each decision area. The specific item statement on the supply chain performance for each of the SCOR decision areas is: "Overall, this decision process area performs very well." The participants were asked to either agree or disagree with the item statement using a five-point Likert scale. Overall performance is the average of the performance from the four SCOR areas.

To analyze the different BA impact on different maturity levels three complementary, approaches were adopted and later combined. Firstly scatter plots were examined due to the simplicity and intuitiveness of the analyses, making it easy to use even by those managers who do not have advanced statistical skills. Secondly Pearson's correlation tests were then conducted in order to measure the impact and direction of the relationships between BA in each SCOR area and performance at each maturity level. Thirdly a stepwise regression for each maturity level, the resulting equations were taken into consideration to identify in which SCOR areas an analytics improvement could be considered to impact on performance for each maturity level.

4   Results

4.1   Different Impacts of BA on Different Maturity Levels

Based on the analysis of the scatter plots and the respective trend lines, the score areas that emerge to more expressively impact on the performance for each maturity level were identified. Pearson's correlation tests were then conducted in order to measure the impact and direction of the relationships between BA in each SCOR area and performance at each maturity level (table 1).

Table 1. Correlations between analytics score and performance at each maturity level

		Analytics Score Level 1	Analytics Score Level 2	Analytics Score Level 3	Analytics Score Level 4	Analytics Score Level 5
Performance	Pearson's correlation	.252	.119	.144	.231	.359
	Sig. (2-tailed)	.071	.138	.038	.000	.000
	N	52	156	206	233	141

The last step was stepwise regression statistics. The stepwise regression is based on a loop procedure in which for each step the independent variable not in the equation that has the smallest probability of F is entered, if that probability is sufficiently small. Variables already in the regression equation are removed if their probability of F becomes sufficiently large. The method terminates when no more variables are eligible for either inclusion or removal. The Overall Performance variable was considered as a dependent variable in the equation and the BA variables for Plan, Make, Source and Deliver were considered as independents. The results of the stepwise regression are shown in Table 2.

Table 2. Regression Table – Stepwise method by maturity level

Maturity Level	Variables Entered	Standardized Coefficients	Sig.
1	Make Analytics	0.287	0.039
2	Deliver Analytics	0.216	0.007
3	Make Analytics	0.166	0.017
	Source Analytics	0.283	0.000
4	Make Analytics	0.189	0.002
	Deliver Analytics	0.181	0.004
5	Source Analytics	0.466	0.000
	Deliver Analytics	0.180	0.180

Criteria: Probability-of-F-to-enter <= .050, Probability-of-F to-remove >= .100. Dependent Variable = Performance

Table 3 summarizes the results from the three used approaches to data analysis. For example, on level 1 scatter plots suggest that BA in Plan and Source have the effect on performance. The correlation analysis suggests that also BA in Make influences performance while multiple regression indicates only the latter. Results are less ambiguous for higher maturity levels.

Table 3. Overview of the impact of BA on various maturity level

level	scatter plot	significant correlations[1]	multiple regression
1	Plan, Source	Source, Make; Plan[2]	Make
2	Plan, Deliver	Deliver	Deliver
3	Make, Deliver	Make	Make
4	Source, Make, Deliver	Source, Make, Deliver	Source, Make, Deliver
5	Source	Source, Make	Source, Deliver

1 At the 0.05 level unless otherwise noted

2 At the 0.10 level

4.2   Discussion

An investment in BA may be beneficial for the performance of companies at all maturity levels as conceptualized in our model. Thus (similarly to the finding in [2]), a relatively low level of process maturity does not preclude a company from generating the benefits of BA. However, the impact at lower levels of maturity is much weaker; further, the area of the BA impact varies considerably.

Interestingly, the results of the analysis with different approaches show the greatest variations for companies at level 1. This shows that at a low level of maturity it is hard to predict if BA will have a positive effect and in which SCOR area the investment would be most beneficial. Based on our results we can stipulate that companies at low maturity levels may benefit from an investment into Plan, Source and partly Make. This is understandable since companies at level 1 have poorly defined (ad hoc) processes and a better approach to and analysis of planning processes can bring substantial benefits to determine to which areas and when to dedicate the company's resources. Other processes may also improve through planning since they have measurable goals.

Further, the development of supplier evaluations in sourcing can bring considerable benefits in the reduction of lead times, an increase in quality and a decrease in inventory [28]. It is well known that relatively small investments in supplier evaluation can considerably improve the quality/lead times/reliability of the supplier and that performance measurement systems directly affect information sharing, problem solving and the willingness to adapt to changes [29].

The companies on level 2 have defined processes and are able to "operate" relatively well and achieve basic cooperation between different functions in an organization. The BA impact now partly shifts from Source to Deliver. The main question is whether the company is able to fulfill the orders of its customers. This supports the commonly held belief that firms need a strong logistics capability to perform well in traditional and e-commerce markets [30]. Companies on level 2 may focus on approaches such as just-in-time and vendor-managed inventories that derive a competitive advantage from accurate and reliable delivery and from an increase in the flexibility of the distribution processes. This follows the finding that the process view improves the reliability of delivery [31]. Further, an investment in Source on level 1 may pay off as supply management (supplier selection and the reduction of the supplier base) is the core prerequisite of just-in-time and similar concepts [32]. Suppliers are now performing efficiently (not necessarily successfully, e.g. companies are probably not cooperating in product development) so a further investment in BA in Source may have a limited effect. The chart also visually suggests a possible relationship between performance and BA in Plan, although this could not be confirmed by the other statistical techniques. We can assert that an investment in BA in Plan still has a sporadic effect which is contingent on several other variables.

The alignment of production and other processes to produce the goods at prices and quality that customers want is crucial at level 3. Various practices such as make-to-order (instead of make-to-stock); a rapid response, flexibility, and lean manufacturing are being used. At level 3, planning is already integral in different processes. An investment in BA in Plan was important at lower levels where this was the only way to at least partly align the business functions. At level 3 specific investments in planning might be unjustified and would lead to analysis-paralysis.

Companies at level 4 have obviously taken cooperation with their customers and suppliers to the process level. Companies need to increase their BPO to build stronger relationships with their trading partners through integrating complex and cross-enterprise processes governed by business logic and rules [33]. Therefore, the shift of the impact on higher levels of maturity (on both the 4th and 5th levels) back to BA in the Source area is logical. Those companies that went after »low hanging fruit« on level 1 by investing in supplier evaluation now take their cooperation with suppliers at the process level and from the supplying of materials to developing final products or services. The basis of the relationship changes from the parts to be supplied to the programs to be developed and marketed [34]. The increase in performance is thus no longer derived from efficient, reliable and high-quality supplies but from strategic cooperation with suppliers, whereby product development, joint projects or even the outsourcing of whole business processes take place. Suppliers gradually receive and share more information and schedules with a focal company and become a co-maker of a product and not just a supplier [35].

Level 5 demonstrates similar impacts of BA as level 4. What is even more visible is that on level 5 the increase in performance is no longer derived from efficient, reliable and high-quality supplies but mainly from strategic partnership/alliances with the use of BA in Source having an undeniable effect well proven by all statistical techniques. The main role of the focal company in the SC is thus to select and coordinate partners. Indeed, if such a network can create a strong identity and coordinating rules, then it will be superior to a firm as an organizational form [36].

Interestingly, our analysis has also revealed either a limited or even nonexisting effect of the use of BA in planning at all levels of BP maturity. While this finding may be surprising at first glance, it is in fact in line with most of the studies in the last two decades which found inconclusive evidence of the effect of planning on performance. Some found low and others no significant relationship, while some studies even found small negative effects [37-39]. The effect on lower levels of maturity indicates that planning may be a surrogate for BPO but on higher levels of maturity planning is integral in other processes.

5   Conclusion

The paper has several practical implications. It shows companies on different maturity levels in which areas they should they focus on. It also provides a general roadmap for development of BA capabilities on different maturity levels. Since validated questionnaires for measuring SCPM exist [24, 40], it is relatively easy to establish the current process maturity level and consequently the proper focus of BA. There may be a smaller impact of implementing BA if the focus is not in line with the maturity level.

The paper has some limitations. The selection of companies in the sample may not be completely random since companies that were more aware of the importance of BA/process improvement might have been more inclined to participate. A refinement of the measurement of BA use in each of the four SCOR areas would also be beneficial. Further, the users' evaluation may not always accurately reflect the real quality of IS [41]. An important limitation is that the impact of BA on performance does not only depend on the SCPM but also on other contingent variables, e.g. the strategy, the type of SC, the industry in question and turbulence in the SC's environment. Finally, since it is quite possible that the use of BA does not bring immediate results, the performance should be measured with a time lag.

Future research should investigate whether the different kinds of IS (e.g. enterprise resource planning, web services/service-oriented architecture) have a different moderating effect on the impact of BA in various areas of SCM on performance. Since performance was treated as a single construct in this paper, a much needed further investigation is how BA in various areas of SC impact different performance metrics, e.g. on-time delivery, quality, costs, reliability and flexibility.

A closely connected topic is an investigation of the development of performance measurement systems and the need for target analytical capabilities in specific areas. The development of analytic capabilities outside a focal company (in e.g. a customer-supplier dyad) could be studied to analyze how value is created in interorganizational networks. Some of those issues along with a more detailed explanation of our results are further explored in [42].

References

1. Trkman, P., Indihar Štemberger, M., Jaklič, J., Groznik, A.: Process approach to supply chain integration. Supply Chain Management - An International Journal 12, 116–128 (2007)
2. Trkman, P., McCormack, K., Oliveira, M.P.V., Ladeira, M.B.: The impact of business analytics on supply chain performance. Decision Support Systems 49, 318–327 (2010)
3. Popovič, A., Coelho, P.S., Jaklič, J.: The impact of business intelligence system maturity on information quality. Information Research 14, paper 417 (2009)
4. Brynjolfsson, E.: The Four Ways IT Is Revolutionizing Innovation. MIT Sloan Management Review 51, 51–56 (2010)
5. Cai, J., Liu, X., Xiao, Z., Liu, J.: Improving supply chain performance management: A systematic approach to analyzing iterative KPI accomplishment. Decision Support Systems 46, 512–521 (2009)

6. Sahay, B.S., Ranjan, J.: Real time business intelligence in supply chain analytics. Information Management & Computer Security 16, 28–48 (2008)
7. Petrini, M., Pozzebon, M.: Managing sustainability with the support of business intelligence: Integrating socio-environmental indicators and organisational context. The Journal of Strategic Information Systems 18, 178–191 (2009)
8. Williams, S., Williams, N.: The Profit Impact of Business Intelligence. Morgan Kaufmann, San Francisco (2007)
9. Ranjan, J.: Business justification with business intelligence. VINE: The Journal of Information and Knowledge Management Systems 38, 461–475 (2008)
10. Fink, L., Neumann, S.: Exploring the perceived business value of the flexibility enabled by information technology infrastructure. Information & Management 46, 90–99 (2009)
11. Stadtler, H.: Supply chain management and advanced planning––basics, overview and challenges. European Journal of Operational Research 163, 575–588 (2005)
12. Burgess, K., Singh, P., Koroglu, R.: Supply chain management: a structured literature review and implications for future research. International Journal of Operations & Production Management 26, 703–729 (2006)
13. Lockamy, A., McCormack, K.: Linking SCOR planning practices to supply chain performance: An exploratory study. International Journal of Operations & Production Management 24, 1192–1218 (2004)
14. Huan, S.H., Sheoran, S.K., Wang, G.: A review and analysis of supply chain operations reference (SCOR) model. Supply Chain Management - An International Journal 9, 23–29 (2004)
15. Valente, P., Mitra, G.: The evolution of web-based optimisation: From ASP to e-Services. Decision Support Systems 43, 1096–1116 (2007)
16. Auramo, J., Kauremaa, J., Tanskanen, K.: Benefits of IT in supply chain management: an explorative study of progressive companies. International Journal of Physical Distribution & Logistics Management 35, 82–100 (2005)
17. McCormack, K.: Business Process Maturity: Theory and Application. BookSurge Publishing Charleston, South Carolina (2007)
18. Reyes, P.M.: Logistics networks: A game theory application for solving the transshipment problem. Applied Mathematics and Computation 168, 1419–1431 (2005)
19. Davenport, T.: Competing on Analytics. Harvard Business Review 84, 150–151 (2006)
20. Watson, H.J., Wixom, B.H., Hoffer, J.A., Anderson-Lehman, R., Reynolds, A.M.: Real-Time Business Intelligence: Best Practices at Continental Airlines. Information Systems Management 23, 7–18 (2006)
21. McCormack, K., Willems, J., Van den Bergh, J., Deschoolmeester, D., Willaert, P., Indihar Štemberger, M., Škrinjar, R., Trkman, P., Ladeira, M.B., de Oliveira, M.P.V., Bosilj Vuksić, V., Vlahović, N.: A Global Investigation of Key Turning Points in Business Process Maturity. Business Process Management Journal 15, 792–815 (2009)
22. Klassen, R.D., Menor, L.J.: The process management triangle: An empirical investigation of process trade-offs. Journal of Operations Management 25, 1015–1034 (2007)
23. Carlsson, S.A., El Sawy, O.A.: Managing the five tensions of IT-enabled decision support in turbulent and high-velocity environments. Information Systems and E-Business Management 6, 225–237 (2008)
24. Oliveira, M.P.V., Ladeira, M.B., McCormack, K.: The statistical analysis of SCM process maturity levels and practices. In: 26th German Logistics Congress, Berlin (2009)
25. Wixom, B.H., Watson, H.J., Reynolds, A.M., Hoffer, J.A.: Continental Airlines Continues to Soar with Business Intelligence. Information Systems Management 25, 102–112 (2008)

26. Lahti, M., Shamsuzzoha, A., Helo, P.: Developing a maturity model for Supply Chain Management. International Journal of Logistics Systems and Management 5, 654–678 (2009)
27. Meixell, M.J., Gargeya, V.B.: Global supply chain design: A literature review and critique. Transportation Research Part E: Logistics and Transportation Review 41, 531–550 (2005)
28. Cormican, K., Cunningham, M.: Supplier performance evaluation: lessons from a large multinational organisation. Journal of Manufacturing Technology Management 18, 352–366 (2007)
29. Mahama, H.: Management control systems, cooperation and performance in strategic supply relationships: A survey in the mines. Management Accounting Research 17, 315–339 (2006)
30. Cho, J.J.-K., Ozment, J., Sink, H.: Logistics capability, logistics outsourcing and firm performance in an e-commerce market. International Journal of Physical Distribution & Logistics Management 38, 336–359 (2008)
31. Armistead, C., Machin, S.: Implications of business process management for operations management. International Journal of Operations & Production Management 17, 886–898 (1997)
32. Kannan, V.R., Tan, K.C.: Just in time, total quality management, and supply chain management: understanding their linkages and impact on business performance. Omega 33, 153–162 (2005)
33. Chen, M., Zhang, D., Zhou, L.: Empowering collaborative commerce with Web services enabled business process management systems. Decision Support Systems 43, 530–546 (2007)
34. Mayer, K.J., Teece, D.J.: Unpacking strategic alliances: The structure and purpose of alliance versus supplier relationships. Journal of Economic Behavior & Organization 66, 106–127 (2008)
35. Bechtel, C., Jayaram, J.: Supply Chain Management: A Strategic Perspective. The International Journal of Logistics Management 8, 15–34 (1997)
36. Dyer, J.H., Nobeoka, K.: Creating and managing a high-performance knowledge-sharing network: the Toyota case. Strategic Management Journal 21, 345–367 (2000)
37. Boyd, B.K.: Strategic planning and financial performance: a meta-analytic review. Journal of Management Studies 28, 353–374 (1991)
38. Falshaw, J.R., Glaister, K.W., Tatoglu, E.: Evidence on formal strategic planning and company performance. Management Decision 44, 9–30 (2006)
39. Miller, C.C., Cardinal, L.B.: Strategic Planning and Firm Performance: A Synthesis of More than Two Decades of Research. The Academy of Management Journal 37, 1649–1665 (1994)
40. Lockamy, A., McCormack, K.: The development of a supply chain management process maturity model using the concepts of business process orientation. Supply Chain Management: An International Journal 9, 272–278 (2004)
41. Goodhue, D., Thompson, R.: Task-technology fit and individual performance. MIS Quarterly 19, 213–236 (1995)
42. Oliveira, M.P.V., McCormack, K., Trkman, P.: Business analytics in supply chains – the contingent effect of business process maturity Expert Systems with Applications (in press, 2012)

Discovering User Communities in Large Event Logs

Diogo R. Ferreira and Cláudia Alves

IST – Technical University of Lisbon, Portugal
{diogo.ferreira,claudia.alves}@ist.utl.pt

Abstract. The organizational perspective of process mining supports the discovery of social networks within organizations by analyzing event logs recorded during process execution. However, applying these social network mining techniques to real data generates very complex models that are hard to analyze and understand. In this work we present an approach to overcome these difficulties by focusing on the discovery of communities from such event logs. The clustering of users into communities allows the analysis and visualization of the social network at different levels of abstraction. The proposed approach also makes use of the concept of modularity, which provides an indication of the best division of the social network into community clusters. The approach was implemented in the ProM framework and it was successfully applied in the analysis of the emergency service of a medium-sized hospital.

Keywords: Process Mining, Social Network Analysis, Hierarchical Clustering, Community Structure, Modularity.

1 Introduction

The goal of process mining [1,2] is to discover, analyze and understand business processes based on the run-time behavior recorded in event logs. Such analysis can be performed on three different perspectives [3]: the *process perspective* focuses on extracting models for the control-flow of the business process; the *case perspective* focuses on the behavior, properties and data elements associated with individual process instances; and the *organizational perspective* focuses on understanding the roles and groups of people participating in the process. Other issues such as performance [4] and conformance [5] can be studied as well.

While much attention has been devoted to the process perspective through several techniques – such as the α-algorithm [6], the Heuristic Miner [7], the Genetic Miner [8], and the Fuzzy Miner [9] –, the organizational perspective is based mostly on techniques developed by [10] and [11]. Also, there has been considerable concern about making control-flow models more understandable [12], but no comparable effort has been done to facilitate the understanding of very large and complex social networks arising from the analysis of real-world event logs.

In this work we describe an approach to deal with such large models by employing a hierarchical clustering technique to discover community structure [13]

F. Daniel et al. (Eds.): BPM 2011 Workshops, Part I, LNBIP 99, pp. 123–134, 2012.

in social networks. Such approach facilitates the analysis and visualization of the social network at different levels of abstraction. It also provides an effective means to discover user groups based on the actual user interactions as in [10], rather than on task similarity as in [11]. The distinction is relevant because although hierarchical clustering has already been used in [11], it has been applied to group users according to the similarity of the tasks they perform. Here we will be interested in applying hierarchical clustering to the social network obtained by considering the *working together* metric [14].

2   Extracting Social Networks from Event Logs

Figure 1 illustrates a purchase process comprising several steps. First, it is necessary to fill out a requisition form and send it for approval. If not approved, the requisition is archived. If approved, the product is ordered from a supplier and two branches will run in parallel: at the warehouse an employee receives the product and updates the stock; at the accounting department someone else will take care of payment. When these two branches complete, the requisition is closed.

Table 1 shows an excerpt of the event log that could be generated by executing this requisition process. There may be several instances of this process, and several participants performing different tasks. Case 1 represents a requisition that was successfully completed, while case 2 is a requisition that was not approved and was afterward resubmitted as case 3.

There are basically two ways to study the interaction between participants recorded in such an event log [14]:

- *Handover of work:* captures the number of times each user performs a task just before another user. This results in a directed graph where nodes represent users and arcs are labeled with the number of times a user hands over work to another user. Figure 2(a) shows the resulting graph for the three cases recorded in the requisition process.
- *Working together:* for each pair of users, it captures the number of cases where these users have worked together. This results in an undirected graph where nodes represent users and arcs are labeled with the number of cases. Figure 2(b) shows the resulting graph for the three complete cases.

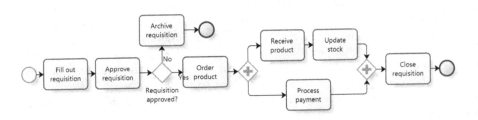

Fig. 1. Purchase process example

Table 1. Example of an event log

case id	task id	user id	timestamp
1	Fill out requisition	John	2010-03-29 10:15
1	Approve requisition	Ann	2010-03-30 09:05
1	Order product	John	2010-03-30 14:20
2	Fill out requisition	Miriam	2010-04-02 11:40
1	Receive product	Peter	2010-04-05 08:00
1	Update stock	Peter	2010-04-05 08:10
2	Approve requisition	Ann	2010-04-05 09:30
2	Archive requisition	Peter	2010-04-06 12:20
1	Process payment	Ann	2010-04-07 08:10
3	Fill out requisition	Miriam	2010-04-09 15:40
...	...	...	...

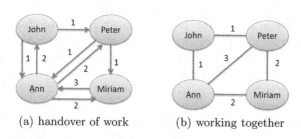

(a) handover of work   (b) working together

Fig. 2. Example networks for three cases of the requisition process

The application of either of these approaches results in a social network (directed or undirected) that depicts the interactions between the participants in a process. For structured processes, the *handover of work* approach may be interesting as it captures some of the control-flow together with the social network. However, for unstructured processes which produce event logs with a lot of ad-hoc behavior, or in the presence of a significant amount of noise, the *working together* metric becomes more useful as it focuses on the social network alone, while the control-flow can be studied with other specialized techniques. For the purpose of understanding large social networks extracted from real-world event logs, we will be using mainly the *working together* metric.

3   Clustering the Social Network

Clustering, and in particular hierarchical clustering [15], is an essential technique to analyze social networks by aggregating nodes that are close together. The distance (actually, similarity) between nodes can be measured according to a number of different metrics, such as the two approaches described above, which represent different ways of capturing the interaction between each pair of users. Once individual nodes have been grouped together to form clusters, it is possible to measure the similarity between clusters to decide whether any pair of clusters should be merged together. Repeating this merging iteratively leads to a hierarchical clustering approach, which provides a range of cluster configurations from having a cluster for each individual node to having a single cluster that contains all nodes.

The similarity between clusters can be computed in different ways based on the similarity between individual nodes. Let c_r and c_s be two clusters with n_r and n_s nodes respectively, and let $d(i, j)$ denote the similarity between node i in c_r and node j in c_s. Then the similarity between the two clusters is given by:

$$D(c_r, c_s) = \frac{1}{n_r n_s} \sum_{i \in c_r} \sum_{j \in c_s} d(i, j) \qquad (1)$$

This equation specifies the well-known *average linkage* function [16] which provides a measure of the average similarity between pairs of nodes in two different clusters. When computing $D(c_r, c_s)$ for every pair of clusters c_r and c_s, one can find the pair of clusters for which the similarity is maximal, and these become the best candidates for being merged in the current iteration. If there are several candidate pairs of clusters with the same maximal similarity, then an untying procedure is required, as will be explained in the next section. For the moment we will assume there are no ties.

Figure 3 shows an example of a small network created using the working together metric. On the right is the adjacency matrix, where A_{ij} denotes is the weight of the arc between nodes i and j. Clustering begins by considering that each individual node is a cluster, and then finding the pair of clusters with maximum similarity in the network.

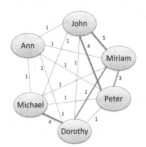

A_{ij}	John	Miriam	Peter	Dorothy	Michael	Ann
John	–	5	4	1	1	1
Miriam	5	–	3	2	1	1
Peter	4	3	–	1	1	1
Dorothy	1	2	1	–	4	1
Michael	1	1	1	4	–	1
Ann	1	1	1	1	1	–

Fig. 3. Diagram and adjacency matrix for a small network

In the first iteration, Equation (1) simplifies to $D(c_i, c_j) = d(i, j) = A_{ij}$ and the best candidate is the pair {John, Miriam} with $D = 5$. These nodes become a single cluster, as shown in Figure 4(a). In the second iteration, the best candidate for merging is {Michael, Dorothy} with $D = 4$. Note that another link with $d = 4$ exists between Peter and John, but since John is part of the cluster

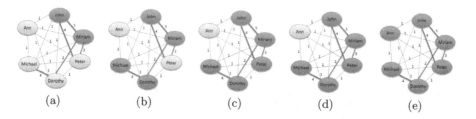

Fig. 4. Clustering of a small network in five iterations

{John, Miriam}, the average similarity between Peter and {John, Miriam} is $D = 3.5$. Therefore, {Michael, Dorothy} with $D = 4$ becomes the second cluster. It is only in the third iteration that Peter joins {John, Miriam} and the cluster becomes {John, Miriam, Peter}, as in Figure 4(c). In the fourth iteration the clusters {Michael, Dorothy} and {John, Miriam, Peter} have $D = 7/6$ and are merged together; at this stage the only other option would be to include Ann in one of these clusters, but $D = 1$ in either case. In the fifth and final iteration, Ann is included in {Michael, Dorothy, John, Miriam, Peter} and the network becomes a single cluster, as shown in Figure 4(e).

4 Using Modularity to Find Communities

Clearly, in going from N clusters to a single cluster one should know where to stop. Between the two extremes there are several possible explanations for the social network. In the example above, it appears that {John, Miriam} form one group, while {Michael, Dorothy} form another, and the question is whether Peter should be included in the group of {John, Miriam} as well. This decision requires a criterion either to stop the clustering algorithm at some point [17,18] or to determine the optimal number of clusters [19,20].

In particular, we are looking for the cluster configuration which best describes the user groups within the social network. A group should contain people who, between themselves, work together more often than they work with people from outside the group or from other groups. Groups should be densely connected on the inside, while on the outside there should be sparse connections between them. A natural way to measure this property is through the concept of *modularity* [21], which can be computed as:

$$Q = \frac{1}{2m} \sum_{ij} \left(A_{ij} - \frac{k_i k_j}{2m} \right) \cdot \delta(c_i, c_j) \qquad (2)$$

where the sum is over each arc ij in the network. In the above equation, m is the sum of the weight of all arcs, A_{ij} is the adjacency matrix, k_i is the *degree* of node i (i.e. the sum of all arcs emanating from node i), and $\delta(c_i, c_j) = 1$ if nodes i and j belong to the same cluster, zero otherwise. Modularity has been successfully used to discover communities in different kinds of networks [13,22].

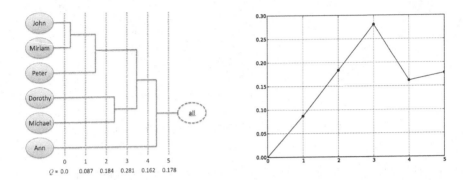

Fig. 5. Dendogram and modularity plot for the small network

In the example from the previous section, the modularity of the initial network is zero since no two nodes belong to the same cluster. After the first iteration, it becomes $Q \simeq 0.087$ and increases to $Q \simeq 0.184$ in the second iteration. It reaches a maximum of $Q \simeq 0.281$ in the third iteration, and in the fourth and fifth it drops to $Q \simeq 0.162$ and $Q \simeq 0.178$, respectively. Figure 5 shows a dendogram and a plot of modularity, where the peak at iteration 3 is clearly visible. The same trend will be observed in practice: modularity keeps increasing monotonically up to a certain point when it reaches a clear maximum, and proceeding further will decrease it. In the small network being used as an example, this means that the best cluster configuration is obtained in iteration 3.

5   Implementation in ProM

We have implemented hierarchical clustering with modularity as a plug-in for the ProM framework [23]. Figure 6 shows a screenshot of the resulting plug-in which, among other features, automatically arranges and colors nodes according to the cluster they belong to. The plug-in is able to build a social network from an event log using either the working together or the similar tasks metric; it is able to perform hierarchical clustering based on single linkage, complete linkage, and average linkage; it is able to decide between several possible merges based on the modularity of the resulting network; and it is able to plot the modularity as well as show the cluster configuration obtained in each iteration.

Internally, the plug-in implements the following algorithm:

1. Let N be the number of nodes in the initial network. Then N clusters are created, each with one individual node.
2. Calculate the similarity $D(c_r, c_s)$ between every pair of clusters c_r and c_s according to the selected linkage function. For average linkage, the similarity is given by Equation (1) with $d(i,j) = A_{ij}$. For single linkage, $D(c_r, c_s) = \min\{d(i,j)\}$, and for complete linkage, $D(c_r, c_s) = \max\{d(i,j)\}$, where i is a node from c_r and j a node from c_s.

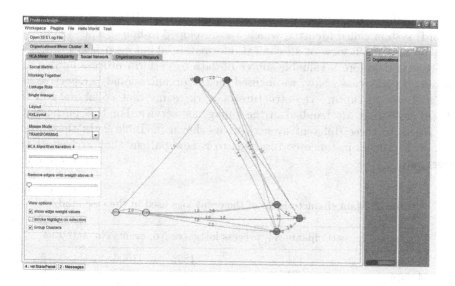

Fig. 6. The hierarchical clustering plug-in implemented in ProM version 6

3. Choose the pair of clusters having maximum similarity D. If several pairs have the same maximum similarity, calculate the modularity of the resulting networks in case each of these pairs is merged; then choose the pair that leads to the highest modularity. In the (rare) event that both similarity and modularity are the same, then choose any of those pairs indifferently.
4. Repeat steps 2 and 3 until the network becomes a single cluster with all nodes. After each iteration, store the resulting cluster configuration and the corresponding value of modularity. Modularity can be computed according to Equation (2).

Besides plotting modularity values, the plug-in also allows an inspection of the cluster configuration obtained after each iteration. This way the user can navigate through all the results produced during clustering and analyze them in terms of structure and modularity.

6   Case Study

The Hospital of São Sebastião (HSS) is a public hospital with approximately 300 beds, located in *Santa Maria da Feira*, Portugal. The hospital provides several medical specialties, namely Anesthesia, Cardiology, Gastroenterology, Gynecology, Immunology, Internal Medicine, Neurology, Obstetrics, Oncology, Ophthalmology, Orthopedics, Otolaryngology, Pediatrics, Pneumology, Psychiatry, Surgery, and Urology. The hospital also has the facilities to carry out medical exams in many of these specialties, and it has an emergency service running 24x7.

In its daily activity, the hospital makes use of an ERP (Electronic Patient Record) system called Medtrix, which was developed in-house. The system provides an integrated view of all clinical information about each patient, and its database is therefore a valuable source of data to perform process mining and analysis. In this case study, we focused on the organizational perspective and our goal was to capture the structure of work teams that collaborate in the clinical cases that are handled in the emergency service. For this purpose, we had access to three different event logs, as shown in Table 2. In these event logs, each process instance corresponds to a new patient that arrived at the emergency.

Table 2. Main characteristics of the event logs used in the case study

Time span	No. participants	No. process instances	No. events	No. activities
12 days	131	1868	11506	18
14 days	231	4851	22803	18
6 months	507	78623	536735	21

We conducted several experiments with these event logs, but here we will focus only on the collaboration between medical doctors. Our goal was to discover which specialists work with other specialists, and for that purpose we did an analysis of the social network based on the working together metric. For this analysis, some preprocessing was applied to the event logs, namely: the activities performed by other members of the staff, such as nurses and medical imaging personnel, were excluded; and all process instances (cases) having a single doctor (i.e. doctors working alone) were excluded as well. Even then, the resulting social network was large and difficult to understand, as shown in Figure 7.

We therefore turned to clustering analysis, and the cluster configurations obtained using different linkage functions were all similar to the one presented in Figure 8. Here, each node corresponds to a doctor or group of doctors, and different colors correspond to different medical specialties. From this and with further analysis we were able to draw conclusions about the following specialties:

- *Emergency*: Emergency doctors are the ones who collaborate the most. Although there are several communities for this specialty, they are all interlinked. The size of these communities may reach as much as 30 elements, which represent the largest communities across all specialties. These specialists also work together with doctors from almost all other specialties. Regardless of how the network is clustered, emergency doctors have always one or two communities that play a central role in the network.
- *Pediatrics*: This is the specialty showing the second highest tendency to work in group, i.e. pediatrics working with other pediatrics. There are several communities comprising only Pediatrics, and they communicate between them.

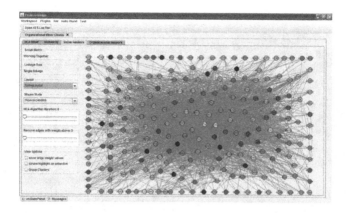

Fig. 7. The initial social network before clustering analysis

There is a certain tendency of this specialty to create islands. We may find a single community of pediatrics isolated from the rest of the social network as in Figure 9(a), or we may find a small group of pediatric communities that communicate between them but are isolated from the rest of the network as in Figure 9(b). The size of these communities goes up to 4 elements.

- *Obstetrics/Gynecology*: This specialty is often isolated from other communities, and these specialists also tend to work in isolation between themselves. The size of these communities is typically 1 or 2 elements. Occasionally, these specialists collaborate with emergency doctors.
- *Orthopedics*: Communities in Orthopedics are very rare. The communities that exist contain a single element, and they always appear at the periphery of the network, as shown in Figure 8. The same applies to the remaining specialties.

In this study we were also able to discover that some specialties never work together, such as: Obstetrics/Gynecology with Orthopedics; Obstetrics/Gynecology with Pediatrics; Orthopedics with Pediatrics; General surgery with Pediatrics; General surgery with Orthopedics.

The results above were all obtained from the iteration (of the clustering algorithm) having the highest value of modularity. It is comforting to realize that this concept works as well in large networks as it did in the small network used as example. In effect, in all experiments of this case study, modularity evolved in a similar way to that depicted in Figure 10. Basically, it keeps increasing monotonically up to a certain point when it reaches a maximum, and proceeding further will decrease it noticeably. The iteration with highest modularity then provides the best cluster configuration. It should be noted that modularity can also be used to compare the results obtained using different linkage functions.

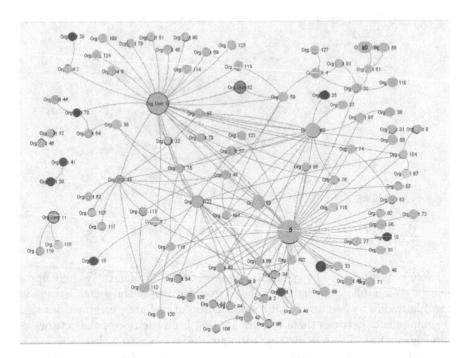

Fig. 8. Results obtained from the event log of 12 days, considering only medical doctors, and using complete linkage (GREEN = Emergency doctors; BLUE = Pediatrics; PINK = Obstetrics/Gynecology, RED = Orthopedics, YELLOW = Emergency relay; DARK PURPLE = General surgery, LIGHT PURPLE = Neurology; GRAY = Internal Medicine)

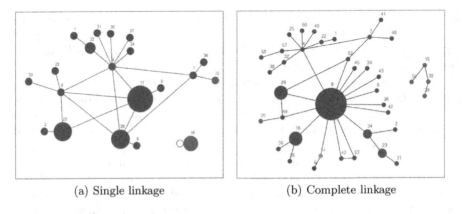

(a) Single linkage   (b) Complete linkage

Fig. 9. Results obtained from the event log of 14 days, considering only medical doctors

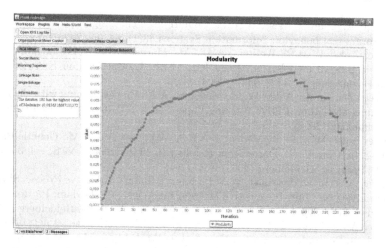

Fig. 10. Modularity per iteration of clustering in an experiment from the case study

7 Conclusion

In this paper we described how to use hierarchical clustering together with the concept of modularity to analyze social networks obtained from large event logs. The clustering iteration with the highest value of modularity determines the best division of the social network into a set of clusters, which correspond to the discovered communities. This approach facilitates the analysis of social networks such as the one that we dealt with in the case study.

There are several metrics than can be used to build social networks from event logs, such as similar tasks and working together. In this case study, it was the working together metric that proved more challenging – and useful – to understand the collaboration between a large set of actors. As future work, we plan to support the handover of work metric as well. The approach has been implemented in ProM version 6 and we hope it will be of interest for other researchers and practitioners in the field of process mining.

References

1. van der Aalst, W.M.P., van Dongen, B.F., Herbst, J., Maruster, L., Schimm, G., Weijters, A.J.M.M.: Workflow mining: A survey of issues and approaches. Data and Knowledge Engineering 47(2), 237–267 (2003)
2. Tiwari, A., Turner, C., Majeed, B.: A review of business process mining: state-of-the-art and future trends. Business Process Management Journal 14(1), 5–22 (2008)
3. van der Aalst, W.M.P.: Business alignment: using process mining as a tool for delta analysis and conformance testing. Requirements Engineering 10(3), 198–211 (2005)
4. Hornix, P.: Performance analysis of business processes through process mining. Master's thesis, Eindhoven University of Technology (2007)

5. Rozinat, A., van der Aalst, W.M.P.: Conformance checking of processes based on monitoring real behavior. Information Systems 33(1), 64–95 (2008)
6. van der Aalst, W.M.P., Weijters, A.J.M.M., Maruster, L.: Workflow mining: Discovering process models from event logs. IEEE Transactions on Knowledge and Data Engineering 16, 1128–1142 (2004)
7. Weijters, A., van der Aalst, W., de Medeiros, A.A.: Process mining with the heuristics miner algorithm. BETA Working Paper Series WP 166, Eindhoven University of Technology (2006)
8. van der Aalst, W.M.P., de Medeiros, A.K.A., Weijters, A.J.M.M.: Genetic Process Mining. In: Ciardo, G., Darondeau, P. (eds.) ICATPN 2005. LNCS, vol. 3536, pp. 48–69. Springer, Heidelberg (2005)
9. Günther, C.W., van der Aalst, W.M.P.: Fuzzy Mining – Adaptive Process Simplification Based on Multi-Perspective Metrics. In: Alonso, G., Dadam, P., Rosemann, M. (eds.) BPM 2007. LNCS, vol. 4714, pp. 328–343. Springer, Heidelberg (2007)
10. van der Aalst, W.M.P., Reijers, H.A., Song, M.: Discovering social networks from event logs. Computer Supported Cooperative Work 14(6), 549–593 (2005)
11. Song, M., van der Aalst, W.M.P.: Towards comprehensive support for organizational mining. Decision Support Systems 46(1), 300–317 (2008)
12. Veiga, G.M., Ferreira, D.R.: Understanding Spaghetti Models with Sequence Clustering for ProM. In: Rinderle-Ma, S., Sadiq, S., Leymann, F. (eds.) BPM 2009. LNBIP, vol. 43, pp. 92–103. Springer, Heidelberg (2010)
13. Girvan, M., Newman, M.E.J.: Community structure in social and biological networks. Proceedings of the National Academy of Sciences of the United States of America 99(12), 7821–7826 (2002)
14. van der Aalst, W.M.P., Song, M.: Mining Social Networks: Uncovering Interaction Patterns in Business Processes. In: Desel, J., Pernici, B., Weske, M. (eds.) BPM 2004. LNCS, vol. 3080, pp. 244–260. Springer, Heidelberg (2004)
15. Johnson, S.C.: Hierarchical clustering schemes. Psychometrika 32(3), 241–254 (1967)
16. Murtagh, F.: A survey of recent advances in hierarchical clustering algorithms. Computer Journal 26(4), 354–359 (1983)
17. Lv, T.-Y., Su, T.-X., Wang, Z.-X., Zuo, W.-L.: An Auto-Stopped Hierarchical Clustering Algorithm Integrating Outlier Detection Algorithm. In: Fan, W., Wu, Z., Yang, J. (eds.) WAIM 2005. LNCS, vol. 3739, pp. 464–474. Springer, Heidelberg (2005)
18. Han, K.J., Narayanan, S.S.: A robust stopping criterion for agglomerative hierarchical clustering in a speaker diarization system. In: Proceedings of InterSpeech, Antwerp, Belgium, pp. 1853–1856 (2007)
19. Milligan, G.W., Cooper, M.C.: An examination of procedures for determining the number of clusters in a data set. Psychometrika 50(2), 159–179 (1985)
20. Jung, Y., Park, H., Du, D.Z., Drake, B.L.: A decision criterion for the optimal number of clusters in hierarchical clustering. Journal of Global Optimization 25(1), 91–111 (2003)
21. Newman, M.E.J.: Modularity and community structure in networks. Proceedings of the National Academy of Sciences 103(23), 8577–8582 (2006)
22. Clauset, A., Newman, M.E.J., Moore, C.: Finding community structure in very large networks. Physical Review E 70(6), 066111 (2004)
23. van Dongen, B.F., de Medeiros, A.K.A., Verbeek, H.M.W., Weijters, A.J.M.M., van der Aalst, W.M.P.: The ProM Framework: A New Era in Process Mining Tool Support. In: Ciardo, G., Darondeau, P. (eds.) ICATPN 2005. LNCS, vol. 3536, pp. 444–454. Springer, Heidelberg (2005)

Supporting the Optimized Execution of Business Processes through Recommendations

Irene Barba[1], Barbara Weber[2], and Carmelo Del Valle[1]

[1] Departamento de Lenguajes y Sistemas Informáticos, University of Seville, Spain
{irenebr,carmelo}@us.es
[2] Department of Computer Science, University of Innsbruck, Austria
barbara.weber@uibk.ac.at

Abstract. In order to be able to flexibly adjust a company's business processes (BPs) there is an increasing interest in flexible Process-Aware Information Systems (PAISs). This increasing flexibility, however, typically implies decreased user guidance by the PAIS and thus poses additional challenges to its users. This work proposes a recommendation system which assists users during process execution to optimize performance goals of the processes. The recommendation system is based on a constraint-based approach for planning and scheduling the BP activities and considers both the control-flow and the resource perspective.

Keywords: Flexible Process-Aware Information System, Declarative Business Processes, Recommendations, Resource allocation, Prediction.

1 Introduction

Nowadays, flexible Process-Aware Information Systems (PAISs) are required to allow companies to rapidly adjust their business processes (BPs) to changes in the environment [10]. The specification of process properties in a declarative way is an important step towards the flexible management of PAISs [3]. Due to their flexible nature, frequently several ways to execute declarative process models exist. Typically, given a certain partial trace (reflecting the current state of the process instances), users can choose from several enabled activities (i.e., activities whose execution does not violate any constraint or only lead to temporary violations [6]) which activity to execute next. This selection, however, can be quite challenging since performance goals of the process (e.g., minimization of overall completion time) should be considered, and users often do not have an understanding of the overall process. Moreover, optimization of performance goals requires that resource capacities are considered. Therefore, recommendation support is needed during BP execution, especially for inexperienced users.

The need for user assistance during the execution of declarative BPs has been picked up in previous work [9,5]. Existing proposals, however, only consider the control-flow perspective for obtaining recommendations, but not resources.

In order to address this gap and to support users of flexible PAISs during process execution in optimizing performance goals like minimizing the overall

F. Daniel et al. (Eds.): BPM 2011 Workshops, Part I, LNBIP 99, pp. 135–140, 2012.
© Springer-Verlag Berlin Heidelberg 2012

completion time (i.e., time needed to complete all process instances which were planned for a certain period), we propose the generation of optimized enactment plans. For this, activities to be executed have to be selected and ordered (planning problem [4]) considering both control-flow and resource constraints (scheduling problem [2]) imposed by the declarative specification.

For planning and scheduling (P&S) the activities in a way that the process goal is optimized, a constraint-based approach is proposed since constraint programming [7] supplies a suitable framework for modeling and solving problems involving P&S [8]. For this, the declarative model is complemented with information related to estimates regarding the number of instances, activity durations, and resource availabilities. Recommendations on possible next steps are then generated considering the partial trace and the optimized plans. Replanning is supported if actual traces deviate from the optimized plans (e.g., because estimates turned out to be inaccurate).

This paper is organized as follows: Section 2 includes an overview of our proposal, Section 3 shows the application of the proposed approach to a running example, and finally, Section 4 includes conclusions and future work.

2   Method for Generating Recommendations

To optimize the overall process performance goals, users of flexible PAISs are supported during BP execution through recommendations. A recommendation is composed by one or more enabled activities (i.e., activities which are allowed to be executed given a declarative process model and a partial trace) to be executed next, together with their resource allocations. Our proposal is based on applying optimization techniques during both build and run-time (cf. Fig. 1).

Build-time. The build-time phase focusses on the generation of optimized enactment plans from declarative BP specifications by P&S the activities.

(1) **Create Declarative Specification.** In a first step, a declarative specification covering both the control-flow and the resource perspective of the BP to be supported is created. We use ConDec [6,11], a declarative language which proposes an open set of constraints for the high-level templates between BP activities (i.e., existence, relation and negation constraints).

(2) **Extend Declarative Specification.** In order to P&S the BP activities, the declarative specification is extended by considering the estimated values for: (i) the duration of the BP activities, (ii) the number of instances executed per planning period, and (iii) resource availabilities.

(3) **Generate Optimized Enactment Plans.** Optimized enactment plans are generated by applying AI techniques for P&S the BP activities, considering the extended declarative specification. In this work, CP is selected for the generation of the optimized plans since it supplies a suitable framework for modeling and solving problems involving P&S [8] (for details see [1]).

The generated plans contain information about the number of times each BP activity is executed, the start and the completion times for each activity execution, and the resource which is used for each activity execution.

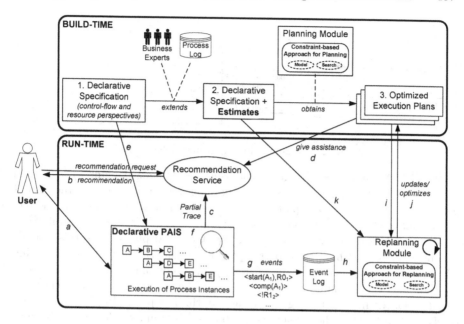

Fig. 1. Overview of our proposal

Since the generation of optimized plans presents NP-complexity, it is not possible to ensure the optimality of the generated plans for all cases. The developed constraint-based approach [1], however, allows solving the considered problems in an efficient way. Despite the NP-complexity of the considered problems, a first feasible solution can be swiftly found by a greedy algorithm.

Run-time. The plans generated in build-time are then used for giving recommendations at run-time. At run-time, process instances are executed by authorized users (a in Fig. 1). At any point during the execution of a process instance, the user can select from the set of enabled activities what to do next. However, to guide the user to optimize the overall process goals, recommendations are provided by the recommendation service (b in Fig. 1), i.e., proposing the most suitable activity to execute next[1]. For this, the recommendation service considers the current partial traces of the process instances (c in Fig. 1) and the best available enactment plan (d in Fig. 1) meeting the constraints imposed by the declarative specification (e in Fig. 1).

As execution proceeds, the enactment of the BP and the resource availabilities are monitored (f in Fig. 1). In particular, information regarding start and completion times of the executed activities, together with the resource availabilities are stored in the event log (g in Fig. 1). This information is analyzed by the Replanning Module (h in Fig. 1) together with the optimized plans (i in Fig. 1) to check if plan updates are required due to unexpected events. The

---

[1] For the current work, the durations of the recommendation request and the response time are considered negligible compared to the duration of the process activities.

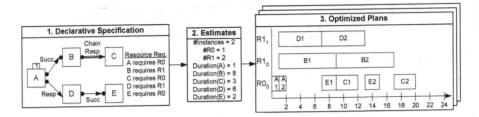

Fig. 2. Build-time for the Running Example

Replanning Module is in charge of updating the optimized plans (j in Fig. 1) in two situations: (1) there are some deviations, i.e., the execution trace is not part of one of the optimized plans (e.g., the user is not always following the recommendations) or estimates are incorrect; and (2) the Replanning Module finds a solution which is better than the current optimized plans, since this module is continuously searching for a better plan by considering the event log during BP execution, provided that the current plan is not optimal. If plan updates are required, the Replanning Module needs to access the extended declarative specification (k in Fig. 1) to generate new optimized plans. In general, despite the NP-complexity of the considered problems, replanning is less time consuming than initial planning, since most of the information about previous generated plans can usually be reused, and CSP variable values become known as execution proceeds.

3   A Running Example

In this section, our approach is used for giving recommendations during a hypothetical execution of a running example. Figure 3 shows the build-time phase for the example. The declarative specification includes 5 activities, A, B, C, D and E, and the following relations (ConDec templates [11]) between the activities (Fig. 2(1)): Exactly_1(A), i.e., activity A must be executed exactly once; Succession(A, B), i.e., to execute activity B, activity A needs to be executed before, and activity A must eventually be followed by activity B; Chain Response(B, C), i.e, immediately after the execution of B, C must be executed; Response(A, D), i.e, eventually after the execution of A, D must be executed; and Succession(D, E), i.e., to execute activity E, activity D needs to be executed before, and activity D must eventually be followed by activity E. For the considered example, resources of two kinds of roles, R0 and R1, are considered. For each BP activity (Fig. 2(1)), a role is defined. In a next step, the declarative specification is extended with estimates (Fig. 2(2)). Lastly, the constraint-based approach is applied to generate optimized enactment plans for the specified problem (Fig. 2(3)). Hereby, label RI_j represents the j-th resource with role i, and label Act_k represents the k-th execution of activity Act.

Figure 3 shows the behavior of the recommendation service when two hypothetical instances with given traces are executed for the declarative specification. At the beginning of the execution, plan P_1 (which has already been generated

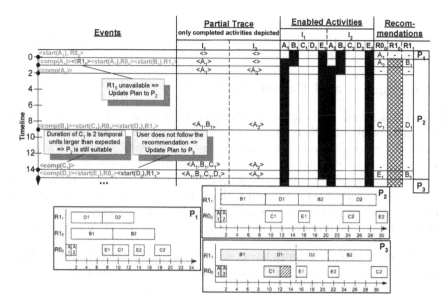

Fig. 3. Run-time for the Running Example

during build-time) is considered for the recommendations. The optimized plan P_1 has been created for two process instances. Initially, the partial trace for both instances I_1 and I_2 is empty (column Partial Trace, where completed events for activity executions are depicted). Furthermore, activities A, C and D of both instances are enabled (reflected by white bars), whereas activities B and E are not enabled (reflected by black bars). Activities B_1 and B_2 are not enabled since A must be executed before executing B (Succession(A, B)). Similarly, activities E_1 and E_2 are not enabled since the execution of E requires a previous execution of D (Succession(D, E)). Considering plan P_1, starting execution of activity A_1 using resource $R0_0$ is suggested. The user follows the recommendation. Due to Exactly_1(A), A_1 is not enabled anymore. At time 1, A_1 is completed, hence activity B_1 becomes enabled, and the partial trace of instance I_1 contains A_1. Furthermore, an unexpected event occurs (i.e., resource $R1_0$ became unavailable), hence plan P_1 is no longer valid, and the replanning module generates plan P_2. At time 1, based on plan P_2, starting execution of activity A_2 using resource $R0_0$ and B_1 using resource $R1_1$ is suggested. The user follows the recommendation. Due to Exactly_1(A), A_2 is not enabled anymore. At time 2, A_2 is completed, hence activity B_2 becomes enabled. At time 9, B_1 is completed, and starting execution of activity C_1 using resource $R0_0$ and D_1 using resource $R1_1$ is suggested. The user follows the recommendation. At time 14, C_1 is completed two time units later than expected. Even with the occurrence of this unexpected event, plan P_2 is still valid due to the slack time between activity C_1 and activity E_1. At time 15, D_1 is completed, and activity E_1 becomes enabled. Starting execution of activity E_1 using resource $R0_0$ and B_2 using resource $R1_1$ is suggested. The user partially follows the recommendation, so that, instead of executing B_2 she starts D_2. After this unexpected decision, plan P_2 becomes invalid, and the replanning module generates plan P_3. From now on, the BP execution proceeds without deviations.

4   Conclusion and Future Work

We propose a recommendation system for giving users assistance during process execution in flexible PAISs to optimize performance goals of the processes (i.e., minimization of overall completion time). The recommendation system is based on a constraint-based approach, which is used for P&S the activities such that the process goal is optimized. In the proposed approach, both control-flow and resources are considered. Furthermore, the optimized enactment plans are updated by replanning techniques when necessary. As for future work, it is intended to extend the proposed approach by considering further objective functions.

Acknowledgments. This work has been partially funded by the Spanish Ministerio de Ciencia e Innovación (TIN2009-13714) and the European Regional Development Fund (ERDF/FEDER).

References

1. Barba, I., Del Valle, C.: A Constraint-based Approach for Planning and Scheduling Repeated Activities. In: Proc. COPLAS, pp. 55–62 (2011)
2. Brucker, P., Knust, S.: Complex Scheduling (GOR-Publications). Springer-Verlag New York, Inc., Secaucus (2006)
3. Fahland, D., Mendling, J., Reijers, H.A., Weber, B., Weidlich, M., Zugal, S.: Declarative versus Imperative Process Modeling Languages: The Issue of Maintainability. In: Rinderle-Ma, S., Sadiq, S., Leymann, F. (eds.) BPM 2009. LNBIP, vol. 43, pp. 477–488. Springer, Heidelberg (2010)
4. Ghallab, M., Nau, D., Traverso, P.: Automated Planning: Theory and Practice. Morgan Kaufmann, Amsterdam (2004)
5. Haisjackl, C., Weber, B.: User Assistance During Process Execution – An Experimental Evaluation of Recommendation Strategies. In: Proc. BPI (2010)
6. Pesic, M., Schonenberg, M.H., Sidorova, N., van der Aalst, W.M.P.: Constraint-Based Workflow Models: Change Made Easy. In: Meersman, R. (ed.) OTM 2007, Part I. LNCS, vol. 4803, pp. 77–94. Springer, Heidelberg (2007)
7. Rossi, F., van Beek, P., Walsh, T. (eds.): Handbook of Constraint Programming. Elsevier (2006)
8. Salido, M.A.: Introduction to planning, scheduling and constraint satisfaction. Journal of Intelligent Manufacturing 21(1), 1–4 (2010)
9. Schonenberg, H., Weber, B., van Dongen, B.F., van der Aalst, W.M.P.: Supporting Flexible Processes through Recommendations Based on History. In: Dumas, M., Reichert, M., Shan, M.-C. (eds.) BPM 2008. LNCS, vol. 5240, pp. 51–66. Springer, Heidelberg (2008)
10. van der Aalst, W.M.P., Jablonski, S.: Dealing with workflow change: identification of issues and solutions. IJCSE 15(5), 267–276 (2000)
11. van der Aalst, W.M.P., Pesic, M.: Specifying, discovering, and monitoring service flows: Making web services process-aware. In: Technical Report BPM-06-09, BPM-center.org (2006)

A Business Process Metric Based on the Alpha Algorithm Relations

Fabio Aiolli, Andrea Burattin*, and Alessandro Sperduti

Department of Pure and Applied Mathematics
University of Padua, Italy

Abstract. We present a metric for the comparison of business process models. This new metric is based on a representation of a given model as two sets of local relations between pairs of activities in the model. In order to build this two sets, the same relations defined for the Alpha Algorithm [2] are considered. The proposed metric is then applied to hierarchical clustering of business process models and the whole procedure is implemented and made publicly available.

1 Introduction

Process mining algorithms [1], designed for real world data, typically cope with noisy or incomplete logs. Because of that, many process models corresponding to different parameters settings can be generated, and the analyst very easily gets lost in such a variety of process models. In [6] a technique for the automatic discretization of the space of the values of the parameters and a technique for selecting one among all the possible models have been proposed. Presenting just a single output model, however, could not be enough informative for the analyst, so the problem is how to find a way of presenting only a small set of informative results, so that the analyst can either point out the one that better fits the actual business context, or extract general knowledge about the business process from a set of relevant extracted models. In this work, we propose a model-to-model metric that allows the comparison between business processes.

2 Comparing Processes

The comparison of two business processes is not trivial as it requires to select those perspective that should be considered relevant for the comparison. For example, we can have two processes having same structure but different activity names: a human will detect the underlying similarity easily, while a machine will hardly be able to capture it.

Comparison of processes has been the focus of several papers, especially in the context of process composition (e.g. in the case of web services), process diagnosis and conformance between a reference model and the result of a process mining

---

* Andrea Burattin (*burattin@math.unipd.it*) is supported by SIAV S.p.A.

F. Daniel et al. (Eds.): BPM 2011 Workshops, Part I, LNBIP 99, pp. 141–146, 2012.

control-flow discovery algorithm. In the context of business process mining, the first papers to propose a process metric are [3,12], where the underpinning idea is that models that differ on infrequent traces should be considered much more similar than models that differ on very frequent traces. In [10], the authors address the problem of detection of synonyms and homonyms that can occur when two business processes are compared and structural similarity is based on the hierarchical structure of an ontology. The work by Bae et al. [5] proposes to represent a process via its corresponding dependency graph. The paper [9] presents an approach for the comparison of models on the basis of "causal footprints", i.e. collections of the essential behavioral constraints that process models impose. The idea behind [8] tries to point out the differences between two processes so that a process analyst can understand them. The proposed technique exploits the notion of complete trace equivalence in order to determine differences. The work by Wang et al. [15] focusses on Petri nets, which are converted into corresponding coverability trees. The comparison is performed on the principal transition sequences. The paper [17] describes a process in terms of its "Transition Adjacency Relations" (TAR). The set of TARs describing a process is the set of pairs of activities that occur one directly after the other. The similarity measure is computed between the TAR sets of the two processes. It is defined as the ratio between the cardinality of the intersection of the TARs and the cardinality of the union of them. A recent work [16] proposes to measure the consistency between processes representing them as "behavioral profiles" that are defined as the set of strict order, exclusiveness and interleaving relations. The approach for the generation of these sets is based on Petri nets (their firing sequences) and the consistency of two processes is calculated as the amount of shared holding relations, according to a correspondence relation, that maps transitions of one process into transitions of the other.

The first step of our approach is to convert a process model into another formalism where we can easily define a similarity measure. We think that the idea of [17] can be refined to better fit the case of business processes. In that work, a process is represented by a set of TARs. Specifically, given a Petri net P, and its set of transitions T, a TAR $\langle a, b \rangle$ (where $a, b \in T$) exists if and only if there is a trace $\sigma = t_1 t_2 t_3 \ldots t_n$ generated by P and $\exists i \in \{1, 2, \ldots, n-1\}$ such that $t_i = a$ and $t_{i+1} = b$.

The main problem with this metric is that, for example, even if from a "trace equivalence" point of view two processes are the same, from a structural point of view (i.e., business processes) they are not.

2.1   Process Representation and Proposal for a Metric

The idea here is to convert a given process model into two sets: one set of relations between activities that *must* occur, and another set of relations that *cannot* occur. In order to better understand the representation of business processes we are introducing, it is necessary to give the definition of *workflow trace*, i.e. the sequence of activities that are executed when a business process is performed. For example, considering the process

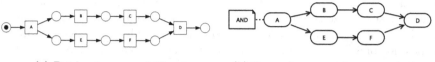

(a) Petri net representation   (b) Dependency graph representation

Fig. 1. Example of process presented as a Petri net and as a dependency graph

in Fig. 1 (it is the same process presented as a Petri net and as a dependency graph), the set of all the possible traces that can be observed is $\{ABCEFD, ABECFD, ABEFCD, AEBCFD, AEBFCD, AEFBCD\}$. We propose to represent such kind of processes by using relations $>$ and $\not>$ introduced in the Alpha Algorithm [2].

More formally, if a relation $A > B$ holds, it means that, in at least one of the workflow traces that the model can generate, activities A and B are adjacent: let W be the set of all the possible traces of a model, then there exists at least one trace $\sigma = t_1 \ldots t_n \in W$, where $t_i = A$ and $t_{i+1} = B$ for some $i \in \{1, \ldots, n-1\}$. The other relation $A \not> B$ is the negation of the previous one: if it holds, then, for any $\sigma = t_1 \ldots t_n \in W$, there is no i for which $t_i = A$ and $t_{i+1} = B$. It is important to note that the above relations describe only local behaviors (i.e., they do not consider activities that occur far apart). Moreover, it must be noticed that our definition of $>$ is the same as the one used in [17]. These relations have been presented in [1,11,2] and are used by the Alpha Algorithm for calculating the possible causal dependency between two activities. In the case of mining, given a workflow log W, the algorithm finds all the $>$ relations and then, according to some predefined rules, these relations are combined to get more useful derived relations. The particular rules which are mined starting from $>$ are: *(i)* $A \rightarrow B$, iif $A > B$ and $B \not> A$; *(ii)* $A\#B$, iif $A \not> B$ and $B \not> A$; *(iii)* $A\|B$, iif $A > B$ and $B > A$. Here, the relations $>$ and $\not>$ will be called *primitive relations*, while $\rightarrow$, $\#$ and $\|$ will be called *derived relations*. The basic ideas underpinning these three rules are that (1) if two activities are observed always adjacent and in the same order, then there should be causal dependency between them ($\rightarrow$); (2) if two activities are never seen as adjacent activities, it is possible that they are not in causal dependency ($\#$) (3) if two activities are observed in no specific order, it is possible that they are in parallel branches ($\|$). The idea of this work is to perform a "reverse engineering" of a process in order to discover which relations must be observed and which relations cannot be observed in an ideal "complete log" (a log presenting all the possible behaviors). The Alpha Algorithm starts from the log (i.e. the set of traces) and extracts the primitive relations that are then converted into derived relations and finally into a Petri net model. In our approach that procedure is reversed: starting from a given model, derived relations are first extracted and then converted into primitive ones; the comparison between business process models is actually performed at this level. The main difference with respect to other approaches in the literature (e.g. [16,17]), is that our approach can be applied on every modeling language and not only Petri net or Workflow net. This is why our approach cannot rely on Petri net specific notions (such as firing sequence). We prefer to just analyze the structure of the process from a "topological" point of view. In order to face this problem, we decided to consider a process in terms of composition of well known patterns. Right now, a small but very expressive set of "workflow patterns" [14] are taken into account. When a model is analyzed, the following derived relations are extracted: *i)* a sequence of two activities A and B (pattern WCP-1^1), will generate a relation $A \to B$; *ii)* every time an AND split is observed and activities A, B and C are involved (WCP-2) the following rules can be extracted: $A \to B$, $A \to C$ and $B \| C$; a similar approach can handle the AND join (WCP-3), generating a similar set of relations: $D \to F$, $E \to F$, $D \| E$; *iii)* every time an XOR split is observed (pattern WCP-4) and activities A, B and C are involved, the following rules can be extracted: $A \to B$, $A \to C$ and $B \# C$; a similar approach can handle the XOR join (WCP-5), generating a similar set of relations: $D \to F$, $E \to F$, $D \# E$. For the case of dependency graphs, this approach is formalized in Algorithm 1 of [4]: the basic idea being that given two activities A and B, directly connected with an edge, the relation $A \to B$ must hold. If A has more than one outgoing or incoming edges $(C_1, \ldots, C_n)$ then the following relations will also hold: $C_1 \rho C_2, \ldots, C_1 \rho C_n, \ldots, C_{n-1} \rho C_n$ (where ρ is $\#$ if A is a XOR split/join, ρ is $\|$ if A is an AND split/join). Once the algorithm has completed the generation of the set of holding relations, this can be split in two sets of positive an negative relations, according to the type of the "derived relations".

Given two processes $P_1 = (R^+, R^-)$ and $P_2 = (R^+, R^-)$, expressed in terms of positive and negative constraints, they are compared according to the amount of shared "required" and "prohibited" behaviors. A possible way to compare these values is the Jaccard similarity J and the corresponding distance J_δ, that are defined as $J(A, B) = \frac{|A \cap B|}{|A \cup B|}$ and $J_\delta(A, B) = 1 - J(A, B) = \frac{|A \cup B| - |A \cap B|}{|A \cup B|}$. In [13] it is proven that the Jaccard is actually a distance measure over sets. Our new metric is built considering the convex combination of the Jaccard distance for the set of positive and negative relations of two processes: $d(P_1, P_2) = \alpha J_\delta \left(R^+(P_1), R^+(P_2) \right) + (1-\alpha) J_\delta \left(R^-(P_1), R^-(P_2) \right)$ where $0 \leq \alpha \leq 1$ is a weighting factor that allows the user to calibrate the importance of the positive and negative relations. Since this metric is defined as a linear combination of distances (J_δ), it is a distance itself. It is important to note that there are couples of relations that are not "allowed" at the same time, otherwise the process is ill-defined and shows problematic behaviors, e.g. deadlocks^2. Incompatible couples are defined as follows: *(i)* if $A \to B$ holds then $A \| B$, $B \| A$, $A \# B$, $B \# A$, $B \to A$ should not hold; *(ii)* if $A \| B$ holds then $A \# B$, $B \# A$, $A \to B$, $B \to A$, $B \| A$ should not hold; *(iii)* if $A \# B$ holds then $A \| B$, $B \| A$, $A \to B$, $B \to A$, $B \# A$ should not hold. Similarly, considering primitive relations, if $A > B$ holds then $A \not> B$ represents an inconsistency so this behavior should not be allowed.

---

^{1} The pattern names are the same as in [14].

^{2} It must be stressed that a process may be ill-defined even if no such couples of relations are present at the same time.

Fig. 2. Two processes that are different and contain contradictions in their corresponding set of relations: they have 0 distance measure

Theorem 1. Two processes composed of different patterns, that do not contain duplicated activities and that do not have contradictions into their set of relations (either derived or primitive), have distance measure greater than 0.

Proof. See [4].

Since the sets of relations are generated without looking at the set of traces, but just starting from the local structure of the process model, if it is not sound (considering the Petri net notion of soundness) it is possible to have "contradictions". There is an important aspect that needs to be pointed out: in the case of contradictions, there may be an unexpected behavior of the proposed metric. For example, the two processes shown in Fig. 2 are "structurally different", but have distance measure 0. This is due to the contradictions contained in the set of primitive relations that are generated because of the contradictions on the derived relations (in both processes $B \| C$ and $B \# C$ hold at the same time). A comparison of values of the current metric and TAR is proposed in [4].

Once the metric on business processes is available, it is possible to perform clustering. Since in general it is difficult to discover how many clusters are present in a set of items, we decided to use an agglomerative hierarchical clustering algorithm with, in this first stage, an average linkage (or average inter-similarity). The entire procedure has been implemented in PLG[3] [7], a software for the generation of random business processes.

3   Conclusions and Future Work

This work presented a new approach for the comparison of business processes. This approach relies on the conversion of a process model into two sets of relations: local relations that must hold; and local relations that must not hold. These two sets are generated starting from the relations of the Alpha Algorithm but, instead of starting from a log, the input is a process model. The proposed metric is based on the comparison of these two sets.

Future work will include further study about the case of contradictory relations as well as considering not only sets of primitive relations, but multisets of relations, eventually considering the distance between the labels of the activities.

---

[3] The PLG software is a free and open source software and can be downloaded at http://www.processmining.it/sw/plg

References

1. van der Aalst, W.M.P.: Process Mining: Discovery, Conformance and Enhancement of Business Processes. Springer, Heidelberg (2011)
2. van der Aalst, W.M.P., van Dongen, B.F.: Discovering Workflow Performance Models from Timed Logs. In: Han, Y., Tai, S., Wikarski, D. (eds.) EDCIS 2002. LNCS, vol. 2480, pp. 45–63. Springer, Heidelberg (2002)
3. van der Aalst, W.M.P., de Medeiros, A.K.A., Weijters, A.J.M.M.: Process Equivalence: Comparing Two Process Models Based on Observed Behavior. In: Dustdar, S., Fiadeiro, J.L., Sheth, A.P. (eds.) BPM 2006. LNCS, vol. 4102, pp. 129–144. Springer, Heidelberg (2006)
4. Aiolli, F., Burattin, A., Sperduti, A.: A Metric for Clustering Business Processes Based on Alpha Algorithm Relations. Tech. rep (2011), http://www.processmining.it
5. Bae, J., Liu, L., Caverlee, J., Zhang, L.-J., Bae, H.: Development of Distance Measures for Process Mining, Discovery, and Integration. International Journal of Web Services Research 4(4), 1–17 (2007)
6. Burattin, A., Sperduti, A.: Automatic determination of parameters' values for Heuristics Miner++. In: IEEE Congress on Evolutionary Computation, pp. 1–8. IEEE, Barcelona (2010)
7. Burattin, A., Sperduti, A.: PLG: A Framework for the Generation of Business Process Models and Their Execution Logs. In: zur Muehlen, M., Su, J. (eds.) BPM 2010 Workshops. LNBIP, vol. 66, pp. 214–219. Springer, Heidelberg (2011)
8. Dijkman, R.: Diagnosing Differences between Business Process Models. In: Dumas, M., Reichert, M., Shan, M.-C. (eds.) BPM 2008. LNCS, vol. 5240, pp. 261–277. Springer, Heidelberg (2008)
9. van Dongen, B.F., Dijkman, R., Mendling, J.: Measuring Similarity between Business Process Models. In: Bellahsène, Z., Léonard, M. (eds.) CAiSE 2008. LNCS, vol. 5074, pp. 450–464. Springer, Heidelberg (2008)
10. Ehrig, M., Koschmider, A., Oberweis, A.: Measuring Similarity between Semantic Business Process Models. In: Proceedings of the Fourth Asia-Pacific Conference on Conceptual Modelling, pp. 71–80 (2007)
11. Mǎruşter, L., Weijters, A.J.M.M., van der Aalst, W.M.P., van den Bosch, A.: Process Mining: Discovering Direct Successors in Process Logs. In: Lange, S., Satoh, K., Smith, C.H. (eds.) DS 2002. LNCS, vol. 2534, pp. 364–373. Springer, Heidelberg (2002)
12. de Medeiros, A.K.A., van der Aalst, W.M.P., Weijters, A.J.M.M.: Quantifying process equivalence based on observed behavior. Data & Knowledge Engineering 64(1), 55–74 (2008)
13. Rajaraman, A., Ullman, J.D.: Mining of Massive Datasets (2010)
14. Russell, N., Ter Hofstede, A.H.M., van der Aalst, W.M.P., Mulyar, N.: Workflow control-flow patterns: A revised view. BPM Center Report BPM-06-22, BPMcenter. org (2006)
15. Wang, J., He, T., Wen, L., Wu, N., ter Hofstede, A.H.M., Su, J.: A Behavioral Similarity Measure between Labeled Petri Nets Based on Principal Transition Sequences. In: Meersman, R., Dillon, T.S., Herrero, P. (eds.) OTM 2010. LNCS, vol. 6426, pp. 394–401. Springer, Heidelberg (2010)
16. Weidlich, M., Mendling, J., Weske, M.: Efficient Consistency Measurement Based on Behavioral Profiles of Process Models. IEEE Transactions on Software Engineering 37(3), 410–429 (2011)
17. Zha, H., Wang, J., Wen, L., Wang, C., Sun, J.: A workflow net similarity measure based on transition adjacency relations. Comp. in Industry 61(5), 463–471 (2010)

Combining Process Mining and Statistical Methods to Evaluate Customer Integration in Service Processes

Michael Leyer and Jürgen Moormann

Frankfurt School of Finance & Management, ProcessLab, Frankfurt, Germany
{m.leyer,j.moormann}@fs.de

Abstract. The integration of customers in service processes leads to interruptions in the processing of customer orders. To still enable an efficient delivery, we propose a new approach combining ideas of process mining and statistical methods. The aim of the paper is to identify patterns of customer integration within event logs of a service process and to make the impact of these patterns on the processing time more transparent and predictable. The approach will be applied to a quantitative case study using a financial service process as an example. The results provide the opportunity for identifying adequate steps for improving the control of service processes.

Keywords: Process mining, services, context-aware BPM, customer integration.

1 Introduction

An important characteristic of services is the integration of customers during delivery [1]. This customer integration implies that the customer provides input (e.g., information) while the service processing takes place. Unfortunately, customers do not necessarily behave as planned or agreed. This often results in delays, i.e., interruptions of processing, and thus the planned schedule of a service process is upset [2]. Therefore, the following research question arises: How can the impact of customer integration on cycle time in service processes be evaluated? To answer this question, this paper proposes a two-stage approach. In the *first stage*, process mining techniques are used to analyse timestamps due to customer integration recorded by process-aware information systems (PAIS). In the *second stage*, statistical methods are applied to the data to analyse the influence of contextual factors on customer integration. The paper is structured as follows: Section 2 discusses related work. Section 3 presents the proposed methodology which is applied in Section 4. The paper concludes with an outlook in Section 5.

2 Related Work

A service process transforms objects or subjects (input) into outputs which represent the process result. This work is performed on process instances that contain the information about the performed activities [3]. A process instance is a customer order,

F. Daniel et al. (Eds.): BPM 2011 Workshops, Part I, LNBIP 99, pp. 147–152, 2012.
© Springer-Verlag Berlin Heidelberg 2012

such as a job application, an insurance claim, or a building permit [4]. The transformation takes place by resources such as customers, employees, and IT systems which are linked to one another in a net of activities [5]. However, in any case the customer will provide the main object or subject incorporating the problems discussed. Furthermore, this customer integration can be differentiated by so called contextual factors. Context is defined as "any information that can be used to characterise the situation of an entity" [6, p. 5]. For processes the following contextual factors should be considered: *Environmental* – (1) the industry such as industry type, information intensity of the industry [7], or competitive pressure [8], (2) customers in terms of their behaviour and expectations [8], (3) general conditions such as the weather or time [9], and (4) characteristics of the process instances [10]. *Internal* – (1) organisational conditions such as the availability of employees [11], and (2) the workload within a process [10].

The first interaction with the customer during a service delivery is the placement of an order. Authors like [12] focus on *predicting the arrival of customer orders*. For our purpose this is not sufficient as the service processing is not considered. Another stream of research focuses on the *isolation of customer integration* by separating tasks into front- (high customer interaction) and back-office (no customer interaction) [13]. However, customer-related and customer-unrelated activities are still cross-linked. Other approaches aim at *identifying general inefficiency drivers* (such as customer integration) affecting the process performance. Here, data envelopment analysis is applied using an input-output-model for efficiency measurement [14]. As the activities of the service delivery are considered as black boxes [15] the integration of customers cannot be further analysed. In the area of *process mining* [16] present an approach to predict cycle times of process instances by applying non-parametric regression and [17] develop a method to predict the remaining cycle time of running process instances. Both approaches focus on analyses of processing times not taking customer integration into consideration. In conclusion, these approaches do not allow a detailed evaluation of customer integration.

3   Methodology for the Analysis of Customer Integration

3.1   Stage 1: Analysing the Impact of Customer Integration on Cycle Time

Within a chosen event log there is a number of events $E_1...E_e \in E$ of finished customer orders in a service process. An event is defined with $E(A, T_b, T_e, O, C)$ when an activity A takes place with T_b for the beginning time stamp and T_e for the end, both with the format "YYYY:MM:DD hh:mm:ss". Originators O performing the activities are divided into O_p indicating personnel executing the activity while O_c stands for customers. Each event takes place for a customer order C_l (l is the number of customer orders). For each C_l there is a certain number of E documented.

Identification of customer integration patterns: The events can be used to identify customer integration patterns, i.e., an activity requiring customer input followed by a customer activity and resulting in an activity receiving this input. These patterns (using the documented information of each E) are formally described as:

$$I_{ij} = \left(E\left(A_i, O_p, C_l\right), E\left(A_{i+1}, O_c, C_l\right), ..., E\left(A_j, O_p, C_l\right) \right) \qquad (1)$$

A_i represents the respective previous activity and A_j the next one after customer activities are finished. To indicate the order of activities $E(T_b)$ is used. This allows identifying the existing number of $I_{ij} \in I$ in E. How often each I_{ij} occurs in the events analysed is described as $N(I_{ij})$. To find these patterns, the events have to be ordered by T_e. For each O_c found the previous event has to be selected; afterwards the following events are checked until an event with an activity O_p. The result is a table containing each I_{ij}, i.e., every combination of demanding and receiving activities.

Occurrence of customer integration patterns: The impact of each I_{ij} is determined by their relative occurrence with regard to the one of A_i. This is done for every I_{ij}, because each A_i can be part of several I_{ij}. Thus, $A_i(I_{ij})$ is calculated as follows:

$$A_i(I_{ij}) = N\left(I_{ij}\right) / N\left(A_i\right) \qquad (2)$$

Beyond descriptive measurements, the aim is to find distributions that explain the occurrence of I_{ij}, which is indicated by $E(A_i, T_e)$ and termed as $OC(I_{ij})$. Here, the modified Kolmogorov-Smirnov test of goodness of fit (K-S test) is recommended [18]. The test allows to check for typical statistical distributions of every $OC(I_{ij})$.

Duration of customer integration patterns: If a customer input is required, the service delivery is delayed. The waiting time for each I_{ij} in E is calculated as follows:

$$WT(I_{ij}) = Z_e \left| \left\{ Z_e : E\left(A_i, I_{ij}\right) \right\} \right| - Z_e \left| \left\{ Z_e : E\left(A_{j-1}, I_{ij}\right) \right\} \right| \qquad (3)$$

The average waiting time of an I_{ij} is denoted as $\varnothing WT(I_{ij})$. For each calculated value of $WT(I_{ij})$ the K-S test can be applied to test for typical statistical distributions.

3.2   Stage 2: Analysis of the Impact of Contextual Factors

The contextual factors CF_m (m is the running number) have to be defined as nominal variables. The identification of CF_m is highly dependent on the concrete service process. There has to be an assumption using the categories presented in Section 2 as guidance. Two generic ways for assigning contextual factors are available: (1) The usage of a certain activity of a process instance indicates CF_m. For each C_l incorporating such an A, every I_{ij} of C_l has to be assigned with the relevant characteristic of CF_m. (2) Date or time of an event incorporating A_i indicates a certain characteristic of each CF_m. Here, the information has to be assigned to the respective I_{ij}. Next, each $A_i(I_{ij})$ and each $WT(I_{ij})$ have to be assigned to the relevant characteristic of CF_m. The analysis of the impact of CF_m on the occurrence of customer integration is performed by a chi-square test.

For analysing the influence of CF_m on the waiting time $WT(I_{ij})$ it first has to be tested whether the data is normally distributed (using the K-S test) and if homoscedasticity occurs (Levene test) [19]. If both conditions are fulfilled (parametric), a one-way analysis of variance (ANOVA) can be performed. The ANOVA tests whether the average value of a metric variable (waiting time) is dependent on a nominal variable (contextual factor). If the data is non-parametric, the Mann-Whitney U test has to be applied for a CF_m with two characteristics and the Kruskal-Wallis test for more than two characteristics. These tests perform the same analysis as the ANOVA but for non-parametric data [19]. If statistically significant results are detected, $WT(I_{ij})$ and $A_i(I_{ij})$ should be calculated again for each CF_m.

4   Application of the Methodology within a Case Study

For evaluation purposes the methodology is applied to real data of a loan application process from a bank for small and medium sized enterprises (SMEs). Customers of this process are 22 branches of a bank; sales is separated from processing due to legal requirements. Thus, each part can be understood as an independent service process. Missing information and documents from SMEs are demanded via the branches. For six months data of 266 completely processed loan applications was collected.

4.1   Results of Stage 1

The results for detecting customer integration patterns are contained in the first two columns and the last one of Table 1. While calculating $A_i(I_{ij})$ it occurred that $I_{13,10}$, $I_{13,14}$, and $I_{13,18}$ had a value of 100 per cent. Therefore, A_{13} is only an activity after customer input is demanded from another A_i. Thus, the algorithm was adapted to incorporate A_{i-1} in the respective I_{ij}. The result lead to a split up of $I_{13,10}$, $I_{13,14}$, and $I_{13,18}$ in two parts as indicated in the table. The further data of Table 1 shows the results of analysing occurrence and duration of waiting times due to customer integration (in case of "-" the number of observations was too small for an analysis). It is revealed that customer integration has quite a considerable impact. However, the occurrence of interruptions and the long waiting times can be explained with statistical distributions.

4.2   Results of Stage 2

There are three CF_m potentially having an influence on customer integration available for the loan application process and their relevant characteristics: (1) Type of loan: Normal loans / Special loans (non-standard conditions); (2) Level of approval: Front office clerk / Front office manager / Back office clerk / Board of management; (3) Holiday time: Holiday time / No holiday time. Concerning CF_1, the characteristic "special loans" can be assigned to process instances incorporating timestamps of the activities related to special processing. The level of approval CF_2 indicates the potential risk of the loan; the higher the risk (e.g., due to a high loan amount), the higher the level of approval needed. Process instances incorporating the respective activity were assigned to the relevant characteristics. For CF_3, information about school holiday times was assigned using $E(A_i, T_b)$.

Combining Process Mining and Statistical Methods to Evaluate Customer Integration 151

Table 1. Quantitative measures of customer integration patterns

A_i [N(A_i)]	I_{ij}	$A_i(I_{ij})$	Best fitting distribution for OC(I_{ij})	$\varnothing$WT (I_{ij})	Best fitting distribution for WT(I_{ij})	A_j
Pre-check [390]	$I_{1,1}$	93 [23.9 %]	Wakeby	4.5 days	Pearson 6	
Processing of incomplete applications [53]	$I_{2,1}$	11 [20.8 %]	Wakeby	7.7 days	Frechet (3P)	Pre-check
Processing of applications [164]	$I_{10,1}$	1 [0.6 %]	-	3.1 days	-	
	$I_{10,11}$	1 [0.6 %]	-	10 min	-	Processing of reply
	$I_{10,10}$	13 [7.9 %]	Wakeby	5.9 days	Cauchy	Processing of applications
	$I_{10,13}$	24 [14.6 %]	Generic extreme value	16.7 days	Lognormal (3P)	Rework
	$I_{10,14}$	29 [17.7 %]	Johnson SB	9.5 days	Frechet	Archiving
Check of applications [248]	$I_{9,10}$	3 [1.2 %]	-	6.4 days	-	Processing of applications
	$I_{9,13}$	6 [2.4 %]	Wakeby	10.7 days	Gen. Logistic	Rework
	$I_{9,14}$	16 [6.5 %]	Johnson SB	8.1 days	Log-Logistic (3P)	Archiving

The analysis of contextual influences on the occurrence of waiting times OC(I_{ij}) revealed that only $I_{1,1}$ ($\chi^2(3) = 26.351$, p < .0001, Contingency Coefficient = .30) and $I_{2,1}$ ($\chi^2(3) = 10.574$, p < .02, Contingency Coefficient = .196) are influenced by CF_2. A further quantification of statistical significant results shows, that loans approved by front-office clerks (66.7 %) are the major reason that $I_{1,1}$ occurs. Concerning $I_{2,1}$ $CF_2(1)$ and $CF_2(2)$ (each count for 45.5 %) are the major causes but never $CF_{2,3}$.

5 Conclusion

The presented methodology enables the evaluation of customer integration in service processes in terms of waiting time. Activities affected by interruptions due to required customer input can be identified and the impact of customer integration can be made transparent. Nevertheless, one has to keep in mind that activities of employees like informal phone calls are not documented. If a service provider applies the proposed methodology, the heterogeneous customer integration becomes considerably more transparent and easier to schedule. The results can also be used as starting point for improvements of the service process analysed. Further research will concentrate on overcoming the existing limitations, enhancing the methodology and identifying possibilities to improve the handling of customer integration.

References

1. Sampson, S.E., Froehle, C.M.: Foundations and implications of a proposed unified services theory. POM Journal 15, 329–343 (2006)
2. Heckl, D., Moormann, J.: Operational Process Management in the Financial Services Industry. In: Wang, M., Sun, Z. (eds.) Handbook of Research on Complex Dynamic Process Management. Techniques for Adaptability in Turbulent Environments, pp. 529–550. IGI Global, Hershey (2010)
3. Davenport, T.H., Short, J.E.: The New Industrial Engineering. Information Technology and Business Process Redesign. SMR 31, 11–27 (1990)
4. van der Aalst, W.M.P., Reijers, H.A., Weijters, A.J.M.M., van Dongen, B.F., de Medeiros, A.K.A., Song, M., Verbeek, H.M.W.: Business Process Mining. An Industrial Application. IS 32, 713–732 (2007)
5. Kim, K.H., Bae, J.W., Song, J.Y., Lee, H.Y.: A distributed scheduling and shop floor control method. Comput. Ind. Eng. 31, 583–586 (1996)
6. Dey, A.K.: Understanding and using context. PUC 5, 4–7 (2001)
7. Bhatt, G.D.: Exploring the relationship between information technology, infrastructure and business process re engineering. BPMJ 6, 139–163 (2000)
8. Jelinek, R., Ahearne, M., Mathieu, J., Schillewaert, N.: A longitudinal examination of individual, organizational, and contextual factors on sales technology adoption and job performance. JMTP 14, 7–23 (2006)
9. Rosemann, M., Recker, J., Flender, C.: Contextualization of Business Processes. IJBPIM 3, 47–60 (2008)
10. Doerr, K.H., Arreola-Risa, A.: A worker-based approach for modeling variability in task completion times. IIE Transactions 32, 625–636 (2000)
11. Davies, M.N.: Bank-office process management in the Financial Services. A Simulation Approach Using a Model Generator. JORS 45, 1363–1373 (1994)
12. Klassen, K.J., Rohleder, T.R.: Demand and capacity management decisions in services. Int. J. Oper. Prod. Manag. 22, 527–548 (2002)
13. Fliess, S., Kleinaltenkamp, M.: Blueprinting the service company. Managing service processes efficiently. JBR 57, 392–404 (2004)
14. Burger, A., Moormann, J.: Performance analysis on process level. Benchmarking of transactions in banking. IJBAAF 2, 404–420 (2010)
15. Frei, F.X., Harker, P.T.: Measuring the Efficiency of Service Delivery Processes. An Application to Retail Banking. JSR 1, 300–312 (1999)
16. van Dongen, B.F., Crooy, R.A., van der Aalst, W.M.P.: Cycle Time Prediction: When Will This Case Finally Be Finished? In: Meersman, R., Tari, Z. (eds.) OTM 2008. LNCS, vol. 5331, pp. 319–336. Springer, Heidelberg (2008)
17. van der Aalst, W., Schonenberg, M., Song, M.: Time prediction based on process mining. IS 36, 450–475 (2011)
18. Yazici, B., Yolacan, S.: A comparison of various tests of normality. JSCS 77, 175–183 (2007)
19. Ruxton, G.D., Beauchamp, G.: Some suggestions about appropriate use of the Kruskal-Wallis test. Animal Behaviour 76, 1083–1087 (2008)

Applying Clustering in Process Mining to Find Different Versions of a Business Process That Changes over Time

Daniela Luengo and Marcos Sepúlveda

Computer Science Department
School of Engineering
Pontificia Universidad Católica de Chile
Vicuña Mackenna 4860, Macul, Santiago, Chile
dlluengo@uc.cl, marcos@ing.puc.cl

Abstract. Most Process Mining techniques assume business processes remain steady through time, when in fact their underlying design could evolve over time. Discovery algorithms should be able to automatically find the different versions of a process, providing independent models to describe each of them. In this article, we present an approach that uses the starting time of each process instance as an additional feature to those considered in traditional clustering approaches. By combining control-flow and time features, the clusters formed share both a structural similarity and a temporal proximity. Hence, the process model generated for each cluster should represent a different version of the analyzed business process. A synthetic example set was used for testing, showing the new approach outperforms the basic approach. Although further testing with real data is required, these results motivate us to deepen on this research line.

Keywords: Temporal dimension, Clustering, Process Mining.

1 Introduction and Related Work

Real-life business processes are dynamic, flexible and adaptable over time, so in different periods of time could exist different execution versions of a given process. For example, the sales process of a retail store may vary its operation between the Christmas season and the summer holidays. It can also happen that a process changes over time in order to adapt to market conditions. By having a model that describes the behavior of each version separately, it is possible to analyze them separately.

A challenge that has arisen in the literature is how to use the time recorded in the event logs to improve Process Mining techniques. In [1], the authors propose the use of time for two purposes: adding information to the process model, and improving the quality of process model discovery.

In this article, we present an approach that uses the starting time of each process instance as an additional feature to those considered in traditional Clustering in Process Mining approaches, in order to group in different clusters, process instances that are apart in time. By combining control-flow features with the starting time, the clusters formed share both a structural similarity and a temporal proximity.

F. Daniel et al. (Eds.): BPM 2011 Workshops, Part I, LNBIP 99, pp. 153–158, 2012.
© Springer-Verlag Berlin Heidelberg 2012

Different approaches of Clustering in Process Mining have been developed to solve the problem of getting "spaghetti" process models. The clustering algorithms instead of generating a single model to explain the behavior of the process, as traditional approaches do, generate several models simpler to understand [2][3]. Clustering algorithms group together in the same cluster a consistent set of process instances based on common control-flow features, so that each cluster could later on be used to generate a more understandable process model.

In Process Mining, interest in Clustering techniques is becoming ever stronger. There are several approaches to Clustering in Process Mining, some of them are: Bag of Activities and K-gram model, which are techniques that analyze each process instance by transforming it into a vector, where each dimension of the vector corresponds to an activity instance. These techniques lack information about the context and the order in which the activities are performed. Some authors [4] have proposed that the vectors be considered as a combination of different perspectives (such as control-flow, data, performance, etc.), which could lead to better results than approaches that consider isolated perspectives, but does not solve the problem of lack of context. Another set of techniques have tried to solve this problem using the complete sequence of activities. One technique is Edit Distance that compares two process instances, assigning a cost to the difference between the two sequences [2]. On the other hand, Sequence Clustering assigns an instance to a cluster according to the probability that the cluster is capable of producing the sequence [3].

Trace Clustering is a technique that uses a robust set of features for measuring the similarity between the process instances to create the different clusters [6]. This approach assumes that if two or more instances of the process share a subset of activities, there is evidence that they have common features and have similar functionalities and could be in the same cluster. This approach, like Bag of Activities and K-gram model, maps every process instance to a vector.

In [5], a general schema is presented that proposes features and a statistical technique to detect changing points and to identify regions of change in a process based on the control-flow perspective. Instead, our work is based on Trace Clustering techniques, mainly because they add context information and they consider the order in which activities are performed, but also because the time it takes to compute is linear, unlike the techniques that work with the complete sequences. Additionally, our approach consider the different type of changes that may occur in a process according to [5], including sudden, recurring, gradual and incremental changes.

This article is organized as follows. Section 2 presents the extensions made to the Clustering in Process Mining techniques. Section 3 shows the performed experiments and main results. The final section presents the findings of our research and future work.

2   Extending Trace Clustering Techniques to Include the Temporal Dimension

Our work is based on the Trace Clustering approach proposed by Bose and van der Aalst [6]. A trace is defined as an ordered list of activities (a sequence) invoked by a process instance from its start to its end. This approach uses the sequence of activities to group the traces in different clusters. In [6] different types of activity sequences are discussed. We consider only one of them, called *Maximal Repeat (MR)*. A *MR* in a sequence T is defined as a substring that occurs in a *Maximal Pair (MP)* in T. A *MP* in a sequence T is a pair of identical substring such that the symbol to the immediate left (right) of the substring are different.

This approach uses each *MR* found in the event log as a dimension of the vector space used to find clusters. We will call the set of all *MRs* found in the event log as Feature Set, and this baseline approach as Approach A.

Our approach adds an additional dimension to the vector space of Approach A, which is the starting time of each process instance (trace) in the event log, calculated as the number of days that have elapsed since a reference timestamp, e.g., January 1st, 1970, to the timestamp in which starts the first activity of the trace.

As a clustering strategy we use the Agglomerative Hierarchical Clustering (AHC) with the minimum variance criterion, using the Euclidean distance between vectors.

Based on the Approach A and the new dimension time, we developed two new approaches, which we call Approach B and Approach C. For all approaches, the distance between two traces (T_A and T_B) is calculated as shown in Eq. 1.

$$dist\ T_A\,T_B = \sqrt{\sum_{i=1}^{n}\left(\frac{T_{Ai}-T_{Bi}}{\max_{j\in T}(T_{ji})-\min_{k\in T}(T_{ki})}\right)^2 + \left(\frac{T_{A(n+1)}-T_{B(n+1)}}{\max_{j\in T}(T_{j(n+1)})-\min_{k\in T}(T_{k(n+1)})}\right)^2 \bullet \mu} \tag{1}$$

Where T_{ij} corresponds to the trace i and the feature j in the Feature Matrix [6]. The number of elements in the feature set is represented by n and the time weight by μ. The basic approach A considers μ as 0. Approach B uses as time weight the number of elements in the *Feature Set* ($\mu = n$); this approach is aimed at giving the same weight to the control-flow features and the time feature. Finally, approach C uses as time weight the factor α described in Eq. 2 with the purpose of giving an equivalent average weight to the control-flow features and the time feature.

$$\mu = \alpha = \frac{average\ distance\ between\ traces\ considering\ only\ the\ Feature\ Set}{average\ distance\ between\ traces\ considering\ only\ the\ Time\ dimension} \tag{2}$$

3   Experimental Set and Result Analysis

To test the new approaches we used three synthetic examples created with CPN Tools [7]; as seen in Fig.1. Each example consists of 2000 process instances executed over a period of one year. In example 1, we consider a process with two very similar versions. In example 2, the process has four versions, in which some are very similar and the other ones are not. Finally, in example 3, the process has three very unlike versions. In all cases, the different versions correspond to different time periods, but there is some overlap between some versions.

For each example, we used the three approaches described previously. The clusters generated by each approach are evaluated based on a metric that measures the accuracy with which each approach is able to classify the different traces; the metric varies from 0% to 100%. A 100% value is obtained when all traces assigned to a cluster correspond to the same version of the process. The accuracy metric is calculated as the sum of all true positive and true negative in the confusion matrix, divided by the total number of traces.

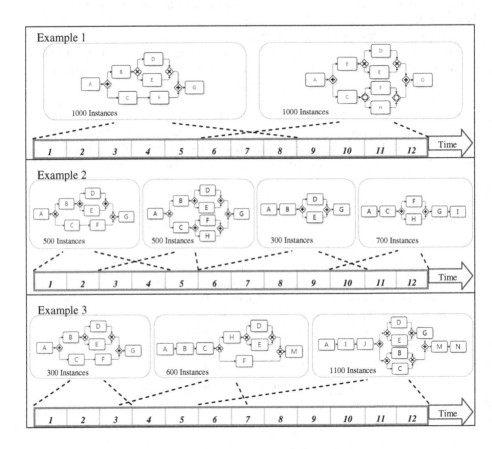

Fig. 1. Experimental set. Numbers represents the months of a year

Each approach is able to split the event log in n different clusters, where n varies from 1 to the number of process instances contained in the event log. In the results outlined, we have partitioned the event logs for each example in a number of clusters equal to the amount of original models (versions) that each example has (Fig.1). This simplification illustrates the quality of the three different approaches (Fig.2).

Example 1 consists of two different versions of a process; however, both versions differ only in one activity and run on different time periods, but during three months of the year (June, July and August) these versions overlap. Looking at the generated models with the three different approaches, we can see the Approach A, which does not consider the time dimension, does not work very well. Of the two approaches that consider the time dimension, only the Approach C is able to separate correctly the traces in the two clusters, so as to allow discovering exactly the two original models.

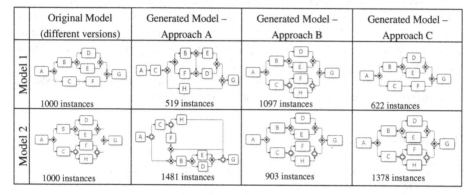

Fig. 2. Original models (corresponding to different versions of the process) and models generated using the three different approaches on Example 1. Models were generated with the Heuristic Miner Algorithm in ProM 6, the same method used in [6] to generate the process models, and then transformed into the BPMN notation.

The accuracy of each approach to correctly classify the different traces in the corresponding versions of each process can be seen in Table 1.

Table 1. Accuracy metric of the different approaches for examples 1, 2 and 3

	Approach A	Approach B	Approach C
Example 1	57%	81%	81%
Example 2	55%	81%	70%
Example 3	99%	74%	100%

In Example 1 and 2, important improvements are achieved in the accuracy by the incorporation of time, due to the similarity among the original process models. But in Example 3, where exists structural differences among the different models, it is not necessary to incorporate time to obtain satisfactory results. Manually, it is possible to observe and analyze the differences between the obtain process models; or analyze the time distribution of the generated clusters to detect changing points.

4   Conclusions

In this paper, we proposed a new strategy for using existing clustering algorithms in Process Mining for analyzing processes that change over time. By incorporating the temporal dimension to the control-flow perspective traditionally considered by these algorithms, it is possible to find different versions of a process that changes over time.

This is relevant because the real-life business processes are dynamic in time, and over a long period of time may have different versions.

The incorporation of the time dimension to the Trace Clustering technique, shows positive results when the different versions of the process are similar in the control-flow perspective. When there is a greater difference, all approaches (A, B and C) show good results. This represents a motivation to deepen on this research line.

Our future work in this research line is testing this novel strategy with real processes. We would also like to enhance the clustering algorithm so as it is able to decide which approach (A, B or C) provides the best results automatically and also that is able to determine automatically the optimal number of clusters. These enhancements require defining new metrics that do not depend on a priori knowledge of the process versions, such as the accuracy metric used in this article.

References

1. van der Aalst, W.M.P.: Process Mining: a research agenda. Computers and Industry 53, 231–244 (2004)
2. Jagadeesh Chandra Bose, R.P., van der Aalst, W.M.P.: Context Aware Trace Clustering: Towards Improving Process Mining Results. In: Proceedings of the SIAM International Conference on Data Mining, SDM, pp. 401–412 (2009)
3. Veiga, G.M., Ferreira, D.R.: Understanding Spaghetti Models with Sequence Clustering for ProM. In: Rinderle-Ma, S., Sadiq, S., Leymann, F. (eds.) BPM 2009. LNBIP, vol. 43, pp. 92–103. Springer, Heidelberg (2010)
4. Song, M., Günther, C.W., van der Aalst, W.M.P.: Trace Clustering in Process Mining. In: Ardagna, D., Mecella, M., Yang, J. (eds.) BPM 2008. LNBIP, vol. 17, pp. 109–120. Springer, Heidelberg (2009)
5. Bose, R.P.J.C., van der Aalst, W.M.P., Žliobaitė, I., Pechenizkiy, M.: Handling Concept Drift in Process Mining. In: Mouratidis, H., Rolland, C. (eds.) CAiSE 2011. LNCS, vol. 6741, pp. 391–405. Springer, Heidelberg (2011)
6. Bose, R.P.J.C., van der Aalst, W.M.P.: Trace Clustering Based on Conserved Patterns: Towards Achieving Better Process Models. In: Rinderle-Ma, S., Sadiq, S., Leymann, F. (eds.) BPM 2009. LNBIP, vol. 43, pp. 170–181. Springer, Heidelberg (2010)
7. Alves de Medeiros, A.K., Günther, C.W.: Process Mining: Using CPN Tools to Create Test Logs for Mining Algorithms. In: Jensen, K. (ed.) Proceedings of the Sixth Workshop and Tutorial on Practical Use of Coloured Petri Nets and the CPN Tools, pp. 177–190 (2005)

Making Compliance Measures Actionable: A New Compliance Analysis Approach

Nour Damer*, Mieke J. Jans, Benoît Depaire, and Koen Vanhoof

Faculty of Business Economics
Hasselt University
3590 Diepenbeek – Belgium
{nour.damer,mieke.jans,benoit.depaire,koen.vanhoof}@uhasselt.be

Abstract. Process mining can be used to measure the compliance between the actual behavior and the designed process. Traditionally, a single figure expressing the overall process compliance has only limited value to managers trying to improve their processes. This article proposes a new compliance methodology which first clusters the event log into homogeneous groups of event traces and then computes the compliance degree for each cluster separately. Additionally, each cluster is profiled by means of case information, which allows the discrimination between less and more compliant parts of the process. The benefits of this new compliance methodology in a business context are illustrated by means of a case study.

1 Introduction

The procedure of ensuring that actual behavior of processes is in accordance with the prescribed processes is referred to as process compliance [5]. Process mining is an interesting technique for compliance checking as it analyzes the behavior of executed process instances recorded in a log file. Examples of compliance checking techniques based on process mining are [3,1]. Some process mining techniques not only measure the compliance but also locate the deviation between the executed process and the designed process such as [2,8].

Traditional compliance checking methodologies, including process mining, provide one "average" compliance degree for the entire process. The compliance degree computed by these techniques cannot distinguish between process executions that are more compliant with the designed process and those which are less compliant. Revealing common characteristics among less compliant process executions would be a good start for process managers to investigate these cases in depth.

In this paper, we present such a methodology to do this type of analysis in a (semi-) automatic manner. The proposed methodology incorporates a clustering technique based on the similarity of the sequence of events. The compliance for

---

* Corresponding author.

F. Daniel et al. (Eds.): BPM 2011 Workshops, Part I, LNBIP 99, pp. 159–164, 2012.

each cluster is analyzed separately and then each cluster is profiled according to case attributes to find the common characteristics. The methodology is applied to a real life case study and results are presented.

The remainder of the paper is structured as follows: The proposed clustering based compliance methodology is presented in Section 2. The proposed methodology is applied to a real life case study and results are documented in Section 3. Finally the conclusion is discussed in Section 4.

2   Clustering Based Process Compliance Methodology

This paper introduces a compliance checking methodology, based on process mining techniques. In a first step we cluster the log file to divide it into a set of clusters (sub log files) of similar cases and then compute a compliance degree for each cluster separately. By analyzing the characteristics of each cluster, insights on compliance determinants are developed.

2.1   Clustering the Log File

Real life data usually represents heterogeneous behavior because of the dynamic nature when executing business processes which generates a set of different workflow sequences. To overcome this problem, we first split the heterogeneous group of cases (the log file) into subgroups with a more homogeneous character [4]. For this purpose sequence clustering algorithm was selected among other clustering algorithm in process mining [9, 7] because it focuses on the execution order of events in an individual trace. Moreover, it is robust to noise and able to deal with very large volumes of data with different behaviors [4, 10].

The sequence clustering algorithm generates a predefined k number of clusters with a model associated with each cluster. It goes beyond the scope of this paper to present the details of the algorithm, so interested readers may refer to [4, 10]. Since there is no information about the optimal number of clusters, we suggest running the algorithm with different values of k and select the optimal solution. To measure the quality of a cluster solution, we first check the conformity between the process instances assigned to this specific cluster and its model. Next, we combine the k cluster quality measures using a weighted average model with the cluster sizes as the respective weight.

2.2   Measuring Compliance

Here, we measure the compliance of each cluster generated in the previous step. For this purpose we use the Conformance Checking technique presented in [8]. The technique provides a fitness metric which measures how much the cases of one log file matches a petri net model. We use the technique to check the conformity between each cluster log file and the designed model. The technique measures the fitness between the event log and a petri net process model and then locates the deviations. To measure the compliance, each executed process recorded in the log file is replayed in the provided model in a non-blocking way. This means that if there are missing tokens to fire a transition, this is detected as a location of non-compliance and missing tokens are created artificially to proceed running the replay algorithm.

2.3 Profiling the Clusters

In this step, we profile the clusters by means of case information to have a closer look at the characteristics of the clusters. The selected information depends on the case under study. However, some recommendations from the process managers would be a good start. The recommendations in this case will be a set of attributes that the process manager thinks might affect the compliance degree either positively or negatively. The output of this step will be a set of relations between the compliance degree and the selected attributes' values.

3 Case Study: Procurement Process

We applied the proposed methodology to a real life data set. The cooperative organization is an international financial services provider. The input data file is an example of a large log file with high diversity of behavior. It was derived from the procurement process cycle configured in an SAP system. The cycle starts with creating a purchase order and ends with the payment of the associated invoice(s). Each trace in the log file, where 10,000 process instances are recorded, represents an item line of a purchase order. The procedure of process selection and data preparation was described thoroughly in the work of Jans [6].

3.1 Clustering the Log File

As a first step, we use sequence clustering algorithm to divide the log file into a set of clusters of similar sequences. We run the algorithm 7 times with predefined number of clusters ranging from two to eight. Next, we measured the cluster solutions quality. By comparing the overall quality measures of all solutions, we found that splitting the entire log file in four clusters reveals the best compliance between the cluster models and the associated cases.

3.2 Checking the Compliance

In this step, the conformance checking algorithm is used to check the compliance between the designed process model and each cluster generated in the previous step separately. Table 1 shows the compliance degree of the four clusters with the designed model as well as the compliance degree of the original log file.

The result indicates that the cases assigned to clusters 3 and 4 are less compliant than the cases assigned to clusters 1 and 2. Note that this is not revealed in the overall compliance degree. The next step is to profile the clusters to have a closer look at the common characteristics in the different clusters.

Table 1. Compliance degree measured by Conformance Checker

Cluster	Compliance Degree	Frequency
Cluster 1	99.60	901
Cluster 2	99.50	7617
Cluster 3	86.60	797
Cluster 4	80.05	685
Original log file	96.60	10000

3.3 Profiling the Clusters

In this phase, we analyzed the attributes of all cases assigned to one cluster to indicate whether there are common characteristics between them. For this study the process manager recommended analyzing four attributes: the document type, the purchasing group (PG), the purchase order (PO) creator and the purchase order (PO) value. In the original log file, there are mainly four document types, seven purchasing groups and four categories of purchasing values. The purchasing values are categorized according to the recommendation from the procurement process manager. As for the PO creator attribute, there are 81 different creators, most of them are less frequent (74 creators). However, these 74 creators together created 17% of the total number of purchases. So, we treated them as one group called 'others'. We profiled the four clusters according to the values of these four attributes. Profiling results show some remarkable results in the distribution of document types, PO creators and PO vales as discussed below. However, no interesting results were found concerning the distribution of purchasing groups. The profiling results are shown in Table 2.

Profiling Document Types. The most outstanding feature in the distribution of document types is the distribution of document type 4. Both clusters 1 and 2, which do not have document type 4 as one of the most dominant documents types, have the highest compliance degree. However, this document type has a slightly higher probability in cluster 3 and a significant higher probability in cluster 4 with respect to the distribution in clusters 1 and 2. Considering the different compliance degree, we assume that there is a relation between the absence of document type 4 and compliance degree so that further analysis is required to uncover this relation.

Profiling PO Creators. Looking at Table 2 we could notice that 67% of the cases assigned to cluster 4 are created by 'others', the group of creators who are less frequent in the original log file. The same group has the second highest distribution in cluster 3. Another noticeable remark is that creator C dominates the distribution in cluster 3 significantly and it has the second highest distribution in cluster 4. However, none of them, creator C and others, has a high probability in clusters 1 and 2 which have high compliance degree. Accordingly, we assume that there is a relation between the presence of creator C and compliance degree

Table 2. The distribution of document types, purchasing groups, PO value categories and PO creators in the four clusters

Attributes	Cluster 1	Cluster 2	Cluster 3	Cluster 4
# of cases	901	7 617	797	685
Document Type				
Doc. Type 1	1%	8%	0%	9%
Doc. Type 2	57%	81%	86%	33%
Doc. Type 3	38%	4%	2%	9%
Doc. Type 4	4%	7%	10%	48%
Purchasing Group				
PG 1	1%	2%	1%	11%
PG 2	4%	9%	3%	28%
PG 3	0%	1%	3%	3%
PG 4	26%	0%	2%	1%
PG 5	0%	2%	1%	1%
PG 6	14%	1%	4%	14%
PG 7	54%	84%	86%	38%
PO Creator				
Creator A	1%	33%	3%	3%
Creator B	16%	16%	3%	3%
Creator C	9%	7%	75%	11%
Creator D	16%	12%	0%	4%
Creator E	25%	8%	2%	9%
Creator F	1%	10%	0%	1%
Creator G	11%	2%	1%	1%
Others	21%	11%	17%	67%
PO Value				
Category 1	21%	25%	48%	8%
Category 2	1%	2%	2%	1%
Category 3	48%	53%	31%	29%
Category 4	30%	20%	19%	61%

so that the cases created by this person should be investigated in depth. As for the group of others, we think that there is a relation between the number of cases created by one person and the compliance of the created PO. This seems to be logical since the more PO's someone creates, the more experience he/she gains and the more compliant their cases will be.

Profiling PO Values. Results show that category 3 has the highest probability in both clusters 1 and 2 which is not the case in clusters 3 and 4. In cluster 3, category 1 dominates the distribution while in cluster 4 category 4 dominates the distribution. According to these remarks, we assume that there exists a relation between the compliance degree and PO value. Cases with very low (below 1,000 €) and very high (above 12,500 €) PO values are assigned to the clusters which are less compliant. Again, this requires further attention from the company.

4   Conclusion

In this paper we propose a clustering based analysis approach to check business process compliance. We believe that clustering log files as a preparatory step to compliance checking can reveal important insights which might remain hidden otherwise. Accordingly, the whole log file is first divided into clusters of similar sequences. Next, the compliance degree of each cluster is measured. The importance of this methodology is to have a closer look at the characteristics of the clusters with low and high compliance degrees.

The proposed methodology was applied to a real life procurement process. Results show that there is a deviation, which is sometimes significant, between the distribution of some attributes' values in the generated clusters. Remarkable results appear in the distribution of three out of the four attributes selected for profiling. Therefore, we can assume that there are relations between some values and the compliance degree. The proposed methodology indeed revealed that although the overall compliance degree was reasonably good, there were various cases whose behavior substantially deviated from the designed process resulting in a lower compliance level.

References

1. Adriansyah, A., van Dongen, B.F., van der Aalst, W.: Cost-based conformance checking using the a* algorithm. Bpm-11-11, BPM Center (2011)
2. van der Aalst, W.M.P., de Beer, H.T., van Dongen, B.F.: Process Mining and Verification of Properties: An Approach Based on Temporal Logic. In: Meersman, R. (ed.) OTM 2005. LNCS, vol. 3760, pp. 130–147. Springer, Heidelberg (2005)
3. Adriansyah, A., van Dongen, B.F., van der Aalst, W.M.P.: Towards Robust Conformance Checking. In: zur Muehlen, M., Su, J. (eds.) BPM 2010 Workshops. LNBIP, vol. 66, pp. 122–133. Springer, Heidelberg (2011)
4. Ferreira, D., Zacarias, M., Malheiros, M., Ferreira, P.: Approaching Process Mining with Sequence Clustering: Experiments and Findings. In: Alonso, G., Dadam, P., Rosemann, M. (eds.) BPM 2007. LNCS, vol. 4714, pp. 360–374. Springer, Heidelberg (2007), ACM ID: 1793147
5. Governatori, G., Sadiq, S.: The journey to business process compliance. In: Handbook of Research on BPM, pp. 426–454. IGI Global (2009)
6. Jans, M.: A Framework for Internal Fraud Risk Reduction: The IFR^2 Framework. Ph.D. thesis, Hasselt University, Diepenbeek, Belgium (2009)
7. Jung, J., Bae, J., Liu, L.: Hierarchical business process clustering. International Journal of Innovative Computing, Information and Control 5(12), 1349–4198 (2009)
8. Rozinat, A., van der Aalst, W.M.P.: Conformance checking of processes based on monitoring real behavior. Information Systems 33, 64–95 (2008)
9. Song, M., Günther, C.W., van der Aalst, W.M.P.: Trace Clustering in Process Mining. In: Ardagna, D., Mecella, M., Yang, J. (eds.) BPM 2008. LNBIP, vol. 17, pp. 109–120. Springer, Heidelberg (2009)
10. Veiga, G.M., Ferreira, D.R.: Understanding Spaghetti Models with Sequence Clustering for ProM. In: Rinderle-Ma, S., Sadiq, S., Leymann, F. (eds.) BPM 2009. LNBIP, vol. 43, pp. 92–103. Springer, Heidelberg (2010)

Analysis of Patient Treatment Procedures

R.P. Jagadeesh Chandra Bose[1,2] and Wil M.P. van der Aalst[1]

[1] Eindhoven University of Technology, The Netherlands
[2] Philips Healthcare, Veenpluis 5–6, Best, The Netherlands
{j.c.b.rantham.prabhakara,w.m.p.v.d.aalst}@tue.nl

Abstract. A real-life event log, taken from a Dutch Academic Hospital, provided for the BPI challenge is analyzed using process mining techniques. The log contains events related to treatment and diagnosis steps for patients diagnosed with cancer. Given the heterogeneous nature of these cases, we first demonstrate that it is possible to create more homogeneous subsets of cases (e.g., patients having a particular type of cancer that need to be treated urgently). Such preprocessing is crucial given the variation and variability found in the event log. The discovered homogeneous subsets are analyzed using state-of-the-art process mining approaches. More specifically, we report on the findings discovered using *enhanced fuzzy mining* and *trace alignment*. A dedicated preprocessing ProM plug-in was developed for this challenge. The analysis was done using recent, but pre-existing, ProM plug-ins. The high-level view of our approach is depicted in Fig. 1. Using this approach we are able to uncover many interesting findings that could be used to improve the underlying care processes.

Fig. 1. Overview of the approach followed

1 Preprocessing: Dissecting the Event Log

Process mining results are affected by the heterogeneity in event logs, e.g., the discovered control-flow models can be spaghetti-like. The event log contains rich information stored as attributes both at the event level and at the case level. We exploit this information and propose five perspectives for preprocessing that can be used in creating more homogenous subsets of cases. We mention three of the five perspectives in this paper.

- *Diagnosis Perspective:* Each case contains a few attributes that provide information on the illness the patient is diagnosed with. These attributes can be broadly classified into two categories (i) diagnosis code and (ii) diagnosis. Each case may contain up to 16 attributes of each type. One can filter the event log based on a particular value for any of the diagnosis codes or diagnosis attributes or a combination of them.
- *Organizational Perspective:* The 'org:group' attribute of each event captures the department/lab where the activity corresponding to the event was performed. Continuous sequence of activities executed in a department/lab can be considered as a notion of artifacts. We propose the transformation of

F. Daniel et al. (Eds.): BPM 2011 Workshops, Part I, LNBIP 99, pp. 165–166, 2012.
© Springer-Verlag Berlin Heidelberg 2012

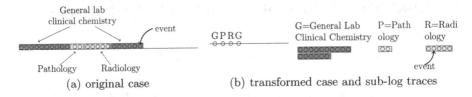

Fig. 2. Transformation of the original log into an abstraction log using the notion of artifacts on the organizational perspective

the original log into an *abstraction log* where the activities correspond to the organization names. Each continuous sequence of one or more events pertaining to the same organization in the process instance of the original log is replaced by a single event with the organization name as its activity. At the same time, we create one sub-log for each organization whose process instances correspond to the replaced sequence of events. The process of transformation is illustrated in Fig. 2.

– *Urgent and Non-Urgent Cases:* The event log contains certain activities that are classified as urgent. Ordinary counterparts to such activities also exist. This indicates that certain cases (patients) are considered as emergency cases and are treated in an expedited manner. This enables the partitioning of a log into two categories: urgent and non-urgent cases.

2   Analysis

We focus on the control-flow and process diagnostics aspects and use the *enhanced* Fuzzy Miner plugin (to mine hierarchical workflow models) for control-flow analysis, and the 'Trace Alignment with Guide Tree' plugin for process diagnostics. The control-flow model mined using the organizational perspective creates the flow of patients across different departments/labs. Each department can be seamlessly zoomed in to view the sub-process for that department. Our analysis revealed that the processes are in fact simple and sequential. Trace alignment enables the *inspection of event logs by grouping and aligning the traces*. Trace alignment can be used to explore the process in the early stages of analysis and to answer specific questions in later stages of analysis, e.g., are there common patterns of execution?, are there any anomalies?, are there any distinguishing aspects with respect to the treatment procedures followed among cases?, etc. Based on trace alignment, we noticed that not only are the treatment procedures simple and sequential but also the cases share a lot in common with very little deviations from the main path. The reader is referred to [1] for a comprehensive report on the approach, analysis, and results.

Reference

1. Bose, R.P.J.C., van der Aalst, W.M.P.: Analysis of Patient Treatment Procedures: The BPI Challenge Case Study. Technical Report BPM-11-18, BPMCenter.org (2011),
   http://bpmcenter.org/wp-content/uploads/reports/2011/BPM-11-18.pdf

Advanced Care-Flow Mining and Analysis

Filip Caron, Jan Vanthienen, Jochen De Weerdt, and Bart Baesens

K.U. Leuven, Faculty of Business and Economics, Leuven Institute for Research on
Information Systems (LIRIS), Naamsestraat 69, Leuven, Belgium
{Filip.Caron,Jan.Vanthienen,Jochen.DeWeerdt,
Bart.Baesens}@econ.kuleuven.be

Abstract. Health-care processes are typically human-centric processes characterized by heterogeneity and a multi-disciplinary nature. This contribution gives an executive summary of our submission for the 2011 Business Process Intelligence Challenge. We proposed both the department-based sub processes and specific treatement/drug focus as new process mining techniques that result in useful information.

1 Introduction

While business process support for structured business processes has always been an important research topic, the growing importance of service organizations (e.g. in health-care) with their human-centric processes has triggered the need for different approaches/focuses. In our submission we introduced the following approaches for care-flow mining:

- Analyzing **department-based sub processes** (e.g. radiotherapy)
- Analyzing the use of a **specific therapy** (e.g. Paclitaxel).

The next paragraphs present a brief overview of the results of these approaches on an event log obtained from the Department of Gynaecology at a Dutch Hospital [1]. Note that in order to use these conclusions the medical correctness and relevance must be determined by a professional. The full contribution can be found on http://www.econ.kuleuven.be/public/N09032/publications/BPIC2011_Caron.pdf.

2 Analyzing Department-Based Sub Processes

In general it can be concluded that most of the contemporary business processes are not isolated, instead they are interlinked and synchronized with other processes. Instead of analyzing the gynaecology superprocess, this section will focus on the specific radiotherapy process. The obtained results tend to be more useful, as comprehensibility increases and the focus is placed on a specific profession.

- Observation 1: Placing the focus on Radiotherapy made it possible to *obtain an understandable process model* for the treatment of multiple and very different cancers from the perspective of this single entity.
- Observation 2: The originator-by-task matrix clearly *confirms the layered structure of the Dutch health-care system*, a distinction is made between second and third order medical care.

F. Daniel et al. (Eds.): BPM 2011 Workshops, Part I, LNBIP 99, pp. 167–168, 2012.
© Springer-Verlag Berlin Heidelberg 2012

- Observation 3: With the social network miner in combination with the handover metric we were able to uncover *interactions* between radiotherapy and other sub processes.
- Observation 4: A *common sequence between treatments* (i.e. teletherapy followed by hyperthermia therapy and finally Brachytherapy) was identified and confirmed.

3 Analyzing the Use of Specific Therapies

For the second set of analyses we opted to focus on the combination of innovative medical knowledge and process mining, more in particular we investigate the use of Paclitaxel (i.e. a mitotic inhibator used in cancer chemotherapy).

- Observation 1: Although several sources (e.g. [2]) indicate the benefits of the sequential use of AC and Paclitaxel, *no patient received the innovative treatment combination.*
- Observation 2: A significant *deviation between the average number of treatment cycles* prescribed in [2] and the actual number of treatment cycles was concluded. The absence of the AC-Paclitaxel treatment can have serious cost repercussions.
- Observation 3: The Paclitaxel drug is mostly administered at the *nursing ward.*
- Observation 4: According to the National Cancer Institute, Paclitaxel is approved by the Food and Drug Administration (FDA) to treat ovarian, breast cancer and AIDS-related Kaposi sarcoma [3]. A close inspection of the event log uncovers an even more *versatile use of paclitaxel,* for malignancies at the uterus, the endometrium and the cervix.

4 Conclusion

Our submission aimed at stimulating the development of new perspectives on care-flow mining. We introduced and investigated both the specific department and the specific drug perspective. This resulted in the retrieval of comprehensible and usefule information in a health-care setting.

References

1. Van Dongen, B.: Real-life event logs: hospital log (2011), doi:10.4121/d9769f3d-0ab0-4fb8-803b-0d1120ffcf54
2. National Institute for Health and Clinical Excellence: NICE Guidance TA108 (2007), http://www.nice.org.uk/nicemedia/live/11596/33590/33590.pdf
3. National Cancer Institute: Cancer Drug Information: Paclitaxel (2011), http://www.cancer.gov/cancertopics/druginfo/paclitaxel

Process Mining Manifesto

Wil van der Aalst[1,2,*], Arya Adriansyah[1], Ana Karla Alves de Medeiros[50],
Franco Arcieri[26], Thomas Baier[11,53], Tobias Blickle[6],
Jagadeesh Chandra Bose[1], Peter van den Brand[4], Ronald Brandtjen[7],
Joos Buijs[1], Andrea Burattin[28], Josep Carmona[29], Malu Castellanos[8],
Jan Claes[45], Jonathan Cook[30], Nicola Costantini[21], Francisco Curbera[9],
Ernesto Damiani[27], Massimiliano de Leoni[1], Pavlos Delias[51],
Boudewijn F. van Dongen[1], Marlon Dumas[44], Schahram Dustdar[46],
Dirk Fahland[1], Diogo R. Ferreira[31], Walid Gaaloul[49], Frank van Geffen[24],
Sukriti Goel[12], Christian Günther[5], Antonella Guzzo[32], Paul Harmon[17],
Arthur ter Hofstede[2,1], John Hoogland[3], Jon Espen Ingvaldsen[14], Koki Kato[10],
Rudolf Kuhn[7], Akhil Kumar[33], Marcello La Rosa[2], Fabrizio Maggi[1],
Donato Malerba[34], Ronny S. Mans[1], Alberto Manuel[20], Martin McCreesh[15],
Paola Mello[38], Jan Mendling[35], Marco Montali[52], Hamid R. Motahari-Nezhad[8],
Michael zur Muehlen[36], Jorge Munoz-Gama[29], Luigi Pontieri[25], Joel Ribeiro[1],
Anne Rozinat[5], Hugo Seguel Pérez[23], Ricardo Seguel Pérez[22],
Marcos Sepúlveda[47], Jim Sinur[18], Pnina Soffer[37], Minseok Song[39],
Alessandro Sperduti[28], Giovanni Stilo[26], Casper Stoel[3], Keith Swenson[13],
Maurizio Talamo[26], Wei Tan[9], Chris Turner[40], Jan Vanthienen[41],
George Varvaressos[16], Eric Verbeek[1], Marc Verdonk[19], Roberto Vigo[21],
Jianmin Wang[42], Barbara Weber[43], Matthias Weidlich[48], Ton Weijters[1],
Lijie Wen[42], Michael Westergaard[1], and Moe Wynn[2]

[1]Eindhoven University of Technology, The Netherlands
w.m.p.v.d.aalst@tue.nl
[2]Queensland University of Technology, Australia
[3]Pallas Athena, The Netherlands
[4]Futura Process Intelligence, The Netherlands
[5]Fluxicon, The Netherlands
[6]Software AG, Germany
[7]ProcessGold AG, Germany
[8]HP Laboratories, USA
[9]IBM T.J. Watson Research Center, USA
[10]Fujitsu Laboratories Ltd., Japan
[11]BWI Systeme GmbH, Germany
[12]Infosys Technologies Ltd, India
[13]Fujitsu America Inc., USA
[14]Fourspark, Norway
[15]Iontas/Verint, USA
[16]Business Process Mining, Australia
[17]Business Process Trends, USA
[18]Gartner, USA
[19]Deloitte Innovation, The Netherlands
[20]Process Sphere, Portugal

* Corresponding author.

F. Daniel et al. (Eds.): BPM 2011 Workshops, Part I, LNBIP 99, pp. 169–194, 2012.

[21]Siav SpA, Italy
[22]BPM Chile, Chile
[23]Excellentia BPM, Chile
[24]Rabobank, The Netherlands
[25]ICAR-CNR, Italy
[26]University of Rome "Tor Vergata", Italy
[27]Università degli Studi di Milano, Italy
[28]University of Padua, Italy
[29]Universitat Politècnica de Catalunya, Spain
[30]New Mexico State University, USA
[31]IST - Technical University of Lisbon, Portugal
[32]University of Calabria, Italy
[33]Penn State University, USA
[34]University of Bari, Italy
[35]Vienna University of Economics and Business, Austria
[36]Stevens Institute of Technology, USA
[37]University of Haifa, Israel
[38]University of Bologna, Italy
[39]Ulsan National Institute of Science and Technology, Korea
[40]Cranfield University, UK
[41]K.U. Leuven, Belgium
[42]Tsinghua University, China
[43]University of Innsbruck, Austria
[44]University of Tartu, Estonia
[45]Ghent University, Belgium
[46]Technical University of Vienna, Austria
[47]Pontificia Universidad Católica de Chile, Chile
[48]Hasso Plattner Institute, Germany
[49]Telecom SudParis, France
[50]Capgemini Consulting, The Netherlands
[51]Kavala Institute of Technology, Greece
[52]Free University of Bozen-Bolzano, Italy
[53]Humboldt-Universität zu Berlin

Abstract. Process mining techniques are able to *extract knowledge from event logs* commonly available in today's information systems. These techniques provide new means to *discover, monitor, and improve processes* in a variety of application domains. There are two main drivers for the growing interest in process mining. On the one hand, more and more events are being recorded, thus, providing detailed information about the history of processes. On the other hand, there is a need to improve and support business processes in competitive and rapidly changing environments. This manifesto is created by the *IEEE Task Force on Process Mining* and aims to promote the topic of process mining. Moreover, by defining a set of guiding principles and listing important challenges, this manifesto hopes to serve as a *guide for software developers, scientists, consultants, business managers,* and *end-users*. The goal is to increase the maturity of process mining as a new tool to improve the (re)design, control, and support of operational business processes.

1   IEEE Task Force on Process Mining

A *manifesto* is a "public declaration of principles and intentions" by a group of people. This manifesto is written by members and supporters of the *IEEE Task Force on Process Mining*. The goal of this task force is to promote the research, development, education, implementation, evolution, and understanding of process mining.

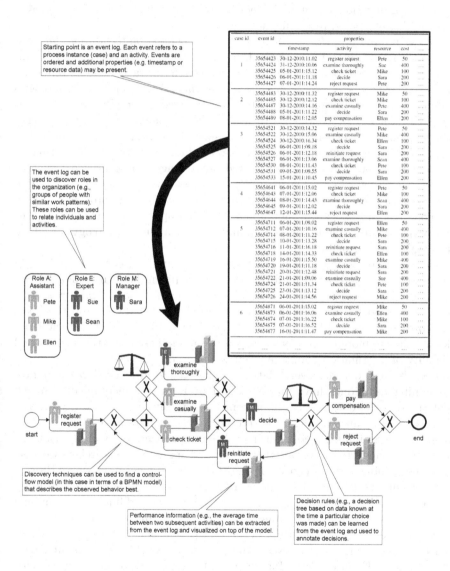

Fig. 1. Process mining techniques extract knowledge from event logs in order to discover, monitor and improve processes [1]

Process mining is a relatively young research discipline that sits between computational intelligence and data mining on the one hand, and process modeling and analysis on the other hand. The idea of process mining is to *discover, monitor and improve real processes* (i.e., not assumed processes) *by extracting knowledge from event logs* readily available in today's (information) systems (see Fig. 1). Process mining includes (automated) process discovery (i.e., extracting process models from an event log), conformance checking (i.e., monitoring deviations by comparing model and log), social network/organizational mining, automated construction of simulation models, model extension, model repair, case prediction, and history-based recommendations.

Process mining provides an important bridge between data mining and business process modeling and analysis. Under the *Business Intelligence* (BI) umbrella many buzzwords have been introduced to refer to rather simple reporting and dashboard tools. *Business Activity Monitoring* (BAM) refers to technologies enabling the real-time monitoring of business processes. *Complex Event Processing* (CEP) refers to technologies to process large amounts of events, utilizing them to monitor, steer and optimize the business in real time. *Corporate Performance Management* (CPM) is another buzzword for measuring the performance of a process or organization. Also related are management approaches such as *Continuous Process Improvement* (CPI), *Business Process Improvement* (BPI), *Total Quality Management* (TQM), and *Six Sigma*. These approaches have in common that processes are "put under a microscope" to see whether further improvements are possible. Process mining is an enabling technology for CPM, BPI, TQM, Six Sigma, and the like.

Whereas BI tools and management approaches such as Six Sigma and TQM aim to improve operational performance, e.g., reducing flow time and defects, organizations are also putting more emphasis on *corporate governance, risks*, and *compliance*. Legislations such as the Sarbanes-Oxley Act (SOX) and the Basel II Accord illustrate the focus on compliance issues. Process mining techniques offer a means to more rigorously check compliance and ascertain the validity and reliability of information about an organization's core processes.

Over the last decade, event data have become readily available and process mining techniques have matured. Moreover, as just mentioned, management trends related to process improvement (e.g., Six Sigma, TQM, CPI, and CPM) and compliance (SOX, BAM, etc.) can benefit from process mining. Fortunately, process mining algorithms have been implemented in various academic and commercial systems. Today, there is an active group of researchers working on process mining and it has become one of the "hot topics" in Business Process Management (BPM) research. Moreover, there is a huge interest from industry in process mining. More and more software vendors are adding process mining functionality to their tools. Examples of software products with process mining capabilities are: ARIS Process Performance Manager (Software AG), Comprehend (Open Connect), Discovery Analyst (StereoLOGIC), Flow (Fourspark), Futura Reflect (Futura Process Intelligence), Interstage Automated Process Discovery (Fujitsu), OKT Process Mining suite (Exeura), Process Discovery Focus

(Iontas/Verint), ProcessAnalyzer (QPR), ProM (TU/e), Rbminer/Dbminer (UPC), and Reflect|one (Pallas Athena). The growing interest in log-based process analysis motivated the establishment of a Task Force on Process Mining.

The task force was established in 2009 in the context of the Data Mining Technical Committee (DMTC) of the Computational Intelligence Society (CIS) of the Institute of Electrical and Electronic Engineers (IEEE). The current task force has members representing *software vendors* (e.g., Pallas Athena, Software AG, Futura Process Intelligence, HP, IBM, Infosys, Fluxicon, Businesscape, Iontas/Verint, Fujitsu, Fujitsu Laboratories, Business Process Mining, Stereologic), *consultancy firms/end users* (e.g., ProcessGold, Business Process Trends, Gartner, Deloitte, Process Sphere, Siav SpA, BPM Chili, BWI Systeme GmbH, Excellentia BPM, Rabobank), and *research institutes* (e.g., TU/e, University of Padua, Universitat Politècnica de Catalunya, New Mexico State University, Technical University of Lisbon, University of Calabria, Penn State University, University of Bari, Humboldt-Universität zu Berlin, Queensland University of Technology, Vienna University of Economics and Business, Stevens Institute of Technology, University of Haifa, University of Bologna, Ulsan National Institute of Science and Technology, Cranfield University, K.U. Leuven, Tsinghua University, University of Innsbruck, University of Tartu).

Concrete objectives of the task force are:

- To make end-users, developers, consultants, business managers, and researchers aware of the state-of-the-art in process mining,
- To promote the use of process mining techniques and tools and stimulate new applications,
- To play a role in standardization efforts for logging event data,
- To organize tutorials, special sessions, workshops, panels, and
- To publish articles, books, videos, and special issues of journals.

Since its establishment in 2009 there have been various activities related to the above objectives. For example, several workshops and special tracks were (co-) organized by the task force, e.g., the workshops on Business Process Intelligence (BPI'09, BPI'10, and BPI'11) and special tracks at main IEEE conferences (e.g. CIDM'11). Knowledge was disseminated via tutorials (e.g. WCCI'10 and PMPM'09), summer schools (ESSCaSS'09, ACPN'10, CICH'10, etc.), videos (cf. www.processmining.org), and several publications including the first book on process mining recently published by Springer [1]. The task force also (co-)organized the first Business Process Intelligence Challenge (BPIC'11): a competition where participants had to extract meaningful knowledge from a large and complex event log. In 2010, the task force also standardized *XES* (www.xes-standard.org), a standard logging format that is extensible and supported by the *OpenXES library* (www.openxes.org) and by tools such as ProM, XESame, Nitro, etc.

The reader is invited to visit http://www.win.tue.nl/ieeetfpm/ for more information about the activities of the task force.

2 Process Mining: State of the Art

The expanding capabilities of information systems and other systems that depend on computing, are well characterized by Moore's law. Gordon Moore, the co-founder of Intel, predicted in 1965 that the number of components in integrated circuits would double every year. During the last fifty years the growth has indeed been exponential, albeit at a slightly slower pace. These advancements resulted in a spectacular growth of the "digital universe" (i.e., all data stored and/or exchanged electronically). Moreover, the digital and the real universe continue to become more and more aligned.

   The growth of a digital universe that is well-aligned with processes in organizations makes it possible to record and analyze *events*. Events may range from the withdrawal of cash from an ATM, a doctor adjusting an X-ray machine, a citizen applying for a driver license, the submission of a tax declaration, and the receipt of an e-ticket number by a traveler. The challenge is to exploit event data in a meaningful way, for example, to provide insights, identify bottlenecks, anticipate problems, record policy violations, recommend countermeasures, and streamline processes. Process mining aims to do exactly that.

   Starting point for process mining is an *event log*. All process mining techniques assume that it is possible to *sequentially* record *events* such that each event refers to an *activity* (i.e., a well-defined step in some process) and is related to a particular *case* (i.e., a process instance). Event logs may store additional information about events. In fact, whenever possible, process mining techniques use extra information such as the *resource* (i.e., person or device) executing or initiating the activity, the *timestamp* of the event, or *data elements* recorded with the event (e.g., the size of an order).

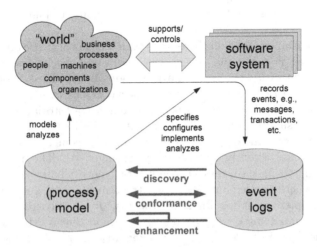

Fig. 2. Positioning of the three main types of process mining: (a) *discovery*, (b) *conformance* checking, and (c) *enhancement* [1]

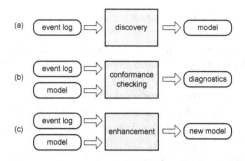

Fig. 3. The three basic types of process mining explained in terms of input and output: (a) discovery, (b) conformance checking, and (c) enhancement

As shown in Fig. 2, event logs can be used to conduct three types of process mining. The first type of process mining is *discovery*. A discovery technique takes an event log and produces a model without using any a-priori information. Process discovery is the most prominent process mining technique. For many organizations it is surprising to see that existing techniques are indeed able to discover real processes merely based on example executions in event logs. The second type of process mining is *conformance*. Here, an existing process model is compared with an event log of the same process. Conformance checking can be used to check if reality, as recorded in the log, conforms to the model and vice versa. Note that different types of models can be considered: conformance checking can be applied to procedural models, organizational models, declarative process models, business rules/policies, laws, etc. The third type of process mining is *enhancement*. Here, the idea is to extend or improve an existing process model using information about the actual process recorded in some event log. Whereas conformance checking measures the alignment between model and reality, this third type of process mining aims at changing or extending the a-priori model. For instance, by using timestamps in the event log one can extend the model to show bottlenecks, service levels, throughput times, and frequencies.

Figure 3 describes the three types of process mining in terms of input and output. Techniques for discovery take an event log and produce a model. The discovered model is typically a process model (e.g., a Petri net, BPMN, EPC, or UML activity diagram), however, the model may also describe other perspectives (e.g., a social network). Conformance checking techniques need an event log and a model as input. The output consists of diagnostic information showing differences and commonalities between model and log. Techniques for model enhancement (repair or extension) also need an event log and a model as input. The output is an improved or extended model.

Process mining may cover different perspectives. The *control-flow perspective* focuses on the control-flow, i.e., the ordering of activities. The goal of mining this perspective is to find a good characterization of all possible paths. The result is typically expressed in terms of a Petri net or some other process notation (e.g., EPCs, BPMN, or UML activity diagrams). The *organizational perspective* focuses on information about resources hidden in the log, i.e., which actors (e.g., people, systems, roles, or departments) are involved and how are they related. The goal is to either structure the organization by classifying people in terms of roles and organizational units or to show the social network. The *case perspective* focuses on properties of cases. Obviously, a case can be characterized by its path in the process or by the actors working on it. However, cases can also be characterized by the values of the corresponding data elements. For example, if a case represents a replenishment order, it may be interesting to know the supplier or the number of products ordered. The *time perspective* is concerned with the timing and frequency of events. When events bear timestamps it is possible to discover bottlenecks, measure service levels, monitor the utilization of resources, and predict the remaining processing time of running cases.

There are some common misconceptions related to process mining. Some vendors, analysts, and researchers limit the scope of process mining to a special data mining technique for process discovery that can only be used for offline analysis. This is *not* the case, therefore, we emphasize the following three characteristics.

– *Process mining is not limited to control-flow discovery.* The discovery of process models from event logs fuels the imagination of both practitioners and academics. Therefore, control-flow discovery is often seen as the most exciting part of process mining. However, process mining is not limited to control-flow discovery. On the one hand, discovery is just one of the three basic forms of process mining (discovery, conformance, and enhancement). On the other hand, the scope is not limited to control-flow; the organizational, case and time perspectives also play an important role.
– *Process mining is not just a specific type of data mining.* Process mining can be seen as the "missing link" between data mining and traditional model-driven BPM. Most data mining techniques are not process-centric at all. Process models potentially exhibiting concurrency are incomparable to simple data mining structures such as decision trees and association rules. Therefore, completely new types of representations and algorithms are needed.
– *Process mining is not limited to offline analysis.* Process mining techniques extract knowledge from historical event data. Although "post mortem" data is used, the results can be applied to running cases. For example, the completion time of a partially handled customer order can be predicted using a discovered process model.

To position process mining, we use the Business Process Management (BPM) life-cycle shown in Fig. 4. The BPM life-cycle shows seven phases of a business process and its corresponding information system(s). In the *(re)design phase* a new process model is created or an existing process model is adapted. In the *analysis phase* a candidate model and its alternatives are analyzed. After the (re)design phase, the model is implemented (*implementation phase*) or an existing system is (re)configured (*reconfiguration phase*). In the *execution phase* the designed model is enacted. During the execution phase the process is *monitored*. Moreover, smaller adjustments may be made without redesigning the process (*adjustment phase*). In the *diagnosis phase* the enacted process is analyzed and

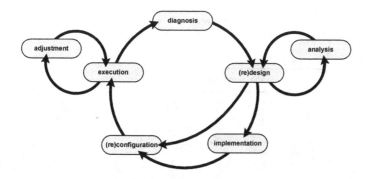

Fig. 4. The BPM life-cycle identifying the various phases of a business process and its corresponding information system(s); process mining (potentially) plays a role in all phases (except for the implementation phase)

the output of this phase may trigger a new process redesign phase. Process mining is a valuable tool for most of the phases shown in Fig. 4. Obviously, the diagnosis phase can benefit from process mining. However, process mining is not limited to the diagnosis phase. For example, in the execution phase, process mining techniques can be used for *operational support*. Predictions and recommendations based on models learned using historic information can be used to influence running cases. Similar forms of decision support can be used to adjust processes and to guide process (re)configuration.

Whereas Fig. 4 shows the overall BPM life-cycle, Fig. 5 focuses on the concrete process mining activities and artifacts. Figure 5 describes the possible stages in a process mining project. Any process mining project starts with a planning and a justification for this planning (Stage 0). After initiating the project, event data, models, objectives, and questions need to be extracted from systems, domain experts, and management (Stage 1). This requires an understanding of the available data ("What can be used for analysis?") and an understanding of the domain ("What are the important questions?") and results in the artifacts shown in Fig. 5 (i.e., historical data, handmade models, objectives, and questions). In Stage 2 the control-flow model is constructed and linked to the event log. Here automated process discovery techniques can be used. The discovered process model may already provide answers to some of the questions and trigger redesign or adjustment actions. Moreover, the event log may be filtered or adapted using the model (e.g., removing rare activities or outlier cases, and inserting missing events). Sometimes significant efforts are needed to correlate events belonging to the same process instance. The remaining events are related to entities of the process model. When the process is relatively structured, the control-flow model may be extended with other perspectives (e.g., data, time, and resources) during Stage 3. The relation between the event log and the model established in Stage 2 is used to extend the model (e.g., timestamps of associated events are used to estimate waiting times for activities). This may be used to answer additional questions and may trigger additional actions. Ultimately, the

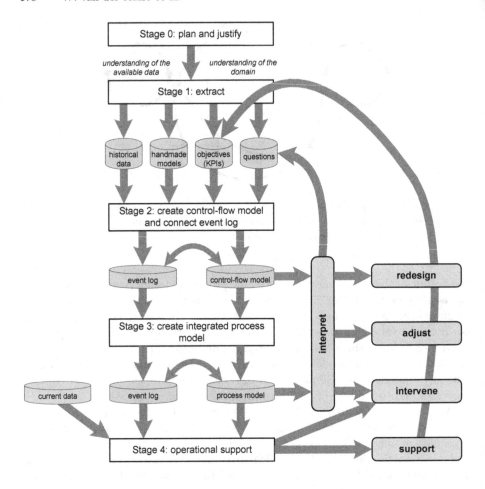

Fig. 5. The L^* life-cycle model describing a process mining project consisting of five stages: plan and justify (Stage 0), extract (Stage 1), create a control-flow model and connect it to the event log (Stage 2), create an integrated process model (Stage 3), and provide operational support (Stage 4) [1]

models constructed in Stage 3 may be used for operational support (Stage 4). Knowledge extracted from historical event data is combined with information about running cases. This may be used to intervene, predict, and recommend. Stages 3 and 4 can only be reached if the process is sufficiently stable and structured.

Currently, there are techniques and tools that can support all stages shown in Fig. 5. However, process mining is a relatively new paradigm and most of the currently available tools are still rather immature. Moreover, prospective users are often not aware of the potential and the limitations of process mining. Therefore, this manifesto catalogs some guiding principles (cf. Section 3) and challenges (cf. Section 4) for users of process mining techniques as well as researchers and developers that are interested in advancing the state-of-the-art.

3 Guiding Principles

As with any new technology, there are obvious mistakes that can be made when applying process mining in real-life settings. Therefore, we list six *guiding principles* to prevent users/analysts from making such mistakes.

3.1 GP1: Event Data Should Be Treated as First-Class Citizens

Starting point for any process mining activity are the events recorded. We refer to collections of events as *event logs*, however, this does not imply that events need to be stored in dedicated log files. Events may be stored in database tables, message logs, mail archives, transaction logs, and other data sources. More important than the storage format, is the *quality* of such event logs. The quality of a process mining result heavily depends on the input. Therefore, event logs should be treated as *first-class citizens* in the information systems supporting the processes to be analyzed. Unfortunately, event logs are often merely a "by-product" used for debugging or profiling. For example, the medical devices of Philips Healthcare record events simply because software developers have inserted "print statements" in the code. Although there are some informal guidelines for adding such statements to the code, a more systematic approach is needed to improve the quality of event logs. Event data should be viewed as first-class citizens (rather than second-class citizens).

There are several criteria to judge the quality of event data. Events should be *trustworthy*, i.e., it should be safe to assume that the recorded events actually happened and that the attributes of events are correct. Event logs should be *complete*, i.e., given a particular scope, no events may be missing. Any recorded event should have well-defined *semantics*. Moreover, the event data should be *safe* in the sense that privacy and security concerns are addressed when recording the events. For example, actors should be aware of the kind of events being recorded and the way they are used.

Table 1 defines five event log maturity levels ranging from excellent quality (★★★★★) to poor quality (★). For example, the event logs of Philips Healthcare reside at level ★★★, i.e., events are recorded automatically and the recorded behavior matches reality, but no systematic approach is used to assign semantics to events and to ensure coverage at a particular level. Process mining techniques can be applied to logs at levels ★★★★★, ★★★★ and ★★★. In principle, it is also possible to apply process mining using event logs at level ★★ or ★. However, the analysis of such logs is typically problematic and the results are not trustworthy. In fact, it does not make much sense to apply process mining to logs at level ★.

In order to benefit from process mining, organizations should aim at event logs at the highest possible quality level.

Table 1. Maturity levels for event logs

Level	Characterization
★★★★★	Highest level: the event log is of excellent quality (i.e., trustworthy and complete) and events are well-defined. Events are recorded in an automatic, systematic, reliable, and safe manner. Privacy and security considerations are addressed adequately. Moreover, the events recorded (and all of their attributes) have clear semantics. This implies the existence of one or more ontologies. Events and their attributes point to this ontology. *Example:* semantically annotated logs of BPM systems.
★★★★	Events are recorded automatically and in a systematic and reliable manner, i.e., logs are trustworthy and complete. Unlike the systems operating at level ★★★, notions such as process instance (case) and activity are supported in an explicit manner. *Example:* the events logs of traditional BPM/workflow systems.
★★★	Events are recorded automatically, but no systematic approach is followed to record events. However, unlike logs at level ★★, there is some level of guarantee that the events recorded match reality (i.e., the event log is trustworthy but not necessarily complete). Consider, for example, the events recorded by an ERP system. Although events need to be extracted from a variety of tables, the information can be assumed to be correct (e.g., it is safe to assume that a payment recorded by the ERP actually exists and vice versa). *Examples:* tables in ERP systems, events logs of CRM systems, transaction logs of messaging systems, event logs of high-tech systems, etc.
★★	Events are recorded automatically, i.e., as a by-product of some information system. Coverage varies, i.e., no systematic approach is followed to decide which events are recorded. Moreover, it is possible to bypass the information system. Hence, events may be missing or not recorded properly. *Examples:* event logs of document and product management systems, error logs of embedded systems, worksheets of service engineers, etc.
★	Lowest level: event logs are of poor quality. Recorded events may not correspond to reality and events may be missing. Event logs for which events are recorded by hand typically have such characteristics. *Examples:* trails left in paper documents routed through the organization ("yellow notes"), paper-based medical records, etc.

3.2 GP2: Log Extraction Should Be Driven by Questions

As shown in Fig. 5, process mining activities need to be driven by questions. Without concrete questions it is very difficult to extract meaningful event data. Consider, for example, the thousands of tables in the database of an ERP system like SAP. Without concrete questions it is impossible to select the tables relevant for data extraction.

A process model such as the one shown in Fig. 1 describes the life-cycle of cases (i.e., process instances) of a particular type. Hence, before applying any process mining technique one needs to choose the type of cases to be analyzed. This choice should be driven by the questions that need to be answered and this may be non-trivial. Consider, for example, the handling of customer orders. Each customer order may consist of multiple order lines as the customer may order multiple products in one order. One customer order may result in multiple deliveries. One delivery may refer to order lines of multiple orders. Hence, there is a many-to-many relationship between orders and deliveries and a one-to-many relationship between orders and order lines. Given a database with event data related to orders, order lines, and deliveries, there are different process models that can be discovered. One can extract data with the goal to describe the life-cycle of individual orders. However, it is also possible to extract data with the goal to discover the life-cycle of individual order lines or the life-cycle of individual deliveries.

3.3   GP3: Concurrency, Choice and Other Basic Control-Flow Constructs Should Be Supported

A plethora of process modeling languages exists (e.g., BPMN, EPCs, Petri nets, BPEL, and UML activity diagrams). Some of these languages provide many modeling elements (e.g., BPMN offers more than 50 distinct graphical elements) whereas others are very basic (e.g., Petri nets are composed of only three different elements: places, transitions, and arcs). The control-flow description is the backbone of any process model. Basic workflow constructs (also known as *patterns*) supported by all mainstream languages are sequence, parallel routing (AND-splits/joins), choice (XOR-splits/joins), and loops. Obviously, these patterns should be supported by process mining techniques. However, some techniques are not able to deal with concurrency and support only Markov chains/transition systems.

Figure 6 shows the effect of using process mining techniques unable to discover concurrency (no AND-split/joins). Consider an event log $L = \{\langle A, B, C, D, E \rangle, \langle A, B, D, C, E \rangle, \langle A, C, B, D, E \rangle, \langle A, C, D, B, E \rangle, \langle A, D, B, C, E \rangle, \langle A, D, C, B, E \rangle\}$. L contains cases that start with A and end with E. Activities B, C, and D occur in any order in-between A and E. The BPMN model in Fig. 6(a) shows a compact representation of the underlying process using two AND gateways. Suppose that the process mining technique does not support AND gateways. In this case, the other two BPMN models in Fig. 6 are obvious candidates. The BPMN model in Fig. 6(b) is compact but allows for too much behavior (e.g., cases such as $\langle A, B, B, B, E \rangle$ are possible according to the model but are not likely according to the event log). The BPMN model in Fig. 6(c) allows for the cases in L, but encodes all sequences explicitly, so it is not a compact representation of the log. The example shows that for real-life models having dozens of potentially concurrent activities the resulting models are severely underfitting (i.e., allow for too much behavior) and/or extremely complex if concurrency is not supported.

As is illustrated by Fig. 6, it is important to support at least the basic work-flow patterns. Besides the basic patterns mentioned it is also desirable to support

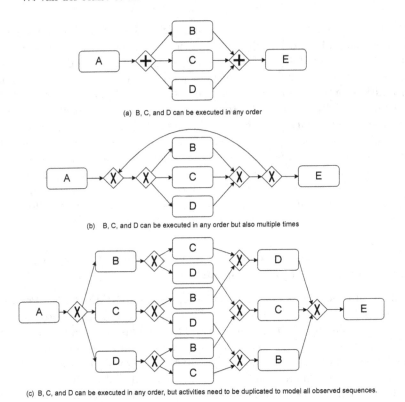

(a) B, C, and D can be executed in any order

(b)   B, C, and D can be executed in any order but also multiple times

(c) B, C, and D can be executed in any order, but activities need to be duplicated to model all observed sequences.

Fig. 6. Example illustrating problems when concurrency (i.e., AND-splits/joins) can-not be expressed directly. In the example just three activities (B, C, and D) are con-current. Imagine the resulting process models when there are 10 concurrent activities ($2^{10} = 1024$ states and $10! = 3,628,800$ possible execution sequences).

OR-splits/joins, because these provide a compact representation of inclusive de-cisions and partial synchronizations.

3.4   GP4: Events Should Be Related to Model Elements

As indicated in Section 2, it is a misconception that process mining is limited to control-flow discovery. As shown in Fig. 1, the discovered process model may cover various perspectives (organizational perspective, time perspective, data perspective, etc.). Moreover, discovery is just one of the three types of process mining shown in Fig. 3. The other two types of process mining (conformance checking and enhancement) heavily rely on the relationship between *elements in the model* and *events in the log*. This relationship may be used to "replay" the event log on the model. Replay may be used to reveal discrepancies between an event log and a model, e.g., some events in the log are not possible according to the model. Techniques for conformance checking quantify and diagnose such discrepancies. Timestamps in the event log can be used to analyze the temporal behavior during replay. Time differences between causally related activities can be used to add expected waiting times to the model. These examples show that the relation between events in the log and elements in the model serves as a starting point for different types of analysis.

In some cases it may be non-trivial to establish such a relationship. For example, an event may refer to two different activities or it is unclear to which activity it refers. Such ambiguities need to be removed in order to interpret process mining results properly. Besides the problem of relating events to activities, there is the problem of relating events to process instances. This is commonly referred to as *event correlation*.

3.5   GP5: Models Should Be Treated as Purposeful Abstractions of Reality

Models derived from event data provide *views on reality*. Such a view should provide a purposeful abstraction of the behavior captured in the event log. Given an event log, there may be multiple views that are useful. Moreover, the various stakeholders may require different views. In fact, models discovered from event logs should be seen as "maps" (like geographic maps). This guiding principle provides important insights, two of which are described in the remainder.

First of all, it is important to note that there is no such thing as "the map" for a particular geographic area. Depending on the intended use there are different maps: road maps, hiking maps, cycling maps, etc. All of these maps show a view on the same reality and it would be absurd to assume that there would be such a thing as "the perfect map". The same holds for process models: the model should emphasize the things relevant for a particular type of user. Discovered models may focus on different perspectives (control-flow, data flow, time, resources, costs, etc.) and show these at different levels of granularity and precision, e.g., a manager may want to see a coarse informal process model focusing on costs whereas a process analyst may want to see a detailed process model focusing on deviations from the normal flow. Also note that different stakeholders may want to view a process at different levels: *strategic level* (decisions at this level have long-term effects and are based on aggregate event data over a longer period), *tactical level* (decisions at this level have medium-term effects and are mostly based on recent data), and *operational level* (decisions at this level have immediate effects and are based on event data related to running cases).

Second, it is useful to adopt ideas from cartography when it comes to producing understandable maps. For example, road maps abstract from less significant roads and cities. Less significant things are either left out or dynamically clustered into aggregate shapes (e.g., streets and suburbs amalgamate into cities). Cartographers not only eliminate irrelevant details, but also use colors to highlight important features. Moreover, graphical elements have a particular size to indicate their significance (e.g., the sizes of lines and dots may vary). Geographical maps also have a clear interpretation of the x-axis and y-axis, i.e., the layout of a map is not arbitrary as the coordinates of elements have a meaning. All of this is in stark contrast with mainstream process models which are typically not using color, size, and location features to make models more understandable. However, ideas from cartography can easily be incorporated in the construction of discovered process maps. For example, the size of an activity can be used to reflect its frequency or some other property indicating its significance (e.g., costs or resource use). The width of an arc can reflect the importance of the corresponding causal dependency, and the coloring of arcs can be used to highlight bottlenecks.

The above observations show that it is important to select the right representation and fine-tune it for the intended audience. This is important for visualizing results to end users and for guiding discovery algorithms towards suitable models (see also Challenge C5).

3.6 GP6: Process Mining Should Be a Continuous Process

Process mining can help to provide meaningful "maps" that are directly connected to event data. Both historical event data and current data can be projected onto such models. Moreover, processes change while they are being analyzed. Given the dynamic nature of processes, it is not advisable to see process mining as a one-time activity. The goal should not be to create a fixed model, but to breathe life into process models so that users and analysts are encouraged to look at them on a daily basis.

Compare this to the use of mashups using geo-tagging. There are thousands of mashups using Google Maps (e.g., applications projecting information about traffic conditions, real estate, fastfood restaurants, or movie showtimes onto a selected map). People can seamlessly zoom in and out using such maps and interact with them (e.g., traffic jams are projected onto the map and the user can select a particular problem to see details). It should also be possible to conduct process mining based on real-time event data. Using the "map metaphor", we can think of events having GPS coordinates that can be projected on maps in real time. Analogous to car navigation systems, process mining tools can help end users (a) by navigating through processes, (b) by projecting dynamic information onto process maps (e.g., showing "traffic jams" in business processes), and (c) by providing predictions regarding running cases (e.g., estimating the "arrival time" of a case that is delayed). These examples demonstrate that it is a pity to not use process models more actively. Therefore, process mining should be viewed as a continuous process providing actionable information according to various time scales (minutes, hours, days, weeks, and months).

4 Challenges

Process mining is an important tool for modern organizations that need to manage non-trivial operational processes. On the one hand, there is an incredible growth of event data. On the other hand, processes and information need to be aligned perfectly in order to meet requirements related to compliance, efficiency, and customer service. Despite the applicability of process mining there are still important challenges that need to be addressed; these illustrate that process mining is an emerging discipline. In the remainder, we list some of these challenges. This list is not intended to be complete and, over time, new challenges may emerge or existing challenges may disappear due to advances in process mining.

4.1   C1: Finding, Merging, and Cleaning Event Data

It still takes considerable efforts to extract event data suitable for process mining. Typically, several hurdles need to be overcome:

- Data may be *distributed* over a variety of sources. This information needs to be merged. This tends to be problematic when different identifiers are used in the different data sources. For example, one system uses name and birthdate to identify a person whereas another system uses the person's social security number.
- Event data are often "object centric" rather than "process centric". For example, individual products, pallets, and containers may have RFID tags and recorded events refer to these tags. However, to monitor a particular customer order such object-centric events need to be merged and preprocessed.
- Event data may be *incomplete*. A common problem is that events do not explicitly point to process instances. Often it is possible to derive this information, but this may take considerable efforts. Also time information may be missing for some events. One may need to interpolate timestamps in order to still use the timing information available.
- An event log may contain *outliers*, i.e., exceptional behavior also referred to as *noise*. How to define outliers? How to detect such outliers? These questions need to be answered to clean event data.
- Logs may contain events at *different levels of granularity*. In the event log of a hospital information system events may refer to simple blood tests or to complex surgical procedures. Also timestamps may have different levels of granularity ranging from milliseconds precision (28-9-2011:h11m28s32ms342) to coarse date information (28-9-2011).
- Events occur in a particular *context* (weather, workload, day of the week, etc.). This context may explain certain phenomena, e.g., the response time is longer than usual because of work-in-progress or holidays. For analysis, it is desirable to incorporate this context. This implies the merging of event data with contextual data. Here the "curse of dimensionality" kicks in as analysis becomes intractable when adding too many variables.

Better tools and methodologies are needed to address the above problems. Moreover, as indicated earlier, organizations need to treat event logs as first-class citizens rather than some by-product. The goal is to obtain ⋆ ⋆ ⋆ ⋆ ⋆ event logs (see Table 1). Here, the lessons learned in the context of datawarehousing are useful to ensure high-quality event logs. For example, simple checks during data entry can help to reduce the proportion of incorrect event data significantly.

4.2   C2: Dealing with Complex Event Logs Having Diverse Characteristics

Event logs may have very different characteristics. Some event logs may be extremely large making it difficult to handle them whereas other event logs are so small that not enough data is available to make reliable conclusions.

In some domains, mind-boggling quantities of events are recorded. Therefore, additional efforts are needed to improve performance and scalability. For example, ASML is continuously monitoring all of its wafer scanners. These wafer scanners are used by various organizations (e.g., Samsung and Texas Instruments) to produce chips (approx. 70% of chips are produced using ASML's wafer scanners). Existing tools have difficulties dealing with the petabytes of data collected in such domains. Besides the number of events recorded there are other characteristics such as the average number of events per case, similarity among cases, the number of unique events, and the number of unique paths. Consider an event log $L1$ with the following characteristics: 1000 cases, on average 10 events per case, and little variation (e.g., several cases follow the same or very similar paths). Event log $L2$ contains just 100 cases, but on average there are 100 events per case and all cases follow a unique path. Clearly, $L2$ is much more difficult to analyze than $L1$ even though the two logs have similar sizes (approximately 10,000 events).

As event logs contain only sample behavior, they should not be assumed to be complete. Process mining techniques need to deal with incompleteness by using an "open world assumption": the fact that something did not happen does not mean that it cannot happen. This makes it challenging to deal with small event logs with a lot of variability.

As mentioned before, some logs contain events at a very low abstraction level. These logs tend to be extremely large and the individual low-level events are of little interest to the stakeholders. Therefore, one would like to aggregate low-level events into high-level events. For example, when analyzing the diagnostic and treatment processes of a particular group of patients one may not be interested in the individual tests recorded in the information system of the hospital's laboratory.

At this point in time, organizations need to use a trial-and-error approach to see whether an event log is suitable for process mining. Therefore, tools should allow for a quick feasibility test given a particular data set. Such a test should indicate potential performance problems and warn for logs that are far from complete or too detailed.

4.3   C3: Creating Representative Benchmarks

Process mining is an emerging technology. This explains why good benchmarks are still missing. For example, dozens of process discovery techniques are available and different vendors offer different products, but there is no consensus on the quality of these techniques. Although there are huge differences in functionality and performance, it is difficult to compare the different techniques and tools.

Therefore, good benchmarks consisting of example data sets and representative quality criteria need to be developed.

For classical data mining techniques, many good benchmarks are available. These benchmarks have stimulated tool providers and researchers to improve the performance of their techniques. In the case of process mining this is more challenging. For example, the relational model introduced by Codd in 1969 is simple and widely supported. As a result it takes little effort to convert data from one database to another and there are no interpretation problems. For processes such a simple model is missing. Standards proposed for process modeling are much more complicated and few vendors support exactly the same set of concepts. Processes are simply more complex than tabular data.

Nevertheless, it is important to create representative benchmarks for process mining. Some initial work is already available. For example, there are various metrics for measuring the quality of process mining results (fitness, simplicity, precision, and generalization). Moreover, several event logs are publicly available (cf. www.processmining.org). See for example the event log used for the first Business Process Intelligence Challenge (BPIC'11) organized by the task force (cf. doi:10.4121/uuid:d9769f3d-0ab0-4fb8-803b-0d1120ffcf54).

On the one hand, there should be benchmarks based on real-life data sets. On the other hand, there is the need to create synthetic datasets capturing particular characteristics. Such synthetic datasets help to develop process mining techniques that are tailored towards incomplete event logs, noisy event logs, or specific populations of processes.

Besides the creation of representative benchmarks, there also needs to be more consensus on the criteria used to judge the quality of process mining results (also see Challenge C6). Moreover, *cross-validation* techniques from data mining can be adapted to judge the result. Consider for example k-fold checking. One can split the event log in k parts. $k-1$ parts can be used to learn a process model and conformance checking techniques can be used to judge the result with respect to the remaining part. This can be repeated k times, thus providing some insights into the quality of the model.

4.4   C4: Dealing with Concept Drift

The term *concept drift* refers to the situation in which the process is changing while being analyzed. For instance, in the beginning of the event log two activities may be concurrent whereas later in the log these activities become sequential. Processes may change due to periodic/seasonal changes (e.g., "in December there is more demand" or "on Friday afternoon there are fewer employees available") or due to changing conditions (e.g., "the market is getting more competitive"). Such changes impact processes and it is vital to detect and analyze them. Concept drift in a process can be discovered by splitting the event log into smaller logs and analyzing the "footprints" of the smaller logs. Such "second order" analysis requires much more event data. Nevertheless, few processes are in steady state and understanding concept drift is of prime importance for the management of processes. Therefore, additional research and tool support are needed to adequately analyze concept drift.

4.5   C5: Improving the Representational Bias Used for Process Discovery

A process discovery technique produces a model using a particular language (e.g., BPMN or Petri nets). However, it is important to separate the visualization of the result from the representation used during the actual discovery process. The selection of a target language often encompasses several implicit assumptions. It limits the search space; processes that cannot be represented by the target language cannot be discovered. This so-called "representational bias" used during the discovery process should be a conscious choice and should not be (only) driven by the preferred graphical representation.

Consider for example Fig. 6: whether the target language allows for concurrency or not may have an effect on both the visualization of the discovered model and the class of models considered by the algorithm. If the representational bias does not allow for concurrency (Fig. 6(a) is not possible) and does not allow for multiple activities having the same label (Fig. 6(c) is not possible), then only problematic models such as the one shown in Fig. 6(b) are possible. This example shows that a more careful and refined selection of the representational bias is needed.

4.6   C6: Balancing between Quality Criteria Such as Fitness, Simplicity, Precision, and Generalization

Event logs are often far from being complete, i.e., only example behavior is given. Process models typically allow for an exponential or even infinite number of different traces (in case of loops). Moreover, some traces may have a much lower probability than others. Therefore, it is unrealistic to assume that every possible trace is present in the event log. To illustrate that it is impractical to take complete logs for granted, consider a process consisting of 10 activities that can be executed in parallel and a corresponding log that contains information about 10,000 cases. The total number of possible interleavings in the model with 10 concurrent activities is $10! = 3,628,800$. Hence, it is impossible that each interleaving is present in the log as there are fewer cases (10,000) than potential traces (3,628,800). Even if there are millions of cases in the log, it is extremely unlikely that all possible variations are present. An additional complication is that some alternatives are less frequent than others. These may be considered as "noise". It is impossible to build a reasonable model for such noisy behaviors. The discovered model needs to abstract from this; it is better to investigate low frequency behavior using conformance checking.

Noise and incompleteness make process discovery a challenging problem. In fact, there are four competing quality dimensions: (a) fitness, (b) simplicity, (c) precision, and (d) generalization. A model with good *fitness* allows for most of the behavior seen in the event log. A model has a perfect fitness if all traces in the log can be replayed by the model from beginning to end. The *simplest* model that can explain the behavior seen in the log is the best model. This principle is known as Occam's Razor. Fitness and simplicity alone are not sufficient to judge the quality of a discovered process model. For example, it is very easy to construct an extremely simple Petri net ("flower model") that is able to replay all traces in an event log (but also any other event log referring to the same set of activities). Similarly, it is undesirable to have a model that only allows for the exact behavior seen in the event log. Remember that the log contains only example behavior and that many traces that are possible may not have been seen yet. A model is *precise* if it does not allow for "too much" behavior. Clearly, the "flower model" lacks precision. A model that is not precise is "underfitting". Underfitting is the problem that the model over-generalizes the example behavior in the log (i.e., the model allows for behaviors very different from what was seen in the log). A model should generalize and not restrict behavior to just the examples seen in the log. A model that does not *generalize* is "overfitting". Overfitting is the problem that a very specific model is generated whereas it is obvious that the log only holds example behavior (i.e., the model explains the particular sample log, but a next sample log of the same process may produce a completely different process model).

Balancing fitness, simplicity, precision and generalization is challenging. This is the reason that most of the more powerful process discovery techniques provide various parameters. Improved algorithms need to be developed to better balance the four competing quality dimensions. Moreover, any parameters used should be understandable by end-users.

4.7   C7: Cross-Organizational Mining

Traditionally, process mining is applied within a single organization. However, as service technology, supply-chain integration, and cloud computing become more widespread, there are scenarios where the event logs of multiple organizations are available for analysis. In principle, there are two settings for *cross-organizational process mining*.

First of all, we may consider the collaborative setting where different organizations work together to handle process instances. One can think of such a cross-organizational process as a "jigsaw puzzle", i.e., the overall process is cut into parts and distributed over organizations that need to cooperate to successfully complete cases. Analyzing the event log within one of these organizations involved is insufficient. To discover end-to-end processes, the event logs of different organizations need to be merged. This is a non-trivial task as events need to be correlated across organizational boundaries.

Second, we may also consider the setting where different organizations are essentially executing the same process while sharing experiences, knowledge, or a common infrastructure. Consider for example Salesforce.com. The sales processes of many organizations are managed and supported by Salesforce. On the one hand, these organizations share an infrastructure (processes, databases, etc.). On the other hand, they are not forced to follow a strict process model as the system can be configured to support variants of the same process. As another example, consider the basic processes executed within any municipality (e.g., issuing building permits). Although all municipalities in a country need to support the same basic set of processes, there may be also be differences. Obviously, it is interesting to analyze such variations among different organizations. These organizations can learn from one another and service providers may improve their services and offer value-added services based on the results of cross-organizational process mining.

New analysis techniques need to be developed for both types of cross-organizational process mining. These techniques should also consider privacy and security issues. Organizations may not want to share information for competitive reasons or due to a lack of trust. Therefore, it is important to develop privacy-preserving process mining techniques.

4.8   C8: Providing Operational Support

Initially, the focus of process mining was on the analysis of historical data. Today, however, many data sources are updated in (near) real-time and sufficient computing power is available to analyze events when they occur. Therefore, process mining should not be restricted to off-line analysis and can also be used for on-line operational support. Three operational support activities can be identified: *detect*, *predict*, and *recommend*. The moment a case deviates from the predefined process, this can be detected and the system can generate an alert. Often one would like to generate such notifications immediately (to still be able to influence things) and not in an off-line fashion. Historical data can be used to build predictive models. These can be used to guide running process instances. For example, it is possible to predict the remaining processing time of a case. Based on such predictions, one can also build recommender systems that propose particular actions to reduce costs or shorten the flow time. Applying process mining techniques in such an online setting creates additional challenges in terms of computing power and data quality.

4.9   C9: Combining Process Mining with other Types of Analysis

Operations management, and in particular operations research, is a branch of management science heavily relying on modeling. Here a variety of mathematical models ranging from linear programming and project planning to queueing models, Markov chains, and simulation are used. Data mining can be defined as "the analysis of (often large) data sets to find unsuspected relationships and to summarize the data in novel ways that are both understandable and useful to the data owner". A wide variety of techniques have been developed: classification (e.g., decision tree learning), regression, clustering (e.g., k-means clustering) and pattern discovery (e.g., association rule learning).

Both fields (operations management and data mining) provide valuable analysis techniques. The challenge is to combine the techniques in these fields with process mining. Consider for example simulation. Process mining techniques can be used to learn a simulation model based on historical data. Subsequently, the simulation model can be used to provide operational support. Because of the close connection between event log and model, the model can be used to replay history and one can start simulations from the current state thus providing a "fast forward button" into the future based on live data.

Similarly, it is desirable to combine process mining with *visual analytics*. Visual analytics combines automated analysis with interactive visualizations for a better understanding of large and complex data sets. Visual analytics exploits the amazing capabilities of humans to see patterns in unstructured data. By combining automated process mining techniques with interactive visual analytics, it is possible to extract more insights from event data.

4.10   C10: Improving Usability for Non-experts

One of the goals of process mining is to create "living process models", i.e., process models that are used on a daily basis rather than static models that end up in some archive. New event data can be used to discover emerging behavior. The link between event data and process models allows for the projection of the current state and recent activities onto up-to-date models. Hence, end-users can interact with the results of process mining on a day-to-day basis. Such interactions are very valuable, but also require intuitive user interfaces. The challenge is to hide the sophisticated process mining algorithms behind user-friendly interfaces that automatically set parameters and suggest suitable types of analysis.

4.11   C11: Improving Understandability for Non-experts

Even if it is easy to generate process mining results, this does not mean that the results are actually useful. The user may have problems understanding the output or is tempted to infer incorrect conclusions. To avoid such problems, the results should be presented using a suitable representation (see also GP5). Moreover, the trustworthiness of the results should always be clearly indicated. There may be too little data to justify particular conclusions. In fact, existing process discovery techniques typically do not warn for a low fitness or for overfitting. They always show a model, even when it is clear that there is too little data to justify any conclusions.

5   Epilogue

The IEEE Task Force on Process Mining aims to (a) promote the application of process mining, (b) guide software developers, consultants, business managers, and end-users when using state-of-the-art techniques, and (c) stimulate research on process mining. This manifesto states the main principles and intentions of the task force. After introducing the topic of process mining, the manifesto catalogs some guiding principles (Section 3) and challenges (Section 4). The guiding principles can be used in order to avoid obvious mistakes. The list of challenges is intended to direct research and development efforts. Both aim to increase the maturity level of process mining.

To conclude, a few words on terminology. The following terms are used in the process mining space: workflow mining, (business) process mining, automated (business) process discovery, and (business) process intelligence. Different organizations seem to use different terms for overlapping concepts. For example, Gartner is promoting the term "Automated Business Process Discovery" (ABPD) and Software AG is using "Process Intelligence" to refer to their controlling platform. The term "workflow mining" seems less suitable as the creation of workflow models is just one of the many possible applications of process mining. Similarly, the addition of the term "business" narrows the scope to certain applications of process mining. There are numerous applications of process mining (e.g., analyzing the use of high-tech systems or analyzing websites) where this addition seems to be inappropriate. Although process discovery is an important part of the process mining spectrum, it is only one of the many use cases. Conformance checking, prediction, organizational mining, social network analysis, etc. are other use cases that extend beyond process discovery.

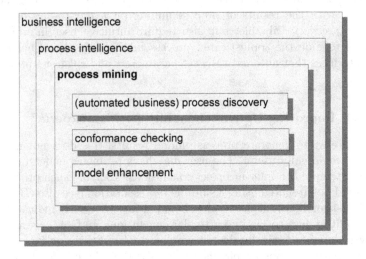

Fig. 7. Relating the different terms

Figure 7 relates some of the terms just mentioned. All technologies and methods that aim at providing actionable information that can be used to support decision making can be positioned under the umbrella of Business Intelligence (BI). (Business) process intelligence can be seen as the combination of BI and BPM, i.e., BI techniques are used to analyze and improve processes and their management. Process mining can be seen as a concretization of process intelligence taking event logs as a starting point. (Automated business) process discovery is just one of the three basic types of process mining. Figure 7 may be a bit misleading in the sense that most BI tools do not provide process mining functionality as described in this document. The term BI is often conveniently skewed towards a particular tool or method covering only a small part of the broader BI spectrum.

There may be commercial reasons for using alternative terms. Some vendors may also want to emphasize a particular aspect (e.g., discovery or intelligence). However, to avoid confusion, it is better to use the term "process mining" for the discipline covered by this manifesto.

Open Access. This chapter is distributed under the terms of the Creative Commons Attribution Noncommercial License which permits any noncommercial use, distribution, and reproduction in any medium, provided the original author(s) and source are credited.

Reference

1. van der Aalst, W.M.P.: Process Mining: Discovery, Conformance and Enhancement of Business Processes. Springer, Berlin (2011)

Glossary

- **Activity**: a well-defined step in the process. Events may refer to the start, completion, cancelation, etc. of an activity for a specific process instance.
- **Automated Business Process Discovery**: see **Process Discovery**.
- **Business Intelligence** (BI): broad collection of tools and methods that use data to support decision making.
- **Business Process Intelligence**: see **Process Intelligence**.
- **Business Process Management** (BPM): the discipline that combines knowledge from information technology and knowledge from management sciences and applies both to operational business processes.
- **Case**: see **Process Instance**.
- **Concept Drift**: the phenomenon that processes often change over time. The observed process may gradually (or suddenly) change due to seasonal changes or increased competition, thus complicating analysis.
- **Conformance Checking**: analyzing whether reality, as recorded in a log, conforms to the model and vice versa. The goal is to detect discrepancies and to measure their severity. Conformance checking is one of the three basic types of process mining.
- **Cross-Organizational Process Mining**: the application of process mining techniques to event logs originating from different organizations.
- **Data Mining**: the analysis of (often large) data sets to find unexpected relationships and to summarize the data in ways that provide new insights.
- **Event**: an action recorded in the log, e.g., the start, completion, or cancelation of an activity for a particular process instance.

- **Event Log**: collection of events used as input for process mining. Events do not need to be stored in a separate log file (e.g., events may be scattered over different database tables).
- **Fitness**: a measure determining how well a given model allows for the behavior seen in the event log. A model has a perfect fitness if all traces in the log can be replayed by the model from beginning to end.
- **Generalization**: a measure determining how well the model is able to allow for unseen behavior. An "overfitting" model is not able to generalize enough.
- **Model Enhancement**: one of the three basic types of process mining. A process model is extended or improved using information extracted from some log. For example, bottlenecks can be identified by replaying an event log on a process model while examining the timestamps.
- **MXML**: an XML-based format for exchanging event logs. XES replaces MXML as the new tool-independent process mining format.
- **Operational Support**: on-line analysis of event data with the aim to monitor and influence running process instances. Three operational support activities can be identified: *detect* (generate an alert if the observed behavior deviates from the modeled behavior), *predict* (predict future behavior based on past behavior, e.g., predict the remaining processing time), and *recommend* (suggest appropriate actions to realize a particular goal, e.g., to minimize costs).
- **Precision**: measure determining whether the model prohibits behavior very different from the behavior seen in the event log. A model with low precision is "underfitting".
- **Process Discovery**: one of the three basic types of process mining. Based on an event log a process model is learned. For example, the α algorithm is able to discover a Petri net by identifying process patterns in collections of events.
- **Process Instance**: the entity being handled by the process that is analyzed. Events refer to process instances. Examples of process instances are customer orders, insurance claims, loan applications, etc.
- **Process Intelligence**: a branch of Business Intelligence focusing on Business Process Management.
- **Process Mining**: techniques, tools, and methods to discover, monitor and improve real processes (i.e., not assumed processes) by extracting knowledge from event logs commonly available in today's (information) systems.
- **Representational Bias**: the selected target language for presenting and constructing process mining results.
- **Simplicity**: a measure operationalizing Occam's Razor, i.e., the simplest model that can explain the behavior seen in the log, is the best model. Simplicity can be quantified in various ways, e.g., number of nodes and arcs in the model.
- **XES**: is an XML-based standard for event logs. The standard has been adopted by the IEEE Task Force on Process Mining as the default interchange format for event logs (cf. www.xes-standard.org)

Assessing Support for Community Workflows in Localisation

Aram Morera, Lamine Aouad, and J.J. Collins

Localisation Research Centre - Centre for Next Generation Localisation (CNGL)
Dept. of Computer Science and Information Systems
University of Limerick, Limerick, Ireland
{aram.morera-mesa,lamine.aouad,j.j.collins}@ul.ie

Abstract. This paper identifies a set of workflow patterns necessary to support community-oriented localisation. Workflow pattern discovery is based on use case analysis of five community translation tools, and modelled using the Yet Another Workflow Language (YAWL) notation. An analysis is presented of the support for these baseline patterns in two mainstream enterprise-oriented Translation Management Systems (TMS) - GlobalSight and WorldServer. A gap is identified with respect to the emerging need for community-oriented workflows and their potential support in mainstream enterprise localisation architectures.

Keywords: crowdsourcing, workflows, workflow patterns, localization, automation.

1 Introduction

The Localization Industry Standards Association (LISA) describe localisation as "the process of modifying products or services to account for differences in distinct markets" [1]. Localisation also includes infrastructural support such as project management, engineering, quality assurance, and human-computer interface design issues [2]. Globalisation and pervasive internet access are driving demand for localised content at lower cost without sacrificing quality. However, this demand is not currently satisfied, and the resulting deficit is referred to as the *digital divide*. Overcoming this challenge will require higher levels of automation [3], such as the use of workflow enactment engines to support the business processes. In addition, it is argued that use of the crowdsourcing paradigm through community-oriented localisation infrastructures will be necessary [3]. Combining crowdsourcing and automation through workflows requires the specification of community-oriented localisation workflows.

Traditional approaches to localisation as embodied in enterprise level platforms have embraced automation support at various points in the workflow. For example, Translation Memory (TM) tools such as TRADOS, Deja vu, and Wordfast, to name a few, facilitate increasing consistency within and across projects, and free translators from manually intensive operations such as copying and pasting of text that had already been

F. Daniel et al. (Eds.): BPM 2011 Workshops, Part I, LNBIP 99, pp. 195–206, 2012.

translated. Machine Translation has made it possible to deliver lower quality translation at almost no cost in near real-time. In addition, Translation Management Systems (TMS) orchestrate the business functions, project tasks, process workflows and language technologies that underpin large-scale translation activity [4].

These systems were designed to help enterprise level Language Service Providers (LSPs) to translate large amounts of content using a predominantly freelance workforce [5]. The emergence of the crowdsourcing paradigm and Web 2.0 has allowed companies and NGOs to leverage the community to do the translation [6]. Two examples of NGOs doing this are The Rosetta Foundation and Translate.org.za. Facebook [7] and PcTools [8] are for profit companies that have developed proprietary tools in order to leverage their communities to translate their strings for free. Other examples include open source projects such as Ubuntu [9], LibreOffice and Firefox that are localized by their communities [10]. This community-based approach is seen as a necessary tactic to address the ever growing demand for localised content [3].

Different strategies and technologies have been adopted by these organizations to carry out their community-oriented localisation projects. This paper analyzes the community-oriented approaches enabled by the localisation technologies of Crowdin, Facebook, Asia Online, Pootle, and LaunchPad. Use cases are recovered for these community translation tools through manual screen scrapes and/or analysis of user manuals. Workflow patterns are suggested for these use cases that will best support the desired functionality, with some additional patterns incorporated to enhance the quality of the service. These patterns discovered through use case analysis constitute a baseline for community-oriented localisation workflows. This baseline is used for comparison with the patterns supported in two mainstream enterprise-oriented localisation industry TMS tools - GlobalSight and WorldServer. This facilitates the identification of the gap in workflow support between enterprise and the emerging community-oriented paradigm based on crowdsourcing.

Section 2 of this paper presents a series of use cases for community translation tools and the workflows that emerge from them. Section 3 presents the TMSs that were used; and a mapping study showing their support for the patterns that were discovered in section 2. The paper concludes with a discussion in section 4 that outlines future research directions.

2   Discovering Community-Oriented Workflows

Use cases are captured in order to identify the patterns that should be supported. Use cases are descriptions of sequences of interactions between the system and its users [11]. If a pattern can be mapped to the actions in a use case, it is deemed necessary to support it for community translation. The sequence pattern is not included in these use cases as it is an implicit requirement for any kind of workflow. For Asia online and Facebook, the process was followed as captured from talks given by Losse [7] and Vashee [12]. For Crowdin, Pootle, and LaunchPad, a number of projects and user accounts were created. Projects were executed by simulating a crowd using the different user accounts that were harnessed to provide translations, votes and comments by iterating through the fields in the screens presented. These screens were used to specify use cases. The use cases are the basis for workflows that are modelled using Yet Another Workflow Language (YAWL) [13] with the notation shown in figure 1. Note that the OR Join and the OR Split can map to different patterns, that the shading does not carry any implicit semantics, and that the sequence pattern has not been made explicit in the use cases.

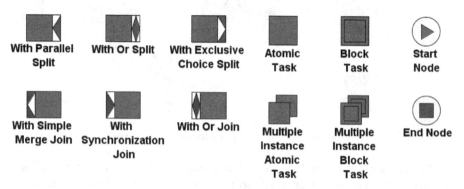

Fig. 1. Workflow notations

2.1   Use cases

The use cases are presented next for a subset of the targeted platforms.

Crowdin

Crowdin has been used to localize products such as the Android app Titanium Backup that has 0.5 - 1 million users. Three different accounts were created, one for the project manager and the other two in order to simulate a crowd. A project can be configured as *managed* in that members of the crowd have to be accepted by the project manager; or *open* in that anyone can participate. The crowd has access to the source text, translations from Crowdin's TM, and translations from Google's and Microsoft's Machine Translation (MT) systems, once the source files have been uploaded in the designated file format. They can then suggest alternative translations or vote for or against other translations. The project creator can give extra rights at any time to any user who then becomes a group leader. The project creator and the group leaders can also approve translations that are then hidden from the crowd. This system creates a *Multiple Instances without Synchronization* task for each new file. Each instance corresponds to a translation unit, their number is known at run time and each instance is an independent thread that does not block the progress of the workflow if it is not executed. These instances consist of a subworkflow that commences with a pre-translation stage that has three tasks: Google MT translation, Bing MT translation and Crowdin's TM leverage. These three tasks happen in parallel and thus a *Parallel Split* must precede them. Crowdin's TM may present none or more matches, this means that it is a *Multiple Instances without a priori Run-Time Knowledge* task. Because the MT systems may fail and the TM may produce no results, the control thread must converge over an *Acyclic Synchronizing Merge*.

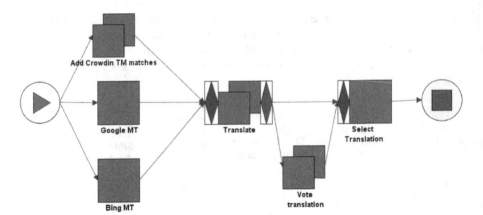

Fig. 2. YAWL representation - Crowdin's translate and vote subworkflow

After the merge, the crowd can suggest their own translations. Since multiple users can suggest translations and any single user can suggest a number of translations, this is a *Multiple Instances without a priori Run-Time knowledge* task. A translation can be voted upon until it is approved. As with the suggest-translation task, the number of votes that a translation will receive before it is approved is not known and it is therefore modelled as a *Multiple Instances without a priori Run-Time knowledge* task. Since a translation can be approved before it receives any votes, the split that follows the suggest-translation task must be a *Multichoice Split*. As the control flow can pass directly from the suggest-translation task to the approve-translation task, the approve translation task must be preceded by an *Acyclic Synchronizing Merge*, so that an absence of votes does not stall the flow. At any time a user with the right permissions can declare the project finished. To be able to react to this signal the system must support the *Transient Trigger* pattern. This triggers the cancellation of all the activities in the case without making the case unsuccessful, thus requiring the *Cancel Region* pattern. The cancellation of tasks prevents the creation of new work items and causes the implicit termination of the case, which requires support for the *Implicit Termination* pattern.

Figure 2 illustrates a YAWL representation of the translate-and-vote subworkflow.

Asia Online
Asia Online has translated part of the content of English Wikipedia to Thai using MT and a selected community of users [12]. Each document goes through an MT translation process. After this 3 instances of a post-edition task are created. To support this it is necessary to use the *Multiple Instances with a priori Design-Time Knowledge* pattern. These post-edition instances are carried out by one community member each. Then, their corrections are compared. As waiting for the three instances to finish is required, this means that support for the *Synchronization* pattern is also required. If two corrections are the same they are automatically sent to the authoritative translation database, otherwise, the corrections go to an administrator. To support this you must support the *Exclusive choice* pattern. The administrator selects the

authoritative version, the alternative translations for storage and the bad translations that are discarded. This is an example action requiring the support of the *Multichoice* split pattern. In the case of the alternative translations, there could be one, two or none being sent for storage and that requires supporting the *Multiple Instances without a priori Run-Time knowledge* pattern.

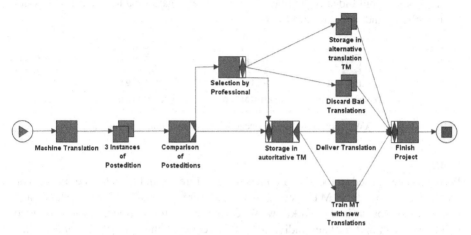

Fig. 3. YAWL representation of Asia Online's workflow

The case of the bad translations being discarded is the same. Zero or more translations could be discarded thus requiring the *Multiple Instances without a priori Run-Time knowledge* pattern. The translations that are added to the authoritative TM are then used in the delivered translation to train the MT. This means that the *Parallel Split* pattern is required. The delivery of the translation, discarding the bad translation(s), storing the alternative translations, and training the MT engine all happen before closing the project. However, the project could close without any translation being stored in the alternative translation TM or being discarded. To support this, one must use the *Acyclic Synchronizing Merge*. After this is done, the project is closed in an explicit manner. This requires support for the *Explicit Termination* pattern. A YAWL representation of this workflow is depicted in figure 3.

Facebook

Facebook uses different models for localisation depending on the language [7]. One of their models lets the users suggest translations for the strings in the User Interface (UI). Because we have a known number of strings and they may individually undergo the translation and voting subworkflow, we need a *Multiple Instances without Synchronization* task where each TU corresponds to an instance.

Each string can receive multiple translation suggestions from an unknown number of users in the subworkflow. Supporting this requires supporting the *Multiple Instances without a priori Run-Time Knowledge* pattern. Once a translation is suggested, an unknown number of users will rate it. This again requires supporting the *Multiple Instances without a priori Run-Time Knowledge* pattern. The suggestion with the highest rating is selected and becomes the translation that appears on the UI, but this may be replaced later by a more popular translation. In order to support the translations being replaced over time, we need once more support for the *Multiple Instances without a priori Run-Time Knowledge* pattern. A YAWL representation of the translate and vote subworkflow in Facebook is depicted in figure 4.

Facebook's would ideally support the implicit termination pattern, but this has not been explicitly indicated by Losse [7].

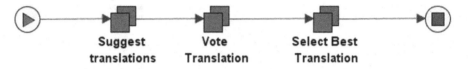

	Suggest	Vote	Select Best
	translations	Translation	Translation

Fig. 4. YAWL representation of Facebook's translate and vote subworkflow

Pootle

Pootle has been used to localize products such as Firefox and LibreOffice. Pootle can obtain suggestions from MT systems, but these were not enabled in our instance and hence do not appear in the workflow. When a user creates a project, a file is divided in TUs that can be translated individually thus requiring the *Multiple Instances without Synchronization* pattern.

The subworkflow starts with a pre-translation task that leverages Pootle's TM. Two tasks can happen concurrently after the leverage: translation suggestion and translation submission. To support this concurrency we need to precede the tasks with a *Parallel Split*. The translation-suggestion task can be carried out an unknown number of times by an unknown number of users. The *Multiple Instances without a priori Run-Time Knowledge* pattern is required to support this interaction. The submit translation task can be carried out directly after the leverage, or after some translations have been suggested. This implies the need for an *Acyclic Synchronizing Merge* where the arches from the leverage and suggest translation tasks meet. After the submission forty seven automatic quality checks are concurrently carried out. Concurrence of different tasks again requires support for the *Parallel Split* pattern. The system waits until all the tests are finished to display the errors, thus requiring the *Synchronization* pattern. The number of errors is not known until the checks are carried out and displayed, and implies support for the *Multiple Instances without a priori Run-Time Knowledge* pattern. To allow users with the right permissions to solve zero or more of the issues the system must support the *Multiple Instances without a priori Run-Time Knowledge* pattern. A YAWL representation of this subworkflow is shown in figure 5.

At any time a user with the right permissions can declare the project finished. To be able to react to this signal the system must support the *Transient Trigger* pattern. This triggers the cancellation of all the activities in the case without making the case unsuccessful, thus requiring the *Cancel Region* pattern. The cancellation of tasks prevents the creation of new work items and causes implicit termination of the case, which requires support for the *Implicit Termination* pattern.

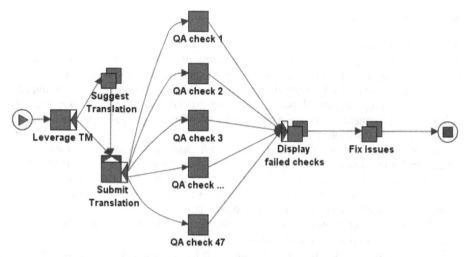

Fig. 5. YAWL representation of Pootle's translation subworkflow

3   Mapping Study and Analysis

A set of control flow patterns have emerged from the use cases above. In this section, the support for those patterns in the workflow engine of two TMSs is analysed. TMSs were developed to satisfy the automation needs of traditional LSPs; however their workflow modules may not be flexible enough to render them suitable for community localisation. A number of additional patterns are identified and added to the list because of their potential suitability for crowdsourcing in an enterprise workflow.

3.1   TMS Selection

According to Rinsche [5] eighty eight out of five hundred and sixty two companies claim to be using a TMS. Of these, eighty six stated that they were using systems developed in-house. While these numbers agree with Sargent [18], the report questions the validity of these responses given the confusion with respect to the description of a TMS. Two of the systems named in the report will serve as a reference - GlobalSight and WorldServer. These systems were chosen because both of them fit the description given by Sargent and DePalma [4], and their support for workflow configurations that go beyond the lineal workflow.

Both GlobalSight and WorldServer include a series of workflows by default and have workflow management engines that can be used to enact any other workflow that they support. Russell [14] suggested that the support for certain patterns could be used to assess the suitability of a workflow system for a project. This suggestion is followed by analysing the suitability of these off-the-shelf products for localisation projects that involve a community.

3.2   Relevant Patterns

Basic Control Patterns

Table 1 shows support for basic control patterns in GlobalSight and WorldServer. Only *Parallel Split* and *Synchronization* are not supported by GlobalSight. This is due to GlobalSight's inability to support concurrent tasks, and does not negatively impact its suitability for enterprise based localisation workflows. There are examples of successful deployments in companies such as salesforce.com [15], Spartan Consulting, and YYZ Translations [16].

WorldServer's support for the *Parallel Split* and *Synchronization* patterns is limited and offered via its parallel revision and parallel subworkflow constructs. The parallel review construct ties each *Parallel Split* to a *Synchronization* that is always followed by an *Exclusive Choice* split. The construct limits thus the power of these patterns that could have been combined in other manners.

Although its functionality differs, from the point of view of control the control flow patterns works like the parallel review construct.

In the context of crowdsourcing, it would also be necessary to support parallelism followed by a free choice of joins, specially the *Acyclic Synchronizing* merge for crowdsourcing. WorldServer's support for the *Parallel Split* is therefore considered incomplete.

Table 1.

Basic Control	GlobalSight	WorldServer
Parallel Split	0	1*
Synchronization	0	1*
Exclusive Choice	1	1

Advanced Branching and Synchronizing Patterns

Table 2 shows support for advanced branching and synchronization patterns in GlobalSight and WorldServer. Neither of the systems supports any of the advanced branching patterns that emerged from the use cases. This illustrates that traditional TMSs are probably not suited for the management of community translations efforts. Supporting the *Acyclic Synchronizing Merge* appears to be a pre-requisite, given that, in crowdsourcing, tasks may be delayed or not undertaken for long periods of time.

Table 2.

Advanced Branching	GlobalSight	WorldServer
Multichoice	0	0
Acyclic Synchronizing Merge	0	0

Structural Patterns

Table 3 shows support for structural patterns in GlobalSight and WorldServer. Although no use cases brought up any of the two looping patterns, one can argue that support for them would be useful in crowdsourcing scenarios and both TMSs support these constructs. Where in traditional localisation workflows it is common to find a translate-review loop, crowdsourcing processes replace this with multiple instances that include the corrections that would usually emerge from the reviews. This system prevents collaborators from finding out why their translation was not approved and hinders thus their learning experience. Although support for the structured loop pattern is a requirement for traditional translation/review loop, none of the TMSs has functionality to count the number of iterations carried out that would be necessary in community workflows. This issue is implicitly acknowledged by GlobalSight as none of its preconfigured workflows uses any kind of loop. Also in the case of the *Arbitrary Cycle* pattern, the issue of the lack of a counter means that the use of this pattern could result in an infinite loop.

Table 3.

Structural Patterns	GlobalSight	WorldServer
Arbitrary Cycles	1	1
Structured Loop	1	1
Recursion	0	1
Implicit Termination	0	0
Explicit Termination	1	1

The use case analysis did not demonstrate a need for the *Recursion* pattern, but it could be useful for crowdsourcing. For example, it would be useful to let testing call themselves, if during a bug test another bug emerged. Although it is not apparent, WorldServer supports *Recursion* through the subworkflow and parallel subworkflows constructs. Both systems support the explicit termination pattern that appeared only in the Asia Online use case, but neither implements the implicit termination pattern that appears in several of the other use cases.

Multiple Instance Patterns
Table 4 shows support for multiple instance patterns in GlobalSight and WorldServer, again emphasizing the fact that GlobalSight and WorldServer are traditional TMS systems developed to support LSP project management practices. Only WorldServer supports one of the multiple instance patterns - *Multiple Instances with a priori Design-Time Knowledge* pattern. This makes perfect sense with respect to the use cases of traditional localisation where resource utilization is maximized by having a one-to-one mapping only, for example, between translators and files.

The *Multiple Instances with a priori Run-Time Knowledge*, like the *Multiple Instances with a priori Design-Time Knowledge* pattern, implies a need for synchronization later on. If these patterns are used in crowdsourcing, they may cause a stall of the progression of the workflow as the more difficult tasks may not be tackled by any member. However, applying them implies guaranteeing that tasks involved in the pattern are completed before moving on to the next step. This feature is potential useful and the reason why the pattern has been added to the list of required patterns.

Table 4.

Multiple Instances	GlobalSight	WorldServer
Multiple Instances without Synchronization	0	0
Multiple Instances with a priori Design-Time knowledge	0	1
Multiple Instances with a priori Run-Time knowledge	0	0
Multiple Instances without a priori Run-Time knowledge	0	0

Supporting *Multiple Instances without Synchronization* allows a number of activities to start and be carried out independently without blocking the progress of other activities at any point.

Cancellation Patterns
Both systems support cancelling a case, but only in reaction to a trigger given by the project administrators.

Table 5.

Cancellation Patterns	GlobalSight	WorldServer
Cancel Case	1	1
Cancel Region	0	0

Trigger patterns
Both systems support triggers from manual cancellation signals, and this does not constitute proper support of the pattern.

Table 6.

Trigger Patterns	GlobalSight	WorldServer
Transient Trigger	1	1

4   Conclusion and Discussion

This comparative study identifies a list of seventeen patterns with thirteen emerging from the use cases and the remaining four being added for completeness of the specification. GlobalSight has partial/full support for six of these patterns, of which four appear in the use cases. Likewise, WorldServer has partial/full support for ten, seven of which were recovered from use cases. While this coverage is incomplete, Van Der Aalst states that none of the general purpose workflow systems offer support for all the patterns in the catalogue [17]. Furthermore, TMSs being specialized tools are invariably developed using a subset of patterns in this catalogue. Both systems can be extended by means of their Application Programming Interfaces (API) potentially enabling support for missing patterns. The mapping study demonstrates that TMSs designed to support traditional enterprise-oriented localisation workflows do not map cleanly to crowdsourced localisation scenarios because of the gaps identified.

A limitation of this comparative study is the number of systems evaluated. Enterprise tools such as Lingotek support a workflow that uses crowdsource-like translation, and MemoQ with its online document management module allows a type of interaction that fits with the crowdsourcing approach to localisation [18]. Furthermore, GlobalSight has been extended with a module called CrowdSight that intends to make it suitable to support crowdsourcing.

Besides this limitation, the community tools discussed focus on the translation task. The crowdsourcing model, with processes unmarred by deadlines, executed by many actors and tasks that can be left incomplete, if applied to them, will probably generate the same set of patterns for other processes, like terminology and QA, however, at the time of this writing, no tools or data were available to back up this claim.

The next phase of this research will expand the number of subjects and include the platforms mentioned. However, initial modelling of the patterns required to support the use cases of the community tools reveal that a crowdsourcing workflow system would have to implement several patterns for parallel tasks, multiple instance tasks, and advanced merging patterns that allow the progression of the workflow without the tasks being complete.

Acknowledgement. This research is supported by the Science Foundation Ireland (Grant 07/CE/I1142) as part of the Centre for Next Generation Localisation (www.cngl.ie) at University of Limerick.

References

[1] Lommel, A.: The Localization Industry Primer. 2nd edn., SMP Marketing and LISA (2003),
http://www.cit.griffith.edu.au/~davidt/
cit3611/LISAprimer.pdf

[2] Schaeler, R.: Communication as a Key to Global Business. Connecting People with Technology: Issues in Professional Communication. In: Hayhoe, G.F., Grady, H.M. (eds.) Baywood Publishing Company (2008)

[3] Van Genabith, J.: Next Generation Localisation. Localisation Focus 8(1), 4–10 (2009)

[4] Sargent, B., DePalma, D.: Translation Management Systems: Assessment of Commercial and LSP specific TMS Offerings. Common Sense Advisory (2008)

[5] Rinsche, A., Portera-Zanotti, N.: Study on the size of the language industry in the EU. European Commission (2009)

[6] Ray, R., Kelly, N.: Crowdsourced Translation Best Practices for Implementation. Common Sense Advisory (2011)

[7] Losse, K.: Facebook - Achieving Quality in a Crowd-sourced Translation Environment. In: LRC XIII Localisation4 All Conference, Ireland (2008)

[8] Rickard, J.: Translation in the Community. In: LRC XIV Localisation in The Cloud Conference, Limerick, Ireland (September 2009)

[9] Mackenzie, A.: Internationalization: software, universality and otherness. Internationalizatio In Java (2006)

[10] Dalvit, L., Terzoli, A., et al.: Opensource software and localisation in indigenous South African languages with Pootle. In: SATNAC 2008 (2008)

[11] Cockburn, A.: Writing effective use cases. Addison-Wesley (2001)

[12] Vashee, K.: MT Technology in the Cloud - An evolving model. In: LRC XIV, Localisation in The Cloud Conference, Limerick, Ireland (2009)

[13] Russell, N., ter Hofstede, A.H.M., et al.: newYAWL: achieving comprehensive patterns support in workflow for the control-flow, data and resource perspectives. BPM Center, Report BPM-07-05, BPMcenter.org (2007)

[14] Russell, N., ter Hofstede, A.H.M., et al.: Workflow Control-Flow Patterns: A Revised View. BPM Center Technical Report BPM-06-22 (2006)

[15] Wunderlich, M.: Our Globalsight migration - lessons learnt (June 2011), http://www.martinwunderlich.com/?p=48

[16] Ghaznawi, S.: GlobalSight and LSPs. ELIA Networking Days, Istanbul (2010)

[17] Van Der Aalst, W.M.P., ter Hofstede, A.H.M., et al.: Workflow patterns. Distributed and Parallel Databases 14(1), 5–51 (2003)

[18] Sargent, B.: Translation Management Systems and Subcategories. Multilingual 18(3), 83–86 (2007)

Non-intrusive Capture of Business Processes Using Social Software
Capturing the End Users' Tacit Knowledge

David Martinho[1,2] and António Rito Silva[1,2]

[1] IST/Technical University of Lisbon, Av. Rovisco Pais, 1049-001, Lisbon, Portugal
{davidmartinho,rito.silva}@ist.utl.pt
[2] ESW Software Engineering Group - INESC-ID, Rua Alves Redol 9, Lisbon, Portugal

Abstract. The participation of end users on the collaborative design of business process models is particularly challenging because they do not master the existing formal business process modeling languages, and they regard business processes on a case-by-case perspective. On the other hand, end users wish to focus their efforts on their daily work and do not want to be interrupted with peculiar modeling tasks. However, regarding the importance of tacit knowledge about business processes, how can this end users' knowledge be captured non-intrusively?

This paper presents an ad-hoc workflow system that focus on supporting and capturing human-interactions while using a non-intrusive strategy in the context of end users' daily operations, and with the support of social software features. Additionally, the information collected through this approach can readily be provided to other stakeholders, including other end users, fostering an implicit collaboration among them.

Keywords: BPM, LAP, End Users, Tacit Knowledge, Social Software, Bottom-Up, Collaboration.

1 Introduction

Even in organizations that provide workflow systems to support the execution of their business processes, there are informal flows of work concurrently occurring. A common example of these "off-the-record" flows of work is the email messages that employees use to easily coordinate themselves and exchange information.

Currently, business process mining efforts try to extract business process models from the existing interaction patterns between the employees, which are captured in email logs. However, given the unstructured nature of email, and the consequent incompleteness of their logs, there are some limitations in relying solely on such mining techniques to build reliable and complete business process models [1].

Concerning these limitations, new socially-empowered Business Process Management Systems (BPMSs)[1] are emerging, claiming to improve collaborative

---

[1] (e.g. ArisAlign (http://www.arisalign.com/), Activiti (http://www.activiti.org), IBM BPM BlueWorks (http://www.blueworkslive.com)).

F. Daniel et al. (Eds.): BPM 2011 Workshops, Part I, LNBIP 99, pp. 207–218, 2012.

modeling among business process stakeholders given their use of social software features. Nevertheless, the explicit addition of social software functionalities is somehow considered intrusive[2] not only because it requires for end users[3] to make a direct use of those features, but also because modeling is an exogenous activity to the execution of business processes.

In this paper, we present a non-intrusive ad-hoc workflow system enriched with social software features, which allows the capture of human-interactions within the organization, and across organizations.

The system is defined as non-intrusive since it does not require for end users to know and use formal business process modeling languages to participate in modeling sessions, and neither to explicitly use social software features.

The system design is based on the Language-Action Perspective (LAP) model constructs, which is enriched with social software features that are embedded and contextualized seamlessly in the BPMS proposed.

In Section 2, we contextualize and identify the problem of capturing the important end user's empirical knowledge. Then, in Section 3, a set of required qualities is identified and the model, which is supported by the LAP, is explained. Then, in Section 4, the system's implementation is depicted. Section 5 introduces some related work, and finally, in Section 6, some concluding remarks and future work directives are highlighted.

2   Problem

We have identified the existence of perspective, language and skill gaps between the different business process stakeholders [11]. Hence, to provide a business process management system that supports different type of stakeholders to collaborate in a more fruitful manner, we must acknowledge for such gaps without requiring the stakeholders to bridge the gaps by themselves. In this paper, we focus on the end users and on the potential contribution supported by the important tacit knowledge they own. The term *tacit knowledge* was initially conceptualized by Polanyi when he described it as the fact that *"we can know more than we can tell or knowing how to do something without thinking about it"* [12]. Later on, Polanyi stated that tacit knowledge is closely related to the concept of skill, and is acquired essentially through practical experience in different contexts, being extremely difficult to externalize [13].

The tacit knowledge owned by end users is important when constructing business process models, however, those who execute business processes are not expected to understand and use formal business process modeling languages such as the Business Process Modeling Notation (BPMN) or Event-driven Process Chain (EPC) [14], and neither to perform tasks (e.g. modeling tasks) which are

---

[2] We refer to intrusive as the enforcing of competencies that are peculiar or unfamiliar to the subject.

[3] We refer to end users as those who are concerned solely with the execution of business processes.

peculiar to their competencies [16]. Such expectations would result in requirements considered to be intrusive to the end user, whose daily core activity is, and should continue to be, the execution of business processes.

The main problem this paper focus on resides on how can that important end users' knowledge be captured in a non-intrusively manner.

Currently, there are solutions based on business process mining techniques that intend to capture the end users' knowledge without being intrusive: the mining of email logs [1]. Through the mining of email logs, human interactions between end users can be captured, and patterns of execution can be identified to build business process models. Another emerging solution that aims to capture this tacit knowledge focus on empowering end users with social software features within their working environments. The addition of social software features (e.g. activity streams, tagging, commentaries, blogs, wikis, etc...) intends to enrich the information concerning the execution of business processes.

The main problem with the log mining solution is that email mainly consists of unstructured data, thus, their respective logs provide poor and incomplete information about the flow of work and its inherent data structure [2]. Also, the main objective of the information sources from which the logs are created is not the capture of workflow, a fact that biases the qualities supporting the business process model's completeness.

On the other hand, the other solution intends to compensate the model incompleteness issue by requiring end users to explicitly provide enriched information about what they are doing, through the use of social software features. However, despite the fact that stakeholders of business processes perceive some benefits between the classical and new socially-empowered BPMS, they still regard the explicit use of social software features as intrusive.

This paper proposes to tackle the identified problems by presenting a pure ad-hoc workflow system that focus on simultaneously supporting and capturing human-interactions within the organization, while concerning the important aspect of being non-intrusive when gathering important information needed to build more complete and structured business process models.

3   Human-Driven Business Processes Model

In our previous research, we already regarded the importance of the end users' contribution to the modeling of business processes. We suggested the embedding of social software features into business process tools, aiming to involve both the end users and the modelers [18]. Aware of the importance of end users' contribution, we proposed an implementation model in [17], which empowered end users to execute business processes in a flexible way while capturing their implicit knowledge in a more structured manner.

In this paper, we acknowledge the intrusiveness issues associated to the collaboration of different business process stakeholders, and while focusing on the end user, we present a system that aims for a more structured and complete capture of their important tacit knowledge. However, before introducing such system, we need to identify which qualities are required given the problems identified in the previous section:

Non-Intrusiveness
When capturing the tacit knowledge owned by the end users, we must ensure that such capture is done in a non-intrusive manner, i.e., that end users are not exposed to the use and understanding of formal notations (e.g. BPMN, EPC, etc...), that end users are not required to make direct usage of social software to enrich the execution supporting entities, and neither interrupted from their daily work to participate on formal process modeling sessions.

Structured Data
End users usually exchange artifacts in a unstructured manner, facing issues such as the poor-management of replicated data (e.g. email messages). In order to provide structure to the entities supporting the flow of work, we must identify what data is exchanged, and, more importantly, how is that data structured so that we can support their associated lifecycle.

Completeness
Capturing human-interactions and the structure of exchanged data is not sufficient to obtain complete information about the underlying business process model and its respective set of business rules capable of supporting those work coordinations. The system must support the semantic enrichment of that information by end users, using embedded social software features, while sustaining the intrusiveness qualities that we focus on.

Synthesization
Ad-hoc workflows can result on a wide variety of cases that may be similar, but end users are not able to identify them as such. We claim that the use of awareness mechanisms on top of the semantic information provided by end users will promote the sharing of work practices. This will also help on the identification of a set of generic tasks that are executed by the end users, and how those tasks are structured and related in order to provide a more detailed information to the modeling efforts.

In order to achieve the qualities described above, while setting the non-intrusiveness quality as our architectural driver, we devise our system to embrace the LAP. The LAP acknowledges how important communication is within organizations, focusing on how people communicate, on how language is used to create a common shared reality, and on how people communicate when coordinating their activities [15]. By embracing this LAP, we propose a model which empowers our system to non-intrusively capture the human-interactions required to execute a particular business process. In order to provide flexibility and not constrain those human-interactions, the model is based in a pure ad-hoc strategy, allowing end users to dynamically create the entities that support their flow of work. To better explain this model and relate it to the required qualities identified above, we consider four aspects of our model: interaction, data, social and awareness.

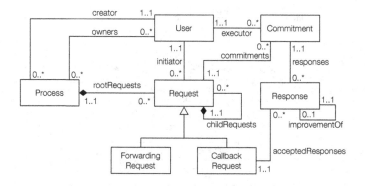

Fig. 1. Interaction Aspect Model

3.1 Interaction Aspect

If we want to capture the tacit knowledge that end users own about business processes, we must provide support for their interaction. The interaction aspect, illustrated in Figure 1, supports and captures the interactions between end users during the execution of a business process. Following a request-response mechanism, an end user (*initiator*) asks another end user (*executor*) to perform some particular work (*request*). To support this, we consider two types of requests: when using a *callback request*, the initiator expects the executor to commit into providing a response to his request; on the other hand, when the initiator uses the *forwarding request*, he expects for its executor to commit to that thread of execution of the business process, i.e, there is no response and the respective workflow responsibility thread of the initiator is completely delegated to the executor. Depending on the claiming policy defined by the initiator of a request, multiple commitments to the same request may exist. Also, executors may improve their responses until they are accepted by the initiator.

With this interaction aspect, we can provide non-intrusiveness to the end user since callback and forwarding request concepts basically conceal workflow patterns such as parallel and sequential execution of work, respectively. Hence, the end users' work is supported by ad-hoc sequential and parallel executions masked as a natural and simple request-response mechanism similar to the one supporting the exchange of email messages.

3.2 Data Aspect

The main objective of the data aspect of our model is to support the definition and evolution of the business process data elements. We have seen that end users work by mainly providing and requesting data. Thus, we need to define how that data is structured and integrated with the entities presented in the interaction aspect of our model.

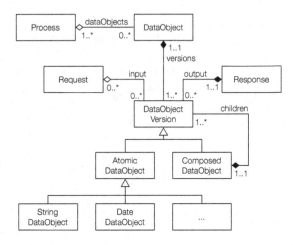

Fig. 2. Data Aspect Model

In Figure 2, it is depicted the data aspect that supports the artifacts produced during the execution of a business process. Although the data object entities are aggregated in the business process concept, capturing their association at the request entity level allows us to identify in which request the data object was created and new versions were defined. When initiating a request, the end user may select some data objects as input for that request, i.e., data which the initiator knows that the executor will require to execute the request. On the other hand, a response to a particular request must always define a new data object version.

Capturing this information is important to later identify the data inputs and outputs of a request when specifying its underlying business process model. It also supports the organization of data, complying with the identified quality regarding structured data. Finally, this aspect also empowers the synthesization of the captured information during the execution of ad-hoc workflows, as it fosters the reuse and share of the same structured data entities with all the business process participants.

3.3   Social Aspect

The social aspect allows the enrichment of the workflow entities supporting the interaction and data aspects of the system's model. Such enrichment is achieved through the implicit association of tags and commentaries to the main primitives of our model as end users provide titles to identify processes, subjects and descriptions to identify and explain requests, and labels to identify data objects.

In Figure 3, it is depicted the social aspect entities that will enrich the interaction and data aspects supporting entities. The *title* of a process is supported by a tag. Similarly to email, end users provide a simple *subject* to identify a request, which is also supported by the tag entity. When creating such requests, end users

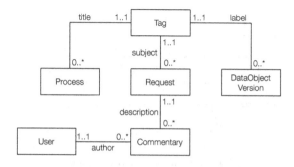

Fig. 3. Social Aspect Model

may need to provide a more detailed description of the request, supported by the commentary entity, which can be replied to discuss the request goals. Also, defining a new label or updating the one associated with a data object is in fact the same as annotating the new version with a tag.

The non-intrusiveness quality is achieved in part by this aspect because the end user does not know that he is in fact tagging and commenting the workflow entities as he points out titles, subjects or labels, and descriptions respectively. Such seamless embedding of social software features fosters the completeness quality as it allows us to capture enriched information concerning the execution of business processes. Also, the enriched information enables the construction of a folksonomy that will help us achieve the synthesization quality by providing the awareness that enables the share of work practices among end users. Such folksonomy identifies patterns of tagging, suggesting similar tags to the end users accordingly to their current execution context.

The separation between the entities supporting execution and the social software features supporting their enrichment allows us to detach the ad-hoc execution workflow concerns from the possible information that is important to be capture. Given that separation, we are empowered not only to seamless embed new social software features in the future, which can capture new information proven to be useful to the design of business process models, but also to bridge concerns from other business process stakeholders (e.g. modeling concerns).

3.4   Awareness Aspect

The awareness aspect provides additional knowledge to the end user about the business processes they are executing. However, that extra knowledge is not provided in a intrusive way, i.e., the end user is not confronted with input forms to provide additional information.

In Figure 4, it is depicted the awareness aspect of the model. During the execution of a request, all the relevant events associated to the construction of a response are captured by the awareness aspect. This capture of information is non-intrusive and allows to better identify the structure of data as it considers

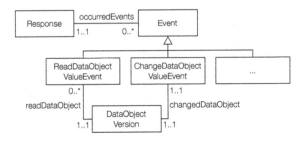

Fig. 4. Awareness Aspect Model

references to the target entities affected in the event. Concerning the complete-ness quality, the awareness aspect provides a detailed description of the process state, listing all the relevant events within a timeline. Finally, the set of iden-tified events will provide us means to use Complex Event Processing (CEP) techniques in order to provide suggestions to the end users when creating new requests. Such suggestions will synthesize the existing tags and comments iden-tifying and describing the workflow entities.

3.5 Solution Overview

The concepts just introduced are illustrated in Figure 5. For the sake of sim-plicity, other aspects supported by our model, such as the identification of data requirements through the awareness aspect, or the more semantic relation be-tween the end user executing a particular request (*to* relation) featuring both the existence of a commitment and response(s), were omitted. When compared to an email system, the solution here proposed mainly differs in four points: (1) exchanged data is structured since it is defined as a composition of atomic data types (e.g. string, integer, date, etc...); (2) data objects are versioned and shared across the process instance; (3) requests, and their respective responses, identify which data was used (input) and created (output); (4) social software is transparently embedded and provides support for labeling (tags) the execu-tion supporting entities, and for describing and clarifying (commentaries) the requests' goals.

4   Implementation

Regarding the benefits of separation of concerns while concerning a functional view of our system, as depicted in Figure 6, we divided its implementation into five different functional modules.

The *Seamless User Interface Integration Module* allows the definition of a unique interface to the end user, with the objective of not disrupting him from his daily work activities. There are no modeling views or tools, only the environment which the end user is used to: the execution environment. Such environment is

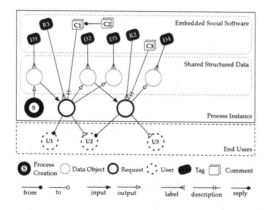

Fig. 5. Generic example of a process instance

supported in part by social software features that are seamless integrated with the objective of causing no intrusion to the end user. Hence, end users can, while coordinating work, enrich the execution information with social software features without knowing that they are in fact associating tags or comments to the business process entities supporting the process' execution.

This enriched information is then integrated and organized by the *Enriched Info Database Module*, which allows the construction of a more semantically detailed instance model of the executed business processes. From such enriched and better structured model, one could better identify patterns of execution and enable the *Execution Guidance Module* to provide collaborative filtering empowerment to the *Seamless User Interface Integration Module*.

The *Seamless User Interface Integration Module* provides a new embedded social software feature to the end users based on collaborative filtering: the suggestion of subjects (tags) for newly created requests, and their respective input and output data configuration. Such suggestions are built according to patterns identified in previous collaborations that occurred within a similar execution context, fostering the synthesization of the entities supporting the execution of business processes.

Additionally, the separation of concerns depicted by the *Execution Module* and the *Social Software Features Module* allows to easily integrate the system with other existing tools while maintaining the important seamless user interface integration.

5   Related Work

An extended set of studies [5, 8, 10, 20] have focused on identifying the purpose for which people use their email, and its importance as a coordination tool for their daily work activities. Contrarily to the attempts in combining speech

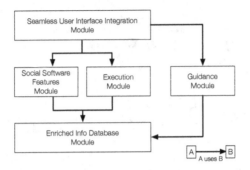

Fig. 6. Module Usage Diagram

act theory with email [21, 9], Cohen et al. [4] proposed a system which passively observes email and automatically classifies it by intention. By using such passive approach, Cohen et al. [4] claim to reduce the burden on the users of the system, and to avoid sacrificing the flexibility and socially desirable aspects of informal, natural language communication. Such effort is aligned with the non-intrusiveness quality while aiming for completeness.

In order to identify an email's intention automatically, Cohen et al. [4] proposed an ontology of email acts, which is composed by nouns (e.g. information, activity, data, opinion, etc...) and verbs (e.g. propose, request, commit, refuse, deliver, remind, etc...). Nevertheless, apart from the automation issues of classification, none of the algorithms or representations presented in [4] take into account the context of the email message. Aware of that context issue, Carvalho and Cohen [3] extended their work in [3] by acknowledging the relation between an email message intention and the sequential information correlation to its replies. In [7], several algorithms for automatically recognizing emails as part of an ongoing activity are presented. However, a completely automated approach in the recognition of activities hinders the enrichment information advantages and benefits of collaborative software.

Another popular workflow system, known as Lotus Notes, makes use of email system and other social tools (e.g. email, calendars, blogs, etc..) as backbones for work interaction support. Nevertheless, apart from their lack of data structure, the evidence of collaboration improvement is not quite clear as stated in [19].

Other current formal methodologies concerning the modeling of business processes, such as the Design and Engineering Methodology for Organizations (DEMO) [6], also have their foundations rooted in the Language-Action Perspective (LAP). However, Dietz [6], apart from concerning a static view of the organization and their respective business processes, currently focus on the modeling of business processes, disregarding the dynamics and complementing information inherent to their execution.

This work is developed within the project Processpedia [16]: a business process management system which contemplates the different business process stakeholders and their particular concerns and perspectives. As a complete business process management system, Processpedia acknowledges the need for business rules to constraint the set of possible executions, however, this paper only focus on providing support for the perspective of unconstrained coordinations of work, aiming to capture the human-interactions and their inherent important tacit knowledge in a non-intrusive manner.

6   Conclusions and Future Work

In this paper, we referred to the problem concerning the fact that business process information extracted from mining approaches to email logs is error-prone given their reliability on unstructured data [2]. Also, the addition of social software features directly into workflow systems for end users to explicitly use is intrusive as it represents, just like modeling, a peculiar task in the context of their daily activities. As a solution, we presented an ad-hoc workflow system which allows for a non-intrusive capture of the end users' interactions and tacit knowledge, an asset considered important to the modeling of business processes.

The model used to capture the human-interactions is based in the LAP, empowering end users to coordinate work in a natural way, just as if they were exchanging emails. Additionally, the request and response constructs provide support for the exchange and definition of structured data elements. All in all, end users are in fact transparently feeding an instance model by effectively executing the business process, as they are simultaneously enriching the execution information through the use of seamlessly integrated social software features.

Our future efforts will be focusing on the empirical evaluation of the system here proposed and its validation through deployment in real organizations. During that field work, we will be continuously studying and classifying the evolving community, identifying further requirements and issues associated to the objectives intended by the solution here presented, and tuning the aspects that compose its model.

Acknowledgements. This work was supported by FCT (INESC-ID multi-annual funding) through the PIDDAC Program funds.

References

1. Aalst, W., Nikolov, A.: Mining e-mail messages: Uncovering interaction patterns and processes using e-mail logs. International Journal of Intelligent Information Technologies 4(3), 27–45 (2008)
2. Aalst, W., Vandongen, B., Herbst, J., Maruster, L., Schimm, G., Weijters, A.: Workflow mining: A survey of issues and approaches. Data & Knowledge Engineering 47(2), 237–267 (2003)
3. Carvalho, V., Cohen, W.: On the collective classification of email '"speech acts". In: SIGIR 2005: 28th ACM SIGIR Conference on Research and Development in Information Retrieval (2005)
4. Cohen, W., Carvalho, V., Mitchell, T.: Learning to classify email into "speech acts". In: EMNLP (2004)

5. Dabbish, L., Venolia, G., Cadiz, J.: Marked for deletion: An analysis of email data. In: CHI 2003 Extended Abstracts on Human Factors in Computing Systems, pp. 924–925. ACM, NY (2003)
6. Dietz, J.: Enterprise Ontology: Theory and Methodology. Springer-Verlag New York, Inc. (2006) ISBN 3540291695
7. Dredze, M., Lau, T., Kushmerick, N.: Automatically classifying emails into activities. In: IUI 2006: Proceedings of the 11th International Conference on Intelligent User Interfaces (2006)
8. Ducheneaut, N., Bellotti, V.: Email as habitat: An exploration of embedded personal information management. ACM Interactions 8(5), 30–38 (2001)
9. Flores, F., Ludlow, J.J.: Doing and speaking in the office. In: Fick, G., Sprague, R.H. (eds.) Decision Support Systems: Issues and Challenges, pp. 95–118. Pergamon Press, New York (1980)
10. Kraut, R., Attewell, P.: Media use in a global corporation: Electronic mail and organizational knowledge. In: Research Milestones on the Information Highway. Erlbaum (1997)
11. Martinho, D., Silva, A.R.: ECHO: An Evolutive Vocabulary for Collaborative BPM Discussions. In: zur Muehlen, M., Su, J. (eds.) BPM 2010. LNBIP, vol. 66, pp. 408–419. Springer, Heidelberg (2011)
12. Polanyi, M.: The Tacit Dimension. Doubleday & Co (1966)
13. Polanyi, M.: Knowing and Being: Essays by Michael Polany. University of Chicago Press (1969)
14. Scheer, A., Thomas, O., Adam, O.: Process Modeling using Event-Driven Process Chains, pp. 119–145. John Wiley & Sons, Inc. (2005)
15. Schoop, M.: An introduction to the language-action perspective. SIGGROUP Bull. 22(2), 3–8 (2001)
16. Silva, A., Rosemann, M.: Processpedia – an ecological environment for bpm stakeholders collaboration. Business Process Management Journal, Emerald (to appear, 2011)
17. Silva, A., Martinho, D., Aguiar, A., Flores, N., Ferreira, H., Correia, F.: An implementation model for agile business process tools. In: IWODE 2009, Lisbon, Portugal (2009)
18. Silva, A.R., Meziani, R., Magalhães, R., Martinho, D., Aguiar, A., Flores, N.: AGILIPO: Embedding Social Software Features into Business Process Tools. In: Rinderle-Ma, S., Sadiq, S., Leymann, F. (eds.) BPM 2009. LNBIP, vol. 43, pp. 219–230. Springer, Heidelberg (2010b)
19. Vandenbosch, B., Ginzberg, M.: Lotus notes and collaboration: Plus ça change... J. of Management Information Systems (1997)
20. Venolia, G., Dabbish, L., Cadiz, J., Gupta, A.: Supporting email workflow (2001)
21. Winograd, T.: A language/action perspective on the design of cooperative work. In: Proceedings of the 1986 ACM Conference on Computer-Supported Cooperative Work, pp. 203–220. ACM (1986)

BPMN and Design Patterns for Engineering Social BPM Solutions

Marco Brambilla, Piero Fraternali, and Carmen Vaca

Politecnico di Milano, Piazza L. da Vinci 32, Milano, Italy,
name.surname@polimi.it

Abstract. The integration of social software and BPM can help organizations harness the value of informal relationships and weak ties, without compromising the consolidated business practices embedded in conventional BPM solutions. This paper presents a process design methodology, supported by a tool suite, for addressing the extension of business processes with social features. The social process design exploits an extension of BPMN for capturing social requirements, a gallery of social BPM design patterns that represent reusable solutions to recurrent process socialization requirements, and a model-to-model and mode-to-code transformation technology that automatically produces a process enactment Web application connected with mainstream social platforms.

Keywords: Model-Driven Engineering, BPM, BPMN, Social Software, Design Patterns, Generative Development.

1 Introduction

Social BPM fuses BPM with social software, with the aim of enhancing performance by means of a controlled participation of external stakeholders to process design and enactment [5,12,17].

In classical BPM, processes are defined centrally by the organization and deployed for execution by *internal performers*, i.e., actors formally entitled to execute the activities and directly produce the advancement of a process case. This closed-world approach can be opened with social features at different levels of control [2]: *Participatory Design* opens the *process design* to multiple actors, including end users; the resulting process is then executed in the traditional way; *Participatory enactment* shifts socialization from design to enactment and allows the participation of *internal observers*, i.e., actors known at design time (e.g., internal to the organization) but different from the internal performers formally entitled to activity execution; these subjects can interact with (observe) the process only indirectly, via the intermediation of messages and artifacts; finally, *Social enactment* enlarges even more the process execution, by allowing the participation of *external observers*, i.e., actors not known at process deployment time and dynamically signed-up to the process.

This paper focuses on participatory and social enactment and contributes:

F. Daniel et al. (Eds.): BPM 2011 Workshops, Part I, LNBIP 99, pp. 219–230, 2012.

- A summarization of the main factors that drive the socialization of a business process (socialization goals).
- An extension of BPMN 2.0 enabling the specification of social roles, activities, events, and process flows (Social BPMN).
- A gallery of design patterns, expressed in Social BPMN, that represent archetypal solutions to recurrent process socialization problems (social process patterns). Social patterns are referred to the goals they contribute to solve, to support the construction of process models from requirements.
- A technical framework for generating Social BPM applications from specifications encoded in Social BPMN, based on model transformations and on a runtime architecture integrating business process execution and social task enactment, implemented in a commercial tool suite called WebRatio BPM [1].

The paper is organized as follows: Section 2 provides an overview of the approach; Section 3 proposes some BPMN language extensions; Section 4 presents the social BPM design patterns; Section 5 provides an example; Section 6 describes the toolsuite supporting the approach; Section 7 discusses the related work; and Section 8 concludes.

2   Overview of the Approach

Figure 1 positions the contributions of the paper with respect to the phases the BPM lifecycle.

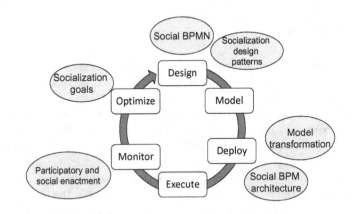

Fig. 1. The BPM lifecycle and the contributions of Social BPM

The social extension of a business process can be regarded as a specific optimization phase, where the organization seeks efficiency by extending the reach of a business process to a broader class of stakeholders. This general objective articulates into different optimization goals, which constitute the motivation of the process socialization effort:

– *Exploitation of weak ties and implicit knowledge*: the goal is discovering and exploiting informal knowledge and relationships to improve activity execution.
– *Transparency*: the goal is making the decision procedures internal to the process more visible to the affected stakeholders.
– *Participation*: the goal is engaging a broader community to raise the awareness about, or the acceptance of, the process outcome.
– *Activity distribution*: the goal is assigning an activity to a broader set of performers or to find appropriate contributors for its execution.
– *Decision distribution*: the goal is eliciting opinions that contribute to the making of a decision.
– *Social feedback*: the goal is acquiring feedback from a broader set of stakeholders, for process improvement.
– *Knowledge sharing*: the goal is disseminating knowledge in order to improve task execution; at an extreme, this could entail fostering mutual support among users to avoid performing costly activities (e.g., technical support).

Once the optimization goals are established, they must be incorporated into the process design phase. This poses a linguistic problem (how to express socialization in the process model) and a procedural problem (how to design the process model so that it fulfills the socialization goals). BPMN 2.0 native extension mechanism can be exploited to provide a quite natural answer to the former issue: the main concepts of the language can be stereotyped to convey their social extension. To support the designer in constructing process models that meet the socialization goals, pattern-based design can be exploited [8]. A design pattern is *general reusable solution to a commonly occurring problem*; by identifying social process design patterns and matching them to socialization goals, it is possible to assist developers in the modeling of social BPM solutions that meet their process socialization requirement. Section 4 lists the collection of design patterns that we have derived by an extensive literature review and by the available descriptions of implemented social BPM products and solutions.

When the model of the social process is consolidated, the *deployment* consists of a the technical phase that produces the actual executable version of the social process enactment application. This task is complicated by the need of interacting at runtime with social software to support the social interactions required by the process model; these platforms are available online and can be used as a service in the enactment of the process (e.g., LinkedIn for skill and people search, Doodle for decision distribution, etc.). However, the integration of the BPM runtime to the social services is a nontrivial task, complicated by the absence of an interoperability standard masking the technical details of the APIs of each different platform. To face this problem and support deployment, Section 6 illustrates a technical architecture and development tools that automate the generation of process enactment applications from Social BPMN process models. The architecture and tools use the WebML Domain Specific Language (DSL) [3] and model transformations to first map Social BPMN models into platform-independent WebML application models and then the WebML models into Java components connected to social software APIs.

Role type	Internal performer	Internal Observer	External Observer
Icon			
Description	Directly affect case and activity advancement	May produce events and artifacts that indirectly affect case and activity advancement	Can be informed and participate through social network platforms

Fig. 2. BPMN lanes and pools stereotyped to denote social actors

3 Social BPMN Extensions

Process design benefits from visual languages that convey the process structure and constraints in an clear way, immediately communicable also to non-technical stakeholders. Social process design should preserve the intuitiveness and expressivity of state-of-the-practice visual languages and possibly be based on standard notations. To this end, social extensions of business processes can be conveyed using the BPMN standard[1] as a linguistic base. BPMN 2.0 incorporates a native extension mechanism that makes the language well suited for the adaptation to special process requirements, like those arising in Social BPM. By enriching the existing BPMN concepts with a social meaning, it is possible to achieve a visual language that is both familiar to BPMN practitioners and possess enough expressive power to convey social design patterns. Our proposal does not alter the semantics of the BPMN elements and interactions, because it simply defines some new annotations for events, tasks and lanes/pools, representing stereotyped definition of these items.

The main social extensions refer to the possibility of assigning work to users different from internal performers, and on the special semantics attached to some community-performed activities and events. Figure 2 shows the notation for *social pools*: social users are denoted by a stereotype icon adorning the BPMN pool, so to distinguish internal performers (corresponding to the standard semantics of BPMN pools) and the pools formed by the social communities of internal and external observers.

Social activities are activities executed by multiple actors; they can be represented with the BPMN 2.0 concept of ad hoc parallel task (the social pool of Figure 8 contains several examples). In particular, *Social tasks* specialize the BPMN task concept to denote a process action with a social semantics: they are denoted by an icon that suggest the social meaning of the task, as exemplified in Figure 3: the broadcasting of messages/contents from a task to the entire social network (or a subset thereof), the posting of messages/contents to one member of the network, the invitation of people from the social network to perform a specific task, the invitation to comment or vote on a task or on its outcomes, the login of users in the BPM system using credentials from a social network, and the search for user's skills or reputation within a social network (e.g., for

---

[1] http://www.bpmn.org/

Task type	Social broadcast	Social posting	Invitation to activity	Commenting	Voting	Login to join	Invitation to join a network	Search for actor's information
Annotation icon								
Description	Data flow to a community pool	Data flow to a single user in a comm. pool	Dynamic enrolment to a task in the process case	Comment the activity	Voting (y/n) on an activity, either within a social network platform or directly in the BPM system	Login using a social profile	Invitation between community users	Lookup query to the community to search for an actor with specific profile attributes

Fig. 3. BPMN tasks stereotyped to denote social activities

Requirement	Community-generated events	Event: New user engaged in the social community	Event: New social relationship link	Event: Invitation acceptance/rejection
BPMN notation				
Comment	(Generic) events raised by the community	An event is raised when a user dynamically enrolls to the process case	An event is raised when a user establishes a social relationship with another user	An event is raised when a user accepts/rejects an invitation

Fig. 4. BPMN event types supporting social interactions

checking recommendations before assigning tasks to users). As shown in Figure 4, specialized event types can be used to denote case advancement triggered by social interactions. A generic social event concept represents any kind of occurrence within the social network; this can be specialized to express more detailed event types like: the addition of a new user to the community, the establishment of a new social relationships, the notification of acceptance/rejection of a social request (e.g., for friendship, invitation to groups or applications), and so on. Social pools, actor categories, social tasks and events are the linguistic building blocks for expressing social design patterns, that are archetypal process model fragments representing recurrent process socialization solutions. They are the subject of Section 4.

4   Social Design Patterns

Social design patters are solutions to recurrent scenarios where cooperative tasks are executed using social software. This section illustrates an initial gallery of design patterns, collected by a broad review of social BPM literature and from an ongoing experience of analysis with process owners in companies and public administrations. For brevity, every pattern is introduced by a statement of the

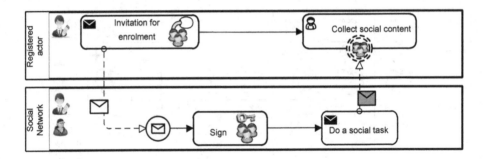

Fig. 5. Dynamic enrollment pattern

problem it addresses, the sub-patterns specializing it or used by it, and a short description explaining the supported social interaction.

Dynamic enrollment: Involving people external to the process.
Sub-patterns: Open invitation for external observers; Closed invitation for internal observers, Self-enrollment.
Description: platforms like enterprise and public social networks[2] are exploited for dynamically adding new actors to social activities. Internal/external observers (not a priori registered to the process) are invited through social software to sign into the process. Figure 5 shows the BPMN representation of the open invitation pattern using the annotation icons to denote social activities. Internal performers generate an invitation by sending a message to a social pool, and internal/external observers sign and start contribute to some social task.

Poll: Cooperating to a social decision.
Description: An internal performer publishes to a social platform a question (e.g., an open or closed list of options to choose from). Internal/external observers receive an invitation to participate in the poll [9], with a termination condition (e.g., a deadline). After the termination event, the internal performer collects the contributions and uses them to produce the decision, which can be published back to the social platform. Figure 6 shows the BPMN representation.

People/skills search: Finding competencies for an activity.
Description: A social community, inside and/or outside the enterprise, is exploited to find people with required expertise and a choice is made trading competence and social distance. The process usually starts by publishing a call for people, to which internal/external observers respond. The internal performer selects the right candidate(s) and publishes the final decision.

Social publication: Making a process artifact visible to social actors.
Description: Content (e.g., a public directive) is published to internal and external observers, e.g., by posting a document to a social platform [9]. Artifacts

---

[2] Example of enterprise social network are Yammer and Jive; of public ones are Facebook, LinkedIn and Twitter.

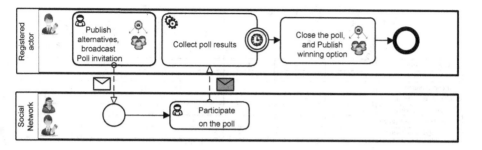

Fig. 6. Poll pattern

contain limited views of the process information. The social task terminates with the production of an advancement event (e.g., a deadline or the achievement of a required number of content views/comments).

Social sourcing: Delegating an activity to social actors.
Sub-patterns: Content creation, Content enrichment
Description: Internal/external observers contribute to the execution of an activity, e.g., by co-authoring socially produced documents [9,17]. Internal performers publish the description of the work and share a resource link to start contributions. It is possible also to enrich already existing content: creating metadata, tagging people/artifacts, e.g., a user finds a relevant colleague's profile, adds it to a bookmark collection and tag it [6,7,16].

Advancement notification: Informing social actors about advancement.
Description: Social contribution to the process can be fostered by delivering timely information on the progress status of activities. Using micro-blogging platforms [15], for example, it is possible to keep the users updated on limited views reflecting activity/case advancement making process execution more transparent. This design pattern lets an internal performer mark an activity as socially notified, so to generate automatic progress messages to selected social networks.

Feebdack: Acquiring qualitative/quantitative feedback from social actors.
Description: The internal performers may produce artifacts in the process execution and evaluate them by asking internal/external observers to rate them or to insert comments into the social platform [9].

Figure 7 shows how the defined social patterns address the optimization goals listed in Section 2 and can be used to drive the construction of a social process model after the process improvement analysis phase.

5   A Complete Example

To illustrate the pattern-based modeling approach, an example of process socialization is presented. A multinational software firm has formalized the process of

	Weak ties/ Tacit knowledge exploitation	Transparency	Participation	Activity distribution	Decision distribution	Social feedback	Knowledge sharing
Dynamic enrolment			X				
Poll					X	X	
People/skill search	X			X	X		
Social content publication		X					X
Social sourcing				X			
Advancement notification		X					
Ranking/Commenting	X				X	X	X

Fig. 7. Principal goals covered by each social pattern

team creation for projects requiring software architects, developers, system specialists and domains experts. In the traditional process, a senior manager of the Business Unit (BU) where the project is conducted is appointed as a team leader and s/he constructs the team based on staff availability and personal relationships; however, past experience has demonstrated that a more flexible approach is desirable, not to overlook hidden skills that may not be apparent from the project definition and to cope with projects in sectors new to the responsible BU. To this end, several of the socialization goals introduced in Section 2 are relevant: *participation*, to involve other BUs as advisors in the team formation; *exploitation of weak ties and tacit knowledge*, to make hidden skills surface; *decision distribution*, to exploit knowledge external to the BU in the team building; and *Advancement notification*, to make the process transparent to contributors. The identification of the primary socialization goals allows the process designer to select a candidate set of patterns, using a relevance matrix like the one shown in Figure 7; these patterns form an initial base for process improvement. Figure 8 shows the (simplified) outcome of process re-design, where the Dynamic Enrollment, Poll, People/skill Search and Advancement Notification patterns are used to meet the socialization goals.

In this version, the actors belong to the owner BU pool, denoting internal performers, and to a social pool of internal observers, denoting managers of other BUs and all the employees of the company. The Project Leader starts the process by creating a project description and an initial skill set; then s/he starts a poll on the skill list and submits it to the social pool (this can be realized by a post on the enterprise social network with a link to an external poll service). Other BU managers act as internal observers; they enroll dynamically to the process and propagate the invitation to other relevant colleagues thanks to the friendship mechanism of the enterprise social software. Comments can be added after completing the poll, so that colleagues from other BUs can suggest skills that have not yet been considered. After a fixed time, the Project Leader collects the feedback on the skill's list, closes the poll and publishes a Call for people to all the employees. The call for people is also a socialized activity; employees can suggest other colleagues or can promote themselves by giving information about their professional experience in similar areas. After a period of time, the

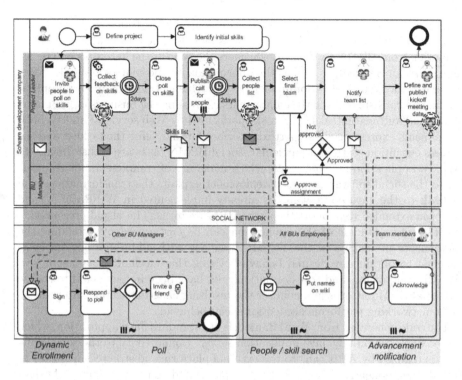

Fig. 8. The socialized Meeting definition process, with highlighted design patterns

Project Leader defines the composition of the team, shares it for approval with the managers of the responsible BU that will work in the project, notifies the selected team members, and finally publishes the kickoff meeting date.

6 Automatic Generation of Social BPM Solutions

The proposed framework has been implemented in WebRatio [1], a Model-Driven Web application development tool allowing one to edit BPMN models and automatically transform them into running JEE applications. The code generation exploits an intermediate platform-independent application model, expressed in the WebML language [3], so that application developers can fine-tune the Web application for enacting the process, by enriching the skeleton application model produced automatically from the BPMN process diagram.

A rapid prototyping function applies directly to the social process model and lets a business analyst or a stakeholder: 1) impersonate any actor of the process, at all the levels of social interaction; 2) start/suspend/resume/terminate the process activities; 3) create and inspect project artifacts and parameters, according to the process specification; 4) impersonate external user roles and play social actions. The prototype can be refined at the WebML modeling level by editing the BPMN or WebML models and then re-executing the model transformations, until the resulting application meets the requirements for deployment.

Figure 9 provides an overview of the implementation framework. At design time, the analyst creates the BPMN process models. Then, the automatic transformation from BPMN to WebML considers the type of the gateways and of the tasks (User or Service), as well as the information on the control and data flows, to generate a Web application model for process enactment. The Web application model consists of: WebML components expressing the business logic of user-driven and automatic tasks (e.g., tasks performed by Web services) and WebML components expressing the hypertext interface for managing the tasklist and the process execution status. In particular, social BPMN tasks are transformed into WebML application-level patterns, which make use of components for connecting to the social software. Process deployment exploits the transformation from WebML to the Java code, which is already implemented in WebRatio [1] and has been extended to support the social BPM patterns. The visual presentation and the business logic of the application can be customized by extending the components predefined in the WebML language with additional custom components, to obtain any desired behavior. Using this mechanism, a set of new WebML components and transformation rules have been implemented to realize the social BPM patterns and connect the resulting enactment application to the social networking platforms needed for social behavior.

The code generated from WebML models is a standard Java application, which can be deployed on any Java application server. Connectivity to the social software is realized by APIs calls to the external platforms, abstracted by means of WebML components. Examples of the implemented connectors include bridges to popular social software like Twitter, Facebook and LinkedIn, wrappers of open authentication systems like OAuth, and connectors to Web utility services like Doodle for polls. For instance, to implement the example described in Section 5, the system connects to two public social networks: LinkedIn and Doodle. At The integration is obtained by exploiting the public APIs of the two platforms: the respective WebML components allow to perform a set of operations on the remote systems, so as to achieve the desired behaviour. A simplified prototype of this application, together with an explanatory video, is available online at: http://www.bpm4people.org/demos.

The design patterns proposed in this paper can be intended as a methodological guideline for the design of social applications with any kind of BPM tools. In case the designer adopts WebRatio, he can combine them together with the rest of the WebML methodology presented in [3].

7   Related Work

Social BPM goals and impact have been deeply investigated in a variety of business sectors. A prominent case is people and skill search, which has been addressed in several contexts as a means to complement data in HR systems [11]. For instance, people tagging has been applied to BluePages, the corporate directory at IBM, to improve information quality on people and skills [7]; similarly, [16] proposes an approach for building competence ontologies in a collaborative way for a repository of people's skills; [6] describes Fringe Contact,

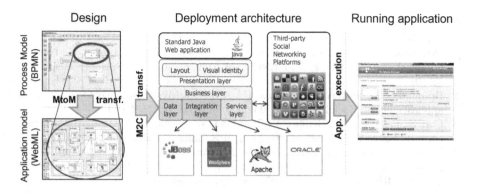

Fig. 9. Overview of the implementation of the approach within WebRatio

a system for collecting tags for an employee from his peers. Previous works on tools for social BPM focus on supporting the process modeling phase [4,13,18] and the execution phase [10,14,17,18]. For example, [9,13] discuss how social modeling tools allow multiple designers to register the design interactions so to produce recommendations for future projects. In the execution phase instead, the goal is to make information available to the users affected by the process even if these users were not identified at the definition stage [17]. In the process deployment field, social and business process integration is emerging also in the industry, as several vendors are proposing integrated social BPM suites. Among them, Appian, IBM BlueWorks Live, Oracle BPM Suite 11g, Software AG AlignSpace, Intalio and a few others. The approach illustrated in this paper focuses on socializing process execution, and is the first attempt at devising a linguistic instrument (Social BPMN) and a systematic method based on design patterns for expressing social process models. With respect to existing design and deployment tools, the architecture and toolsuite illustrated in Section 6 apply for the first time the pattern-driven development paradigm to the life-cycle of social BPM solutions; they support the specification of social process models and the collection and reuse of social design patterns, and provide a high level of automation to the process prototyping and deployment phases.

8 Conclusions

This paper has presented an approach for supporting the design and deployment of social BPM solutions through an extension of BPMN with primitives expressing social interactions, a set of reusable design patterns for process socialization, and a supporting toolsuite enabling integration between the process engine and the external social software. Ongoing work is focusing on the collection of a large gallery of social design patterns, on the implementation of further components in the WebRatio tool suite for integration of more social interactions and services.

230   M. Brambilla, P. Fraternali, and C. Vaca

References

1. Brambilla, M., Butti, S., Fraternali, P.: WebRatio BPM: A Tool for Designing and Deploying Business Processes on the Web. In: Benatallah, B., Casati, F., Kappel, G., Rossi, G. (eds.) ICWE 2010. LNCS, vol. 6189, pp. 415–429. Springer, Heidelberg (2010)
2. Brambilla, M., Fraternali, P., Vaca, C.: A model-driven approach to social BPM applications. In: Social BPM, pp. 95–112. FutStrat WfMC (2011)
3. Ceri, S., Fraternali, P., Bongio, A., Brambilla, M., Comai, S., Matera, M.: Designing Data-Intensive Web Applications. Morgan Kaufmann Publishers Inc. (2002)
4. Dengler, F., Koschmider, A., Oberweis, A., Zhang, H.: Social Software for Coordination of Collaborative Process Activities. In: zur Muehlen, M., Su, J. (eds.) BPM 2010. LNBIP, vol. 66, pp. 396–407. Springer, Heidelberg (2011)
5. Erol, S., Granitzer, M., Happ, S., Jantunen, S., Jennings, B., Johannesson, P., Koschmider, A., Nurcan, S., Rossi, D., Schmidt, R.: Combining BPM and social software: contradiction or chance? J. Softw. Maint. Evol. 22, 449–476 (2010)
6. Farrell, S., Lau, T.: Fringe contacts: People-tagging for the enterprise. In: Proc. of the Collaborative Web Tagging Workshop at WWW 2006 (2006)
7. Farrell, S., Lau, T., Nusser, S., Wilcox, E., Muller, M.: Socially augmenting employee profiles with people-tagging. In: Proceedings of the 20th Annual ACM Symposium on User Interface Software and Technology, pp. 91–100 (2007)
8. Fowler, M.: Analysis Patterns: Reusable Object Model. Addison-Wesley (1996)
9. Holtzblatt, L., Tierney, M.L.: Measuring the effectiveness of social media on an innovation process. In: Proceedings of the 2011 Annual Conference Extended Abstracts on Human Factors in Computing Systems, CHI EA 2011, pp. 697–712. ACM (2011)
10. Huiming, Q., Sun, J., Jamjoom, H.T.: SCOOP: Automated social recommendation in enterprise process management. In: IEEE SCC, vol. 1, pp. 101–108 (2008)
11. Jansen, E.A.: A semantic web based approach to expertise finding at KPMG. Master's thesis, Delft University of Technology (August 2010)
12. Johannesson, P., Andersson, B., Wohed, P.: Business Process Management with Social Software Systems – A New Paradigm for Work Organisation. In: Ardagna, D., Mecella, M., Yang, J. (eds.) BPM 2008 Workshops. LNBIP, vol. 17, pp. 659–665. Springer, Heidelberg (2009)
13. Koschmider, A., Song, M., Reijers, H.A.: Social Software for Modeling Business Processes. In: Ardagna, D., Mecella, M., Yang, J. (eds.) BPM 2008 Workshops. LNBIP, vol. 17, pp. 666–677. Springer, Heidelberg (2009)
14. Neumann, G., Erol, S.: From a Social Wiki to a Social Workflow System. In: Ardagna, D., Mecella, M., Yang, J. (eds.) BPM 2008 Workshops. LNBIP, vol. 17, pp. 698–708. Springer, Heidelberg (2009)
15. Riemer, K., Richter, A.: Tweet inside: Microblogging in a corporate context. In: Proceedings 23rd Bled eConference, eTrust, BLED 2010, paper 41 (2010)
16. Schmidt, A., Braun, S.: People tagging & ontology maturing: Towards collaborative competence management. In: 8th International Conference on the Design of Cooperative Systems (COOP 2008), Carry-le-Rouet (2008)
17. Schmidt, R., Dengler, F., Kieninger, A.: Co-creation of Value in IT Service Processes Using Semantic MediaWiki. In: Rinderle-Ma, S., Sadiq, S., Leymann, F. (eds.) BPM 2009. LNBIP, vol. 43, pp. 255–265. Springer, Heidelberg (2010)
18. Silva, A.R., Meziani, R., Magalhães, R., Martinho, D., Aguiar, A., Flores, N.: AGILIPO: Embedding Social Software Features into Business Process Tools. In: Rinderle-Ma, S., Sadiq, S., Leymann, F. (eds.) BPM 2009. LNBIP, vol. 43, pp. 219–230. Springer, Heidelberg (2010)

Applying Social Technology to Business Process Lifecycle Management

Paul Mathiesen, Jason Watson, Wasana Bandara, and Michael Rosemann

Faculty of Science and Technology, Queensland University of Technology, Brisbane, Australia
QUT@qut.edu.au

Abstract. In recent years social technologies such as wikis, blogs or microblogging have seen an exponential growth in the uptake of their user base making this type of technology one of the most significant networking and knowledge sharing platforms for potentially hundreds of millions of users. However, the adoption of these technologies has been so far mostly for private purposes. First attempts have been made to embed features of social technologies in the corporate IT landscape, and Business Process Management is no exception. This paper aims to consolidate the opportunities for integrating social technologies into the different stages of the business process lifecycle. Thus, it contributes to a conceptualization of this fast growing domain, and can help to categorize academic and corporate development activities.

Keywords: Business process management, lifecycle, social technology, Web 2.0, collaboration, model-reality divide, innovation.

1 Introduction

Organizations are currently undergoing a paradigm shift where existing Business Process Management (BPM) methodologies and organizational structures are being enhanced by emerging social technology such as wiki's, blogs, micro-blogs and instant messaging. Business Process Management can be defined as *"the discipline that improves measurable business performance for stakeholders through ongoing optimization and synchronization of enterprise-wide process capabilities."* (Burlton, 2001). Classically, the focus of BPM has been on transactional, highly repetitive processes that can be predicted and executed according to a schema, i.e. a process model. This traditional value proposition of BPM is constrained in environments that require complementary diverse, emerging and less predictable conversations in the context of process executions.

Drawing upon this statement we assert that social technology can support a more flexible, humanistic approach to Business Process Management, designed around the agile software development concept and supported by collaborative and incremental process design as proposed by Erol et al., (2010). The movement to social BPM is

F. Daniel et al. (Eds.): BPM 2011 Workshops, Part I, LNBIP 99, pp. 231–241, 2012.

evidenced in the literature by Silva et al., (2010) who discuss the view that business processes should not hinder human intervention, and that social technology should be embedded within BPM initiatives, especially in the modeling and execution phases of the processes lifecycle. This integration of social collaboration to crowd-source expertise and crowd-solve process issues (potentially from sources external to the organization) supports improved knowledge exchange, process requirements integration, application of situational context and increased process transparency.

The integration of social technologies in BPM is currently conducted in a number of 'trial-and-error' attempts. However, so far, and to the best of our knowledge, there is no holistic framework that summarizes the possible opportunities along the main stages of the process lifecycle. Thus, this paper is driven by the research question *"How do social technology characteristics relate to Business Process Management lifecycle activities?"*

In our quest to answer this question, we comprehensively studied related work and embedded existing practices and case studies where appropriate. This exploratory paper is structured as follows. First, we will present the selected Business Process Management lifecycle to introduce the key stages and activities that could benefit from the application of social technology. Second, we will characterize the two generic capabilities of social technology platforms that deserve attention in BPM. Third, we will interrelate the identified process lifecycle stages and these two capabilities of social technologies in an attempt to characterize the existing potential. Fourth, and finally, we will summarize our findings and put them into the context of our future work.

2   The Process Management Lifecycle

Business Process Management (BPM) is a set of structured methods and technologies for managing the operations of an organization (ABPMP, 2009). *"The goal of BPM is to create a process-centric, customer-focused organization that integrates management, people, process and technology for both operational and strategic improvement"* (Goeke & Antonucci, 2011). BPM encompasses methodologies and technologies for process definition (e.g. process modeling), process analysis (e.g., Six Sigma, Lean Management), process improvement (e.g., BPR, Process Innovation), process execution (e.g., Process-aware Information Systems) and process monitoring and control (e.g., Business Activity Monitoring) (Hammer & Champy, 1993; Spanyi, 2008). Originating from early organizational improvement efforts of (Demming, 1986; Taylor, 1911) the quality and improvement approach of Business Process Re-engineering (BPR) introduced process orientation to these initiatives (Goeke & Antonucci, 2011). As outlined by Silva et al., (2010), a key factor for the more recently emerging Business Process Management methodologies will be agility (Dreiling, 2010).

Business Process Management is divided into enterprise-wide and project-specific BPM (Hammer, 2007). The focus of this paper is on the latter, i.e. the way social technologies can be introduced into a project dedicated to the improvement of a business process. As the foundation of our analysis, we refer to the proposed process lifecycle model by Becker, Kugeler, & Rosemann (2001).

This model was selected on the basis of comprehensiveness, suitability to the research as well as the close alignment to the Six Sigma process improvement model DMAIC[1] (Harmon, 2007). This process lifecycle model has been applied in other published empirical studies such as Arora & Bandara (2006), Forster (2006) and Reiter et al., (2010) since it was first published in 2003.

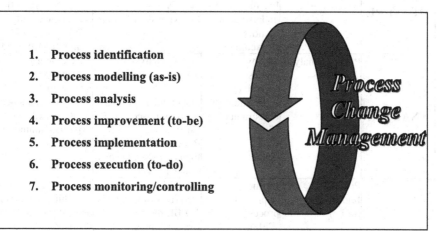

1. **Process identification**

2. **Process modelling (as-is)**

3. **Process analysis**

4. **Process improvement (to-be)**

5. **Process implementation**

6. **Process execution (to-do)**

7. **Process monitoring/controlling**

Fig. 1. The BPM Process Lifecycle (Becker, Kugeler, & Rosemann, 2001)

Table 1 shows the core phases of the life cycle [(column 2), also relating them to the phases of the Six Sigma life cycle phases (column 1)] and describes the objectives (via a list of core targeted tasks) associated with each phase (column 3). As specified in Table 1 (column 4), various tools and techniques can be applied in support of these tasks. From this perspective it is asserted that these tasks and associated enabling methods can benefit from a collaborative approach with the potential for introducing feedback and knowledge from outside of the modeling team. In addition, each lifecycle step has inherent risk associated with the tasks (see column 5 of Table 1) such as; process stakeholder expertise, organizational knowledge and stakeholder expectations. We believe that a more social, collaborative approach will mitigate these risks and improve the overall quality of the process improvement initiative.

---

[1] DMAIC – Define; Measure; Analyse; Improve; Control.

Table 1. BPM Lifecycle definitions (Becker, et al., 2001)

Six Sigma	Process Life-Cycle	Objectives	Methods	Issues & Risks
DEFINE	Process Identification	Identify process priority/ Stakeholders Define process goals/metrics	Stakeholder objectives matrix SWOT analysis Interviews/workshops	Incorrect process scope Unknown process ecosystem Limited participant knowledge
MEASURE	Process Modelling (as-is)	Document the process Establish shared understanding Identify shortcomings	Modelling notation AS-IF & AS-IS models Interviews/workshops	Model – Reality divide Syntactic, semantic & pragmatic quality Narrow focus of design (constrained)
ANALYSE	Process Analysis	Discover - Process objectives Accountability Constraints Risk Cost Value	SWOT analysis Six Sigma analysis Scenario & Stakeholder analysis Activity Based Costing Root Cause analysis Interviews/workshops Issues Register	Stakeholder expectation management Model completeness Analysis skills & expertise limited to team
IMPROVE	Process Improvement (to-be)	Define improved process Within constraints Too expectations Minimize risk Process Innovation	Interviews/workshops Derived from analysis TO-BE models Brainstorming Reference models	Incremental/redesign or rethink – outcome driven/limited by team Differing outcome perceptions Poor process analysis Ideas generation – lack of creativity
CONTROL	Process Implementation	Embed improved process Change Management	Force Field Analysis Project plan	Incomplete issue assessment Improvements & objectives disconnect Poor Stakeholder communication
	Process Execution (to-do)	Capture process enhancements	Automation	Technology adoption
	Process Monitoring and Control	Supervise & review process Map process capability	Process flow audit data & log files Service level agreements	Stakeholder signoff Team member re-assignment

3   The Social Media Landscape

Social software has been defined by Schmidt & Nurcan (2009) as "software that supports the interaction of human beings and production of artifacts by combining the input from independent contributors without predetermining the way to do this". The key outputs from this statement are that the contributors are independent, don't necessarily know each other and there is no prescribed process of interaction to follow. It is through this knowledge exchange process that social technologies can be applied to overcome deficiencies with traditional BPM methodologies. The characteristics of social technology such as the power of social interactions and the strengths of weak ties have been debated and discussed since the 1960's (Granovetter, 1983). A key development since then is that we now posses the technology to implement these characteristics.

The concept of weak ties of individuals who do not have immediate, close connections, is powerful as it can provide alternate viewpoints and divergent thinking. According to Neumann and Erol (2009), the demand for social technologies such as blogs/wikis/tagging/document sharing etc is evidenced by the introduction of these social components to leading business software applications. The authors assert that the intent is to provide more ease of use/networking/communication/sharing, accessibility & visibility, amongst other drivers.

Table 2. The Eight Core Patterns of Web 2.0 applications (O'Reilly & Musser, 2006)

The Eight Core Patterns of Web 2.0 applications		
Pattern	**Description**	**Example(s)**
1. Harnessing Collective Intelligence	User participation based on the network effect where the outputs improve as more people contribute. i.e. "crowdsourcing"	Linux Wikipedia
2. Data Is the Next "Intel Inside"	Use of unique data sources (knowledge) that is as important as functionality	Amazon.com
3. Innovation in Assembly	Fosters innovation to create new opportunities i.e. Enterprise SOA	Google maps
4. Rich User Experiences	Provide a rich user experience based on best practice software	Google maps
5. Software Above the Level of a Single Device	Use of pervasive online software i.e. location aware software	iTunes
6. Perpetual Beta	Adoption of continuous improvement approach i.e. SaaS	Google
7. Leveraging the Long Tail	Leverage off broad reach & identify niche opportunities	eBay
8. Lightweight Models and Cost-Effective Scalability	Agile development model for efficiency	Flickr

It is in part because of these characteristics that social technology has boomed in recent years. Yet there is still no common taxonomy of capabilities that can be used to clearly define this technology landscape. Currently, the closest accepted framework is that of O'Reilly & Musser (2006) who offer a list of characteristics (presented as social network 'patterns') that define what social technology can offer. These emerging social technology platforms can be grouped under a definition of Web 2.0 as proposed by O'Reilly & Musser (2006) where *"Web 2.0 is a set of social, economic, and technology trends that collectively form the basis for the next generation of the Internet—a more mature, distinct medium characterized by user participation, openness, and network effects."* O'Reilly & Musser (2006) lists these key principles as eight core interdependent patterns (see Table 2) which support the network effect of collaborative interaction for richer knowledge creation.

We can briefly apply each of these patterns against the process modeling phase to demonstrate the value of adopting social technology:

1. Harnessing Collective Intelligence: The overarching principle here is to establish an environment that provides an "architecture of participation (O'Reilly & Musser, 2006) where participants can add value through interaction and benefits from the network effect.

2. Data is the next "Intel Inside": This pertains to the use of the captured data (or knowledge) and using this for competitive advantage. This data could take the form of geo-location based information such as that used by the Foursquare social network (foursquare, 2011) and applied as a strategic corporate asset.

3. Innovation in Assembly: Emerging social technologies offer a diverse range of capabilities that may be distinctly appropriate at specific BPM lifecycle phases. The use of a wiki or blog could be the collaboration platform typical for the process modeling phase whereas an activity stream (e.g. Twitter) may be more applicable for the final step of process monitoring and control.

4. Rich User Experiences: Provide process model participants with best practice online applications which promote usability and a design which compels high user engagement.

5. Software above the level of a single device: The emerging use of smart-phones and other mobile devices will continue to simplify content creation and therefore provide support for data and media rich sources of information. By tapping into this ecosystem, process model participants now have access to more context sensitive information, on demand and extendable using the Web as a platform.

6. Perpetual Beta: The concept of software as a service that is always available and in a constant state of improvement provides the incentive for the process modeling team to follow the same design and adopt a continuous improvement philosophy.

7. Leveraging the Long Tail: Relates to using the Web to capture those pockets of knowledge and innovation that may not necessarily be available to a traditional process modeling environment. This 'democratized' approach of connecting both internally and externally to an organization may uncover expertise and requirements that provide innovative points of differentiation and create new market opportunities.

8. Lightweight Models and Cost Effective Scalability: Social technology platforms typically have no financial cost for access and minimal barriers to participation. This concept of doing 'more with less' via an outsourced infrastructure supports agility and mitigates the risk of expensive, unwieldy collaboration tools.

The following section looks to apply these concepts to the different phases of the BPM lifecycle and to provide some initial insights to determine a "best fit" for social technology capability applicable within BPM initiatives. The issues and benefits that can be addressed through the adoption of social technology platforms are also discussed, from this perspective.

4   Social Media Applied across the BPM Lifecycle

Schmidt & Nurcan (2009) have explored the different phases of the BPM lifecycle and how Web 2.0 concepts such as wiki's, blogs, and recommender and reputation systems could be used to enhance the steps of: process design; implementation and deployment; and evaluation and improvement.

Based on a comprehensive analysis of current literature, we mapped the identified process lifecycle stages against the eight core patterns of Web 2.0. The outcomes of this mapping exercise are captures in Table 3.

Table 3. BPM Lifecycle and Web 2.0 patterns

Lifecycle Phase	Phase Descriptions	O'Reilly's Core Patterns for Web 2.0 Success							
		Collective Intelligence	"Intel inside"	Innovation	User Experience	Pervasive Software	Perpetual Beta	Long Tail	Scalable
Process Identification	Understand the process scope and ecosystem in detail	✓	✓					✓	
Process Modelling	Represent the identified process via a modeling language	✓							
Process Analysis	Analyse process performance and issues	✓	✓	✓					
Process Improvement (to-be)	Identify and evaluate options for process improvement, consider constraints/resources	✓	✓	✓	✓	✓	✓	✓	✓
Process Implementation	Embed improved process in the Organisation				✓	✓	✓	✓	✓
Process Execution (to-do)	Perform the processes manually or automatically				✓	✓		✓	✓
Process Monitoring & Control	Guiding and controlling the daily operations	✓				✓	✓	✓	

From this Table, it is evident that the emerging field of social technologies can have a tremendous impact on the adoption of social technology to existing BPM practices. Current literature in the field presents how this approach is key to providing not only the software required but also a culture of collaboration and continuous, user driven process improvement.   Some potential benefits of the introduction of social technology to the BPM lifecycle are discussed below. However, what is also evident from Table 3 is that not all phases are suitable for a more collaborative approach. Each lifecycle step is now presented with discussion on the issues and benefits that can be addressed through the adoption of social technology platforms.

1. Process Identification

In this lifecycle phase, modeler collaboration to identify process priority, goals and metrics is a crucial task prior to documenting the as-is model. This concept is referred to by Magdaleno, et al., (2008) who discuss how collaboration is viewed as a distributed collective activity amongst several Actors, each performing tasks in alignment with a shared objective (Clarke and Smyth, 1993). As each person involved in the collaborative activity holds information important to the group, problem solving potential is enhanced (Marwell and Schmitt, 1975). A key point though is the importance of selecting the right process as the addition of collaboration activities may be time consuming and increase process cost for little return (Magdaleno, et al., 2008).

2. Process Modelling

The key benefits of a collaborative approach to this lifecycle phase are a more inclusive integration of process stakeholder requirements, detailed aggregation of process impediments, improved codification of knowledge and an enhanced process improvement cycle (Schmidt & Nurcan, 2009). It is their belief that this improved knowledge exchange will enhance business processes and models. The collaborative benefits of social technology are discussed in the work of Neumann and Erol (2009) who present an approach of using wiki applications to develop a collaborative open-source work-flow system. The authors believe that recent developments of social software are an extension of existing collaborative applications currently inplace to support unstructured communication and knowledge/information sharing. If a collaboration element can be incorporated in the modeling process, the benefits will be: an improved process understanding; higher quality process models; an established path for process improvement; and supports the sharing of knowledge (Magdaleno, et al., 2008).

An assertion by Rossi & Vitali (2009) is that one of the main strengths of social technologies is that they provide an array of collaboration tools (blogs, wikis, forums) that support user interaction. In support of this, Dollmann, et al., (2009) discuss how BPM can be enhanced by Web 2.0 concepts by integrating functions of cooperative modeling and using the collective intelligence of the process model user group. By employing a folksonomy approach, process stakeholders can tag their activities, share and search these tags, for the activities and comments of others (Silva, et al., 2010). Process modelers can then analyze these activities and create a new, improved version of the process model.

3. Process Analysis

Proposed by Schmidt and Nurcan (2009), the basic success factors of social technology are the creation of weak ties; the wisdom of the crowds; social production; and the view that the model consumer is a co creator of value. Erol, et al., (2010) assert that *"social software provides a better integration of all stakeholders into the business process life-cycle and offers new possibilities for a more effective and flexible design of business processes"*. These social technology factors provide benefit to this phase of the BPM lifecycle. This analysis heavy, discovery phase utilizes a wide range of tools and techniques, results of which are richer for a wider range of contributors. A key risk that a social approach will mitigate is to extend the analytical expertise of the process modeling team to potentially include those with a more appropriate skill-set.

4. Process Improvement

Some key benefits from incorporating social technologies into the BPM lifecycle include the integration of process knowledge from all stakeholders; continuous process improvement opportunities due to community intelligence; workflow support; and stakeholder digital identity and reputation (Erol, et al., 2010). As discussed by Schmidt and Nurcan (2009), the intent of social software is to facilitate social interaction and collaborative production. This social production occurs without a predetermined mechanism and is driven by independent collaborators (Erol, et al., 2010). Examples of incorporating social production into business processes include the integration of Customer feedback into the product development cycle or using wikis & blogs to speed up knowledge exchange and decision making (Schmidt & Nurcan, 2009).

As presented by Schmidt and Nurcan (2009), the success of the social software and social production approach is evidenced by wikipedia.org and other open source software initiatives such as the Linux operating system.

Derived from the above discussion is that incremental, innovative process redesign or indeed process transformation can be supported by social collaboration platforms either in the form of blogs, wiki's or indeed instant messaging (e.g. Yammer). Other benefits of this self-organizing, bottom-up approach to process modeling, supported by the collective intelligence of the user community, is that the contents of process models are more visible and the opportunity for continuous process improvement by the community. Further research by Neumann & Erol (2009) has highlighted *"a shift from top down approaches in business process design and deployment to an approach where bottom-up reengineering and adaption from the user side is welcomed"*. This requirement for agility is an outcome of a rapidly changing business environment and the need to quickly adapt to process and organizational changes. Erol et al., (2010) believe that through the application of the "collective intelligence" of a process user group, in lieu of formally defining the user inputs, model users are encouraged to provide inputs in a bottom-up manner without an existing overall plan. The concept of bottom-up modeling, based on the collective intelligence of the user community, is an integral part of a social BPM methodology as it removes the hierarchical divide between process model developer and model consumer, which is often a barrier to model adoption.

5. Process Implementation

An important feature of social technologies is the ability to apply situational context through extended functionalities such as tags, links and bookmarks. It is through the retention of this contextual information that meaning can be associated with the digital artifact (Erol, et al., 2010). Through facilitating an improved exchange of knowledge and information within a user community, there will be new opportunities to improve existing business processes (Schmidt & Nurcan, 2009). According to Jennings & Finkelstein (2009), incorporating social technologies within an Organisation has two key benefits: firstly business processes can be improved through socially supported interactions and secondly, by providing a means for human knowledge to be captured and reused by the organization. The Authors also discuss the theoretical use of "social software data artifacts" to trace data creation back to a unique digital identity so that individuals can be linked to a specific activity, expertise or knowledge. The above capabilities will assist with embedding an improved process with innovative, knowledge enhanced, practices.

6. Process Execution
During the process execution phase, a number of opportunities exist to involve social technologies. This could be the inclusion of external stakeholders in the act of voting on which path to take during a process execution or the inclusion of external stakeholders as part of the automated staff resolution.

7. Process Monitoring and Control
Similar to the preceding phase, this lifecycle step may not receive direct benefits from social technology. However, communication of process review and monitoring steps may be enhanced by the use of automated system updates or activity streams e.g. Twitter or Facebook status updates.

5   Conclusion

The preceding discussion has highlighted the key research areas and possible opportunities when a social technology approach is applied to a Business Process Management lifecycle. Consequently we propose that a higher degree of collaboration supported by appropriate tools will lead to improved communication and coordination of knowledge intensive tasks.

This exploratory paper presents a snapshot of current research in the BPM and social technology space and as such there are inherent limitations. The research landscape is in a state of rapid change as new technologies and business models emerge, impacting upon organizational capabilities and requirements. Further, the BPM community will face the challenges of social technology adoption, and difficulties with the facilitation and measurement of any process improvements that these technologies may bring. Future research can extend upon the discussed BPM and social technology convergence.

References

ABPMP, Guide to the Business Process Management Common Body of Knowledge (BPM COK), 2nd edn. (2009)
Arora, A., Bandara, W.: IT Service Desk Process Improvement – A Narrative Style Case Study. In: Pacific Asia Conference on Information Systems (PACIS), vol. (78) (2006)
Becker, Kugeler, Rosemann, M.: Business Process Lifecycle Management, White paper (2001)
Burlton, R.: Business process management: profiting from process. SAMS (2001)

Demming, W.E.: Out of the crisis. MIT Press, Cambridge (1986)

Dollmann, T., Fettke, P., Loos, P.: Web 2.0 Enhanced Automation of Collaborative Business Process Model Management in Cooperation Environments. In: ACIS 2009 Proceedings, vol. 41 (2009)

Dreiling, A.: Business Process Management and Semantic Interoperability. In: vom Brocke, J., Rosemann, M. (eds.) Handbook on Business Process Management, pp. 497–512. Springer, Heidelberg (2010)

Erol, S., Granitzer, M., Happ, S., Jantunen, S., Jennings, B., Johannesson, P., et al.: Combining BPM and social software: contradiction or chance? Journal of Software Maintenance and Evolution: Research and Practice 22(6-7), 449–476 (2010)

Forster, F.: The Idea behind Business Process Improvement: Toward a Business Process Improvement Pattern Framework. BPTrends (April 2006)

Foursquare (2011), https://foursquare.com/about (accessed May 13, 2011)

Goeke, R.J., Antonucci, Y.L.: Antecedents to Job Success in Business Process Management: A Comparison of Two Models. Information Resources Management Journal (IRMJ) 24(1), 46–65 (2011)

Granovetter, M.: The strength of weak ties: A network theory revisited. Sociological Theory 1, 201–233 (1983)

Hammer, M., Champy, J.: Reengineering the Corporation (1993)

Harmon, P.: Business process change: a guide for business managers and bpm and six sigma professionals (2007)

Jennings, B., Finkelstein, A.: Digital Identity and Reputation in the Context of a Bounded Social Ecosystem. In: Ardagna, D., Mecella, M., Yang, J. (eds.) BPM 2008. LNBIP, vol. 17, pp. 687–697. Springer, Heidelberg (2009)

Magdaleno, A.M., Cappelli, C., Baiao, F.A., Santoro, F.M., Araujo, R.: Towards Collaboration Maturity in Business Processes: An Exploratory Study in Oil Production Process. Information Systems Management 25(4), 302–318 (2008)

Neumann, G., Erol, S.: From a Social Wiki to a Social Workflow System. In: Ardagna, D., Mecella, M., Yang, J. (eds.) BPM 2008. LNBIP, vol. 17, pp. 698–708. Springer, Heidelberg (2009)

O'Reilly, T., Musser, J.: Web 2.0 Principles and Best Practices. O'Reilly Radar (2006)

Reiter, S., Stewart, G., Bruce, C., Bandara, W., Michael, R.: The Phenomenon of Business Process Management: Practitioners' Emphasis. In: European Conference on Information Systems (ECIS), vol. (28) (2010)

Rossi, D., Vitali, F.: Workflow Enactment in a Social Software Environment. In: Ardagna, D., Mecella, M., Yang, J. (eds.) BPM 2008. LNBIP, vol. 17, pp. 716–722. Springer, Heidelberg (2009)

Schmidt, R., Nurcan, S.: BPM and Social Software. In: Ardagna, D., Mecella, M., Yang, J. (eds.) BPM 2008. LNBIP, vol. 17, pp. 649–658. Springer, Heidelberg (2009)

Silva, A.R., Meziani, R., Magalhães, R., Martinho, D., Aguiar, A., Flores, N.: AGILIPO: Embedding Social Software Features Into Business Process Tools. In: Rinderle-Ma, S., Sadiq, S., Leymann, F. (eds.) BPM 2009. LNBIP, vol. 43, pp. 219–230. Springer, Heidelberg (2010)

Spanyi, A.: More for Less: The Power of Process Management. Meghan-Kiffer Press, Tampa (2008)

Taylor, F.W.: Scientific Management. Harper & Brothers, New York (1911)

A Framework for the Support of Value Co-creation by Social Software

Rainer Schmidt

HTW-Aalen, Anton-Huber-Str. 25
73430 Aalen
Rainer.Schmidt@htw-aalen.de

Abstract. For a long time, business process management has been based on the understanding that the single point of interaction between the producer and the consumer is at the end of the business process. Products and services are exchanged against the payment. However, there is a growing conviction that both the producer and the consumer can profit from intensifying the interaction during the business process. Value can be co-created between producer and an active consumer, called prosumer. This active involvement of the prosumer is done by ad-hoc asynchronous interactions between producer and a now prosumer called consumer. Social software is an ideal means for supporting these value-providing asynchronous interactions.

Keywords: Social software, business process management, value co-creation.

1 Introduction

There are a number of benefits of using social software combined with business process management [1]: Social software integrates stakeholders into the business process in a better way and offers new possibilities for a more effective and flexible design of business processes. Alleviating the integration of process knowledge from all stakeholders improves the quality of business process models. During the business process lifecycle, social software allows to collect valuable information for continuous business process improvement. An analysis of social software showed that four principles support business processes. These principles are weak ties [2], egalitarianism [3], social production [4] and service-dominant logic [5]. In [6] four benefits of social software for internal business processes are identified: Better meeting of customer needs, increased knowledge of employees and sustained performance improvement. Social software creates these benefits by amplifying connections between the employees and increasing the company's opportunities for serendipity. Social software is capable to overcome limitations of present enterprise infrastructure and create an Enterprise 2.0 [7].

In spite of these benefits from combining social software and business process management, a new challenge arises out of the changing roles of producer and consumer in modern business processes. For a long time, the understanding prevailed, that the single locus of interaction between the producer and the consumer is at the end of the business processes [8]. That means business processes provide goods or

F. Daniel et al. (Eds.): BPM 2011 Workshops, Part I, LNBIP 99, pp. 242–252, 2012.
© Springer-Verlag Berlin Heidelberg 2012

services to the customer in exchange for payment. Following the ideas of Taylorism [9] and Fordism [10], [11], goods and services are produced in an industrialized way and separated from the customer in order to achieve high economies of scale. In the past, industrialization has led to enormous gains in efficiency of production.

However, this approach to differentiate strictly between an active, value-creating producer and a passive, value-destroying consumer is questioned increasingly. Instead, the producer is a partner of an increasingly active prosumer, interacting with the producer in order to create value. In this way, the former unidirectional structure is transformed to a bidirectional and dynamic one.

The traditional role model of industry is further questioned by new business models such as group purchases [12]. They profit from the rise of socials networks [12] [13]. Thus, the flow-oriented structures of retail become more and more network ones.

Therefore it does not surprise that many enterprises strive for integrating their customers more intensively into the value chain: an active role of the consumer is demanded [8] in order to leverage the innovative power of the consumer. The customer is always involved into the creation of value [14]. Such an active consumer is called prosumer [4]. Enterprises aim to leverage the potential to co-create value together with their prosumers. The prosumers engage in dialog with enterprises during each stage of the product lifecycle[15]. Based on this change of the roles of producer and the consumer, now prosumer, business processes have to be adapted and the involvement of social software has to be rethought. However, the mechanisms how social software provides support for business processes in order to co-create value with the prosumer is not well explored.

Therefore, this paper will investigate the possibilities to support business process management by social software in order to enable the co-creation of value. The paper proceeds as follows: First, an analysis of industrialized business processes is made. Based on this analysis, the support of social software for the co-creation of value is shown. Also, the influence on business process management is illustrated. Other research in this area is discussed in the following section related work. Finally, a conclusion and outlook is given.

2   Industrialized Business Processes

Present business process management is strongly influenced by the ideas of industrialization. Goods are produced in a highly efficient manner by separating the production from the customer, as shown in the scenario below. The single locus of interaction between customer and produces it at the end of the value chain and the relationship between to the customer is restricted to a single transaction [8]. The separation from the consumer and standardized production make it possible to concentrate production to one or only few productions sites. By this, huge scaling effects are possible that allow offering the produced good at a low price [9]. However, this view – later evolving into Fordism [10] – also contradicts to individual products. Individual wishes of the customer are not taken into account, or as Ford expressed it in [16]: "Any customer can have a car painted any color that he wants so long as it is black."

To illustrate the following considerations, the production of frozen food shall be used, as shown in figure 1. The production of frozen foods shows all advantages of an industrialized production. Instead of employing hundreds of cooks preparing the consumers' meals individually, only one cook prepares the meal on the frozen food production site. Thus, high economies of scale can be leveraged.

The core process starts with the development of the recipe. Then the packaging is designed. Before the production can start the ingredients and the packaging has to be procured. Finally, the produced frozen food is delivered to the shops. The only interaction with the customer is at the end of the business process, when he – hopefully – buys the frozen product.

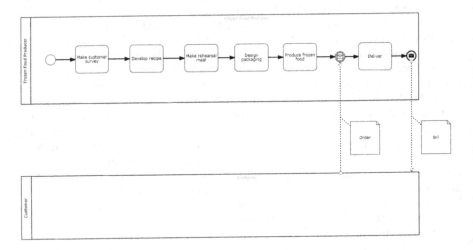

Fig. 1. Frozen food production

It quickly became obvious, that such an isolated process is not very sustainable. Therefore, synchronous interactions have been introduced in order to know more about the customer preferences. E.g. in the scenario above, the customer survey and the rehearsal meals are such synchronous points of interaction. Customer surveys are made to capture the consumers' expectations and to "repair" the deficits of industrialized production. However, the producer has to do large investments without knowing whether the customer will accept his product offering in the end. It is necessary to ask a large number of people to get representative results; you have to pay probands for tasting the meal etc. Nevertheless, such measures always imply the danger of ignoring important facts, because it is not known who has to be asked in the survey etc.

3   Co-creation of Value Using Social Software

The separation of the producer from the customer introduced by industrialized processes is no longer feasible. According to [8] companies can no longer act autonomously. The strict separation of the role of the producer and consumer cannot be maintained [4]. The high effort for capturing consumers' requirements as shown above is not the only disadvantage. Consumers strive for a more active role, or as expressed in [8]: "consumers want to interact with firms and thereby co-create value".

There are five basic types of value co-creation: innovation, co-production, customization, integration and personalization [17], [18], as shown in figure 2. All types of value co-creation imply that interactions take place between producer and prosumer. Most of them cannot be predetermined regarding both their number and their temporal relation to the business process. Thus, value co-creation implies the support for ad-hoc, asynchronous interactions between producer and prosumer. Important to note is that these interaction may overlap. E.g. the production of the food starts in the factory of the producer and ends on the plate of the prosumer. The asynchronous interactions for supporting value co-creation are more than only a bi-directional information exchange with the customer, but the creation of a learning relationship [8] between producer and prosumer as peers.

To illustrate asynchronous interactions, examples shall be given. Innovation is the first interaction co-creating value. The prosumer may provide his ideas for new meals and changes in the recipe. Also, the production of the meal can be used to co-create value. Instead of completely finishing the production of the meal, some very last steps of production may be given to the prosumer. E.g. he may add further ingredients, which are not possible to freeze such as fresh eggs. In this way producer and prosumer may leverage benefits. The producer may offer an additional product; the prosumer can reduce his effort for this meal. A customization interaction between producer and prosumer may be the definition of appropriate unit sizes. It has to be decided how many package sizes shall be produced. Also integration is a possibility to co-create value by an interaction between producer and prosumer. The prosumer may communicate to the producer the available to prepare the meal. Finally personalization is another interaction which enables value co-creation. The producer may collect ideas how to add a personal touch to the meals and distribute them to the other prosumers. Thus, the producer is able to increase the intrinsic value for the prosumer. The prosumer gets meals which are more than heated-up frozen food.

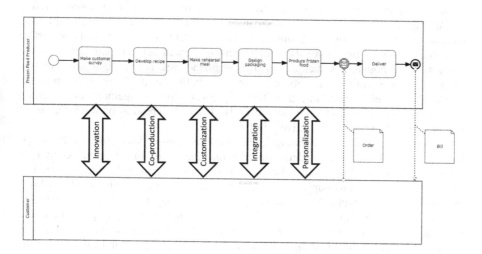

Fig. 2. Value co-creation interactions

Business processes are extended by asynchronous interactions for integrating consumers as prosumers. They may strongly influence the value created by a business process. These interactions may happen anywhere and anytime [8] as shown in figure 2. It is not possible to predetermine these interactions, which may be initiated by the producer or prosumer and which may also include multiple prosumers. Thus, interactions are not restricted to one-to-one interactions. Instead, one-to-many interactions are found quite frequently.

Complaints and suggestions are conveyed by the prosumer independently and not synchronized with the proceeding of the process. E.g. complaints concerning the frozen food may be raised before delivery of a good due to late delivery, during delivery and after delivery. The customer may complain about a lack of supply, high prices or sickness after consuming the frozen food. Another difference of such asynchronous interactions is that many of them cannot be predetermined in their structure or content. This has the consequence that such contributions cannot be checked for quality as synchronous contributions. On the other hand, especially such unforeseen propositions may provide the greatest value by providing unforeseen ideas and improvements.

3.1   Interaction Support by Social Software

The four principles in social software: weak ties, social production, egalitarianism and mutual service provisioning are able to support such ad-hoc, asynchronous interactions. Weak ties allow finding new interaction partners; social production enables the interaction with them. Egalitarianism avoids information asymmetry. Finally, social software is a platform for the exchange of ad-hoc defined services between the interaction partners.

A precondition for the initiation of not predefined interactions in parallel to the predefined process schema is the support for so-called weak-ties [19]. Weak ties are spontaneously established contacts between individuals. They are not initiated by the management or induced by organizational structures such as department. Before social software weak-ties have been created by incident. Social software enables the creation of weak ties by the visibility of the engagement of individuals in certain subjects. Activities indicating the engagement in certain subjects are visible across organizational boundaries such as department boundaries. E.g. an individual writing to a blog or giving comments is visible to both the producer and prosumer organization. Very important, activities expressing the engagement in a certain subject can now be found using search tools. Thus, the creation of weak ties is no longer by incident but can be actively initiated.

As identified above, co-creating value requires non-predetermined interactions. However, due to lacking predetermination the quality of the outcome cannot be enforced as it is done in standard business process management. Social software can fill this gap by providing support for social production. Social Production [3], [20] is the creation of artifacts, by combining the input from independent contributors without predetermining the way to do this. It is possible to integrate new and innovative contributions not identified or planned in advance in a very flexible way by these means. Because nothing is defined in advance, changes can be done until the last possible moment. Very important, social production helps to solve the dilemma created by the need for not pre-determined interactions. Social production uses a holistic, a-posteriori approach for quality control. Quality is not enforced by deliberately defining quality controls for the single step of production in advance, but by using collective evaluation of the overall result after production. This collective evaluation is done by comments, recommendation and reputation mechanisms, which are widespread in social software. Valuable contributions are commented positive and increase the reputation of the contributor.

The co-creation of value also implies the increasing equalization of the producer and prosumer role. This is achieved by an egalitarian [20] approach. Social software highly relies on egalitarianism and therefore strives for giving all participants the same rights to contribute. The goal is to encourage a maximum of contributors and to get the best solution by fusioning a high number of contributions, thus enabling the "wisdom of the crowds" [20]. Social software realizes egalitarianism by abolishing hierarchical structures, merging the roles of contributors and consumers and introducing a culture of trust. The egalitarianism inherent to social software also supports the one-to-many and many-to-many interaction patterns necessary for the co-creation of value. It is not possible to predetermine all valuable contributions to improve a product. Thus an open approach is necessary, allowing each participant to contribute equally assures to collect a maximum of input. The following quality enforcement by recommendations and comments assures the quality of the contributions.

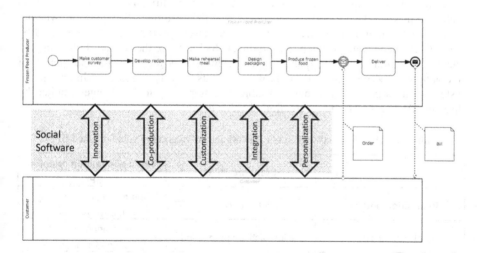

Fig. 3. Social Software support for value co-creating interactions

Concerning the scenario introduced above, the customer can contribute ideas etc. not only during the customer survey and the rehearsal meal, but anytime, as shown in figure 3. Furthermore, these contributions become immediately visible to all participants. This reduces the reaction time to complaints, e.g. No complaint-processing workflow has to be passed. Furthermore, delays due to false assignments of complaints are also avoided, because all participants see the complaint at the same time and are able to check whether there is a fault in their domain. The public documentation of complaints may surprise at first sight; however it helps the enterprise to quickly detect if there is really something wrong with a product. Furthermore, a bad-willing comment often stirs up positive comments. Such positive comments are of special value because they are read by other consumers and have a high degree of credibility. Furthermore, engaged prosumers also provide suggestions to improve the product, e.g. they may provide interesting new recipes the learned about or they may give hints how to improve packaging. Another kind of value contributing interactions are suggestions for cross- and up-selling. In the scenario, the consumers of certain types of meals, e.g. Italian meals, may receive notice about new products of the same or similar kind such as other meals from the Mediterranean.

4   Value Co-creation Oriented Business Process Management

The support of value co-creation by social software has side-effects on business process management and foster the creation of a value co-creation oriented Business Process Management. First, there is no completely predefined process schema anymore, instead, the interactions between producer and prosumer that are not known in advance. Second, the interactions are asynchronous and cannot be assigned to a certain point in the process. Third these interactions are not only one-to-one but also one-to-many.

Value co-creation also influences the manner how quality and thus customer (prosumer) satisfaction is achieved. In former times, quality has been achieved by an elaborate product design, mostly separated from the customer. The question, whether the customer's requirements have had been correctly captured, had been answered by the market. Inadequate products and producers had to leave the market. Following the value co-creation approach, quality is also achieved by the intensity and quality of interactions between producer and prosumer. Thus, quality is achieved in an a-priori instead of an a-posteriori manner. In table 1, a summary of the changes implied by directing BPM towards the co-creation of value is given.

Table 1. Differences between classical BPM and co-creation of value oriented BPM

	Standard BPM	Value co-creation oriented BPM
Interaction patterns	One-to-one	One-to-one, one-to-many, many-to-many
Predefined	All interactions predefined	Predefined and not predefined interactions
Synchronous / asynchronous interactions	Synchronous interactions	Synchronous and asynchronous interaction
Quality	Quality-by-design, a posteriori	Quality-by-interaction, a-priori

5   Related Work

Related work can be found in both in the research about augmenting of business process management by ad-hoc mechanisms and basic research about value-co-creation.

The support of value-co-creation has overlapping requirement with the support of an agile BPM lifecycle. Nevertheless Agile BPM has another intention. In [21] three prerequisites for an agile BPM lifecycle are identified: responsiveness, organizational and semantic integration. Responsiveness is the capability of the BPM lifecycle to adapt in reaction to external events. Organizational integration denotes the capability of the BPM lifecycle to receive input from all stakeholders of the business process. Semantic integration stands for the ability to merge the different views of the stakeholders to a common body of knowledge.

The conceptual handling of ad-hoc mechanisms as extensions of business processes is part of the study done in [22]. The ADEPT approach introduces concepts and tools to handle exceptions during process execution. Based on a set of rules, the ad-hoc change of the process change is allowed or denied [23]. This approach is very useful, if the rules for valid ad-hoc changes can be determined in advance. E.g. in the medical area. However, in business the truly innovative ideas often break with rules, hitherto taken for fixed. In [24] a constraint-based language is used to handle instance-related exceptions. It has to be known a-priori which kind of exception will appear. However, this is not a realistic precondition in the business area. A constraint-based approach for handling exceptions in business processes is also proposed in [25]. The problems created when supporting ad-hoc processes in the public sector are discussed in [26]. Business process modeling approaches such as BPMN [27] offer so called ad-hoc sub processes. However, they have to be known in advance to be handled properly. Worklets [28] are set of self-contained, generic workflows to handle exceptions.

A conceptual analysis of co-creation of value is made in [29]. A fundamental analysis of value and value co-creation in services is done in [14]. The debate of value-in-use vs. value-in-exchange is considered in a very detailed manner. Especially the importance to interact with the customer and to use small steps for innovation is emphasized. Differences between goods and service innovation are analyzed in [30]. The importance to collaborate and to co-create value in services to achieve a strategic advantage is examined in [31]. The importance to interact with the customer in general is shown in [8]. The nature of value co-creation in services is analyzed in [32]. In [33] the role of the customer in new service development is discussed. In [34] a model of value co-creation using service systems [35] is developed. However, it is too abstract to give concrete hints for the design of business processes. In [36] the service system approach is used to analyze the value-provided in several IT service engagements. However, no hints for designing value co-creation arrangement are given.

A conceptual approach for managing the co-creation of value is introduced in [37]. It is based on SD-Logic [38] and differentiates a customer value-creating, supplier value-creating and an encounter process. However, no concrete means for enabling co-creation are presented. In [17] social networks are proposed as infrastructure for value co-creation. However, no concrete processes are defined.

6   Conclusion and Outlook

For a long time, business process management followed the ideas of Taylorism and Fordism. An unidirectional model of producer consumer interaction has been inherent. The only locus of interaction had been at the end of the value chain, where the product had been exchanged for money. However, this view does not take into account that the customer – or better prosumer – can – and wants – to contribute value too. In order to enable value co-creation, business process management has to support asynchronous, not predetermined interactions between producer and consumer. These interactions follow not only a one-to-one pattern, but also a one-to-many or many-to-many pattern.

Social software is capable to support such interactions between producer and prosumer by the four principles realized in social software: weak ties, social production, egalitarianism and mutual service provisioning. Weak ties allow finding new interaction partners. Social software supports the initiation of weak ties by making visible the engagement for a certain subject. Social production enables the interaction between producer and prosumer by providing an a-posterori quality enforcing mechanism using recommendations and evaluations. Egalitarianism avoids information asymmetry and facilitates one-to-many and many-to-many interaction patterns. Finally, social software is a platform for the exchange of ad-hoc defined services between the interaction partners. The activities in social software represent micro-services in order to provide a larger composed service or support the production of a good.

The support of value co-creation will influence social software itself. In the beginning, social software had been used only for exchanging simple chunks of information and knowledge. However, over time the information and knowledge exchanged become more and more complex and effective. Thus the exchange of information and knowledge morphed to the provisioning of services. These services may complement or replace services. E.g. complaints and suggestions collected in the product blog can be used by many enterprises as a supplement to customer surveys and research. In this way, the platform for information exchange has become an innovation service for enterprises. Social software becomes a platform for the exchange of ad-hoc defined services. Both functional and non-functional properties of services are defined in an ad-hoc manner.

This can be further enhanced by promoting the dialogue between customers. To create a trustful relationship between producer and prosumer it is necessary to provide access to information and tools. The access to information and tools is essential for the prosumer to contribute and create value. However, value co-creation also raises the question, how risks are handled, which are created by the integration of the prosumer. It has to be defined, what happens if false or lacking input of the customer creates damage. Transparency is the fourth element of value co-creation. The producer cannot profit from an information asymmetry. Instead, in order to maximize the co-creation of value, he has to enhance the information flow between provider and prosumer.

Further research has to cope with the question, how to augment existing conceptual approaches for business process management in order to integrate asynchronous, not pre-determined activities. E.g. many modeling methods only support synchronous interactions.

A very broad are of future research are possible negative consequences of using social software. Business processes with the involvement of social mechanisms may not be as fast, reliable, secure etc. as traditional business processes. An example is the detection and handling of malicious actions. The openness of social software allows introducing false or misleading information, possibly leading the enterprise in wrong directions. Therefore, recommendation and reputation mechanisms have to be further developed. This and the effort needed to implement social mechanisms may lead to increased cost.

Future work should also be done concerning the process characteristics which influence the effectiveness of social software either positively or negatively. Vice versa, the question has to be answered, which social software suits best to support which kind of processes.

References

[1] Erol, S., et al.: Combining BPM and social software: contradiction or chance? Journal of Software Maintenance and Evolution: Research and Practice 22(6-7), 449–476 (2010)
[2] Granovetter, M.: The strength of weak ties: A network theory revisited. Sociological Theory 1(1), 201–233 (1983)
[3] Benkler, Y.: The Wealth of Networks: How Social Production Transforms Markets and Freedom. Yale University Press (2006)
[4] Tapscott, D., Williams, A.: Wikinomics: How Mass Collaboration Changes Everything. Portfolio Hardcover (2006)
[5] Lusch, R.F., Vargo, S.L.: Service-dominant logic: reactions, reflections and refinements. Marketing Theory 6(3), 281 (2006)
[6] Hagel III, J., Brown, J.S.: The Enterprise Value of Social Software. Harvard Business Review,
http://blogs.hbr.org/bigshift/2010/09/social-software.html
(accessed November 08, 2010)
[7] McAfee, A.P.: Enterprise 2.0: The dawn of emergent collaboration. MIT Sloan Management Review 47(3), 21 (2006)
[8] Prahalad, C.K., Ramaswamy, V.: Co-creating unique value with customers. Strategy & Leadership 32(3), 4–9 (2004)
[9] Taylor, F.W.: The Principles of Scientific Management. General Books LLC (2010)
[10] Shiomi, H., Wada, K.: Fordism transformed: the development of production methods in the automobile industry. Oxford University Press, USA (1995)
[11] Fordismus – Wikipedia,
http://de.wikipedia.org/wiki/Fordismus (accessed: April 26, 2011)
[12] Wei, Y., Straub, D.W., Poddar, A.: The Power Of Many: An Assessment Of Managing Internet Group Purchasing. Journal of Electronic Commerce Research 12(1), 19–43 (2011)
[13] Dennis, C., Morgan, A., Wright, L.T., Jayawardhena, C.: The influences of social e-shopping in enhancing young women's online shopping behaviour. Journal of Customer Behaviour 9, 151–174 (2010)
[14] Vargo, S.L., Maglio, P.P., Akaka, M.A.: On value and value co-creation: a service systems and service logic perspective. European Management Journal 26(3), 145–152 (2008)
[15] Payne, A.F., Storbacka, K., Frow, P.: Managing the co-creation of value. Journal of the Academy of Marketing Science 36(1), 83–96 (2008)
[16] Henry, F.: My Life and Work (2005)
[17] Fragidis, G., Ignatiadis, I., Wills, C.: Value Co-creation and Customer-Driven Innovation in Social Networking Systems. In: Morin, J.-H., Ralyté, J., Snene, M. (eds.) IESS 2010. LNBIP, vol. 53, pp. 254–258. Springer, Heidelberg (2010)

[18]   Tarabanis, K.: Business Models for the Co-Creation of Value with the Customer. Journal of e-Business, 17

[19]   Granovetter, M.: The Strength of Weak Ties. The American Journal of Sociology 78(6), 1360–1380 (1973)

[20]   Surowiecki, J.: The Wisdom of Crowds. Anchor (2005)

[21]   Bruno, G., et al.: Key challenges for enabling agile BPM with social software. Journal of Software Maintenance and Evolution: Research and Practice 23(4), 297–326 (2011)

[22]   Nurcan, S.: A survey on the flexibility requirements related to business processes and modeling artifacts. In: HICSS, p. 378 (2008)

[23]   Dadam, P., Reichert, M., Rinderle-Ma, S., Goeser, K., Kreher, U., Jurisch, M.: Von ADEPT zur AristaFlow BPM Suite - Eine Vision, wird Realität: 'Correctness by Construction' und flexible, robuste Ausführung von Unternehmensprozessen (January 2009), http://dbis.eprints.uni-ulm.de/489/ (accessed: May 30, 2010)

[24]   Pesic, M., Schonenberg, M.H., Sidorova, N., van der Aalst, W.M.P.: Constraint-Based Workflow Models: Change Made Easy. In: Meersman, R. (ed.) OTM 2007, Part I. LNCS, vol. 4803, pp. 77–94. Springer, Heidelberg (2007)

[25]   Sadiq, S.W., Orlowska, M.E., Sadiq, W.: Specification and validation of process constraints for flexible workflows* 1. Information Systems 30(5), 349–378 (2005)

[26]   Gilmore, T.N., Krantz, J.: Innovation in the public sector: dilemmas in the use of ad hoc processes. Journal of Policy Analysis and Management 10(3), 455–468 (2007)

[27]   BPMN 2.0 draft, OMG, http://www.omg.org/cgi-bin/doc?dtc/09-08-14 (accessed: February 23, 2010)

[28]   Adams, M., ter Hofstede, A.H.M., Edmond, D., van der Aalst, W.M.P.: Facilitating flexibility and dynamic exception handling in workflows through worklets. In: Proceedings of the CAiSE, vol. 5, pp. 45–50 (2005)

[29]   Kambil, A., Friesen, G.B., Sundaram, A.: Co-creation: A new source of value. Outlook Magazine 3(2), 23–29 (1999)

[30]   Tether, B.: Do Services Innovate (Differently)? Insights from the European Innobarometer Survey. Industry and Innovation 12(2), 153–184 (2005)

[31]   Lusch, R.F., Vargo, S.L., Brien, M.: Competing through service: Insights from service-dominant logic. Journal of Retailing 83(1), 5–18

[32]   Payne, A., Storbacka, K., Frow, P.: Managing the co-creation of value. Journal of the Academy of Marketing Science 36(1), 83–96 (2008)

[33]   van der Wind, B.S.F.: The Use of Customers in the New Service Development Process. Writer 4, 9 (2007)

[34]   Vargo, S.L., Maglio, P.P., Akaka, M.A.: On value and value co-creation: A service systems and service logic perspective. European Management Journal 26(3), 145–152 (2008)

[35]   Spohrer, J., Vargo, S.L., Caswell, N., Maglio, P.P.: The Service System Is the Basic Abstraction of Service Science. In: Proceedings of the 41st Annual Hawaii International Conference on System Sciences, p. 104 (2008)

[36]   Stucky, S., Cefkin, M., Rankin, Y., Shaw, B., Thomas, J.: Business Value in Complex IT Service Engagements: Realization is Governed by Patterns of Interaction. In: HICSS, pp. 1–10 (2010)

[37]   Payne, A.F., Storbacka, K., Frow, P.: Managing the co-creation of value. Journal of the Academy of Marketing Science 36(1), 83–96 (2008)

[38]   Vargo, S.L., Akaka, M.A.: Service-Dominant Logic as a Foundation for Service Science: Clarifications. Service Science 1(1), 32–42 (2009)

Using Status Feeds for Peer Production by Coordinating Non-predictable Business Processes

Simon Vogt and Andreas Fink

Institute of Computer Science
Faculty of Economics and Social Sciences
Helmut-Schmidt-Universität Hamburg
Holstenhofweg 85, 22043 Hamburg, Germany
{simonvogt,andreas.fink}@hsu-hamburg.de

Abstract. Peer production uses the collaborative intelligence of its environment by relying on self-managed, decentralized coordination. Social software offers a broad variety of methods and applications for simplifying communication and harnessing collective intelligence. Status feeds, which are regularly used within social networks, may be considered as an important feature of these approaches. This article examines the use of status feeds for supporting the execution of non-predictable business processes. Given the context of Enterprise 2.0, existing business process management approaches will be discussed before developing resulting requirements for a feed-based system which will then be implemented as a prototype and showcased via an exemplary peer production process. The implementation is followed by an evaluation of the findings and results.

Keywords: peer production, business process management, status feeds, flexible workflows, Enterprise 2.0.

1   Introduction

"The term 'peer production' characterizes a subset of commons-based production practices. It refers to production systems that depend on individual action that is self-selected and decentralized, rather than hierarchically assigned" ([1] p. 62). Benkler's concept of peer production (also known as "social production") is based on the benefits that effective collective action brings to production processes. The recent progress in web technology and resulting new use cases open up a new horizon for the IT-based support for collaboratively executing business processes, summarized by the expression "Enterprise 2.0". This article focuses on the flexible and adaptive execution of business processes in the context of Web 2.0 and social software in a self-managed and decentralized environment. We take a design-oriented approach by identifying gaps in the current literature and then discussing new opportunities for the coordination of business processes, which will be realized and implemented by using a showcase example.

Section 2 starts by briefly outlining Enterprise 2.0 and discussing its use for supporting business process execution. This leads to new requirements and objectives (Section 2.1) and the design of the software architecture for the execution of business

F. Daniel et al. (Eds.): BPM 2011 Workshops, Part I, LNBIP 99, pp. 253–265, 2012.

processes (Section 2.2). In Section 3, we will describe the concept and the implementation of a status-feed-based system for supporting the execution of business processes. The resulting concept will be demonstrated using an exemplary implementation and finally be reviewed and evaluated (Section 4). Conclusions are summarized in Section 5.

2   Business Process Management in the Era of Enterprise 2.0

When Web 2.0 first rose, it primarily provided techniques and addressed applications for private users, not yet aiming at organizations and enterprises, but focusing on the communication and collaboration of multiple users ("social software"). Recently, especially short personal status updates became more and more relevant and popular. Wikis and blogs (weblogs) have already been transferred into the organizational context, named as Enterprise 2.0 ([2] p. 4, [3] p. 121ff., [4]), but the area of process management had nearly been untouched. The resulting needs for research have now been identified and several valuable approaches have been developed [5] [6].

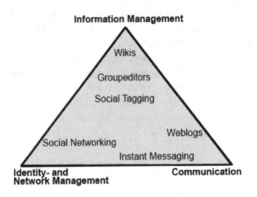

Fig. 1. Social software use cases ([7] p. 45)

A classification of typical social software use cases is given by Koch as presented in Fig. 1 ([7] p. 45, and [4]). Additionally, important usage areas may also be: management of knowledge and information, distribution of knowledge and information, management of experts and contacts, common creation of documents and project management and finally business process management (BPM). While the first four areas have already been covered by Enterprise 2.0 applications, BPM is still dominated by proprietary and custom-tailored systems, even though a few approaches and thoughts aiming to bridge this gap can already be found ([2] p. 645–722). Komus discusses the use of wikis for the collective development of instructions and procedural requirements ([8] p. 38), Neumann and Erol are using wikis to control business processes and develop the organizational requirements of enterprises and the system architecture [6]. Koch and Richter refer to the use of Atom/RSS to disseminate status updates of resources ([9] p. 125). This is where our following approach and the concept of a feed-based system for business process support start of. Therefore, we will discuss the aspect of IT-based BPM, before we describe the design and implementation of a system using status feeds.

2.1   IT-Based Support for the Execution of Business Processes

Business processes, as associated sequence of enterprise tasks (functions, activities) for the purpose of generating a valuable output ([11] p. 10f.), can be divided in four classes ([12] p. 3ff.). *Production workflows* contain repetitive and highly predictable business processes and implement the core processes of an enterprise. *Administrative workflows* are also predictable and repetitive but of a simple structure and do not touch the core processes. *Collaborative workflows* may include several iterations over one task and are impossible to be predefined. *Ad hoc workflows* have no predefined structure at all, support is limited to documentation and offering communication channels, exceptions are very common. In this work, we focus on the aspect of supporting the execution of not completely predictable business processes (collaborative and ad hoc workflows) which are found in heterogeneous organizations as well as in interorganizational relations [13].

Concerning production and administrative workflows, companies mainly trust on partially adapted workflow management systems (WfMS) ([5] p. 11). They basically provide automatic coordination of business processes while distributing information or tasks to participating resources ([10] p. 50). WfMS are based on formal process models, created by arranging tasks in the correct sequence and connecting them with resources (human or machine). These workflows can then be handled by process engines, which interpret the specification and use it for a case-specific coordination and interaction of the required resources ([10] p. 50). As practical experience shows, WfMS may lead to several problems. These can be imprecise parameters, "overengineering", a lack of planning, a variety of interfaces, a deficit in information, non-transparent action and interdependencies between instances of one process ([14] p. 2). Many software solutions try to solve these challenges, but there are several problems in the appliance of WfMS which are connected with the behavior of the company's employees ([14] p. 1f). In particular, WfMS require a behavior of participants that conforms to the process specification ([14] p. 97, [5] p. 3ff). This often leads to a "model-reality-divide" between the assumed model on the one hand and the actual reality on the other hand. This may also involve that innovations and positive developments are inhibited because of strictly predefined processes ([10] S. 55). A lack of responsibility, complicated decision-making procedures, incomplete flows of information, division-oriented thinking, and orientation to one's function alone may be the consequences that lead to deficits in innovation ([14] p. 2, [5] p. 3ff). A strictly hierarchical organization will empower these tendencies. Considering these difficulties, Benkler places emphasis on decentralization as "conditions under which the actions of many agents cohere and are effective despite the fact that they do not rely on reducing the number of people whose will counts to direct effective action" ([1], p. 62). Therefore, the involved employees and participants of one workflow can be described as a defined common/group, since they are not completely open for everyone (see [1], p. 61).

Collaborative and ad hoc workflows have so far mainly been addressed by using groupware software, which does not aim at automation but primarily at supporting the participant's communication ([7] p. 45). They can therefore create and exchange documents or get in contact via instant-messaging. The participants are self-organized; that is, there is no obvious structure or process for spectators to identify. Groupware has been existing before the rise of Web 2.0 which now brings in new opportunities and applications to harness collaborative intelligence and make use of collective action (for examples and studies see [15]), but is still unusual in the enterprise context.

Considering this gap, we aim at an Enterprise 2.0-based system for supporting and coordinating the execution of business processes. This should on the one hand displace groupware-solutions and its deficits. On the other hand it should create space for innovation and out-of-the-box thinking by establishing a structured, open and easy to follow platform for decentralized collaboration and peer production.

2.2   Software Architectures for the Execution of Business Processes

In the everyday use, software is often seen as a black box, though a closer look reveals a system of different involved and interacting components. The structured alignment of these system components as well as the description of their relations is covered by software architecture [16]. This section briefly introduces and compares the concepts of Service Oriented Architecture (SOA) and Event Driven Architecture (EDA).

The idea of the SOA is to connect and coordinate existing systems or components in a company instead of replacing them by a completely new homogenous system ([17] p. 89). Therefore, the SOA uses loose links of existing functions and applications by making them accessible via standardized protocols, independent of the used platform or language (e.g., web services). To provide extendibility, scalability and flexibility, the involved components do not communicate directly with each other but by using a service-bus.

The SOA is suitable for process-oriented workflows that can be described by requests, loops and single working steps ([17] p. 119). In contrast, the EDA provides a structure to support event-oriented processes, where an event can be described as a change of state ([18] p. 1). The EDA is not to be seen as a rival to the SOA but as an extension ([17] p. 121). Its software structure describes the so-called middleware (often message-oriented, MOM) as core element which can also be named as event-processor ([17] p. 121). The involved components send an event of a special type to this middleware where other components have previously registered themselves for special event-types. As soon as an event arrives at the middleware it sends a message to the registered components that will then pick up that event. Besides the middleware as event-processor there are event-publishers and registered event-consumers which will then continue with the next event on their part (event-reaction) [18]. This architecture determines some fundamental characteristics ([17] p. 122f.): The MOM works as mediator. Thus, an event-publisher does not know where and how the event is preceded next. The participating components do not communicate directly but in an asynchronous manner, while the semantic of the exchanged messages has to be platform independent and standardized to be understandable for everyone. The event-consumers work autonomously and can decide themselves which events to take and what to do with them.

3   Design of a Feed-Based BPM-System

3.1   Requirements and Fundamental Architecture

According to the previous sections, our scientific objective is to develop a system to support the execution of collaborative and ad hoc workflows which provides a high level of flexibility and interoperability by using Web 2.0 elements and works as a platform for coordinating the process by considering the advantages of peer production. Therefore, the following requirements are set up for this artifact: i) According to the principles of Web 2.0: simple concept, low requirements for the technical infrastructure, low barriers for the users to participate, usage of collective intelligence, simple implementation and administration, open source-code. ii) Following the findings in BPM: flexibility against changes and deviations, simple adoption to inter- and intraorganizational conditions, low implementation and operating costs, usage of innovation conducted by employees, space for self-management, extendibility and interfaces for linkage and combining the software with existing systems.

To meet these requirements and achieve the scientific objective, we propose an approach which is inspired by social network's status feeds: it uses these feeds as description of events or transitions. Since we are trying to support the execution of collaborative and ad hoc workflows and to provide space for employees' innovations, ideas and synergetic effects, the approach synthesizes the EDA and the capability- and behavior-oriented process organization [14] along with the concept of peer production [1].

The general system design is based on three fundamental components and their interaction (see Fig. 2). The underlying structure corresponds to the EDA as described in Section 2.2, to meet the requirements as stated above, especially concerning the ad hoc characteristics of the processes that should be supported.

A crucial part of our approach is the message-oriented middleware (MOM) in the mediating role which creates and receives events on the one hand and publishes them on the other hand. Hence the MOM works as information platform of the event-consumers (participating components). The MOM itself is not able to manipulate an event, nor knows which event-consumers process what task. To manage the communication with the participating components, a publishing protocol becomes necessary which routes the MOM's information to the event-consumers as fast as possible. Since the consumers may be humans or machines, this protocol needs to be platform-independent which can be achieved by a well-defined syntax and semantic. The third component of the system is a protocol for publishing the executed transitions to the MOM that must be platform-independent for the same reason. Using these standards enables the communication and the execution of procedure-calls in heterogeneous systems.

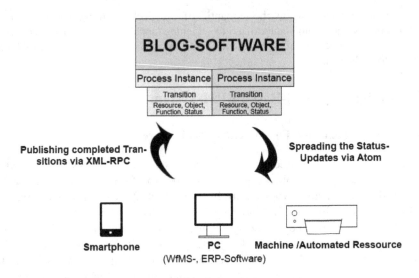

Fig. 2. Composition of the blog- and Atom-based system

3.2   Technical Design

A blog software (e.g., the Wordpress software) is well suited to represent the MOM.
A new instance of a process is realized by a post, a new blog entry which can contain
information about required steps, descriptions, remarks and a URL-based reference to
the considered object. The standardized publishing protocol is realized by the Atom
publishing protocol which had been launched in 2003 to establish a copyright-
independent, extendible format. It has been developed under special consideration of
the characteristics of blog systems ([19] p. 36). In most cases, one feed (a specific
information channel of one provider) consists of article-related entries with the
following elements: a title, a summary, and the content of one article itself, the link to
the website of this article, and eventually some further extensions.

Publishing updates via Atom feeds will be designed in the style of the "Activity
Streams" project which aims at a common, open, standardized protocol for status
feeds of social networks. Its fundament is the Atom format, extended by a custom
namespace [3] whose elements structure a status post into verbs (e.g. "post", "share"),
objects ("blog entry" or "photo"), actors, time, and target. The application focus is on
private status posts in social networks. However, the general idea of the common
standardized grammar might be adapted to the actual context, especially because it
enables that computers and machines react to some predefined vocabulary. This
approach is related to the "Semantic Web" concept which tries to establish XML-
based semantics for information to make it interpretable for machines [20].

For each post processed by the blog software, users are able to post comments. We
will use them as notification of transitions or events, published via the blog by the
involved event-publishers. Therefore they do not have to load some HTML document
into their browser but can publish the notification via remote procedure call (XML-
RPC). The typical interaction of the system is as follows: The participating resources
for a process register at the MOM by subscribing the Atom feed of one specific post

(representing a new process instance) and become event-consumers. The blog software automatically generates this feed from the published comments for one post (in this case: notifications of transitions or events), so that registered users and devices are informed about new updates. They can then decide how to deal with this event, for example by taking it over (event reaction) and work on it. The resulting transition (changed state of the considered object) can then be published via XML-RPC – a simple implementation of the web service concept. It is basically a remote procedure call, coded in XML and transported via HTTP ([9] S. 214). This enables the communication and procedure-calling between heterogeneous systems. Notifications of a transition contain information about the considered object, the executing resource, its relating function, and its status.

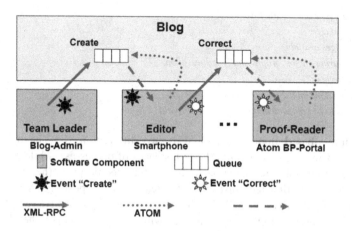

Fig. 3. System from the EDA-perspective (on the basis of [17], p. 122)

By the described arrangement, the system complies with the EDA: the MOM works as mediator and does not know where and how an event is processed. The required common semantic on the technical level is assured by using the Atom protocol and XML-RPC. The participators decide autonomously and are not directed by a central engine. Fig. 3 shows the system from the process-view, based on the EDA. Because Atom, as well as XML-RPC, is based on the platform-independent XML, all participating resources can interact with each other. It is possible to link this system and the conducted process to some WfMS or ERP-software via XML-interfaces. For example, a new sub-process can be started by the responsible WfMS by creating a new post in the blog via XML-RPC. As soon as this sub-process is completed, this information can also be forwarded to the WfMS in XML. The integration of machines could be achieved similarly.

4   Implementation and Case Study

In this section we explain the implementation of our concept by discussing an exemplary use case and describing the developed software artifacts.

4.1   Use Case Scenario

A publishing house's department for a monthly released magazine plans articles for the next issue. The team consists of employed but also freelancing journalists, graphic artists, photographers, editors, and proofreaders. A team leader sets broad guidelines for each issue and its content, in reconciliation with the departments for marketing and controlling. Apparently the team is of a heterogeneous, interorganizational structure without a strict hierarchical order. In this example, the December issue shall (amongst others) feature a detailed article covering the peace-process in the Middle-East. The initial blog post in the category "Articles" is created by the team leader and at first only contains the following information:

Peace-process in the Middle East

By Teammanager:

- *8 pages available*
- *featuring photos, graphs and rich illustration*
- *interviews?!*
- *to be done until 20th November*
- *files to be uploaded and shared in http://[path]*

The Wordpress-based implementation uses two different feeds: The more general feed publishes incoming new posts (here: instances of processes), while post-oriented feeds spread comments that have been entered for specific posts (here: notifications for transitions). The first feed distributes the team leader's post and is modified in a way that makes it deliver the URL of the post-oriented feed (see below). Thus, team members can subscribe to the comment feed without having to open the blog website in a browser.

The recipients of this feed can decide self-responsibly if they will take part in the creation of this article. If an editor is already busy doing research for two other projects, he may just write the subtexts for the photo story. Another editor may instead have enough capacity and is an expert for Middle-East topics. He works in Istanbul in an agency of this publisher and sees the team leader's new post about this article in his modified newsreader. He subscribes to the specific feed and uses the built-in XML-RPC interface for publishing his notification *"started research"*. An independent photographer, who already owns pictures for this topic, reads about this article on his smartphone's RSS-reader. Via a web browser he opens the blog website and writes (below the editor's notification): *"started illustration"*. The posted status notifications are immediately spread via the specific feed of this article so that other potential participants can see if a task is already executed. As a next step, the editor and the photographer can report their activities as *"finished research"* and *"finished illustration"*, so the proofreader is able to start his work (*"started correction"*). As soon as he has posted his notification *"finished correction"*, the publishing house's printers will recognize this because of the standardized vocabulary and can immediately start printing or buffering the article until the remaining content of this issue arrives as completed event. In the same way, the printer publishes its status report via XML-RPC.

This example shows how the resources of a creative process which is highly flexible can be coordinated using a modified blog, Atom, and XML-RPC to enable the communication. The underlying simple implementation will be described in the following section.

4.2   Changes in Wordpress

Wordpress has been developed as blog software, thus is not designed for BPM. However, the number of required changes for the concept as described above is surprisingly small. The Wordpress XML-RPC-interface can be activated via its administration-interface ("Dashboard"). The existing simple text field for comments has been changed to two lines – one for the current status of a function, and one for the function itself (like "correction" and "finished"). Because the username of each comment-author is automatically taken over by Wordpress and a comment can only refer to one specific post, a notification accordingly contains the considered object (represented by the post), the operating resource of a task (the author of one comment), its function as well as its status. In the following step, the automatically generated Atom feed that gives an overview of the existing posts has been modified and now also comes with an URL of the related comment-feed for each post. Thereby the participants do not have to load the blog website to subscribe to one specific feed. They immediately receive the required address. This procedure also simplifies the integration of machines and automated resources.

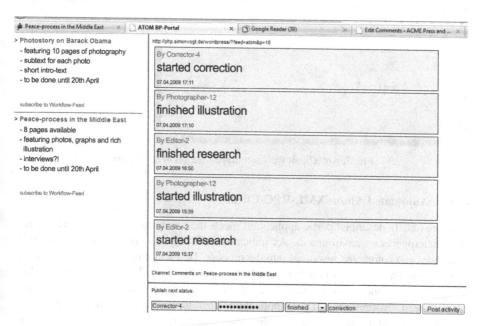

Fig. 4. Atom BP-Portal with selected process-feed

4.3   Browser-Based Atom-/XML-RPC-Client

To ensure that the participants have an overview about the existing and currently relevant feeds and have the opportunity to publish their own updates (without having to open the blog), we prototypically implemented a web-based and thus platform- and location independent user interface using PHP/HTML ("Atom BP-Portal"), as shown in Fig. 4. This application consists of three major parts: At first, an Atom parser for the general Wordpress feed which contains all existing posts (in our case: all existing process instances) and has been modified as described in the previous section. At second, a parser for the specific post that shows the progress of one process, and, at third, a form that enables the publishing of updates to the considered feed directly from this user interface using XML-RPC.

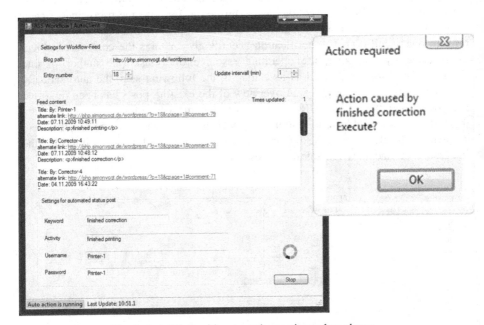

Fig. 5. AutoClient with automatic reaction to key phrase

4.4   Automated Atom-/XML-RPC-Client

The previously described portal application meets the requirements of human resources in a heterogeneous environment. As indicated before, it also is possible to integrate machines and automated resources into the process. That will now be demonstrated by a C#-application ("AutoClient") that simulates a printing unit. It reacts as soon as the proofreader or the team manager publish their final notification, enabled by the standardized vocabulary. The application therefore includes the XML-RPC-functionality and an Atom parser. Furthermore, it has a GUI to set the preferences (see Fig. 5), like the ID of the considered process, the update-interval of the feed, the key phrase that causes the action (e.g. "correction finished") as well as the status notification that will be published in reaction to that (e.g. "printing finished"). After the Start-button has been clicked, the application periodically reloads the specific feed of the process and as soon as it reads the key phrase it automatically starts its action (represented by a dialog box) and publishes the new status via XML-RPC.

These applications along with the use case example give an impression of the abilities that the combination of a blog, Atom and XML-RPC offer. This system can easily be adjusted to one company's circumstances by adapting the Wordpress software or custom client software, since all elements are open source and platform independent.

5   Conclusions

„Given what we're trying to do now, what is the simplest thing that could possibly work?" [21]

This question was Ward Cunningham's guiding credo while developing the Wiki-concept. The Web 2.0 does not consist of complex new developments but of a new composition of existing methods and techniques. So does our system. Blogs and feeds are already common in the enterprise context but in most cases just for simple news-publishing and marketing purposes.

Evaluating the developed software artifact against the scientific objective shows that the requirements as constituted in Section 3.1 are fulfilled: The concept is simple and only few changes to existing software have been made; the infrastructural requirements are low since only a web server is needed; the applications are platform-independent, open source and can be linked to existing WfMS or ERP-software. The barriers for user-participation are kept low as well, since blogs and feeds are a common feature in the everyday internet-use. The collective intelligence is used by letting the employees manage the process themselves. The implementation and customization of the software is easy and cheap, since it is open source and XML-based.

Taking the EDA as architectonical fundament enables full flexibility for the sequences of a process and conforms to the concept of peer production. However, because of the self-management within the EDA concept, complex events that involve multiple resources are difficult to coordinate. In addition the blog does not provide a discussion platform for the participants, since the comment feature is used for status notifications. This might be compensated by an additional forum/wiki. Additionally, monitoring can be ensured by using a Wordpress rating-plug-in. Since the Atom protocol is based on a pull-mechanism, delays may occur in spreading the status notifications to the resources. To minimize this delay, the Pushbutton-Web-concept as well as Pubsubhubbub may be used. These (still experimental) techniques create a hub between publisher and clients to provide a real-time circulation of feeds [22]. The system that has been developed in this article is only one of multiple opportunities to achieve the required functionality and architecture. It is also possible to use other platforms than Wordpress.

A software solution can only be effectively assessed and improved when used in reality. Practical experience enables to draw valid conclusions considering the suitability and the potential. From a research perspective we envision the use of the focus group approach for artifact refinement and evaluation [23]. The future development of social software in general as well as this particular system in the context of BPM has to be monitored. Hence, this article offers an approach for further development and amends the repertoire of Enterprise 2.0-tools and methods to coordinate business processes.

References

1. Benkler, Y.: The Wealth of Networks: How Social Production Transforms Markets and Freedom. Yale University Press (2006)
2. Ardagna, D., Mecella, M., Yang, J. (eds.): Business Process Management Workshops. LNBIP, vol. 17. Springer, Heidelberg (2009)
3. Atkins, M., Norris, W., Messina, C., Wilkinson, M., Dolin, R.: Atom Activity Extensions 1.0 (February 13, 2011), http://activitystrea.ms/spec/1.0/
4. Hippner, H.: Bedeutung, Anwendung und Einsatzpotentiale von Social Software. HMD – Praxis der Wirtschaftsinformatik 252, 6–16 (2006)
5. Erol, S., Granitzer, M., Happ, S., Jantunen, S., Jennings, B., Johannesson, P., Koschmider, A., Nurcan, S., Rossi, D., Schmidt, R.: Combining BPM and Social Software: Contradiction or Chance? Journal of Software Maintenance and Evolution: Research and Practice 22(6-7), 449–476 (2010)
6. Neumann, G., Erol, S.: From a Social Wiki to a Social Workflow System. In: Ardagna, D., Mecella, M., Yang, J. (eds.) BPM 2008 Workshops. LNBIP, vol. 17, pp. 698–708. Springer, Heidelberg (2009)
7. Koch, M.: Lehren aus der Vergangenheit – Computer-Supported Collaborative Work & Co. In: Buhse, W., Stamer, S. (eds.) Enterprise 2.0 – Die Kunst, loszulassen, pp. 17–35. Rhombos, Berlin (2008)
8. Komus, A.: Social Software als organisatorisches Phänomen – Einsatzmöglichkeiten in Unternehmen. HMD – Praxis der Wirtschaftsinformatik 252, 36–44 (2006)
9. Koch, M., Richter, A.: Enterprise 2.0. Oldenbourg, München (2009)
10. Weske, M.: Business Process Management. Springer, Berlin (2007)
11. Scheer, A.-W.: ARIS – vom Geschäftsprozess zum Anwendungssystem. Springer, Berlin (1999)
12. Alonso, G., Agrawal, D., El Abbadi, A., Mohan, C.: Functionality and Limitations of Current Workflow Management Systems. IEEE Expert 12(5) (1997)
13. Vogt, S., Fink, A.: Status-Feeds zur flexiblen Koordinierung nicht vollständig voraussehbarer Geschäftsprozesse. Working Paper (2011)
14. Bartelheimer, G.: Leistung nicht aus Zufall – Verhaltensorientiertes Prozessmanagement. Tectum, Magdeburg (2009)
15. Swenson, K. (ed.): Mastering the Unpredictable – How Adaptive Case Management Will Revolutionize the Way That Knowledge Workers Get Things Done. Meghan-Kiffer Press, Tampa (2010)
16. Balzert, H.: Lehrbuch der Software-Technik. Spektrum Akademischer Verlag, Heidelberg (2001)
17. Dunkel, J., Eberhart, A., Fischer, S., Kleiner, C., Koschel, A.: Systemarchitekturen für verteilte Anwendungen. Hanser, München (2008)
18. Taylor, H., Yochem, A., Phillips, L., Martinez, F.: Event-Driven Architecture – How SOA Enables the Real-Time Enterprise. Pearson Education, Boston (2009)
19. Wittenbrink, H.: RSS and Atom – Understanding and Implementing Content Feeds and Syndication. Packt Publishing, Birmingham (2005)

20. Berners-Lee, T., Hendler, J., Lassila, O.: The Semantic Web: A New Form of Web Content that is Meaningful to Computers Will Unleash a Revolution of New Possibilities. Scientific American 284(5), 34–43 (2001)
21. Venners, B.: The Simplest Thing that Could Possibly Work – A Conversation with Ward Cunningham, Part V (January 19, 2004),
    http://www.artima.com/intv/simplest3.html
22. Dash, A.: The Pushbutton Web: Realtime Becomes Real (July 24, 2009),
    http://dashes.com/anil/2009/07/
    the-pushbutton-web-realtime-becomes-real.html
23. Tremblay, C.M., Hevner, A.R., Berndt, D.J.: Focus Groups for Artifact Refinement and Evaluation in Design Research. Communications of the Association for Information Systems 26(27) (2010), http://aisel.aisnet.org/cais/vol26/iss1/27

Cross Enterprise Collaboration in Multi-Sourcing Service Engagements

Hamid R. Motahari-Nezhad

Hewlett Packard Laboratories
Palo Alto, CA, USA
hamid.motahari@hp.com

Abstract. This talk discusses the challenges of enabling and supporting cross enterprise collaboration (CEC) from a technology perspective. We use the collaboration requirements of multiple service providers in the context of multi-sourcing service engagements as an exemplary scenario to study this problem. We provide a conceptual model for examining CEC from various stakeholders' perspectives, collaboration at the business process level and technology enablement requirements at different level of the stack. Finally, we present a vision and technical architecture for offering the technology support to facilitate cross enterprise collaboration, offered as a service (called CEC as a Service).

Keywords: Cross Enterprise Collaboration, CEC as a Service.

1   Summary

Collaboration of different business entities to achieve a common goal (e.g., deliver a product or a service to a customer jointly) is becoming a necessity. This is attributed not only to customer demands but also to businesses looking to achieve business agility and competitiveness and to acquire complementary portfolio or expertise. The collaboration requires people-level interactions and execution, and also technology support to enable and facilitate the collaboration. Offering the technology support for CEC is challenging today mainly due to the current setup of the technology and IT support in the organizations that treat them as guarded castles to protect data, intellectual property and other business advantages. In this talk, we use a scenario in the domain of service outsourcing, and in particular mutli-sourcing services in which multiple providers need to collaboratively offer a single service experience to a customer. We study the technological issues that hinder cross enterprise collaboration including data and process interoperability, secure data sharing and support for people collaboration at the collaborating entities to frame and drive the collaboration.

We provide a conceptual framework for understanding the CEC issues, and present an overview of the state of the art using this framework. We then provide a vision and technical architecture for a technology solution to support CEC, which is offered as a service (we refer to it as CEC as a Service). This solution could be offered by a new role in the service outsourcing world, namely a multi-sourcing service integrator (MSI).

F. Daniel et al. (Eds.): BPM 2011 Workshops, Part I, LNBIP 99, p. 266, 2012.
© Springer-Verlag Berlin Heidelberg 2012

Technology for Supporting Collaboration across Enterprise Boundaries

Kelly Dempski and Alex Kass

Accenture Technology Labs
50 West San Fernando Street, San Jose, CA 95113
{kelly.1.dempsky,alex.kass}@accenture.com

Abstract. This position paper provides an informal framework for thinking about Cross-Enterprise Collaboration (CEC), which is an increasingly crucial factor in driving business results. We argue that sustaining effective CEC generally requires careful consideration of technology to support *both* person-to-person *and* system-to-system interaction. We outline the main ingredients of CEC, identify common CEC patterns, and discuss some key technologies that enable collaboration across enterprise boundaries.

Keywords: Collaboration, integration, process coupling, extended enterprise.

1 Introduction

This position paper presents an informal framework intended to help organize thinking about how to support effective collaboration across enterprise boundaries. The growing importance of *Cross-Enterprise Collaboration (CEC)* is well documented (see, for example, [1] and [2]). This trend is known to have many causes, such as the increased complexity of modern products and services; ongoing pressure to cut costs and improve agility; globalization of markets; and – critically - the emergence of new technologies that make it possible for individuals within business partners to collaborate at a distance. While the factors driving CEC have crept along incrementally, the cumulative effect has been a strategic shift of focus from the individual enterprise as an encapsulated monolith, to an *extended* enterprise made up of independent organizations able to accomplish more together than they could alone.

Unfortunately, it remains quite challenging to support effective CEC. We believe that one reason many organizations are challenged by CEC is that they fail to develop an approach that will systematically address *both* system inter-operation challenges, *and* inter-personal issues such as establishing trust and developing a common understanding of shared objectives. To make CEC work, it is crucial to address both system-to-system and person-to-person issues. We also believe that while technology alone cannot drive effective collaboration, new and existing technologies can play a bigger role than many expect – even in relation to aspects that don't initially appear to be technological. In some cases effective technological solutions can directly address a key problem, as with, for instance, open standards and accessible Web Services,

F. Daniel et al. (Eds.): BPM 2011 Workshops, Part I, LNBIP 99, pp. 267–279, 2012.
© Springer-Verlag Berlin Heidelberg 2012

which are used to address interoperability issues. In other cases, the effect is more indirect, but still crucial. For instance, federated instant messaging can increase informal communication between individuals in different organizations; over time this can help address interpersonal barriers to collaboration by making it easier for collaborators to build trust.

To present our CEC framework, we begin with a discussion of the main modes CEC and three key functions that support CEC in those modes. We then turn to a discussion of how those functions come together in some common CEC patterns. Finally, we turn to a discussion of some established and emerging technological capabilities that can be employed to enable those patterns of collaboration.

2   What Cross-Enterprise Collaboration Involves

Enterprises interact every time they conduct a transaction, but not every interaction fits our definition of collaboration. When we talk about cross-enterprise collaboration we mean organizations, or individuals within, making an explicit decision to work together toward overlapping objectives, *more closely* than the minimum required to conduct transactions. They do this, despite the inevitable added complexity, costs and risks involved.

Carrying out these collaborations involves various kinds of *sharing* and *coupling*, which we will analyze a bit later in this paper. These common elements take on very different forms in various collaborations because the underlying collaborations they support vary quite a bit. For example, CECs can sometimes involve relatively small, tightly- compartmentalized commitments, such as participating with competitors in a marketing campaign that promotes an entire industry, or forming a short-term consortium to pursue a specific government contract. Other CECs involve longer-term commitments: For example, forming a long-term alliance that merges significant operations or creates jointly-controlled business processes with complex hand-offs and interweaving of day-to-day operations.

While each collaboration is different, we find common recurring patterns in how the elements are combined. Understanding these patterns can provide a framework for thinking about the needs of potential new collaborations, and especially for thinking about the technological capabilities that will be most important for supporting the success of that collaboration.

2.1   Two Main Modes of CEC

The role of technology is dramatically different in the two primary forms of collaboration:

1. *Collaboration between people:* All cross-enterprise collaborations have some aspects that are essentially collaborations between individuals in the collaborating enterprises working to get something specific done together. Person-to-person collaboration (P2P-CEC) often faces challenges rooted in the separation in

geography, culture or objectives between collaborators in various organizations. These challenges can be mitigated with the use of technologies to support three main functions: 1) rich communication 2) coordination, 3) knowledge sharing. Although these are the same functions that need to be supported to facilitate collaboration within an enterprise [3], special considerations often involved in supporting these functions across enterprise boundaries.

2. *Collaboration between systems*: Some forms of CEC are driven by large-scale inter-operation between IT systems (S2S-CEC). For example, when large scale business processes are outsourced, or when business partners decide to operate in close collaboration to make a large-scale, joint process more efficient, the execution of this form of collaboration is generally automated, involving transfer of data streams between the enterprises.

Table 1. Supporting CEC at the Person-to-Person and System-to-System Levels

	Collaboration between people	Collaboration between systems
Key IT functions	• Synchronous and asynchronous communication • Coordination • Shared online storage	• Federated databases and data streams • Shared processes
Key IT Challenges	• Identity federation • Platform interoperability • Governing information access	• Data interoperability • Application interoperability • Balancing access and security

It is important to note that the two modes of cross-enterprise collaboration are not mutually exclusive; instead, a given collaboration pattern will typically mix and match S2S- and P2P collaboration. The patterns we'll discuss below include examples of small-scale P2P-CEC without S2S-CEC being involved at all, (Consider, for instance, two companies deciding to pursue a joint marketing campaign). However, the reverse, S2S-CEC without P2P, is pretty much impossible: it typically requires an intensive P2P-collaboration at design time to define the S2S-collaboration approach up front, as well as ongoing P2P collaboration to maintain it over time. In the section on representative scenarios, we'll discuss some common contexts in which these two forms of CEC show up in various combinations.

2.2   Three Main Ingredients of CEC

CEC involves three main functional ingredients: (1) knowledge sharing, (2) data coupling, and (3) process coupling.

1. *Knowledge sharing:* Knowledge sharing is a core part of P2P-CEC. Collaborators can share knowledge and expertise on either an episodic or an ongoing basis in order to create a value chain that is lower cost, higher quality, or more innovative than it would be if the collaborators kept their knowledge to themselves. Doing this requires trust, both between the individuals involved, and between the management stakeholders within the collaborating organizations.

   Therefore, to facilitate knowledge sharing between enterprises, the supporting technology needs to do at least two things: 1) Provide the mechanisms for doing the sharing itself. These mechanisms can include synchronous communication channels such as audio or video conferencing, or asynchronous mechanisms, such as online file-sharing repositories. And, 2) provide that mechanisms for making the people on both sides of the collaboration comfortable enough with each other that they are willing to share. This second goal is best served by technologies such as high-fidelity video conferencing, screen-sharing, and other tools that support rich interaction at a distance. These can help collaborators build trust, hammer out detailed plans, and develop common objectives at a distance.

2. *Data coupling:* Data coupling is about automated sharing of data at industrial scale. For example, a retailer and a supplier might share fine-grained data about their respective inventory, and supply/demand forecasts in order to improve overall efficiency and profitability of the overall value chain. Data coupling is primarily a S2S-CEC function at execution time, though success requires intensive P2P-CEC at design time, as collaborators negotiate both what to share and how to share. Data coupling requires agreement on data format, access privileges, usage restrictions, etc. Collaborators must be able to access, translate, and use each other's data, and they need to trust that the shared data will be use protected appropriately.

3. *Process coupling:* Process-coupling is required for effective P2P-CEC and S2S-CEC, though it takes different forms in the two cases:

   a. Smaller-scale, *P2P process coupling* is about individuals agreeing on processes they will follow to achieve joint objectives, and then communicating effectively as they execute those processes.

   b. Larger-scale, *S2S process-coupling* is about adapting automated processes and making them interoperable with complementary processes that may be owned by another collaborator.

   In both cases, the collaborating entities invest in adapting/merging their internal processes to support the collaboration. In most cases, this involves some negotiation and compromise, where each party accepts a process that may not be what it would choose as optimal if operating on its own, in order to get the advantages that the collaboration brings.

To summarize: The two primary modes of cross-enterprise collaboration, which we have identified as person-to-person-CEC and System-to-system-CEC, take on different flavors, and can be delivered by a variety of technical means, depending on the specific needs of the collaboration. Conceptually, they are enabled by three main ingredients: Knowledge sharing (for P2P), process coupling (for both P2P and S2S), and data coupling.

3   Five Cross-Enterprise Collaboration Patterns

In this section, we'll describe some CEC patterns that seem to be typical. We highlight the kinds of coupling required to achieve various patterns and to identify some of the risks and rewards of each. This is definitely not an exhaustive discussion either in terms of identifying all CEC patterns, or exhaustively examining the ones we do discuss, but merely an initial discussion of some common patterns. We've divided them into established patterns, which we believe are in common use among collaborating enterprises, and emerging patterns, which leverage newer – often lighter-weight – technologies. The emerging technologies are just starting to be leveraged by large enterprises. They may involve technologies that are not as tried and true, but are worth exploring either because they offer new forms of CEC or the possibility of supporting CEC with less overhead.

In this section, we'll describe several representative CEC scenarios, highlighting the degree of coupling that each pattern typically entails, and some of the risks and rewards of each. In the section after that, we'll highlight several technical capabilities that could be employed to support the different degrees of coupling.

3.1   Three Established Patterns

3.1.1   Collaborative R&D
Many companies who have occasional need for a certain type of R&D sometimes find it useful to form collaborations with external labs that specialize in that form of R&D rather than to do all R&D internally since the specialized skills needed to carry out the R&D may not all exist in house. The open innovation movement has spotlighted the advantages of forming R&D collaborations.

While R&D can take many forms, typical R&D initiatives have certain characteristics that lend themselves to a particular CEC pattern: They are typically decoupled from day-to-day operations of the larger organization since R&D functions are targeted at creating the organization's *future* products and services. Many R&D projects can be characterized as involving a small group of highly-trained, highly specialized people working to solve poorly-structured problems of longer-term value in a large R&D organization. The emphasis within CEC efforts in this space is more on P2P collaboration than S2S, since industrialized, automated processes are typically not a big part of the picture.

Key elements of success: The main elements of success for this kind of collaboration are person-to-person issues: Promoting sharing of knowledge; facilitating the communication needed to build trust and to agree on a process to work together and to execute that process. Joint ideation, debate, and analysis are common activities that put stress on the coupled P2P processes when the collaborators are separated by distance, organizational culture, and IT firewalls. Because intellectual property is a key outcome of R&D, joint R&D efforts involving multiple IP owners often struggle to balance the need to protect each organization's individual IP while encouraging the sharing of knowledge needed to support creation of joint IP. The knowledge sharing necessary to drive this form of CEC can therefore be difficult to encourage and to govern because information shared across enterprise boundaries typical leaves the initiator's control.

Given the keys to success outlined above, at least three functions become critical pieces of a cross-enterprise R&D solution: 1) technology that makes the needed knowledge sharing across the enterprise boundary as easy as possible. 2) technology that aids with tracking of and protection of knowledge that has been shared beyond the enterprise boundary, and 3) technology that allows for rich, convenient, relationship-building interaction between the people involved in establishing and executing the collaboration, to allow them to build trust, and formulate specific knowledge-sharing and governance agreements.

3.1.2 Collaborative Design

Aspects of collaborative design can look a lot like collaborative R&D, especially the need to share knowledge freely between organizations, but the key differences arise when focusing on design activities that are more closely enmeshed with day-to-day operations than R&D. For instance, consider ongoing collaborative design that is part of a continuous improvement regime, in which operational data is constantly being reviewed in order to identify opportunities to make cost or quality improvements by tweaking the product or process designs. Collaborative design such as this, targeted at nearer-term impact, often involves larger groups of practitioners, and sometimes involves sharing of operational data to inform the design in addition to the kinds of knowledge and expertise involved in R&D. In other words, these design collaborations involve person-to-person issues similar to R&D collaborations, though often at a larger scale, and then they can also often involve system-to-system issues related to sharing of operational data needed to inform the design process.

Two typical examples of collaborative design scenarios:

1. Collaboration between various entities participating in a supply chain, who share information about their internal processes and challenges so that participants can make design changes that improve the effectiveness (in terms of cost and/or quality) of the overall chain.

2. Collaboration between companies forming an alliance to go to market with an offering that combines elements of their respective product lines.

In the typical supply chain case, a common pattern is for a manufacturer to work very closely with select component suppliers to form an integrated design team. This contrasts with an arms-length supplier relationship in which a customer might design the parts they need, then put out a spec for bids. In collaborative design, the joint design team shares a lot of information and expertise about the needs of the product in which the part will be used, as well as the options for the design and manufacture of the product, such that the product company's knowledge can influence the design of the part, and the manufacturer of the part can influence the design of the product. When successful, this can lead to an overall product that is more efficient to produce, and perhaps more functional, than if the designs had been modularized in the traditional way.

Key elements of success: Since collaborative design involves high-stakes commitments, the first element of success is a mechanism to ensure rich and effective person-to-person collaboration can be supported between the architects of the strategic relationships, ensuring that they have high-touch interaction needed to build trust, as well as an ability conduct fine-grained discussion needed to get details right. It is common for such collaborations to be formed between companies that also maintain active relationships with the competitors of their collaborators, which means that collaborators expose themselves to the risk that proprietary information will be shared with competitors. Careful agreements, a jointly-managed governance model, and mechanisms for protecting against data loss are key elements of success.

Additional elements of success involve supporting the design process itself with convenient means to share status, ideas, and feedback. In addition to supporting initial design, a crucial concerns is supporting maintenance, which is can be where cross-enterprise feedback loops can be crucial; light process coupling can provide continuous sharing of information about design issues.

3.1.3 Collaborative Operations

When we talk about collaborative operations, we're referring to two organizations forming a joint operational team whose combined resources are able to achieve objectives more effectively than could be performed by a team drawn from just one of the collaborating organizations. Joint task forces in military operations are dramatic examples, as are disaster response operations bringing together police, fire, EMT and other first responders. Large consulting companies also often perform joint operations with clients, with project teams comprised of individuals or subgroups from both the consulting firm and the client.

Characteristics of this form of CEC include the following: 1) these joint teams must often be formed very quickly, knit together, perform a high-stakes, short-term task very effectively, and then disband. 2) Collaboration tends to very fine-grained and synchronous. The joint team really has to work as a single team, not two groups who happen to be pushing toward the same objective; ideally, this form of CEC should be indistinguishable from a single organization's team.

Key elements of success: Fine-grained process-coupling is at the core of many successful joint operations. For the scenario in which ad-hoc collaborative operations must be up and running quickly, as with emergency response, there is no time to prepare the ground for effective collaboration, so much depends on advanced planning, including processes, protocols, and interfaces that are open and inter-operable between all likely collaborators. Joint operations typically require very high process coupling, and very free and rapid knowledge sharing. Close data coupling is also a critical factor in some forms of collaborative operations, such as sharing of reconnaissance data, for example, or resource inventory data. Joint operations can represent a very challenging form of CEC, often demanding high degrees of knowledge sharing, data coupling, and process coupling.

3.2   Two Emerging Cross-Enterprise-Collaboration Patterns

In addition to the well-established patterns discussed above, there seem to be new patters emerging based on newer, social technologies. These include some relatively light-weight approaches that can be used to share knowledge and data within a cross-enterprise community.

3.2.1 Cross-Enterprise Ideation

Historically, value chains have typically lacked a rich feedback loop that tells companies how their products are being used, perceived, or modified by once they go out the door. Companies might share structured about the pipeline, but there was no channel for individual employees "on the shop floor" to share experience and ideas.

New social technologies and sharing behaviors can create that feedback loop directly between individuals anywhere in the supply chain. For example, a manufacturer of industrial equipment can now get feedback from an assembly line worker at an automotive company, resulting in new designs for the manufacturer, better equipment for the car company, and a better employee satisfaction.

This kind of CEC is a kind of mass P2P collaboration. It does not require any process coupling, or even require organizational support. Though less systematic than other CEC patterns, it can pay off through ideas harvested, and also by strengthening the sense of community between collaborating enterprises.

Key elements of success: Although the social applications needed to support sharing of this sort are relatively easy to set up, there are two distinct challenges that need to be addressed: 1) how to incent sufficient participation, and 2) how to make use of large numbers of contributions. Strong social search, which classifies, indexes, and retrieves relevant contributions, along with rating of contributions, are important for avoiding information overload.

3.2.2 Collaborative Optimization

Collaborative optimization involves trading partners sharing data in order to promote shared operational objectives. For instance, a retailer might be incented to share real time sales data to eliminate stock outs and improve customer experience.

Collaborative optimization is a lighter-weight cousin of collaborative operations. It requires a high degree of data coupling, unlike collaborative operations, doesn't require process coupling; each collaborator decides how to act on the shared data on its own, without having to get involved in each other's internal processes. This looser coupling makes collaborative optimization feasible in situations where the relationship between the collaborating companies may not be close enough to support deep process coupling.

Key elements of success: Three keys to collaborative optimization are: 1) knowing what data will be important to share, 2) having technology that can share securely, and 3) being willing to share. Being willing to share data that may be sensitive, and may contain proprietary value is often the biggest barrier, as the business case must be strong enough to balance the significant risks of sharing. Risks can also be reduced through the application of security technologies (discussed below) that reduce the chances of data leaking into the wrong hands.

3.3   Summary of Cross-Enterprise-Collaboration Patterns

In the collaboration patterns discussed above, data coupling, knowledge sharing, and process coupling are combined in various different combinations to achieve objectives that are difficult to achieve without collaborating. Of course all of these patterns also involve costs, and risks. Data coupling requires access to, and in some cases, redesign of IT systems, which can be expensive. Process coupling requires changing the ways the members do business, which involves both technical and non-technical costs. Knowledge sharing events themselves are not costly, but laying the groundwork for knowledge sharing - creating the incentives to share, establishing IP agreements and security measures that make sharing safe – can be. One of the appeals of the newly-emerging CEC patterns is that the cost and risks can be considerably less. And, as we shall discuss in the next section, while technology provides no silver bullet, there are existing technologies and capabilities can help reduce the costs and risks of all the CEC patterns.

4   Six Capabilities That Support CEC

This section highlights 6 different capabilities that support CEC scenarios like those we have discussed above. It is not an exhaustive list of all possible technologies. It instead focuses on newer technologies and approaches that support CEC in new and better ways.

4.1   Effective Web Services

For any form of S2S collaboration, the members of a cross-enterprise relationship need to have effective ways to have systems on opposite sides of enterprise boundaries interoperate. They will need to coordinate to execute coupled processes and expose data services to achieve data coupling. For example, one enterprise may need to access data from both new and legacy systems owned by a collaborator, requiring federation of data and systems with fine-grained access controls. In recent years, an increase in the maturity of technologies related to web services, SOA, and legacy integration have made this a solvable, if not solved problem.

By opening up key systems through web services (with appropriate levels of security), organizations will enable themselves to take advantage of collaboration scenarios like those described above. The interoperability that web services can provide are also a prerequisite to some of the other capabilities described below; web services often form the underlying foundation for richer forms of analytics, visualization, process optimization, and cloud platform integration.

4.2   Federated Identity Management and Communications

Person-to-person collaboration with most enterprises relies on various forms of digital communication and information sharing. These include everything from instant (text) messaging to tele-presence, and from email to threaded discussion groups to online file sharing. With the exception of email, which was federated early on, most of these technologies are, by default accessible only within an enterprise. However, vendors of these technologies are increasingly able to support federation of identity and communications channels between organizations. For instance, two companies who have federated their instant messaging services (such as Microsoft Office Communicator or Cisco's Unified Communications platform) allow individuals who are working with collaborators their company has federated with to exchange instant messages, easily engage in audio/ video conferences, share desktops, and determine presence. Federating communications services can go a long way to supporting richer communication across enterprise boundaries, helping to establish a 'one team' atmosphere in which individuals build the awareness and trust necessary support knowledge and process sharing.

4.3   Security Beyond the Enterprise Border

In the world of the monolithic enterprise it was possible to at least imagine that security could be maintained by stopping intruders at the border – providing physical and network defenses that allowed only authorized persons to access sensitive systems and data. In reality, this may never have been a very feasible approach (hence the rise of defense-in-depth approaches to security), but limitations of security at the border becomes even more pressing for CEC because the very essence of the data coupling required by many forms of CEC is to let outsiders to come inside and/or to transmit sensitive data outside the enterprise boundary. It doesn't necessarily work to extend the boundary to include the collaborating organizations – one always give up some measure of control when one shares with another organization.

What's required to support data security in the context of CEC are approaches that go beyond security at the border to not just control who can get at the data, but also to track and control who does what with it. Digital Rights Management (DRM) and Data Loss Prevention (DLP) technologies are designed to help organizations limit the ways technology is used, and to track the ways it is distributed, even after it has left the owner's control. DRM and DLP complement each other.

DRM takes many forms, but generally involves encryption schemes that restrict data access to certain authorized hardware devices. The authorized devices implement various safeguards at the hardware level, such as requiring the presence of an authorizing dongle, or requiring authorization over the internet from a machine controlled by the data owner.

DLP can be implemented in various ways, including 1) network-based approaches, which involve monitoring network traffic to detect sensitive data (perhaps tagged as such using DRM technology) that is being transmitted; 2) storage-based DLP, which involves scanning storage locations to detect sensitive data store in unauthorized or unsecured places; and 3) application-based DLP, which involves building access restriction directly into the applications that access the data, and ensuring that access is limited to those applications.

4.4   Cloud Data Platforms

This recent interest in cloud computing began as an interest in some of the cost saving opportunities afforded by infrastructure as a service. However, new opportunities become apparent when we shift our thinking higher up the stack of services. As enterprises begin to put their data into cloud based services, such as CRM systems and more, they begin to create more opportunities for cross-enterprise collaboration. The most obvious example is that they give the cloud provider the means to optimize the service that they provide to the enterprise. However, they also offload some of the system integration work to the cloud provider. A cloud provider who mediates the data transfer between two organizations will be in the position of creating and managing the technical linkage between the two companies. They are also in the position of handling the security and monitoring the data flows, a role that might be outside the expertise of the collaborators. Therefore, cloud providers have the opportunity to provide the service of connecting, mediating, and supporting intra-enterprise collaboration. Enterprises using such services could immediately benefit in the form of streamlined collaboration and data sharing.

4.5   Crowdsourcing Platforms

The cross-enterprise ideation pattern discussed in section 3.2.1 can be enabled by various kinds of crowdsourcing technologies [4], such as Wiki platforms and other distributed ideation tools. These are designed to allow a large, distributed group to debate ideas and work together to co-create artifacts that bring together contributions from many group members without requiring intensive top-down organization. Crowdsourcing platforms vary considerably in their details, but can generally be characterized by two key elements: 1) They make contributing content and ideas very easy for individual users, and 2) they include some mechanisms for bottom-up quality control. These mechanisms can be as simple as supporting meta-conversations about the content (as in Wikipedia 'discussion' pages about each article), or allowing users to rate the quality of each other's contributions (as with Dell's IdeaStorm).

Crowdsourcing platforms have the advantage that they are relatively easy to create and deploy since they do not require intensive integrations, and there are number of off-the-shelf options available to serve as the foundation. On the other hand, deploying a crowdsourcing tool is not sufficient to create a thriving community of users on it: The successful use of crowdsourcing tools seems to depend on at least three factors: 1) Making it very easy to contribute, without requiring extra steps or approvals; 2) actively recognizing valuable contributions, to provide incentive for getting involved; and 3) accomplishing the cultural shift needed to make users comfortable with sharing issues in a forum accessible to external collaborators.

On the recognition front, approaches vary: Some crowdsourcing systems reward good ideas with tangible benefits such as cash or prizes. Others focus on intangible rewards such as recognition by the community. Different approaches seem to work in various contexts. Successful crowdsourcing solutions are based on developing the right incentive structure for the desired outcomes.

4.6 Process-Driven Collaboration Tools

Many so-called collaboration tools are really just general-purpose communication tools. They can be convenient, but do not use the structure of the work process to shape that communication. For example, getting input on a document often involves sending it to a collaborator over email, crafting a message requesting feedback, and perhaps calling to receive the feedback. Outside of highly-structured workflows, there is little support for structuring these collaborative activities, or making them visible to those engaged in related activities. Complications increase when crossing enterprise boundaries: Collaborators are often left wondering if the recipient read the document, if progress is being made, or if everyone understands the current status. Process-Driven Collaboration (as discussed, for instance, in [3]) is an approach that focuses on integrating collaboration tools as deeply as possible with business applications and processes. It generalizes the idea of the workflow engine with support for less structured processes, and dynamic analysis to support search for relevant assets and expertise. Process driven collaboration tools, properly federated between enterprises, could streamline cross-enterprise processes.

5 Conclusion

Cross-enterprise collaboration is too complex to allow for a comprehensive discussion in a paper of this length. Our goal has been to provide an informal framework to help the reader *begin* organizing their thinking about the established and emerging CEC patterns we hear about most often, and the technologies that support them. One key point about of our argument is that almost all cross-enterprise collaborations require support for both system-to-system and person-to-person collaboration in mind.

Of course, we make no claim that patterns we have discussed represent a comprehensive set or that we've fully analyzed those patterns. Our purpose has been to provide a foundation for future work, which we expect would include the following: 1) conducting a comprehensive inventory of all the important CEC patterns; 2) analyzing those patterns more formally; and 3) providing a more rigorous analysis of the technologies that can be used to support those patterns.

References

1. Stephenson, C., et al.: Cross-Enterprise Leadership: Business Leadership for the Twenty-First Century. Wiley and Sons, Canada (2010)

2. Dyer, J.H.: Collaborative Advantage: Winning through Extended Enterprise Supplier Networks. Oxford University Press, New York (2000)
3. Kass, A.: Making Collaboration Technology Work for the Enterprise. Accenture White Paper, available from the author, San Jose, CA (2010)
4. Howe, J.: Crowdsourcing: Why the Power of the Crowd is Driving the Future of Business. Three Rivers Press, New York (2008)

Towards Collaborative
Cross-Organizational Modeling*

Christian Pichler[1], Manuel Wimmer[2], Konrad Wieland[2],
Marco Zapletal[2], and Robert Engel[2]

[1] Research Studios Austria Forschungsgesellschaft mbH
Research Studio Inter-Organizational Systems
Vienna, Austria
christian.pichler@researchstudio.at
[2] Vienna University of Technology
Institute of Software Technology and Interactive Systems
Vienna, Austria
{wimmer,wieland}@big.tuwien.ac.at, {marco,engel}@ec.tuwien.ac.at

Abstract. Standardized business documents are a prerequisite for successful electronic information exchange in inter-organizational systems. These documents are typically defined through Standard Developing Organizations (SDOs) such as the United Nations Centre for Trade Facilitation and eBusiness (UN/CEFACT). In today's highly dynamic environment with ever-changing market demands, SDOs are confronted with the need to constantly evolve their standardized business documents based on the needs of business partners utilizing these documents. However, the business document development process between SDOs and business partners is currently lacking efficient collaborative support. In this position paper, we present (i) a reference model supporting hierarchical, collaborative and cross-organizational business document modeling, (ii) a conflict resolution model to find a consolidated version of a new business document model as well as (iii) our vision of a Configurable Collaboration-Aware Online Model Repository.

Keywords: cross-organizational, collaboration, reference model, conflict resolution, business document model, model repository.

1 Introduction

Seamless information exchange between business partners is a prerequisite for successful collaboration in cross-organizational scenarios enabling electronic business transactions. Nowadays, systems and applications facilitating cross-organizational information exchange tend to be implemented following the service-oriented architecture paradigm. One important aspect of such systems includes

* The work of Research Studios Austria is funded by the Austrian Federal Ministry of Science and Research. Furthermore, this work has been carried out under the research grant Public Private Interoperability (No. 818639) of the Austrian Research Promotion Agency (FFG).

F. Daniel et al. (Eds.): BPM 2011 Workshops, Part I, LNBIP 99, pp. 280–292, 2012.

specifying the structure and the semantics of the information exchanged. This may be achieved through business documents defining service interfaces.

In general, there are two different approaches for defining business documents. First, business documents may be specified on the transfer syntax level meaning that a particular notation, such as XML Schema, is used for defining the format. Second, business documents may be created on the conceptual level utilizing a particular modeling language, such as UML class diagrams. These conceptual business document models serve as a basis for generating implementation artifacts such as Web Service Description Language (WSDL) files.

Such a conceptual business document modeling approach is envisioned by the Core Component technology [18] of the United Nations Centre for Trade Facilitation and eBusiness (UN/CEFACT), which became generally known for maintaining the United Nations Directories for Electronic Data Interchange for Administration, Commerce and Transport (UN/EDIFACT) standards [21]. In a nutshell, Core Components represent standardized, domain-independent, customizable, as well as reusable building blocks for defining business document models (cf. Fig. 1, Mark 1). Furthermore, UN/CEFACT provides these reusable building blocks through the publicly available Core Component Library (CCL)[17]. Business partners as well as Standard Developing Organizations (SDOs) may then define their business document models through customizing the building blocks provided in the CCL (cf. Fig. 1, Mark 2).

However, in such a highly dynamic environment with ever-changing market needs, the requirements of market participants typically change. As a consequence, business partners are often confronted with the need to adapt the business documents in use. For requesting changes to standardized business documents created and maintained through SDOs, business partners typically have to follow standardization processes dictated through SDOs. For fostering agile standardization efforts as well as for reaching broader acceptance of standardized business documents, support for hierarchical, collaborative, and cross-organizational modeling is needed.

Therefore, the remainder of this paper is structured as follows: Section 2 stresses on state-of-the-art in collaborative, cross-organizational modeling motivated through UN/CEFACT's standardization process for Core Components. In Section 3, we present our reference model for hierarchical, collaborative, cross-organizational modeling. Section 4 discusses our Conflict Resolution Model and Section 5 presents our vision of a Configurable Collaboration-Aware Online Model Repository.

2   State of the Art

In the following, we motivate the need for cross-organizational collaborative development of business document models as well as present an overview on related work in the area of cross-organizational collaboration. In particular, we support the discussion with our running example based on UN/CEFACT's standardization process for Core Components.

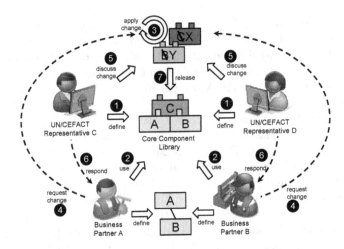

Fig. 1. Using Core Components - at a Glance

2.1   Current Procedures at UN/CEFACT

For changing standardized business documents, business partners typically have to follow a certain processes dictated through SDOs. Considering business documents based on the CCL, changing the structure and semantics of a particular business document, may require adapting the underlying Core Components used for defining the business document model. However, business partners may not directly adapt the underlying Core Components but they have to follow a standardization process for Core Components [19], as illustrated in Fig. 1.

In order to add new as well as to change existing Core Components (cf. Mark 3), business partners have to propose the change to UN/CEFACT (cf. Mark 4). Based on the proposed change, the SDO processes the changes on a regular basis in order to reflect the business partners needs (cf. Mark 4). This is achieved through discussing the proposed changes among the members of the SDO whether a change is incorporated into the business document format or not (cf. Mark 5). Alternatively, instead of incorporating the change as requested, the SDO may propose an substitute solution to the corresponding business partners (cf. Mark 6). Business partners may either accept or reject the proposal. In the latter case, business partners typically submit another alternative change request (cf. Mark 3). Once an agreement is found, UN/CEFACT refines the business document format by incorporating relevant proposed changes. Subsequently, a new version of the business document format is released (cf. Mark 7).

However, the standardization process is currently not formalized, but is described through a textual specification only. In [20], it is stated that UN/CEFACT currently struggles with the governance of the CCL and that a process supporting the management of the CCL is needed. To address these shortcomings, we define a reference model supporting hierarchical, cross-organizational development of business document models. Though the reference model is inspired by

UN/CEFACT's standardization process, we argue that the proposed reference model is generally applicable to similar cross-organizational modeling scenarios.

2.2   Limitations of Current Technology

In this subsection, we elaborate on existing technologies for collaborative development which may be employed to better support the needs of SDOs.

Version Control Systems. During the software development lifecycle, software artifacts are subject to successive changes. Consequently, tool support for managing the evolution of these artifacts is indispensable [7]. To this end, the discipline of Software Configuration Management provides tools and techniques for making evolution manageable [15]. Amongst others, these tools include Version Control Systems. So far, versioning research mainly focused on the management of textual artifacts like source code. For textual artifacts, a line-wise processing of files has proven to be adequate in the past. The situation is different when the artifacts put under version control are graph-based artifacts like models. Here, a more precise consideration of model elements is necessary to obtain accurate reports on the performed modifications and potential conflicts between concurrently performed changes. In [1], different state-of-the-art tools are compared. Since model versioning is urgently needed in practice, much effort is spent in this research area, resulting in a rapid evolution and of model versioning approaches.

Collaborative Ontology Editors. In the ontology engineering community the need for collaborative development has arisen as well. In fact, ontologies are becoming so large that they cannot be built by a single person. Furthermore, ontologies have to represent an accepted terminology for a particular community. Thus, the community should be involved in the ontology development – so to say gaining acceptance by participation. To tackle these issues, several approaches have been proposed such as Wiki-based environments [2]. For instance, LexWiki[1] supports to extend and refine terminologies by making comments and proposing changes in a text-based manner by annotations. These annotations are later examined by curators which are editing the ontologies in standard ontology editors separated from LexWiki. A step further goes OntoWiki which allows to change and rate ontology definitions [3]. However, OntoWiki only supports limited capabilities for explicitly representing conflicting changes. Besides these generic approaches for ontology engineering, there are some approaches tailored to a particular development workflow such as [12]. However, these specific approaches are not adaptable to other workflows. Furthermore, Collaborative Protégé [16] allows for collaborative ontology development by using annotations for changes, proposals, votings, and discussions. All the mentioned approaches only support the collaborative development of structured information expressed in OWL and RDFs, but models are not considered.

Although, in the papers of Collaborative Protégé the need for synchronous and asynchronous development is mentioned as one of the main requirements

---

[1] http://biomedgt.org

for ontology engineering, currently only synchronous development is supported. Thus, the conflict detection and resolution does not explicitly support what is needed for cross-organizational collaborative modeling of business documents.

Collaborative Modeling Environments. The need for collaborative modeling environments with special focus on negotiation gained academic relevance already in the 80ies [11]. In 2005, Lippe et al. [6] presented an extensive evaluation of state-of-the-art approaches in cross-organizational modeling, where the requirement for model management and for collaborative modeling has been investigated. However, their conclusion was that current technologies fail to support all stated requirements for cross-organizational modeling. More recently, Rittgen [10] presents a process for collaborative modeling and a collaborative modeling tool. Although, this work tackles various interesting points, currently the collaborative support is limited for only some modeling languages and one dedicated process. Furthermore, the collaborative modeling infrastructure is hard-wired with the proposed tool and is therefore not generally applicable. Over the years, several dedicated environments for real-time collaboration have been proposed (for textual artifacts as well as for models) which provide sophisticated notification and communication mechanisms indicating that a resource is currently touched by another team member (e.g., [13]). Examples of collaborative modeling editors are SLIM [14] and DAWN [4]. These tools only allow for synchronous modeling, that is again not suitable for cross-organizational, collaborative modeling of business documents.

3   Reference Model

Our reference model is designed for collaborative scenarios meeting the following two characteristics. First, the reference model addresses a *cross-organizational* aspect meaning that the different stakeholders involved in the collaborative process are spread across different organizations and institutions. Second, the stakeholders form a *hierarchy*, i.e., one stakeholder may overrule decisions of another stakeholder involved in the same development process. Based on these needs, we define a generic reference model supporting hierarchical, cross-organizational, collaborative modeling, as illustrated in Fig. 2. The reference model describes a generic workflow as well as offers variability aspects for customizing the workflow for a particular collaboration scenario. Generally speaking, the workflow comprises three different phases, namely the *Revision* phase, the *Consolidation* phase, as well as the *Release* phase. Furthermore, two different stakeholders are involved in the different phases whereas each stakeholder takes on a particular role. The roles defined in our reference model are *Participant* as well as *Facilitator*, forming a hierarchical relationship. In other words, the *Participant* may propose changes to a particular model and the *Facilitator* reviews the proposed changes and decides whether the changes are applied to the model.

Revision. Throughout the *Revision* phase, different *Participants* may propose changes for a model in parallel and independently from each other (cf. Mark 1).

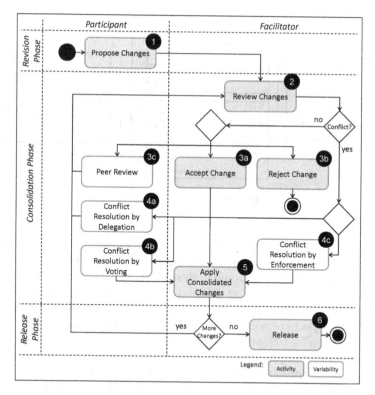

Fig. 2. Generic Reference Model

Considering our running example, business partners would take on the role of *Participant* and propose changes to Core Components contained in the CCL.

Consolidation. At a given point in time, the *Facilitator* brings the *Revision* phase to an end and initiates the *Consolidation* phase. In this phase, the *Facilitator* reviews the proposed changes, indicated through *Review Changes* (cf. Mark 2). Applied to our example, UN/CEFACT takes on the role of the *Facilitator*.

In case the proposed change is not conflicting with any other changes, the *Facilitator* decides whether to *Accept* (cf. Mark 3a), *Reject* (cf. Mark 3b), or *Peer Review* (cf. Mark 3c) a particular change. In case the change is *Accepted* it is then ready to be incorporated into the model. However, the *Facilitator* may as well decide to *Reject* a particular change. Furthermore, the *Facilitator* may want to discuss the proposed change with the *Participant*, indicated through the activity *Peer Review* which represents the first variability aspect within our reference model. This means that the detailed workflow within the activity can be customized to fit the requirements of a particular scenario. For example, in the *Peer Review* activity, the *Participant* may then either accept or reject the *Facilitator*'s alternative, as well as suggest another alternative to the *Facilitator*.

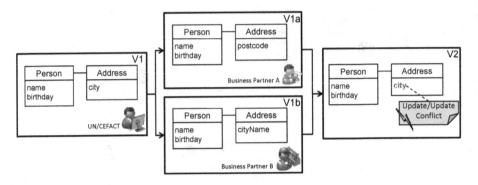

Fig. 3. Conflict Example

However, it may occur that two different *Participants* propose changes resulting in a conflict. In this case we have provided three options for handling conflicting changes including *Conflict Resolution by Delegation* (cf. Mark 4a), *Conflict Resolution by Voting* (cf. Mark 4b), as well as *Conflict Resolution by Enforcement* (cf. Mark 4c). All three options for resolving conflicts represent further variability aspects of our reference model. In utilizing the first option, i.e., *Conflict Resolution by Delegation*, the *Facilitator* does not influence the decision process, but leaves the process of resolving the conflict up to the *Participants*. For instance, in a customized reference model fitting a certain business scenario, *Participants* may utilize synchronous collaboration techniques for resolving conflicts. In the second option, the *Facilitator* provides several alternatives for resolving the conflict to the *Participants*. The *Participants* may then vote for a particular conflict resolution. In pursuing the third option, the *Facilitator* resolves the conflicting changes and makes a decision, which may overrule change requests of the *Participants*. After completing the first or second option, the Facilitator reviews the outcome of the conflict resolution strategy. In case the pursued conflict resolution strategy resulted in another conflict, a new review cycle is started (cf. Mark 2).

Regardless, whether a change has been accepted at the very beginning, has been peer reviewed, or has been resolved following a particular conflict resolution strategy, once an agreement between the *Facilitator* and the *Participant* is found, the consolidated change is incorporated into the model (cf. Mark 5).

Release. Assuming that all changes are consolidated, the *Facilitator* introduces the *Release* phase. In this phase, a new, consolidated, version of the model is released (cf. Mark 6).

4   Conflict Resolution

Following UN/CEFACT's approach, business partners may request changes to the Core Components provided through the CCL. Furthermore, change requests may be submitted on the property level or on the Core Component level, as

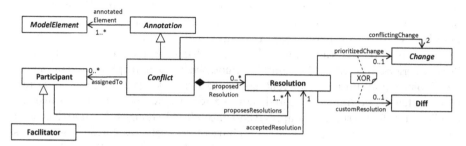

Fig. 4. Conflict Resolution Model

illustrated in the following. As elaborated on earlier, it may occur that different business partners submit change requests resulting in a conflict. For instance, consider the example scenario illustrated in Fig. 3. It is assumed, that the CCL provided by UN/CEFACT contains two reusable building blocks, namely, Person as well as Address having different attributes. Due to changing market requirements and evolving business needs, business partners are confronted with the need to update their business documents often requiring to update the underlying CCL. Following UN/CEFACT's approach, business partners have to submit their change requests to UN/CEFACT. For instance, as illustrated in Fig. 3, *Business Partner A* proposes to change the attribute city to postcode resulting in an intermediary version *V1a*. At the same time, *Business Partner B* proposes changing the same attribute from city to cityName resulting in version *V1b*. Consequently, UN/CEFACT reviews the change requests and plans to release a new version thereof. However, as illustrated in Fig. 3, the changes proposed by both business partners result in an *Update/Update* conflict since the same attribute is renamed differently.

As discussed earlier, our reference workflow model provides three different options for resolving conflicts. For all three options, we present a *Conflict Resolution Model* defining the relevant information about a concrete conflict resolution. A generic conflict resolution model is presented in [22], which we have adopted and extended in this paper to satisfy the needs of cross-organizational, collaborative modeling. In particular, one option of the reference workflow is to involve the business partners themselves in resolving the conflict represented through *Conflict Resolution by Delegation*. This option has the advantage, that business partners may discuss changes amongst themselves for reaching an ideal agreement fitting the requirements of both business partners. Therefore, we firstly present the Conflict Resolution Model supporting cross-organizational modeling and, secondly, we demonstrate the *Conflict Resolution by Delegation* pattern based on the example presented above.

4.1   Conflict Resolution Model

For supporting the consolidation phase, we have developed a dedicated model defining the relevant information about a concrete conflict resolution. The resulting *Conflict Resolution Model* is depicted in Fig. 4. A `ModelElement` may be annotated by a `conflict`. A `conflict` links two conflicting `changes` and may be assigned to different `participants`, i.e., business partners, which are responsible to resolve the conflict. In case multiple conflicts exist for the same `ModelElement`, the `ModelElement` is annotated with multiple conflicts. These participants may propose different `resolutions`, but exactly one of these resolutions has to be finally accepted by the `facilitator` in order to resolve the conflict and, furthermore, to apply the consolidated changes. No matter which consolidation strategy is chosen, two kinds of concrete resolution possibilities exist: (1) either select *one* out of the conflicting changes, or (2) discard both and perform a custom resolution, which may contain several changes. In the latter case, the modeled resolution is stored as its own `Diff` to comprehend afterwards what happened to the conflict in the resolution process.

4.2   Conflict Resolution by Example

In Fig. 5, we present the *Conflict Resolution by Delegation* process on the basis of the example presented before. Please note, that due to readability, only the most important relationships are illustrated. In this concrete example, a conflict occurred due to concurrent changes of the attribute `city`. Again, Business Partner A (`BPA`) has renamed the attribute to `postcode`, whereas Business Partner B (`BPB`) has renamed the same attribute to `cityName` leading to a so-called `Update/Update` conflict. The facilitator decides to delegate the resolution of this conflict to both business partners and, thus, `BPA` and `BPB` are assigned to the `Update/Update` conflict to collaboratively propose a resolution. They decide to prioritize the update of `BPA`, i.e. `up2`. The facilitator may now accept or reject the proposed resolution. In our example, the proposed resolution, i.e., the rename of the attribute `city` to `postcode`, is accepted and, thus, the change is applied to the model.

5   Vision

Our vision is a Configurable Collaboration-Aware Online Model Repository. In other words, we aim at creating a repository configurable through workflows describing a collaborative modeling process whereas the workflows represent instances of the customized reference model. The repository is considered to provide the infrastructure for supporting the collaborative modeling process. In the following, we define a set of requirements that such a repository must fulfill for supporting customized workflows. The requirements are designed based on the shortcomings discussed earlier. However, the totality of these requirements has to be verified after completing the research proposed in this paper.

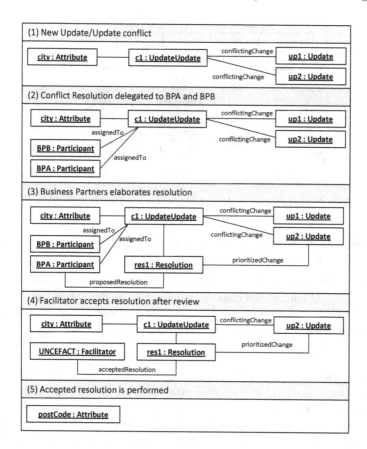

Fig. 5. Conflict Resolution by Delegation

5.1 Requirements of a Collaboration-Aware Model Repository

Model Data Management

Models. For supporting cross-organizational, collaborative modeling, the repository must be capable of handling model-based artifacts. In particular, the repository has to support the metamodeling standard MOF [8].

Changes. *Participants* submit adapted models to the repository. Thus, the repository must be able to exactly calculate the applied changes between a particular model and an adapted version of the same model, forming a change.

Conflicts. The repository should be able to calculate conflicting changes for supporting the conflict resolution process between *Participants* and *Facilitators*. This is of major importance, because the conflicts indicate parts in the models which need further discussions to reach a consolidated version.

Tolerance. Different *Participants* may propose changes resulting in a conflicting change. Therefore, the repository must be able to mark and track conflicting

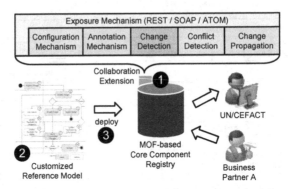

Fig. 6. Collaboration-Aware Model Repository Architecture

changes throughout the *Revision* phase until the conflicting changes are resolved in the *Consolidation* phase.

Provenance. It is often the case that *Participants* and *Facilitators* have the need to investigate back-dated changes applied to a model. Therefore, the repository must be able to provide provenance information, i.e., meta-information regarding the changes applied to the models stored in the repository.

Model Data Access

Autonomy. Development environments for Model-Driven Engineering as well as for traditional software engineering often rely on domain-specific tools and implementations. Thereby, interoperability between different tools is often inhibited. Hence, one requirement is that the repository is autonomous, i.e., it is independent from the use of any particular client. For example, *Participants* and *Facilitators* may use different development environments for participating in the process of collaborative, cross-organizational modeling.

Roles. The reference model defines different roles forming a hierarchical relationship. However, each role, namely the *Participant* as well as the *Facilitator*, has different responsibilities and authorities. Therefore, the repository must provide mechanisms for enabling such role-based concepts to allow for different access and change rights.

Model Data Manipulation

(A)synchronicity. *Participants* must be able to propose changes independently from the *Facilitator* and other *Participants*. Also, *Participants* may resolve conflicts through synchronous collaboration. Therefore, the repository must be capable of handling synchronous as well as asynchronous collaboration.

5.2   Architecture of a Collaboration-Aware Model Repository

For realizing our vision, we extend our existing Core Component Registry [9], based on MOF, through a Collaboration Extension (cf. Fig. 6, Mark 1). The

Configuration Mechanism is responsible for configuring the registry to support a collaborative modeling process. One prerequisite for configuration is to customize the reference model to fit a particular scenario which also implicates assigning roles and authorities to participants of the business scenario (cf. Fig. 6, Mark 2). Consequently, the adapted reference model needs to be deployed to the registry (cf. Fig. 6, Mark 3). Based on proposed changes, the *Annotation Mechanism* adds change and conflict information to the model, where the information is calculated through the *Change Detection* and the *Conflict Detection*. These annotations allow tolerating conflicts as well as serve as a basis for deriving provenance information. The *Change Propagation* serves as a mediator for editing models simultaneously as it is required for synchronous conflict resolution. The *Exposure Mechanism* exposes all functionality through Web-based protocols for gaining independence from any particular clients. In fact, clients rather act as consumers of functionality provided through the repository.

Future work, based on the findings presented in this paper, includes the following. First, we are currently evaluating the *Jazz* platform [5] regarding its applicability for extending the platform to support hierarchical, cross-organizational, and collaborative modeling. Second, we continue implementing the components of the *Collaboration Extension*.

References

1. Altmanninger, K., Seidl, M., Wimmer, M.: A Survey on Model Versioning Approaches. International Journal of Web Information Systems 5, 271–304 (2009)
2. Auer, S., Dietzold, S., Lehmann, J., Riechert, T.: OntoWiki: A Tool for Social, Semantic Collaboration. In: Workshop on Social and Collaborative Construction of Structured Knowledge, Banff, Alberta, Canada (May 8, 2007)
3. Auer, S., Dietzold, S., Riechert, T.: OntoWiki – A Tool for Social, Semantic Collaboration. In: Cruz, I., Decker, S., Allemang, D., Preist, C., Schwabe, D., Mika, P., Uschold, M., Aroyo, L.M. (eds.) ISWC 2006. LNCS, vol. 4273, pp. 736–749. Springer, Heidelberg (2006)
4. Fluegge, M.: Entwicklung einer kollaborativen Erweiterung fuer GMF-Editoren auf Basis modellgetriebener und webbasierter Technologien. Master's thesis, University of Applied Sciences Berlin (2009)
5. IBM: About Jazz
6. Lippe, S., Greiner, U., Barros, A.: A Survey on State of the Art to Facilitate Modelling of Cross-Organisational Business Processes. In: 2nd GI-Workshop XML4BPM, Karlsruhe, Germany (March 1, 2005)
7. Mens, T., Demeyer, S. (eds.): Software Evolution. Springer, Heidelberg (2008)
8. OMG: OMG's MetaObject Facility
9. Pichler, C., Langer, P., Wimmer, M., Huemer, C., Hofreiter, B.: Registry Support for Core Component Evolution. In: International Conference on Service-Oriented Computing and Applications, Perth, Australia, December 13-15 (2010)
10. Rittgen, P.: Collaborative Modeling - A Design Science Approach. In: 42nd Hawaii International Conference on Systems Science, Waikoloa, HI, USA, January 5-8 (2009)

11. Samarasan, D.: Collaborative Modeling and Negotiation. In: ACM SIGOIS and IEEE CS TC-OA 1988 Conference on Office Information Systems, Palo Alto, CA, USA, March 23-25 (1988)
12. Sebastian, A., Noy, N.F., Tudorache, T., Musen, M.A.: A Generic Ontology for Collaborative Ontology-Development Workflows. In: 16th International Conference on Knowledge Engineering and Knowledge Management, Acitrezza, Italy, September 29-October 3 (2008)
13. Shen, H.: Internet-Based Collaborative Programming Techniques and Environments. Ph.D. thesis, Griffith University (2003)
14. Thum, C., Schwind, M., Schader, M.: SLIM—A Lightweight Environment for Synchronous Collaborative Modeling. In: Schürr, A., Selic, B. (eds.) MODELS 2009. LNCS, vol. 5795, pp. 137–151. Springer, Heidelberg (2009)
15. Tichy, W.F.: Tools for Software Configuration Management. In: International Workshop on Software Version and Configuration Control, Grassau, Germany, January 27-29 (1988)
16. Tudorache, T., Noy, N.F., Tu, S., Musen, M.A.: Supporting Collaborative Ontology Development in Protégé. In: Sheth, A.P., Staab, S., Dean, M., Paolucci, M., Maynard, D., Finin, T., Thirunarayan, K. (eds.) ISWC 2008. LNCS, vol. 5318, pp. 17–32. Springer, Heidelberg (2008)
17. UN/CEFACT: Core Component Library
18. UN/CEFACT: Core Components Technical Specification 3.0
19. UN/CEFACT: Submission Guidelines
20. UN/CEFACT: TBG Steering Committee Call Minutes (November 30, 2009)
21. UN/CEFACT: United Nations Directories for Electronic Data Interchange for Administration, Commerce and Transport
22. Wieland, K., Langer, P., Seidl, M., Wimmer, M., Kappel, G.: Turning Conflicts into Collaborations. Submitted to Computer Supported Collaborative Work: The Journal of Collaborative Computing (2011)

A Verification Method for Collaborative Business Processes

Jorge Roa[1], Omar Chiotti[2], and Pablo Villarreal[1]

[1] CIDISI, Universidad Tecnológica Nacional - Facultad Regional Santa Fe, Lavaisse
610, S3004EWB, Santa Fe, Argentina
jroa, pvillarr@frsf.utn.edu.ar
[2] INGAR-CONICET, Avellaneda 3657, S3002GJC, Santa Fe, Argentina
chiotti@santafe-conicet.gov.ar

Abstract. The verification of collaborative processes is a key issue to consider in cross-organizational modeling methodologies. Some of the existing verification approaches provide only partial support, whereas others impose some restrictions to verify models with advanced control flow, compromise (completely or partially) the enterprise autonomy, or are focused on technology-dependent specifications. In order to deal with these issues we introduce Global Interaction Nets, which are based on Hierarchical and Colored Petri Nets, and the Global Interaction Soundness property, which was adapted from the classical definition of soundness, as the main correctness criterion. The method can be used to formalize and verify models defined with different modeling languages. In addition, we apply the method through a case study modeled with UP-ColBPIP, which is a modeling language for collaborative processes, and formalize its constructs by means of Global Interaction Nets.

Keywords: Verification, Collaborative Business Processes, Petri Nets, B2B Collaborations.

1 Introduction

Nowadays, organizations are being encouraged to integrate their business processes and adapt themselves to dynamic market opportunities by setting up Business-to-Business (B2B) and cross-organizational collaborations. Collaborative Business Processes (CBPs) define the global view (choreography) and the behavior of the interactions of cross-organizational collaborations, as well as the way the organizations B2B systems will interact [1,2]. Errors in the behavior of a CBP may affect several internal processes and cause an error propagation across the boundaries of an organization. In addition, any error in the business solution would be propagated to the technological solution of a B2B collaboration. Therefore, it is essential to provide a verification method which guarantees the control flow of CBPs is well-defined. Thus, business analysts and system designers can get quick feedback regarding the correctness of the behavior of the collaboration, previous to the generation of the organizations private processes and the corresponding technological solution [1].

F. Daniel et al. (Eds.): BPM 2011 Workshops, Part I, LNBIP 99, pp. 293–305, 2012.
© Springer-Verlag Berlin Heidelberg 2012

Currently, several modeling languages can be used to model the control flow of CBPs, such as BPMN [3], UMM [4], UP-ColBPIP [2,1], IOWF [5]. Providing formal semantics of such languages is an important task to eliminate language's ambiguities and enable the definition of formal verification methods. At present, there is no agreement on the proper construct to represent interactions in CBPs: interaction activities [3], business transactions [4], or messages [5,2]. Thus, to enable the verification of different representations of CBPs and make the reuse of verification methods easier, it is important to abstract methods from such differences and make them independent of modeling languages.

In addition, important aspects to consider in verification methods include the fulfillment of requirements for CBPs [1,2], the support to models with advanced control flow such as cancellation regions and advanced synchronization [6,7], and a good performance in process analysis. However, existing verification approaches for CBPs [5,8,9,10] do not tackle all these issues.

Therefore, in this work we propose a verification method for the global view of interactions of CBP models that copes with the above issues. The purpose is to detect errors in technology-independent CBP models. The method is independent of the modeling language whose models are going to be verified. To this aim, we introduce a Global Interaction Net, which is a particular type of Hierarchical and Colored Petri Net, and the Global Interaction soundness property as the main correctness criterion. We apply the method to UP-ColBPIP [1,2] and use CPN Tools [11] to formalize and verify UP-ColBPIP models, which may have advanced control flow, by means of Global Interaction Nets and the Global Interaction soundness property. From now on, we use GI to denote Global Interaction.

This work is structured as follows. Section 2 describes the verification method. Section 3 apply the method to UP-ColBPIP models. Section 4 presents some related work. Finally, section 5 presents the conclusions and future work.

2   Verification Method for CBP models

We define the verification method for CBPs as follows.

Definition 1. *The verification method for the global view of interactions of CBP models is an eight-tuple* $V_{CBP} = (\lambda, GI_M^a, \phi, GI_M^c, GI_N, R, P, A)$, *where*

1. λ *is a finite set of modeling constructs that defines a conceptual modeling language for CBPs,*
2. GI_M^a *is a finite set of abstract GI Modules where each* $am \in GI_M^a$ *formalizes a set of constructs* $C \subset \lambda$,
3. ϕ *is a CBP model defined by an ordered finite set of model elements such that each element* $e \in \phi$ *is associated with a construct* $c \in \lambda$,
4. GI_M^c *is a finite set of concrete GI Modules where each concrete GI module* $cm \in GI_M^c$ *formalizes a set of model elements* $E \subset \phi$ *and each cm is associated with an abstract GI module* $am \in GI_M^a$,

5. GI_N *is a GI Net defined by an ordered finite set of concrete GI Modules* GI_M^c *that formalize the model* ϕ,

6. $R : \phi \rightarrow GI_M^c$ *is a mapping function that defines a transformation from a set of model elements* $E \subset \phi$ *to a concrete GI Module* $cm \in GI_M^c$,

7. P *is a finite set of correctness properties,*

8. $A : GI_M^c \rightarrow \phi$ *is a relation function that associates each concrete GI module* $cm \in GI_M^c$ *with a set of CBP model elements* $E \subset \phi$.

The aim of the proposed method is to verify the global view of interactions of a CBP model ϕ, defined with a language λ. A set of constructs of λ can be formalized with an abstract GI Module GI_M^a, whereas a set of elements of the CBP model ϕ can be formalized with a concrete GI Module GI_M^c. The difference between abstract and concrete GI module is analogous to that of a class and its instances in the object oriented paradigm. To apply this method and verify models of a specific CBP modeling language, formal semantics of each construct must be defined with abstract GI modules. The GI Net, which formalizes a CBP model, is composed of a set of concrete GI Modules, and is generated by applying the function R to the CBP model. Retrieving the element $e \in \phi$, which is the source of an error in a CBP model ϕ, is possible by means of function A, which establishes a direct association between each concrete GI module and its corresponding element of the CBP model. The output of this method is the set of model elements of ϕ that do not hold the correctness properties P. If no error is found, an empty set is returned. Following, the elements and main features of this method are described.

2.1   Preliminaries

A *Colored Petri Net (CP-Net)* [11] is a nine-tuple $CPN = (P, T, A, \Sigma, V, C, G, E, I)$, where P is a finite set of *places*, T is a finite set of *transitions*, and A is a finite set of directed *arcs* that connects places to transitions (and vice versa). A CP-Net has a finite set of *color sets* Σ, a finite set of variables V of one type (color) of Σ, and a *color set function* C that assigns a color set to each place. Transitions may have a *guard function* G, and arcs may have an *arc expression function* E. I is an *initialization function* of the CP-Net. $\bullet p$ is the set of input transitions $t \in T$ of the place p, and $p \bullet$ is the set of output transitions of p. $\bullet t$ is the set of input places of the transition t, and $t \bullet$ is the set of output places of t. $\mid \bullet p \mid$ and $\mid p \bullet \mid$ are the number of input and output transitions of place p respectively. $\mid \bullet t \mid$ and $\mid t \bullet \mid$ are the number of input and output places of transition t respectively. For any two markings $M1$ and $M2$, $M1 \geq M2$ iff for each $p \in P : M1(p) \geq M2(p)$. $M1 > M2$ iff $M1 \geq M2$ and $M1 \neq M2$. For a place p and marking M, $\mid M(p) \mid$ is the number of tokens on p in marking M.

A *CP-Net module* [11] is a tuple $CPN_M = (CPN, T_{sub}, P_{port}, PT)$, where CPN is a CP-Net that has a set of *port places* P_{port}, which have a *port type* PT (IN,OUT,I/O). It may also have a set of *substitution transitions* T_{sub}.

A *Hierarchical and Colored Petri Net (HCP-Net)* [11] is a four-tuple $CPN_H = (S, SM, PS, FS)$, where S is a finite set of *CP-Net modules*. Each substitution transition have its corresponding CPN-Net module by means of the *submodule function SM*. The input and output places of a CP-Net module are associated with their corresponding places of the substitution transition by means of a *port-socket relation function PS*. *FS* is a set of *fusion sets* of places. P^s is the set of places of the module $s \in S$. T^s is the set of transitions of the module $s \in S$. $PT(p)$ is the port type of a place p. $E(p,t)$ is the arc expression on the input arc from p to t. $E(t,p)$ is the arc expression on the output arc from t to p. $Var[e]$ is the set of *free variables* in an expression e, and $Type[v]$ is the type (color) of a variable v. $Var(t)$ denotes the variables of a transition $t \in T$. Let K be a set of tokens. A *multiset* over K is a function $t : K \Rightarrow \mathbb{N}$ that maps each element $k \in K$ into the number of appearances $t(k) \in \mathbb{N}$ of k in t.

2.2   A Formal Language for Global Interactions of CBPs

A CBP model is composed of a choreography of interactions between organizations. In this work, we introduce a Global Interaction Net (GI-Net), which is a type of HCP-Net, to formalize CBP models. In addition, we introduce a Global Interaction module (GI module) to represent an interaction or a set of control flow elements of a CBP model. Since a GI-Net defines the control flow and interactions from a global (synchronous) point of view, interacting roles of a CBP are not represented. A GI-Net is a structured tree whose elements are GI modules. GI-Nets and GI modules have two types of places: *interaction place*, which represents the expected state of interactions and its color set is *GINT*, and *control place*, which is used to restrict and control the advanced control flow of interactions and its color set is *CTRL*. Control places could be used, for instance, in exception constructs (see section 3.1) to block the control flow of parallel interactions while the exception is being executed. To this aim, different modules are connected through control places. A GI-Net allows the connection of different modules only through their corresponding input and output interaction places, or by a set of control places that are part of the same fusion set. We define GI-Net and GI module as follows.

Definition 2. *A CP-Net module $GI_M = (CPN, T_{sub}, P_{port}, PT)$ is a GI module iff:*

1. *$P_I \subset P$ is a non-empty set of interaction places such that for each $p \in P_I$ the color set of p is GINT,*
2. *$P_C \subset P$ is a set of control places such that for each $p \in P_C$ the color set of p is CTRL,*
3. *There is only one input place $ip \in P_I$ such that $PT(ip) = IN \wedge \bullet ip = \emptyset$,*
4. *There is only one output place $op \in P_I$ such that $PT(op) = OUT \wedge op\bullet = \emptyset$,*
5. *For each element $n \in (P \cup T) \wedge n \neq op$, there is a direct path from ip to n.*

Definition 3. *Given a CP-Net module $r \in S$, a HCP-Net $GI_N = (S, SM, PS, FS)$ is a GI-Net iff:*

1. *GI_N is an ordered finite set of GI modules which is structured as a tree, such that the root of the tree is the module $r \in S$,*

2. *For each transition $t \in T^r$, t is associated with a GI module by means of the submodule function SM,*
3. *For each GI module $s \in S$ such that $s \neq r$, there is a direct path from r to s,*
4. *$P_I \subset P^r$ is a non-empty set of interaction places such that for each $p \in P_I$ the color set of p is GINT,*
5. *$P_C \subset P^r$ is a set of control places such that for each $p \in P_C$ the color set of p is CTRL,*
6. *There is only one input place $ip \in P_I$ such that $\bullet ip = \emptyset$,*
7. *There is only one output place $op \in P_I$ such that $op\bullet = \emptyset$, and op is a member of the fusion set $End \subset FS$,*
8. *For each element $n \in (P \cup T)$, n is on a directed path from ip to op,*
9. *For each place $p \in P^r$ and $t \in T^r$ such that $p \neq ip \wedge p \neq op$, $\mid p\bullet \mid = \mid \bullet p \mid = \mid t\bullet \mid = \mid \bullet t \mid = 1$,*
10. *For each $s1, s2 \in S$ and each $p1 \in P^{s1}, p2 \in P^{s2}$ such that $s1 \neq s2$, if $p1, p2$ are members of the fusion set $f \subset FS$, then $Type[p1] = Type[p2] = CTRL$.*

2.3 Correctness Properties for Global Interactions

Formalizing advanced control flow constructs with Petri nets may imply tokens in different places in the final marking of a net. The classical soundness definition [7] is too restrictive and does not support this. Other variants of soundness relax this restriction [7], but they do not guarantee that places (different from the final place) have a proper state in the final marking. In a GI-Net, we want to be sure that, in the final marking, all the *interaction places*, except the final place, are in the empty state, and *control places* are in a predefined state (may be different from empty). To deal with these issues, we propose GI soundness as follows.

Definition 4. *(GI soundness) Let $GI_N = (S, SM, PS, FS)$ be a GI-Net. Let M_E, M_0 be the empty and initial markings respectively of GI_N, such that $\forall_{p\in P_c} \mid M_E(p) \mid \geq 0 \wedge \forall_{p\in P_I} \mid M_E(p) \mid = 0 \wedge M_0 = M_E + M(ip)$. Furthermore, let M_F be the final marking of GI_N, such that $M_F = M_E + M(op)$. Then, GI_N is GI sound iff:*

1. *Option to complete: $\forall_M (M_0 \xrightarrow{*} M) \Rightarrow (M \rightarrow M_F)$.*
2. *Proper completion: $\forall_M (M_0 \xrightarrow{*} M \wedge M \geq M_F) \Rightarrow (M = M_F)$.*
3. *No dead transitions: $\forall_{t\in T} \exists_{M,M'} M_0 \xrightarrow{*} M \xrightarrow{t} M'$.*

In order to determine if a given GI-Net GI_N is GI sound, we define the extended net $\overline{GI}_N$ by adding a transition t^* which connects op and ip to GI_N.

Theorem 1. *If $(\overline{GI}_N, ip)$ is live and bounded, then GI_N is GI sound.*

Proof. $(\overline{GI}_N, ip)$ is live. Since op is the input place of t^*, for any marking M reachable from marking M_0 it is possible to reach a marking with at least one token in place op. Consider an arbitrary reachable state $M'+M(op)$, i.e. a marking with one token in place op. In this marking t^* is enabled. If t^* fires, the marking $M'+M(ip)$ is reached. Since $(\overline{GI}_N, ip)$ is also bounded, M' should be equal to M_0. Hence requirements 1 and 2 hold and proper termination is guaranteed. Requirement 3 holds since $(\overline{GI}_N, ip)$ is live. Hence, GI_N is GI sound.

In case a GI-Net is not GI sound, we want to determine the reasons. For a sound GI-Net GI_N the following rules hold: 1) There must be exactly one dead marking [11] M_D and one home marking [11] M_H, such that both markings are the same, and they are also the final marking M_F of GI_N. i.e., $M_D = M_H = M_F$, 2) For each transition $t \in T$, t is not dead. If the first rule does not hold, then there is at least one deadlock different from the final marking M_F in the GI-Net. The location of the deadlock is determined by checking each marking M' which is part of the set of deadlock markings M_{dl}, such that $M' \neq M_F$. For each place $p \in P^s$ and module $s \in S$, if $M'(p) \neq M_F(p)$ there is a deadlock originated in module s, and at least one of the transitions $p\bullet$ is the source of the deadlock. If the second rule does not hold, it means that there is at least one interaction that will not be carried out. The GI module causing the unexpected behavior is determined by checking the set of dead transitions T_d of the GI-Net.

GI soundness is determined with CPN Tools by inspecting the properties of the report that it generates as follows. Given a non-negative integer $n \in \mathbb{N}$, if each place p in the report holds that $\mid M(p) \mid \leq n$ then the GI-Net is bounded. Liveness is determined by checking if t^* is a member of the set of "live transition instances". CPN Tools also reports the sets of "dead markings" and "dead transitions", so if a GI-Net is not GI sound, the reasons can be determined by inspecting these sets.

3   Applying the Verification Method to UP-ColBPIP

The UP-ColBPIP language [1,2] extends the UML2 semantics and encourages the modeling of technology-independent CBPs in a top-down approach. UP-ColBPIP supports the modeling of interaction protocols to represent the global view of interactions through a choreography of business messages between organizations who play different roles. In interaction protocols, internal activities of organizations cannot be defined; hence, the organizations autonomy is preserved.

In UP-ColBPIP, *Organizations and the Role* they fulfill are represented through lifelines. The basic building blocks of an interaction protocol are the business messages. A *Business Message* defines a one-way asynchronous interaction between two roles: a sender and a receiver. Protocols have an implicit termination. A *Termination* represents an explicit end event of a protocol, which can be labeled *Success* or *Failure*. A *Control Flow Segment (CFS)* represents complex message sequences. It contains a *Control Flow Operator* and one or more interaction paths. An *Interaction Path* contains an ordered sequence of protocol elements: messages, termination events, protocol references, and nested CFSs. The semantics of a CFS depends on the operator used. The control flow operators of UP-ColBPIP are: And, Xor, Or, If, Loop, Exception, Cancel, and Multiple Instances. Further details of this language can be found in [1,2].

3.1   Formal Semantics for the UP-ColBPIP Language

To represent a UP-ColBPIP model with a GI-Net GI_N, for each construct of UP-ColBPIP an abstract GI module $am \in GI_M^a$ must be defined. The input and output places of each GI module are ip and op respectively, and their port types are $PT(ip) = IN$ and $PT(op) = OUT$. If the color set of a place $p \in P$ is not defined, then $Type[p] = GINT$ must be assumed. Following the abstract GI modules for UP-ColBPIP are described. We omit modules for simple control flow constructs (Xor, And, etc.) since they can be easily inferred from [12].

Interaction Protocol, Business Message, Interaction Path, and Termination. Let $r = $ InteractionProtocol be a module of S such that r is the root of the tree that defines the GI-Net GI_N. Let $s = $ BusinessMessage be a GI module of S where $bmt \in T^s$ is a transition such that $bmt \in ip \bullet \wedge bmt \in \bullet op \wedge \mid ip\bullet \mid = \mid \bullet bmt \mid = \mid bmt\bullet \mid = \mid \bullet op \mid = 1$. Let $ip = $ InteractionPath be a GI module of S where for each place $p \in P^{ip}$ and $t \in T^{ip}$, p, t are on directed path from ip to op, and if $p \neq ip \wedge p \neq op$ then $\mid p\bullet \mid = \mid \bullet p \mid = \mid t\bullet \mid = \mid \bullet t \mid = 1$. Let $t = $ Termination be a GI module of S where $tt \in T^s$ is a transition such that $tt \in ip \bullet \wedge \mid ip\bullet \mid = \mid \bullet tt \mid = 1 \wedge \mid tt\bullet \mid = \mid \bullet op \mid = 0$.

Or. The complete GI module for the Or construct is composed of a split and a synchronization part. Since the Or construct can be synchronized in different ways, the common part of the Or split is first formally described.

Let $s \in S$ be a GI module in which the Or split is defined. Given a non-negative integer $m \in \mathbb{N}$ that represents the max number of parallel paths, the transition $it \in T^s$ is connected to the place $ip \in \bullet it$ such that $\mid \bullet it \mid = 1$ and $\mid it\bullet \mid = m$. Let V' be a subset of the set of variables V such that $V' \subseteq Var(it)$. Let $EXPR_{V'}$ be the set of expressions $se \in EXPR$ such that $Var[se] \subseteq V'$. Let A' be a subset of the set of arcs A such that $A' \subseteq it \times it\bullet$. For each place $ipp \in it\bullet$ there is an arc $a \in A'$, a substitution transition $t \in T^s_{sub}$ that represents an interaction path, a place $opp \in P^s$, an arc expression $e = E(a) = E(it, ipp) \in EXPR_{V'}$, and a variable $v \in Var[e]$ such that $Type[v] = BOOL \wedge ipp \in \bullet t \wedge opp \in t\bullet \wedge \mid \bullet t \mid = \mid t\bullet \mid = 1$, and the multiset of tokens K added to the place ipp is given by the evaluation of the arc expression e, where

$$e = E(a) = E(it, ipp) = \begin{cases} k \in K & \text{if } v = true \\ \emptyset_{MS} & \text{if } v = false \end{cases}$$

Following, the Or's synchronization types are described. Both the split and synchronization descriptions must be read together as a whole

Or with Synchronizing Merge Let $s = $ OrSyncMerge be a GI module of S. For each place $opp \in \bullet ot$ there is an arc $a \in A'$, an arc expression $e1 = E(a) = E(it, opp) \in EXPR_{V'}$ such that the multiset of tokens $k1$ added to the place opp is given by the evaluation of the arc expression $e1$, where

$$e1 = E(a) = E(it, opp) = \begin{cases} k \in k1 & \text{if } v = false \\ \emptyset_{MS} & \text{if } v = true \end{cases}$$

Or with N-out-of-M Let $s = $ Or-N-out-of-M be a GI module of S. Let the non-negative integer $n \in \mathbb{N}$ be the number of interactions to be synchronized. Let

$p1 \in P^s$ be a place such that $\mid \bullet p1 \mid = M$. For each place $opp \in P^s$ there is
a transition $ot \in T^s$, such that $ot \in \bullet p1$ and $ot \in opp\bullet$. Transition $ct \in T^s$ is
connected to places $p3, rp \in ct\bullet$ and places $p1, p2 \in \bullet ct$. Transition $rt \in T^s$ is
connected to places $p2, p4 \in rt\bullet$ and places $p1, rp \in \bullet rt$. Transition $bt \in T^s$ is
connected to $p3, p4 \in \bullet bt$ and $op \in bt\bullet$. Let $A^{'}$ be a subset of the set of arcs A
such that $A^{'} \subseteq (p1 \times \bullet rt)$. The arc $a \in A^{'}$ has an arc expression $e = E(a) =$
$E(p1, rt) \in \text{EXPR}_{V'}$, such that the multiset of tokens K removed from the place
$p1$ is given by the evaluation of the arc expression $e = E(a) = E(p1, rt) = t(k)^{'}k$
such that $k \in K$ and $t(k) = m - n$.

Multiple Instances With a Priori Design-Time Knowledge. Let $s =$
MI-DT be a GI module of S. Let the non-negative integer $n \in \mathbb{N}$ be the number
of multiple instances known at design time. Let transitions $it, ot \in T^s$ and the
place $p1 \in P^s$ be given such that $it \in ip \bullet \wedge it \in \bullet p1$ and $ot \in p2 \bullet \wedge ot \in \bullet ot$. Let
$t \in T^s_{sub}$ be a substitution transition representing an interaction path such that
$t \in p1 \bullet \wedge t \in \bullet p2$. Let $A^{'}$ be a subset of the set of arcs A such that $A^{'} \subseteq (it \times \bullet p1)$.
The arc $a \in A^{'}$ has an arc expression $e = E(a) = E(it, p1) \in \text{EXPR}_{V'}$, such
that the multiset of tokens K added to the place $p1$ is given by the evaluation
of the arc expression e, where $e = E(a) = E(p1, rt) = t(k)^{'}k$ such that $k \in K$
and $t(k) = n$. The arc $a1 \in A^{'}$ has an arc expression $e1 = E(a1) = E(p2, ot) \in$
$\text{EXPR}_{V'}$, such that the multiset of tokens $K1$ removed from place $p2$ is given by
the evaluation of the arc expression $e1$, where $e1 = E(a1) = E(p2, ot) = t(k)^{'}k$
such that $k \in K1$ and $t(k) = n$.

Exception. Let $s = \text{Exception}$ be a GI module of S. Let transitions $it, ot1, ot2 \in$
T^s be given such that $it \in ip \bullet \wedge ot1 \in \bullet op \wedge ot2 \in \bullet op$. Let the substitution
transition $exct \in T^s_{sub}$ be the expected control flow of the module and let the
set of substitution transitions $T_{trigt}, T_{handt} \subseteq T^s_{sub}$ be the exception triggers and
handlers respectively. $exct$ is connected to places $eip, eep \in P^s$ such that $it \in$
$\bullet eip \wedge exct \in it\bullet$ and $exct \in \bullet eep \wedge ot1 \in eep\bullet$. For each transition $handt \in T_{handt}$
there is a transition $trigt \in T_{trigt}$ such that there is a place $hip \in \bullet handt \wedge hip \in$
$trigt\bullet$, and a place $hop \in handt \bullet \wedge hop \in \bullet ot2$. Let $Reset, Ctrl \subset FS$ be sets
members of the set of fusion places. Let $rp \in \bullet ot2$ be a place member of the fusion
set $Reset$ such that $Type[rp] = CTRL$. Let $ctrp \in ot2\bullet$ be a place member of
the fusion set $Ctrl$ such that $Type[ctrp] = CTRL$. Let the non-negative integer
$n \in \mathbb{N}$ be the max number of parallel paths within the exception scope. The
output transition $ot2$ has a guard expression $G(ot2)$, such that the multiset
of tokens K removed from the place rp is given by the evaluation of the arc
expression e, where $e = E(a) = E(p1, rt) = n^{'}k$ such that $k \in K1$ and $t(k) = n$.

Let $se = Excc$ be a GI module of S associated with transition $exct \in T^s$.
Let $q \subset S$ be the set of submodules of s. For each transition $t \in T^q$ there is
a place $c \in P^q$ member of the fusion set $Ctrl$ such that $Type[c] = CTRL$ and
$c \in \bullet t \wedge t \in c\bullet$. Let the set of fusion sets $epfs \subset FS$ be given. For each place
$p \in P^q$ that is a trigger place, i.e. a point where an exception can occur, p is
member of the fusion set $epfs$ such that $Type[c] = GINT \wedge p \neq ip \wedge p \neq op$.

Let $st = Trig$ be a CP-Net module of S associated with transition $trigt \in T^s$. Let the sets of fusion sets $rpfs, ctrlfs \subset FS$ be given. Let $rp, ctrlp \in P^{st}$ be places members of the fusion sets $Reset$ and $Ctrl$ respectively, such that $Type[rp] = Type[ctrlp] = CTRL$. For each trigger place in se, there are a place $ep \in P^{st}$ and transitions $ct, et \in T^{st}$ such that ep is member of the fusion set $epfs$ and $Type[ep] = GINT \wedge ep \neq op \wedge ep \in \bullet et \wedge ep \in \bullet ct \wedge et \in ctrlp \bullet$ $\wedge et \in \bullet op \wedge et, ct \in \bullet rp \wedge ct \in rp\bullet$. Transition et represents the raising of an exception. The place $ctrlp$ guarantees that only one exception can be raised at any given time within the exception scope. The place rp enables the cleaning of tokens after the exception was raised. Finally, let $sh = Hand$ be a GI module of S associated with transition $handt \in T^s$ where for each place $p \in P^{sh}$ and $t \in T^{sh}$, p, t are on directed path from ip to op, and if $p \neq ip \wedge p \neq op$ then $| p\bullet | = | \bullet p | = | t\bullet | = | \bullet t | = 1$.

Cancel. The difference between this module and the Exception module is that the arc going from transition $ot2$ to place op is not part of the Cancel GI module. Then, when an exception occurs, the Cancel finishes the process execution.

3.2   Applying the Verification Approach to an Example

We applied the verification method to a collaborative model for the supply chain management of desktop computers and notebooks, taken from a real world case study. In this scenario, there are two organizations collaborating to agree on a demand forecast. Fig. 1a shows the interaction protocol for this process. The *Success* element in the Or construct was intentionally added to show the results of the verification approach. Fig. 1b shows the GI-Net that represents the interaction protocol of the scenario in CPN Tools. The left part of Fig. 1b shows the tree structure of the GI-Net. Fig. 1c shows three concrete GI modules of the GI-Net: Or with Synchronizing Merge, Business Message, and Exception. The last one is composed of three main modules: the expected (normal) interaction flow (exct), the exception trigger (trigt) (which is also shown in Fig. 1c), and the exception handler (handt). The report generated by CPN Tools returned three dead markings. One of them represents the proper termination of the CBP, whereas the other two represent a deadlock caused by the definition of the termination "Success" in one of the interaction paths of the Or construct. The semantics defined for the Or construct establishes that once a path has been enabled, it must be synchronized. In the example, the synchronization will never occur since the termination construct "Success" finishes the CBP before the synchronization can be realized. Furthermore, since both paths in the Or construct are concurrent, interactions may occur even when the CBP has already finished through the termination "Success". We get similar results if we define a Cancel construct within a path of the Or construct. In larger CBPs, this could be a recurrent problem without the aid of a verification method.

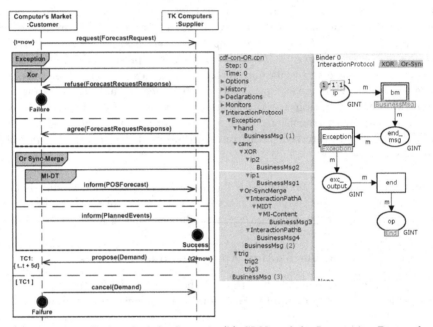

(a) Interaction Protocol of the Scenario (b) GI-Net of the Interaction Protocol

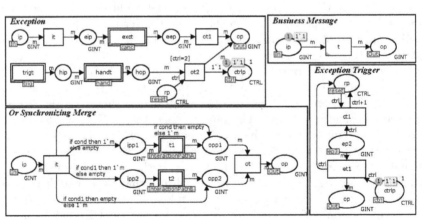

(c) Concrete GI Modules Defined in the GI-Net

Fig. 1. Collaborative Demand Forecast Process

4 Related Work

In [5,8], the verification of IOWFs was proposed, but these approaches compromise (completely or partially) the enterprises' autonomy. The method we are proposing verifies the choreography of interactions before public and private views are generated, which is appropriate in a top-down approach for modeling CBPs [13] and do not compromise the enterprises' autonomy. A verification approach based on HCP-Nets was presented in [9]. However, it does not guarantee that CBP models are deadlock-free neither it provides any support for advanced control flow. Other approaches are based on technology-specific languages [10], but they focus on verifying process specifications instead of process models when the business solution is defined. The use of structured processes was proposed to improve the performance of verification methods [14]. However, a structured formalization of advanced control flow constructs is not easy to accomplish. We showed that the structure of a GI-Net enables the reuse of formal definitions and delimits the scope of a problem in a module.

5 Conclusions and Future Work

In this work, we proposed a method for the verification of technology-independent CBP models. It enables the detection of errors in the global view of interactions of CBPs keeping the organizations' autonomy safe, since no private aspects of the participating organizations are considered. The method is independent of the semantics of any specific CBP modeling language, which makes it flexible and adaptable to be used with different CBP modeling languages. To this aim, it provides mechanisms to formalize the constructs of a language and verify its models. In particular, it allows the representation of the formal semantics of the cross-organizational message exchange that any CBP language should provide.

To support the method, we defined Global Interaction Nets (GI-Nets), which are based on Hierarchical and Colored Petri Nets, and are used to formalize CBP models. A GI-Net is composed of concrete GI modules that formally represent the elements of a CBP model, i.e. interaction or control flow elements. Concrete GI modules are derived and defined according to abstract GI modules that formalize the constructs of a CBP modeling language. Abstract GI-modules of a language can be used to develop a transformation process that generates a GI-Net from a model defined with such a language.

Since a GI-Net is a structured tree of GI modules, its corresponding CBP model must be structured as well. In block-based languages, which only generate structured models such as UP-ColBPIP, this is direct. However, to apply this method to a non-structured CBP model, e.g. BPMN-based choreographies, it has to be first transformed into a structured one before deriving its corresponding GI-Net. The structure of a GI-Net makes the reuse of formal definitions easier and delimits the scope of a problem to a module. GI modules for simple control flow constructs (and, xor, etc.) can be structurally defined according to [14] to reduce the analysis complexity. GI-Nets for models with advanced control flow constructs can be defined as structured as possible by decomposing the solution into modules.

In addition, we proposed GI soundness as the main correctness criterion. With this property, the final marking is not restricted to having a token only in the final place, as it happens in the classical soundness definition. Furthermore, a random final marking, which could stem from miss-behaved situations, is avoided since it has a predefined set of control tokens in the control places and no tokens in the interaction places, except for the final (interaction) place.

The proposed verification method was applied to UP-ColBPIP. Constructs for advanced synchronizations, cancellation and exception management were formalized with abstract GI modules, and a verification example of a UP-ColBPIP model was given. We showed that GI-Nets can be used to formalize these constructs in a modular way. In addition, we described how to use CPN Tools to define GI-Nets that formalize CBP models, verify them according to the GI soundness property, and detect the modules that cause errors in a GI-Net.

Ongoing work is concerned with the empirical validation of this method and its implementation into an Eclipse-based tool for modeling and verifying CBPs. We are also going to apply this method to BPMN-based choreography models. Technical and performance aspects are also part of future work.

References

1. Villarreal, P., Salomone, H., Chiotti, O.: Modeling and specifications of collaborative business processes using a MDA approach and a UML profile. In: Enterprise Modeling and Computing with UML, pp. 13–45. Idea Group Inc. (2007)
2. Villarreal, P.D., Lazarte, I., Roa, J., Chiotti, O.: A Modeling Approach for Collaborative Business Processes Based on the UP-ColBPIP Language. In: Rinderle-Ma, S., Sadiq, S., Leymann, F. (eds.) BPM 2009. LNBIP, vol. 43, pp. 318–329. Springer, Heidelberg (2010)
3. OMG, BPMN 2.0: http://www.omg.org/spec/BPMN/2.0/
4. Huemer, C., Liegl, P., Motal, T., Schuster, R., Zapletal, M.: The development process of the UN/CEFACT modeling methodology. In: ICEC, pp. 1–10. ACM (2008)
5. van der Aalst, W.M.P.: Modeling and analyzing interorganizational workflows. In: Proc. of the ACSD, pp. 262–272. IEEE Comp. Soc., Washington, DC (1998)
6. Aalst, W.M.: Discovery, verification and conformance of workflows with cancellation. In: Ehrig, H., Heckel, R., Rozenberg, G., Taentzer, G. (eds.) ICGT 2008. LNCS, vol. 5214, pp. 18–37. Springer, Heidelberg (2008)
7. van der Aalst, W., van Hee, K., ter Hofstede, A., Sidorova, N., Verbeek, H., Voorhoeve, M., Wynn, M.: Soundness of workflow nets: classification, decidability, and analysis. Formal Aspects of Computing, 1–31 (2010)
8. Norta, A., Eshuis, R.: Specification and verification of harmonized business-process collaborations. Information Systems Frontiers 12, 457–479 (2010)

9. Stuit, M., Szirbik, N.: Towards Agent-Based Modeling and Verification of Collaborative Business Processes: an Approach Centered on Interactions and Behaviors. Int. Journal of Cooperative Information Systems (IJCIS) 18, 423–479 (2009)
10. Breugel, F., Koshkina, M.: Models and Verification of BPEL, http://www.cse.yorku.ca/~franck/research/drafts/tutorial.pdf
11. Jensen, K., Kristensen, L.M.: Coloured Petri Nets: Modelling and Validation of Concurrent Systems, 1st edn. Springer Publishing Company, Incorporated Heidelberg (2009)
12. Workflow Patterns: http://www.workflowpatterns.com
13. Lazarte, I., Tello-Leal, E., Roa, J., Chiotti, O., Villarreal, P.: Model-Driven Development Methodology for B2B Collaborations. In: EDOCW, pp. 69–78. IEEE (2010)
14. Vanhatalo, J., Völzer, H., Leymann, F.: Faster and More Focused Control-Flow Analysis for Business Process Models Through SESE Decomposition. In: Krämer, B.J., Lin, K.-J., Narasimhan, P. (eds.) ICSOC 2007. LNCS, vol. 4749, pp. 43–55. Springer, Heidelberg (2007)

Towards an Integrated Simulation Approach for Planning Logistics Service Systems

Stefan Mutke, Christopher Klinkmüller, André Ludwig, and Bogdan Franczyk

University of Leipzig, Grimmaische Str. 12,
04109 Leipzig, Germany
{mutke,klinkmueller,ludwig,franczyk}@wifa.uni-leipzig.de

Abstract. The planning of complex logistics service systems is increasingly characterized as a collaborative process with various participants involved. The planning process of a logistics service system can be rendered by a Fourth Party Logistics Service Provider (4PL) together with an existing network of logistics partners. Simulation can be used to improve the decision-making process in the planning phase and to detect errors that can become cost intensive in the future. This paper outlines how simulation is integrated into a planning approach for a 4PL. The focus is on the derivation of goals and requirements from the specific characteristics of a 4PL. Based on these goals and requirements an initial integrated planning and simulation procedure is presented.

Keywords: simulation, logistics service systems, Fourth Party Logistics Service Provider.

1 Introduction

Enterprises are faced with new challenges such as increasing complexity, dynamic sampling of markets, globalization of competition, and ever-changing customer requirements. Hence, the ability to adapt to fast changing environmental conditions becomes increasingly important and the ability to generate competitive advantages highly depends on the level of flexibility an enterprise is able to support in its business processes [1] [2] [3]. Staying abreast of this development and in order to reach the required flexibility value creation increasingly takes place collaboratively by several organizations in which business activities and processes are assigned to the most capable business partners. While the number of corporations that are directly or indirectly involved in the development of goods and services increases this change leads to a better exploitation of specialization advantages and core competency concentration with the integrated partners.

Among other industries the shift towards cross-enterprise collaboration especially affects the logistics service sector [4]. An increasing number of manufacturers outsource their formerly internal logistics functions and require that outsourced logistics services need to be customized to their individual needs. Therefore, it is necessary for logistics service providers (LSP) to become more flexible by collaboratively offering their services.

F. Daniel et al. (Eds.): BPM 2011 Workshops, Part I, LNBIP 99, pp. 306–317, 2012.

Such logistics services are usually provided by companies like *Second* (2PL) and *Third Party Logistics Service Providers* (3PL). They typically offer logistics services like transport, handling, picking and warehousing or a more complex combination. Commonly 2PL and 3PL are not involved in the planning of the logistics service system, but their core competencies are to perform certain services. In the context of this paper a logistics service system on business level is defined as a combination of different LSP for a customer specific logistics contract. A role which pre-dominantly concentrates on the integration and management of complex value added logistics services is the *Fourth Party Logistics Service Provider* (4PL). A 4PL acts as a requester of logistics services from different providers, like 2PL and 3PL, and as a provider of integrated services towards shippers and their customers. For this task, a 4PL does not even have to possess logistics resources but rather needs to concentrate on the management of value added logistics service in terms of planning, configuration, monitoring and optimization [5]. Thus, for a 4PL an inter-organizational end-to-end perspective is of main importance, for developing a whole supply chain regarding to the customers need. To be competitive it is necessary to provide complex logistics with better quality and lower costs, compared with other LSP. This requires a quick and flexible implementation of the customer requirements. An important precondition for this is an existing logistics network and knowledge about their offered services. A logistics network in this context means a pool of LSP with the aim to strengthen their market position. For the 4PL this logistics network is of major importance in order to offer a wide range of logistics services and to improve the flexibility to provide them to their customers.

The planning of a whole logistic service system including the LSP is one of the 4PL's core competence [6]. Within the planning process an important task is how a 4PL can control the planned configuration of a customer specific logistics service system with reference to "forward-looking statements", including but not limited to statements that are predictions of indicated future events, trends or plans, based on certain assumptions.

Simulation has been widely recognized as a suitable methodology for analyzing and problem-solving in real-world complex systems in order to understand the system, explore possibilities, detect bottlenecks, identify potential towards optimization and transfer the results to real systems [7]. Especially in the field of logistics, simulation techniques are helpful to avoid bad investments, to increase planning security, to reduce lead times and to increase delivery reliability. All these general simulation objectives are necessary for the 4PL, to be competitive compared to other LSP. One of the crucial issues for the use of simulation in this context is the importance of the collaborative aspects within a logistics network, which has to be considered within the development of a customer specific logistics service system.

In order to avoid cost-intensive errors during the planning phase, our work-in-progress research efforts towards an integrated simulation approach for a 4PL to secure a logistics service system on business level is presented in this paper. It gives a motivation and points out, why simulation is important in logistics and especially for 4PL (chapter 2). The paper furthermore presents a first sketch of a solution for simulating logistics services (chapter 3) and provides further background in terms of related work (chapter 4). Finally a summary and an outlook on future work are given (section 5).

2   Motivation

A contract-specific logistics system of a 4PL is a collaborative, dynamic, stochastic and complex structure. It is very expensive and often consumes an enormous amount of resources and efforts to plan complex logistics service. The performance of such a contract-specific system depends to a large extent on the behavior of all participants. For improving the overall performance of this system, it is necessary to view the system as a whole and as a collaboration between all participants [8]. Furthermore, a logistics service system is established for a long period of time. Therefore, radical changes during the operation phase are very expensive and often consume an enormous amount of time [9]. For that reasons the simulation methodology for securing the planning, management and monitoring of material, personnel and information flows on business level now takes an important place in the field of logistics.

"Simulation is the imitation of the operation of a real-world process or system over time. [...] Simulation is an indispensable problem-solving methodology for the solution of many real-world problems. Simulation is used to describe and analyze the behavior of a system, ask what-if questions about the real system, and aid in the design of real systems. Both existing and conceptual systems can be modeled with simulation. " [7]

Simulation models of logistics networks can be used to improve the decision-making process in the planning phase. The feasibility of a newly designed logistics system can be evaluated prior to its implementation. There are different goals which are pursued by the use of simulation concepts within the planning process of a 4PL. All of these objectives are aimed at general logistics topics, like minimization of cycle time, maximization of the service level, maximization of utilization and minimization of stock [10]. The following goals of a simulation approach address the specific characteristics and needs of a 4PL.

G1: Optimal arrangement of the logistics service system
The first goal of simulation in the 4PL context is to find the optimal arrangement of a whole system with all participants involved to improve the dynamic system behavior providing the best strategy. For this, simulation offers an efficient way of identifying, studying and comparing different strategic options, e.g. shortest processing time, highest quality, lowest cost etc. This provides the possibility to select the best combination of logistics service provider for specific customer needs. For example, a delivery without warehousing can help to save storage costs but reduces the reliability of delivery in terms of fluctuating customer demands. In order to achieve this objective it is particularly important that the optimal strategy is developed together with the customer.

G2: Identification of bottlenecks in logistics service system
The second goal aims the dynamic observation of a logistics service system in order to get more accurate predictions for the future and to optimize the whole logistics service system. In particular, simulation techniques support the identification of bottlenecks (e.g. capacity constraints) and prevent them from being implemented in the real world system. Capacity constraints, for example in the provision of storage

services, can thus be identified at an early stage. In this case, the distribution functions of the different logistics service providers participating in the logistics network need to be considered.

G3: Verification of a planned logistics service system

The third goal of a 4PL's simulation approach is the verification of the planned logistics service system considering defined criteria (e.g. process lead-time, costs) and different fluctuations (e.g. fluctuations in demand, seasonal variations). Thus, the 4PL is able to analyze the robustness of the logistics service system under different extreme conditions. For example, the effect resulting in an increased demand in Christmas season or a constantly increasing sales volume for several years can be examined with simulation.

These goals are especially important for a 4PL, because its core competence is the management of value added logistics service in terms of planning, configuration and optimization. In the following, the most important requirements to a simulation approach for a 4PL, which were derived from the goals, are pointed out.

R1: Integrated planning and simulation

An important requirement for a simulation approach to the 4PL is the integrated use of simulation techniques in the planning process. It must be ensured that the created process models within the planning process, based on a separate description of each logistics service and the different fluctuation of the whole logistics service system, which can probably occur, can be transferred automatically into a simulation model. One the one hand, this requirement aims the goal to minimize the planning effort of a 4PL. On the other hand, manual errors in the creation of a simulation model should be avoided.

R2: Reuse of simulation components

Another requirement concerns the reuse of simulation components to ensure that the planning effort is minimized for individual contracts [11]. Each participant (LSP) of the 4PL's logistics network provides a distinct set of activities (logistics services) and could perform this set of activities in various supply chains [8]. The structure of the different logistics services (e.g. transport, handling, picking and warehousing) remains the same for all LSP, only the concrete characteristic (e.g. means of transport, delivery area, freight goods) is different. A structured description of the logistics services is a precondition for the development of domain-specific simulation components. The reuse of simulation model components is not a simulation requirement in general. But it is especially important and useful for a 4PL in terms of increased flexibility and a minimized use of resources, time and costs.

R3: Collaboration with partner

The third requirement refers to the collaboration between customer, a 4PL and the different participating LSP. Stefansson emphasizes the importance of collaboration between companies participating in supply chain setups to increase efficiency and decrease costs [12]. Especially information asymmetries within the planning process should be avoided. Therefore, it is necessary to ensure that the different partners in both, the creation of the simulation model and in the evaluation of results, are involved. Through a collaborative approach catastrophic misunderstandings can be prevented.

The majority of logistics simulation approaches is rather static and offers insufficient flexibility and variability [13]. Specifically for the business model of a 4PL these approaches are not suitable and do not fully meet the specific characteristics and demands. Therefore, this paper presents an initial approach that is adapted for the requirements of a 4PL mentioned above.

This section pointed out how the simulation techniques can support the planning of value added logistics services for a 4PL and which objectives are pursued. Furthermore, the most important requirements to a simulation approach for a 4PL has been defined. To achieve these requirements an initial approach is presented in the following chapter.

3   Integrated Simulation Approach for Logistics Service Systems

In this section an initial approach to the use of simulation techniques in the planning process of a 4PL is shown. The goals and requirements illustrated in the previous section are taken up in this approach.

To clarify which activities are performed previously and which the simulation approach is based on the simulation is classified into the planning process of a 4PL. The following Fig. 1 shows the planning procedure of a 4PL.

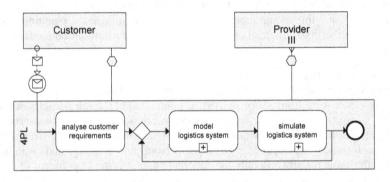

Fig. 1. Planning procedure of a 4PL

At first, the 4PL analyzes the customer requirements and derives a first description (e.g. required cycle time, types of goods, start and end point of the whole logistics service system etc.) of the complex logistics service. Afterwards the logistics service system is modelled by decomposing the customer requirements. Thereby the *Business Process Model and Notation* (BPMN) is used as the notation for modeling the processes [14]. The aim is the identification of partial services, to integrate them along the main process and the selection of suitable partners. Based on the process model the simulation methodology is used for securing the planning by studying the behavior of the system concerning the requirements.

An important precondition for planning a logistics service system is an existing network of LSP's and knowledge about their offered services. The knowledge about the logistics services must be available to the 4PL in a structured way. So, the LSP's have to describe their services using a template provided by the 4PL, which is derived from a service meta-model. For example, if a LSP offer a storage service, they have to describe this service with a template for a storage service. The description includes parameters like location of warehouse, storage capacity, types of goods they can store, technical equipment of the warehouse, specific permissions for dangerous goods, etc. As a result, all services offered by the partner network are consistent specified and a 4PL is able to search for specific services and to compare them. Furthermore, the reuse of these services within the planning process and the collaborative development of a complex logistics service system with the customer and the involved LSP is enabled.

The concept of service-orientation, as known from the IT level, addresses the needs for flexibility and reuse [15]. Some authors also emphasize the potential of adapting the concept analogously on the business level [16] [17]. A company "*expose[s] and offer[s] operations as business services to business partners in order to facilitate on-demand collaboration opportunities. A business service is the outcome of a specific* "chunk of operation" *that is performed by an organisation*" [18]. Thereby, the realisation of a business service (BS) is not limited to IT, so that it also might be implemented using real world resources like humans und machines. In the context of logistics domain business services referred to as logistics services. In this paper it is assumed, that "simple" logistics services (e.g. transport, handling, storage, quality control, labeling etc.) are provided by different LSP from a 4PL's logistics network. In the modelling process, these logistics services need to be composed and assigned to the most capable, best-in-class partners with the goal to optimize the self-enclosed service offering together with the customer. By integrating both the customer and the LSP within the whole planning process information deficits should be avoided. The result of the process modeling is a concrete logistics service system to provide a value added logistics service for a customer, consisting of different logistics services, which are performed by different LSP.

To describe the logistics services with concepts of service-orientation in a structured and formalized way a first draft of a meta-model has been developed based on different existing approaches such as USDL [19] and USM [17] (Fig. 2).

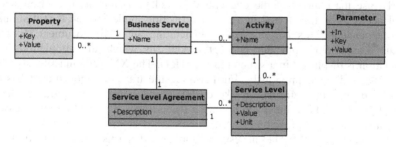

Fig. 2. First draft of BS meta-model

A service (BS) consists of a number of properties, activities and a service level agreement. A service level agreement is a contractually agreement between a service provider (LSP) and a customer (4PL), in which a guaranteed service quality is defined prior to service provisioning. They are a base for monitoring the provisioning and consumption of the service in business interaction between the involved parties. The individual quality parameters are described in terms of the service level (e.g. performance, security, dependability). A property describes the characteristic of a service more specifically, such as the means of transport etc. Activities specify individual tasks provided by a service. The individual activities can be further specified by other parameters. This meta-model is a first draft and still under development.

The description of the logistics services represents the link between process modeling and simulation, since relevant information is shared. The challenge is to transfer this process model into a simulation model to achieve the goals of simulation mentioned in the previous section. Thereby, various alternatives can be evaluated and adjusted efficiently. In the design of the simulation model and the evaluation of the simulation results, all partners are involved. This ensures that the logistics service system can be adjusted by all participants. The simulation procedure within the planning process of a 4PL is illustrated in Fig. 3.

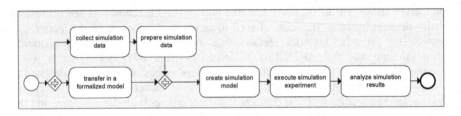

Fig. 3. Simulation procedure within the planning process of a 4PL

The designed process model of the logistics service system is used for the simulation approach as a conceptual model. *"The conceptual model is a non-software specific description of the simulation model that is to be developed, describing the objectives, inputs, outputs, content, assumptions and simplifications of the model."* [20] To use the content of the conceptual model in a simulation environment, the model needs to be transferred into a transformation model, which is still simulation tool independent. This is achieved by generating an XML document (Extensible Markup Language) from the concept model, in which the simulation-relevant information is displayed in a structured way (**R1**). The XML file must be conform to a Schema as defined previously. Furthermore, the transformation model has to be extended by missing information like customer requirements, (required cycle time, types of goods etc.) and other requirements (time issues, start and end points of each BS, means of transport, load units etc.).

At the same time all further necessary simulation data (distribution functions of the processing times of each logistics services provided by the LSP, fluctuations in demand, seasonal variations, purchase order lifecycle, etc.) are collected and prepared for the simulation model, if they are not already included in the process model. This data has to be provided by the customer and LSP's themselves or it can be extracted from past expired contracts stored in a simulation repository. By providing precise information and the maintenance of them, the LSP is able to engage actively in the simulation process and help to improve the quality of the simulation results (**R3**). The acquisition and preparation of simulation data is not part of this work and will not be further deepened. Further information on acquisition of simulation data in logistics networks can be found in [21] and [22].

After generating a formalized XML based model, the simulation model is developed using a simulation tool. To minimize the cost of creating a simulation model, the simulation environment itself is adapted in the run-up. Within our research, the domain-specific simulation tool *Enterprise Dynamics*[1] (ED) is used. This simulation environment is suitable for the use in the logistics domain. Therefore, a set of pre-defined simulation model components is provided within a simulation library to increase the usability and enable a quick construction of simulation models. These simulation model components (conveyors, storage, robots, etc) encapsulate certain functions and logics from the logistics domain. These predefined components do not reflect all the requirements of the presented service-oriented approach and the BS meta-model. Therefore, the authors extend the ED simulation library for the 4PL's simulation approach by components (logistics services) including the service-oriented description of the logistics services provided by the LSP (BS meta-model). New components will be created, which represent the characteristics of the logistics services that are offered by the LSP. Thus, the reuse for creating simulation models for a wide range of different logistics contracts is enabled (**R2**). Due to the fact that these BS templates were used when designing the process model and integrated in the simulation environment in the run-up, the creation of the simulation model is facilitated because the whole planning procedure employs the same structure.

After the simulation model is created a simulation experiment can be executed. The results of the simulation experiments have to be prepared in an appropriate structure for all participants, so they can optimize collaboratively the logistics system. If changes are necessary, the process model has to adapt or corrected before a new simulation model can be created. In order to share simulation models with other users, some simulation software tools provide a special viewer tool to allow all participants to load and run a simulation model. In addition, methods for a realistic 3D visualization improve the validation and presentation of simulation models [23] (**R3**).

Following, the first steps on our ongoing work creating a transformation model are presented (**R1**). In order to develop the structure of a transformation model it is necessary to analyze the central concepts of simulation. As a result, these concepts can be matched with the service-oriented description of each BS within the process model and with the appropriate representation in the simulation environment. Each discrete event simulation model is made up by system state variables, entities, attributes, lists processing, activities and delays. Banks described the concepts underlying simulation as follows [9].

Events
An event is an occurrence that changes the state of the simulation system and is the beginning and ending of an activity or delay (e.g. freight is loaded).

System state variables
The system state is a collection of variables (system state variables) necessary to describe the system at a certain time. In a discrete-event model the system state variables remain constant over intervals of time. The value of these variables change

---

[1] http://www.incontrolsim.com/en

only at certain well defined points called event times. Examples for system state variables are *number of customer in the queue* (an integer from 0 to n) and *status of entities* (busy, idle, blocked, full, load etc.). If all storage locations are occupied, the status is *full*.

Entities
An entity represents real-world objects or components. Entities that move through the system (e.g. products, customer) are dynamic and entities that serve other entities (e.g. conveyors, machines, warehouse) are static. Static entities are also called **resources**. There are different possible states of a resource (e.g. idle, busy, failed, and blocked).

Attributes
Attributes describe the characteristics of an entity (e.g. time of arrival, due date, priority, color). A set of entities may have same attribute slots but different values for different entities, so the attribute value is tied to a specific entity. Attributes of a warehouse are for example capacity, types of goods that can be stored, technical equipment of the warehouse, specific permissions for dangerous goods, etc.

List processing
Lists are used to represent queues (a warehouse in the domain of logistics) in a simulation model. There are different possible processing lists, e.g. FIFO (first in, first out), LIFO (last in, first out), according to the value of an attribute or randomly.

Activities
An activity is a specific period of time. The duration of this time period is known prior and can be a constant, a random value from a statistical distribution, input from a file, etc. For example, a *service time* of a resource managing an entity (order picking) is an activity.

Delays
A delay is an indefinite period of time. The duration is caused by some combination of system conditions. For example, a delay is the time that an entity will remain in the queue for a resource (e.g. the freight is waiting for loading). Discrete-event simulations contain delays as entities wait.

These central simulation concepts must be taken up by creating a transformation model for the 4PL's simulation approach. On the one hand the designed process model of the logistics service system including the service-oriented description of each BS has to be transferred in the formalized model using these simulation concepts. Therefore, the description of the BS has to be adapted in advance to that effect. On the other hand, for the development of the simulation model based on the transformation model, the representations of the simulation concepts used in the simulation tool (ED) need to be identified. How a matching between the BS description, the simulation concepts, and the representation in the simulation tool can be realized has to be worked out in the next step of the ongoing research.

This section presented an initial approach to the use of simulation techniques in the planning process of a 4PL. Therefore, the goals and requirements illustrated in chapter 2 were taken up.

4   Related Work

There are many approaches relevant in the context of using simulation for designing logistics systems.

Ingalls discussed the use of simulation as a analysis methodology to evaluate supply chains [24]. In addition, a complete list of advantages and disadvantages against other analysis methodologies is provided. A concrete simulation approach is not provided. In [25] Cimino et al. presented a general simulation framework for modeling supply chains. The paper provides an overview of different discrete event simulation software in terms of domains of applicability, types of libraries, input-output functionalities, animation functionalities, etc. Moreover, the use of general programming languages as an alternative to discrete event simulation software is proposed. A modeling approach and a simulation model for supporting supply chain management is presented by Longo et al. in [13]. In addition, to developing a discrete event simulation tool for a supply chain simulation using eM-Plant[2] and including a modeling approach, they provide a decision making tool for supply chain management.

All these approaches are relevant for developing an integrated planning and simulation approach. However, all these approaches satisfy the 4PL's specific requirements (chapter 2) only partially. The development of simulation models based on process models is not considered. Other works interesting in the context of this research deal with the transformation of process models in simulation models.

Petsch et al. presented in [26] a transformation model as an intermediate in the transfer of process models in simulation models with a practical example for process improvement in a hospital. It is assumed that process models are created to increase process transparency, shorten the training period for new employees and prepare businesses for certification. The transformation model is derived under consideration of process modeling using event-driven process chain (EPC) notation and two simulation software systems.

Kloos et al. presented another interesting transformation model approach in [27], which can be used to convert process models to simulation software systems. This approach also derives the transformation model using EPC notation. To transfer the EPC process models to the transformation models a flow chart notation and transformation rules were developed.

Both transformation approaches use existing process models to create simulation models. But the use of EPC notation for process modeling does not meet the 4PL's requirements in this approach.

---

[2] http://www.emplant.de/

5   Conclusion

Due to the structural change towards cross-enterprise collaboration in the logistics LSP need to become more flexible by collaboratively offering their services. This article presented our work-in-progress research efforts towards developing an integrated planning and simulation approach based on service-oriented logistics description for 4PL. It was shown why and how simulation can ease and improve the collaborative planning process. Therefore, specific goals and requirements related to the 4PL characteristics, which represent the basis for simulation of logistics service systems, were outlined. By taking up these goals and requirements an integrated planning procedure was presented. Subject to future work is the development of a transformation model to convert the process model to a simulation model. Therefore, the first draft of BS meta-model needs to be worked out in detail. Furthermore, the matching between the BS description, the simulation concepts, and the representation in the simulation tool has to be worked out.

Acknowledgement. The work presented in this paper was partly funded by the German Federal Ministry of Education and Research under the projects InterLogGrid (BMBF 01IG09010F) and Logistics Service Bus (BMBF 03IP504).

References

1. Saxena, K.B.C.: Business process management in a smart business network environment. In: The Network Experience, pp. 69–81. Springer, Berlin (2009)
2. Wang, X., Meng, Q.: Outsourcing and Third-Party Logistics. In: Logistics Engineering Handbook, pp. 27-21–27-13. CRC Press (2007)
3. Rinsler, S.: Outsourcing: the result of global supply chains? Global Logistics: New Directions in Supply Chain Management, 164–177 (2010)
4. Sahay, B.: Supply chain collaboration: the key to value creation. Work Study 52, 76–83 (2003)
5. Thiell, M., Hernandez, S.: Logistics services in the 21st century: supply chain integration and service architecture. In: Service Science and Logistics Informatics, pp. 359–378. Business Science Reference, Hershey (2010)
6. Kutlu, S.: Fourth Party Logistics: Is It the Future of Supply Chain Outsourcing? Best Global Pub. Ltd. (2007)
7. Banks, J., Knovel (Firm): Handbook of simulation principles, methodology, advances, applications, and practice. Wiley Co-published by Engineering & Management Press, New York (1998)
8. Pundoor, G., Herrmann, J.W.: A hierarchical approach to supply chain simulation modeling using the Supply Chain Operations Reference model. International Journal of Simulation and Process Modeling 2, 124–132 (2006)
9. Alves, G., Roßmann, J., Wischnewski, R.: A discrete-event-simulation approach for logistic systems with real time resource routing and VR integration. In: International Conference on Computational Systems Engineering (ICCSE 2009), pp. 476–481. World Academy of Science, Engineering and Technology WASET, Venedig (2009)
10. Christopher, M.: New directions in logistics. Kogan Page, London (2010)

11. Chen, G., Szymanski, B.K.: Reusing simulation components: cost: a component-oriented discrete event simulator. In: Winter Simulation Conference, pp. 776–782 (2002)
12. Stefansson, G.: Collaborative logistics management: the role of third-party service providers and the enabling information systems architecture. Chalmers Univ. of Technology, Göteborg (2004)
13. Longo, F., Mirabelli, G.: An advanced supply chain management tool based on modeling and simulation. Comput. Ind. Eng. 54, 570–588 (2008)
14. OMG: Notation (BPMN) 2.0. Object Management Group (2009)
15. Erl, T.: SOA Design Patterns. Prentice Hall, Upper Saddle River (2009)
16. Jones, S.: Enterprise SOA Adoption Strategies (2006)
17. Nayak, N., Nigam, A., Sanz, J., Marston, D., Flaxer, D.: Concepts for Service-Oriented Business Thinking. In: Proceedings of the IEEE International Conference on Services Computing, pp. 357–364. IEEE Computer Society (2006)
18. Kohlborn, T., Korthaus, A., Rosemann, M.: Business and software service lifecycle management. In: IEEE International Conference on Enterprise Distributed Object Computing, Auckland, New Zealand (2009)
19. Cardoso, J., Barros, A., May, N., Kylau, U.: Towards a Unified Service Description Language for the Internet of Services: Requirements and First Developments. In: Proceedings of the 2010 IEEE International Conference on Services Computing, pp. 602–609. IEEE Computer Society (2010)
20. Robinson, S.: Simulation: the practice of model development and use. Wiley, Chichester (2004)
21. Bernhard, J., Wenzel, S.: Information Acquisition for Model-based Analysis of Large Logistics Networks. In: Proceedings of SCS-ESM (2005)
22. Kuhnt, S., Wenzel, S.: Information acquisition for modelling and simulation of logistics networks. J. of Sim. 4, 109–115 (2010)
23. Kamat, V.R., Martinez, J.C.: Enabling smooth and scalable dynamic 3D visualization of discrete-event construction simulations, pp. 1528–1533. IEEE Computer Society (2001)
24. Ingalls, R.G.: The value of simulation in modeling supply chains, pp. 1371–1376. IEEE Computer Society Press (1998)
25. Cimino, A., Longo, F., Mirabelli, G.: A general simulation framework for supply chain modeling: state of the art and case study. Arxiv (2010)
26. Petsch, M., Schorcht, H., Nissen, V., Himmelreich, K.: Ein Transformationsmodell zur Überführung von Prozessmodellen in eine Simulationsumgebung. In: Loos, P., Nüttgens, M., Turowski, K., Werth, D. (eds.) Modellierung Betrieblicher Informationssysteme - Modellierung Zwischen SOA Und Compliance Management, Saarbrücken, Germany, pp. 209–219 (2008)
27. Kloos, O., Nissen, V., Petsch, M.: From process to simulation - a transformation model approach. Ges. für Informatik, Bonn (2009)

Building a Bridge between Information and Process Management

Jörg Wurzer

iQser AG, Chlupfgasse 2, 8303 Bassersdorf, Switzerland
joerg.wurzer@iqser.net

Abstract. Semantic technology enables a bridge between the currently isolated worlds of information retrieval and process management. Relevant and required information is selected and assigned to any process instance by automatically and dynamically linked enterprise data to support each process participant. This approach consequently implements the idea of automized information logistics.

Keywords: information logistics, information retrieval, business process management, semantic technology.

1   Challenges of Practice

Today the world of information retrieval and process management are isolated. While process management is characterized by management advice, information retrieval requires usually inefficient search. There is no solution for context aware information distribution on the level of process instances.

While the challenge of information retrieval are an increasing number of distributed data and sources, the challenge of process management is the gap and delay between process models and the execution of lived processes.

2   Information Logistics for Process Management

Intelligent information logistic enables a paradigm shift, where people do not need to search any more but selected, relevant, personalized information is provided and delivered automatically in a given context. This context could be represented by any information like a received message or an opened document. Therefore any process instance could either represent a context for information logistics, which may include additional parameters like the user's role, location, device and time.

A system for information logistics selects and assigns dynamically information from distributed sources, which is related to the concrete process instance. Each information is strictly filtered by a relevance score and linked to options for interaction. These bridge between information retrieval and process management does not only significantly improve the efficiency of the workflow but also takes care of the awareness of corporate compliance rules.

F. Daniel et al. (Eds.): BPM 2011 Workshops, Part I, LNBIP 99, pp. 318–319, 2012.

3 Semantic Technology as Enabler for Information Logistics

For the implementation of information logistic in a process context semantic technology can be used, which is based on automized, scalable, robust and real-time procedures. In this case each part of a process instance represents a content object like other information objects with are assigned to the parts of the process instance.

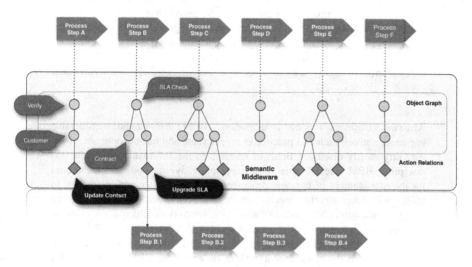

Fig. 1. Dynamically linked process instance with information objects and interaction options for an incoming call in a customer care scenario

Each new process instance as well as any new or modified information object trigger instantly a semantic analysis process to find, qualify and quantify relations to other content objects. This pro-active, event-driven analysis ensures the availability of current information for each user context.

Beyond the object relations the objects are linked to interaction options, which enables direct information processing and triggering sub-processes.

References

1. Mutschler, Wurzer.: Bringing Innovative Semantic Technology to Practice: The iQser Approach and its Use Cases, AST (2009)
2. Smolnik, Wurzer: Towards an automatic semantic integration of information (2008)

On Theoretical Foundations of Empirical Business Process Management Research

Constantin Houy, Peter Fettke, and Peter Loos

Institute for Information Systems (IWi)
at the German Research Center for Artificial Intelligence (DFKI GmbH) and
Saarland University, Campus, Building D3$_2$
66123 Saarbrücken, Germany
{Constantin.Houy,Peter.Fettke,Peter.Loos}@iwi.dfki.de

Abstract. Business Process Management (BPM) has gained considerable importance in research and practice in recent years and has become one of the currently mostly discussed fields of research in the Information Systems (IS) discipline. BPM research aims to develop innovative methods and techniques for the management of business processes in the first place and, moreover, to build and further develop theory, which is an important objective of every scientific discipline. The state of theory is commonly considered a significant indicator for the maturity and grounding of a field of research. This article investigates theoretical foundations of empirical BPM research based on conceptual considerations and a review of empirical BPM literature. Our analysis shows that empirical BPM research is only to a certain extent guided by existing theory. Furthermore, the investigated contributions often refer to theories originating from different other fields of research, like economics or sociology. Implications and the potential of dedicated BPM theory development by means of empirical research are discussed.

Keywords: Business Process Management, BPM, Empirical Research, Theory, Theoretical Foundations, Theory Building, Design Theory.

1   Introduction

Business Process Management (BPM) has become an intensely discussed topic in the Information Systems (IS) discipline. Besides the growing maturity of concepts, methods and techniques of BPM, the field of research has gained tremendous importance in research as well as in organizational practice [1]. A growing research community develops BPM-related knowledge, publishes it in specialized journals; e.g., the Business Process Management Journal, and discusses the research results on dedicated conferences; e.g., the BPM-Conference (meanwhile in the ninth year). Furthermore, the institutionalization of BPM-focused degree programs at several universities (e.g., the Masters programme in Business Process Engineering at the University of Liechtenstein or the Masters programme in IS focussing on Business Process Management at Saarland University, Germany) evidence that BPM is not a

F. Daniel et al. (Eds.): BPM 2011 Workshops, Part I, LNBIP 99, pp. 320–332, 2012.
© Springer-Verlag Berlin Heidelberg 2012

temporary fashion but an evolving trend. In addition, BPM methods and techniques are increasingly applied in organizations and a further growth of the market for Business Process Management Systems (BPMS) can be expected [2]. Although being an important sub-area of the IS discipline, which generally aims at building theory for the description, explanation, prediction and for the support of IS design [3], BPM research has always rather been constituted by its designed artefacts, like modeling methods; e.g., the Business Process Modeling Notation (BPMN), Unified Modeling Language (UML), Petri Nets, Event-driven Process Chains (EPC), or frameworks like the Architecture of Integrated Information Systems (ARIS) [4] which are of high practical relevance. This practical relevance of BPM approaches, techniques and tools has resulted in the outstanding significance of design-oriented research for BPM. Design Science Research (DSR) in IS strives for engineering innovative and useful IS artefacts like software prototypes, methods etc. and for simultaneously developing new and reliable artefact-related knowledge [5-7].

However, as already mentioned, being an important part of the IS discipline, BPM research also aims to develop fundamental theory in the sense of true and justified knowledge representing generally admitted (and "universally valid") relationships in a domain. This is one of the most important tasks of every scientific discipline. Furthermore, the advancement of a discipline's theory building process is commonly considered an important indicator describing its maturity. In IS research, theory building is supported by different scientific approaches. Besides behavioral science approaches, design-oriented research methods can contribute to theory building and the development of fundamental knowledge [7, 8].

In recent years, empirical research methods have gained more and more relevance for BPM research, and methods like experiments, surveys, case studies, action research or empirical multi-method approaches are increasingly used [9]. Empirical research methods are both important in the context of behavioral as well as design science research. In the behavioral science context, empirical research serves for theory building and testing in the first place. In the design science context, empirical methods are important for the investigation of the actual effects, the efficiency and other characteristics concerning the practical usage of innovative design artefacts [6]. In both behavioral and design science research, theoretical foundations gain more and more importance [10]. Both the fundamental development of dedicated BPM theories as well as the empirical investigation of design artefact characteristics considerably profit from, respectively necessitate theoretical foundations [7]. Current empirical BPM contributions, both in the context of developing theoretical frameworks as well as in the context of design artefact evaluation, pay special attention to theoretical foundation; e.g., the articles of Trkman [11] or Recker and Dreiling [12]. The grounding and further development of BPM knowledge based on "established" theories and commonly accepted knowledge bears considerable potential for BPM research as a discrete research discipline.

However, it remains unclear which theoretical foundations are the most important for current BPM research and which dedicated theories are used as a foundation for empirical BPM research endeavors. Against this background, this article has *two goals*. Firstly, the theoretical foundations of empirical BPM research are investigated in order to identify theories which are relevant for BPM. Secondly, implications of the findings for design-oriented research are discussed. The following *research questions* are of particular importance for our article:

1. Which specific theories are of significance for empirical BPM research?
2. Which implications result from the theoretical foundations of empirical BPM research?

In order to answer these research questions, this article is based on conceptual analyses and considerations [13] as well as on a review of empirical BPM literature [14]. Based on these findings, we deduce, analyze and discuss resulting implications for future BPM research.

Our contribution is structured as follows: in section two the underlying concepts of BPM, the term "theory" in the IS discipline and the relevance of theories for design-oriented research are presented and discussed. Section three introduces and explains the applied research methodology as well as the findings of our study. Thereby, theories which are important for current empirical BPM research and different trends are identified. Section four discusses the findings and presents implications for future BPM research before section five summarizes and concludes the paper.

2   Terminology and Conceptual Foundations

2.1   Business Process Management

Although BPM has been defined very differently in literature since the concept's introduction, it can be understood as an approach which supports organizations in sustaining their competitive advantage [15]. BPM focuses on business processes as sequences of executions for the purpose of creating goods and services [4]. It subsumes a set of methods, techniques and tools supporting the design, enactment, control and analysis of business processes in order to facilitate an optimized value creation [16]. Today, BPM is commonly understood as an evolutionary improvement process [1] which can be described by a life cycle with the following phases: process strategy development, process definition and modeling, implementation, process execution, process monitoring and controlling as well as process optimization and improvement [9].

2.2   Theory in the Information Systems Discipline

Scientific disciplines, like the IS discipline, aim to develop knowledge on the basis of scientific standards [17]. However, the term "knowledge" has been controversial for as long as researchers have been thinking about it and there is still no consistent understanding. In our contribution, we understand knowledge in the "classical" sense as a belief or opinion which is justified on the basis of acceptable justification standards and, furthermore, satisfies the claim of being true. A common term for a structured representation of knowledge created by scientific disciplines is "theory"

[18]. This term is still intensely discussed in many disciplines as well as in the IS discipline, and several different forms of theory exist. In IS research, especially empirical theories describing phenomena and relationships which can be observed in reality are important. In order to be able to identify and investigate such phenomena, empirical research methods are needed which support the systematic gathering and analysis of observable data about IS in reality.

One framework describing the nature of theory which is widely applied in the IS discipline has been introduced by Gregor [3]. It provides a valuable overview on the characteristics of theory in IS. Gregor has identified five different types of theory:

(I)   *theory for analyzing* which describes the "lowest level" of theory that is concerned with properly defining a theory's constructs without describing relationships between them (*terminology*),

(II)   *theory for explaining* which aims at the explanation of phenomena by providing a deeper understanding of how and why a relationship between two or more constructs exists,

(III) *theory for predicting* which supports the prediction of what will be, not necessarily based on a deeper understanding of why this happens,

(IV)   *theory for explaining and predicting* (EP Theory) which supports both the prediction of what will happen as well as the explanation for how and why it will happen and

(V)   *theory for design and action* which supports the design, construction and usage of IS artefacts.

While the first type is concerned with the fundamental definition and description of concepts, type II to IV can be seen as *theories in the classical sense* which are also of high relevance for different other academic disciplines, like natural sciences. As already mentioned, these theory types specify and explain law-like relationships between well-defined constructs. Type V describes so called design theories which are of special interest in Sciences of the Artificial and engineering disciplines aiming to develop innovative artificial objects [19]. These theory types will be investigated in more detail in the following.

Theory in the classical sense (type II – IV, building on type I). These theory types represent systems of law-like statements, so called nomological hypotheses ("if-then-statements"), aiming to represent cause-effect relationships between dedicated constructs mainly supporting the description, explanation and prediction of observable phenomena [20]. According to this understanding, the most important components of a theory are well-defined constructs (Gregor's "type-I-theories" or Dubin's "units") (X and Y) which are put into a relationship by law-like statements ("If X then Y") [21]. In some cases these statements can describe cause-effect relationships between observed constructs. Such statements can, for example, be found in the context of natural sciences; e.g., chemical or physical laws. However, in other cases, especially in social sciences, it is debatable if such hypotheses can be regarded as causal or strictly deterministic relationships because of the complex dependencies in studied systems. The latter aspect is fully valid for the IS discipline [22]. In the IS context hypotheses rather describe statistical correlations. An example of an IS theory in the classical sense is the Technology Acceptance Model (TAM) which formulates law-like relationships between the constructs of "perceived ease of use" (X_1) and "perceived usefulness" (X_2) of a certain technology and its actual usage (Y) [23].

Design Theories. Against the background of the growing importance of design-oriented research in the IS discipline [7], so called design theories [24] are currently intensely discussed in leading IS journals, e.g., MISQ, JAIS etc. [25, 26]. According to the first contribution on design theories by Walls et al. [24], design theories support the design of IS artefacts by formulating prescriptive or normative statements. Design theories contain theories in the classical sense as an important part ("kernel theories") and furthermore consist of other components; e.g., design methods, meta-requirements, design hypotheses. However, a closer examination of three current design theories shows that the central statements in such theories have different characters and are formulated very differently. Design theory statements can be expressed in the form of *technological rules* [27] with prescriptive character; e.g. in [28] ("If you want to improve software processes…, then choose…"), in the form of classical hypotheses with descriptive character ("The more consistent and concordant the processes… the more successful…") or in the form of *factual statements with normative character* ("It is feasible and practicable to…") both in [29]. The latter kind of statements is also discussed under the term of *technical norms* for design sciences ("You should do X. It is rational for you to do X. It is profitable for you to do X.") [5]. Although structured and scientifically founded knowledge in this form seems to be very useful for effective and efficient IS design, it remains unclear what kind of knowledge and which types of statements are constitutive for design theories. As the structure of design theories proposed by Walls et al. is rather complicated, different research contributions try to simplify the definition of design theories, e.g. [30]. Although design theories are gaining importance and are increasingly investigated, the discipline's understanding of design theories is still evolving and, thus, no agreement of what is constitutive for design theories exists up to now.

2.3   On the Relevance of Theory for Design-Oriented Research

Empirical theories and scientific knowledge created by the application of empirical research methods play an important role in the context of design-oriented research [30]. More and more current research contributions investigate the role of theoretical knowledge for the construction of design artefacts; e.g. [6, 31]. The theoretical foundation of design-oriented research in the IS discipline is not only important in order to further strengthen Design Science as a discrete academic research stream in IS which also contributes to theory development. Furthermore, underlying theoretical or at least empirically observed relationships can considerably support the design, construction and evaluation of innovative IS artefacts [30]. Empirical methods in the context of design-oriented research can moreover serve for the investigation of hypothesized (means-end) relationships which can be useful on the quest for underlying cause-effect relationships in a domain (Krcmar in [32]). In conclusion, design-oriented research can profit from (theoretical) knowledge about artefacts and their domain of usage which can inform the artefact design and construction process. Furthermore, design-oriented research can also support the creation and development of theoretical knowledge and empirical theories. These two facets of design-oriented research which are equally important for BPM research are visualized in figure 1. In the following, concrete theories used in empirical BPM research are investigated.

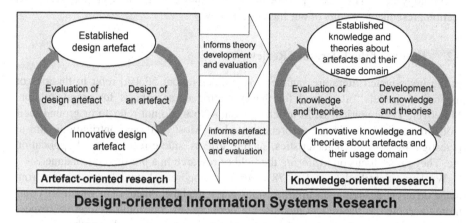

Fig. 1. On the relevance of theory for design-oriented research, inspired by [6] and [31]

3   Analysis of Theoretical Foundations of Empirical BPM Research

3.1   Research Methodology

In order to analyze the role and character of theories in empirical BPM research we have conducted a review of empirical BPM literature. In our research, we take the working hypothesis as a basis which assumes that the theoretical foundations of a scientific discipline increase over the years, resulting in the assumption that a sample of current contributions can give an adequate overview. Thus, we have analyzed a comprehensive sample of 251 empirical journal articles on BPM taken from a current ten-year time frame (2000-2009). These articles have been systematically retrieved in two internationally leading literature databases (Science Citation Index by Thomson Scientific and Business Source Premier/EBSCOhost). Systematic retrieval supports the avoidance of subjective decisions and coincidence. Moreover, the reproducibility of research results can be considerably improved. The articles were retrieved by searching for constitutive terms of BPM in their title, abstract and keywords; e.g., "business process modeling", "business process monitoring" and further relevant terms according to the BPM life cycle (section 2.1). Within this amount of articles, empirical contributions have been identified by searching for typical terms describing empirical research methods; e.g., "survey", "experiment", "case study" etc. These 251 contributions have been analyzed regarding their theoretical foundations. Firstly, explicit theories have been searched in the full texts by means of the truncated search term "theor*". Moreover, the articles have also been "manually" scanned for potential theories and models which represent systems of law-like statements but do not carry the label "theory"; e.g., the Technology Acceptance Model (TAM) [23], the Task-Technology Fit (TTF) model [33] or the Transaction Cost Economics [34]. The next section presents the results of our literature review.

3.2   Results of the Literature Review

In the investigated literature sample, 134 articles (about 53,4%) refer to theories or theoretical models, often used for theory testing or as a basis for argumentation. Moreover, 117 empirical BPM articles (about 46,6%) do not refer to or ground their work in existing theories or theoretical models. Most of these contributions aim at investigating artefact characteristics, such as effects, side-effects, costs of application etc. They rather focus on *exploring* the field of research in a pre-theoretic manner.

We have identified a total of 78 theories or theoretical models originating from many different academic disciplines which carry the label "theory" or which are commonly accepted as theoretical models. Furthermore, 24 contributions refer to, respectively develop new research models which formulate nomological hypotheses but do so far not have the label of a theory. Due to space limitations not the whole amount of identified theories can be presented here. Most of the theories have been referenced only once in the sample. In order to present the chronological development of theory usage in empirical BPM research, we give an overview of the citation development concerning the mentioned 78 identified theories in figure 2. Each referenced theory has been counted once per article. Especially from 2002 up until 2008 the usage of existing theories has gained importance. An exception to this trend is the decline in the year 2009 which can not be explained in this article. However, an increase of references to existing theories in empirical BPM contributions can be stated, which suggests a growing importance of theories in recent years.

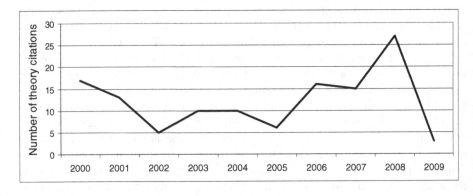

Fig. 2. Chronological development of theory citations in empirical BPM research

In order to give an overview of the *most important theories* in the context of empirical BPM research, we present a list of 11 theories which have been referenced at least twice in the investigated literature sample (table 1). According to table 1, it can be stated that many of the most often referenced theories in empirical BPM research originate from different scientific disciplines, which is equally valid for the rest of identified theories in our literature sample.

Furthermore, we noticed in our research that other types of theories; e.g., from the field of mathematics have been used in empirical BPM research, like Queueing Theory, Fuzzy Set Theory or Graph Theory. These theories cannot be considered theories in the sense of our given definition ("systems of law-like statements") as they do not contain nomological hypotheses or prescriptive respectively normative statements which are typical for design theories. Therefore, we have not considered them in our overview. Moreover, we have noticed that some articles reference *the* organizational theory without further specifying which dedicated theory from the field of organizational research is meant. It has to be further noticed that the empirical or law-like character of some of the identified theories is still under discussion. For example, some authors assign an important empirical character to the General System Theory (GST) because it serves for the explanation and prediction of system-related empirical phenomena. But it is also stated that GST should be classified as a theory for analysis (Gregor's type I) in the first place (Zelewski in [32]).

We have mostly found theories in the classical sense (type II – IV) to be used in current empirical BPM research. Although some contributions develop "theoretical frameworks" in which they provide technological rules; e.g., Wu [35], or in which systematic normative statements on BPM topics are formulated; e.g., in Ursic et al. [36], the concept of design theories does so far obviously not play an important role in current empirical BPM research.

Table 1. Overview of important theories used in empirical BPM research

	Name of Theory	Sources	x times identified	Original Area
1	Transaction Cost Economics (TCE)	Coase (1937) [34], Williamson (1975, 1979) [37, 38]	8	Microeconomics
2	General System Theory (GST)	von Bertalanffy (1946, 1968) [39]	6	Philosophy, Mathematics, Cybernetics
3	Resource-based View (RBV, RBT)	Penrose (1959) [40], Wernerfelt (1984) [41]	5	Strategic Management, Microeconomics
4	Contingency Theory	Fiedler (1964, 1967) [42, 43]	4	Organizational Theory, Psychology, Strategy
5	Agency Theory	Alchian / Demsetz (1972) [44], Jensen / Meckling (1976) [45]	4	Economics
6	Theory of Reasoned Action (TRA)	Fishbein / Ajzen (1975) [46], Ajzen / Fishbein (1980) [47]	3	Social Psychology
7	Task-Technology Fit (TTF)	Goodhue / Thompson (1995) [33]	2	Information Systems
8	Technology Acceptance Model (TAM)	Davis (1989) [23]	2	Information Systems
9	Knowledge-based Theory of the Firm	Conner (1991) [48], Kogut / Zander (1992) [49]	2	Strategic Management
10	Resource Dependency Theory (RDT)	Pfeffer / Salancik (1978) [50]	2	Sociology, Political Science
11	Speech Act Theory	Searle (1969) [51]	2	Linguistic, Philosophy of Language

4   Discussion of the Results and Implications

The systematic review of the 251 journal articles has shown that current empirical BPM research is only to a certain extent based on established theories or theoretical research models. Nevertheless, the theoretical foundation of empirical BPM research has gained importance in recent years, which is indicated by the growing number of theory citations. Almost half of the investigated literature sample did not refer to existing theories or theoretical models but aimed at exploring the field of research and developing starting points for theory building in BPM. Furthermore, it can be stated that the most important and most frequently used theories in empirical BPM research do not originate from the IS context but from different other scientific disciplines, like economics, strategic management or sociology. In addition, used IS-related theories have not been adapted to BPM-specific requirements so far. They are predominantly used in their original form. These findings suggest that the development process of original BPM theories is still in its early stages.

It has furthermore become clear that empirical BPM research up to now has mainly focused on theories in the classical sense. The concept of design theories does so far not play an important role in this context. However, the concept is still in its early stages. Although the idea of design theories has already been introduced in the early 1990s [24], IS research has started to intensely discuss the topic and to develop dedicated design theories no more than a few years ago.

Taking a closer look at the used theories, it becomes clear that empirical BPM research mostly focuses on established theories which are also used in different subareas of IS research; e.g., the resource-based view [52]. The frequently discussed lack of IS theories is thus also especially valid for BPM research. However, as already mentioned, BPM is rather constituted by its artefacts; e.g., the BPMN or the ARIS framework, than by theories in the classical sense. In BPM, design-oriented research and the development of artefacts which are useful for practical application are more in focus than building theory in the classical sense. This seems to be characteristic for many engineering disciplines, too. Nevertheless, the building of original BPM theories or the further development and BPM-related adaption of established theories can support and improve the construction of BPM artefacts, as has been argued in section 2.3. In order to support this, future BPM research and especially empirical BPM research should put a stronger focus on the theoretical foundations of research. Besides explanation and prediction, scientific knowledge about reliable relationships of BPM-related concepts and constructs can also support the design and construction of innovative BPM artefacts. Therefore, further research into fundamental relationships will be necessary in the future in order to develop original theories in the further growing area of BPM. Moreover, the potential of theories in the classical sense as well as design theories, which have been touched on in this article, should be investigated in order to further clarify the role and the arising opportunities of theoretical research for design-oriented research disciplines.

Our contribution has, however, some *limitations* which shall be mentioned. First of all, we have only studied a limited sample of empirical BPM literature. Anyhow, the systematic review approach chosen in our article allows for meaningful analyses and a high inter-subjective reproducibility of results. A second limitation lies in the fact that we relied on one IS theory conceptualization framework for the explication of our understanding of the term theory, although other theory conceptualizations exist. The chosen framework furthermore contains ideas which have not been fully clarified, like the concept of design theories. Future IS research has to work on the further clarification of these concepts and the understanding of IS theory in general. Nevertheless, Gregor's framework has oftentimes been applied in current IS research and can thus serve as a reliable reference point. Although it would have been interesting to give a more detailed overview of the chronological development of the usage of every single theory or certain topical clusters, the strong diversity and the timely distribution of usage of the different theories has not allowed for more detailed and at the same time meaningful analyses. However, the presented research describes interesting tendencies and developments in the context of theoretical foundations of current empirical BPM research.

5   Conclusion and Outlook

The presented article has investigated the theoretical foundations of empirical BPM research and furthermore discussed the potential and implications of the results for future empirical BPM research. At first, we have motivated the topic by explicating the relevance of theory building in the IS discipline in general. Then, we have introduced fundamental concepts, like BPM and Gregor's IS theory conceptualization. We have furthermore discussed the relevance of theories for design-oriented research. In the third section, the used review methodology and our findings were presented. It was shown that existing theories have gained importance for empirical BPM research in recent years. However, almost half of the empirical research articles have not referred to existing theories or theoretical models but rather focused on exploring the field of research in order to develop starting points for new original BPM theories or to investigate artefact characteristics. Moreover, it was found that the used theories mostly originate from different fields of research and that common IS theories are seldom used or adapted for BPM. Section four has discussed the results and presented implications for future research, especially the potential and the need for further theory building in BPM.

Future BPM research, and especially empirical research endeavors should focus on a stronger theoretical foundation in order to strengthen the quality of BPM research. Original BPM theories could be developed besides the existing BPM artefacts and techniques and could thereby improve the theoretic grounding of the discipline. With our overview of theoretical foundations of empirical BPM research we hope to contribute to a fruitful discussion on the topic of theory building which can significantly further the development of BPM as a discrete research discipline.

Acknowledgements. The research described in this paper was supported by a grant from the German Federal Ministry of Education and Research (BMBF), project name: "Process-oriented   Web-2.0-based   Integrated   Telecommunication   Service" (PROWIT), support code FKZ 01BS0833. The authors would also like to thank the anonymous reviewers and the workshop participants for their valuable comments which helped to improve this paper.

References

1. Scheer, A.-W., Brabänder, E.: The Process of Business Process Management. In: vom Brocke, J., Rosemann, M. (eds.) Handbook on Business Process Management 2 - Strategic Alignment, Governance, People and Culture, pp. 239–265. Springer, Berlin (2010)
2. Ko, R.K.L., Lee, S.S.G., Lee, E.W.: Business process management (BPM) standards: A survey. Business Process Management Journal 15, 744–791 (2009)
3. Gregor, S.: The Nature of Theory in Information Systems. MIS Quarterly 30, 611–642 (2006)
4. Scheer, A.-W.: ARIS - Business Process Frameworks. Springer, Berlin (1999)
5. Niiniluoto, I.: The Aim and Structure of Applied Research. Erkenntnis 38, 1–21 (1993)
6. Fettke, P., Houy, C., Loos, P.: On the Relevance of Design Knowledge for Design-Oriented Business and Information Systems Engineering. Business and Information Systems Engineering 2, 347–358 (2010)
7. Hevner, A.R., March, S.T., Park, J., Ram, S.: Design Science in Information Systems Research. MIS Quarterly 28, 75–105 (2004)
8. Carlsson, S.A.: Developing Knowledge Through IS Design Science Research. Scandinavian Journal of Information Systems 19, 75–86 (2007)
9. Houy, C., Fettke, P., Loos, P.: Empirical Research in Business Process Management - Analysis of an emerging field of research. Business Process Management Journal 16, 619–661 (2010)
10. Weber, R.: Theoretically Speaking. MIS Quarterly 27, iii–xii (2003)
11. Trkman, P.: The critical success factors of business process management. International Journal of Information Management 30, 125–134 (2010)
12. Recker, J., Dreiling, A.: The Effects of Content Presentation Format and User Characteristics on Novice Developers Understanding of Process Models. Communications of the Association for Information Systems 28, 65–84 (2011)
13. Sloman, A.: The Computer Revolution in Philosophy: Philosophy, Science and Models of Mind. Harvester, Hassocks (1978)
14. Cooper, H., Hedges, L.V.: Research Synthesis As a Scientific Enterprise. In: Cooper, H., Hedges, L.V. (eds.) The Handbook of Research Synthesis, pp. 3–14. Russell Sage Foundation, New York (1994)
15. Hung, R.Y.: Business Process Management as Competitive Advantage: a Review and Empirical Study. Total Quality Management 17, 21–40 (2006)
16. van der Aalst, W.M.P., ter Hofstede, A.H.M., Weske, M.: Business Process Management: A Survey. In: van der Aalst, W.M.P., ter Hofstede, A.H.M., Weske, M. (eds.) BPM 2003. LNCS, vol. 2678, pp. 1–12. Springer, Heidelberg (2003)
17. Chalmers, A.F.: What is This Thing Called Science? University of Queensland Press, St. Lucia (1999)
18. Thagard, P.: Computational Philosophy of Science. The MIT Press, Cambridge (1988)
19. Simon, H.A.: The Sciences of the artificial. MIT Press, Cambridge (1996)
20. Dubin, R.: Theory Building. Free Press, London (1978)
21. Wacker, J.G.: A definition of theory: research guidelines for different theory-building research methods in operations management. Journal of Operations Management 16, 361–385 (1998)
22. Frank, U.: Towards a Pluralistic Conception of Research Methods in Information Systems Research. ICB-Research Report Nr. 7, Institut für Informatik und Wirtschaftsinformatik (ICB) der Universität Duisburg-Essen, Essen (2006)

23. Davis, F.D.: Perceived Usefulness, Perceived Ease of Use, and User Acceptance of Information Technology. MIS Quarterly 13, 319–340 (1989)
24. Walls, J., Widmeyer, G., Sawy, O.E.: Building an information systems design theory for vigilant EIS. Information Systems Research 3, 36–59 (1992)
25. Gregor, S., Jones, D.: The Anatomy of a Design Theory. Journal of the Association for Information Systems 8, 312–335 (2007)
26. Pries-Heje, J., Baskerville, R.: The Design Theory Nexus. MIS Quarterly 32, 731–755 (2008)
27. Bunge, M.: Scientific Research II: The Search for Truth. Springer, Berlin (1967)
28. Pries-Heje, J., Baskerville, R.: A Design Theory for Managing Software Process Improvement. In: Proceedings of the 4th International Conference on Design Science Research in Information Systems and Technology (DESRIST 2009), Philadelphia, Pennsylvania (2009)
29. Siponen, M., Baskerville, R., Heikka, J.: A Design Theory for Secure Information Systems Design Methods. Journal of the Association for Information Systems 7, 725–770 (2006)
30. Venable, J.R.: The Role of Theory and Theorising in Design Science Research. In: Chatterjee, S., Hevner, A.R. (eds.) Proceedings of the First International Conference on Design Science in Information Systems and Technology (DESRIST 2006), Claremont, California, pp. 1–18 (2006)
31. Patas, J., Milicevic, D., Goeken, M.: Enhancing Design Science through Empirical Knowledge: Framework and Application. In: Jain, H., Sinha, A.P., Vitharana, P. (eds.) DESRIST 2011. LNCS, vol. 6629, pp. 32–46. Springer, Heidelberg (2011)
32. Winter, R., Krcmar, H., Sinz, E.J., Zelewski, S., Hevner, A.R.: What in Fact is Fundamental Research in Business and Information Systems Engineering? Business and Information Systems Engineering 1, 192–198 (2009)
33. Goodhue, D.L., Thompson, R.L.: Task-technology fit and individual performance. MIS Quarterly 19, 213–236 (1995)
34. Coase, R.H.: The Nature of the Firm. Economica 4, 386–405 (1937)
35. Wu, I.L.: A model for implementing BPR based on strategic perspectives: an empirical study. Information & Management 39, 313–324 (2002)
36. Ursic, D., Anteric, S., Mulej, M.: Business process re-engineering in practice - An example of a medium-sized Slovenian company in difficulties. Systemic Practice and Action Research 18, 89–117 (2005)
37. Williamson, O.E.: Market and Hierarchies: Analysis and Antitrust Implications. Free Press, New York (1975)
38. Williamson, O.: Transaction-Cost Economics: The Governance of Contractual Relations. Journal of Law and Economics 22, 233–261 (1979)
39. von Bertalanffy, L.: General System Theory: Foundations, Development, Applications. George Braziller, New York (1968)
40. Penrose, E.T.: The Theory of the Growth of the Firm. Wiley, New York (1959)
41. Wernerfelt, B.: A Resource Based View of the Firm. Strategic Management Journal 5, 171–180 (1984)
42. Fiedler, F.E.: A Contingency Model of Leadership Effectiveness. In: Berkowitz, L. (ed.) Advances in Experimental Social Psychology, vol. 1, pp. 149–190. Academic Press, New York (1964)
43. Fiedler, F.E.: A Theory of Leadership Effectiveness. McGraw-Hill, New York (1967)
44. Alchian, A., Demsetz, H.: Production, information costs, and economic organization. American Economic Review 62, 777–795 (1972)

45. Jensen, M., Meckling, W.: Theory of the firm: Managerial behavior, agency costs, and ownership structure. Journal of Financial Economics 3, 305–360 (1976)
46. Fishbein, M., Ajzen, I.: Belief, Attitude, Intention and Behaviour: An Introduction to Theory and Research. Addison-Wesley, Reading (1975)
47. Ajzen, I., Fishbein, M.: Understanding Attitudes and Predicting Social Behaviour. Prentice-Hall, Englewood Cliffs (1980)
48. Conner, K.R.: A Historical Comparison of the Resource-Based Theory and Five Schools of Thought Within Industrial Organization Economics: Do We Have a New Theory of the Firm? Journal of Management 17, 121–154 (1991)
49. Kogut, B., Zander, U.: Knowledge of the Firm, Combinative Capabilities, and the Replication of Technology. Organization Science 3, 383–397 (1992)
50. Pfeffer, J., Salancik, G.: The external control of organizations: A resource dependence perspective. Harper and Row, New York (1978)
51. Searle, J.R.: Speech Acts: An Essay in the Philosophy of Language. Cambridge University Press, Cambridge (1969)
52. Wade, M., Hulland, J.: The Resource-based View and Information Systems Research: Review, Extension, and Suggestions for Future Research. MIS Quarterly 28, 107–142 (2004)

On Handling Process Information: Results from Case Studies and a Survey*

Bernd Michelberger[1], Bela Mutschler[1], and Manfred Reichert[2]

[1] University of Applied Sciences Ravensburg-Weingarten, Germany
{bernd.michelberger,bela.mutschler}@hs-weingarten.de
[2] Institute of Databases and Information Systems, University of Ulm, Germany
manfred.reichert@uni-ulm.de

Abstract. An increasing data overload makes it difficult to provide the needed information to knowledge-workers and decision-makers in today's process-oriented enterprises. The main problem is to identify the information being relevant in a given process context. Moreover, there are new ways of collaboration in the context of distributed processes (e.g., automotive engineering, patient treatment). The goal is to provide the right process information, in the right format and quality, at the right place, at the right point in time to the right people. Picking up this goal, enterprises crave for an intelligent and process-oriented information logistics. In this paper we investigate fundamental issues enabling such information logistics based on two exploratory case studies in the automotive and the clinical domain. Additionally, we present results of an online survey with 219 participants supporting our case study findings. Our research does not only reveal different types of process information, but also allows for the derivation of factors determining its relevance. Understanding these factors, in turn, is a fundamental prerequisite to realize effective process-oriented information logistics.

Keywords: information logistics, process information, empirical study.

1 Introduction

Market globalization has led to increasing competitive pressure for enterprises. Products and services must be developed in ever-shorter cycles. New forms of collaboration within enterprises and between organizations are continuously emerging. As examples consider distributed engineering processes in the automotive domain [1] or the treatment of patients in healthcare networks [2]. To cope with these challenges, effective *business process management* (BPM) [3] becomes more and more success-critical for enterprises.

So far, supporting business processes through information technology has focused on modeling, analyzing, and executing processes (e.g., using BPM technology) [4]. What has been neglected so far is the support of knowledge-workers

---

* This research was performed in the niPRO project. This project is funded by the German Federal Ministry of Education and Research (BMBF) under grant number 17102X10. More information can be found at http://www.nipro-project.org

F. Daniel et al. (Eds.): BPM 2011 Workshops, Part I, LNBIP 99, pp. 333–344, 2012.

and decision-makers with personalized and contextualized process information. More attention to this challenge will become necessary, however, as an extensive amount of process information is exchanged within enterprises and between organizations using techniques and tools such as e-mail, Web 2.0 applications or enterprise information systems (e.g., enterprise resource planning (ERP) systems, customer relationship management (CRM) systems) [5].

More specifically, we apply the definition of *information* by Bocij et. al [6] as well as Rainer and Turban [7], and define the term *process information* as follows: *process information* refers to data that have been processed to support process users in the modeling, execution, monitoring, optimization, and design of processes, so that data has a meaning and a value with respect to the process users' activities. Examples of process information include textual process descriptions, working guidelines, graphical processes models, operational instructions, forms, checklists, lessons learned, and best practices (documented in text documents, spreadsheets, or e-mails).

Note that the mere availability of process information is not sufficient to adequately support knowledge-workers and decision-makers as requested above. Only when considering a user's process context it becomes possible to effectively provide personalized and contextualized process information. In practice, many problems arise in this context, e.g., revision control of process information, archiving of process information, inter-departmental exchange of process information, and handling of distributed process information. Further, inconsistencies (schematic and semantic) occur and an increased communication overhead can be observed due to the different structures of digital and paper-based process information. *Process-oriented information logistics* [8] can help to overcome these issues and to effectively manage and distribute process information.

Following these considerations, we investigate the handling of process information in enterprises based on three empirical studies. Thereby, our research has been guided by the following three research questions:

- **RQ1**: In what different forms is process information specified?
- **RQ2**: How can a process context be determined?
- **RQ3**: How can the relevance of process information be determined?

RQ1 and RQ2 are addressed by means of two exploratory case studies. Based on an online survey we answer RQ3 and further concretize RQ1.

The presented research is performed in the niPRO project. In this project we apply semantic technology to integrate both unstructured and structured process information within intelligent, user-adequate *process information portals*. The overall goal is to support knowledge-workers and decision-makers with the needed process information depending on their preferences and current process context. So far, both research and practice have not addressed how processes and related process information can be effectively merged. Currently, conventional methods of information retrieval or enterprise search engines are mainly used for this purpose. The niPRO process information portal, by contrast, aims at determining required information for knowledge-workers and decision-makers dynamically and automatically. Key challenges include the role-oriented provision of process information, a flexible visualization of process information, and the design of innovative approaches for different levels of information granularity.

This paper is organized as follows. Section 2 presents the results of our empirical studies. Section 3 discusses related work. Section 4 concludes the paper with a summary and an outlook.

2   Empirical Studies

Our empirical studies comprise two parts (cf. Figure 1). First, we performed two qualitative exploratory case studies based on face-to-face interviews and questionnaires. Second, we conducted an online survey to collect further data.

2.1   Research Design

Our case study research is of explorative nature. According to Yin [9] case studies are a research method to answer *why* and *how* research questions. Kitchenham et. al [10] add to this statement that case studies usually investigate what is happening in "typical" project settings, so it is *research-in-the-typical*. For *research-in-the-large*, i.e., to capture what is happening broadly over large groups, surveys are used. We therefore additionally conduct an online survey to collect further data that helps us to generalize our case study results.

Part 1: Case Studies. Two organizations are involved: one from the automotive domain (cf. Section 2.2) and one from the clinical sector (cf. Section 2.3).

In the first case study eight persons have been interviewed, nine in the second one. The interviewees work in different areas of their respective organizations. Both knowledge-workers and decision-makers are involved. Participants were selected in consultation with contact persons from each organization. None of the participants was a member of the research team.

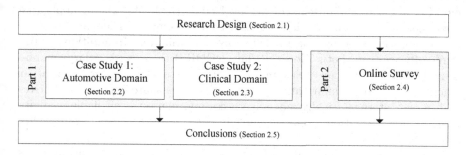

Fig. 1. Our empirical studies

The interviews addressed three major topics: (a) the *processes* in which the interviewees participate, (b) the *types of process information* (RQ1) needed, and (c) the factors determining a *process context* (RQ2). The interviews were conducted in November 2010. Each of them lasted about 90 minutes.

In both case studies, data was gathered through face-to-face interviews following a semi-structured interview guideline. After each interview, an additional questionnaire had to be filled out by each interviewee to collect further data.

Part 2: Online Survey. The online survey was conducted via a web questionnaire (cf. Section 2.4). The survey was accessible from mid-December 2010 to late January 2011. 219 users from different enterprises participated. The online survey was advertised via private contacts, business contacts, mailing lists, and groups in social platforms (e.g., LinkedIn). The questionnaire comprised 23 questions on (a) *demographic issues*, (b) *business process management in general*, and (c) *handling of process information* (in order to pick up RQ1 and RQ3).

2.2   Case Study 1: Automotive Domain

Our first case study was conducted in the automotive industry. The participants mainly stem from electric/electronic engineering departments, but also from the departments responsible for project management and safety planning. These departments were selected because of the knowledge-intense business processes they are involved in.

RQ1. Yin [9] states that research questions in case studies are usually too abstract and broad. Therefore, we divide our first research question *"In what different forms is process information specified?"* into three sub-research questions:

- **SRQ1**: Where is process information located?
- **SRQ2**: What are important file formats/systems during daily work?
- **SRQ3**: How is the quality of the available process information?

To answer the first sub-research question we consider the Information Technology (IT) application landscape of the involved departments. The IT application landscape in the automotive industry is extremely complex. There are numerous applications in use providing needed process information. In addition to standard software (e.g., Lotus Notes, RPlan, DOORS) there exists a large number of individual applications (e.g., process portals, Visual Basic for Applications macros etc.). Process information is also available on shared drives, local drives, and in the Internet. Finally, not all process information is available in digital form. Some information is only available in paper form (e.g., technical drawings or circuit diagrams).

Participants confirmed that most process information is available in databases, in applications, in the Internet, and on shared drives. Due to the extensive use of shared drives, a revision control system not officially supported (so far:

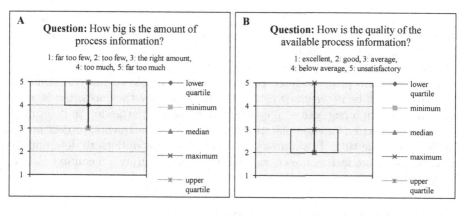

Fig. 2. A) Quality and B) amount of process information

Subversion, in future: MKS Integrity) is used. The file explorer and the Intranet are the most common ways to access process information. Information access via applications is not always possible since not all employees typically have needed licenses. Hence, system discontinuities occur, as information is often printed, manually processed, re-entered in enterprise information systems, and further processed.

To answer the second sub-research question we examined file formats and existing information systems. All participants stated that they use Excel files, PowerPoint files, and PDF files. 7 out of 9 participants said that diagrams (e.g., circuit diagrams, technical drawings) are relevant as well. To establish an order of priority, we asked for the three most important file formats during daily work. The result: Excel files, PDF files, and PowerPoint files are most important.

To answer the last sub-research question we take a closer look at the quality of process information. Because the structure and quantity of process information affect its quality [11], we also want to investigate these factors. Most process information is available in unstructured form. However, as unstructured process information is difficult to handle, employees often try to store process information in a structured way (e.g., via templates, databases, applications). In seven of our interviews it was said that the existence of process information is more important than its quality in daily work. However, the interviews also showed that employees often have no overview on available process information due to its large amount; i.e., they often cannot say whether they have all necessary process information. This, in turn, leads to decreased process quality. Not surprisingly, the amount of process information is classified by most participants as too much (cf. Figure 2A). By contrast, the quality of process information was rated differently (cf. Figure 2B). Some process information is rated as being very good (e.g., databases, own documents, information about own tasks). Other information is rated as being very poor (e.g., process documentation, information on tasks).

RQ2. To investigate the employees' process context we ask for factors that can be used to identify a specific process context.

The participants confirmed that the process context is determined based on the progress of a process; specifically by milestones or quality gates (specific milestones) for instance. Some interviewees said that some documents have metadata in which the relation to process steps is noted. Another possibility, also used, is the information progress (e.g., customer data available to 80%). A context, for example, can be determined by folder names because they are often labeled with the name of a respective milestone. Other useful information to determine a specific context is, for example, user names, roles, departments, project memberships, and the time. In summary, there exist various options to determine a context. The more factors are considered, the more accurately a context can be determined.

2.3   Case Study 2: Clinical Domain

In our second case study we considered a process of an unplanned, stationary hospitalization in a surgical clinic. It includes the patient admission, the medical indication in the anesthesia, the surgical intervention, the post-surgery stay on the ward, patient discharge and the financial accounting and management.

RQ1. Like in Case Study 1, we investigate our first research question based on the sub-research questions introduced in Section 2.2.

In the clinical sector, both standard software (e.g., SAP ERP) and individual applications are in use. Clinical staff interacts with them using fat-clients (e.g., DIACOS) and thin-clients (e.g., iMED, CIRS). Process information is available in shared drives, in local drives, in the Internet, in digital archives, and in paper form (e.g., patient files, medical reports, and patient checklists). Our study has revealed that a large amount of process information is not available in electronic form at all. Therefore, exchange of process information between departments is often done manually and only automated to a limited degree. In addition, much process information is available on the Internet, in the Intranet, and in clinical databases or applications (e.g., CIRS). Typically, the processes are not implemented but scattered over multiple more or less integrated systems (e.g., after computer-aided enrollment of patient data via SAP the data is printed and further processed manually by different departments).

To answer sub-research question SRQ2 we analyzed file formats and information systems. 6 out of 8 interviewees confirmed that they mainly use PDF files and Word files. None of the participants uses audio files and only one of them uses video files (medical tutorials). Like in Case Study 1 we asked for the three most important file formats the participants need during daily work. The formats most frequently used are paper-based documents, Word files, and SAP data records.

To answer sub-research question SRQ3, we address quality issues of process information. Like in Case Study 1 we also consider the structure and quantity of process information. Analogous to Case Study 1 most process information is only available in unstructured form. Further Case Study 2 shows that daily problems are the poor quality (e.g., poorly maintained data about utilization

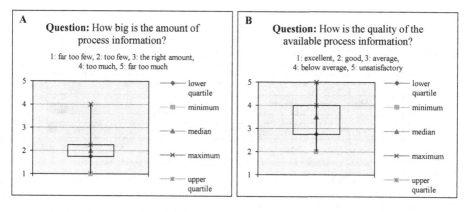

Fig. 3. A) Quality and B) amount of process information

of hospital beds) and the incompleteness (e.g., not all necessary information is available on the emergency protocol) of process information. Besides, process information is often outdated mostly due to the lack of responsibilities concerning information maintenance. The amount of process information is classified by most interviewees as too low (cf. Figure 3A). Reason is that process information is typically paper-based and only one person at a certain point in time can access this information (e.g., the patient file is needed for preliminary investigations, medical reporting, patient care, medical surgery, accounting, etc.). Quality of process information is rated different (cf. Figure 3B). Finally, self-made process information is ranked higher than third-party process information.

RQ2. Useful information to determine a context can be time, users or individual computers (because some computers are only used for certain tasks). Also, user location can be helpful, e.g., with the help of mobile devices. Based on the GPS-location of a user, it can be determined, for example, whether a doctor is currently on ward or in the operating theatre. However, 4 out of 8 interviewees believe that is very difficult to determine a process context in healthcare processes. In particular there are no fully pre-specified processes, instead they dynamically evolve and many tasks are performed manually without any IT support. Concerning tasks supported by information systems, the process context can be determined based on information progress (e.g., is a patient ready for accounting or is the patient already settled). Information state changes (e.g., State 1: "patient is in the operating room" or State 2: "patient is on ward") in information systems also occur and can be used to determine the process context.

2.4 Online Survey

In our online survey, 219 employees from more than 100 enterprises participated. 26% of the participants were decision-makers and 57% were knowledge-workers.

In the first part of the online survey (cf. Section 2.1), we wanted to know whether or not business processes are documented. Obviously, most business

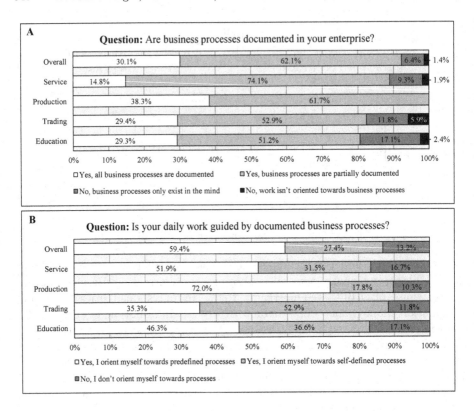

Fig. 4. Documentation of business processes

processes are fully or partially documented (cf. Figure 4A). Only a small group of participants reported that their work does not take into account business processes or that business processes do only exist in their mind. No one from the production industry reported that processes are undocumented.

We also wanted to know whether the employees' daily work is guided by documented business processes (cf. Figure 4B). More than a half of the respondents stated that they follow predefined business processes. 27.4% of the respondents follow at least self-defined processes. Only 13.2% of respondents said that they perform their work without considering pre-specified business processes.

Interesting results were also given by means of individual statements of survey participants. Several participants confirmed that people are the most important information source since they can deal with difficult questions or explain other people's work processes. Participants also pointed out that inexperienced staff will benefit most from process information portals. Another participant said that if processes are undocumented, the identification of a process context gains importance.

The first questionnaire block concludes with the question whether an information portal providing needed information could help employees during daily work (cf. Figure 5A). Most of the respondents (85.8%) somewhat or totally agreed.

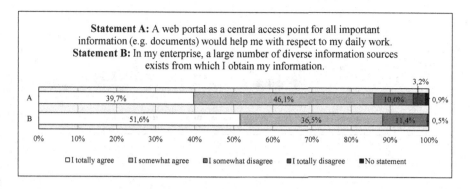

Statement A: A web portal as a central access point for all important information (e.g. documents) would help me with respect to my daily work.
Statement B: In my enterprise, a large number of diverse information sources exists from which I obtain my information.

Fig. 5. Information portal and information sources

Respondents also agreed that there exists a large number of diverse information sources from which they obtain their information (cf. Figure 5B).

RQ1. We asked where needed process information is located. Most participants referred to databases, applications, shared and local drives, and the Internet as the most important sources of process information. When comparing shared and local drives it becomes evident that the majority of process information is stored on shared drives (86%). Furthermore, several participants pointed out that people represent an important source of information as well (e.g., experts, colleagues or hotlines). The most important file formats are PDF, Excel, PowerPoint, and Word.

RQ3. We also investigated the relevance of process information. Many participants stated that self-made process information (e.g., own documents, e-mails) have a greater relevance than third-party information. Our survey results also show a direct relationship between the frequency a particularly information is accessed and its relevance. The more frequent a particular process information is accessed the higher is its relevance. Hence, participants confirmed that standardized process information (e.g., forms) is more relevant than non-standardized one. In this context participants confirmed that the relevance of process information is significantly influenced by the reliability of the information source. Additionally relevance factors mentioned include the number of changes of an information, the date of the last access, the amount of metadata assigned to a process information, and the file size. As far as temporal consideration is concerned, recurring information and timeliness of process information influences its relevance as well. Most participants stated that only up-to-date and complete process information can be relevant. The accessibility to process information is denoted as a basic requirement.

We also analyzed the available amount of process information (cf. Figure 6). Obviously, decision-makers are confronted with too much information. 45.1% of the decision-makers confirm that they have too much or far too much process information (knowledge-workers: 24%). Knowledge-workers, by contrast, have

342   B. Michelberger, B. Mutschler, and M. Reichert

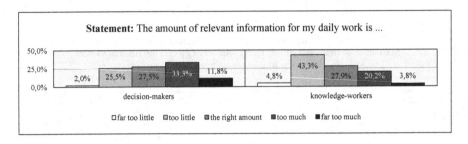

Fig. 6. Amount of process information

the problem of being confronted with insufficient information. 48.1% of the
knowledge-workers mentioned that they have too little or far too little process
information (decision-makers: 27.5%).

2.5 Conclusions

Regarding research questions RQ1-RQ3 we can draw the following conclusions:

RQ1. *"In what different forms is process information specified?"* The majority of process information in enterprises is available in Word files, Excel files,
PowerPoint files, PDF files, and in paper form. In addition, there are many
enterprise-specific file formats. The most common information sources are the
Internet, shared and local drives, and non-electronic information sources (e.g.,
documents in paper form). Significant problems in enterprises are the poor quality and timeliness of process information. Finally, access problems (e.g., lack of
licenses) to process information sources are reported.

RQ2. *"How can a process context be determined?"* Our results show that a
process context can be determined through various factors, e.g., by considering
the progress of processes, information progress, data associated with processes
(e.g., folder names, metadata), and specific computers for certain tasks. Other
useful information to determine a specific context includes, for example, the user
name, the role, the department, the project membership, and the time.

RQ3. *"How can the relevance of process information be determined?"* The results show that self-made process information has a much greater relevance than
third-party process information. This relevance is affected by many factors: access frequency, standardization, reliability of information sources, number of
changes, date of last access, available metadata, and size. Another important
factor is the quality of process information, which can be determined based on
characteristics such as periodicity, precision, and granularity. Process information must be up-to-date and complete to increase its relevance for employees'
daily work.

3 Related Work

There are studies dealing with process-oriented information logistics in enterprises. Dinter and Winter [12] analyze current information logistics strategy practices by means of a survey. Their findings show that information logistics strategy is linked to company size and governance type. Bucher and Dinter [13] provide another empirical analysis to assess benefits, design factors, and realization approaches for process-oriented information logistics. The study of Lahrmann and Stroh [14] identifies typical scenario patterns in information logistics. A case study in a tourism setting is performed by Landqvist and Stenmark [15]. They investigate portal information integration and ownership misfits. Hristidis et. al. [16] conduct a survey about data management and analysis. They achieved the same results as in our study: Data are available in many different formats, have varying characteristics, and stem from different sources.

All these studies analyze process-oriented information logistics with different emphasis (e.g., strategy, design factors, scenarios, and misfits). However, the combination of different types of process information, process context, and process information relevance is addressed by none of them.

4 Summary and Outlook

This paper summarizes the results of two case studies and one online survey. We investigate different types of process information and factors determining the relevance of process information and process context. We further identify the most important characteristics of process information like source, location, and quality of the process information. In addition, we investigate how a specific process context can be determined.

Future research will include additional studies to investigate quality dimensions of process information such as periodicity, granularity, and completeness. These quality dimensions of process information need to be analyzed as they strongly influence overall quality of process information.

References

1. Müller, D., Herbst, J., Hammori, M., Reichert, M.: IT Support for Release Management Processes in the Automotive Industry. In: Dustdar, S., Fiadeiro, J.L., Sheth, A.P. (eds.) BPM 2006. LNCS, vol. 4102, pp. 368–377. Springer, Heidelberg (2006)
2. Lenz, R., Reichert, M.: IT Support for Healthcare Processes - Premises, Challenges, Perspectives. Data and Knowledge Engineering 61(1), 39–58 (2007)
3. Weske, M.: Business Process Management: Concepts, Languages, Architectures. Springer, Heidelberg (2007)
4. Mutschler, B., Reichert, M., Bumiller, J.: Unleashing the Effectiveness of Process-oriented Information Systems: Problem Analysis, Critical Success Factors and Implications. IEEE Transactions on Systems, Man, and Cybernetics (SMC) - Part C 38(3), 280–291 (2008)

5. Laudon, K., Laudon, J.: Management Information Systems: Managing the Digital Firm. Pearson/Prentice Hall (2009)
6. Bocij, P., Chaffey, D., Greasley, A., Hickie, S.: Business Information Systems: Technology, Development and Management for the E-Business. Prentice Hall (2006)
7. Rainer, R.K., Turban, E.: Introduction to Information Systems: Supporting and Transforming Business. Wiley & Sons (2008)
8. Meissen, U., Pfennigschmidt, S., Voisard, A., Wahnfried, T.: Context- and Situation-Awareness in Information Logistics. In: Lindner, W., Fischer, F., Türker, C., Tzitzikas, Y., Vakali, A.I. (eds.) EDBT 2004. LNCS, vol. 3268, pp. 335–344. Springer, Heidelberg (2004)
9. Yin, R.K.: Case Study Research: Design and Methods. Sage Publications (2009)
10. Kitchenham, B., Pickard, L., Pfleeger, S.L.: Case Studies for Method and Tool Evaluation. IEEE Software 12(4), 52–62 (1995)
11. Wang, R.Y., Strong, D.M.: Beyond Accuracy: What Data Quality Means to Data Consumers. J. of Management Information Systems 12(4), 5–34 (1996)
12. Dinter, B., Winter, R.: Information Logistics Strategy - Analysis of Current Practices and Proposal of a Framework. In: Proc. of the 42nd Hawaii Int'l Conf. on System Sciences (HICSS-42), Hawaii, pp. 1–10 (2009)
13. Bucher, T., Dinter, B.: Process Orientation of Information Logistics - An Empirical Analysis to Assess Benefits, Design Factors, and Realization Approaches. In: Proc. of the 41st Annual Hawaii Int'l Conf. on System Sciences, pp. 392–402 (2008)
14. Lahrmann, G., Stroh, F.: Towards a Classification of Information Logistics Scenarios - An Exploratory Analysis. In: Proc. of the 42nd Hawaii Int'l Conf. on System Sciences (HICSS-42), Hawaii (2009)
15. Landqvist, F., Stenmark, D.: Portal Information Integration and Ownership misfits: A Case Study in a Tourism Setting. In: Proc. of the 39th Annual Hawaii Int'l Conf. on System Sciences (HICSS 2006) (2009)
16. Hristidis, V., Chen, S.C., Li, T., Luis, S., Deng, Y.: Survey of data management and analysis in disaster situations. J. of Systems and Software 83(10), 1701–1714 (2010)

Investigating Process Elicitation Workshops Using Action Research

Alexander Luebbe and Mathias Weske

Hasso-Plattner-Instittute, 14482 Potsdam, Germany
{alexander.luebbe,mathias.weske}@hpi.uni-potsdam.de
http://bpt.hpi.uni-potsdam.de

Abstract. We develop a workshop technique for process co-creation with domain experts called tangible business process modeling. After assessing the idea in a laboratory experiment, we started workshops with professionals in the field. This paper illustrates how we used action research in two subsequent studies in which groups modeled BPMN and EPCs using tangible tiles on a table.

The practical result is best practice guidance for moderators applying tangible process modeling. Our research interest is to investigate the differences between tangible modeling and other techniques. In the lab experiment we found that tangible modeling supports user engagement and validated results. In the field, we compare the workshop performance and outcome to software-supported workshops. We found tangible modeling to be competitive in speed and result.

Keywords: business process elicitation, workshops, process modeling, tangible business process modeling, field research, action research.

1 Introduction and Background

Business process modeling is the act of capturing domain knowledge about work activities, their interdependencies, and responsibilities, in a graphical representation. Process models are used to analyze current business operations, communicate requirements for IT systems, or discuss alternatives to the current way of doing business. Typically, domain experts share their knowledge with a process analyst in interviews or workshops. The model is either created after the interview or in parallel during the workshop by a dedicated tool expert [1]. Domain experts review the results but do not actively participate in process model creation. This practice detaches the domain expert from the process model with problems such as misunderstandings and limited commitment [2].

We have created a modeling approach to engage the domain expert with the act of process modeling. The approach covers a toolkit and a method to apply it. In the first phase we developed the toolkit as a set of transcribable plastic tiles to be used on a table for process modeling [3], see Fig. 1. In the second phase we assessed the effect of modeling with tangible tiles by comparing individuals in interview situations with tangible process modeling sessions. Subjects were

F. Daniel et al. (Eds.): BPM 2011 Workshops, Part I, LNBIP 99, pp. 345–356, 2012.
© Springer-Verlag Berlin Heidelberg 2012

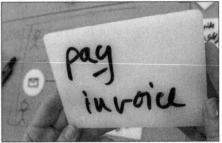

Fig. 1. tangible modeling tool set: transcribable plastic tiles reflecting the BPMN iconography

more engaged with the task. Moreover, they reviewed and corrected the model more often leading to more validated results [4].

The lab experiment showed positive effects of tangible modeling on individuals. The current research interest is the efficiency of group modeling workshops in reality. We aim to assess the applicability of tangible modeling in real environments and compare tangible modeling workshops with other techniques in place today.

The practical goal is to derive guidance for professionals who want to leverage the theoretical potential [4] of tangible business process modeling in their workshops, namely stronger engagement and validated results. Since practical guidance can only be derived from practice, we choose action research as a method to guide our cooperation with professionals in the field.

In Section 2 we introduce the idea of action research. Afterwards, we apply action research in Section 3 and Section 4 in two subsequent iterations and discuss our learnings in Section 5. Finally, we look at related empirical research in Section 6 and conclude the paper in Section 7.

2   Action Research – An Iterative Learning Cycle

Action research (AR) is a class of research approaches in which researchers collaborate with practitioners to act in or on a social system [5]. The goal is to solve practical problems and generate scientific knowledge. Action research assumes that complex social problems cannot be reduced to meaningful controllable studies. They need to be investigated within the context in which they appear. Therefore the system is studied, changed, and the effect of change is studied again. It is an iterative learning cycle. We adopt a five stage process proposed by e.g. Baskerville [6], see Figure 2. We also follow the principles for AR defined by Davison et al. [7] such as multiple iterations, the principle of theory, and learning through reflection.

In the *diagnosing* step the context and problem statement are described. In *action planning* the desired future state and proposed changes are introduced based on theoretical background. The first two steps are carried out in close

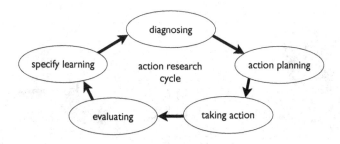

Fig. 2. Action research cycle used to guide the field studies in this paper

collaboration with practitioners. In *taking action* the practitioners act alone while the researchers observe and collect data for the *evaluating* phase. This phase analyses whether the proposed changes realized the intended effect and whether the practitioners' problems were solved. The results are used to *specify learning* as more general knowledge, practically and scientifically. In this last step, we also develop research questions for the next iteration.

3   BPMN Process Modeling Workshop with Clinical Staff

In mid 2009, a consultant used the tangible toolkit (see Fig. 1) to capture clinical paths in a hospital with medical staff. A clinical path is a treatment process for a class of patients with a similar disease, in this case for a certain type of cancer. It was the first application of our tangible modeling approach in the field. As researchers, we observed the situation and framed it as a case study [2]. Within one week, twenty BPMN processes were modeled together with three doctors using the tangible modeling toolkit. The workshop was considered a success by the consultant. In mid 2010, the same consultant approached us again with the same request. The setting was very similar, only the participants and the clinical path were changed. This was the starting point for the first action research cycle.

Diagnosing. When reviewing the workshop from 2009 together with the consultant, we agreed that the introduction was not optimal. Originally, a one-day introduction to BPM and BPMN was given. Modeling only started on the second day. A further problem was that the workshop in 2009 got confused with different media. Tangible tiles, paper printouts, and software were all present during the workshop. Jumping between media created different embodiments with different versions of the same process model. A clear guideline was needed that matches the media with the purpose of the modeling phase. Finally, as researchers, we wanted to investigate to which extend data collection is feasible in such a research environment and what can be traced from the data. Up to this point, we were not sure which data to trace in order to characterize modeling sessions and results.

Fig. 3. Modeling (left) and reviewing (right) clinical processes using BPMN

Action planning. We developed a shorter BPMN introduction with the consultant and proposed warm-up excercises to enable a quicker start with process modeling. This was based on the idea of learning by doing [8]. We collected modeling exercises from consultants and literature such as 'withdrawing money from an ATM' inspired by Rittgen [9]. These scenarios enable participants to get familiar with process modeling without getting lost in domain specific discussions. We also defined a media framework that proposes to (1) complement discussions with drawings, (2) use tangible tiles on a table to generate models, (3) use printouts for reviews, and (4) use software to store models. This was inspired by the research of Edelman [10] on the role of media in steering conversations. For data collection, we sent an observer to take photos and detailed notes during the workshop.

Action taking. Again, a one-week workshop was conducted. Three participants from the hospital worked out the clinical paths for liver transplantation together with the consultant. The introduction to BPM and BPMN was shortened to half a day. The second half of the first day was used to model a pizza-ordering process and discuss modeling decisions. In the following four days, the doctors modeled thirteen processes together with the consultant. Fig. 3 shows some impressions from the workshop. In total we collected more than six hundred pictures, nine pages with observer notes and interviews with the consultant and each participant. From the modeling sessions we collected six snapshots of the project to document the progress during the week.

Evaluating. In interviews at the end of the week, the participants qualified tangible modeling as well suited to adopt process thinking. The modeling exercise in the beginning was perceived as a logical part of the introduction. The consultant liked the way in which the modeling exercise complemented the introduction and activated participants early. In his opinion the contribution to learning BPMN is not very high, but the modeling exercise reduces the barrier to start creating. All together, the introduction and modeling exercise consumed the first day of the workshop.

The consultant also classified the media framework as a nice idea to keep in mind. However, it is not a golden rule and does not necessarily match the practical situation. For example, on day three people added role information to all existing models. They did this by coloring process steps in printed models. Strictly following our media framework would have implied recreating tangible models to add this information. Participants said to have experienced the media choices as natural.

The observer notes and photos were analyzed to identify patterns. We distinguished four working modes during the workshop week. People got introduced to new modeling knowledge, participants modeled, the consultant digitalized the models in the evenings and everybody reviewed results. These modes happened in a cyclic pattern: (1) introduce, (2) model, (3) digitalize, and (4) review.

Additionally, we used process model metrics by Mendling [11] to explore characteristics of the models and the modeling progress. Model metrics that showed a high dynamic were considered as candidate KPIs. We concluded the amount of information pieces to be characteristic for the modeling progress of the project. The amount of information mapped per hour in a modeling session seemed to be a good indicator for productivity. These metrics do not tell all the truth about a workshop. They are an abstraction to compare workshop outcomes in relation to the time spent. However, in this special case there was no data to compare with.

Finally, we asked the consultant for his preferred alternative to tangible modeling and he responded: "There is no alternative. I knew it would work from our previous workshop. If I did not have this option then I would have to do interviews. But if you are not an expert in the domain – which I am not – good luck understanding your client."

Specify learning. From this field study, we learned that participants and the consultant perceived the warm-up exercise as positive. It did shorten the time to start modeling but overall it did not save time in comparison to the previous workshop. The actual modeling of content started in both cases at the second day.

We also learned that the media framework is a good idea to guide consultants in the selection of media for the workshop. But it is not a golden rule and the media must be chosen specific to the situation. Observation notes and photos enabled us to trace phases, productivity and modeling progress. From the transition of phases, we identified a natural modeling cycle. The productivity and process data itself, however, is meaningless without a proper data set to compare with.

By reviewing the workshops in 2009 and 2010 we identified themes that worked well. From that we derived the first practical guidance for moderators and iterated it with the consultant. The guidance was on topics such as the right setting, the media framework and the warm-up exercises. To broaden our results, we identified the following research questions to be most pressing for a subsequent AR study:

1. Is the idea specific to BPMN as a process notation?
2. Does tangible modeling create results different from other techniques?
3. How productive is tangible modeling compared to other group workshops?

4   EPC Modeling at an Energy Provider

In early 2011, an in-house consultant working for a subsidiary of a large energy provider in Germany contacted us. The company is responsible to develop and test new ideas for the energy market such as smart home devices and e-mobility concepts. Within this company, our contact captures and improves organizational processes in workshops together with domain experts. He approached us because he saw a need for tangible modeling in specific workshop situations.

Diagnosing. Two people typically run the process elicitation workshops at this company as a team, a moderator and a software tool expert. While the moderator elicits information in a conversation with the participants, the tool expert translates the information into a process model in the background. The computer screen is simultaneously projected to a wall. The participants can see the process model evolving and review it. In this case the process notation is EPC and the modeling tool is ARIS [12]. A modeling workshop lasts three hours. The process modeling team worked on more than six hundred process models together in the last years.

The modeling team faced some problems, which they wanted to tackle with tangible models. For one, the projector limits the overview. A typical screen resolution for projectors is 1024 by 768 pixels but even a full HD resolution would not enable to see the large models all at once. Thus, participants can lose the overview. A further aspect is the very limited involvement of the participants, especially, if the model is not that clear but has to be discussed and developed together. The moderator felt that some conflicts are not expressed because the participants have no means to do that. These conflicts pop up in subsequent workshops when the previous workshop result is reviewed. For us, as researchers, the setting was excellent to tackle our open research questions.

Action planning. We wanted a similar setting but change the modeling tool. Instead of ARIS and a dedicated tool expert, we proposed to use a tangible version of EPCs, see Fig. 4 (left). The moderator insisted on the software and the tool expert as a backup. Thus, the model was created on the table and digitalized for documentation by a dedicated ARIS modeler in parallel.

It was clear that not all workshops would equally benefit from tangible modeling. We looked for processes with lots of need for discussion and people open-minded towards active workshop participation. The department for idea management was identified within the company. This department was formed one year earlier and just grew from two to three knowledge workers. The processes were not modeled yet but the department looked for software to support their work. Two workshop sessions were scheduled at two subsequent days. The goal was to create an overview of the existing processes in this department and to model the core process that would benefit from software support.

To collect data, we sent two observers to the workshop. Furthermore, we got access to the organizational handbook of this company with 22 processes of a similarly structured department. It serves as a reference point for typical processes captured by this team of process modeling experts in this company. To trace productivity, we collected effort estimations for a recently finished modeling project from a different department. This project spanned 18 models and served as a reference point for the productivity of the process modeling team.

Action taking. The first workshop started late and ended early due to other commitments of the participants. Two out of three hours actually remained. Within that time, the moderator gave a standard ten-minute introduction about the need for process modeling. In the first step a map of processes for this department was created. In a brainstorming manner, all processes were collected on Post-Its at a flip-chart. Subsequently, the workshop participants consolidated the process landscape by re-arranging the Post-Its. Here, it already turned out that the scope of this department was not entirely clear. Creating this map consumed the first workshop hour. In the remaining time, the tangible EPC set was introduced and the first steps for the 'idea creation and evaluation' process were mapped.

Fig. 4. tangible EPC toolkit (left) and modeling idea management (right) at energy provider

The next day started with a review of the existing process snippet. The main path was completed and two alternative paths were modeled. Iteratively, each path was enriched with roles, documents and IT systems. Three explicit reviews were done during the workshop, after each completed path. Many more small reviews happened in the form of mental leaps during discussions. We collected three pages of observer notes and 112 photos including four snapshots of intermediate modeling results. We interviewed the moderator, the software tool expert and one of the participants after the workshops.

Evaluating. The interviewees expressed satisfaction with the workshop result. The software tool expert attributed the stronger activation of participants to the non-technical, puzzle-like nature of tangible modeling. The moderator classified the stronger participation as an expected result. For him, standing, pointing, and talking already adds value to the workshop. The additional option to move around tiles and try out alternatives replaces review discussions at later stages, he said. The participant liked playing an active role in the workshop. For him, being an active workshop participant was not a new experience. When asked about the next steps of reviewing the digitalized EPC model, he said "I won't look at it. There is nothing to gain. I was here. I know what is in the model." Limited review interest might apply to all types of workshops making active participation and corrections during the workshop even more relevant.

The digital EPC printed on A3 paper was hardly readable. A graph with 126 nodes in total. The same model as a tangible representation was overlooked on a three by one meter table. Both observers took notes of events where participants leaped from one end of the model to the other in order to add or correct information.

We evaluated the workshop result by quantifying the information in the model. In Figure 5 (left) we compare this with a box-plot derived by evaluating 22 processes modeled by the same BPM experts in a similar department. For this statistic we counted the amount of node type occurrences in the models. The values from tangible modeling are in range except for role information.

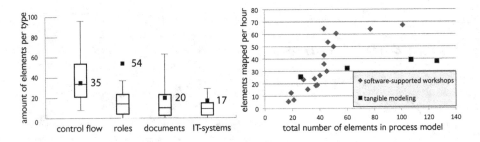

Fig. 5. Left: boxplot characterizing 22 models of a similarly structured department. The data points characterize the tangible EPC workshop result; Right: workshop productivity related to model size for 18 models derived in software-supported workshops and the four modeling phases observed in the tangible modeling workshops.

We also quantified the delta of information added in each tangible modeling session as the amount of nodes in the resulting EPC graph. We compared our productivity (25-39 elements mapped per hour) to 18 processes from a recently finished modeling project (6-67 elements/hour). In Fig. 5 (right) the modeling speed is related to the size of the model. The 'tangible modeling' data points represent the modeling speed in the four modeling phases related to the size of the growing model. Fig. 5 (right) shows that tangible modeling is competitive to the software-supported approach for small model sizes. The productivity does not change with larger models, in particular it does not get slower. But as models grow in size the productivity of software-supported workshops goes up dramatically. The reason we found is copy-and-paste. In big models, substructures get re-used. As an example, in accounting the invoicing is handled differently according to the contract type. After the process for one contract type is modeled, it gets copied and adapted for the other case. In the end, the different paths involve different IT systems but do not differ much in the steps taken. Here a digital modeling tool can speed up the creation of model parts dramatically with up to 67 elements modeled in one hour in the analyzed sample set. This relation was an unexpected finding. We see model size as a candidate to determine the tool choice for modeling workshops.

Specify learning. For the practitioners the modeling workshop was successful. As researchers, we realized that standing, pointing and discussing are important aspects, no matter which media is in place. Tangible media adds additional value because it enables the participants to express ideas by directly interacting with the model. We have chosen the idea management department because they are familiar with interactive workshops and they had a need for clarifying discussions. We learned that those situations welcome the use of shared tangible media.

Our measures indicate that tangible modeling creates similar results when compared to the established software-supported modeling technique. In our data set, tangible modeling is also faster for smaller models. Larger models benefit from a digital tool because it allows copying, pasting, and adapting model parts. Despite this restriction, we think the tangible modeling productivity is astonishing. Especially because the additional software modeling tool expert is not required during tangible workshops. But we are also aware that the numbers we compare with represent a range of cases from a different department. They were modeled by the same team of process experts but with other participants.

Although we provided our existing best practice knowledge from the first AR study, the moderator in charge at the energy provider did not look at them prior to the workshop. As a result, there was e.g. no warm-up exercise. Instead the moderator improvised a variant of his existing workshop technique. We reviewed both AR studies and complemented our best practice knowledge with new insights about setting and group facilitation. As examples, the modeling session should be well scoped. Especially, the modeling goal to create an as-is or a to-be model must be defined upfront.

5   Result Discussion

As a practical result of this work, we identified guidelines in the categories of setting, media framework, modeling cycles, warm-up exercises and group facilitation. Experienced modeling experts might ignore the advice entirely and run the workshop by their intuition. But some good practices, like scoping the modeling session to as-is vs. to-be models, have also been forgotten by the experts in our studies. Thus, these guidelines can serve as a reminder even for experienced modeling professionals. The guidelines for setting and media framework are of particular importance to tangible modeling.

The workshops were able to deliver the expected strong engagement of participants. The benefits are inline with findings from our lab experiment [4]. For example, participants said that this type of modeling helped them to learn process thinking. This is strongly related to 'more insights into process modeling' measured in the lab experiment when comparing interviews with tangible modeling. We also found in the same experiment that participants do many more reviews and corrections when the process is mapped on the table. In the second AR study, reviews and corrections were noticed as mental leaps by the workshop moderator and by both observers independently.

We answer our research questions as follows:

1. Tangible process modeling is not specific to a process notation but to the people and the process to be discussed. People need to be open for the technique and see a need to discuss the process.
2. Tangible modeling can be used to produce models competitive to software-supported modeling workshops.
3. Tangible modeling productivity is competitive to software-supported modeling for models that cannot take advantage of re-use through copy and paste.

We want to draw the attention to some limitations of this research. One particular aspect to point out are the measurement instruments used to compare productivity and outcome. They are new instruments which need further testing. Our testing compared workshops from different departments with different participants. Nevertheless, all data comes from the same team of process modeling experts that ran the AR study with us. Therefore we think the data is valuable to build insights and hypotheses. Further investigations with larger and more homogeneous data sets are needed to strengthen or disprove our conclusions with statistical expressiveness. For now, we can only make transparent the path taken for readers to follow or challenge our conclusions.

The two field studies reported in this paper were the main drivers for insights into the technique and the basis to answer our research questions. But this paper can only tell a subset of the overall story. As an example, we discussed our guidelines with more practitioners and researchers to form a stable opinion on relevance.

6   Related Action Research

Action research is quite well adopted in information systems science to guide researchers working with professionals [13]. As examples, it was used to improve the process of software development in coordination with the client organization [14], increase the value of existing information systems [15] or use software to create social impact [16].

A typical action research publication mentions the research method but focuses on problem descriptions and findings from multiple iterations. This is complemented by theoretical papers on the action research cycle [6] or general AR principles [7]. In this paper, we use these theoretical guidelines and show their operationalization in two subsequent action research cycles.

In business process management, action research is not mainstream yet. Practitioners are typically involved in research through surveys and case studies [17]. If solutions are developed together with practitioners, this is framed as or combined with design science research (DSR) [18]. Indeed both research approaches have a lot in common [19], in particular the iterative refinement and assessment of the research artifact, in our case the method.

The nearest relative to our work is the research done by Rittgen [9,20]. He designed and implemented software to engage people in group modeling workshops. The fundamental difference to our work is the assumption that people can be engaged with computer-based modeling. Our tangible approach targets people who do not want to work with computers in group workshops.

Rittgen describes his research method as design science research(DSR) in [20] or a combination of DSR and action research in [9]. In [20], he presents three years of research as a single execution of the design science cycle. We illustrate our research journey in this paper using two concrete AR iterations to spread knowledge about the operationalization of action research.

7 Conclusion

We created a modeling approach to engage domain experts in the creation of their process models. In previous work [4], we determined the effect of tangible media on individuals in a lab experiment. In this paper, we present field research with groups. We opt for a five-step action research model to guide our cooperation with practitioners. We successfully applied tangible modeling with doctors and businessman using BPMN or EPC as process notations.

In cooperation with the professional partners, we developed guidance for moderators facilitating tangible modeling workshops. This guidance spans the areas of setting, media framework, modeling cycles, warm-up exercises and group facilitation. The knowledge we bring into the scientific discussion evolves from our case data. We claim that (1) tangible process modeling is not restricted to a process notation but to the people willing to do it. Furthermore, (2) tangible modeling does not produce a different type of process model and (3) it is not slower than software-supported modeling as long as model re-use is not common practice.

Our conclusions are based on qualitative research meaning they are the result of interpretation. Further investigations with larger and more homogeneous data sets may strengthen or disprove our claims. In this paper, we present the observations that led to these interpretations. We also provide a sample for other BPM researchers that want to work with practitioners to generate both, practical and scientific knowledge.

Acknowledgement. We are grateful to the BPM practitioners that fearlessly tried out new ideas at work. We also acknowledge the support by Markus Guentert who helped to collect and evaluate data.

References

1. Stirna, J., Persson, A., Sandkuhl, K.: Participative Enterprise Modeling: Experiences and Recommendations. In: Krogstie, J., Opdahl, A.L., Sindre, G. (eds.) CAiSE 2007 and WES 2007. LNCS, vol. 4495, pp. 546–560. Springer, Heidelberg (2007)

2. Luebbe, A., Weske, M.: Designing a tangible approach to business process modeling. Electronic Colloquium on Design Thinking Research (2010)
3. Grosskopf, A., Edelman, J., Weske, M.: Tangible Business Process Modeling – Methodology and Experiment Design. In: Rinderle-Ma, S., Sadiq, S., Leymann, F. (eds.) BPM 2009. LNBIP, vol. 43, pp. 489–500. Springer, Heidelberg (2010)
4. Luebbe, A., Weske, M.: Tangible Media in Process Modeling – A Controlled Experiment. In: Mouratidis, H., Rolland, C. (eds.) CAiSE 2011. LNCS, vol. 6741, pp. 283–298. Springer, Heidelberg (2011)
5. Brydon-Miller, M., Greenwood, D., Maguire, P.: Why action research? Action Research 1(1), 9 (2003)
6. Baskerville, R.: Investigating information systems with action research. Communications of the AIS 2(3es), 4 (1999)
7. Davison, R., Martinsons, M., Kock, N.: Principles of canonical action research. Information Systems Journal 14(1), 65–86 (2004)
8. Anzai, Y., Simon, H.: The theory of learning by doing. Psychological Review 86(2), 124 (1979)
9. Rittgen, P.: Success Factors of e-Collaboration in Business Process Modeling. In: Pernici, B. (ed.) CAiSE 2010. LNCS, vol. 6051, pp. 24–37. Springer, Heidelberg (2010)
10. Edelman, J.: Hidden in plain sight: Affordances of shared models in team based design. In: Proceedings of the 17th International Conference on Engineering Design, ICED 2009 (2009)
11. Mendling, J.: Metrics for process models: empirical foundations of verification, error prediction, and guidelines for correctness. Springer, Heidelberg (2008)
12. Scheer, A.: ARIS-business process modeling. Springer, Heidelberg (2000)
13. Chiasson, M., Germonprez, M., Mathiassen, L.: Pluralist action research: a review of the information systems literature*. IS Journal 19(1), 31–54 (2009)
14. Baskerville, R., Stage, J.: Controlling prototype development through risk analysis. Mis Quarterly, 481–504 (1996)
15. Lindgren, R., Stenmark, D., Ljungberg, J.: Rethinking competence systems for knowledge-based organizations. European Journal of IS 12(1), 18–29 (2003)
16. Wastell, D., Kawalek, P., Langmead-Jones, P., Ormerod, R.: Information systems and partnership in multi-agency networks: an action research project in crime reduction. Information and Organization 14(3), 189–210 (2004)
17. Bandara, W., Tan, H.M., Recker, J., Indulska, M., Rosemann, M.: Bibliography of process modeling: An emerging research field. Technical report, QUT (2007)
18. Hevner, A., March, S., Park, J., Ram, S.: Design science in information systems research. MIS Quarterly 28(1), 75–106 (2004)
19. Cole, R., Purao, S., Rossi, M., Sein, M.: Being proactive: where action research meets design research. In: 26th ICIS, pp. 325–336 (2005)
20. Rittgen, P.: Collaborative Modeling–A Design Science Approach. In: Proceedings of the 42nd Hawaii International Conference on System Sciences, pp. 5–8 (2009)

Towards Understanding the Process of Process Modeling: Theoretical and Empirical Considerations

Pnina Soffer[1], Maya Kaner[2], and Yair Wand[3]

[1]University of Haifa, Carmel Mountain 31905, Haifa 31905, Israel
[2]Ort Braude College, Karmiel 21982, Israel
[3]Sauder School of Business, The University of British Columbia, Vancouver, Canada
spnina@is.haifa.ac.il, kmaya@braude.ac.il, yair.wand@ubc.ca

Abstract. Empirical studies of business process modeling typically aim at understanding factors that can improve model quality. We identify two limitations of such studies. First, the quality dimensions usually addressed are mainly syntactic and pragmatic, not addressing semantic quality sufficiently. Second, while findings related to model understanding have been anchored in cognitive theories, findings related to model construction have remained mostly unexplained. This paper proposes to study the process of process modeling, based on problem solving theories. Specifically, the work takes the approach that problems are first conceptualized as mental models, to which solution methods are applied. The paper suggests that investigating these two phases can help understand and hence improve semantic and syntactic quality of process models. The paper reports on an empirical study addressing the mental model created during process model development, demonstrating the feasibility of such studies. It then suggests designs for other studies that follow this direction.

Keywords: Process modeling, Problem solving, Empirical study.

1 Introduction

The importance of empirical studies in general and experimental studies in particular in the area of business process modeling has been recently acknowledged, giving rise to increasing body of such reported experiments. These experiments promote the understanding of how better support can be given to the human tasks involving the use of process models and increase the quality of the outcomes of these tasks. Following the SEQUAL framework [7], quality dimensions of models include syntactic, semantic, and pragmatic quality. Syntactic and semantic quality relate to model construction, and address the correct use of the modeling language and the extent to which the model truthfully represents the real world behavior it should depict, respectively. Pragmatic quality addresses the extent to which a model supports its usage for purposes such as understanding behavior or developing process aware systems. Considering process models whose purpose is to develop an understanding of real world behavior, pragmatic quality is typically related to the understandability of the model [6].

F. Daniel et al. (Eds.): BPM 2011 Workshops, Part I, LNBIP 99, pp. 357–369, 2012.

Following this, experimental studies in the area of conceptual process modeling can be classified as studies addressing model construction, and studies addressing model understanding. The former are intended to improve syntactic and semantic model quality. The latter are intended to increase pragmatic model quality. Empirical investigations of process understanding rely on theories related to the cognitive processes involved in this task (e.g., [12]). The underlying assumption of such studies is that understanding the cognitive processes involved in reading and comprehending a model can lead to models that better support these tasks and hence improve pragmatic quality of process models.

The situation regarding model construction is different. Reviewing empirical investigations of process model construction, this paper indicates two gaps. First, the main quality attribute investigated is syntactic quality. Syntactic quality often refers to formal model correctness in terms of properties such as soundness. Such properties do not address the extent to which the model truthfully represents domain behavior. Clearly, an unsound model is both semantically and syntactically incorrect. However, sound models can still be semantically incorrect, inaccurately depicting the domain they intend to represent. To the best of our knowledge, this issue has hardly been investigated so far. Second, empirical investigations have identified correlations between process models properties such as size and complexity and quality attributes (measured by error probability). However, most of these observations are still unexplained theoretically. In other words, we are aware of certain phenomena and can derive practical conclusions from them (e.g., the seven process modeling guidelines – 7PMG [11]), but we do not understand *why* they exist.

We suggest that deeper understanding of the process of process model creation can be obtained by making a clear distinction between two phases in the modeling process. The first phase is the creation of a mental model of the domain, where observed behavior is conceptualized and abstracted. The second phase involves mapping the mental model to a process model. We suggest that using this two-phase approach in empirical studies of model creation can result in better understanding of difficulties and of opportunities for improving the quality of process models.

In the following, Section 2 reviews empirical studies of process modeling. Section 3 discusses cognitive theories as a basis for empirical studies of process modeling. Section 4 discussed the implications of the theories on empirical studies and describes an empirical study following this approach to demonstrate the feasibility of such studies and their potential benefit. Section 5 concludes the paper.

2   Empirical Studies in Business Process Modeling

Several empirical studies investigated the quality of process models, mainly focusing on syntax and pragmatics. For example, the impact of structural model properties on pragmatic quality has been studied [17, 23]. Significant correlations between control flow complexity (i.e., structural complexity in terms of split and join types) and process understandability and modifiability in BPMN models with different structural characteristics is reported in [19]. Another structural metric, termed cross connectivity, has been found to affect model understanding [26]. These findings have been explained based on cognitive considerations.

A number of studies (e.g., [12][13][22][10]) focused on factors of the modeler and of model representation, including labels, icons, and layout. They found significant connection between these factors and model understandability. These studies, as well as others, used the theory of multimedia learning, originating from cognitive science [8]. According to this theory, content, content presentation, and user characteristics can influence pragmatic quality [12].

Several empirical studies deal with content representation in terms of modeling languages and their connection to pragmatic quality. For example, [21] compared EPC with Petri Nets, finding that end users considered the EPC approach of using connectors superior to the token game, but the EPC OR-connector has a negative impact on model comprehension. In another experiment, students were trained in EPC and then given either EPC models or BPMN models (a language they were not trained in) [17]. No significant differences were found between the groups in terms of model comprehension (recall questions about basic features of the process model) and problem solving (questions that require solutions to problems based on the process models, but not directly included in them). The authors concluded that the knowledge required for model understanding is of conceptual nature rather than syntactic one.

As opposed to the relative abundance of empirical studies of model understanding, only few have addressed model creation. The main property that has been investigated is error probability, which basically relates to syntactic quality. Findings indicate that certain properties of a model increase the likelihood of syntax and logical errors (e.g., deadlocks, lack of soundness). Some studies [9][14] identified types of error patterns in SAP reference model and linked them to the model size (e.g., number of functions) and to model complexity metrics (e.g., split-join ratio). Note that a trivial explanation to these findings is that as there are more elements in a model, its error probability increases. Yet, some of these findings have been explained using cognitive theories about the process of model construction. For example, the cognitive load theory was used for explaining the increase of error probability with model size, implying that human modelers lose track of interrelations in large models due to their limited cognitive capabilities. This can lead to errors that would be avoided in smaller models [3]. However, no comprehensive cognition-based explanation has addressed the correlation between numbers of splits and joins in a model and its error probability. Pragmatically, guidelines such as the 7PMG [11] exist, following empirical findings to increase model quality (syntactic and pragmatic). However, we are still far from understanding why these practices can promote quality.

A study to understand the creation of a model by novices with no knowledge in modeling languages [18] identified five process design types ranging from purely textual to purely graphical representation forms. The authors evaluated the semantic quality of the models, and found that over a certain level of graphics use, the quality of the models decreases with the increased use of graphics. The "optimal" level was of hybrid designs, featuring appropriate text labels and abstract graphical forms.

Other empirical studies aimed at understanding model creation in the context of model variations. When a modeling language has more than one construct for expressing a certain phenomenon (construct overload), the modeler needs to decide which of these options to use. The result is variations among different models of the same domain. While this is not usually perceived as a model quality problem, it can impose difficulties on model understanding and on specific uses of models. Studies addressing this issue measure the number and types of variations (e.g., [23] with respect to conceptual models, followed by [1] with respect to process models), and use it as a predictor for possible difficulties in the process of modeling.

Summarizing the current state of empirical studies, we found two main gaps. First, the studies focus on syntactic and pragmatic quality, and hardly on semantic quality, namely, the extent to which the model truthfully represents domain behavior. Second, cognition-based explanations are mainly related to how a process model is read and understood, identifying affecting factors such as content (e.g., model size, complexity), content representation (modeling language, labeling) and user characteristics. In contrast, extant studies approach model creation by practical guidelines rather than based on cognitive considerations of process modeling.

3   The Process of Process Modeling

We turn to research in the area of human cognition and problem solving for guidance in gaining better understanding of the cognitive processes involved in model creation. According to [16], when facing a task, the problem solver first formulates a mental representation of the problem, also termed "the problem space", and then uses it for reasoning about the solution. The cognitive fit theory [5][27] adopts on this view, stressing that matching information types along this process support high performance in the problem solving task. In process modeling, the task is to create a model which represents the behavior of a domain. We therefore distinguish two phases in the construction of a process model. First, the modeler forms a mental model[1] of domain behavior. Second, the modeler maps the mental model to modeling constructs. Each of these steps may incur specific difficulties. Thus, to identify problems that arise in process model construction and find how the construction process can be supported, it would be logical to study the two phases separately.

Two characteristics of problem solving, indicated by [16], are of particular interest. First, the shape of the mental model is affected by the characteristics of the task and the methods for achieving it. Hence, the concepts available to the modeler for reasoning about the domain may affect the mental modeling process even before an actual mapping to constructs is performed. Second, the process of forming mental models and applying methods for achieving the task is not done in one step applied to the entire problem. Rather, due to the limited capacity of short term memory, the problem is broken down to pieces that are addressed sequentially, chunk by chunk.

Consider now the formation of a mental model of the process behavior. This requires gaining an understanding of the domain and its behavior, conceptualizing and abstracting this behavior so it can then be mapped to modeling constructs. Different types of domain information may require different levels of effort. For example, an actor performing a task is a concrete part of the domain, easy to recognize and conceptualize in terms which are possible to include in a process model. An activity is

---

[1] Note, we use the terms mental model and mental representation interchangeably.

also observable and easy to identify as such, but there might be different ways of scoping it and different granularity levels by which it can be addressed. Routing decisions, on the other hand, are not directly observable. Rather, they abstract different possible occurrences of the process (this is why they are considered decisions). Hence, conceptualizing routing decisions might require a higher cognitive effort than conceptualizing actors or activities. In terms of the cognitive fit theory, the fit between domain concepts and modeling concepts for actors and activities is better than for routing decisions. To illustrate, consider the commonly used token semantics of process modeling languages. When the intended model is based on token semantics, the modeler needs to conceptualize domain behavior in terms of tokens. However, tokens are abstractions rather than observable phenomena. They do not have a good fit with domain concepts. Hence, additional effort might be needed.

Consider now the phase of mapping the mental representation into modeling constructs. This task follows conceptualization and is of a more technical nature. This is where the expressiveness of modeling languages and modeling practices may play a role. For example, construct overload may impose a difficulty in deciding whether to represent an organizational unit as a pool or as a lane in BPMN. In contrast, token semantics, which, as mentioned, may impose difficulties in conceptualization, can make the mapping itself easy to achieve. As well, as discussed, the problem is usually not addressed at once in its full scope. Rather, it is broken down to chunks that are addressed sequentially, so the process model is gradually constructed. Modeling practices such as constructing well-structured or block-structured processes may support the formation of "natural" problem chunks, easier to map to a process model.

It follows that a variety of research questions can guide empirical studies that may promote the understanding of process modeling and help improve the quality of the resulting models. In particular, mental model formation is related to the semantic quality of process models because imprecision and incompleteness of mental representations will be carried through the mapping phase. In comparison, the actual mapping to modeling constructs is mainly associated with syntactic quality (incorrect mapping may however also result in reduced semantic quality).

Given the different impacts of conceptualization and mapping, we are faced with the challenge of how to differentiate these impacts in empirical studies. One possible way is through think-aloud exercises with protocol analysis to distinguish the two phases. However, such techniques are mostly appropriate in exploratory studies and are less suitable when seeking quantitative results and hypotheses testing. We now describe an empirical approach that can isolate the effects of conceptualization.

4   Empirical Research Directions

This section discusses possible directions for empirical research that may emerge when considering the two phases of model construction separately. We start by describing an empirical study which has already been performed following this line of research, as an example demonstrating how such studies can be performed. In particular, we provide an in-depth discussion of the considerations that drove the experimental design. We then suggest how these ideas can be generalized and suggest other research questions about model construction and principles for designing empirical studies to address such questions.

4.1   Empirical Study Addressing Mental Models

Focus and hypotheses: The focus of the empirical study described here is on the mental model formed before the actual creation of a process model. Two assumptions underlie the study. First, for the resulting process model to represent domain behavior completely and accurately (namely, to be of high semantic quality) the mental model must reflect this behavior faithfully. Second, the faithfulness of the mental model to the actual behavior will be affected by the reasoning "tools" used by the modeler.

The first assumption implies that the quality of the mental model can be measured in terms of domain understanding gained while developing a process model. In studies of conceptual modeling, domain understanding has been measured by comprehension and problem solving questions [4]. Since the purpose is to measure domain understanding prior to model creation, this approach requires testing understanding of domain behavior *independent of the model*. The empirical task can be performed before or after a process model has been constructed, but must be done after subjects have engaged in cognitive processing activities related to domain behavior in a process. Considerations as to when evaluation of the mental model should take place are discussed later with respect to our specific study and on a general level.

Our study focuses on situations modeled as split and merge structures in process models. Empirical studies reviewed in Section 2 (e.g., [15]) have indicated that these situations are associated with high error probability in the resulting models. While this phenomenon has been observed and corroborated, its roots have not been explained theoretically so far. Following the above two assumptions, we suggest that (a) this high error probability is related to difficulties in forming a complete and accurate mental model of branching situations, and (b) the outcome of modeling can be improved by supporting the reasoning process with appropriate "thinking tools".

Cognitive fit theory [5] [27] indicates that a good fit between concepts used in problem domain description and concepts used for problem solving can improve problem solving performance. For split and merge structures, the concepts modelers typically use to reason about behavior are driven by the commonly used modeling language constructs (mainly AND, OR, XOR). We posit, however, that node types available in process modeling languages do not match the full range of actual behaviors which should be represented by branching nodes. It follows that a poor fit exists between problem domain phenomena and problem solving concepts.

Based on this, we hypothesize that a set of concepts which better represent real world behavior at split and merge situations would better support the creation of the mental model. Such a set of concepts has been theoretically developed [25] based on ideas presented in [24]. It has resulted in a catalog of split and merge behaviors, which includes four split types and eight merge behaviors for binary nodes (two branches). In comparison to the Workflow patterns collection [20], which is the most comprehensive set of behaviors available so far, the catalog includes split and merge types which are not recognized there.

We propose that the catalog can help analysts conceptualize branching situations by classifying them in terms similar to human perceptions of domain behavior. Classifying a situation, an analyst can infer additional information about it and possibly ask additional questions to better understand it.

Method: The catalog was evaluated in an experiment that measured domain understanding. The treatment group received the catalog, and the control group a comparable list of split and merge cases taken from the workflow patterns collection [20]. The study focused on the mental model created while developing a process model. Since the purpose was to compare the "sets of tools" used (the catalog and the workflow patterns list) independent of any modeling language, we tested domain understanding without asking subjects to create a process model.

A main challenge faced when designing the experiment was to design a task that would enable assessing the quality of the mental model while ensuring that it relies on the "set of tools" given. To address this challenge, we designed a task focusing on understanding the situations without actually modeling them. In particular, we tested the success in classifying control flow situations and the understanding developed following this classification. Understanding was evaluated by asking subjects to make inferences about the situations, not directly answerable from the material.

The task comprised two types of assignment that had to be done in sequence for five short cases (an example case is given in Fig. 1).

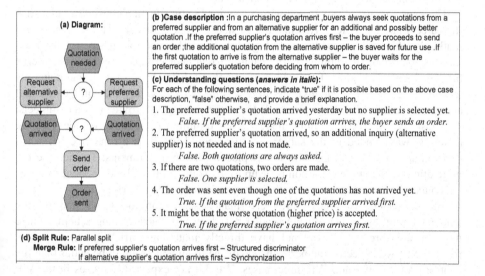

Fig. 1. An example case including: (a) Diagram, (b) Case description, (c) Understanding questions and expected answers (in italics), (d) Logical rules as can be specified using the workflow patterns list

Each case included a textual description (Fig. 1(b)) and an EPC-like diagram, where the logical connectors were left blank (Fig. 1(a)). The EPC representation was chosen since the subjects were familiar with this notation, but it could be replaced by any other graphical notation.

The first part of the task (sub-task "Rule") required the subjects to assign the correct logical rule to each connector using one of two methods: (1) identifying the specific case (from the catalog or from the workflow patterns list, for the treatment and control groups respectively), or (2) providing a logical expression specifying the behavior of the process at the specific node in a process model fragment (for example, see Fig. 1(d)). The Rule task, done first, "forced" subjects to engage with the details of the case and with the concepts of the list they were given, and to actually use these concepts in the mental model they were forming.

The second part of the task performed for each case (sub-task "Understanding") was intended to evaluate the understanding the subjects had gained while forming the mental model. It included five "true/false" questions relating to possible process behavior (when enacted). For example, see Fig. 1(c). The subjects were also required to explain their answers. While the Rules task used the catalog or the workflow patterns list as a classification scheme for the situation at hand, the Understanding task could be viewed as reflecting inferences based on the classification. The task materials were designed to include some cases which were directly available as entries in both the catalog and the workflow patterns list (termed the "WF direct set"), and some cases which were only directly available in the catalog (termed "non WF direct set"). When not directly available in a given list, the cases could be described by combining up to three entries in a logical rule.

The experiment was conducted with 54 senior IS students in a course on Enterprise Resource Planning (ERP) systems and business process design. The students were randomly assigned to the treatment group or to the control group. Each group received one hour of training on the catalog (treatment group) or workflow patterns list (the control group). To avoid any effect of differences of training materials (except differences in contents), an effort was made to maximize the equivalence and appearance of the workflow pattern list and the catalog as provided to the subjects. The task was performed immediately after training. A printout of the training materials was handed to the subjects so they could use it as a reference list when performing the task. No time limit was placed for the assignments. To increase the motivation of the students, a bonus of up to 10 points in the lab component (30% of the course grade) was promised to the students, based on their performance.

The dependent variables were performance scores on the Rules and on the Understanding tasks. These were graded based on a defined grading scheme. Since the non WF direct cases did not have directly matching entries in the workflow patterns list, we expected the performance of the treatment group to be better than the control group in the non WF direct cases. We did not expect differences in the WF direct ones. Accordingly, we formulated two sets of hypotheses, considering the two sub-tasks and the two sets of cases.

Findings: The findings, reported in detail in [25], supported our hypotheses. Considering the non WF direct set of cases, the treatment group outperformed the control group with a high level of significance for the Rule assignment (P-value =0.000) and with significance for the Understanding assignment (P-value = 0.017). As expected, no significant performance differences were found for the WF-direct cases, directly available in both lists. These findings are not surprising with respect to the Rule sub-task. Clearly, conceptualizing a situation is easier when a matching concept is available in a given list than when an appropriate rule combining several concepts needs to be logically defined. However, considering the Understanding sub-task, the findings indicate that the quality of the mental model is affected by the set of concepts used. This was not a predictable result, as it indicated the understanding gained of the situations was not the same. This goes against the common belief that process models are constructed based on deep understanding of the behavior to be depicted. This understanding directly affects the semantic quality of the resulting process model. Our findings indicate that domain understanding cannot be taken for granted. Furthermore, the study shows that understanding can be improved when using an appropriate set of "thinking tools" or concepts. These indications are obtained despite the small scale of the study, which is its main limitation. In addition, the results provide an explanation for the difficulties found in other works with respect to correctly modeling routing situations. The concepts "borrowed" from modeling languages might not support conceptualization well enough.

4.2   Designing Empirical Studies to Separately Address Modeling Phases

The empirical study described above demonstrates how studies to test understanding of domain behavior can be designed and the non-trivial results that can be obtained, leading to improved model quality. We now generalize these ideas by outlining possible research questions about mental model formation (independent of the process model), and suggesting experimental designs to address them.

Empirical evaluations related to model construction have so far focused on the properties of a developed process model to form dependent variables. This approach does not allow separating the two phases – domain conceptualization and model construction. Hence, the effect of modeling languages, domain knowledge, model size and model complexity, cannot be attributed to a specific phase. However, as shown, such differentiation can provide useful (and even unexpected) results. Evaluating each phase separately gives rise to a variety of research questions that can be studied by experiments, whose possible variables and measurement points are now discussed.

Independent variables: various factors may affect the mental model, its mapping to a process model, or both. These include modeling languages, conceptualization tools (e.g., tokens, catalog), problem characteristics (e.g., process size and complexity), modeling practices, and modeler's experience.

Dependent variables: the mental model can be evaluated by the level of domain understanding the modeler gains. Domain understanding, as a dependent variable, can be measured as performance in answering questions about the domain, either before or after the actual process model is constructed. Given an accurate and complete mental model, mapping to modeling constructs may still yield errors. These errors might be of two origins [2]. First, they may be syntactic, suggesting syntactic quality as a second type of dependent variable, which can be evaluated by itself or with respect to domain understanding. Second, expressiveness deficiencies of modeling grammars might affect semantic quality. Finally, dependent variables might relate to the process of modeling rather than the outcome (the model). In particular, the effort required for mapping the mental model to a process model (e.g. measured by time required) might depend on various factors. This indicates a third type of dependent variable.

Table 1. Possible experimental studies

Research question	Independent variable	Dependent variable	Point of measurement	Comments
How to support mental model creation	Conceptualizing tools (tokens, catalog)	Domain understanding	Prior to model construction	Measure deep understanding by problem solving questions not directly answerable from the materials, related to the domain.
	Modeling language	Domain understanding	After model construction	
How is the mental model affected by process size and complexity	Process size and complexity	Domain understanding	Prior to model construction	Relates to the domain behavior – requires suitable process metrics
Do modeling practices (e.g., well structuredness) affect the mental model	Modeling practices	Domain understanding	After model construction	Task should be related to domain understanding
Is poor syntactic quality attributed to problems of conceptualization or of mapping		Correlation of domain understanding and syntactic model quality	After model construction	Test correlation between variables (use "difficult" – error prone processes)
Conceptualization effect on the mapping	Conceptualizing tools (tokens, catalog)	Domain understanding	Prior to model construction	Evaluate syntactic quality with respect to domain understanding and the modeling time.
		Modeling time	During model construction	
		Model correctness	After model construction	Evaluate model correctness (e.g. by subject matter expert)
		Syntactic quality		

Point of measurement: domain understanding can be evaluated prior to or after model construction. If the manipulation is related to the modeling language or practice, evaluation should be done after model construction. Since the phases of modeling may apply separately to chunks of the process, the full effect of the treatment can only be measured after a model has been constructed, but should reflect domain understanding. If the manipulation is not related to modeling language or process, domain understanding may be evaluated before model construction.

Examples of research questions that can be asked together with basic features of possible experimental designs are summarized in Table 1. The table presents for each research question possible independent and dependent variables, and specifies when the dependent variable should be measured.

5   Conclusion

Empirical studies of process modeling are aimed at gaining an understanding that can guide the development of higher quality models. However, the quality dimensions usually addressed are mainly syntactic and pragmatic, while semantic quality has not been addressed sufficiently. In addition, while empirical findings related to model understanding have been anchored in cognitive theories, findings related to model construction have remained mostly unexplained.

In this paper, we propose based on cognitive theories of problem solving, to view the process of process modeling as comprising two phases *conceptualization* (creation of a mental model), and *mapping* of the mental model to process modeling constructs. We suggest that empirical investigations separating these phases can lead to a better understanding of process modeling rather than relying on the final model created. Furthermore, we claim that improving the quality of the mental model formed is a key to achieving semantic quality, since a mental model reflecting flawed domain understanding will result in a semantically flawed process model.

To demonstrate how such research can be done, the paper described an experiment to test process domain understanding. The results of the study showed the feasibility of such studies and their potential benefits. We discussed the considerations that drove the experimental design of the reported study, in particular, the operationalization of evaluating the mental model separately from a process model. These considerations were then generalized to other experimental designs that can be used for addressing various research questions that emerge from the two-phase view.

References

1. Breuker, D., Pfeiffer, D., Becker, J.: Reducing the Variations in Intra- and Interorganizational Business Process Modeling – An Empirical Evaluation. Wirtschaftsinformatik (1), 203–212 (2009)
2. Burton-Jones, A., Wand, Y., Weber, R.: Informational Equivalence, Computational Equivalence, and the Evaluation of Conceptual Modelling. Journal of the Association for Information Systems 10(6), 495–532 (2009)
3. Figl, K., Mendling, J., Strembeck, M., Recker, J.: On the Cognitive Effectiveness of Routing Symbols in Process Modeling Languages. In: Abramowicz, W., Tolksdorf, R. (eds.) BIS 2010. LNBIP, vol. 47, pp. 230–241. Springer, Heidelberg (2010)
4. Gemino, A.: Comparing Object Oriented with Structured Analysis Techniques in Conceptual Modeling (PhD Thesis), Sauder School of Business, University of British Columbia, Vancouver (1998)
5. Khatri, V., Vessey, I., Ram, S., Ramesh, V.: Cognitive Fit Between Conceptual Schemas and Internal Problem Representations: The Case of Geospatio–Temporal Conceptual Schema Comprehension. IEEE Transactions on Professional Communication 49(2), 109–127 (2006)
6. Krogstie, J., Sindre, G., Jorgensen, H.: Process Models Representing Knowledge for Action: A Revised Quality Framework. Eur. J. of IS 15, 91–102 (2006)
7. Lindland, O., Sindre, G., Solvberg, A.: Understanding Quality in Conceptual Modeling. IEEE Software 11, 42–49 (1994)

8. Mayer, R.E.: Models of Understanding. Review of Educational Research 59, 43–64 (1989)
9. Mendling, J., Moser, M., Neumann, G., Verbeek, H.M.W., Dongen van, B.F., Aalst van der, W.M.P.: Faulty EPCs in the SAP Reference Model. In: Dustdar, S., Fiadeiro, J.L., Sheth, A.P. (eds.) BPM 2006. LNCS, vol. 4102, pp. 451–457. Springer, Heidelberg (2006)
10. Mendling, J., Recker, J.: Towards Systematic Usage of Labels and Icons in Business Process Models. In: Halpin, T., Proper, H.A., Krogstie, J. (eds.) EMMSAD 2009, Montpellier, France, pp. 1–13 (2009)
11. Mendling, J., Reijers, H., van der Aalst, W.: Seven Process Modeling Guidelines (7PMG). In: Qut eprint (2008)
12. Mendling, J., Reijers, H.A., Recker, J.: Activity Labeling in Process Modeling: Empirical Insights and Recommendations. Information Systems 35, 467–482 (2010)
13. Mendling, J., Strembeck, M.: Influence Factors of Understanding Business Process Models. In: Abramowicz, W., Fensel, D. (eds.) Proc. Conference on Business Information Systems (BIS 2008). LNBIP, vol. 7, pp. 142–153 (2008)
14. Mendling, J., Verbeek, H.M.W., van Dongen, B.F., van der Aalst, W.M.P., Neumann, G.: Detection and Prediction of Errors in EPCs of the SAP Reference Model. Data and Knowledge Engineering 64, 312–329 (2008)
15. Mendling, J.: Empirical Studies in Process Model Verification. In: Jensen, K., van der Aalst, W.M.P. (eds.) ToPNOC II. LNCS, vol. 5460, pp. 208–224. Springer, Heidelberg (2009)
16. Newell, A., Simon, H.A.: Human Problem Solving. Prentice Hall, Englewood Cliffs (1972)
17. Recker, J., Dreiling, A.: Does It Matter Which Process Modelling Language We Teach or Use? An Experimental Study on Understanding Process Modelling Languages without Formal Education. In: 18th Australasian Conference on Information Systems, Toowoomba, Australia, pp. 356–366 (2007)
18. Recker, J., Safrudin, N., Rosemann, M.: How Novices Model Business Processes. In: Hull, R., Mendling, J., Tai, S. (eds.) BPM 2010. LNCS, vol. 6336, pp. 29–44. Springer, Heidelberg (2010)
19. Rolón, E., Cardoso, J., García, F., Ruiz, F., Piattini, M.: Analysis and Validation of Control-Flow Complexity Measures with BPMN Process Models. In: Halpin, T.A., Krogstie, J., Nurcan, S., Proper, E., Schmidt, R., Soffer, P., Ukor, R. (eds.) Enterprise, Business-Process and Information Systems Modeling. LNBIP, vol. 29, pp. 58–70. Springer, Heidelberg (2009)
20. Russell, N.C., Hofstede, A.H.M., van der Aalst, W.M.P., Mulyar, N.: Workflow Control-Flow Patterns: A Revised View, BPM Center Report BPM-06-22, BPMcenter.org (2006)
21. Sarshar, K., Loos, P.: Comparing the Control-Flow of EPC and Petri Net from the End-User Perspective. In: van der Aalst, W.M.P., Benatallah, B., Casati, F., Curbera, F. (eds.) BPM 2005. LNCS, vol. 3649, pp. 434–439. Springer, Heidelberg (2005)
22. Schrepfer, M., Wolf, J., Mendling, J., Reijers, H.A.: The Impact of Secondary Notation on Process Model Understanding. In: Persson, A., Stirna, J. (eds.) PoEM 2009. LNBIP, vol. 39, pp. 161–175. Springer, Heidelberg (2009)
23. Soffer, P., Hadar, I.: Applying Ontology-Based Rules to Conceptual Modeling: A Reflection on Modeling Decision Making. European Journal of Information Systems 16(4), 599–611 (2007)
24. Soffer, P., Wand, Y., Kaner, M.: Semantic Analysis of Flow Patterns in Business Process Modeling. In: Alonso, G., Dadam, P., Rosemann, M. (eds.) BPM 2007. LNCS, vol. 4714, pp. 400–407. Springer, Heidelberg (2007)

25. Soffer, P., Wand, Y., Kaner, M.: Conceptualizing Control Flows in Business Processes Using a Catalog of Branching Possibilities, Working paper (2011)
26. Vanderfeesten, I.T.P., Reijers, H.A., Mendling, J., van der Aalst, W.M.P., Cardoso, J.: On a Quest for Good Process Models: The Cross-Connectivity Metric. In: Bellahsène, Z., Léonard, M. (eds.) CAiSE 2008. LNCS, vol. 5074, pp. 480–494. Springer, Heidelberg (2008)
27. Vessey, I.: Cognitive fit: A theory-based analysis of graphs vs. tables literature. Decision Science 22(2), 219–240 (1991)

Tracing the Process of Process Modeling with Modeling Phase Diagrams

Jakob Pinggera[1], Stefan Zugal[1], Matthias Weidlich[2], Dirk Fahland[3], Barbara Weber[1], Jan Mendling[4], and Hajo A. Reijers[3]

[1] University of Innsbruck, Austria
{jakob.pinggera,stefan.zugal,barbara.weber}@uibk.ac.at
[2] Hasso-Plattner-Institute, University of Potsdam, Germany
matthias.weidlich@hpi.uni-potsdam.de
[3] Eindhoven University of Technology, The Netherlands
{d.fahland,h.a.reijers}@tue.nl
[4] Humboldt-Universität zu Berlin, Germany
jan.mendling@wiwi.hu-berlin.de

Abstract. The quality of a business process model is presumably highly dependent upon the modeling process that was followed to create it. Still, there is a lack of concepts to investigate this connection empirically. This paper introduces the formal concept of a phase diagram through which the modeling process can be analyzed, and a corresponding implementation to study a modeler's sequence of actions. In an experiment building on these assets, we observed a group of modelers engaging in the act of modeling. The collected data is used to demonstrate our approach for analyzing the process of process modeling. Additionally, we are presenting first insights and sketch requirements for future experiments.

Keywords: business process modeling, modeling phase diagrams, process model quality, empirical research, modeling process.

1 Introduction

Considering the heavy usage of business process modeling in all types of business contexts, it is important to acknowledge both the relevance of process models and their associated quality issues. On the one hand, it has been shown that a good understanding of a process model has a positive impact on the success of a modeling initiative [1]. On the other hand, actual process models display a wide range of problems that impede upon their understandability [2]. Clearly, an in-depth understanding of the factors of process model quality is in demand.

The quality of process models can be evaluated along a wide spectrum of properties, such as syntactic correctness or semantic accuracy [3]. Most research in the field puts a strong emphasis on the *product* or *outcome* of the process modeling act [4,5]. For this category of research, the resulting model is the object of analysis. Many other works—instead of dealing with the quality of individual

F. Daniel et al. (Eds.): BPM 2011 Workshops, Part I, LNBIP 99, pp. 370–382, 2012.

models—focus on the characteristics of modeling languages [6,7]. However, these studies put less emphasis on the fact that model quality is presumably dependent upon the modeling process that was followed to create it. While there is work on micro-management of creating models [8], there is a notable research gap on how the process of process modeling can be analyzed quantitatively.

In this paper, we address this specific problem. In particular, we focus on the *formalization phase* in which a process modeler is faced with the challenge of constructing a syntactically correct model that reflects a given domain description (cf. [9]). This appeals to one's *ability to model* [10], arguably the most important capability of a modeler according to its expected effect on the quality of the ensuing model. The formalization of process models—which can be considered a *process in itself*—is crucial for obtaining a good modeling result and to overcome quality problems right from the start [2].

Given this context, we introduce an analysis technique called *modeling phase diagram*. The technique supposes to record all modeling activities throughout the creation of a process model in a log. Our technique classifies the recorded modeling activities according to cognitive research; the classification, in turn, allows to visualize and analyze the process of modeling itself in a diagram. The technique has been implemented in a graphical modeling tool that logs a user's modeling activities in the background. We conducted a modeling session with graduate students to demonstrate the feasibility of our approach; we present first insights and outline requirements for further experiments.

The paper is structured accordingly. We continue with a discussion of the fundamental cognitive considerations about the process of process modeling. Then, Sect. 3 presents our general approach along with the corresponding algorithms to generate modeling phase diagrams. The setup of the modeling experiment and its results are described in Sect. 4, along with a discussion of lessons learned. Then, Sect. 5 discusses related research before Sect. 6 concludes the paper.

2 Cognitive Foundations of the Process of Modeling

Before investigating the process of process modeling, a discussion of its cognitive foundations is required. Sect. 2.1 introduces a basic model for understanding information processing within the human mind. In particular, the concept of "chunking" is introduced. The different phases of this process are described in Sect. 2.2, namely comprehension, modeling, and reconciliation.

2.1 A Model of the Mind

A central insight from cognitive research is that the human brain contains specialized regions that contribute different functionality to the process of *solving complex problems*. The *modal model* describes the mind as being separated into different types of memory, the most important for our research being *working memory*, the place where comparing, computing and reasoning takes place [11]. Although working memory is the main working area of the brain, it can store only a limited amount of information, which is forgotten after 20–30 seconds

if not refreshed [12]. The working memory's span is measured in chunks, being
able to store a more or less constant number of items [13]. Although this capacity is reduced while performing difficult tasks, the span of working memory
can be increased by suitable organization of information [11]. For example, when
asked to repeat the sequence "U N O C B S N F L", most people miss a character or two as the number of characters exceeds the working memory's span.
However, people being familiar with acronyms might recognize and remember
the sequence "UNO CBS NFL", effectively reducing the working memory's load
from nine to three so-called "chunks" [11,14,15]. As modeling is related to problem solving [14], modelers with a better understanding of the modeling tool, the
notation, or a superior ability of extracting information from requirements can
utilize their working memory more efficiently when creating process models [16].

2.2   Process of Process Modeling — An Iterative Process

During the formalization phase process modelers are working on creating a syntactically correct process model reflecting a given domain description by interacting with the process modeling tool [9]. This modeling process can be described
as an iterative and highly flexible process [14,17], dependent on the individual
modeler and the modeling task at hand [18]. At an operational level, the modeler's interactions with the tool would typically consist of a cycle of the three
successive phases of comprehension, modeling, and reconciliation.

Comprehension. In the comprehension phase modelers try to understand the
requirements to be modeled as well as the model that has been created so far.
Consequently, working memory is filled with knowledge extracted from the requirements and, if available, from the process model itself. The amount of information stored in working memory depends on the modeler's abilities and her
knowledge organization (cf. Section 2.1).

Modeling. The modeler uses the information acquired and stored in working memory during the previous comprehension phase for changing the process
model. The process modeler's utilization of working memory influences the number of modeling steps executed during the modeling phase before forcing the
modeler to revisit the requirements for acquiring more information.

Reconciliation. After the modeling phase, modelers reorganize the process
model (e.g., renaming of activities) and utilize the process model's *secondary notation* (e.g., notation of layout, typographic cues) to enhance the process model's
understandability [19,20]. However, the number of reconciliation phases in the
process of process modeling is influenced by a modeler's ability of placing elements correctly when creating them, alleviating the need for additional layouting.
Furthermore, the factual use of secondary notation is subject to the modeler's
personal style [19]. The improved understandability supports the comprehension
phase of the subsequent iteration, as the process model becomes more comprehensible for the modeler when coming back to it [19]. In particular, during the
subsequent comprehension phase the modeler has to identify the part of the
model to work on next. A better laid out model helps identifying a suitable area

of the model, causing less distraction and therefore enables the modeler to store more information in working memory that can be incorporated in the process model.

3 Investigating the Process of Process Modeling

This section introduces a method to investigate the process of process modeling via *modeling phase diagrams*. Sect. 3.1 describes how the modeling process can be captured, providing the basis for its analysis in Sect. 3.2. Finally, Sect. 3.3 illustrates how the modeling process can be measured.

3.1 Capturing Events of the Process of Process Modeling

In order to get a detailed picture of how process models are created, we use the Cheetah Experimental Platform (CEP). CEP has been specifically designed for investigating the process of process modeling in a systematic manner [21]. In particular, we instrumented a basic process modeling editor within CEP to record each user's interactions together with the corresponding time stamp in an event log, describing the creation of the process model step by step.

When focusing on the process modeling environment, the development of process models consists of adding nodes and edges to the process model, naming or renaming these activities, and adding conditions to edges. In addition to these interactions a modeler can influence the process model's secondary notation, e.g., by laying out the process model using move operations for nodes or by utilizing bendpoints to influence the visualization of edges. A complete overview of the possible interactions is provided in Table 1.

3.2 Analyzing the Process of Process Modeling

By capturing all of the described interactions with the modeling tool, we are able to *replay* a recorded modeling process at any point in time without interfering with the modeler or her problem solving efforts. This allows for observing how the process model unfolds on the modeling canvas. A demonstration of the replay function is available at http://cheetahplatform.org. Fig. 1 illustrates the basic idea of our technique. Fig. 1a shows several states of a typical modeling

Table 1. User Interactions Recorded by Cheetah Experimental Platform

User Interaction	Description	User Interaction	Description
CREATE NODE	Create activity or gateway	RENAME	Rename an activity
DELETE NODE	Delete activity or gateway	UPDATE CONDITION	Update an edge's condition
CREATE EDGE	Create an edge connecting two nodes	MOVE NODE	Move a node
DELETE EDGE	Delete edge	MOVE EDGE LABEL	Move the label of an edge
CREATE CONDITION	Create an edge condition	CREATE/DELETE/MOVE EDGE BENDPOINT	Update the routing of an edge
DELETE CONDITION	Delete an edge condition		
RECONNECT EDGE	Reconnect edge from one node to another		

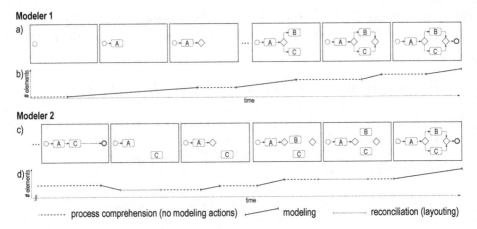

Fig. 1. Two Different Processes of Process Modeling to Create the Same Process Model

process as it can be observed during replay. Fig. 1c shows the states of a different modeling process that nonetheless results in the *same* model. This replay functionality of CEP allows to observe in detail how modelers create the model on the canvas.

We postulate that observations made for the process of modeling at a syntactic level can be traced back to the various phases of the modeling process (cf. Section 2.2). Clearly, modeling manifests in the creation of model elements. Hence, (1) a *modeling phase* consists of a sequence of interactions to create or delete model elements such as activities or edges. (2) A modeler usually does not create a model in a continuous sequence of interactions. She rather pauses after several interactions to inspect the intermediate result of her modeling and to plan the next steps. Syntactically, this manifests in reduced modeling activity or even inactivity. We refer to such a phase as a *comprehension phase*. (3) Besides modeling and thinking, a modeler also needs to *reorganize* the model. Reconciliation interactions manifest in moving or renaming model elements to prepare the next modeling interactions or to support her comprehension of the model. A sequence of such interactions is a *reconciliation phase*.

To obtain a better understanding of the modeling process and its phases, we supplement model replay with a *modeling phase diagram*. Such a diagram quantitatively highlights the three phases of modeling, comprehension, and reconciliation. It primarily depicts how the size of the model (vertical axis) evolves over time (horizontal axis), as can be seen in Fig. 1b and Fig. 1d for the modeling processes in Fig. 1a and Fig. 1c, respectively. The graph partitions the user interactions into the three phases, based on the kind of interactions and their frequencies in the modeling process.

So, we can read from Fig. 1b that the modeler created the model in a straightforward series of modeling steps interrupted by periods of comprehension. The modeling process in Fig. 1d shows a different approach. After some modeling, the modeler removes parts of the created model and moves an activity to make

Table 2. Identification of Phases of the Process of Process Modeling

Phase	Identification Criteria
Comprehension	no interaction with the system for longer than a predefined threshold
Modeling	creating modeling elements (activities, gateways, edges), deleting modeling elements, reconnecting edges, adding/deleting edge conditions
Reconciliation	layouting of edges, moving of modeling elements, renaming of activities, updating edge conditions

space for some control-flow constructs, as indicated by the reconciliation phase. Then, several model elements are placed and laid out before the model is completed. Note that the resulting models are identical. Yet, the phase diagrams show significant differences between both modeling processes. This illustrates the value of analyzing the modeling process in the described manner beyond the inspection of the process models themselves.

3.3   Measuring the Process of Process Modeling

Based on the theoretical background regarding the process of process modeling, we developed an algorithm for automatically extracting *modeling phase diagrams* (cf. Fig. 1) from the logs created by CEP. For this purpose, the user interactions depicted in Table 1 are categorized into modeling and reconciliation interactions as listed in Table 2. Comprehension phases are determined by measuring the time when no interaction with the system is recorded.

Algorithm 1. Extracting the Process of Process Modeling

Require: *interactions* $[I_1, I_2, \ldots I_n]$
Require: *threshold$_c$, threshold$_d$*
1: *phases* $\leftarrow$ [new comprehension phase]
2: **for all** i such that $1 \leq i \leq n$ **do**
3:     **if** $i > 1$ and durationBetween(I_{i-1}, I_i) > *threshold$_c$* **then**
4:         add new comprehension phase to *phases*
5:     *previousPhase* $\leftarrow$ *last(phases)*
6:     *upcomingPhase* $\leftarrow$ *identifyUpcomingPhase(interactions, I_i)*
7:     **if** *upcomingPhase = previousPhase* **then**
8:         add I_i to *previousPhase*
9:     **else**
10:         *durationOfUpcomingPhase* $\leftarrow$ *duration(upcomingPhase)*
11:         **if** *durationOfUpcomingPhase* > *threshold$_d$* **then**
12:             add *upcomingPhase* to *phases*
13:         **else**
14:             add I_i to *previousPhase*

Algorithm 1 shows the procedure for extracting the phases of the modeling process from the user interactions logged by CEP. Comprehension phases are identified in lines 3–4 of the algorithm by evaluating the time between interactions and comparing it to the minimal duration of a comprehension phase defined by *threshold$_c$*. Line 6 calculates the upcoming phase by integrating all following interactions that are of the same type as the current interaction until a different interaction type is found. The upcoming phase is subsequently compared to the previous phase and, in case they match, added to the previous phase. Otherwise, the duration of the upcoming phase is assessed by computing the time between the first interaction and the last interaction of the identified phase (line 10). If the duration is longer than $threshold_d$ a new phase is added to the list of identified phases (line 12). Otherwise, the interaction is added to the previous phase. Time periods between two phases, being shorter than $threshold_c$, are indicated as gaps in the phase diagrams as it cannot be determined whether the user was still in the first phase or already in the second one.

Additionally, comprehension phases which are interrupted by short modeling or reconciliation phases are merged, as users sometimes move single elements of the process model or add single elements (e.g. a start event) while making sense of the requirements. Using the phases extracted by Algorithm 1, Algorithm 2 identifies situations comprising two comprehension phases being separated by an intermediary modeling or reconciliation phase. If the duration of the intermediary phase is smaller than the $threshold_a$ the two comprehension phases and the intermediary phase are merged to a single comprehension phase.

Algorithm 2. Merging of Comprehension Phases

Require: $phases\ [P_1, P_2, \ldots P_n]$
Require: $threshold_a$
1: **for all** i such that $1 \leq i \leq n - 2$ **do**
2:     **if** P_i and P_{i+2} are comprehension phases **and** $duration(P_{i+1}) < threshold_a$ **then**
3:         merge phases P_i, P_{i+1} and P_{i+2}

---

4 Experimental Investigation

This section describes a modeling session conducted to collect modeling processes for demonstrating our technique. Sect. 4.1 introduces the setup used for data collection. Sect. 4.2 describes the execution while Sect. 4.3 presents two of the collected modeling processes. Sect. 4.4 presents first insights into the process of process modeling and outlines lessons learned.

4.1 Preparing the Experiment

The main goals of the described experiment have been (1) to investigate the process of creating a formal process model in BPMN from an informal description, and (2) to assess the applicability of the described approach. The object that was to be modeled is an actual process run by the "Task Force Earthquakes" of the German Research Center for Geosciences (GFZ). The task force runs in-field missions after catastrophic earthquakes [22]. Subjects were asked to model the "Transport of Equipment" process based on a structured description of how the task force transports its equipment from Germany to the disaster area[1].

---

[1] Material download: http://pinggera.info/experiment/ModelingPhaseDiagrams

To mitigate the risk that the modeling processes were impacted by complicated tools or notations [14], we decided to use a subset of BPMN for our experiment. In this way, modelers were confronted with a minimal number of distractions, but the essence of how process models are created could still be captured. A pre-test was conducted at the University of Innsbruck to ensure the usability of the tool and the understandability of the task description. This led to further improvements of CEP and minor updates to the task description.

4.2   Conducting the Experiment

The experiment was conducted in November 2009 with students of a graduate course on Business Process Management at Eindhoven University of Technology and students from Humboldt-Universität zu Berlin following a similar course. The modeling session at each university started with a demographic survey, followed by a modeling tool tutorial explaining the basic features of CEP. After that, the actual modeling task was presented in which the students had to model the above described "Transport of Equipment" process. This was done by 20 students in Eindhoven and 6 students in Berlin. By conducting the experiment during class and closely monitoring the students, we mitigated the risk of falsely identifying comprehension phases due to external distractions. No time restrictions were imposed on the students.

4.3   Modeling Phase Diagram Examples

This section presents two modeling processes and the corresponding modeling phase diagrams from the experiment[2]. Recall that in such a diagram the horizontal axis represents time and the vertical axis the number of elements in the process model. Differences in the number of elements in the process models can be attributed to superfluous activities, missing activities or different usage of gateways among our subjects. We explicitly connect each example to the modeling phase diagram, and to observations that we obtained by replaying each of the modeling process in CEP.

Example 1. The modeling phase diagram of Example 1 (cf. Fig. 2) shows a rather long initial comprehension phase after which alternating comprehension and modeling phases can be observed. All modeling phases are very long and steep, i.e., much model content is added per iteration. Virtually no reconciliation can be observed.

Modeling Style. Replaying the modeling process in CEP shows that the modeler appears to have a clear conception of the model to be created. Elements are placed on the canvas in large chunks, while all elements are being placed to appropriate positions so that no movement of elements is required.

Modeling Result. The created process model moderately approximates the expected modeling outcome in terms of graph edit distance (cf. [23]), due to

---

[2] We used $threshold_c = 30s$; $threshold_d = 2s$; $threshold_a = 4s$

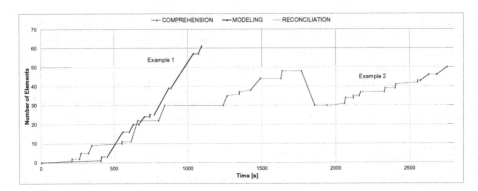

Fig. 2. Two Processes of Process Modeling

some superfluous activities. The created model is, however, free of syntax errors and behavioral anomalies, such as deadlocks.

Example 2. The modeling phase diagram of Example 2 is depicted in Fig. 2. This process starts very similar to Example 1 by adding model elements in large chunks after average comprehension phases. At around 800s, the process starts to deviate by a very long comprehension phase. After this phase, modeling continues similarly to the beginning of the process until a large part of the model is removed (falling iteration around 1800s). The modeling process completes in iterations with significantly longer comprehension phases, short modeling phases, and some time spent on reconciliation.

Modeling Style. The replay shows that the modeler started modeling with a clear idea of the model to be created in mind. However, the modeler used some BPMN modeling elements wrongly, i.e., start events as intermediate states. At about 2/3 of the model created, the modeler realizes the mistake, removes all intermediate states, inserts missing gateways and arcs, and completes the model.

Modeling Result. The model shows an above average similarity to the expected modeling result in terms of graph edit distance. While the model is syntactically correct, it contains two deadlocks due to a wrong pairing of gateways.

4.4   Lessons Learned

The main purpose of our experiment was to validate the feasibility of using modeling phase diagrams for gaining insights into the process of process modeling, more specifically into the formalization of process models. We could demonstrate that our technique allows to empirically investigate aspects of modeling that could not be observed or analyzed earlier. In particular, we witnessed different approaches on layouting the process models. Some of the modelers placed many of the key activities at strategic places on the canvas *right from the start*, without ever having to change their position again, alleviating the need for further reconciliation. Others were more careless when placing modeling elements on the canvas, but continuously invested into improving the process model's optical appearance, resulting in many short reconciliation phases. Interestingly, when replaying the modeling processes we observed that all modelers seemed to dislike activities disappearing from sight. By placing elements far apart, a modeler can in principle span up a 'virtual' canvas beyond the size of the physical dimensions of the computer display. However, many modelers—when reaching the bounds of the physical canvas—spent much time on reconciliation exactly to prevent such a situation. Besides these principle observations on layouting, we were also able to track when a modeler faced difficulties as this directly manifests in the modeling phase diagram, for instance in phases where elements are removed (cf. Fig. 2). A subsequent replay usually allowed us to understand very well the nature of the difficulty, such as an improper use of gateways. Observations like these would not have been possible without the specific setup employed, allowing us to investigate the process underlying the creation of the process model. Therefore, we conclude that modeling phase diagrams and CEP's replay feature constitute valuable assets for further research on understanding the factors influencing the process of creating process models.

5 Related Work

Our work is essentially related to three streams of research: model quality frameworks, research on the process of modeling, and insights into modeling expertise.

There are different frameworks and guidelines available that define quality for process models. Among others, the SEQUAL framework uses semiotic theory for identifying various aspects of process model quality [3], the Guidelines of Process Modeling describe quality considerations for process models [25], and the Seven Process Modeling Guidelines define desirable characteristics of a process model [26]. While each of these frameworks has been validated empirically, they rather take a static view by focusing on the resulting process model, but not on the act of modeling itself. Our research complements these works by providing the methodological means for tracing model quality back to different modeling strategies and competence.

Research on the process of modeling typically focuses on the interaction between different parties. In a classical setting, a system analyst directs a domain expert through a structured discussion subdivided into the stages elicitation, modeling, verification, and validation [9,27]. The procedure of developing process models in a team is analyzed in [8] and characterized as a negotiation process. Interpretation tasks and classification tasks are identified on the semantic level of modeling. Participative modeling is discussed in [28]. These works build on the observation of modeling practice and distills normative procedures for steering the process of process modeling towards a good completion. Our tool-based approach focuses on the formalization of process models by generating fine-granular phase diagrams from event logs, inspired by process mining techniques. In a similar vein, the replay function of ProcessWave has been used to analyze the modeling collaboration support provided by BPM tools [29].

Finally, research has discussed various aspects of modeling expertise. Results of a survey on process modeling success establish modeler expertise as a critical success factor [30]. On the one hand, different experiments have shown that expertise is a key factor for comprehension performance [20,24]. On the other hand, expert modelers spend much more time and dedicate more attention to an appealing layout of the models [19]. Our research design provides means for making modeling phases visible based on log data. In this way, this work offers a way to observe how variations in expertise translate into models of different quality by using different modeling strategies.

6   Summary, Conclusions and Future Work

In this paper, we motivated the need for a detailed understanding of the process of process modeling and provided the conceptual background to analyze the modeling process itself. Through the unique setup of the described modeling environment involving Cheetah Experimental Platform, we have been able to observe under experimental conditions the process of process modeling at close quarters. In particular, we presented a technique for extracting modeling phase diagrams and demonstrated the feasibility of our approach in an experiment from which we presented insights into the creation of two example process models.

Requirements for Experiments. In addition to presenting lessons learned with respect to the act of modeling, we collected requirements for future empirical experiments investigating the process of modeling. Besides standard requirements such as a significant number of participants with representative skills, some specific requirements can be postulated. While the modelers that participated in this study are not representative for the modeling community at large, the question can be raised whether experienced modelers exhibit the same style of modeling observable with our technique as skillful yet inexperienced modelers; observing differences may yield fruitful insights regarding teaching modeling. In addition, it has to be recognized that there are some aspects of the process of process modeling that cannot be measured using solely the modeling tool (e.g., sense making of an informal process description). For this purpose, think-aloud protocols and/or eye tracking technologies might be considered.

Future Work. In the short term, our follow up research will be concerned with collecting additional data, identifying different modeling practices and developing a categorization of different modeling styles. Furthermore, we are planning to develop measurements to quantify the modeling process that might be connected to the quality of the resulting process model. In addition, we are planning to extend the basis for our findings by involving modeling experts. In the longer term, our interest is with how superior modeling styles can be acquired or trained, if at all. Even if we understand that experts increase their cognitive capacity through a masterly organization of knowledge, i.e., chunking, a question with a high practical relevance is how such techniques can be developed and trained.

Acknowledgements. This research was funded by the Austrian Science Fund (FWF): P23699-N23.

References

1. Kock, N., Verville, J., Danesh-Pajou, A., DeLuca, D.: Communication flow orientation in business process modeling and its effect on redesign success: results from a field study. DSS 46, 562–575 (2009)
2. Mendling, J.: Metrics for Process Models: Empirical Foundations of Verification, Error Prediction, and Guidelines for Correctness. Springer, Heidelberg (2008)
3. Krogstie, J., Sindre, G., Jørgensen, H.: Process models representing knowledge for action: a revised quality framework. EJIS 15, 91–102 (2006)
4. Van der Aalst, W., ter Hofstede, A.: Verification of workflow task structures: A petri-net-baset approach. IS 25, 43–69 (2000)
5. Gruhn, V., Laue, R.: Complexity metrics for business process models. In: Proc. BIS 2006, pp. 1–12 (2006)
6. Siau, K., Rossi, M.: Evaluation techniques for systems analysis and design modelling methods-a review and comparative analysis. ISJ (2007)
7. Moody, D.L.: The "Physics" of Notations: Toward a Scientific Basis for Constructing Visual Notations in Software Engineering. IEEE Trans. Software Eng. 35, 756–779 (2009)
8. Rittgen, P.: Negotiating Models. In: Krogstie, J., Opdahl, A.L., Sindre, G. (eds.) CAiSE 2007 and WES 2007. LNCS, vol. 4495, pp. 561–573. Springer, Heidelberg (2007)
9. Hoppenbrouwers, S.J.B.A., Proper, H.A(E.), van der Weide, T.P.: A Fundamental View on the Process of Conceptual Modeling. In: Delcambre, L.M.L., Kop, C., Mayr, H.C., Mylopoulos, J., Pastor, Ó. (eds.) ER 2005. LNCS, vol. 3716, pp. 128–143. Springer, Heidelberg (2005)
10. Persson, A., Stirna, J.: Towards Defining a Competence Profile for the Enterprise Modeling Practitioner. In: van Bommel, P., Hoppenbrouwers, S., Overbeek, S., Proper, E., Barjis, J. (eds.) PoEM 2010. Lecture Notes in Business Information Processing, vol. 68, pp. 232–245. Springer, Heidelberg (2010)
11. Gray, P.: Psychology. Worth Publishers (2007)
12. Tracz, W.: Computer programming and the human thought process. Software: Practice and Experience 9, 127–137 (1979)
13. Miller, G.: The Magical Number Seven, Plus or Minus Two: Some Limits on Our Capacity for Processing Information. The Psychological Review 63, 81–97 (1956)
14. Crapo, A.W., Waisel, L.B., Wallace, W.A., Willemain, T.R.: Visualization and the process of modeling: a cognitive-theoretic view. In: Proc. KDD 2000, pp. 218–226 (2000)
15. Newell, A.: Unified Theories of Cognition. Harvard University Press (1990)
16. Shanteau, J.: How much information does an expert use? Is it relevant? Acta Psychologica 81, 75–86 (1992)
17. Morris, W.T.: On the Art of Modeling. Management Sc. 13, B-707-B-717 (1967)
18. Willemain, T.R.: Model Formulation: What Experts Think about and When. Operations Research 43, 916–932 (1995)
19. Petre, M.: Why Looking Isn't Always Seeing: Readership Skills and Graphical Programming. Commun. ACM, 33–44 (1995)

20. Mendling, J., Reijers, H.A., Cardoso, J.: What Makes Process Models Understandable? In: Alonso, G., Dadam, P., Rosemann, M. (eds.) BPM 2007. LNCS, vol. 4714, pp. 48–63. Springer, Heidelberg (2007)
21. Pinggera, J., Zugal, S., Weber, B.: Investigating the process of process modeling with cheetah experimental platform. In: Proc. ER-POIS 2010, pp. 13–18 (2010)
22. Fahland, D., Woith, H.: Towards Process Models for Disaster Response. In: Proc. PM4HDPS 2008, pp. 254–265 (2008)
23. Dijkman, R., Dumas, M., García-Bañuelos, L.: Graph Matching Algorithms for Business Process Model Similarity Search. In: Dayal, U., Eder, J., Koehler, J., Reijers, H.A. (eds.) BPM 2009. LNCS, vol. 5701, pp. 48–63. Springer, Heidelberg (2009)
24. Reijers, H., Mendling, J.: A study into the factors that influence the understandability of business process models. IEEE Trans. Sys. Man & Cybernetics, A (2011)
25. Becker, J., Rosemann, M., von Uthmann, C.: Guidelines of Business Process Modeling. In: van der Aalst, W.M.P., Desel, J., Oberweis, A. (eds.) BPM 2000. LNCS, vol. 1806, pp. 241–262. Springer, Heidelberg (2000)
26. Mendling, J., Reijers, H.A., van der Aalst, W.M.P.: Seven process modeling guidelines (7pmg). Information & Software Technology 52, 127–136 (2010)
27. Frederiks, P., Weide, T.: Information modeling: The process and the required competencies of its participants. DKE 58, 4–20 (2006)
28. Stirna, J., Persson, A., Sandkuhl, K.: Participative Enterprise Modeling: Experiences and Recommendations. In: Krogstie, J., Opdahl, A.L., Sindre, G. (eds.) CAiSE 2007 and WES 2007. LNCS, vol. 4495, pp. 546–560. Springer, Heidelberg (2007)
29. Hahn, C., Recker, J., Mendling, J.: An exploratory study of it-enabled collaborative process modeling. In: Proc. BPD 2010 (2010)
30. Bandara, W., Gable, G., Rosemann, M.: Factors and measures of business process modelling: model building through a multiple case study. EJIS 14, 347–360 (2005)

Imperative versus Declarative Process Modeling Languages: An Empirical Investigation

Paul Pichler[1], Barbara Weber[1], Stefan Zugal[1], Jakob Pinggera[1],
Jan Mendling[2], and Hajo A. Reijers[3]

[1] University of Innsbruck, Austria
paul.pichler@student.uibk.ac.at
{barbara.weber,stefan.zugal,jakob.pinggera}@uibk.ac.at
[2] Humboldt-Universität zu Berlin, Germany
jan.mendling@wiwi.hu-berlin.de
[3] Eindhoven University of Technology, The Netherlands
h.a.reijers@tue.nl

Abstract. Streams of research are emerging that emphasize the advantages of using declarative process modeling languages over more traditional, imperative approaches. In particular, the declarative modeling approach is known for its ability to cope with the limited flexibility of the imperative approach. However, there is still not much empirical insight into the actual strengths and the applicability of each modeling paradigm. In this paper, we investigate in an experimental setting if either the imperative or the declarative process modeling approach is superior with respect to process model understanding. Even when task types are considered that should better match one or the other, our study finds that imperative process modeling languages appear to be connected with better understanding.

Keywords: Imperative and Declarative Business Process Models, Cognitive Dimensions Framework, Empirical Research.

1 Introduction

At the present stage, formal properties of business process models like liveness and boundedness are quite well understood [1]. In contrast to these aspects, we know rather little about theoretical foundations that might support the superiority of one process modeling language in comparison to another one. There are several reasons why suitable theories are not yet in place for language design, most notably because the discipline is still rather young. Only little research has been conducted empirically in this area so far, e.g., [2,?] which relate model understanding to the modeling language and to model complexity.

The lack of empirical research on language quality has contributed to a notable, continuous invention of new techniques and to the claims on the supposed superiority. For instance, Nigam and Caswell introduce the OpS technique in which *"the operational model is targeted at a business user and yet retains the*

F. Daniel et al. (Eds.): BPM 2011 Workshops, Part I, LNBIP 99, pp. 383–394, 2012.

formality needed for reasoning and, where applicable, automated implementation" implying that existing languages fall short on these characteristics [3, p. 429]. In a Poplin white paper, Owen and Raj claim a general superiority of one modeling language over another, i.e., BPMN over UML Activity Diagrams, because *"[BPMN] offers a process flow modeling technique that is more conducive to the way business analysts model"* [4, p.4]. As a final example, Smith and Fingar state in their book that *"BPML is the language of choice for formalizing the expression, and execution, of collaborative interfaces"* [5, p.205]. We do not want to judge on the correctness of these statements here. Rather, we wish to emphasize that a clear and objective baseline to judge such claims is in demand.

The matter of understanding is well-suited to serve as a pillar for discussing process modeling language quality. Insights from cognitive research on programming languages point to the fact that 'design is redesign' [6]: A computer program is not written sequentially; a programmer typically works on different chunks of the problem in an opportunistic order which requires a constant reinspection and comprehension of the current work context. If we assume that process modelers design their models in a similar fashion, we clearly have to accept the importance of *understanding* as a quality factor. In other words, characteristics of a process modeling language presumably facilitate comprehension to differing degrees in a particular context.

To investigate whether process modeling languages actually offer different levels of support for sense-making, we will necessarily need to limit our scope. One of the important watersheds that exists between process modeling languages is the one between *imperative* and *declarative* process modeling languages. For the recently developed ConDec, a declarative process modeling language, its first design criterion has been that *"the process models developed in the language must be understandable for end-users"* [7, p.15]. While it is claimed in the same work that imperative languages, in comparison, deliver larger and more complex process models, only anecdotic evidence is presented to support this. Also, in the practitioner community opinions are manifold about the advantages of declarative and imperative languages to capture business processes, see for example [8,?,?]. These claims and discussions clearly point to the need for an objective, empirically founded validation of the presumed advantages of the different types of process modeling languages, which motivates the scope of our research.

The contribution of this paper is that it empirically examines if either imperative or declarative process models are superior with respect to understanding matters. To this purpose, we will test a set of theoretically grounded propositions about the differences between the imperative and declarative process modeling approach. The paper is structured as follows. Sect. 2 provides the background for our research. Sect. 3 describes the experimental definition and planning, covering the experimental setup and design. Sect. 4 presents the experimental execution and the analysis of collected data. Furthermore, the results are discussed in this section. Sect. 5 concludes the paper by providing a summary and an outlook.

2   Background

The differentiation between imperative and declarative languages has its roots in computer programming. Imperative programming implies to *"say how to do something"* [9, p.406], whereas declarative programming implies to *"say what is required and let the system determine how to achieve it"* [9, p.406]. Similar to imperative programming, imperative process modeling is characterized by a so-called 'inside-to-outside' approach. It primarily specifies the procedure of how work has to be done. Simply put, imperative modeling languages require all execution alternatives to be explicitly specified in the model before the execution of the process. All new alternatives must be added to the model during build-time. It is argued that this results in process models being over-specified [7]. Declarative process modeling, by contrast, is referred to as an 'outside-to-inside' approach. In contrast to imperative languages, declarative languages do not specify the procedure *a priori*. Instead of determining how the process has to work exactly, only its essential characteristics are described. Adding new constraints to the model limits the number of execution alternatives [7]. This may be understood as follows: Initially, only the process activities are in the model, allowing every possible execution behavior. By adding constraints to the model, execution alternatives are discarded step by step. Figure 1 shows an example of a declarative process model consisting of three activities A, B, and C and two constraints. The constraint attached to activity C specifies that it has to be executed at least once. The constraint between activities A and B requires that the execution of activity B is preceded by activity A. Except for these restrictions, the activities in the model can be executed arbitrarily often and in any order.

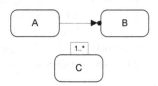

Fig. 1. Declarative Process Model

Clearly, the above mentioned claims need to be substantiated in terms of appropriate theories. The Cognitive Dimensions Framework (CDF) offers a reference for discussing and evaluating various types of notations based on their cognitive effectiveness [10]. Its development is based on the 'mental operations theory' [6], which in essence states that a notation performs better if fewer mental operations are required to perform a task. In this way, a "matched pair" between particular, notational characteristics and a specific task gives the best performance. This view has evolved and matured over the years towards the CDF [10,?], which contains many different characteristics to distinguish notations from each other. In particular, the dimensions *hard mental operations* (to understand a model) and *hidden dependencies* (between notation elements) directly apply to process modeling understanding [10].

In line with the CDF, different notations should be judged *relatively*, i.e., in terms of their aptitude towards different types of understanding tasks. *"A notation is never absolutely good, therefore, but good only in relation to certain tasks"* [10, p.3]. In this vein, it seems appropriate to investigate whether imperative languages are better understandable with tasks containing a particular type of information and declarative languages with tasks containing another type of information [10]. For such a distinction, the classification between sequential and circumstantial information is relevant.

Sequential information explains how input conditions lead to a certain outcome. An example of a statement containing sequential information is: "Activity X must be directly preceded by activity Y". As this example demonstrates, sequential information often concentrates on what actions could be either next or previous in a model [6]. In other words, sequential information typically relates to actions immediately *leading to* or *following from* a certain outcome. On the other hand, *circumstantial information*, given an outcome, relates to the overall conditions that produced that outcome. An example of a statement containing circumstantial information is: "If activity X or Y has been executed, it is possible to terminate a process instance by executing at least one additional activity". As this example demonstrates, circumstantial information frequently corresponds to what (combination of) circumstances will cause a particular outcome or action [6]. In this context, circumstantial information typically relates to conditions that *have* or *have not* occurred.

Empirical evidence has already been established that imperative programming languages display sequential information in a readily-used form, while declarative languages display circumstantial information in a readily-used form [6]. Based on the similarities between software programs and process models, it may be assumed, therefore, that a similar, relativist viewpoint could also provide a theoretical basis for the comparison of imperative versus declarative process modeling languages [11]. Consequently, the following set of propositions may be advanced, which are in line with those proposed in an earlier paper [11]:

P1. Given two semantically equivalent process models, establishing sequential information will be easier on the basis of the model that is created with the process modeling language that is relatively more imperative in nature.

P2. Given two semantically equivalent process models, establishing circumstantial information will be easier on the basis of the model that is created with the process modeling language that is relatively more declarative in nature.

To test these expectations, we will next describe an experimental design for that purpose.

3   Experimental Definition and Planning

This section introduces the hypotheses, describes the subjects, objects, factors, factor levels and response variables of our experiment. It will also present the instrumentation, data collection procedure, and experimental design. Finally, the parameters we controlled for in our experiment are discussed.

Factor and Factor Levels. The considered factors were *model type* and *task type*, with two factor levels each. For the model type factor, we considered the factor levels of *imperative* and *declarative*. For the task type factor, we considered the factor levels *sequential* versus *circumstantial*.

Subjects. Students enrolled in classes on business process management were participating as subjects in the experiment.

Objects. In preparation for the experiment, four semantically equivalent process model pairs were created[1]. Semantic equivalence was ensured by testing valid traces based on both model variants. BPMN was used to create the imperative models, and ConDec to create the declarative models. Both imperative and declarative process models were created considering the following criteria: 1) Correctness, 2) Executability and 3) Representativeness. *Correctness* is the precondition of executability, a characteristic of understandable process models defined by the SEQUAL Framework [12]. For imperative models soundness and structuredness were considered as correctness notions [13]. For declarative models, in turn, absence of dead activities and conflicts was required [7]. To ensure *executability* we transformed the imperative models to Petri nets allowing us to apply the token game. For declarative models, in turn, we tested executability using the in-built verification functionality of DECLARE [7]. To ensure content validity, i.e., the *representativeness* of the experimental objects, we ensured that the four model pairs covered the core concepts of both the imperative and declarative paradigm. Imperative process models covered the five basic control flow patterns (i.e., sequence, exclusive choice, simple merge, parallel split and synchronization) [14] as well as loops. Declarative models, in turn, covered all major constraint groups (i.e., existence, relation and negation constraints [15]).

Tasks. For each of the model pairs, i.e., a declarative versus an imperative model, four sequential and four circumstantial tasks had to be created (comprising understandability questions) considering the following criteria: 1) Typical constructs, 2) Model parts, 3) Difficulty and 4) Consistency. To maintain content validity it had to be ensured that the experimental tasks cover all relevant aspects of understandability for each modeling language. In [16], the four constructs order, concurrency, exclusiveness, and repetition are mentioned as being crucial for the understanding of imperative process models and were therefore considered for creating the sequential tasks. Circumstantial tasks, in turn, were adjusted in terms of the constraints groups which determine declarative representativeness (i.e., existence, relation, and negation constraints).

Sequential information usually affects local parts of a process model [17]. Consequently, sequential tasks were formulated with reference to local actions (e.g., next or previous) in the model. Contrary to sequential information,

---

[1] The material used for this study can be downloaded from:
http://barbaraweber.org/experiments/2010_Declarative_vs_Imperative.pdf

circumstantial information tends to affect the process model rather globally [17]. Therefore, circumstantial tasks were formulated such that they ask for (the combination of) circumstances that caused or will cause a particular action within the process. To establish a balanced level of difficulty among the experimental tasks, and hence avoid that tasks which are either too easy or too difficult impact the result of the experiment, a pre-test was conducted. To ensure that only the information captured by the tasks is of relevance for the experimental outcome, the tasks were formulated consistently in respect of their structure and the use of terms.

Response Variables. To compare declarative and imperative modeling languages we defined the following response variables: 1) *accuracy* as measured by the number of correctly answered questions (tasks) and 2) *speed* by measuring the time needed to complete the tasks. Since four sequential and four circumstantial tasks had to be completed for each model pair, accuracy values could range between 0 and 4 for sequential and circumstantial tasks respectively.

Hypotheses. A statistical test with two factors is always associated with three null hypotheses [18], one for each factor and one for the interaction between the factors:

- *Null Hypothesis H_1: There is no significant difference in the performance (in terms of accuracy and speed) of imperative and declarative models.*
- *Null Hypothesis H_2: There is no significant difference in the performance (in terms of accuracy and speed) of sequential and circumstantial tasks.*
- *Null Hypothesis H_3: There is no significant interaction between the factor model type and the factor task type (in terms of accuracy and speed).*

Parameters. In addition to the described factors other variables can affect the response variables under examination and therefore need to be controlled [19]. For this experiment we considered three main parameters that can influence the understandability of process models, i.e., model characteristics, domain knowledge and personal factors [20]. *Model characteristics* we controlled involved visual layout and structural attributes. To control *visual layout* we maximized symmetry, minimized bends and minimized edge crosses for both model variants (i.e., imperative and declarative), since they are known factors which influence model understandability [21]. To control the *structural attribute* size, which has significant impact on model understandability [22], we had to ensure that the imperative and declarative variants have equal size. Consequently, to avoid size rather than the used modeling paradigm dictating the outcome, the used model pairs comprised two small and two large models for each factor level. Fig.2 shows an experimental model pair consisting of a small imperative and a small declarative model.

To eliminate the influence of *domain knowledge*, activities of the process models were labeled with random letters. To control *personal factors*, the selection of experimental subjects comprised preferably persons with uniform knowledge regarding business process modeling. Nevertheless, the subjects had to complete

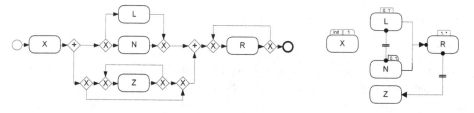

Fig. 2. Imperat. BPMN model (left) and equivalent, declarat. ConDec model (right).

a questionnaire at the beginning of the experiment allowing us to analyze how possible variations between the individual modeling knowledge influenced the model understanding and quantify the distribution of modeling experience between the imperative and declarative modeling approach.

Experimental Design. The experimental design is based on the guidelines for designing experiments from [19]. Following these guidelines, a *randomized 2x2 factorial experiment* has been designed, which investigates the influence of two factors with two factor levels each. The experiment is called *randomized*, since subjects are assigned to groups randomly. Fig. 3 illustrates the described setup: Overall, the experiment comprised four model pairs. Depending on their group, subjects either started with the imperative variant of Model Pair 1 or with the semantically equivalent declarative variant. For two of the remaining model pairs, the levels of factor model type were switched for the two groups, i.e., overall, every subject worked on two declarative and two imperative process models. Regarding factor task type every subject worked on both factor levels (i.e., sequential and circumstantial tasks) for each model pair. To ensure independence of samples, both sequential and circumstantial tasks were presented in a random, and thus unique order to each subject.

Instrumentation and Data Collection Procedure. The participants conducted the experiment using the Cheetah Experimental Platform [23], which guided them through the experiment. The tool also automatically logged the given answers, as well as the time that was needed to accomplish the experimental tasks.

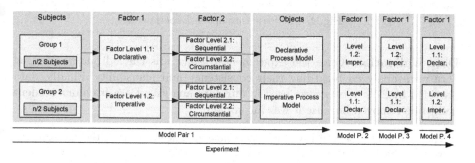

Fig. 3. Experimental Design

4   Performing the Experiment

This section deals with the experiment's execution. Sect. 4.1 covers operational aspects, i.e., how the experiment has been executed. Then, in Sect. 4.2 data is analyzed and subsequently discussed in Sect. 4.3.

4.1   Experimental Operation

Experimental Preparation. Four semantically equivalent model pairs were created for the empirical test. Additionally, for each model pair a set of four sequential and four circumstantial tasks was developed (cf. Sect. 3). To ensure the overall understandability of the experimental setup and a balanced degree of difficulty, a pre-test was conducted.

Experimental Execution. The experiment was conducted in July 2010. In sum, 28 subjects from the Humboldt Universität zu Berlin and the University of Innsbruck participated in this empirical test. Subjects had one week time to complete the experiment in an "offline" mode, i.e., they were not constantly monitored.

Fig. 4 shows the structure of the experiment by means of a complete run: Each student received a PDF file containing the introduction, hints for the experiment and troubleshooting as well as specific instructions on how to download and execute it.[2] Having downloaded the experiment, the subjects had to complete the questionnaire about their personal modeling knowledge and experience. An example followed providing the solution as well as the respective explanation to every test task. During the experimental phase, the subjects had to complete eight tasks (four sequential and four circumstantial ones) for each of the four models. A legend with the used modeling elements was attached to every process model.

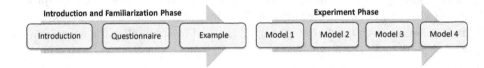

Fig. 4. The Structure of the Experiment

Data Validation. Once the experimental study was carried out, the logged data were analyzed regarding their consistency and plausibility. Finally, data provided by 27 students were used in our data analysis. Data from one student had to be removed because it was incomplete.

---

[2] The version of CEP which was used for the experiment including the experimental workflow can be downloaded from:
http://barbaraweber.org/experiments/2010_Declarative_vs_Imperative.zip

4.2   Data Analysis

In the following we describe the analysis and interpretation of data.

Descriptive Analysis. To give an overview of the experiment's data, Table 1 shows mean values and standard deviation for accuracy and speed.

Table 1. Descriptive Statistics

Model Type	Task Type	N	Accuracy Mean(score)	Accuracy Std. Dev.	Speed Mean(min.)	Speed Std. Dev.
Declarative	Sequential	54	2.61	1.14	2.21[3]	1.13
	Circumst.	54	2.44	1.18	2.79	1.69
Imperative	Sequential	54	3.26	0.89	1.91	0.98
	Circumst.	54	2.87	0.95	2.06	0.80
Declarative		108	2.53	1.16	2.50	1.46
Imperative		108	3.06	0.94	1.98	0.89
	Sequential	108	2.94	1.07	2.06	1.06
	Circumst.	108	2.66	1.10	2.43	1.37

Hypotheses Testing. In a next step, the hypotheses introduced in Sect. 3 were tested. The empirical test in this work was designed as a two-way factorial experiment. Accordingly, a two-way factorial research design requires a statistical analysis method that allows the interpretation of both factors together (i.e., (M)ANOVA). Since the requirements for the application of ANOVA were not satisfied, we applied the Sheirer-Ray-Hare test, a non-parametric alternative for ANOVA [18].

First we discuss the result of testing null hypothesis H_3, since the effect of a factor can be interpreted individually only when there is no evidence that it interacts with another factor [19].

Null Hypothesis H_3: With an obtained p-value (=significance value) of 0.45 (>0.05), null hypothesis H_3 cannot be rejected at a confidence level of 95% for the response variable of accuracy. Also, the results for the response variable of speed turned out to be insignificant (p-value of 0.37, >0.05). Hence, there is no statistically significant interaction between the factors model type and task type. Since there is no evidence of a significant interaction, the effect of the factors can be interpreted individually [19].

Null Hypothesis H_1: With an obtained p-value of 0.001 (<0.05), null hypothesis H_1 has to be rejected for the response variable *accuracy* at a confidence level of 95%. Hence, there is a statistically significant difference between the alternatives of the factor model type: *Imperative models have a better performance in terms of accuracy than declarative models, regardless of the factor task type.* With an obtained

---

[3] A lower number in terms of response variable "speed" implies a better result.

392 P. Pichler et al.

p-value of 0.002 (<0.05), null hypothesis H_1 has to be rejected for response variable *speed*. This result indicates that *imperative models have a better performance in terms of speed than declarative models, regardless of the factor task type.*

Null Hypothesis H_2: With an obtained p-value of 0.06, which just exceeds the 0.05 level, null hypothesis H_2 cannot be rejected at a confidence level of 95%, *i.e., there is no statistically significant difference between the alternatives of the factor task type, i.e., sequential or circumstantial tasks, in terms of accuracy.* Since there is the possibility that one type of process models is significantly better performing with one type of the tasks, and the other type of process models is not, we additionally analyzed this hypothesis separately for each factor level of factor model type using the Mann-Whitney-U test. With an obtained p-value of 0.02 (<0.05), a statistically significant difference between the alternatives of the factor task type could be established when imperative models are used, i.e., *sequential tasks compared to circumstantial tasks lead to a better performance in terms of accuracy when imperative models are used.* For declarative models, in turn, with a p-value of 0.51 >0.05 no statistically significant results could be obtained. For the response variable of speed, null hypothesis H_2 has to be rejected (p-value of 0.01, <0.05): *Sequential tasks compared to circumstantial tasks lead to a better performance in terms of speed than circumstantial tasks, regardless of the factor model type.*

4.3 Discussion

The objective of this paper has been to investigate if either the imperative or the declarative process modeling approach is superior with respect to understanding matters. The set-up for this investigation has been grounded on insights from cognitive research on programming languages. Our findings suggest that imperative process models are significantly better understandable than declarative models, irrespective of the type of tasks involved (sequential vs. circumstantial).

This result, however, must be treated with care, since an ex-post analysis of the process modeling experience of our subjects revealed that the experimental subjects were rather familiar with imperative process modeling, but at best only to a limited extent to declarative modeling. Based on this imbalance, a subsequent analysis was examined. This revealed that a learning effect for declarative models might have occurred during the experiment. Since this affects generalizability of the results, replications regarding this research objective are required with subjects having a more balanced level of familiarity for both modeling paradigms.

In addition to examining imperative versus declarative process models, our goal has been to test if the theoretical axioms of the CDF, which were originally established for computer programming as part of extensive cognitive research, also apply to business process modeling. Based on the obtained data it could only be confirmed that tasks containing sequential information are better understandable using imperative process models, but not that tasks containing circumstantial information are better understandable using declarative models. Regarding the response variable *accuracy*, sequential tasks were easier to understand using imperative models. However, we could not confirm that circumstantial tasks are easier to understand using declarative models. In terms of the response variable *speed*, sequential tasks turned out to be better performing irrespective of the type of model concerned.

We effectively conducted the experiment with a homogeneous group of students. Still, further potential limitations must be considered. In particular, the relatively low number of experimental subjects constitutes a limitation as tests converge towards significant results with more subjects. Moreover, due to the small number of participants in the pre-test, it was not possible to conduct a statistically significant reliability analysis on the internal consistency of the different understandability tasks. Even though we tried to balance the level of difficulty with a pre-test, it cannot be entirely excluded that this issue might have influenced the experimental result. Another limitation regarding the generalizatbility of our results relates to the fact that our experiment only compares one concrete modeling language representing each process modeling approach.

5 Summary and Outlook

In this paper, we compared the imperative process modeling approach with the declarative approach with reference to understanding based on insights from cognitive research on programming. Essentially, imperative process models turned out to be more comprehensible than declarative process models, irrespective of the type of task involved. However, based on the imbalance of subjects' familiarity with imperative and declarative process modeling, this result must be treated with care.

A further insight concerns the theoretical axioms of the Cognitive Dimensions Framework, stating that tasks containing sequential information are better understandable using imperative languages, and tasks containing circumstantial information are better understandable using declarative languages. This could be confirmed partially. Apparently, sequential tasks are better understandable, regardless whether an imperative or declarative process model was used.

The most important direction for future research we identify would be to replicate the experiment in a situation where the participants' knowledge of and experience with both imperative and declarative languages is less skewed. One can argue that this may be hard to establish, given the dominant emphasis in many settings on the use of imperative approaches, for example in academic programs. A step forward here may be taken by involving people with no training or background at all in process modeling, who can be provided equal amounts of training time in both paradigms.

References

1. Reisig, W., Rozenberg, G. (eds.): APN 1998. LNCS, vol. 1491. Springer, Heidelberg (1998)
2. Recker, J., Dreiling, A.: Does It Matter Which Process Modeling Language We Teach or Use? An Experimental Study on Understanding Process Modelling Languages without Formal Education. In: Proc. ACIS 2007, pp. 356–366 (2007)

3. Nigam, A., Caswell, N.: Business artifacts: An approach to operational specification. IBM Systems Journal 42(3), 428–445 (2003)
4. Owen, M., Raj, J.: BPMN and Business Process Management: Introduction to the New Business Process Modeling Standard. Popkin, Technical report (2003), http://whitepaper.talentum.com/whitepaper/view.do?id=7050
5. Smith, H., Fingar, P.: Business Process Management: The Third Wave. Meghan-Kiffer Press (2003)
6. Gilmore, D.J., Green, T.R.: Comprehension and recall of miniature programs. IJMMS 21, 31–48 (1984)
7. Pesic, M.: Constraint-Based Workflow Management Systems: Shifting Control to Users. PhD thesis, TU Eindhoven (2008)
8. Korhonen, J.: Evolution of agile enterprise architecture (April 2006), http://blog.jannekorhonen.fi/?p=11 (retrieved May 10, 2011)
9. Roy, P.V., Haridi, S.: Concepts, Techniques, and Models of Computer Programming. The MIT Press (2004)
10. Green, T.R.: Cognitive dimensions of notations. In: Proc. BCSHCI 1989, pp. 443–460 (1989)
11. Fahland, D., Mendling, J., Reijers, H.A., Weber, B., Weidlich, M., Zugal, S.: Declarative Versus Imperative Process Modeling Languages: The Issue of Understandability. In: Halpin, T., Krogstie, J., Nurcan, S., Proper, E., Schmidt, R., Soffer, P., Ukor, R. (eds.) EMMSAD 2009. LNBIP, vol. 29, pp. 353–366. Springer, Heidelberg (2009)
12. Krogstie, J., Sindre, G., Jørgensen, H.: Process models representing knowledge for action: a revised quality framework. EJIS 15, 91–102 (2006)
13. Mendling, J.: Metrics for Process Models: Empirical Foundations of Verification, Error Prediction, and Guidelines for Correctness. Springer, Heidelberg (2008)
14. Russell, N., ter Hofstede, A.H.M., van der Aalst, W.M.P., Mulyar, N.: Workflow Control-Flow Patterns. A Revised View. BPM Center Report, 6–22 (2006)
15. van der Aalst, W.M.P., Pesic, M.: DecSerFlow: Towards a Truly Declarative Service Flow Language. In: Bravetti, M., Núñez, M., Tennenholtz, M. (eds.) WS-FM 2006. LNCS, vol. 4184, pp. 1–23. Springer, Heidelberg (2006)
16. Melcher, J., Mendling, J., Reijers, H.A., Seese, D.: On Measuring the Understandability of Process Models. In: Rinderle-Ma, S., Sadiq, S., Leymann, F. (eds.) BPM 2009. LNBIP, vol. 43, pp. 465–476. Springer, Heidelberg (2010)
17. Weidlich, M., Zugal, S., Pinggera, J., Fahland, D., Weber, B., Reijers, H.A., Mendling, J.: The Impact of Sequential and Circumstantial Changes on Process Models. In: Proc. ER-POIS 2010, pp. 43–54 (2010)
18. Dytham, C.: Choosing and Using Statistics. A Biologist's Guide. John Wiley & Sons (2003)
19. Juristo, N., Moreno, A.M.: Basics of Software Engineering Experimentation. Kluwer Academic Publishers (2001)
20. Mendling, J., Strembeck, M.: Influence factors of understanding business process models. In: Proc. BIS 2008, pp. 142–153 (2008)
21. Purchase, H.: Which Aesthetic has the Greatest Effect on Human Understanding? In: DiBattista, G. (ed.) GD 1997. LNCS, vol. 1353, pp. 248–261. Springer, Heidelberg (1997)
22. Mendling, J., Reijers, H.A., Cardoso, J.: What Makes Process Models Understandable? In: Alonso, G., Dadam, P., Rosemann, M. (eds.) BPM 2007. LNCS, vol. 4714, pp. 48–63. Springer, Heidelberg (2007)
23. Pinggera, J., Zugal, S., Weber, B.: Investigating the process of process modeling with cheetah experimental platform. In: Proc. ER-POIS 2010, pp. 13–18 (2010)

Emphasizing Events and Rules in Business Processes

Giorgio Bruno

Politecnico di Torino, Torino, Italy
giorgio.bruno@polito.it

Abstract. In the domain of Process-Aware Information Systems, business processes, events, rules and information models appear intertwined and this calls for a representation that integrates different viewpoints. A motivating example is the mapping of several customer orders to one bulk supplier order: a distributor may wait until the number of items needed by customers entitles them to take advantage of a quantity discount. The individual events representing the incoming customer orders need to be mapped to complex events that trigger the submissions of supplier orders. Complex events are defined through rules that must be able to access the properties of the events involved; rules then need an information model providing the relevant information at an adequate abstraction level. This paper presents a notation, called Chant, which consists of three interrelated models, i.e. the process model, the information model and the rule model. Processes imply choices, which can be classified into a number of selection patterns. Two major categories are addressed in this paper: they are referred to as data selection patterns and path selection patterns.

Keywords: information systems, business processes, Petri nets, events, business rules, selection patterns.

1   Introduction

Business Process Management (BPM) [1] and Complex Event Processing (CEP) [2] are two disciplines for which current research is emphasizing the points of contact [3]. The major one is the notion of event. In BPM notations and languages such as BPMN and BPEL, the events are the major factors affecting the control flow, including the instantiation of processes. Events enable business processes to interact with the external world at the very beginning, during their course of action and at their completion; in BPMN, these three categories of events are called start events, intermediate events and end ones. Events are usually associated with the exchange of messages and the firing of timeouts.

However, it may happen that a mismatch occurs between the basic events (i.e. those produced by the actual sources) and those the listeners are really interested in. For example, a listener may not want to receive a whole flow of events but only the abnormal ones, i.e. those violating certain constraints; or they may want to get combinations of events based on certain conditions. The need to extract "interesting"

F. Daniel et al. (Eds.): BPM 2011 Workshops, Part I, LNBIP 99, pp. 395–406, 2012.

events out of the flows of actual events has stimulated the development of an approach called Complex Event Processing (CEP).

Cross-fertilization between BPM and CEP is a growing line of research to which this paper is meant to bring a contribution in the domain of Process-Aware Information Systems [4]. In particular, this paper focuses on the role of endogenous events in the determination of precedence relationships between process elements representing external activities. In BPMN, external activities can be carried out by human performers or services and are represented by process elements called user tasks and service tasks, respectively. The activation of such tasks consists in the emission of one request event followed by the wait for the corresponding reply event; such events are endogenous since they are related to the execution of process-driven activities. The precedence rules provided by BPMN can make the activation of a task depend on the completion of: one previous task, a number of previous tasks or even a number of instances of a previous task. However, in third case, the number of instances is determined once, before the activation of the first instance.

What is difficult to express is the fact that the activation of a task, say, B, depends on the completion of several executions of a previous task, say, A, and the number of instances of A is obtained from a business rule that is a function of the results produced by the instances of A. A motivating example is the mapping of several customer orders to one bulk supplier order: a distributor may wait until the number of items needed by customers entitles them to take advantage of a quantity discount. Therefore, distributors may accept several customer orders (which are handled individually through a task playing the role of task A) before placing a supplier order (with a task playing the role of task B).

In such cases, complex events are needed to aggregate the basic events produced by the instances of task A and to trigger the execution of task B; they are defined through rules that must be able to access the properties of the events involved. In the domain of Process-Aware Information Systems, events point to business entities and rules may be formulated not only on the basis of the specific business entities causing the input events (called primary business entities) but also on other business entities that are interrelated with the primary ones. Rules then need an information model providing the relevant information at an adequate abstraction level.

In situations like the above-mentioned one, business processes, events, rules and information models appear intertwined and this calls for a representation that integrates different viewpoints. This paper presents a notation, called Chant, which consists of three interrelated models, i.e. the process model, the information model and the rule model. The process model links events and tasks, the information model describes the properties of the business entities involved, and the rule model specifies how the events are consumed and produced by the tasks.

Processes imply choices, which can be classified into a number of selection patterns. Two major categories are addressed in this paper: they are referred to as data selection patterns and path selection patterns. The former describe how tasks select the input events needed for their execution; the latter address situations in which the same events may be taken by two or more tasks in competition with each other.

This paper is organized as follows. Section 2 illustrates the Chant notation along with two simple patterns. Section 3 provides an overview of selection patterns. Section 4 is about related work and section 5 presents the conclusion and future work.

2   The Chant Notation

This section introduces the Chant notation and presents some examples of selection patterns.

Chant models consist of three interrelated models, i.e. the process model, the information model and the rule model.

The process model shows the event flow and the related tasks. The control flow and the data flow are integrated in the event flow: events indicate facts about business entities and bring about precedence relationships between tasks, as the input events of a task are usually the output events of a previous task.

The events are then the link between the processes and the underlying information system; their payloads refer to the business entities whose structure is shown in the information model.

An example of Chant model is given in Fig. 1. It describes the behavior of a distribution company that assembles orders from customers into bulk orders for suppliers. The basic requirements are as follows. The process receives orders from customers: it accepts those coming from customers in good credit standing and rejects the others. It combines a number of accepted customer orders into one supplier order, when it can take advantage of a quantity discount.

These basic requirements give rise to the process model shown in Fig. 1a.

The structure of a Chant process model is similar to a Petri net and hence it is made up of places and transitions connected by oriented arcs. Transitions represent tasks, and places are containers of events. Places have two labels separated by a comma: the first label is the name of the events represented by the place and the second label is the type of their payloads. The payload of an event is the business entity related to the event. Two types of business entities are addressed in this process, i.e., customer order and supplier order: they are called CO and SO, respectively.

Incoming customer orders are collected in place co (customer order). Place co has no input arcs because its events come from an external source; it is an input place for the process. Processes have interfaces in charge of handling their input and output events, but their description is beyond the scope of this paper. Customer orders may be accepted (task acceptCO) or rejected (task rejectCO): the orders accepted are collected in the internal place named coa (customer order accepted) while those rejected are put in output place cor (customer order rejected). An output place has no outgoing arcs and its events are handled by the above-mentioned interface. The names of the places are singular as they express the meaning of the individual events they contain.

The process model gives a number of indications on the local event flows, i.e., on the events taken and produced by the tasks. A first distinction concerns the number of events taken from an input place or put in an output one: if there is a label on an arc, this label denotes a group of events. The selection rules, which specify how the events have to be grouped, are defined in the Rules section of the Chant model. If there is no label, only one event is involved and it is referred to with the place name.

Tasks acceptCO and rejectCO take one event, while task genSO takes a group of events called cOrders; as a matter of fact it assembles several customer orders into one supplier order.

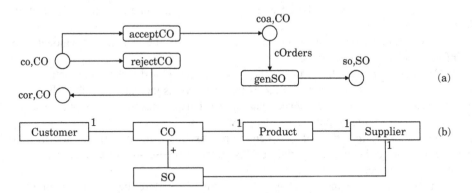

Attributes

Customer: boolean goodStanding. CO: int n. Supplier: int threshold.

Rules   (c)

acceptCO {pri:1. sr: co.customer.goodStanding}

genSO {sr: cOrders (same product.supplier as s) and cOrders.sum(n) >= s.threshold.

post: so = new SO (.cos == cOrders, .supplier == s).}

Fig. 1. A Chant model describing an order-handling process

An output flow primarily shows the events produced by a task and collected in a place; moreover, some considerations can be made on the relationships between the payloads of the output events and those of the input events. The major cases are as follows. If a task is meant to move the payloads from an input place to an output place, then the two places have the same type, say, T, the output arc has no label and the task has no more input or output places of type T. Tasks acceptCO and rejectCO simply move the payload from a co event to either a coa event or a cor event, respectively. If the type of an output place is different from the types of the input places, the output events may refer to new payloads or to existing payloads related to the input payloads: the details are provided in the Rules section of the Chant model.

Rules draw on events and on business entities and therefore an information model is needed, such as the one shown in Fig. 1b, which derives from the additional requirements that follow.

A customer order refers to one product type and includes the number (n) of items needed. A product type is provided by one supplier. The condition of "good credit standing" (mentioned in the basic requirements above) applies to customers and is represented by a simple attribute (goodStanding) so as to keep the information model simple. In fact, an expression involving other business entities is likely to be needed: for example, this condition might call for the total value of the unpaid orders of a customer to be not greater than their credit limit, as suggested in [5]. The process combines a number of accepted customer orders into one supplier order, when it can take advantage of a quantity discount: this occurs when the total number of the items on order is greater than a threshold associated with the supplier. In addition, the customer orders must refer to products provided by the same supplier, which becomes the recipient of the supplier order.

There are many kinds of choices that may take place in a course of action, but they may be classified into two major categories referred to as data selection and path selection. A detailed discussion of these patterns (along with further examples) is given in the next section.

A path selection pattern consists of a number of tasks having at least one input place in common. Place co and tasks acceptCO and rejectCO follow such a pattern: for each incoming customer order (co), the process selects the appropriate task on the basis of the selection rule and the priority of the tasks. As shown in the Rules section (Fig. 1c), task acceptCO has higher priority (pri: 1) than task rejectCO (pri: 0, the standard value) and hence its selection rule is evaluated first. If the rule is successful, the event is acted on by this task; otherwise the event is taken by task rejectCO.

Rules are grouped by tasks and are written between curly brackets after the task name. Selection rules are introduced by keyword "sr" and consist of Boolean expressions including the labels of the input arcs or of the places of the task: such labels act as variables to be matched by events. The matching events are those taken by the task.

Rule "co.customer.goodStanding" in task acceptCO selects a customer order, provided that the corresponding customer is in good standing. Term "co" denotes the payload (i.e., a customer order) of an event in place co, ".customer" returns the customer associated with the order (there is only one as shown in the information model), and ".goodStanding" returns the value of attribute goodStanding of that customer.

Rules in Chant are written in a tailored version of OCL (Object Constraint Language, http://www.omg.org/spec/OCL/). Since events in Chant do not carry specific attributes but only references to business entities (their payloads), event names denote business entities. The conditions expressed by the rules are then based on the attributes of the payloads of the input events and on the attributes of the business entities that can be reached from such payloads through the associations defined in the information model. The information model in Fig. 1b shows that a product is linked to one supplier, which may be linked to several products (the standard multiplicity is 0 .. many); then, if p and s denote a product and a supplier, respectively, p.supplier returns the supplier of p and s.products the collection of products supplied by s. Terms supplier in p.supplier and products in s.products are implicit associative attributes; they are obtained from the corresponding class names. The class name with the initial in lower case is used when the attribute is single-valued, i.e., it refers to one business entity (e.g. attribute supplier in class Product); if the attribute is multi-valued, i.e., it refers to a collection of business entities, the class name in the plural is used (e.g. attribute products in class Supplier).

Names CO and SO are acronyms: the corresponding implicit associative attributes are co and so (single-valued), cos and sos (multi-valued); as a matter of fact, acronyms are turned into lower case.

A data selection pattern characterizes the way a task takes the events needed from its input places. A case of multi-event selection is offered by task genSO. It takes a group of customer orders referred to as cOrders from place coa; the selection rule "cOrders (same product.supplier as s) and cOrders.sum(n) >= s.threshold" indicates what conditions have to be satisfied. A group of customer orders is suitable if it satisfies the expression when it takes the place of label cOrders; then it has to be made up of members pointing to the same supplier and the total sum of items has to be not less than the threshold of the common supplier. A condition to be met by all the members of a group is written between parentheses after the group name; in particular, operator same introduces an expression whose result must be identical for all the members of the group. Clause "as s" keeps the common supplier in local identifier s whose scope includes all the rules of the task.

The post-condition of genSO shows the effects of the execution of the task; the event to be put in place so points to a new payload whose type is SO. Operator new means that the execution of the task results in the generation of a new business entity whose type follows the operator; the parentheses include the conditions to be satisfied by the attributes of the newly generated entity. In this case, two implicit associative attributes are involved: attribute cos (which indicates the collection of customer orders associated with the current supplier order) has to denote the same business entities as the input events (cOrders) and attribute supplier has to refer to the above mentioned common supplier (pointed to by local identifier s).

3   Selection Patterns and Local Event Flows

Processes imply choices, which can be classified into a number of selection patterns. Two major categories are addressed in this paper: they are referred to as data selection patterns and path selection patterns. The former describe how tasks select the input events needed for their execution; the latter address situations in which the same events may be taken by two or more tasks in competition with each other.

Data selection patterns come in three major flavors: single-event selection, multi-event selection and multi-source selection. Single-event selection is exemplified by tasks acceptCO and rejectCO in Fig. 1a, and multi-event selection is exhibited by task genSO in Fig. 1a. Multi-source selection takes place when the events come from several places, as illustrated in Fig. 2.

Each execution of task genTransaction produces one transaction out of one request and one offer, provided that the request and the offer refer to the same product type and the maximum purchase price (maxPrice, an attribute of requests) is not less than the minimum selling price (minPrice, an attribute of offers). Requests come from buyers and offers from sellers.

Path selection patterns occur when there are places with two or more output arcs; then, there are two or more tasks that may take the same events and the choice of the task is determined by the selection rules.

When the choice depends on the events of only one place, it is called free choice in Petri net literature [6]. A free choice is denoted by a place that is the only input place of two or more tasks. An example is given by place co in Fig. 1a. In Chant, free choices are called simple path selections; the other situations are referred to as complex path selections.

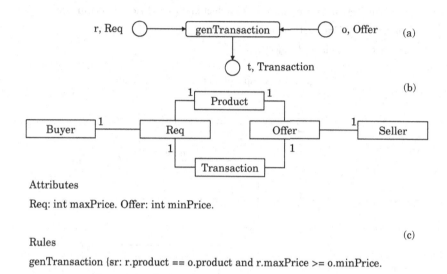

Attributes

Req: int maxPrice. Offer: int minPrice.

Rules

genTransaction {sr: r.product == o.product and r.maxPrice >= o.minPrice.

post: t = new Transaction (.req == r, .offer == o)}

Fig. 2. An example of multi-source selection pattern

A complex path selection is shown in Fig. 3. The situation addressed is an extension of the one illustrated in Fig. 2, as requests and offers are discarded if they are waiting for too long. An additional attribute, i.e., deadline d, is added to requests and offers. Selection rules "r.d elapsed" and "o.d elapsed" include a timing constraint indicated by keyword elapsed: an input even is taken, when its deadline (the value of attribute d) becomes equal to (or less than) the current time.

Local event flows have been introduced in the previous section; they are concerned with the flows of payloads from input events to output events in tasks. An interesting situation addressed in this section is when a group of input payloads has to be distributed to several output places: the corresponding pattern is called distribution pattern. The example shown in Fig. 4 refers to a process handling purchase requisitions. Its requirements are as follows.

When the process receives a purchase requisition (pr) for a given product type, it produces three requests for quote with task genRequests. A request for quote (rfq) is linked to a purchase requisition and a supplier. As shown in the post-condition of the task, the requests are directed to distinct suppliers able to provide the product needed.

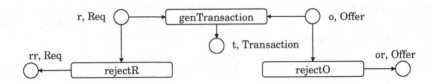

Rules

genTransaction {sr: r.product == o.product and r.maxPrice >= o.minPrice.

post: t = new Transaction (.req == r, .offer == o)}

rejectR {sr: r.d elapsed} rejectO {sr: o.d elapsed}

Fig. 3. An example of complex path selection

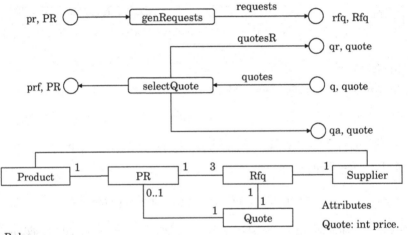

Rules

genRequests {post: requests = 3 new Rfq (.pr == pr, .supplier in pr.product.suppliers); requests.supplier distinct}

selectQuote {sr: quotes (3, same rfq.pr). post: qa = quotes.min(price); quotesR = quotes – qa; qa.pr == qa.rfq.pr; prf = qa.pr}

Fig. 4. An example of distribution pattern

Place q collects the events related to the quotes provided by suppliers; a quote is assumed to be linked to the rfq it is a reply to. Since task genRequests may be performed several times, the quotes may refer to requests originated from different purchase requisitions. For this reason, task selectQuote selects a group (quotes) related to the same pr (reached via the rfq associated with the quote). This group is divided into two parts: the winning quote (i.e., the one with the minimum price) is put in place qa (and is referred to as qa in the post-condition of the task) and the remaining quotes, collected in group quotesR, are put in place qr. Place qa contains the events related to the quotes accepted, and place qr those related to the quotes rejected. In addition, task selectQuote links the winning quote to the purchase requisition and signals its fulfillment with event prf. The payload of event prf is obtained from the implicit associative attribute pr of the winning quote (qa).

Task selectQuote and places q, qa and qr follow a distribution pattern: all these places have the same type, the task takes a group of events from input place q and distributes the related payloads to the other places.

4   Related Work

Various forms of integration between BPM and CEP have been proposed. One line of research is to enable business processes to handle complex events in addition to the basic ones. BEMN (Business Event Modeling Notation) [7] provides a graphical notation to build complex events out of basic ones on the basis of the event patterns defined in [8]. Such complex events can be introduced in BPMN models: for example, the event conjunction pattern can be used to make the execution of a task depend on the occurrence of all the events listed in the conjunction. The use of tailored service tasks is proposed in [9] in order to include event detectors in BPMN models. Such detectors examine input event streams and raise escalation events when conditions expressed in the EPL (Event Processing Language) of Esper (http://esper.codehaus.org/) are violated.

Another line of research addresses event-driven behavior and hence it focuses on how to handle the events and to express their effects. The starting point is usually provided by ECA (Event Condition Action) rules [10], which were originally introduced to add dynamic aspects to database systems. ECA rules can be combined so as to give rise to full-fledged business processes [11], but their major drawback is the lack of a graphical representation. The action of an ECA rule may be the generation of an event that will trigger another ECA rule: a complex reaction path can then be built through the combination of simple rules. A notation for such reaction paths is illustrated in [12], where a process in charge of responding to order delays is presented as a combination of sense and responds rules. Ad hoc processes in the health care domain are addressed in [13], where the actors interact through request events and reply ones.

It is common opinion that BPM and rule languages, since both are aimed at defining organizational policies, have several contact points that are not yet fully understood [14]. Rules can be associated with events (e.g. ECA rules) but, in general, they can be used to define a number of conditions and constraints: in [15], 16 types of business rules are presented. In declarative business process languages such as ConDec [16], the precedence relationships between tasks are defined through rules with the purpose of improving the flexibility of the processes.

Chant addresses the situations in which precedence relationships between tasks are mediated by the data flow. An example shown in this paper is the mapping of several customer orders (each being the output of the execution of a task, say, accept customer order) to one supplier order. In this case, there is a precedence relationship between a number of instances of task accept customer order and one instance of task place supplier order. This relationship can be expressed by means of a selection rule associated with task place supplier order. Selection rules act on the payloads of the input events and for this reason the payloads need to be indicated in the process model. In general, rules are formulated not only on the basis of the specific business entities causing the input events (called primary business entities) but also on other business entities that are interrelated with the primary ones, and therefore an information model is needed. A similar approach to handling events related to business entities is called relation-based semantic correlation in [17].

In Chant, rules are expressed in an OCL-like notation to take advantage of the underlying information model. In alternative, textual representations based on SBVR (Semantics of Business Vocabulary and Business Rules, http://www.omg.org/spec/SBVR/1.0/) can be used so as to make them easier to read by non-technical users; transformations from OCL to SBVR and vice versa have been proposed (an example of the first is given in [18] and of the second in [19]).

5   Conclusion

This paper has presented an approach (called Chant) to business process modeling based on the integration of three components representing complementary viewpoints: the process model addressing tasks and events, the information model and the rule model. Events are explicitly represented in process models as the precedence relationships between tasks may be mediated by the payloads of events. Such payloads are business entities whose properties are described in the information model, which is the second component of the integrated model. The conditions of activation of the tasks and the intended effects of their execution are expressed with rules which may act on the payloads of the input events of the tasks as well as on other business entities on the basis of the relationships defined in the information model.

Current work is going on in two directions. One direction regards the construction and implementation of Chant models. As to the construction, a common repository is needed so as to maintain the links among the three components of Chant. The examples presented in this paper are concerned with automatic tasks and then the decisions to take and the effects to produce are described by rules to be performed automatically. Rules in Chant are written in an OCL-like notation and therefore they can be implemented in relational databases, as shown in several papers, e.g. [20]. However, Chant rules are event-driven in that they are triggered by events entering the input places of tasks and then they can take advantage of rule languages such as Esper (http://esper.codehaus.org/).

The second direction of development is about the architectural relationships between process models and rules. Seven scenarios have been illustrated in [21] and the current state of Chant lies in the third level, called Complex navigation and analysis. The next step is to use rules not only at the task level but also at the process level with the purpose of carrying out dynamic configurations. In addition, it is important to make the appropriate provisions in such a way as to enable designers to easily adapt the rules to the changes in business policies.

Acknowledgments. The author would like to thank the anonymous reviewers for their helpful comments. The work presented in this paper has been partly supported by MIUR under the PRIN 2008 project "Documentation and processes".

References

1. Ko, R.K.L.: A computer scientist's introductory guide to business process management (BPM). ACM Crossroads 15(4), 11–18 (2009)
2. Luckham, D.: The power of events: an introduction to complex event processing in distributed enterprise systems. Pearson Education Inc., Boston (2002)
3. von Ammon, R., Emmersberger, C., Ertlmaier, T., Etzion, O., Paulus, T., Springer, F.: Existing and future standards for event-driven business process management. In: 3rd ACM International Conference on Distributed Event-Based Systems, ACM Press, New York (2009)
4. Dumas, M., van der Aalst, W.M.P., ter Hofstede, A.H.M.: Process-Aware Information Systems: bridging people and software through process technology. Wiley, New York (2005)
5. De Roover, W., Vanthienen, J.: Unified Patterns to Transform Business Rules Into an Event Coordination Mechanism. In: zur Muehlen, M., Su, J. (eds.) BPM 2010 Workshops. LNBIP, vol. 66, pp. 730–742. Springer, Heidelberg (2011)
6. Murata, T.: Petri nets: properties, analysis and applications. Proc. of the IEEE 77(4), 541–580 (1989)
7. Decker, G., Grosskopf, A., Barros, A.: A graphical notation for modeling complex events in business processes. In: 11th IEEE International Enterprise Distributed Object Computing Conference. IEEE Computer Society, Los Alamitos (2007)
8. Barros, A., Decker, G., Grosskopf, A.: Complex Events in Business Processes. In: Abramowicz, W. (ed.) BIS 2007. LNCS, vol. 4439, pp. 29–40. Springer, Heidelberg (2007)
9. Kunz, S., Fickinger, T., Prescher, J., Spengler, K.: Managing Complex Event Processes with Business Process Modeling Notation. In: Mendling, J., Weidlich, M., Weske, M. (eds.) BPMN 2010. LNBIP, vol. 67, pp. 78–90. Springer, Heidelberg (2010)
10. Paton, N.W., Díaz, O.: Active database systems. ACM Computing Surveys 31(1), 63–103 (1999)
11. Bry, F., Eckert, M., Pătrânjan, P.-L., Romanenko, I.: Realizing Business Processes with ECA Rules: Benefits, Challenges, Limits. In: Alferes, J.J., Bailey, J., May, W., Schwertel, U. (eds.) PPSWR 2006. LNCS, vol. 4187, pp. 48–62. Springer, Heidelberg (2006)
12. Schiefer, J., Rozsnyai, S., Rauscher, C., Saurer, G.: Event-driven rules for sensing and responding to business situations. In: 1st ACM International Conference on Distributed Event-Based Systems, pp. 198–205. ACM Press, New York (2007)
13. Alexopoulou, N., Nikolaidou, M., Anagnostopoulos, D., Martakos, D.: An Event-Driven Modeling Approach for Dynamic Human-Intensive Business Processes. In: Rinderle-Ma, S., Sadiq, S., Leymann, F. (eds.) BPM 2009. LNBIP, vol. 43, pp. 393–404. Springer, Heidelberg (2010)

14. zur Muehlen, M., Indulska, M.: Modeling languages for business processes and business rules: a representational analysis. Information Systems 35, 379–390 (2010)
15. Goedertier, S., Haesen, R., Vanthienen, J.: Rule-based business process modelling and enactment. International Journal of Business Process Integration and Management 3(3), 194–207 (2008)
16. Pesic, M., van der Aalst, W.M.P.: A Declarative Approach for Flexible Business Processes Management. In: Eder, J., Dustdar, S. (eds.) BPM Workshops 2006. LNCS, vol. 4103, pp. 169–180. Springer, Heidelberg (2006)
17. Moser, T., Roth, H., Rozsnyai, S., Mordinyi, R., Biffl, S.: Semantic Event Correlation Using Ontologies. In: Meersman, R., Dillon, T., Herrero, P. (eds.) OTM 2009. LNCS, vol. 5871, pp. 1087–1094. Springer, Heidelberg (2009)
18. Cabot, J., Pau, R., Raventós, R.: From UML/OCL to SBVR specifications: a challenging transformation. Information Systems 35, 417–440 (2010)
19. Bajwa, I.S., Bordbar, B., Lee, M.G.: OCL constraints generation from natural language specification. In: 14th IEEE International Enterprise Distributed Object Computing Conference, pp. 204–213 (2010)
20. Demuth, B., Hussmann, H., Loecher, S.: OCL as a Specification Language for Business Rules in Database Applications. In: Gogolla, M., Kobryn, C. (eds.) UML 2001. LNCS, vol. 2185, pp. 104–117. Springer, Heidelberg (2001)
21. Koehler, J.: The process-rule continuum - How can the BPMN and SBVR standards interplay? Submitted for publication (2011)

Interval Logic for Design and Maintenance of Complex Event Processing Systems
(Short Paper)

Jean-René Coffi[1,2], Nicolas Museux[1], and Christophe Marsala[2]

[1] Thales Research and Technology,
1, Avenue Augustin Fresnel 91767 Palaiseau, France
[2] LIP6/UPMC,
4, Place Jussieu 75005 Paris, France

Abstract. We present in this paper logical tools for verification of Complex Event Processing (CEP) system at design time, and maintenance at runtime. Although the framework is general enough for most applications, we focus on its use in Business Process Management (BPM).

Keywords: Complex Event Processing, Interval Logic, Model Checking, Business Process Management.

1 Event Processing in Business Process Management

Event-Driven Architectures - in particular CEP - have become an increasingly popular field of study in various domains. From security systems to production chains, its expressive power - capacity to find correlations between structured objects given a certain context - make it an important tool to extract pertinent information from a cloud of data ([10], [6]).

In Business Process Management, CEP can either be used to analyze events coming from various process in real-time, or to start processes in a BPM after the analysis of external events. Many argue that the use of CEP coupled with business rules represents the future of process management ([9]). Although a lot is known about business rules design and management, the lack of a unified logic for the description of an event-based system limits the possibility to reason about them and predict their behavior beforehand. Anicic proposed an interval logic-based language with backward decomposition which provides efficient tools for data-driven reasoning about complex situations ([2]). Our approach extends the runtime reasoning to *a-priori* verification of a system. Aiming to improve robustness our focus is the detection of inconsistencies in a set of rules.

In this context, independently of the language, timing of events and conditions of rules' satisfaction are primordial. The main concepts in our work are interval based event detection and rule decomposition into subgoals. If a subgoal is unreachable, the rule will never be activated. The method also allows to check for inconsistencies in successive rules and verify at runtime if a rule is still actionable. In the final part of this paper we show our frameworks in the

F. Daniel et al. (Eds.): BPM 2011 Workshops, Part I, LNBIP 99, pp. 407–413, 2012.

field of infrastructures' security and how it can be extend to business process management.

2 Verification of a CEP System

2.1 System Formalization

When describing an event driven system S with reactive rules of type *pattern-conditions-actions*, a few key concepts are necessary.

The ontology of event types where the topmost class describing all event types is represented by the set $\hat{\mathcal{E}}$. Each subclass of the ontology is a subset of $\hat{\mathcal{E}}$. The event class e is denoted with a $\hat{e}$. We can differentiate *virtual event (v-event)*, used to describe a pattern in a rule and therefore have no attribute values yet - denoted $\dot{e}$ and belonging to a set $\dot{\mathcal{E}}$; from *actual event (a-event)* which are records of a particular activity at a particular time - denoted as a small character (e) and belonging to a set $\mathcal{E}$.

An a-event e is a *specification* of a v-event $\dot{e}$ iff the type of e is a subtype of the type of $\dot{e}$: $\forall \hat{e} \in \mathcal{E}, \forall \dot{e} \in \dot{\mathcal{E}}$, $e \sqsubseteq \dot{e} \leftrightarrow \hat{e} \subseteq \hat{\dot{e}}$. If $\hat{e} = \hat{\dot{e}}$, then e is an exact specification of $\dot{e}$, noted $e \doteq \dot{e}$.

In its most basic form, an event has basic attributes: an identifier, a date of occurrence of the instance, the set of events that lead to the creation of that instance (empty if it's a simple event). Those attributes are used for event filtering, but can also be associated with rule operators as we will see later.

To construct CEP rule, the events' classes are connected by operators to form the patterns we expect to be detected. Most operators are specializations of logical conjunctions and disjunctions, and they can be of any arity.

A problem in the literature is that each CEP language has its own set of operators. Among the most frequent, the *sequence, absence, causality, independence* (in terms of cause), *periodicity* or *aperiodicity, re-occurrence, mutual exclusion, ...* Those operators can be defined either in terms of time of occurrence of the events - absolute, or relative to other events - (*sequence*) or in terms of constraints on the values of the attributes, (*causality*).

We denote $\mathcal{O}$ the set of operators used in a system S and $\forall o^k \in \mathcal{O}$, k is the arity of o and $k \geq 1$.

A CEP rule $\mathcal{R}$ in a system S, is a triplet in $\mathcal{M} \times \mathcal{C} \times \mathcal{A}$ such that: $\mathcal{R}(m, c, a) = (m \wedge c \vdash a)$, where $\mathcal{M}$ is the set of all patterns that can be defined with event types $\hat{\mathcal{E}}$ and operators $\mathcal{O}$, $\mathcal{C}$ are the contextual conditions in which the rules can be valid and $\mathcal{A}$ is the set of all possible actions.

The lifetime of S is $\mathcal{D} = [t_0, t_\infty]$, where t_0 is the system's starting time and t_∞ its stopping time. We denote t^* the current time. A pattern m is framed by the first $(\overleftarrow{m})$ and last $(\overrightarrow{m})$ dates of the events occurring in the pattern and $\forall m \in \mathcal{M}, [\overleftarrow{m}, \overrightarrow{m}] \subset \mathcal{D}$.

2.2 Rule Satisfaction/Unsatisfaction

The consistency checking protocol is inspired by elements from *Model Checking* ([5]) and *Interval Temporal Logic* ([12]).

Model Checking is a technique for automatic verification of finite state reactive systems such as sequential circuits design and communication protocols. We propose here a framework in which a user can check the validity of a CEP model, given a specification. The first step to checking a system is to verify the validity of the local conditions composing a rule, if the conjonction of all local conditions is satisfiable then the overall rule will be satisfiable as well.

We consider the local conditions of a rule (subgoals) to be the satisfaction of elementary patterns on intervals and of constraints. We introduce a set of functions to evaluate the satisfiability of an elementary pattern. Then we discuss how composed patterns of a rule can be transformed into subgoals.

The first two predicates verify if an elementary pattern is satisfied or not:

Definition 1 (Satisfaction of an elementary pattern). *An elementary pattern $\dot{e}$ is satisfied on a date interval I iff there is an a-event e specifying $\dot{e}$ with a date in I: $S : \dot{\mathcal{E}} \times \mathcal{D} \longmapsto \{T, F\}$, is true (T) if the pattern is satisfied on I and false (F) otherwise: $S(\dot{e}, I) \equiv \exists e \in \mathcal{E}, (e \sqsubseteq \dot{e}) \wedge (e.date \in I)$*

Definition 2 (Non-satisfaction of an elementary pattern). *An elementary pattern $\dot{e}$ is unsatisfiable on a date interval I iff there is no a-event e specifying $\dot{e}$ with a date in I and the date interval is over (we are sure the pattern will never be satisfied anymore): $NS : \dot{\mathcal{E}} \times \mathcal{D} \longmapsto \{T, F\}$, is true (T) if the pattern is unsatisfiable and false (F) otherwise: $NS(\dot{e}, I) \equiv \forall e \in \mathcal{E}, (e \not\sqsubseteq \dot{e} \vee e.date \notin I) \wedge (t^* > \sup(I))$*

The truth value of those two functions will be used to evaluate the state of an elementary pattern. When both $S(\dot{e}, I)$ and $NS(\dot{e}, I)$ are *false* the state of the elementary pattern is unknown and takes the truth value U. Furthermore $S(\dot{e}, I)$ and $NS(\dot{e}, I)$ cannot both be *true* at the same time. So when the first is *true* (and therefore the second is automatically *false*) the elementary pattern is satisfiable, when the second is *true* (and therefore the first is *false*) the elementary pattern is unsatisfiable. This can be resumed as follows:

Theorem 1 (Evaluation of elementary patterns). *We call $\mathcal{T} : \dot{\mathcal{E}} \times \mathcal{D} \longmapsto \{T, F, U\}$ the evaluation function of a pattern and:*
$\mathcal{T}(\dot{e}, I) = S(\dot{e}, I) \vee (\overline{NS(\dot{e}, I)} \wedge U)$, assuming the trivalent logic rules[1].

We noted before that most CEP operators can be though of in terms of events' time of occurrence or in terms of constraints on events' attributes. A pattern $m \in \mathcal{M}$, composed of multiple events connected with operators, is satisfied if the expected events occur at the right time and some constraints on the attributes are respected, consistently with the semantic of each operators used in the pattern. If we call $\dot{\mathcal{E}}_m$ the set of v-events appearing in the pattern m then:
$$\forall m \in \mathcal{M}, \forall I \subset \mathcal{D}, \mathcal{T}(m, I) \equiv \bigwedge_n (\mathcal{T}(\dot{e}_n, I_{e_n})) \bigwedge_{i,j} (C_j^{o_i^k})$$

where $\dot{e}_n \in \dot{\mathcal{E}}_m$, $I_{e_n} \subseteq \mathcal{D}$ and $C_j^{o_i^k}$ is the jth content based constraint of the ith operator of the pattern.

---

[1] $T \wedge U \Rightarrow U, \quad T \vee U \Rightarrow T, \quad F \wedge U \Rightarrow F, \quad F \vee U \Rightarrow U, \quad \overline{U} \Leftrightarrow U$

The first step in the verification of a rule consists therefore in evaluating the truth value of each individual events on inferred intervals and the content constraints introduced by the operators.

2.3   Explorable Paths

The second step is to verify that all paths, leading to a conclusion, are achievable. We propose to verify that by checking that the interval on which an event is expected is compatible with the interval on which it is created.

The link between a rule generating an event and a rule expecting an event of a sup-type will be made with the evaluation function $\mathcal{T}(.,.)$ and a new function of event generation $\mathcal{G}(.,.)$.

Definition 3 (Event generation). *The boolean function $\mathcal{G}(e, I)$, indicates if an actual instance $e \in \mathcal{E}$ is generated on interval $I \subseteq \mathcal{D}$. For simple events $I = \mathcal{D}$.*

We remind that, a CEP rule $\mathcal{R}$ in a system $\mathcal{S}$, is a triplet in $\mathcal{M} \times \mathcal{C} \times \mathcal{A}$ such that $\mathcal{R}(m, c, a) = (m \wedge c \vdash a)$. If a is the generation of a complex event ec and m has been decomposed into the evaluation of subgoals (elementary patterns $\dot{e}_i \in \dot{\mathcal{E}}_m$ and constraints $C_j^{o_i^k}$), there are two possible situations:

- the rule is satisfied or still undecided. The complex event can be generated at the earliest when the last event can be evaluated, $\max_{e_i}(\inf(I_{e_i}))$, and at the latest when the last event is no longer expected, $\max_{e_i}(\sup(I_{e_i}))$:
$$\bigwedge_n(\mathcal{T}(\dot{e_n}, I_{\dot{e_n}})) \bigwedge_{i,j}(C_j^{o_i^k}) \Rightarrow \mathcal{G}(ec, [\max_{\dot{e}_i}(\inf(I_{\dot{e}_i})), \max_{\dot{e}_i}(\sup(I_{\dot{e}_i}))])$$
- the rule is unsatisfiable. The complex event can never be generated on $\mathcal{D}$:
$$\overline{\bigwedge_n(\mathcal{T}(\dot{e_n}, I_{\dot{e_n}}))} \vee (\bigwedge_{i,j}(C_j^{o_i^k})) \Rightarrow \mathcal{G}(ec, \emptyset)$$

After determining the expected intervals of events' generation and the intervals of expected events' by decomposition, we need to check if the successions of rules in the system are consistent. It is done by verifying that, for all consumers of an event type, there is at least one producer of the same event on compatible intervals. Conversely, we can verify that no resource is lost by checking if all produced events have a compatible consumer.

Proposition 1 (Consistency Check of $\mathcal{S}$). *A CEP system $\mathcal{S}$ is said to be consistent if all paths of the system are achievable and if they all lead to a used information (command action, alert, etc.)*

Let $\mathcal{F}$ the function which for a given virtual events returns the intervals on which it is expected and $\mathcal{G}$ th event generation function.

$\mathcal{F} : \dot{\mathcal{E}} \longmapsto \mathcal{P}(\mathcal{D})/\mathcal{F}(\dot{e}) = I$, *if $\dot{e}$ is expected on I.*
$\mathcal{G} : \mathcal{E} \times I \longmapsto \{true, false\}/\mathcal{G}(e, I) = true$, *if e can be generated on I.*
Now, for the system to be coherent, I and $\mathcal{F}(\dot{e})$ must be compatible:

$$\forall \dot{e}, \forall I' \in \mathcal{F}(\dot{e}), \mathcal{T}(\dot{e}, I') \Rightarrow \exists e, \exists I, e \sqsubseteq \dot{e} \wedge \mathcal{G}(e, I) \wedge I \cap I' \neq \emptyset \tag{1}$$

This ensures that for all expected events, there is an event that can be generated on the same interval. To ensure that every generated event is consumed, the same thing can be done be defining a function F' that does the same for e.

2.4   Runtime Satisfiability

A particularity of our non-satisfaction function (NS) is that it takes into account the current time of the system. For some patterns, such as the ones verifying the *absence* of events, the upper bound of the interval is t_∞ therefore the function can still be verified at design time. For other patterns, the moment t^* is higher than the upper bound at runtime, we know it is no longer satisfiable and a particular thread can be aborted. This will significantly increase the efficiency of the whole system by not having half-verified patterns waiting indefinitely for an event and using processing time.

2.5   Example

Let's consider three operators - one verifying the *absence* of an event, one verifying a *sequence* between two events and the time window - defined as follows:

- sequence: $\forall m, m' \in \mathcal{M}, m \gg m' \equiv$
  $(\mathcal{T}(m, \mathcal{D}) \wedge \mathcal{T}(m', [\overrightarrow{m}, t_\infty])) \vee (\mathcal{T}(m', \mathcal{D}) \wedge \mathcal{T}(m, [t_0, \overrightarrow{m'}]))$
- absence: $\forall m \in \mathcal{M}, \neg m \equiv \overline{\mathcal{T}(m, \mathcal{D})}$
- time frame: $\forall m \in \mathcal{M}, \delta \in I\!N, m : \delta \equiv \mathcal{T}(m, [\overline{m}, \overline{m} + \delta[)$

And the scenario where when a video-camera is not functioning and a maintenance staff is available, a reparation procedure is launched. The malfunction of a video-camera is detected in two ways: *camera one* does not send a signal $(\neg signalDetected[cam1])$ or *camera two* sends a signal that *camera one* did not detect before $((\neg signalDetected[cam1] \gg signalDetected[cam2])$.

According to our definition of an *absence* the first rule will never generate a malfunction event and the reparation will never occur, whereas the second rule is limited by the signal sent by *camera two* therefore the malfunction event may be detected. If the time frame were absolute, instead of relative to another event, we might have even been able to tell when not to expect a malfunction anymore.

The same principle can be applied to business processes, where concepts like events' and operators' hierarchies, events' *start* and *end time* or operators structures are important.

Let's consider, for example, the simple scenario involving a group of three simple events - *order placed, money send, order received* - has seen in [4], and two complex events - *sendReminder* and *contactSupplier*. First a rule is used for reminding the customer that a payement is due:
$(orderPlaced \gg \neg moneySend[id = orderPlaced.id) \rightarrow sendReminder$. If an order is placed and no money has been sent by the customer for that order, a reminder is sent. The rule is invalid since the absence of payment is bounded by t_∞. Introducing a time window fixes the problem has show in the second rule: if an order hasn't been delivered in three days, the supplier must be contacted. $(orderPlaced \gg \neg orderReceived[id = orderPlaced.id) : 3days)$ $\rightarrow contactSupplier$. The rule is valid since the *orderReceived* event will not be waited on indefinitely. The verification can be made on large sets of rules, thus improving the efficiency of business processes that use CEP.

3   Related Works

Many event rule languages exist in the literature, varying in types of operators, representation of events and implementation of the rule engine. COMPOSE [8], for example, uses finite state automata where each event is associated with an automaton which reaches the accepted state exactly when the event appears. SAMOS [7] on the other hand combines Active Objects and object oriented programming; complex events are detected using a Petri's net. SNOOP([1]) defines a language to express conditions based on events in an object oriented structure. This diversity may impose limits on our method. However, if an operator can be expressed in terms of intervals and conditions, any rule using it can be verified.

In BPM more data-oriented tools are used ([11], [3]). In this particular context the management and monitoring of large set of rules has become crtitical, some methodologies were proposed ([14], [13]) using a semantic representation of complex patterns.

4   Conclusion

We present a logical framework for complex event systems conception and management based on concepts of interval logic and model checking. We also show how it can be applied to event-driven business process management, although more practical experiments are needed at this point. The main steps in our coherence checking method are the satisfiability of isolated rules, and the verification of *rule paths*. The full implications and possibilities of this representation of rule-based event architectures have not been thoroughly researched yet, although we can anticipate many applications such as system monitoring, unavailable event sources' detection or machine learning for valid rules' generation.

References

1. Adaikkalavan, R., Chakravarthy, S.: Snoopib: interval-based event specification and detection for active databases. Data Knowl. Eng. 59(1), 139–165 (2006)
2. Anicic, D., Fodor, P., Stuhmer, R., Stojanovic, N.: An efficient logic-based complex event processing and reactivity handling. In: International Conference on Distributed Event-based Systems, DEBS (2009)
3. Barnickel, N., Böttcher, J., Paschke, A.: Incorporating semantic bridges into information flow of cross-organizational business process models. In: I-SEMANTICS (2010)
4. Chen, S.-K., Jeng, J.-J., Chang, H.: Complex event processing using simple rule-based event correlation engines for business performance management. In: Proceedings of the The 8th IEEE International Conference on E-Commerce Technology. IEEE Computer Society (2006)
5. Clarke, E.M., Grumberg, O., Long, D.E.: Model checking and abstraction. ACM Transactions on Programming Languages and Systems 16(5), 1512–1542 (1994)
6. Etzion, O., Niblett, P.: Event Processing in Action. Manning (2010)

7. Gatziu, S., Dittrich, K.R.: Samos: an active object–oriented database system. In: IEEE Bulletin of the TC on Data Engineering (1992)
8. Gehani, N.H., Jagadish, H.V., Shmueli, O.: Event specification in an active object-oriented database. SIGMOD Rec. 21(2), 81–90 (1992)
9. Knolmayer, G., Endl, R., Pfahrer, M.: Modeling Processes and Workflows by Business Rules. In: van der Aalst, W.M.P., Desel, J., Oberweis, A. (eds.) Business Process Management. LNCS, vol. 1806, pp. 16–29. Springer, Heidelberg (2000)
10. Luckham, D.: The Power Of Events. Addison-Wesley (2002)
11. Markovic, I., Jain, S., El-Gayyar, M., Cremers, A.B., Stojanovic, N.: Modeling and Enforcement of Business Policies on Process Models with Maestro. In: Aroyo, L., Traverso, P., Ciravegna, F., Cimiano, P., Heath, T., Hyvönen, E., Mizoguchi, R., Oren, E., Sabou, M., Simperl, E. (eds.) ESWC 2009. LNCS, vol. 5554, pp. 873–877. Springer, Heidelberg (2009)
12. Moszkowski, B., Manna, Z.: Reasonning in interval temporal logic. In: Proceedings of the Carnegie Mellon Workshop on Logic of Programs, pp. 371–382 (1984)
13. Museux, N., Papillon, S., Contat, M.: Managing huge set of complex event processing rules for critical infrastructure protection: An ontology based instrumentation approach. In: Cognitive Systems with Interactive Sensors, Cogis 2009 (2009)
14. Sen, S., Stojanovic, N.: GRUVe: A Methodology for Complex Event Pattern Life Cycle Management. In: Pernici, B. (ed.) CAiSE 2010. LNCS, vol. 6051, pp. 209–223. Springer, Heidelberg (2010)

Event-Driven Exception Handling
for Software Engineering Processes

Gregor Grambow[1], Roy Oberhauser[1], and Manfred Reichert[2]

[1] Computer Science Dept., Aalen University
{gregor.grambow,roy.oberhauser}@htw-aalen.de
[2]Institute for Databases and Information Systems, Ulm University, Germany
manfred.reichert@uni-ulm.de

Abstract. In software development projects, process execution typically lacks automated guidance and support, and process models remain rather abstract. The environment is sufficiently dynamic that unforeseen situations can occur due to various events that lead to potential aberrations and process governance issues. To alleviate this problem, a dynamic exception handling approach for software engineering processes is presented that incorporates event detection and processing facilities and semantic classification capabilities with a dynamic process-aware information system. A scenario is used to illustrate how this approach supports exception handling with different levels of available contextual knowledge in concordance with software engineering environment relations to the development process and the inherent dynamicity of such relations.

Keywords: Complex event processing; semantic processing; event-driven business processes; process-aware information systems; process-centered software engineering environments.

1 Introduction

The development of software is a very dynamic and highly intellectual process that strongly depends on a variety of environmental factors as well as individuals and their effective collaboration. In contrast to industrial production processes that are highly repetitive and more predictable, software engineering processes have hitherto hardly been considered for automation. Existing software engineering (SE) process models like VM-XT [1] or the open Unified Process [2] are rather abstract (of necessity for greater applicability) and thus do not really reach the executing persons at the operational level [3]. In sparsely governed processes without automated data assimilation and process extraction, deviations from the planned process, exceptions, or even errors often remain undetected. Even if detected, an automated and effective exception handling is hard to find.

To increase the level of standardization (i.e., usage, repeatability, conformance, etc.) of process execution, automated support for SE processes is desirable. To enable this in a holistic way, an automated solution should be capable of some kind of

F. Daniel et al. (Eds.): BPM 2011 Workshops, Part I, LNBIP 99, pp. 414–426, 2012.
© Springer-Verlag Berlin Heidelberg 2012

process exception handling so that the occurrence of exceptions does not deteriorate process performance. Further, automated process exception support will only be acceptable if it is not too complex or more cumbersome than manual handling [4]. Automated handling implies automated detection of exceptions that depends on the capabilities of the system managing the processes [5]. However, existing process-aware information systems (PAIS) are still rather limited regarding detection and handling of exceptions [6]. Exceptions can arise for reasons such as constraint violations, deadline expiration, activity failures, or discrepancies between the real world and the modeled process [7]. Especially in the highly dynamic SE process domain, exceptions can arise from various sources, and it can be difficult to distinguish between anticipated and unanticipated exceptions. Even if they are detected, it can be difficult to directly correlate them to a simple exception handler. Due to its high dynamicity, SE has been selected as first application domain, but the generic concept can also be applied to other domains.

Two fictional scenarios from the SE domain illustrate the issues:

- Scenario 1 (Bug fixing): In applying a bug fix to a source code file, the removal of a known defect might unintentionally introduce other problems to that file. E.g., source code complexity might increase if multiple people applied "quick and dirty" fixes. Thus, the understandability and maintainability of that file might drop dramatically and raise the probability of further defects.
- Scenario 2 (Process deviation): In developing new software, the process prescribes the development and execution of a unit test to aid the quality of the produced code. For various reasons, the developer omits these activities and integrates the produced code into the system. This could eventually negatively affect the quality of that system.

These scenarios demonstrate the various challenges an automated process exception handling approach for SE faces: Exceptions can arise relating to various items such as activities, artifacts, or the process itself. Many of these exceptions may be difficult to detect, especially for a PAIS without direct knowledge of the environment. It may also be unclear when exactly to handle the exception and who should be responsible. Generally, the knowledge about the exception can vary greatly, making unified handling difficult and the application of standardized exception handlers unsuitable. Both of the aforementioned scenarios will be used to show the applicability of our approach to SE processes and their exception handling.

The remainder of this paper is organized as follows: Section 2 introduces the novel exception handling approach, followed by Section 3 showing its technical realization. An application scenario is presented in Section 4 and related work is discussed in Section 5. Finally, Section 6 presents the conclusion.

2   Flexible Exception Handling

To respond to the special properties of dynamic SE process execution, this paper proposes an advanced process exception handling approach. It is grounded on two properties: the ability to automatically gather contextual information utilizing special sensors and complex event processing; and second, an enhanced flexibility in the handling of the exceptions is achieved by the separation of different concerns regarding exception handling. These concerns include the determination of the responsible person or concrete insertion of counter measures into the process.

Our approach can be roughly understood as an extended flexible variant of ECA (Event-Condition-Action) [8]. The three phases are called *Recognition, Processing,* and *Action* here, as illustrated in Fig. 2. The steps involved in the phases of this approach rely on the following component definitions:

Event: *Event* is used to capture a multitude of possible events that may occur during an SE project. These include, but are not limited to, events that can be related to various exceptions. Examples include the saving of a source code artifact in an integrated development environment (IDE) or the execution of a static source code analysis tool that provides certain metrics. These metrics can be indicative of an arising problem and thus lead to an exception.

Exception: The notion of *Exception* is utilized to classify a deviation from the planned procedure that was recognized to have a potential negative impact on the process and thus should be dealt with to avoid such an impact. In literature [9], typically there is a distinction between anticipated exceptions, whose occurrence can be easily foreseen, and unanticipated exceptions. For anticipated exceptions, standard exception handlers can be defined. That is usually not possible for the unanticipated ones. Since SE projects typically feature a very dynamic process and it may be difficult so foresee a multitude of possible exceptions, our approach does not discriminate between anticipated and unanticipated exceptions. It also does not use standard exception handlers tied to specific exceptions. Flexibility is improved through the explicit separation of events, exceptions, handling of the exceptions, responsible persons, and the point in the process where a handling is invoked. Thus, occurring events can be classified and it can be separately determined whether exceptions shall be raised, what to do with them, when to do it, and who shall do that. Additionally, the approach manages different levels of knowledge about occurring events. Depending on that level of event knowledge, it can be decided whether a more generic exception shall be raised or rather a specialized one. Fig. 1 exemplifies different hierarchically structured exceptions belonging to three defined exception categories.

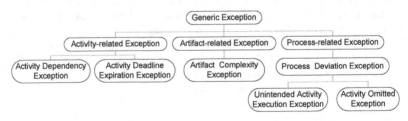

Fig. 1. Exception hierarchy extract

As stated in [7], anticipated exceptions occurring during the execution of pre-specified workflows include the following categories: activity failures, deadline expiration, resource unavailability, discrepancies (between a real-world process and its computerized counterpart), and constraint violations. These can be covered by the exception types *Activity-related Exception, Artifact-related Exception,* and *Process-related Exception* depicted in Fig. 1. Consider Scenario 1 from the introduction: the code complexity of a source code artifact is very high and was introduced by some activity. The problem may be detected much later and relate more to the artifact than to the activity in that case. Furthermore, the appropriate person to deal with the problem could be the one responsible for the entire artifact rather than the last person who worked on it.

Handling: The notion of *Handling* is used to describe activities executed as countermeasures for a triggered exception. Since SE exceptions are usually complex and of semantic nature, no simple rollback of the activities that caused the exception can be done. As an example, consider the activity of bug fixing (Scenario 1): While fixing a bug, this activity can also introduce additional problems to the code such as increased code complexity. This can happen when the person applying the bug fix is not the one responsible for the processed artifact. As a countermeasure, an explicit refactoring can become necessary. *Handling* neither comprises the person to execute these activities nor the time or point in the process where they are to be executed.

Responsible: *Responsible* captures the responsible person for a *Handling*. As in Scenario 1, this can be the one who executed an activity introducing the exception or the one responsible for an artifact related to an exception.

Target: *Target* is the point in the process where the *Handling* is executed. For certain exceptions, it can be suitable to integrate *Handling* directly into the workflow where the exception occurred whereas in other cases a separate exception handling workflow has to be executed.

The procedure is illustrated in Fig. 2 and described in the following phases and steps.

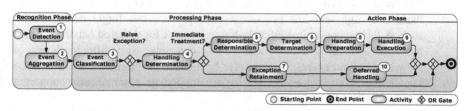

Fig. 2. Abstract Exception Handling Concept

Recognition Phase: In this phase, low and high level events are gathered from the environment in the following steps:

1. **Event Detection**: To enable automated assistance for exception handling, the detection of events related to exceptions must be automated. In a SE project, these events relate to processed activities and artifacts and thus also to supporting tools. Our exception handling approach utilizes a set of sensors that enable gathering of event information from various tools.

2. **Event Aggregation:** Automatically recognized events relating to the tools in an SE project provide information about currently executed activities. Nevertheless, these events are often of rather atomic nature (like saving file) and provide no information about the complex activity a person is processing. Therefore, these atomic events need to be processed and aggregated to derive higher-level events of more semantic value (like the application of a bug fix).

Processing Phase: In this phase, all necessary parameters for the exception handling are determined using the following steps:

3. **Event Classification:** Event classification can be used to gain more knowledge about the event to be able to find a specific handling later. For example, if a static analysis tool detects deterioration in the quality of a source code artifact, it can be classified as to what kind of source code artifact it relates, e.g., an artifact that constitutes an interface of a component or a test code artifact. In order to effectively automatically the usage of the detected events, they must also be related to the current project. The current focus of the project should be considered, like the defined quality goals that can be important in various situations (the modeling of these for use with automated support has been shown in [10].) For example, if a static analysis tool detects a rise in code complexity of certain source code artifacts, and performance is very important for that project this may be no special event. However, it may be an important event if, for example, the most important quality goals are maintainability or reliability. These factors can be incorporated when deciding whether an exception shall be raised according to an event.

4. **Handling Determination:** When an exception has occurred, it has to be decided when and how to take measures against it. This also depends on the current project situation. The situation can be classified using different parameters like risk or urgency (as shown in [11]). If urgency is high, meaning there is a high schedule pressure on the project, one might decide not to address the exception immediately but to retain it for deferred handling. Since our approach, using event classification, can cope with different levels of knowledge about events, it might also be decided to retain an exception if the knowledge about it does not suffice for immediate automatically supported handling.

5. **Responsible Determination:** If it is decided to take immediate action in case of an exception, the person responsible for that action has to be determined. There can be different possibilities: For example, if an exception relating to an activity occurred, the processor of that activity can be responsible or, if an exception occurred relating to an artifact, the responsible person for that artifact (or, e.g. source code package) can be also responsible for handling the exception. There may not be a direct responsible for each processed artifact, but responsibilities can be hierarchically structured to simplify determination of the responsible party (as described in [12]).

6. **Target Determination:** When the responsible party for handling the exception is determined, the concrete point in the process has to be determined where the handling is applied. As in Scenario 1, if a person introduced an exception while performing an activity and the respective workflow is still running, it can be feasible to directly integrate the handling into that workflow. In other cases, a new workflow for the same or another person can be started.

7. **Exception Retainment:** If, due to various parameters of the situation, no immediate handling is favored, the exception is retained in a special exception container. That container can be analyzed, e.g., at the end of an iteration by the project manager.

Action Phase: In this phase the concrete execution of the selected exception handling is done via the following steps:

8. **Handling Preparation:** After all parameters for the handling of an exception are determined, the concrete handling has to be prepared, i.e., a new workflow instance has to be created or the handling has to be integrated seamlessly into a running workflow instance.

9. **Handling Execution:** Finally, the prescribed handling is executed by the chosen person.

10. **Deferred Handling:** When exceptions are retained, a human can decide for which exceptions a deferred handling is preferred. Therefore, an additional GUI will be developed presenting a list of retained exceptions and enabling manual determination of a handling or discarding of the exception.

3   Proof-of-Concept Implementation

The realization of the presented concept is based on our previously developed framework CoSEEEK (Context-aware Software Engineering Environment Event-driven Framework) [13]. The framework is intended to provide holistic support for the software development process and this paper presents the newly added exception handling approach on the process level. The framework features a loosely coupled event-driven architecture incorporating various modules. The modules relevant to this new approach will now be described briefly.

Event Detection: This module builds upon the Hackystat framework [14], which provides a rich set of SE tool sensors, to enable the automatic detection of various SE events. Examples of these tools are IDEs or version control systems.

Event Processing: Complex Event Processing (CEP) is applied in this module utilizing the tool esper [15]. Thus, basic events like saving a file can be consolidated into higher-level events like bug fixing.

Context Management: The *Context Management* module incorporates various types of information concerning users, activities and processes, and aggregated events. It manages the connection between the project context and the workflows and is responsible for determination of the exceptions as well as the handlings to be applied.

Information is managed via semantic web technology: an OWL-DL ontology [16] serves as an information store, while Pellet [17] is used for logical reasoning. Additionally, Pellet executes rules written in the semantic web rule language (SWRL) [18]. Note that the execution of SWRL rules does not endanger the decidability of the OWL-DL ontology in this case, since Pellet supports DL-safe rules execution [19]. For programmatic access to the ontology, the Jena framework [20] is used.

Process Management: The responsibilities of this module, in view of this scenario, include not only guarantees for correct process execution and reliability, but also adaptability of running workflows to be able to integrate contemporaneous measures for triggered exceptions. Therefore, AristaFlow [21] was chosen since it supports dynamic adaptations of running workflow instances. Further information on correctness guarantees, adaptation facilities, and other features can be found in [21]. For CoSEEEK to automatically govern workflow execution, and to connect this with contextual facts and apply automated workflow adaptations, the workflows have been contextually annotated in the ontology. This is illustrated in Fig. 3. The concept of the *Work Unit* maps an activity in process management and the *Work Unit Container* maps a workflow in process management.

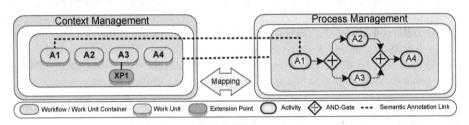

Fig. 3. Contextual process annotations

In the following, the realization of the process illustrated in Fig. 2 shall be briefly described. The process can be initiated by various events detected from tools or triggered by users. These events are aggregated using predefined CEP patterns and then received by the *Context Management* module. Therein, the reasoner further classifies the events as exemplified in the following:

$$SourceCodeEvent \equiv Event$$
$$(\wedge \exists relatedTo \Pr ojectComponent(SourceCodeArtifact)$$
$$\vee \exists relatedToTool(IDE \vee StaticAnalysis))$$

In the given example, a source code event constitutes an event that is related either to a source code file, an IDE, or a static analysis tool. After classification of the event, it is decided if an exception shall be raised due to the event. This is done by SWRL rules and exemplified in the following:

$$SourceCodeComplexityEvent(EventSCE)$$
$$\wedge hasGoal(currentProject, goalMaintainability)$$
$$\rightarrow raisesException(EventSCE, CodeComplexityException)$$

The example illustrates the raising of a 'Code Complexity Exception' if a 'Source Code Complexity' event occurs and one of the goals of the current project is maintainability. The creation of the individual exception in the ontology is done programmatically. Thereafter, it is determined with SWRL rules how this exception shall be handled. This decision can incorporate situational properties. In the aforementioned example of the 'Source Code Complexity Exception', it can be decided to retain the exception, e.g., if 'Urgency' is very high in the current project (or phase or iteration). This will connect the exception to a list associated to the project (or phase or iteration) to be decided upon later by a human. If the situation allows immediate handling, that handling is connected to the exception and the responsible party is determined. This is done with SWRL rules and depends on the type of exception as described in Section 2. The last fact to determine is the concrete target where the handling is to be applied. This is realized by *Extension Points* that are illustrated in Fig. 3. Via *Extension Points*, certain *Work Units* can be defined that enable extending the process. The former have certain properties to distinguish which kinds of extensions are possible (like the application of exception handling - for another example of their use we refer to [22]). CoSEEEK automatically determines the next upcoming *Extension Point* and initiates automated integration into the running workflow as illustrated in Fig. 4.

The contextual extension of the process management concepts does impose additional configuration effort since workflows would have to be modeled as well as concepts in the ontology. However, this effort can be limited: The direct mappings of the process management concepts can be automatically generated. Future work will include the development of web based GUIs to model the other required concepts (e.g., *Extension Points*) and their connections in the ontology.

4   Application Scenario

This section illustrates the application of the approach by means of Scenario 2. In that scenario, new source code is developed and the respective developer omits prescribed testing activities. Fig. 4A shows an excerpt of a workflow governing these activities ('Implement Solution', 'Implement Developer Test', 'Run Developer Test', 'Integrate and Build') modeled in AristaFlow.

After implementing the solution, the developer directly integrates his source code. The steps the system executes to handle that deviation (according to Fig. 2) are explained in the following.

- **Event Detection**: The system detects that the user checks in certain artifacts by sensors in his IDE and the source control system.
- **Event Aggregation**: From the detected events, the system derives the activity 'Integrate and Build' for that user. Since this is not the next intended activity in the workflow, an 'Activity Omitted' event is created.
- **Event Classification**: That event is then contextually classified: the omitted activities relate to testing and thus the event is classified as a 'Testing Activity Omitted' event.

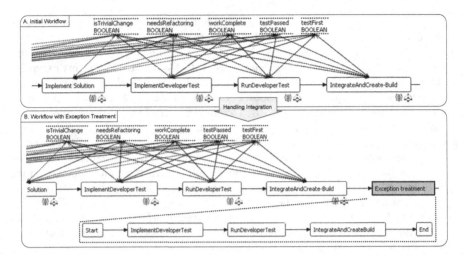

Fig. 4. Exception handling application

- **Handling Determination**: According to this event, an 'Activity Omitted Exception' is raised that includes information about the omitted activities and the executing person from the event.
- **Responsible Determination**: For this type of exception, the developer who omitted the activities is also responsible for the handling.
- **Target Determination**: In the given case, the workflow of the developer is still running. That means the respective *Work Unit* for the activity 'Integrate and Build' is still active. For that *Work Unit*, an *Extension Point* has been defined that can be used for handling extension integration. Thus, a direct integration into that workflow is chosen.
- **Handling Preparation**: Utilizing the dynamic capabilities of AristaFlow, the handling is integrated into the running workflow instance. This is done by the on-the-fly insertion of a new activity during runtime that is connected to a sub-workflow containing the handling as illustrated in Fig. 4B. Activity data dependencies are not shown for clarity and space reasons.

Technical aspects regarding performance and scalability for different components of the CoSEEEK framework have been previously evaluated in prior work [10][11][12].

5   Related Work

For automatically detecting exceptional situations and determining the actions (i.e., workflow adaptations) required to handle them, ECA-based (Event-Condition-Action) models have often been considered. Classically, many of these approaches limit adaptations to currently enabled and running activities (e.g., to abort, redo, or skip activity execution) [23]. One approach to enable automated adaptations of the unexecuted regions of a running workflow (e.g., to add or delete activities) is

AgentWork [24]. It allows process adaptations to be specified at an abstract level and independent from a particular process model based on a temporal ECA rule model. Temporal estimates are made when an ECA rule fires during run-time to determine which parts of a running process instance are affected by the identified exception. For these parts, two types of changes are possible: predictive and reactive change. Predictive changes are applied immediately whereas reactive changes are applied at the time the concerned process fragments are entered. Another modern approach to workflow adaptation is presented in [25]. It consists of a rule-based and data-driven approach to workflow adaptation. Therein, hierarchical context rules are utilized to tailor workflows to changing data-contexts. Additionally, for environments involving eventing paradigms, an event-driven adaptation pattern catalogue is also presented. An example for this is the context-dependent cancelation of a workflow segment and the triggering of a special handler task. These approaches are both event- and rule-based as is CoSEEEK. However, they cannot utilize the variety of contextual events since they lack the environmental sensors integrated via Hackystat. Furthermore, these approaches are rather rigid in the way exceptions are handled since events, conditions, and relating actions are statically connected. CoSEEEK not only separates exception treatment into additional refinement steps, including semantic classification, but also allows for flexible assignment of handlings based on various factors. That way, an appropriate handling can be found for various situations and different levels of knowledge about a situation. CoSEEEK also enables greater flexibility for the handling itself by adaptively combining what is to be done, who shall do it, and where / when it is to be applied.

Classical rule-based approaches concerning SE processes include MARVEL [26], OIKOS [27], or Merlin [28]. In MARVEL, rules are defined in its own language to enable forward and backward chaining. Thus, the system can request additional activities from a user executing an activity to satisfy the preconditions of the desired action. OIKOS features rules defined in Prolog that are utilized by agents. These cooperating agents operate in different workspaces and enable user cooperation. Merlin also processes different contexts that are assigned to roles. Between these contexts, artifacts are distributed to foster collaboration. As opposed to these approaches, CoSEEEK features the combination of an extended flexible rule-based approach with an advanced adaptive PAIS, semantic classification abilities, and sensors providing contextual information. Therefore, process execution is more robust and the discrepancies between the real world and the modeled process are minimized.

Exception handling could be accomplished utilizing only the PAIS. For example, most BPEL workflow engines support so-called fault handlers to enable some kind of exception handling, for instance [29]. However, these engines do not typically possess process adaptation abilities. While AristaFlow supports this capability and enables exception handling [30], yet in contrast to CoSEEEK the automatic exception handling abilities of these systems are rather limited because they lack both access to context information and semantic reasoning or classification capabilities.

6   Conclusion

SE is a very dynamic and yet immature domain and thus poses a significant challenge for process management. Process models are often abstract and document-centric and not directly utilized in process execution. Moreover, processes are dependent on a variety of environmental and contextual factors. Appropriate process automation could enhance quality and repeatability in SE to better connect the abstract processes with the operational level. However, such a process automation system must be able to accommodate these various aspects and be able to deal with a variety of unforeseen situations regarding process execution in order to provide real support and be relevant. This paper presents an extension to the CoSEEEK framework enabling a flexible exception handling approach incorporating diverse features to support the dynamic SE process:

- Exception occurrence detection is supported by a set of sensors gathering environment knowledge and by CEP that combines those events to derive higher-level events with more semantic value.
- Semantic web technology is integrated to enable classification of events based on various factors like the current situation or the goals of a project. The proposed approach can deal with different levels of knowledge concerning events and exceptions and thus does not require the separation between anticipated and unanticipated exceptions.
- The combination of environmental awareness with the semantic capabilities also enables the discovery of links between activities and exceptions that have no direct connection.
- The flexibility of the handling is enhanced by separating the determination of the handling, the responsible party, and the target of the handling.
- Featuring the dynamic adaptation capabilities of AristaFlow, exception handling is automatically and seamlessly integrated into users' running workflows.
- If, due to various reasons, a contemporaneous handling is not favorable, deferred handling and analysis of exceptions are also enabled.

Future work will include the industrial application to evaluate the suitability of the approach for real life projects and to refine and extend the modeling in alignment with industrial requirements. It is also planned to extend the deferred handling with exception grouping and exception filters to cope with very high exception load situations or repetitive exceptions. Finally, the application in other domains is also considered, as the approach itself is generic. Therefore, facilities to gather contextual information in these environments have to be developed or integrated.

Acknowledgement. This work was sponsored by BMBF (Federal Ministry of Education and Research) of the Federal Republic of Germany under Contract No. 17N4809.

References

1. Rausch, A., Bartelt, C., Ternité, T., Kuhrmann, M.: The V-Modell XT Applied - Model-Driven and Document-Centric Development. In: 3rd World Congress for Software Quality, vol. III, pp. 131–138 (2005) (online supplement)
2. OpenUP (May 2011), http://epf.eclipse.org/wikis/openup/
3. Wallmüller, E.: SPI-Software Process Improvement mit Cmmi und ISO 15504. Hanser Verlag (2007)

4. Ellis, C., Keddara, K., Rozenberg, G.: Dynamic change within workflow systems. In: Proc. ACM Conf. on Organizational Computing Systems (COOCS 1995), pp. 10–21 (1995)
5. Luo, Z., Sheth, A., Kochut, K., Miller, J.: Exception handling in workflow systems. Applied Intelligence 13(2), 125–147 (2000)
6. Russell, N., van der Aalst, W.M.P., ter Hofstede, A.H.M.: Workflow Exception Patterns. In: Martinez, F.H., Pohl, K. (eds.) CAiSE 2006. LNCS, vol. 4001, pp. 288–302. Springer, Heidelberg (2006)
7. Russell, N., ter Hofstede, A.H.M., Edmond, D., van der Aalst, W.M.P.: Workflow resource patterns. Tech. Rep. WP 127, Eindhoven Univ. of Technology (2004)
8. Paton, N. (ed.): Active Rules in Database Systems. Springer, Berlin (1999)
9. Reichert, M., Weber, B.: Enabling Flexibility in Process-aware Information Systems – Challenges, Methods, Technologies. Springer, Heidelberg (to appear)
10. Grambow, G., Oberhauser, R.: Towards Automated Context-Aware Selection of Software Quality Measures. In: Proc. 5th Intl. Conf. on SW Eng. Adv. IEEE CS (2010)
11. Grambow, G., Oberhauser, R., Reichert, M.: Semantic Workflow Adaption in Support of Workflow Diversity. In: Proc. 4th Int'l Conf. on Advances in Semantic Processing (2010)
12. Grambow, G., Oberhauser, R., Reichert, M.: Towards Automatic Process-Aware Coordination in Collaborative Software Engineering. In: Proc. of the 6th Int' Conf. on Software and Data Technologies (ICSOFT 2011). NSTICC Press (to appear, 2011)
13. Oberhauser, R.: Leveraging Semantic Web Computing for Context-Aware Software Engineering Environments. In: Wu, G. (ed.) Semantic Web, In-Tech, pp. 157–179 (2010)
14. Johnson, P.M.: Requirement and Design Trade-offs in Hackystat: An In-Process Software Engineering Measurement and Analysis System. In: Proc. of 1st Int. Symposium on Empirical Software Engineering and Measurement. IEEE Computer Society Press (2007)
15. Espertech Event Stream Intelligence, http://www.espertech.com/products/esper.php (retrieved April 2011)
16. World Wide Web Consortium, OWL Web Ontology Language Semantics and Abstract Syntax (2004) (retrieved April 2011)
17. Sirin, E., Parsia, B., Grau, B.C., Kalyanpur, A., Katz, Y.: Pellet: A practical OWL-DL Reasoner. Journal of Web Semantics (2006)
18. World Wide Web Consortium: SWRL: A Semantic Web Rule Language Combining OWL and RuleML W3C Member Submission (2004) (retrieved April 2011)
19. Motik, B., Sattler, U., Studer, R.: Query Answering for OWL-DL with Rules. In: McIlraith, S.A., Plexousakis, D., van Harmelen, F. (eds.) ISWC 2004. LNCS, vol. 3298, pp. 549–563. Springer, Heidelberg (2004)
20. McBride, B.: Jena: a semantic web toolkit. Internet Computing (2002)
21. Dadam, P., Reichert, M.: The ADEPT Project: A Decade of Research and Development for Robust and Flexible Process Support - Challenges and Achievements. Springer, Computer Science - Research and Development 23(2), 81–97 (2009)
22. Grambow, G., Oberhauser, R., Reichert, M.: Employing Semantically Driven Adaptation for Amalgamating Software Quality Assurance with Process Management. In: Proc. 2nd Int'l. Conf. on Adaptive and Self-adaptive Systems and Applications (2010)
23. Casati, F., Ceri, S., Paraboschi, S., Pozzi, G.: Specification and implementation of exceptions in workflow management systems. ACM TODS 24(3), 405–451 (1999)
24. Müller, R., Greiner, U., Rahm, E.: AGENTWORK: A workflow system supporting rule–based workflow adaptation. Data & Knowledge Engineering 51(2), 223–256 (2004)
25. Döhring, M., Zimmermann, B., Godehardt, E.: Extended Workflow Flexibility using Rule-Based Adaptation Patterns with Eventing Semantics. LNIP-175 (2010)

26. Barghouti, N.S.: Supporting cooperation in the marvel process-centered sde. In: Weber, H. (ed.) Fifth ACM SIGSOFT Symposium on Software Development Environments, Special issue of Software Engineering Notes, Tyson's Corner VA, vol. 17, pp. 21–31 (1992)

27. Montangero, C., Ambriola, V.: OIKOS: constructing process-centred SDEs. In: Finkelstein, A., Kramer, J., Nuseibeh, B. (eds.) Software Process Modelling and Technology. Research Studies Press Advanced Software Development Series, pp. 131–151. Research Studies Press Ltd., Taunton (1994)

28. Junkerman, G., Peuschel, B., Schäfer, W., Wolf, S.: Merlin: Supporting cooperation in software development through a knowledge-based environment. In: Software Process Modelling and Technology, ch. 5, pp. 103–130. Research Studies Press Ltd. (1994)

29. Kloppmann, M., Konig, D., Leymann, F., Pfau, G., Roller, D.: Business process choreography in websphere: Combining the power of BPEL and J2EE. IBM Systems Journal 43, 270–296 (2004)

30. Lanz, A., Reichert, M., Dadam, P.: Making Business Process Implementations Flexible and Robust: Error Handling in the AristaFlow BPM Suite. In: CAiSE 2010 Demos, Hammamet, Tunisia (2010)

eduFlow: An Event-Driven Ubiquitous Flow Management System

Jae-Yoon Jung, Pablo Rosales, Kyuhyup Oh, and Kyuri Kim

Department of Industrial and Management Engineering
Kyung Hee University, Republic of Korea
{jyjung,prosales,k8383,kimkyuli}@khu.ac.kr

Abstract. Ubiquitous technologies such as radio frequency identification (RFID) and wireless sensor network (WSN) have enabled companies to realize more rapid and agile manufacturing and service systems. In this paper, we design an event-driven ubiquitous process management system by using complex event processing technology for RFID and WSN. Such ubiquitous process management can be applied to manufacturing, logistics, and supply chain process. In particular, we focus on complex event processing of sensor and RFID events in order to integrate them to business rules of business process. The ubiquitous event processing helps to filter and aggregate ubiquitous events, to detect event patterns from sensors and RFID by means of event pattern languages (EPL), and trigger event-condition-action (ECA) rules in logistics processes.

Keywords: Ubiquitous complex event processing, ubiquitous business process management, event process language, RFID, wireless sensor network.

1 Introduction

Today's dynamic and competitive business environment urges companies to be transformed into real-time enterprises. The realization of enterprise-wide real-time monitoring and rapid decision making requires not only the network of information systems, but also a network of physical objects, the so-called the Internet of Things [1]. Ubiquitous sensor network and RFID are emerging as widely adaptable and also promising technology in industry (e.g. u-manufacturing, u-inventory, u-logistics, u-SCM). Unfortunately, it is too complicated and memory ineffective to store or handle the many heterogeneous events from sensors and RFID in enterprise-wide systems and physical environments.

Complex event processing (CEP) is the research field that deals with diverse and large amount of multiple data and event streams for the purpose of identifying meaningful event patterns within the event cloud [2]. CEP engines can be applied to detect real-time event patterns from RFID and sensor event streams [3, 4] and trigger business rules [2]. In this paper, we present an architecture of complex sensor event processing in ubiquitous manufacturing and service systems. Especially, we concentrate on business process since the technology can maximize business performance only when they are dynamically and seamlessly integrated business processes [5].

F. Daniel et al. (Eds.): BPM 2011 Workshops, Part I, LNBIP 99, pp. 427–432, 2012.

2   Framework of Ubiquitous Business Process Management

The proposed framework is designed to reach the following goals: 1) To create a bridge between the physical world and business information systems. We visualize our approach as a system that enhances service and manufacturing information systems by linking them to sensorial information originated in the physical world. 2) To enable the flow and process of events to derive synthesized and relevant information to drive automated business processes.This goal was set to satisfy two important requirements: a) transforming low level RFID and WSN data into meaningful information and b) the need to deliver relevant information, at the right place and time in a dynamic and fastchanging business environment. To satisfy the goals above, we propose aconceptual frameworkfor ubiquitous business process integration and management.

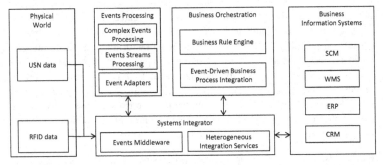

Fig. 1. Conceptual framework for ubiquitous business process management

To gather data from the Physical World, our proposal includes the use of two automatic sensing technologies: RFID and WSN. RFID technology is appropriate for tracking objects in industry such as logistics and manufacturing [6]. Using WSN as a supporting tool has advantages such as usability in static and dynamic domains, low costs, absence of wiring, and automatic reconfiguration [7]. These characteristics have made the adoption of RFID and WSN in many manufacturing and service applications.

3   Ubiquitous Event Processing

In this section, we describe the mechanism of ubiquitous event processing, which is composed of ubiquitous event stream processing, complex sensor event processing, and event-driven rule processing. As example scenario we use cool logistics; RFID and WSN technologies are applied to guarantee the safe delivery of vegetables, fruits, and meat: RFID enables the tracking of products and WSN does the recording of temperature, humidity, and illumination [8]. Moreover, WSN can also send significant information of equipment, such as door locks, gas valves, lights, as well as RFID tag data. The constraints of delivery depend on business policies that are codified as business rules and mapped to each task in the logistics process. For example, meat delivery trucks must maintain the temperature of their containers below 4 degrees centigrade.

3.1   EPL for Sensor Event Stream Processing

The first stage in event processing is to capture events with certain characteristics from sensor event streams, and then to direct them to a new event stream. These two steps can be accomplished by specifying an expression in the CEP engine by using Event Processing Languages (EPL). The expression below conforms to the grammar of EPL of the Esper engine [9].

```
insert into TEMPMON
select containerID, timestamp, temp-prev(count(*)-1,temp)as tempDiff
from Temperature.win:time(5 min)
group by containerID output all every 1 minutes
```

Fig. 2. Example of EPL for Ubiquitous Event Stream Processing

In this example, the container ID, the sensor reading timestamp and the difference between the current and the first temperature readings from the temperature flow, in a time window of five minutes, are put into the TEMPMON flow of events every single minute.

3.2   EPL for Complex Sensor Event Processing

After the sensor event stream processing directs the events of interest into a specific event flow (i.e. TEMPMON), higher level events are created by using complex sensor event processing. The central idea at this stage is to create abstraction hierarchies of relevant events by means of an aggregation process. Such aggregation process is exemplified with the following EPL statement for our cool logistics scenario:

```
insert into SHIPALERT
select * from pattern
        [ every a=Door(state=open) -> (not Door(state=close)
               and (timer:interval(3 min) or TEMPMON(tempDiff>5)) ) ]
```

Fig. 3. Example of EPL for Complex Sensor Event Processing

In this case, a new high level event is inserted in a high level event flow called SHIPALERT; the member event types of each high level event are Door and temperature differences (that were originated in the TEMPMON flow of events). A particular SHIPALERT event is generated when the pattern specified in the CEP statement is matched by a subset of events originated in the above mentioned flows. Informally, the pattern in our example says that a SHIPALERT event must be created when the door of a container has been open for three minutes or the temperature difference is more than five degrees while door is open. In this way, an abstract and relevant event can be generated to trigger actions in the subsequent stage of our proposed system.

3.3   Event-Driven Rule Processing

The last stage in our ubiquitous event processing proposal is the handling of the CEP-derived events to drive business processes with the aid of a rules engine. The specific events and rules to handle these events and other business conditions and trigger specific business actions are specified by using Event-Condition-Action (ECA) rules in a rule engine. As an example for our cool logistics scenario, the following ECA rule is specified in Jess rule language:

```
(defrule Ship_Temp_Alert
(and ?evt<- (SHIPALERT)
     (Activity {name == 'Shipping' && state == 'executing'}))
=> (assert (InvokeService (name 'sendSMS') (to evt.containerID))))
```

Fig. 4. Example of Event-Driven Rule

Informally, this rule indicates that when a shipping activity is executing and a SHIPALERT event is generated, a sendSMS action should be executed; the meaning of this action can be interpreted as the sending of a mobile phone message to the operator whenever the conditions detected in the CEP stage are satisfied. As briefly described in this section, the WSN and RFID events cloud is processed in three main stages to conclude in business relevant actions that allow the fulfilling of business process policies.

4   edUFlow: Ubiquitous Event-Driven BPM System

The concept of ubiquitous complex event processing was implemented as a part of ubiquitous process management system, named edUFlow. The system architecture is shown in Fig. 5.

We used Ubee430-AP-Kit and Alien 9800 Development Kit as real-time event sources of WSN and RFID. We implemented Java program to send sensor events to the Event Middleware. The GlassFish Message Queue 4.4 was implemented as the Event Middleware, which allows other systems to interact with by interchanging messages. The open-source Esper Engine 3.2 was integrated with our CEP application to handle event streams and complex events. In ueFilter, we used Esper's API to create the CEP Engine objects. The system prototype allows users to define both ubiquitous event patterns and event processing rules that guide the CEP Engine's behavior. To codify business rules, we used Jess Rule Engine (BRE). The BRE obtains events from the middleware that are later used as inputs to Jess rules that may trigger relevant actions in application systems.

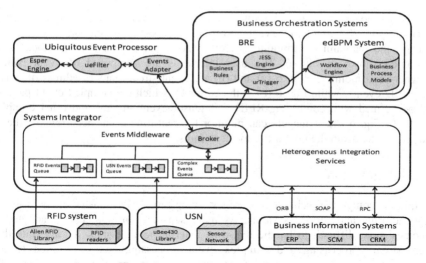

Fig. 5. System architecture of eduFlow

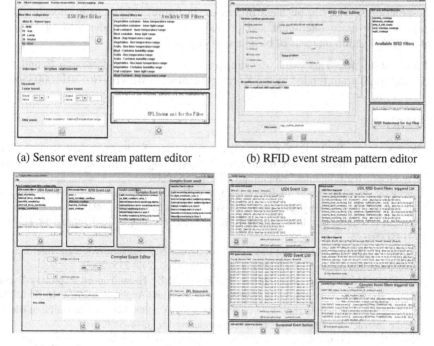

(a) Sensor event stream pattern editor   (b) RFID event stream pattern editor

(c) Complex event pattern editor   (d) Event monitor

Fig. 6. User interfaces for ubiquitous event pattern design and monitoring

The prototype system, eduFlow, provides the platform of integrating event processing of WSN and RFID events to business process management. To effectively manage and maintain the ubiquitous event processing, several user interfaces were developed shown in Fig. 6. The user interfaces are composed of event pattern designers and monitors. Fig. 6 (a) and (b) are event stream pattern editors of sensor and RFID events, while Fig. 6 (c) is the editor by which the complex event patterns can be defined with combining RFID and sensor event streams and other complex events. In Fig. 6 (d), managers can monitor the real-time event occurrences filtered and aggregated from the ubiquitous event streams.

5   Conclusion

Ubiquitous computing technologies are spreading rapidly in industry for purposes of manufacturing and service systems. As more sensor event sources are adopted, it becomes more difficult to handle real-time heterogeneous events. To alleviate this, event stream processing and complex event processing can be applied to this environment. In this paper, a brief introduction to complex event processing for sensor and RFID events was presented in terms of business process integration and management. In the proposed framework, real-time events are filtered and aggregated by the CEP engine; such events later trigger business rules and invoke the corresponding services in business processes. In future, ubiquitous events should be manipulated in more intelligent and proactive manners by understanding business context and situation on basis of business process models.

Acknowledgments. This work was supported by the National Research Foundation of Korea (NRF) grant funded by the Korea government (MEST) (No. 20110003560).

References

1. Welbourne, E., Battle, L., Cole, G., Gould, K., Rector, K., Raymer, S., Balazinska, M., Borriello, G.: Building the Internet of Things Using RFID: The RFID Ecosystem Experience. IEEE Internet Computing 13(3), 48–55 (2009)
2. Luckham, D.: The Power of Events: An Introduction to Complex Event Processing in Distributed Enterprise Systems. Addison-Wesley, Massachusetts (2002)
3. Wang, F., Liu, S., Liu, P.: Complex RFID Event Processing. VLDB Journal 18(4), 913–931 (2009)
4. Dunkel, J.: On Complex Event Processing for Sensor Networks. In: 9th IEEE International Symposium on Autonomous Decentralized Systems, pp. 249–255 (2009)
5. Suntinger, M., Obweger, H., Schiefer, J., Groller, M.E.: Event Tunnel: Exploring Event-Driven Business Processes. IEEE Computer Graphics and Application 28(5), 46–55 (2008)
6. Kortuem, G., Kawsar, F., Fitton, D., Sundramoorthy, V.: Smart Objects as Building Blocks for the Internet of Things. IEEE Internet Computing 14(1), 44–51 (2010)
7. Riem, R.: Cold Chain Management Using an Ultra Low Power Wireless Sensor Network. In: Workshop on Applications of Mobile Embedded Systems, pp. 21–23 (2004)
8. Woo, S.H., Choi, J.Y., Kwak, C., Kim, C.O.: An Active Product State Tracking Architecture in Logistics Sensor Networks. Computers in Industry 60(3), 149–160 (2009)
9. EsperTech, http://www.espertech.com/

A Review of Event Formats as Enablers of Event-Driven BPM

Jörg Becker[1], Martin Matzner[1], Oliver Müller[2], and Marcel Walter[1]

[1] University of Muenster, European Research Center for Information Systems,
Leonardo-Campus 3, 48149 Münster, Germany
[2] University of Liechtenstein, Hilti Chair of Business Process Management,
Fürst-Franz-Josef-Strasse 21, 9490 Vaduz, Liechtenstein
{joerg.becker,martin.matzner}@ercis.uni-muenster.de,
oliver.mueller@uni.li, marcel.walter@uni-muenster.de

Abstract. Event-driven Business Process Management (edBPM) is based upon exchanging and processing business events. As yet, no commonly adopted event format for communicating business events between distributed event producers and consumers has emerged. This paper is an effort to review the status quo of event formats against the requirements of edBPM. We particularly discuss BPAF, CBE, and XES as promising candidates and identify prospects for development.

Keywords: edBPM, Event Exchange Format, EDA.

1   Introduction

In light of today's dynamic business environments, a great share of business processes need to be agile and adaptable in a timely manner. So far, processes are adapted at design time in a cycle of modeling, analysis, implementation, and testing. Today, focus shifts to a continuous and timely feedback on how processes are executed. Further, immediate response capabilities are required to quickly react to business events as they occur. These demands led to the notion of edBPM. edBPM applies Complex Event Processing (CEP) technology and the paradigm of Event-Driven Architecture to Business Process Management (BPM) [1]. edBPM provides a platform for exchanging and processing business events in order to turn insights into immediate actions in a (semi)automated manner. Business events, here, refer to events originating from the execution of a business process. An event denotes something (an activity) that has happened or is considered as having happened [2, p. 4]. For computational processing, such an event is represented and encoded by an event object [3], which is often used synonymously to the notion of event (here also). How event objects are technically realized and which data they contain is specified by an event format.

A crucial challenge in edBPM is the communication of events among several event-producing and event-consuming systems. At this, several event formats have been proposed as means to facilitate loosely-coupled interaction of systems and processes in distributed and heterogeneous IT landscapes [1]. This paper is an effort to review existing event formats against the needs of edBPM. Particularly, we are

F. Daniel et al. (Eds.): BPM 2011 Workshops, Part I, LNBIP 99, pp. 433–445, 2012.
© Springer-Verlag Berlin Heidelberg 2012

interested in the ability to suite three use cases. In *Process Analytics* (U1) the BPM System (BPMS) is the event producer that emits process audit events, e.g. to a CEP infrastructure for calculating and visualizing KPIs. In *Process Intervention* (U2) event analysis leads to (automatic) intervention into business processes in order to influence run time behavior. *Process Interoperability* (U3) coordinates between different business processes possibly running on different BPMS with distinct functional capabilities through event exchange.

This paper proceeds as follows: We first identify classification criteria to purposefully review event formats from several domains (Sec. 2). From these approaches, we extract concepts that together with further BPM-specific aspects qualify as a list of requirements we pose to edBPM event exchange (Sec. 3). We review three promising event formats based on these requirements (Sec. 4) and identify limitations in expressiveness and flexibility. We end with a summary and a research outlook (Sec. 5).

2   Classification of Event Formats

What kind of events are logged, which event data is considered, and how events are technically represented depends on the purpose of an event log, the addressed application domain, the targeted business layer and the logging type. Dependent on an event format *purpose*, certain event data is collected and provided in the log. The event log of a web server, for example, may comprise timestamps, IP addresses, and requested URLs for monitoring traffic and access on server resources. In contrast, an operating system log may focus on application names, threads, and error codes in order to monitor system stability and integrity. As can be seen from these examples, the purpose is closely related to a *domain* as a specific set of cognate purposes. Event formats address different *layers* of an enterprise architecture [4,5]. On a *business* layer, event formats focus on data that typically originates from an enterprise's business processes, such as data about inventories or orders. On an *application* layer, event formats are not embedded into explicit business transactions, but claim for generality. On an *infrastructure* layer, event formats deal with low-level technical event data such as data about networks, routers, or other technical devices. We further distinguish *internal* and *exchange* event formats. While exchange formats have to provide or reference all relevant data explicitly, internal event formats refer to the context of the logging system. Since internal formats are often product-specific, hardly documented, and rarely standardized, we restrict our analyses to exchange formats. We searched for event formats, first in the fields of BPM, BAM and CEP, then in related areas. The classification criteria guided this search. Table 1 presents the identified formats.

3   Requirements for an Event Exchange Format

3.1   Generic characteristics of Event Objects

We analyzed the specifications and data models of the 12 above listed event exchange formats to extract common concepts of an event object. Our results have been rechecked against literature from CEP, EDA, and edBPM. The concepts address in

Table 1. Analyzed event formats

Domain	Name	Purpose	Layer
BPM	Business Process Analytics Format (BPAF)	Analyzing and monitoring of process run time audit data	B
	Common Workflow Audit Data (CWAD)	Analyzing and monitoring of audit data from different workflow related systems	B
	XML Mining Format (MXML)	Analyzing of event logs for process mining	B
	Extensible Event Stream (XES)	Analyzing of event logs, in particular for process mining	B
CEP	RuleCore Event Format (RCEF)	Packaging of arbitrary event data for automatic processing	A
	WebSphere Business Event Format (WBEF)	Packaging of arbitrary event data for automatic processing	A
System Interoperability	Common Base Event (CBE)	Interoperability and communication among different enterprise components and business applications	A
	Common Event Expression (CEE)	Interoperability of electronic systems and devices	I
	Web Services Distributed Management (WSDM) Event Format	Interoperability of communication among different IT resources in a web service based system architecture	A
IT Security	Common Event Format (CEF)	Detection of low-level security relevant events from different kinds of infrastructure devices	I
	Intrusion Detection Message Exchange Format (IDMEF)	Interoperability of intrusion detection systems	I
	Incident Object Description Exchange Format (IODEF)	Intrusion management and collaboration of Computer Security Incident Response teams	B
	Distributed Audit Service (XDAS) Common Audit Event Record Format (XCAERF)	Security auditing across heterogeneous systems and applications	A
	Event Metamodel and Profile (EMP)	-	-

particular the issues of *what* has actually happened (identifier and type), *when* did it happen (time), *where* did it happen (origin), under *which circumstances* did it happen (context), *why* did it happen (cause) and *which effects* may it impose (impact).

Identifier. Business transactions typically include attributes that allow for their accurate identification, e.g. a unique order ID or customerID-time combination. Only few of the analyzed event formats, however, allow for such context-based IDs. CWAD, for example, provides unique instance IDs of business processes and activities to distinguish similar process audit events from a BPMS [6]. Instead, it is more common to use a technical, key-based ID [4]. Such an event ID is often provided natively by event producers. Compared to context-based identifiers, an event ID allows for an easier processing of event objects, a more precise tracing of events, and a consistent description of event associations [2,7]. However, it is harder to relate such technical eventIDs to real life business events. To ensure uniqueness of a system-generated event ID in cross-system event exchange (global validity) further action has to be taken as opposed to system internal use only (local validity). Different approaches exist in practice: WEF specifies a local ID with respect to a source [8]. BPAF requires a global ID that is unique across systems. CBE allows for specifying both, a local and a global event ID to be able to request additional context data from an event log that has not been exchanged as part of an event object.

Type. Assigning a type or class to event objects allows for grouping events with similar semantics or structure. Classification allows for easier comparison, correlation, and processing of event objects. Types also facilitate human interpretation of what has actually happened. Thus, event types are of significance [2,4]. The type of an event results from its context. XES allows for marking context attributes as criteria for grouping event objects. If two events match in all marked attributes, they are considered to be of the same type [9]. However, it is more common to specify the event type explicitly; either codified, as a descriptive text or as a more complex data type. Text-based classifications may also be subject to restrictions in order to increase expressiveness. CWAD dictates a verb-noun syntax (e.g., "Received Order") while CEE proposes an object-action-status (OAS) syntax (e.g., "Order Received Successfully") [6,10]. Domain-specific formats like BPAF or MXML restrict the set of event types by enumeration, while generic formats like RCEF allow for specifying user-defined types [11,12].

Time. The temporal order of events affects the results of their processing [4]. For instance, an event may only be of interest, if it occurs within a certain time span. Particularly in event stream processing, a relative order of incoming events is assumed. All analyzed event formats support indicating time. They differ in the actual points in time that are represented and in the preciseness of the representation [2]. The occurrence time or situation time indicates when an event emerged in real world. BPAF, for example, requires specifying the occurrence time of an event [13]. The detection or observation time, instead, specifies when an event has been discovered by an IT system. CWAD, for instance, indicates when an event has been recorded in an event log [6]. However, different systems detect events in different ways, so that the detection time depends on the specific implementation [2]. Thus, reporting time, i.e. the time an event is sent to an event processing system, is also used, e.g. by WEF [8]. Activities signified by an event might occur over a period of time, featuring start and end time [4]. Thus, events might be specified by time intervals, e.g. as IODEF does for security incidents [14]. Determining the occurrence time of derived events that aggregate several member events can be a complex task. It has been proposed to use either detection time as occurrence time, the occurrence time of the latest member event, or an interval over all member events [2]. In addition, preciseness has to be considered [2]. If events occur at intervals of milliseconds, but event objects only account for seconds, the relative order of events might get lost. Here, WEF and other formats provide additional sequence numbers assigned by the event producing system to event objects with same timestamp. They can be used by event consumers to preserve the relative order of events [7,8].

Origin. Event objects might have different origins such as applications or sensors. Knowing the origin of an event is important for tracing it, distinguishing similar events, and interpreting an event's context [2]. The event source indicates where an event occurred, while the event reporter indicates who published it. Both, source and reporter might be identical since events are often published by dedicated adapters of sources such as devices or applications. Adapters also transform and convert event data according to a certain specification [4]. Whether the source or reporter is indicated by an event object and how detailed they are described depends on the event emitting system and the purpose of the event format. While BPAF provides only an abstract label for the event source, IDMEF and XCAERF also allow for specifying technical attributes such as hostnames or thread IDs [5,13,15]. CBE and WEF even distinguish between source and reporter of an event object explicitly [7].

Context. The context describes the circumstances under which an event of a particular type occurred in more detail. For example, an event of type "order received" may contain an order ID. ETZION AND NIBLETT refer to this contextual data as payload compared, in contrast to the event header and unspecific open content [2]. We distinguish three types of contextual data according to the degree of standardization and domain-specificity of the event format. The explicit payload is closely coupled with an event format by named attributes with well-defined semantics [2]. CWAD allows for explicitly specifying ID and role of a user who is engaged in executing a business process [6]. In contrast, the extendable payload extends the set of meaningful attributes only for certain situations. Generic formats like CBE use extension mechanisms to adapt the event context, while remaining compatible to event objects which signify other situations [7]. Open content contains data that is not subject to any standardization. It typically consists of user-defined key-value-pairs (e.g. BPAF) or key-value-type-tuples (e.g. XES) [9,13]. The event context might also contain pointers to external data sources. Event processors might use this reference to request additional data [2]. XCAERF even allows for referencing entire log files from which an event originates [5].

Cause. Usually, events do not occur in isolation, but in relation to each other. A specific event might be either caused by or aggregated from other occurrences. According to LUCKHAM, analyzing these relationships is a key to understand what actually happened, since the informative content of single events on their own is limited [4]. Thus, relationships between events should be represented by event objects. Making relationships explicit has several advantages. Particularly, analyzing an event trace and performing a drill down in an event hierarchy is possible without a costly reconstruction of event relationships [4]. Dependencies are often indicated by listing event IDs of causing events [4]. CBE, for example, allows for specifying associated events based on their global event IDs, an association engine that established the relationship, and a pre-defined relationship type such as "contains" or "caused by" [7].

Impact. The impact of an event occurrence is less shaped by event objects, since the event producing system typically does not know the consumers of a particular event and their reactions on the occurrence of that event. However, in certain situations it may be reasonable to attach such information to an event object. Actually, there are first attempts to exert influence on how an event object should be processed by a possible consumer. CEF and CBE, for instance, allow specifying the severity and priority of an event [7,16].

3.2   Domain-Specific Requirements to an edBPM Event Exchange Format

Based on the above discussion of general event object concepts, we now explore required properties of domain-specific event exchange formats in an edBPM context. In particular, we focus on the use cases real-time process analytics (U1), automated process intervention (U2), and dynamic process interoperability (U3). We consider two categories of events. BPM events or process audit events originate from BPMS and contain data about the progress of running business processes. Arbitrary business events are derived by an event processor or reported externally. They may indicate business situations that are not related to a specific business process, e.g. traffic or weather events. Furthermore, two interfaces have to be considered in the edBPM architecture. In process analytics (U1), process audit events flow from a BPMS to the event processing system, e.g. to analyze process run times. In process intervention and interoperability (U2 and U3), business events also flow back from the event processing system to the BPMS to influence business processes at runtime.

General requirements

Identifier: BPM audit events typically contain data that is specific for a certain process instance and thus allows for an unambiguous identification of single events. Such identification cannot be presupposed for other types of business events. Thus, we require for an edBPM event exchange format that events can be uniquely and consistently identified.

Time: Besides serving as an ordering relationship, time is also used for different kinds of content analyses. In particular, time is a relevant variable to business process monitoring and is used for measuring, e.g. cycle times of business processes or idle times of resources. Since events in an edBPM system typically occur within and are logged and reported by IT systems, particularly by BPM or CEP engines, a distinction of occurrence, detection, and reporting time is not essential. Since edBPM draws on a real-time architecture, detection time should approximately equal reporting time. Thus, we merely require an edBPM event exchange format to indicate the point in time an event has been recorded.

Origin: Information on the origin of an event facilitates event tracing and the interpretation of contextual event data. In edBPM, a business process or process instance which has caused the occurrence of a certain audit event can be only identified with regard to the BPMS that executed the process. The source BPMS must also be known for intervening into processes at runtime in reaction to events. However, a distinction of event source and reporter seems to be unnecessary. We assume that all systems in the edBPM architecture, particularly BPM and CEP engines including event adapters, are sources and reporters at the same time. We require for an edBPM event exchange format that the source of an event is uniquely identifiable across an event processing system.

Type: Classification allows detecting different situations in event processing, e.g. for filtering or correlating event objects. In edBPM, classification is important for analyzing the progress of business processes based on BPM audit events. A consistent analysis of business processes from several BPMS is only possible if the event data (esp. the event type) is standardized. However, other business events can represent situations which cannot be covered by a single taxonomy in advance. We require for an edBPM event exchange format that event classification must be supported explicitly for any kind of business event. For process audit events, we also require that the BPM event types are prescribed by a taxonomy.

Context: In edBPM the event context has to consider all business data, e.g. about customers, products, or orders. Since not all business situations can be ex-ante defined, predefining contextual event data is impossible. However, BPM audit events need more standardization than other business events since their context enables process run time analyses across several BPMS. At least data such as the business process name has to be accessible in a standardized way. Thus, we require for an edBPM event exchange format to include all kinds of business data. For BPM audit events, we also require that a standardized set of context elements is prescribed by a taxonomy.

Cause: Process audit events typically depend on a process model which determines causal relationships externally to an event processing system. This is not necessarily true for other business events. In process intervention and process interoperability, causal relationships are induced by an event processor at run time. They have to be made visible to improve transparency of the behavior of the event processing system and to facilitate the analysis of cause-and-effect chains. Hence, we require for an edBPM event exchange format that it must be able to explicate induced causal relationships between events.

Impact: The event processing capabilities of some systems in the edBPM architecture might be limited. Thus, events which shall induce a certain behavior at an event consumer have to be interpreted by the event processor in advance. We require for an edBPM event exchange format that it allows for including data which is targeted at a specific event consumer to induce a specific behavior. For BPMS, we additionally require that a standardized set of BPM actions is prescribed explicitly by a taxonomy.

Requirements related to process analytics

Business process definitions consist of several types of interconnected elements (e.g. activities, gateways, events, data objects) that define the business process behavior at design time. Current process auditing standards focus on processes and activities for monitoring and further analytics. Activities are by definition the building blocks of business processes. The sequence of activities describes the run time behavior of the process. A change in the control flow based on a gateway condition is observable through the executed activities. Therefore we focus on situations related to processes and activities in the following.

Processes and activities feature states that change at run time. An activity might be "idle" if no work is performed at that time or might be "in progress" if an employee is working on a task. The transition from state to state is induced by event occurrences. We argue that an analysis of state transitions of processes and activities allows for classifying different BPM audit events and building up a taxonomy of BPM-related event types. The WfMC defined a model that describes different states and state transitions of processes and activities. Table 2 event types that might occur on a process level and maps them to the WfMC state model, if possible. For example, before a process can be executed, a new instance of that process has to be created within a BPMS. A running process instance can be interrupted and sent to hibernation from which it can be recovered later (suspending, resuming). Actions can also be reserved, released, stopped, and expired.

Additional data needs to be provided within the event context to identify, e.g. processes that have been started or activities that have been aborted, so that run time metrics can be calculated or appropriate reactions can be initiated. The WfMC auditing standards specify such data on two levels: definition and case. The definition level includes IDs for process or activity models that are deployed on a BPMS. The case level includes a specific instance ID for a process or activity that has been executed. The WfMC distinguishes different groups of activities in business processes. Manual activities are handled outside a BPMS, automated activities are implemented within a BPMS or related applications. Automated activities might comprise work items, i. e. tasks to be performed by humans. The taxonomy can be further refined. BPMN and BPEL define additional activities for sending or receiving messages, for calling web services, or evaluating business rules. This distinction of activity types is beneficial for process run time analyses since not all activity types support all BPM event types or context elements. For example, reserving or releasing a task does not make sense for application calls. These context elements focus on the process perspective of process analytics applications. The WfMC auditing standards also consider a resource perspective with organizational entities (i.e. user IDs) and IT systems (i.e. application IDs). We include both in the taxonomy of BPM context elements to facilitate analyzing workloads and other resource-related metrics. Table 3 exhibits the resulting context elements for BPM audit events.

Table 2. BPM event types for processes (PI = process instance, partly adopted from [17])

Event	Description	Previous State	Current State
Instantiated	New PI created	-	Open.NotRunning
Started	PI started execution	Open.NotRunning	Open.Running
Suspended	PI was sent to hibernation	Open.Running	Open.Running.Suspended
Resumed	PI awoke from hibernation	Open.NotRunning	OpenNotRunning.Suspended
		Open.Running.Suspended	Open.Running
		Open.NotRunning.Suspended	Open.NotRunning
Completed	PI finished normally	Open.Running	Closed.Completed
Aborted	PI ended gracefully with respect to included resources	Open.	Closed.Cancelled.Aborted
Terminated	PI ended forcibly with respect to included resources	Open	Closed.Cancelled.Terminated
Broken	PI ended due to an error	Open	Closed.Cancelled.Error
Skipped	PI ended due to new version	Open	Closed.Cancelled.Obsolete

Table 3. BPM context elements and their relevance for processes (P) and activities (A)

Context element	P	A	Context element	P	A	Context element	P	A
ProcessDefinitionID	■	■	ActivityDefinitionID	■	■	ActivityType	■	■
ProcessInstanceID	■	■	ActivityInstanceID	■	■	ApplicationID	▨	▨
ProcessName	■	■	ActivityName	■	■	UserID	▨	▨

Requirements related to process intervention and process interoperability
Actively controlling processes and activities at run time requires for an event format to support targeted event data, including a target system, an action that shall be performed, and a set of data elements. To ensure consistent communication with different BPMS, the set of actions and data elements has to be standardized by a taxonomy. Each transition between two states of the WfMC state model can be described as a BPMS operation. The operations might be induced by the system itself, as part of the business process control flow, or it might be initiated externally. WfMC provides two standards that deal with controlling process instances in a BPMS – WAPI for interfaces of workflow-enabled applications and Wf-XML for workflow interoperability. On a *process level* (cf. Table 4), Wf-XML distinguishes creating a new process instance and changing an instance's state. The former operation directly corresponds to the event "process initiated". The latter generically covers all other state transitions. WAPI refines the state change operations to starting, aborting, and terminating process instances. The instantiation of a process requires the identification of the process definition and further input data. Manipulating instances in addition requires the identification of the affected instance. Table 4 also exhibits actions for intervening into running processes on an *activity level*. Initiating or starting activities is not reasonable since the control flow shall be coordinated by the workflow system. Activities with human interaction can be assigned to or unassigned from an owner.

Table 4. BPM actions for influencing processes and activities

Actions on Processes	Instantiate	Start	Suspend	Resume	Abort	Terminate	Skip
Actions on Activities	Reserve	Release	Suspend	Resume	Abort	Terminate	Skip

4   Evaluation of Existing Event Formats

Against the backdrop of the identified requirements, we have identified BPAF, CBE, and XES as the most promising event exchange formats.

4.1   Business Process Analytics Format (BPAF)

As a process auditing standard, BPAF is designed to facilitate the analysis of process run time events. It supports common header data such as event ID, server ID, and timestamp and thereby addresses our requirements for identification, origin, and time. Event types cannot be signified. BPAF implements the WfMC state model. Each event object must at least describe the current state of the event emitting process and may also describe its previous state, so that the event type can be inferred from the transition from one state to another. BPAF is restricted to process audit events and does not allow for indicating other business events. The event context accounts for arbitrary business data by data elements that consist of a descriptive key and a value. Definition ID, instance ID, processes name, and activities are supported. Activity types such as "human" or "application" can only be indirectly signified via key-value-pairs. Since audit events are based on a process definition or model, referencing causing events is not supported. BPAF does not allow for annotating targeted instructions.

4.2   Common Base Event (CBE)

The CBE event header references an event source and an event reporter, the creation time, an optional sequence number for event ordering, and a local and a global instance ID. Thus, CBE fulfills all requirements on identification, origin, and time. CBE focuses on the management of IT components. Thus, each event is classified by a situation type. They comprise, e.g., a start situation indicating that a component finished start-up, a configuration situation indicating that component settings have been changed, or a connection situation indicating that two components established a communication link. In process auditing, IBM recommends to use the report situation and a product-specific extension to the CBE specification. The extension comprises of a name that acts as custom event classifier. IBM FileNet P8 BPM uses several extensions to indicate the start or end of processes and activities by corresponding extension names such as "P8.BPM.Process.Start" or "P8.BPM.Activity.End". Extensions also specify a set of extended data elements which are assumed to be present in a specific event object. IBM FileNet P8 BPM provides process ID, process name, or activity ID. By using the extension mechanism, basically any business or BPM audit event, event type, and business data can be (indirectly) represented. CBE allows for referencing associated events by their global instance IDs. The association engine distinguishes e.g. "contains", "cleared", "caused by", or "correlated" relations. Annotating targeted event data and instructions is not supported.

4.3   Extensible Event Stream (XES)

XES is a generic event log format for exchanging entire event traces, esp. for Process Mining. An event log is a hierarchy of log, traces, and events. The log refers, e.g. to a business process. The traces refer to specific process instances. The events refer to single occurrences within a process instance. Each hierarchy level contains attributes with key, value, and type. On log level, global event and trace attributes can be defined that occur in any event or trace of the log. Global attributes allow for classifying and grouping events. If events are classified by an attribute "name" then all events with the same name are assumed to be of the same type. XES provides extensions for attaching semantics to attributes. Some extensions are included in the standard specification and contain attributes for process auditing. The concept extension specifies a generally understood name attribute for each element in the log hierarchy. A name might indicate the name of a business process, the instance ID of a process, or the name of an activity. The latter may also contain an instance attribute for the related activity instance. Since several names might refer to the same artifact in a process definition, the semantic extension specifies a model reference attribute. The lifecycle extension allows for using a transactional model. Each event may have a transition attribute with values such as start, suspend, or complete. However, the lifecycle and state model in XES only partly fulfills our requirements on BPM event types. Finally, the time and organization extensions deal with timestamp, resource, role, and group attributes. Referencing events and annotating target instructions is not possible. Nevertheless, relationships among events partly result from the log hierarchy.

4.4   Findings

The analysis of BPAF, CBE and XES showed that the domain-specific requirements of edBPM are as yet not fully covered. BPAF and XES are strong in representing BPM-specific event types since both incorporate some kind of state model for processes and activities. While the flexible structure of XES allows for modeling other business events as well, BPAF is restricted to a state model and process audit events. Both formats presuppose the existence of a process definition which prescribes causal dependencies between event occurrences. As a consequence, they do not support referencing causing events explicitly. XES is not designed for exchanging single event objects, but complete event logs. CBE does not stem from process

Table 5. Analysis of selected event formats

Requirement		Event format		
		BPAF	CBE	XES
ID	Glob. unique event ID	● Event ID	● GlobalInstanceID, LocalInstanceID	● Concept ext.
Time	Time of event observation	● Timestamp	● CreationTime	● Time ext.
Origin	Glob. unique source ID	● ServerID	● SourceComponent, Reporter Component	◐ Classifier on log level
Type	Business event types	○ Not supported due to state model	● Report- or OtherSituation + ExtensionName	● Classifier on event level + concept ext.
	BPM event types	◐ PreviousState + CurrentState (state transition)	◐ Report- or OtherSituation + ExtensionName	◐ Classifier on event level + concept/ lifecycle ext.
Context	Business Data	● DataElement (key, value)	● ContextDataElement (name, type, value)	● Attribute (key, type, value)
	BPM-specific data	◐ No support of ActivityType, ApplicationID, UserID	◐ ExtendedDataElement (name, type, value)	◐ Attribute (key, type, value)
Cause	Referencing causing events	○ Not supported	● AssociatedEvents	◐ Partly resulting from log hierarchy
Impact	Targeted actions	○ Not supported	○ Not supported	○ Not supported
	BPM-specific actions	○ Not supported	○ Not supported	○ Not supported

● explicitly supported   ◐ implicitly supported   ○ not supported

auditing. It can be used to indicate any kind of event occurrence and also supports referencing of events. However, CBE provides a huge overhead of data fields that are not relevant to edBPM. This results from the fact that the core specification of CBE such as the specified situation types focus on events in IT management. Any BPM-specific data has to be included via the extension mechanism. In fact, all three event formats support many required data fields either directly or indirectly. Nevertheless, we perceive BPAF as being too narrowly focused on process audit events; XES as not suited for real-time scenarios; and CBE as being at least partially alienated. None of these formats allow for indicating targeted event data or actions (required for use cases U2 and U3). Our findings are summarized in Table 5.

5   Summary and Outlook

State-of-the-art BPMS are limited in their capabilities to detect complex events surrounding the process execution and to trigger immediate reactions in response. Here, edBPM proposes a shift to event-based system architectures that integrate concepts from BPM and CEP. In this paper, we identified concepts to describe event objects from several related domains and added further BPM specific requirements to an event exchange format. These requirements are surely not exhaustive, but heavily depend on the focus of the analyses, e.g. as expressed by our use. However, a feature comparison approach as followed here will always suffer from subjectivity [18].

The contribution of this work is twofold. First, we provided a discussion of three promising approaches. BPAF and XES proved to be strong in representing BPM-specific event types, while being limited in their scope (BFAF) and ability to exchange single event objects (XES). CBE suffers from a huge overhead of irrelevant data. At the same time, the presented concepts illustrate prospects and provide directions for further developments of event exchange formats.

References

1. von Ammon, R., et al.: Existing and future standards for event-driven business process management. In: Proceedings of the ACM International Conference on Distributed Event-Based Systemstributed Event-Based Systems, New York (2009)
2. Etzion, O., Niblett, P.: Event Processing in Action. Manning Publications, Cincinnati (2010)
3. Luckham, D., Schulte, R.: Event Processing Glossary - Version 1.1 (2008)
4. Luckham, D.: The Power of Events: An Introduction to Complex Event Processing in Distributed Enterprise Systems. Addison-Wesley Professional, Boston (2002)
5. The Open Group.: Preliminary Specification: Distributed Audit Service, XDAS (1998)
6. WfMC: Audit Data Specification Version 1.1 (1998)
7. Ogle, D., et al.: Canonical Situation Data Format - The Common Base Event V 1.0.1 (2003)
8. OASIS: Web Services Distributed Management: Management using Web Services (WSDM-MUWS) 1.1 (2006)
9. Günther, C.W.: Extensible Event Stream (XES) Standard Definition (2009)
10. MITRE: Common Event Expression Overview (2010)

11. zur Muehlen, M., Swenson, K.D.: BPAF: A Standard for the Interchange of Process Analytics Data. In: Proceedings of the International Workshop on Business Process Intelligence, Hoboken (2010)
12. von Dongen, B.F., van der Aalst, W.M.P.: A Meta Model for Process Mining Data. In: Proceedings of the CAiSE Workshops, Porto, pp. 309–320 (2005)
13. WfMC: Business process analytics format - draft specification 1.0 (2008)
14. Danyliw, R., Meijer, J., Demchenko, Y.: The Incident Object Description Exchange Format (IODEF), RFC 5070 (2007)
15. Debar, H., Curry, D., Feinstein, B.: The Intrusion Detection Message Exchange Format (IDMEF), RFC4765 (2007)
16. ArcSight: Common Event Format: Event Interoperability Standard (2010)
17. zur Muehlen, M., Shapiro, R.: Business Process Analytics. In: vom Brocke, J., Rosemann, M. (eds.) Handbook on Business Process Management 2: Strategic Alignment, Governance, People and Culture. Springer, Berlin (2010)
18. Siau, K., Rossi, M.: Evaluation techniques for systems analysis and design modelling methods–a review and comparative analysis. Information Systems Journal 21, 249–268 (2007)

A Prototype Tool for the Event-Driven Enforcement of SBVR Business Rules

Willem De Roover, Filip Caron, and Jan Vanthienen

Department of Decision Sciences and Information Management,
Katholieke Universiteit Leuven, Belgium
{willem.deroover,filip.caron,jan.vanthienen}@econ.kuleuven.be

Abstract. Business rules define and constrain various aspects of the business, such as vocabulary, control-flow and organizational issues. Although the presence of many languages for expressing business rules that differ in expressivenes, knowledge representation mechanism and execution model, none of these cover all the necessary business aspects. In this paper, we show how business rules, not only vocabulary rules, but also control-flow rules and organizational rules can be expressed in SBVR and translated using patterns into a more uniform event mechanism, such that the event handling could provide an integrated enforcement of business rules of many kinds. As a proof of concept a prototype tool integrates this pattern mechanism and provides an execution environment in which these rules are enforced.

Keywords: business rules, event coordination, business processes, SBVR, declarative process modeling, prototype.

1 Introduction

Languages for declarative process modeling often do not cover the many real-life business concerns that exist in reality. Some only allow to express business rules about activity sequence and timing constraints, i.e. the control-flow perspective, others include the organizational and vocabulary aspects, but do not provide a temporal logic to express temporal relationships between concepts such as activities or events. Moreover, these languages make use of very different knowledge representation paradigms. These heterogeneous knowledge representation paradigms raise the question how to reason about such heterogeneously expressed knowledge. The enforcement of such wide variety of rules is not straightforward, as each type has its own mechanism for the transformation into a model driven implementation, leading to partial solutions for the vocabulary, control-flow and organizational aspects of the business.

In our approach we extend SBVR (Semantics of Business Vocabulary and Business Rules)[1] with the EM-BrA²CE extension[2] such that vocabulary, control-flow and organizational aspects of a business can all be expressed by SBVR rules. We translate these business rules into a more uniform event mechanism, such that the event handling could provide an integrated enforcement of

F. Daniel et al. (Eds.): BPM 2011 Workshops, Part I, LNBIP 99, pp. 446–457, 2012.

business rules of many kinds. The translation happens by means of a pattern mechanism that transforms SBVR business rules into event-driven enforcement rules. In this paper we propose a tool that implements this pattern mechanism such that business vocabularies and rules of all kind can be defined and enforced at run-time.

This paper is structured as follows. Section 2 outlines the relevant literature on declarative languages in business process modeling. Section 3 gives a summary of the SBVR standard and the EM-BrA²CE extension. In section 4 we introduce the template mechanism to transform SBVR rules into an event-driven enforcement rules. Section 5 provides tool support for this template mechanism such that rules can be defined and enforced. Section 6 details our approach with an example. We conclude in section 7.

2 Related Work

A distinction can be made between several business rules. A total of fifthteen business rule types are identified that can constrain a business, as shown in table 1. Each business rule refers to one of the three aspects of business process modeling that are generally considered [3]: control-flow, vocabulary and organizational aspects.

Control-flow Aspects. Business policy and regulations contain a lot of constraints (partial order, timing, exists, activity pre- and postconditions). In a trade community, for instance, different business protocols lay down the obligations of business partners and can be expressed in the form of temporal deontic rules [4].

Vocabulary aspects. The performer of an activity can perform particular manipulations (addition, removal or update) of business facts. These state transitions can be constrained by integrity constraints and derivation rules.

Organizational aspects. Organizational aspects relate to the visibility of business concepts and events and the authorization to perform particular activities.

In the literature, languages such as the case handling paradigm [7], OWL-S [12], the constraint specification framework of Sadiq et al. [10], the Web Service Modeling Ontology (WSMO) [6], the ConDec language [9] and the PENELOPE language [4] can be categorized as declarative languages.

Many of these languages for declarative process modeling focus on one particular aspect of the business process and thus miss expressivity to cover the many real-life business concerns that exist in reality. For instance, the ConDec language and the PENELOPE language only allow to express business rules about sequence and timing constraints, i.e. the control flow aspects [3]. Web Service Orchestration standards such as OWL-S [12] and WSMO [6], on the other hand, include the organizational and vocabulary aspects, but do not provide a temporal logic to express temporal relationships between concepts such as activities or events.

Table 1. Business rule types

Vocabulary [5,4,6,7,8,9,10]	Control-Flow [8]	Organizational [11]
Static integrity	Activity order rules	Activity authorization rule
Data value constraint	Activity precedence rule	Role based authorization
Data uniqueness constraint	Activity response rule	Separation of duties
Derivation rule	Activity serialism rule	
Comparison rule	Activity cardinality rule	
Calculation rule	Temporal deontic process rules	
Data manipulation rule	Deadline obligations for activities	
Update restriction rule	Activity condition rules	
Removal restriction rule	Activity precondition	
	Activity postcondition	

Moreover, these languages make use of very different knowledge representation paradigms. For instance, the ConDec language is expressed in Linear Temporal Logic (LTL) whereas the PENELOPE language is expressed in terms of the Event Calculus. These heterogenous knowledge representation paradigms raise the question how it will be possible to reason about such heterogeneously expressed knowledge.

Finally, these languages do not have an explicit execution model or have an execution model that explicitly assumes either human or machine-mediated service enactment. The WSMO, for instance, has a specific execution model (WSMX) [13] that is focused on Web service mediated service orchestration. The case handling paradigm, for instance, assumes humans to perform atomic tasks but has an orchestration engine to perform the orchestration (coordination) work.

3   SBVR for Vocabulary and Process Aware Rules

The Semantics of Business Vocabulary and Business Rules (SBVR) [14] is a new standard for business modeling within the Object Management Group (OMG) that is on the one hand comprehensible so that it can be understood by business people and on the other hand formal so that they can be enforced by information systems. SBVR provides several concepts that allow to describe the vocabulary aspects of a business in natural language. However because SBVR lacks process aware concepts it fails to support the control-flow and organizational aspects of the business. This is why SBVR is extended with EM-BrA^{2}CE.

3.1   The Semantics of Business Vocabulary and Business Rules

In SBVR meaning and representation are separated, which makes it possible for a certain meaning to have several representation in the form of words, sounds, figures, etc. Communities play a major part in separating meaning from representations. A community has a set of concepts for which there is a shared

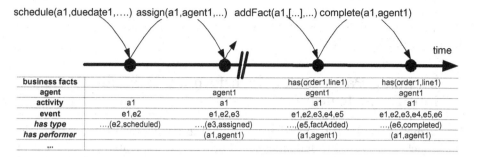

Fig. 1. An illustration of state transitions

understanding. These concepts can be found in the community's body of shared meaning which contains noun concepts, fact types and business rules. Noun concepts represent the meaning of business objects such as Order. In the same manner fact types represent the meaning of a relation between concepts, i.e. Order *contains* OrderLine. Business rules build on top of fact types and allow to constraint these fact types: Order *contains* at least one OrderLine.

Different languages or speech communities can then assign a representation to these concepts making it possible to talk about the same concepts in different languages. One way of representing the concepts in SBVR is by means of a structured, English vocabulary for expressing vocabularies and rules, called SBVR Structured English [14]. SBVR structured English uses font styles to designate statements with formal meaning. The term font (green) is used to designate a noun concept, the name font (green) designates an individual concept, the *verb* font (blue) is used for designation for a verb concept and the keyword font (red) is used for linguistic particles that are used to construct statements.

3.2   Process Aware SBVR Vocabularies and Rules

With concepts and fact types SBVR provides elements that are excellent for specifying the vocabulary aspects of the business. However the lack of elements for specifying process related concepts makes SBVR unsuitable for defining the control-flow and organizational aspects. In order to makes SBVR suitable it needs to be extended with support for concepts as agents, activities, process states and events. EM-BrA^{2}CE [2,15] is an extension that provides SBVR with concepts for expressing these process-related concepts. EM-BrA^{2}CE stands for 'Enterprise Modeling using Business Rules, Agents, Activities, Concepts and Events'.

The EM-BrA^{2}CE vocabulary thinks of a business process instance as a trajectory in a state space. A process consists of several activities that are performed by agents and have a particular duration. Changes to the lifecycle of an activity are reflected by means of activity events. These activity events occur as a result of twelve predefined state transitions e.g. create, assign, complete. Each of these transitions results in a new set of concepts and ground facts and thus a new state. Figure 1 illustrates a few state transitions in a place order activity a1. Business rules constrain the state space such that particular state transitions are not allowed to occur.

4   Example Patterns for Transforming Business Rules into Event Rules

We examine how SBVR business rules can be translated into more uniform event rules, such that the event handling could provide an integrated enforcement of business rules of many kinds, not only vocabulary rules, but also control-flow and organizational rules. To this end, we provide a pattern mechanism to transform SBVR integrity constraints, derivation rules and process rules into event-driven enforcement rules and notifications.

4.1   Data Constraints and Derivations

An example pattern for integrity constraints and derivations are shown in figures 2 and 3. These templates serve as a transformation function from a structured english business rule to a set of event-condition-action rules. The input for this transformation function will be the concepts that the business user enters to complete the business rule. The result is twofold: Firstly, the business user will have written down a rule of the business. Secondly, the system will have the business rule transformed into the corresponding ECA-rules. The sets of ECA rules are equivalent to the business rules that they express. However ECA rules have the advantage that they make clear when they have to be checked. The condition of an ECA rule checks whether the business rule is violated and in case of a violation the system will be notified of this violation.

Vocabulary: Integrity Rule

•Template:
   <Concept1> must be less than <Concept2>
•Translation:
   On isCreated(<Concept1>) or isCreated(<Concept2>):
      if <Concept1> is no less than <Concept2> report violation
   On IsModified(<Concept1>) or IsModified(<Concept2>):
      if <Concept1> is no less than <Concept2> report violation

---

Fig. 2. Integrity Constraint

We have defined templates for a common set of business rules. The use of templates may seem to limit the ways in which rules can be formulated, but provides a uniform way of defining business rules that reduces the possibility of writing the same business rule in different syntactical ways. Templates also allow the easy extraction of information, such as the business rule type and the concepts, from business rules.

Vocabulary: Derivation Rule

•Template:

    <Concept1> must be calculated as <calculation of concept2 and concept3>

•Translation:

    On isCreated(<Concept1>): compute(<Concept1>)
    On isModified(<Concept2>) or isModified(<concept3>): compute(<Concept1>)
    On compute(<Concept1>): signal isModified(<Concept1>)

Fig. 3. Derivation Rule

Process: Precedence Rule

•Template:

    <Activity2> may only happen after <Activity1>

•Translation:

    On start(<Activity2>): if not completed(<Activity1>) then report violation

Fig. 4. Precedence Rule

Organizational: Authorization Rule

•Template:

    <Agent1> that <verb phrase> < Concept1> must be different from <Agent2> *that* <verb phrase> <Concept2>

•Translation:

    On isCreated (<Agent1> <verb phrase> <Concept1>) or isCreated (<Agent2> <verb phrase> <Concept2>) :
      if <Agent1> is equal to <Agent2> then report violation

Fig. 5. Authorization Rule

In some cases business rules also generate events. This happens for example when a business rule changes the value of some concept. Derivation rules e.g. calculate the value of a concept based on other concepts. These rules will generate an event that signals that the value of the calculated concept has changed.

4.2 Control Flow and Organizational Aspects

The approach is not limited to data rules. It is possible to develop patterns for control-flow and organizational rules, as already indicated in [16,17,18,19]. As SBVR does not provide process related concepts, we used the concepts provided by the EM-BA^{2}CE extension. Figure 4 presents a control-flow template for a precedence rule of activities and figure 5 illustrates an organizational template that models a four-eyes principle.

5 Tool Support

As a proof of concept we have developed a tool that allows to construct an environment in which we can test our templated business rules. This tool offers a design-time environment which allows a business user to create business rules that build on a predefined business vocabulary. When the user has defined all the necessary business rules he can switch to the run-time environment in which the user can execute a process that is compliant with the defined business rules.

5.1 Design-Time Environment

In the design-time environment a business user can create the business's vocabulary which consists of activity types, concept types and fact types that relate concept types to each other. Once the business vocabulary has been defined the concepts of the business can be used to constrain the business process with business rules.

The interface of the design-time environment is divided into two parts, a vocabulary part situated at the top of the environment and a business rules part situated at the bottom of the screen. The layout of the business vocabulary part is divided in three areas that are responsible for the management of the business vocabulary by offering an intuitive layout for the definition of activitiy types, concept types and fact types.

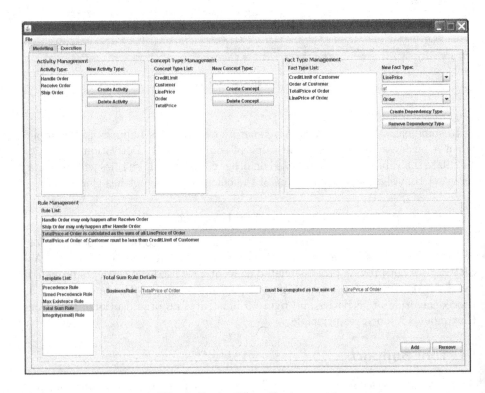

Fig. 6. Design-Time Environment

The business rules part of the design-time environment provides an area that is used for the management of business rules. These rules build on the activities and fact types that are defined by the business vocabulary . The business rule area consists of three interactable elements: a rule list, a template list and a detailed overview of the currently selected rule or template. The rule list comprises a list of all the rules that have been created by the user. The template list contains all the templates that are currently supported by the tool. The selection of such a template results in a detailed overview of the template in the overview element. The overview element allows the user to complete the template with concepts types, fact types and activities and thus adding a new rule to the system. When a new business rule is added to the system then the system generates the corresponding ECA-rules such that they can be used for run-time checking.

5.2   Run-Time Environment

Once the business vocabulary and rules have been defined the user can switch to the run-time environment. The run-time environment allows a user to start and complete instances of activity types , and create, manipulate and remove concept instances. All these actions will result in the triggering of corresponding events that will be evaluated against the created business rules. If no rules are violated then the action is allowed, otherwise the action is not performed.

The run-time environment contains four elements that allow the user to manipulate instances of the business vocabulary. The first element, situated at the top left side of the environment, is a list of activities which can be started or completed. Depending on the current state an activity will be started or completed when the business user selects it. As a result of this actions events are created that are evaluated against the created ECA-rules. If one of the rules is violated then the system cancels the action and notifies the user in the notification area, otherwise the action is performed.

The second element, located in the middle, is responsible for the management of concept instances. These concepts are represented by means of a tree, which orders the instances according to their type. Within the tree, instances can be created, modified and removed. As with activities these action will create events that are evaluated against the ECA-rules that generate violations if the actions are prohibited.

The other elements of the environment, a notification area at the bottom and and an event log at the right side, are non interactable elements that the system uses to communicate to the user. The notification area signals the user that a selected action is in violation with the current rule set. The event log presents a history of the events that have occured during the execution of a process. The events are shown as a combination of the object that was manipulated and the corresponding action.

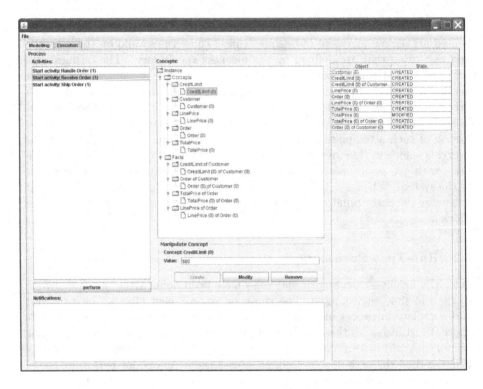

Fig. 7. Run-Time Environment

6 Example

This section illustrate the tool by means of a creditlimit example that permits a customer to place orders provided that they do not exceed the customer's creditlimit.

1. **Designing the business model** We model the following situation: An order consists of one or more orderlines which refer to a product that is requested a certain amount of times. The price of an orderline is calculated as the price of the product times the quantity that the product is requested. The totalprice of an order is calculated as the sum of the price of each orderline. Further we model a customer, which has a creditlimit that can not be exceeded by the order's totalprice. These objects and relations are added to the tool as concepts and facts.

2. **Constraining the business model** The business vocabulary in itself is not a complete representation of the example just described because it lacks information. This information will be described by the following rules:

    Rule 1: The totalprice of an order of a customer must be less than the creditlimit of a customer

    Rule 2: The totalprice of an order is calculated as the sum of the lineprices of the orderLines of the order

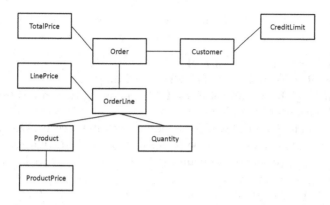

Fig. 8. Model of the creditlimit example

Rule 3: The lineprice of an orderline is calculated as the multiplication of the price of the product of the orderline and the quantity of the orderline
These rules are added to the tool using following steps:
- Select the corresponding template. For business rule 2 this means that a derivation template is selected.
- Enter the correct concepts into the template. The derivation template needs to be completed with two concepts that are related to the business vocabulary. This is done with the help of a conceptbuilder that guides us through the business vocabulary and makes sure we only write down concepts that are allowed by the business vocabulary.
- Add the rule to the system.
3. **Instantiating the business model** – A customer with a creditlimit of 1000 euro places an order for two products. The price for the products is respectively 50 and 150 euro and they are ordered respectively 3 and 4 times. The totalprice equals 750 euro.
- important events and consequences:
   - isCreated(OrderLine): triggers business rule 3, which calculates the lineprice.
   - isModified(LinePrice): triggers business rule 2, which calculates the totalprice.
- The customer decides to add an extra product to the order which creates a new orderline that totals 400 euros.
- important events and consequences:
   - isCreated(OrderLine): triggers business rule 3, which calculates the lineprice.
   - isModified(LinePrice): triggers business rule 2, which calculates the totalprice.
   - isModified(TotalPrice): triggers business rule 1, which checks if the totalprice exceeds the customer's creditlimit. In this case the rule is violated, the user is notified of this violation and the product is not added to the order.

The modeling and execution of activities works in a similar matter. The following example defines a small process in which an order is received and processed.

1. **Designing the business model** We create activity types for the following activities: Receive Order, Handle Order and Ship Order
2. **Constraining the business model** The following rules are entered in the system by means of templates:
   Rule 1 Handle Order may only be performed after Receive Order
   Rule 2 Ship Order may only be performed after Handle Order
   Rule 3 Ship Order must be completed after Receive Order has been completed.
3. **Instantiating the business model** – important events and consequences:
   - isStarted(Handle Order): triggers business rule 1 that allows Handle Order provided that Receive Order has been completed.
   - isStarted(Ship Order): triggers business rule 2 that allowsShip Order provided that Handle Order has been completed.
   - isCompleted(Ship Order): triggers business rule 3 that marks the process as completed as all requirements following the handle order activity are satisfied.

7   Conclusion

In this paper, we demonstrated a tool such that business rules in SBVR, not only vocabulary rules, but also control-flow and organizational rules, can be translated using patterns into a more uniform event mechanism, such that event handling could provide an integrated enforcement of business rules of many kinds. Future work includes the development of new general patterns with a focus on the modeling of the goal driven aspects of process models in a declarative and executable manner. Further we will extend the prototype with database support and research the integration of our event-driven enforcement rules with the database trigger mechanism.

References

1. Object Management Group: Semantics of Business Vocabulary and Business Rules (SBVR) – Interim Specification. OMG Document – dtc/06-03-02 (2006)
2. Goedertier, S., Haesen, R., Vanthienen, J.: EM-BrA^{2}CE v0.1: A vocabulary and execution model for declarative business process modeling. FETEW Research Report KBI_0728, K.U.Leuven (2007)
3. Jablonski, S., Bussler, C.: Workflow Management. In: Modeling Concepts, Architecture and Implementation. International Thomson Computer Press, London (1996)
4. Goedertier, S., Vanthienen, J.: Designing Compliant Business Processes with Obligations and Permissions. In: Eder, J., Dustdar, S. (eds.) BPM Workshops 2006. LNCS, vol. 4103, pp. 5–14. Springer, Heidelberg (2006)

5. Paschke, A., Bichler, M., Dietrich, J.: ContractLog: An Approach to Rule Based Monitoring and Execution of Service Level Agreements. In: Adi, A., Stoutenburg, S., Tabet, S. (eds.) RuleML 2005. LNCS, vol. 3791, pp. 209–217. Springer, Heidelberg (2005)
6. Roman, D., Keller, U., Lausen, H., de Bruijn, J., Lara, R., Stollberg, M., Polleres, A., Feier, C., Bussler, C., Fensel, D.: Web service modeling ontology. Applied Ontology 1(1), 77–106 (2005)
7. van der Aalst, W.M.P., Weske, M., Grünbauer, D.: Case handling: a new paradigm for business process support. Data & Knowledge Engineering 53(2), 129–162 (2005)
8. Wagner, G.: The agent-object-relationship metamodel: towards a unified view of state and behavior. Information Systems 28(5), 475–504 (2003)
9. Pesic, M., van der Aalst, W.M.P.: A Declarative Approach for Flexible Business Processes Management. In: Eder, J., Dustdar, S. (eds.) BPM Workshops 2006. LNCS, vol. 4103, pp. 169–180. Springer, Heidelberg (2006)
10. Sadiq, S.W., Orlowska, M.E., Sadiq, W.: Specification and validation of process constraints for flexible workflows. Information Systems 30(5), 349–378 (2005)
11. Strembeck, M., Neumann, G.: An integrated approach to engineer and enforce context constraints in RBAC environments. ACM Transactions on Information System Security 7(3), 392–427 (2004)
12. The OWL Services Coalition: OWL-S 1.2 Pre-Release (2006), http://www.ai.sri.com/daml/services/owl-s/1.2/
13. Zaremba, M., Bussler, C.: Towards dynamic execution semantics in semantic web services. In: Proceedings of the Workshop on Web Service Semantics: Towards Dynamic Business Integration, International Conference on the World Wide Web (WWW 2005), Chiba, Japan (2005)
14. Object Management Group: Semantics of Business Vocabulary and Business Rules (SBVR), v1.0. OMG Document – dtc/08-01-02 (2008)
15. Goedertier, S., Mues, C., Vanthienen, J.: Specifying Process-Aware Access Control Rules in SBVR. In: Paschke, A., Biletskiy, Y. (eds.) RuleML 2007. LNCS, vol. 4824, pp. 39–52. Springer, Heidelberg (2007)
16. Pesic, M.: Constraint-based workflow management systems: Shifting control to users. PhD thesis, Eindhoven University of Technology (2008)
17. van der Aalst, W.M.P., Pesic, M.: Decserflow: Towards a truly declarative service flow language. In: Leymann, F., Reisig, W., Thatte, S.R., van der Aalst, W.M.P. (eds.) The Role of Business Processes in Service Oriented Architectures. Dagstuhl Seminar Proceedings, vol. 06291. Internationales Begegnungs- und Forschungszentrum fuer Informatik (IBFI), Schloss Dagstuhl, Germany (2006)
18. Wang, M., Wang, H.: From process logic to business logic–A cognitive approach to business process management. Information & Management 43(2), 179–193 (2006)
19. Ceponiene, L., Nemuraite, L., Vedrickas, G.: Separation of event and constraint rules in uml & ocl models of service oriented information systems. Information Technology and Control 38(1), 29–37 (2009)

Applying Complex Event Processing towards Monitoring of Multi-party Contracts and Services for Logistics – A Discussion

Martin Roth and Steffi Donath

Information Systems Institute, Faculty of Economics and Management,
University of Leipzig, Grimmaische Straße 12, 04109 Leipzig
{roth,sdonath}@wifa.uni-leipzig.de

Abstract. As a result of globalization and the falling profit margin, companies started to outsource their processes ensured by contracts. This is also happening within the logistics service sector. The resulting networks, which must be managed and monitored, have a very collaborative and dynamic character. Based on the Fourth Party Logistics Provider business model that aims at establishing as a coordinator of such networks the usability of complex event processing is discussed. A typical workflow exemplifies the challenges in terms of monitoring. Besides the theoretical model a possible solution approach with the use of complex event processing is discussed.

Keywords: Fourth Party Logistics Provider, Complex Event Processing, Contract, Service Level Agreement, Service Level Objective.

1 Introduction

Nowadays companies are faced with unpredictable market changes and the pressure to fulfill their processes faster, better and more flexible. The dynamically changing regulations also complicated a long term planning. To cope with those situations companies outsource their internal processes to external providers. Thus they are able to concentrate on their core processes in order to save costs and assure sustainable competitiveness.

This evolution also takes place in the logistics service sector. Companies are outsourcing their logistics department and the associated services like transportation, cross boarder finance management, material handling and so forth. Additionally, they outsource the closely linked IT functions like logistics information systems. The shift from these internal activities to external providers is based on contracts. A contract records the agreed upon obligations and responsibilities of contractual parties in terms of business process conditions [1, 2]. These conditions are often expressed as goals which must be reached by each party. The goals can be extracted from the customer needs or from law and are known as Service Level Objectives (SLOs).

As the integration of several logistics services is not easy to be managed, a new business model has evolved that is focused on the integration and management of

F. Daniel et al. (Eds.): BPM 2011 Workshops, Part I, LNBIP 99, pp. 458–463, 2012.

different services within the meaning of the outsourcer. The emerge of the fourth party logistics provider (4PLP) business model offers services for integrating and managing complex value added logistics services [3]. A 4PLP acts as a requester and coordinator of quite simple services from different providers, manages these services within a logistics network and provides the resulting services to its customers regarding to the defined SLOs. Due to the collaborative and dynamic character of the 4PLP a traditional Business Process Management (BPM) is not suitable. The collaborative aspect is given due to the need to involve several business partners (BPs) to fulfill a service whereas the dynamic nature is constituted by the appearance and disappearance of BPs. To reach this, BPM is mainly enhanced by concepts of Service Oriented Architecture (SoA) as well as Complex Event Processing (CEP) [4]. On this account this paper discusses the support of CEP regarding to monitor several processes and their SLOs to support the work of a 4PLP.

This paper outlines the 4PLP business model and its characteristics. It derives challenges of the 4PLP related to monitoring exemplified by a short example (section 2). Afterwards, the role that CEP can play to provide support for solving these challenges is discussed. An overview of the related work (section 4) and a conclusion (section 5) finalize this paper.

2   Fourth Party Logistics Business Model and Its Characteristics

To emphasize the challenges of a 4PLP business model a differentiation towards traditional logistics service provider (LSP) is presented. Second, a scenario exemplifies the challenges which are investigated as third.

Outsourced logistics services are mainly processed by Second and Third Party Logistics Provider (2PLP, 3PLP). 2PLP and 3PLP are commonly not involved in the design of a supply chain. Hence the design is often subject to one of the companies inside the supply chain. To foster the concentration on core competencies the outsourcing of such coordinators as 4PLP was discussed in recent years. The differentiation between the 3PLP and 4PLP is the involvement of supply chain management and supply chain integration. This includes the management and integration of several organizations in the supply chain and extended the tasks to the company borders of the customer. The goal is to establish complete supply chains without the use of own assets [5]. A 4PLP can has assets like trucks but ideally uses other LSPs to fulfill a logistics operation to keep his neutrality [7]. Thereby a 4PLP can be defined as an independent, singularly accountable, non-asset based integrator of a client's supply and demand chains [8] by integrating upstream (e.g. suppliers) and downstream (e.g. distributors) actors of the supply chain [7]. To avoid confusions, a 4PLP utilizes 2PLP respectively 3PLP to supply services to customers, possessing only computer systems and domain-specific knowledge.

The following presented service lifecycle consists of the phases: analysis, design, implementation, publishing, operation and retirement and is divided into software and business level [9]. Against the consideration of [9] the business services of the 4PLP are designed with regard to an individual contract. Therefore, the publishing phase is not part of this lifecycle. A deeper view into the software level is given in [10].

A company, further called business customer (BC), wants to transport goods. The BC assigns the 4PLP to fulfill this operation. Both parties, the 4PLP and the BC, draw up a contract with some SLOs, which define measurable indicators like delivery quality, delivery reliability and delivery flexibility. The 4PLP has to ensure the compliance to these during the logistics service execution towards the BC. Regarding to the defined requirements the 4PLP selects the appropriate BPs from a pool with several BPs, which can collaboratively accomplish the contract between the BC and the 4PLP. The BPs also described their capabilities during preliminary stages and draw up a contract. This contract is similar to the contract between the 4PLP and BC. With this step the *analysis* phase ends.

The 4PLP models and simulates a suitable logistics network regarding to the above mentioned constraints. As soon as the simulation is positive the 4PLP has a model with a physical flow and defines the SLOs which must be monitored. Furthermore, the 4PLP knows how to orchestrate and execute the business services offered by the appropriate BPs to accomplish the whole operation towards the BC. The *design* phase ceases with this step.

In the *implementation* phase the 4PLP has to encompass the designed process by the integration of the BPs and the alignment of the existing logistics system and IT support. Besides ensuring suitable information flow to allow coordination between the involved parties, a monitoring system has to be set up. Thus the 4PLP is able to observe the operations and see violations or successful fulfillment.

During the *operation* phase, the 4PLP monitors the business service execution realized by the BPs. In addition the process can be analyzed over a longer period regarding to improvements and optimizations.

With the expiration of the contract, the 4PLP has to terminate the service (*retirement*). If the 4PLP analyzed some lacks within the process execution, it can redesign the logistics network regarding to the next execution.

The next subsection deals with the challenges regarding to monitor several processes and to ensure the fulfillment of the defined SLOs. Challenges like preselecting the appropriate BP or qualified employees are out of scope.

The alignment and management of several services from a variety of different organizations are complex tasks. Therefore a platform for managing all these aspect is necessary. An adequate solution based on service-orientation providing the 4PLP with tools is presented in [10]. Possible challenges within the business model of the 4PLP are shown afterwards with a special focus on monitoring. Thereby the phases *design* and *operation* are in the centre view. The following enumeration shows the prime challenges:

O1: Legal Aspect: The outsourced services are ensured by a contract with SLOs between the 4PLP and the BC. The 4PLP also has similar structured contracts with his BPs. If e.g. a good is delivered too late to the BC, the 4PLP has to pay the defined monetary penalties to the BC. To secure the robustness of the coordinated network, the 4PLP has to pass the penalties to the guilty member in the network. Therefore the 4PLP must be provided with a method to achieve a reliable identification.

O2: Proactive behavior: In contrast to O1 a mechanism to prevent such breaches of contract would be a next step to keep the established network competitively viable. E.g. a BPs only has trucks to execute the transportation service. Due to a delayed delivery of the previous party, the whole operation is vulnerable, because the transport with a truck is too time-intensive. Therefore a method to recognize this situation in an anticipatory manner is needed.

The above described challenges within the *operation* phase can only be countered if the *design* phase (and partially the *analyze* phase) is adapted in the right way. Hence there are some points to emphasize:

A1. Description of the individual goals: A 4PLP has to monitor a multitude of individual business services. To solve the O1 and O2 issues he has to know, which goals must be achieved. Therefore a 4PLP has to be provided with a method to formalize the SLAs and to turn SLOs into an appropriate data format which can be processed by different tools.

D1. Modeling the monitoring system: After the 4PLP has modeled the goods and information flow, he has to define, how to ensure the compliance. Furthermore he has to model the monitoring system regarding to the SLOs. In so doing, he has to describe under which conditions the responsibility of a BP ends and starts.

D2. Notification source: The 4PLP has normally less influence on the used IT-Systems of his BPs caused by the possible short lifespan of the collaboration with the BPs. Therefore he has to model (and certainly monitor) every possible source of notifications. Additionally, aspects about security or distributed sources as well as notification messages, e.g. expression by small data value, must be considered.

D3. Notification accumulation: It is not meaningful to get every single notification. Therefore a filtering, composition and accumulation method must be provided to point out, which information is significant. Additionally, these must be presented in an adequate abstract level to not overwhelm the 4PLP.

D4. Notification assignment: The notification of a violated or successful fulfillment of operations must be reliable. Due to the fact that the 4PLP is searching for synergies within the business services, e.g. two independent transport services can be done within one business service, it must be assured, that the notifications are assigned to the right business service.

3   Discussion of Complex Event Processing Support for 4PLP

CEP is defined as *"a defined set of tools and techniques for analyzing and controlling the complex series of interrelated events that drive modern distributed information systems"* [11]. Therefore the discussion is on an abstract level without going into detail of a particular tool or technique.

To automate the alignment between the SLOs and the processed operation, the formalization of the SLOs (**A1**) is done by using the Unified Service Description Language (USDL). By means of this standard the SLOs can be described in XML whereby these can be processed automatically. The formalized SLOs can be transformed into event patterns, which are responsible to detect violated or successful fulfillments of a certain process. This transformation has to be executed automatically because a human-oriented approach would be too time-consuming and error-prone. Additionally, the XML files are stored in a repository, so they are accessible by other tools.

CEP is also capable, because it is service-oriented [12]. Because of that all notification sources like RFID or ERP can be requested and linked quickly with the platform respectively the monitoring system (**D2**). This fact must be considered during the modeling of the monitoring system by using a CEP-engine conform Event Processing Language (**D1**). The 4PLP has to react in real-time e.g. by integrating new BPs. Using other technologies for notification like the Electronic Data Interchange would be too time-consuming to implement and thus not suitable [13].

In addition CEP enables the opportunity to accumulate simple events to complex events which can be investigated and assigned to an individual business service with the use of the above mentioned description (**D3**). Therefore an alignment from events to every individual business service is possible as well as providing events in a useful granularity (**D3, D4**). With the use of events, the 4PLP can define the responsibilities of each organization within a customer business service (**D1**). By defining pattern based on the automatically extraction of individual SLOs, the monitoring system can assure the assignment of possible penalties to the correct organization (**O1**).

CEP also provides the opportunity to predict what will occur in the future of the business services. By using and applying patterns based on the research of past business services and including other external sources (e.g. traffic) it is possible to predict failures by selecting the events of the pattern (**O2**).

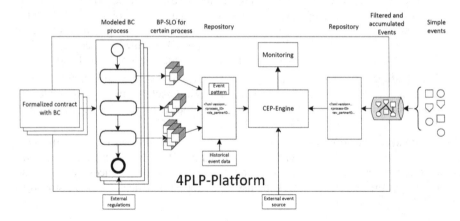

Fig. 1. Conceptual usage of CEP regarding to the 4PLP business model

4   Related Work

Werner et al. covered the monitoring of logistics processes by using RFID. In contrast to the presented solution in this paper, the approach focuses on the integration of distributed RFID data into the EPCGlobal network [13].

Further on, there are some approaches that detect abnormalities in distributed systems or describing the monitoring of quality indicators. These are almost based on static policy descriptions and are not suitable for the challenges described above [13].

Xu investigates how to formulize a contract which could support actual violations and pro-active detection of imminent contract violations. This investigation is focused on e-business and does not meet the requirements of logistics, but the pro-active approach can be adapted [14].

5   Conclusion

In this paper the need to outsource internal activities to external provider within the logistics area is introduced. Arising thereby the business model of the 4PLP is presented and a differentiation to other logistics providers. To point out the challenges in the space of the model, a short scenario describing the work of a 4PLP is given. The resulting challenges regarding to the monitoring are presented. Afterwards a possible solution by using CEP is discussed. Based on these explanations it should be clear, that CEP is a powerful approach to support the work of a 4PLP.

References

1. Weigand, H., Xu, L.: Contracts in e-commerce. In: 9th IFIP 2.6 Working Conference on Database Semantic Issues in e-Commerce Systems, DS-9 (2001)
2. Seaborne, A., Stammers, E., Casati, F., Piccinelli, G., Shan, M.: A Framework for Business Composition. Position Paper, W3C Workshop (2001)
3. Kutlu, S.: Fourth Party Logistics: The Future of Supply Chain Outsourcing? Best Global Publishing, Brentwood (2007)
4. von Ammon, R., Ertlmaier, T., Etzion, O., Kofman, A., Paulus, T.: Integrating Complex Events for Collaborating and Dynamically Changing Business Processes. In: Dan, A., Gittler, F., Toumani, F. (eds.) ICSOC/ServiceWave 2009. LNCS, vol. 6275, pp. 370–384. Springer, Heidelberg (2010)
5. Thiell, T., Hernandez, S.: Logistics Services in the 21st Century: Supply Chain Integration and Service Architecture. In: Luo, Z. (ed.) Service Science and Logistics Informatics: Innovative Perspectives, pp. 359–378. Information Science Reference, Hershey (2010)
6. Marasco, A.: Third-party logistics: A literature review. International Journal of Production Economics 113, 127–147 (2008), doi:10.1016/j.ijpe.2007.05.017
7. Schmitt, A.: 4PL-Providing als strategische Option für Kontraktlogistikdienstleister. Eine konzeptionell-empirische Betrachtung. Gabler Verlag, Wiesbaden (2006)
8. Win, A.: The value a 4PL provider can contribute to an organisation. International Journal of Physical Distribution & Logistics Management 38(9), 674–684 (2008)
9. Kohlborn, T., Korthaus, A., Rosemann, M.: Business and software service lifecycle management. In: IEEE International Conference on Enterprise Distributed Object Computing, Auckland, New Zealand, pp. 87–96 (2009)
10. Klinkmüller, C., Kunkel, R., Ludwig, A., Franczyk, B.: The Logistics Service Engineering and Management Platform: Features, Architecture, Implementation. In: Abramowicz, W. (ed.) BIS 2011. Lecture Notes in Business Information Processing, vol. 87, pp. 242–253. Springer, Heidelberg (2011)
11. Luckham, D.: The power of events. Addison-Wesley Longman, Amsterdam (2002)
12. Buchmann, A., Koldehofe, B.: Complex Event Processing. It-Information Technology 5/2009, 241–242 (2009)
13. Werner, K., Schill, A.: Automatic Monitoring of Logistics Processes using Distributed RFID based Event Data. In: 3rd International Workshop on RFID Technology, Milan, pp. 101–108 (2009)
14. Xu, L.: Monitoring Multi-party Contracts for E-business: An approach to e-contracting that enables pro-active and reactive monitoring. VDM Verlag, Saarbrücken (2009)

Nuclear Crisis Use-Case Management in an Event-Driven Architecture

Sebastien Truptil[1], Anne-Marie Barthe[1], Frederick Benaben[1], and Roland Stuehmer[2]

[1] Université de Toulouse – Mines Albi, Campus Jarlard – Route de Teillet,
81000 Albi, France
[2] FZI Forschungszentrum Informatik,
Karlsruhe, Germany
{sebastien.truptil,anne-marie.barthe,
frederick.benaben}@mines-albi.fr,
roland.stuehmer@fzi.de

Abstract. The European PLAY project aims at providing an event management platform. That platform should be tested and stimulated through use-cases. Obviously, these use-cases should be relevant on the business point of view, but to make them relevant, it could be interesting to be able to redesign them as often as required (to improve their business context). This article presents a specific use-case for the PLAY platform evaluation and also a technical framework dedicated to make this use-case as agile as possible. The general principle is to bridge the gap between business level (process models) and technical level (workflows definition and web-services implementation). The way the use-case will be simulated (to stimulate the PLAY platform) and the way the use-case will be designed and potentially re-designed (to be simulated) are described in this article.

Keywords: events, web-services, use-case, nuclear crisis, SOA, business processes, workflows.

1 Introduction

The European PLAY project (FP7-ICT-2009-5) aims at designing an event management platform. Any event provider (for instance, electronic devices, information systems, etc.) would be able to send its events to the PLAY platform through a cloud infrastructure. The PLAY platform provides an event market place containing (i) the events received from event providers and (ii) new events generated by the Complex Event Processing tool (CEP layer) from the combination of the previous ones (rule-based deduction). Any event consumer would then receive the events from the type it has subscribed for. Event consumers could finally use these events to act on a better way, according to the way the situation evolves.

This article aims at presenting the way one specific use-case could be implemented to stimulate the PLAY platform and demonstrate its features. This use-case concerns a nuclear crisis. The global objective is to define workflows and web-services simulating the crisis management and using the PLAY platform to run and adapt the overall behavior. Furthermore, in order to match with the business level definition of

F. Daniel et al. (Eds.): BPM 2011 Workshops, Part I, LNBIP 99, pp. 464–472, 2012.

the crisis management, this article introduces the mechanisms in charge of ensuring the direct generation of these workflows and web-services from the process models and activities.

The first section of this article introduces the global architecture of the demonstration platform and the way workflows and web-services will be used in a SOA context. The second section presents the use-case scenarios. The third section describes the automatic transformation of business models (process cartography) into technical components (workflows and web-services) that will be implemented in the demonstration platform of the first section.

2   Overview of the Global Architecture

In our use-case of a nuclear crisis management, the scenarios are very complex and a lot of sub-processes are involved. One of the objectives of our current research work is to simulate this use-case through a demonstration platform. This platform will be based on the Service Oriented Architecture (SOA) principles [1] and will be able to run the three levels of processes (decisional, operational, support). Technically, we will use the Enterprise Service Bus (ESB) PETALS developed by the French open-source software editor PETALS Link [2]. Such a technical infrastructure requires the description of the processes as workflows in a runnable language (Business Process Execution Language (BPEL) [3] for instance). In order to make this task easier, all the sub-processes will be described with Business Process Modeling Notation (BPMN) [4]. Furthermore, considering the fact that we have to describe the event exchanges between actors during the crisis response, BPMN is a good choice: this language is not only strongly aligned with computer implementation of workflows, but also structurally event-oriented (events are represented via circles and can be typed). BPMN is at the intersection between our need to represent events and the technical requirements of our demonstration platform (proximity between BPMN and workflow language).

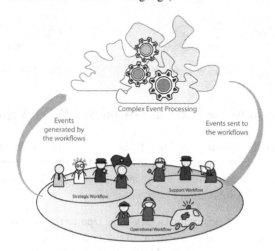

Fig. 1. Nuclear Crisis Use Case, Actors and Events

Basically, the structure of the demonstration platform will be the following: several ESBs will run, thanks to their workflow engine, several workflows (representing decisional, operational or support processes) among several web-services (representing activities of actors that might be invoked in a crisis management context). Each web-service will be able to generate events (such as status but also business events like radiation measures or requested resources) that will be sent to a special service of ESB. This special service (event manager or event proxy) is in charge of gathering events, translating them into an appropriate format for further processing (in the case of PLAY this is an RDF Schema) and sending them to the cloud platform of PLAY. The PLAY platform can use these events to generate new events and enrich the event market place. The event manager is also in charge of receiving new events from the cloud PLAY platform in order to send them to the web-services that are subscribers for that type of event. The following figure illustrates that architecture:

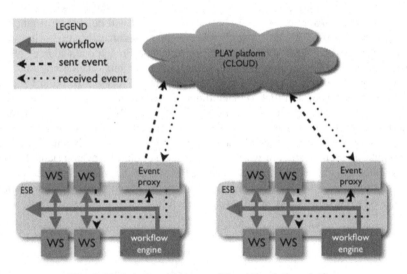

Fig. 2. Technical architecture of the s(t)imulation platform

3   Description of the Use-Case through a BPM Approach

The considered crisis situation use-case takes place in a French nuclear plant. The studied nuclear reactor is a water-pressurized reactor, the type used for all nuclear reactors in France, exception made for a single reactor [5]. The radiation leak in our scenario results of the combination of two issues:

1. The metal of the steam generator is very thin. Due to the wearing effect of time, a leak appeared in the steam generator. As a consequence, the water within the primary loop, which is contaminated, spreads through the secondary loop.

Consequences: The steam (and the water) of the secondary loop are contaminated and the pressure within the secondary loop increases.

2. The throttle valve, a safety device of the secondary loop, opens due to the increased pressure inside the secondary loop. Unfortunately, it does not respond to the manual bypass of the safety loop, requiring its closure.

Consequences: The steam of the secondary loop, contaminated, escapes from the secondary loop to the atmosphere.

To solve, or at least reduce, this crisis situation, several stakeholders are involved. They are grouped into an organization called "crisis cell", which is in charge of the crisis response. This crisis cell is piloted by the representative of the French national authority (the prefect), outside the nuclear plant. Delegates of each actor are present in the crisis cell. Firemen, policemen, weather survey network, scientists, emergency medical service, and any other actor involved in response process has one representative in the crisis cell. The delegates validate the feasibility of the decisions, ensure link with actors on the field and ensure communication between actors.

Each actor involved in the crisis response has its own abilities, the events it is listening to and the events it is able to generate and to send to the cloud (i.e. the technological platform that manages the events) (cf. Fig. 1.).

The crisis cell is structured according to three kinds of process, regarding the standards of business process cartography (as defined by the European standard NF EN ISO 9001 version 2000 [6]): decisional process, operational process and support process. These three processes may be detailed through seven sub-processes, as shown on Fig.3.

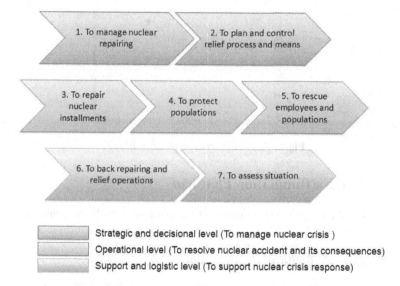

Fig. 3. Nuclear Crisis Overall Treatment/ Management

For the rest of this article, we will focus on a simplified version of that process cartography, partially covering decisional process number 2 (plan and control relief process and means), operational process number 4 (protect population) and support process number 7 (assess situation).

The following Fig. 4 presents several swim lanes (horizontal containers) that represent the involved actors (army, policemen, office of infrastructure e.g.) and the PLAY system. Each pool embeds its own activities and flows, while exchanges between pools are represented through flows generating events.

The matching workflow of the previous BPMN process will be run on our simulation platform. Now, we have developed a demonstration that shows the future execution of the corresponding workflow.

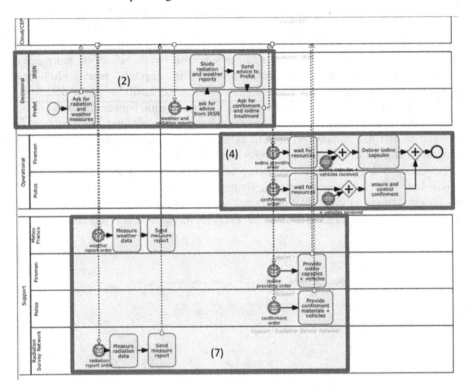

Fig. 4. Part of the crisis response in BPMN

4   Use of the s(t)imulation Platform

In this section, the overall configuration of the platform will be presented first. The previous example will be used to illustrate the behavior of the platform second.

4.1   S(t)imulation Platform Configuration

The input of this step is a set of ordered business activities, each under the responsibility of an actor. Nevertheless the business activities could not be directly used by the platform, it is necessary to match these business activities with technical services (as an operation of web-services). Research works try to define semantics service search engine, like [7] or [8], in charge of realizing automatically this kind of matching. Since the aim of our work is to configure a technical platform which has to simulate a business description, we decided at first to manually realize this matching before improving our work with any semantics service search engine.

Based on this choice, the automatic configuration of the technical platform, represented by the fig. 5, is divided in eight steps for each business process:

Step 1: The Manual matching operation consists in extracting from a business process, the set of business activities. Then for each business activity, the user has to make the link with an operation of a web-service. If the link already exists, the user has to provide the WSDL file of this web-service. In other case, the business service is added to the list of services that need to be created.

Step 2: All services, which need to be created, are grouped according to the actor they depend on. Then a WSDL file is created for each identified actor (a lane in the BPMN diagram). Consequently, a web-service could correspond to several business services.

Step 3: This step consists in generating the BPEL file corresponding to the business process. This step is based on the result of [9] & [10] which defines a model driven engineering to transform a BPMN model in a BPEL file based on the WSDLs files and the matching between business activities and web-services operations.

After this step, two operations are realized. The first one, divided in step 4 and 5, consists in generating all the artifacts required to configure an ESB based on JBI standard [11]. The second one, divided in step 6 and 7, consists in creating the web-services.

Step 4: The aim of this step is to generate some artifacts needed to execute the workflow in a JBI environment. As explained in [10], it is necessary to generate service Assemblies (SA) and Service Units (SU) to allow the ESB to communicate with any web-service. A SU is composed of the WSDL of the service and a JBI file that defines, in a unique way for the ESB, the web-service. A SA makes the link between a protocol (SOAP, HTTP, ...) and the web-services through the SU. So this step consists in creating all the necessary SAs and SUs

Step 5: This step consists in deploying all the artifacts on the ESB. These artifacts are composed of, on the one hand all the SAs and SUs created during the previous step, and, on the other hand all the binding component (BC) needed to communicate with the web-services (one BC per protocol) and the potentially requires service engine (for instance a workflow engine).

Step 6: This step uses a tool, named EasiestDemo, proposed by PEtALS Link [12]. EasiestDemo creates the SOAP shell of WebServices from the BPEL file and all the WSDL files. However, the main functions of the operations are not created, it is the subject of the following step.

Step 7: our work consists in simulating the execution of a crisis response. Consequently for each operation of a WebService, corresponding to a WSDL file created at step 2, a graphical interface is build. A graphical interface is composed of TextBox for each input and output elements of the operation and the colors of the interface are defined for each actor in a XML file.

Step 8: At the end of the Step 5 and 7, the simulated crisis response can be launched.

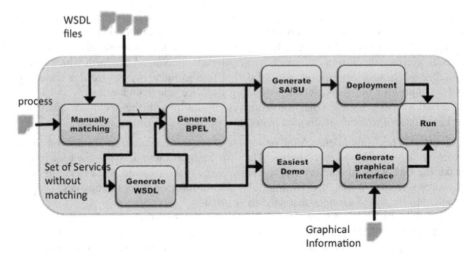

Fig. 5. Overview of the S(t)imulation Platform configuration

4.2   S(t)imulation Platform Execution

Once the technical platform is configured, the simulation is launched. The following of the simulation is realized thanks to a screen divided in four parts represented in Fig. 6. Part (1) is a picture of the executed business process. Part (2) represents the area where all the decisional services, which are created in step 6 & 7, will appear. Part (3) is dedicated to operational services while Part (4) is for support services.

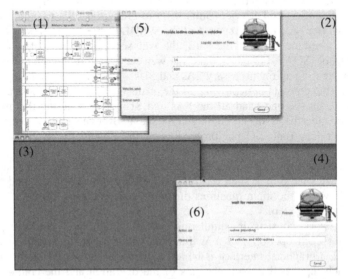

Fig. 6. Example of a s(t)imulation platform execution

During this simulation, the prefect is asking support services about radioactivity and weather measures. Then, he asks for advice about the situation to IRSN (scientific institute specialist in nuclear context). Afterwards, the prefect decides to follow the received and to protect people (instead of massive evacuation). Thanks to the cloud, this event triggers some activity execution and some additional information requests (required resources for example). This specific time of the simulation is represented on Fig. 6. A support service (5) and an operational service (6) are invoked: the logistic section of firemen has to provide 14 vehicles and 600 iodine capsules. This service will finish when the delegate of this actor will write the number of vehicles and iodine capsules really sent. At the same time, the firemen are informed that they have to deliver iodine capsules and the theoretical quantity they have to deliver.

5   Conclusion

To demonstrate the powerful capabilities of the PLAY platform, and especially the way interactions and interconnections of events could be handled, complex workflows must be designed. These workflows must also be directly connected to the cloud infrastructure of PLAY. There are two main issues in this objective: (i) the quality of the considered use-case (and of the associated workflows) and (ii) the way these use-cases can be easily executed to stimulate the PLAY platform. This article tried to deal with both these issues. The presented use-case is a very complete one that could be easily made simpler or more complex. The technical infrastructure presented in section three is a concrete step to bridge the gap between business description of use-cases and implementation of these use-cases. Based on these results, it is easy to understand that use-cases will be easily adapted or re-designed, at business level, and almost instantaneously ready to be experimented on the simulation platform to stimulate the PLAY platform, at technical level.

However, there are still a lot of questions concerning the capabilities of these tools and especially on non-functional aspects. For instance, scalability of the simulation platform will be a crucial issue in order to evaluate scalability of the PLAY platform. Some other points like quality of service or security, even if less crucial, are also to be considered.

Acknowledgments. The authors would like to thank very gratefully the members of the PLAY consortium (FZI, Karlsruhe; PetalsLink, Toulouse; ICCS, Athens; CIM, Nis; INRIA, Sofia-Antipolis; Orange-Labs, Sophia-Antipolis).

References

1. Vernadat, F.: Interoperable enterprise systems: Principles, concepts, and methods. Annual Reviews in Control 31(1), 137–145 (2007)
2. PEtALS Link (2010), http://www.petalslink.com
3. OASIS, Web Services Business Process Execution Language Version 2.0 (2007), http://docs.oasis-open.org/wsbpel/2.0/OS/wsbpel-v2.0-OS.html

4. Object Management Group, Business Process Model And Notation (BPMN), Version 1.2 (2009), http://www.omg.org/spec/BPMN/1.2/PDF/
5. Electricité de France (EDF), Panorama de l'électricité: les différents types de réacteurs nucléaires, http://www.edf.com/html/panorama/production/industriels/nucleaire/types_reacteurs.html
6. Norme européenne NF EN ISO 9001 version 2000, Systèmes de management de la qualité – Exigences, AFNOR (2000)
7. Bénaben, F., Boissel-Dallier, N., Lorré, J.-P., Pingaud, H.: Semantic Reconciliation in Interoperability Management Through Model-Driven Approach. In: Camarinha-Matos, L.M., Boucher, X., Afsarmanesh, H. (eds.) PRO-VE 2010. IFIP AICT, vol. 336, pp. 705–712. Springer, Heidelberg (2010)
8. Dong, H., Hussain, F.K., Chang, E.: A service search engine for the industrial digital Ecosystems. IEEE Trans. on Industrial Electronics 99 (2009)
9. Touzi, J., Benaben, F., Pingaud, H., Lorré, J.P.: A model-drivenapproach for collaborative service-oriented architecture design. International Journal of Production Economics 121(1), 5–20 (2009)
10. Truptil, S.: Etude de l'approche de l'interopérabilité par médiation dans le cadre d'une dynamique de collaboration appliquée à la gestion de crise. PhD, Université de Toulouse (2011)
11. JSR 208: The Java Community Process(SM) Program - JSRs: Java Specification Requests - detail JSR# 208 (2005)
12. EasiestDemo (2011), http://research.petalslink.org/display/easiestdemo/EasiestDemo+-+Open+source+BPEL+to+Java+generator

Event-Driven Process-Centric Performance Prediction via Simulation

David Redlich and Wasif Gilani

SAP Research Center Belfast, United Kingdom
{david.redlich,wasif.gilani}@sap.com

Abstract. Today's fast, competitive and extremely volatile markets exert a great deal of pressure on businesses to react quicker against the changes, and sometimes even before the changes actually happen. A late action can potentially result in a legal compliance failure or violation of service level agreements (SLA's). A business analyst needs to be notified before these failures and violations occur. This paper proposes an approach that enables real-time and process-centric decision support in the form of performance prediction as an application of Event-Driven Business Process Management (EDBPM). The ability of simulations to produce future-events, which are of the same type like the live-events generated by the really executed business process, is utilised. Live-events and simulated future-events can therefore be treated by a Complex-Event Processing (CEP) engine in the same way and parameters representing the historic, current, and future performance of the business process can be easily computed.

Keywords: event-driven business process management, business process simulation, performance decision support, operational excellence, complex event processing.

1 Introduction

In order to achieve an organisation's objectives, tasks are usually carried out in certain ways, i.e. workflows are defined to express activities and their order of execution. This behavioural information is captured in business process models [1].

Business processes need to change and evolve continuously in order to meet the rapidly changing market contexts, user requirements and business imperatives. The ability of reacting pro-actively on these changes is a crucial feature for an organisation. Additionally, business processes are typically composed of parts offered by different providers, spread across different geographical locations, and are managed with different modelling and execution environments. One step towards a continuous Business Process Management (BPM) for such distributed and heterogeneous businesses is the application of Event-Driven Business Process Management (EDBPM) techniques.

F. Daniel et al. (Eds.): BPM 2011 Workshops, Part I, LNBIP 99, pp. 473–478, 2012.
© Springer-Verlag Berlin Heidelberg 2012

In this paper an EDBPM solution for process-centric performance prediction in real-time is proposed in which simulation is utilised for the purpose of prediction. With this approach it is possible to provide a rather process-centric than data-centric view. The process-centric approach embeds the information into the actual business process context, thereby enables the identification of the root causes of deviations from SLA's by the detection of bottlenecks, exceptions, risks and non-compliances at the process activity level.

This paper is structured as follows: In Section 2, essential background information about BPM in general and EDBPM in particular is provided. Then in Section 3, a solution for event-driven and process-centric performance prediction in real-time is proposed. Work related to that topic is discussed in the following Section 4. The paper is concluded thereafter in Section 5.

2   Event-Driven Business Process Management

Event-Driven Business Process Management (EDBPM) is a recently coined term that emerged from the combination of the two disciplines Business Process Management (BPM) and Complex Event Processing (CEP) [2].

BPM is defined in [3] as follows: *"Supporting business processes using methods, techniques, and software to design, enact, control, and analyze operational processes involving humans, organizations, applications, documents, and other sources of information."*. Part of the definition is BPM's lifecycle which essentially includes four phases as shown in Figure 1: First is the *Configure* phase where the business processes are orchestrated and configured. Second is the *Execute* phase in which the business process is actually executed. Third is the *Analyse* phase where the running business process is monitored and data is collected for quantitative process analysis, process efficiency analysis, etc. The last phase is the *Decide* phase where decisions about the resolution of the identified problems are made and then implemented again in the configuration phase.

CEP, on the other hand, deals with the event-driven behaviour of large, distributed enterprise systems [5], i.e. events produced by the system are captured, selected, aggregated, and eventually abstracted to generate complex events representing high-level information about the situational status of the system. To put it into the BPM lifecycle perspective, a business process is executed as part of the second phase and produces events whenever a state change in the business process occurs. These events are usually of a simple nature and often only comprise raw and direct data information, like process instance id, timestamp, and type of the state change, e.g. 2011-05-26 T 10:45 CET: Activity ''Check availability'' completed, pi-id: 253, but not the state of the whole system [6]. With CEP these events can be processed and information about the business performance can be computed, e.g. process instance occurrence, activity net working time.

The extraction of performance parameters from live-events is a common application of real-time monitoring of business processes, which is in general called Business Activity Monitoring (BAM) and constitutes the third phase of the

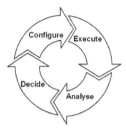

Fig. 1. Loop for continuous business process improvement [4]

BPM lifecycle [6]. BAM, in turn, is often related to EDBPM as the real-time or near real-time approach of monitoring of events with a CEP engine to support BPM suits this task perfectly. Usually single live-events are not of interest in the context of BAM, instead the aggregation of these into performance related parameters is carried out [7]. In this way, flaws within a business process can be detected in real-time and responsible entities can be notified immediately.

As stated in the beginning of this section, EDBPM is an approach to link BPM and CEP. Practically, this is realised by two individual platforms interacting with each other through interfaces or events, one a BPM system, which is to model, manage, and optimise a business, and the other one a CEP engine [8].

3   Event-Driven Performance Prediction via Simulation

The solution proposed in this paper enhances the BAM capabilities of producing real-time performance parameters related to business processes with the ability to further predict the future trends of these parameters. One first approach would be using the existing traditional data-centric Business Intelligence (BI, [9]) tools to predict each parameter individually based on its history only. However, this approach does not consume the workflow information of the business processes, provided by the BPM suites. A number of the performance parameters, such as *process instance occurrence* and *activity net working time*, are workflow independent, i.e. there future development can be predicted directly by analytical approaches. In contrast, other performance parameters, such as *activity throughput* and *end-to-end processing time*, are dependent on the workflow. The beneficial effect of using simulation for predicting these parameters is illustrated in Figure 2. The predicted throughput of *Activity 2* (bottom right graph) is more accurate as it takes the throughput of *Activity 1* into account, which supposedly has a delayed impact on the throughput of *Activity 2*. This way, predictions based on simulations that utilise not only the history data but the workflow information potentially produce better results.

In Figure 3 the framework for providing real-time analytics in the sense of performance predictions via simulation is depicted along with data flow and involved components; Flows of raw data events like live- and future-events are depicted as fine grained arrows; processed performance data as coarse grained arrow; common

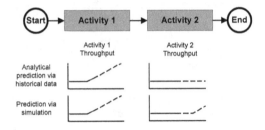

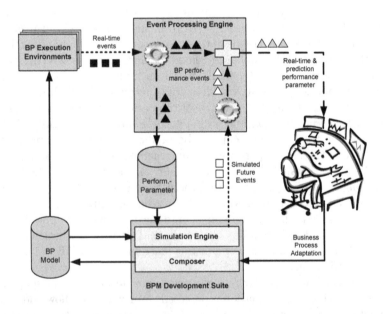

Fig. 2. Beneficial effect of prediction via simulation exemplified

data exchange via services as uninterrupted arrows. In this framework the simulation's ability to produce future-events, which are of the same type as the live-events, is utilised in a way that requires only minimal adaptations in the CEP engine.

The prediction framework operates as follows: The business processes are executed by the "BP Execution Environments" where live events are produced continuously. These real-time events contain raw data like discussed in the previous section. The "Event Processing Engine" captures and aggregates these events to compute the current state of the system as well as performance related data independent from the workflow information. As these parameters change over time, their future development has to be predicted by analytical methods based on their historical data. A simulation engine, e.g. implemented as discrete event simulation [10], takes the current state of the system, the potential devel-

Fig. 3. Data flow of the event-based framework for real-time performance prediction

opment of the workflow independent performance parameters, and the workflow information provided by the business process model as input to simulate the near future. The results are passed in form of raw data events directly back to the "Event Processing Engine". There, these future-events are processed just like the live-events. The available historic, current, and future performance data is then merged and further processed, e.g. by presenting the results in a dashboard, sending warning notifications if a future SLA violation is predicted, or trigger more complex events. The self-adaptation of both, the business processes or the analysis engine would be possible examples for these complex events. Based on the predicted results, responsible causes can be determined and the business process can be pro-actively adapted, accordingly. This way, SLA violations can be avoided and continuous performance decision support for operational excellence is provided.

4 Related Work

Before an event processing is possible the events have to be made available, i.e. the "BP Execution Environment" needs to be able to produce events. Some execution environment do not offer this possibility but only create business logs. To address this problem in [11], the Slipstream framework is introduced which enables event-driven business activity monitoring, taking business logs as input and creating real-time events whenever a state change is noticed.

Also closely related to the paper's topic is the research work in [12]: A business process optimisation loop including simulation as a mean for performance parameter computation and process adaptation is proposed. In this solution a simulation engine is interposed into the event processing in a similar way as proposed in our approach. However, only performance ascertainments and what-if analyses are supported but no predictions.

Common BI tools already offer many possibilities for data-centric performance predictions. These predictions are, however, based on mathematically extracted functions of the historical development of corresponding parameters and do not normally take the workflow information into account [13].

5 Conclusion and Outlook

In this paper an EDBPM solution for process-centric performance prediction in real-time is proposed, for which the ability of simulations to produce future-events similar to live-events is utilised to additionally provide future trend information. The general design benefit of our proposed performance prediction approach is the straightforward integration of the simulation engine: It consumes the processed performance data to create future-events that are transmitted back into the CEP engine.

In contrast to existing performance prediction solutions in BI the paper's approach takes the workflow information available via the business process models into account and is event-driven, i.e. offers process-centric performance prediction in real-time. However, it has not yet been evaluated if and in which way the prediction via simulation is a better approach than a direct parameter prediction based on the parameter's historical data. This examination is considered to be future work.

Furthermore, the next step would be to integrate advanced analyses like optimisations into the loop and, based on their results, an intelligent adaptation of the business process would be performed. Rather than just providing manual decision support, this approach would then enable the framework to automatically react on changes or avoid future violations without any human interaction, e.g. by instant resource rescheduling. The realisation of a feedback loop for this purpose is, however, a very intricate issue in general, e.g. because of the fact that design tools used for adaptation and reconfiguration of business processes are commonly operated manually.

References

1. Object Management Group Inc: Business Process Modeling Notation (BPMN) Specification 1.0 (2006)
2. von Ammon, R., Ertlmaier, T., Etzion, O., Kofman, A., Paulus, T.: Integrating Complex Events for Collaborating and Dynamically Changing Business Processes. In: Dan, A., Gittler, F., Toumani, F. (eds.) ICSOC/ServiceWave 2009. LNCS, vol. 6275, pp. 370–384. Springer, Heidelberg (2010)
3. van der Aalst, W.M.P., ter Hofstede, A.H.M., Weske, M.: Business Process Management: A Survey. In: van der Aalst, W.M.P., ter Hofstede, A.H.M., Weske, M. (eds.) BPM 2003. LNCS, vol. 2678, pp. 1–12. Springer, Heidelberg (2003)
4. Fritzsche, M., Gilani, W., Picht, M.: Process-Centric Decision Support. In: Rosenberg, A., von Rosing, M., Chase, G., Omar, R., Taylor, J. (eds.) Applying Real-World BPM in an SAP Environment. SAP PRESS (2011)
5. Luckham, D.: The Power of Events: An Introduction to Complex Event Processing in Distributed Enterprise Systems. Addison-Wesley Professional, Reading (2002)
6. van der Aalst, W.: Process Mining: Discovery, Conformance and Enhancement of Business Processes. Springer, Heidelberg (2011)
7. Eckert, M.: Complex Event Processing with XChange EQ: Language Design, Formal Semantics, and Incremental Evaluation for Querying Events. LMU München (2008)
8. von Ammon, R.: Event-Driven Business Process Management. In: Proceedings of Encyclopedia of Database Systems, pp. 1068–1071. Springer, US (2009)
9. WebFinance, Inc.: Busines Dictionary (2011), http://www.businessdictionary.com/
10. Robinson, S.: Simulation: The Practice of Model Development and Use. John Wiley & Sons (2004)
11. Janiesch, C., Matzner, M., Müller, M., Vollmer, R., Becker, J.: Slipstream: architecture options for real-time process analytics. In: Chu, W., Wong, W., Palakal, M., Hung, C. (eds.) Proceedings of the 2011 ACM Symposium on Applied Computing (SAC), TaiChung, Taiwan, March 21-24. ACM (2011)
12. Solomon, A., Litoiu, M., Lau, A.: Business Process Adaptation on a Tracked Simulation Model. In: ACM IBM Center for Advanced Studies Conference (2010)
13. SAP AG, Business Analytics Solutions, http://www.sap.com/solutions/sapbusinessobjects/index.epx

Author Index